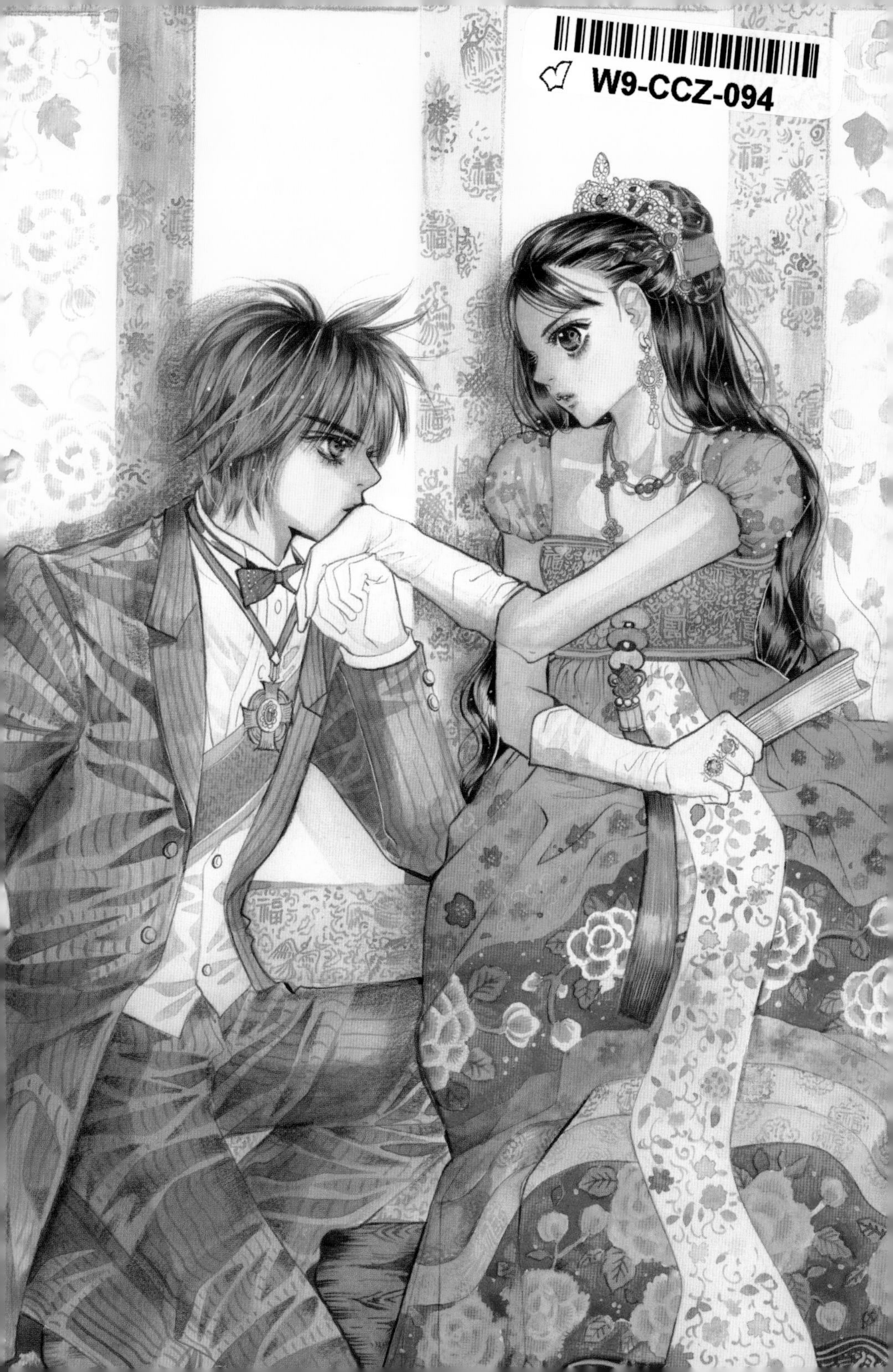

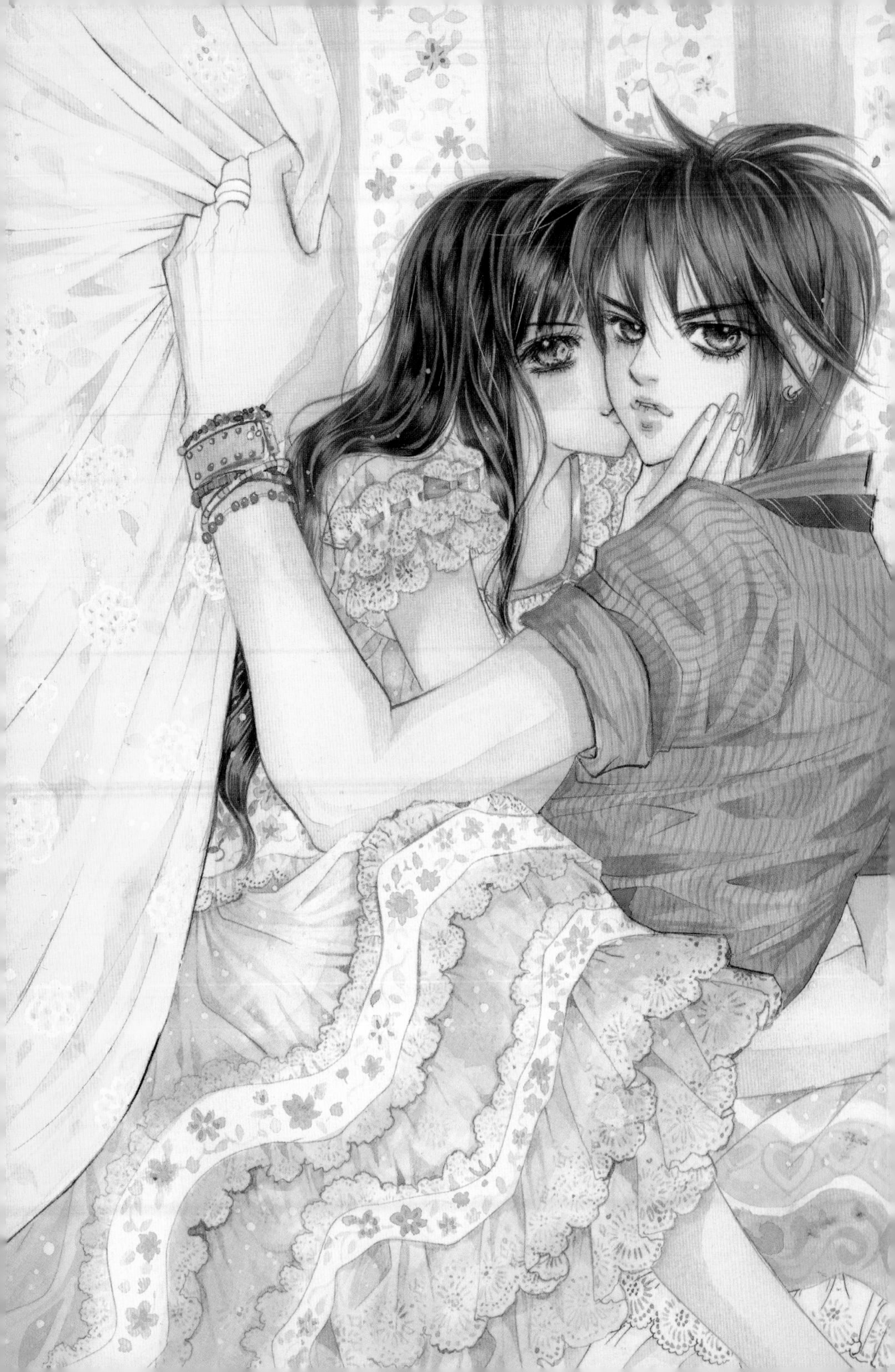

THE ROYAL PALACE

Goong

vol. 10

Park SoHee

Yen Press

Words from the Creator

Volume 11

Working on **Goong** has been like a long climb up
a mountain. While I was putting together Volume
11, I felt like a climber who kept only the mountain
peak within her sights throughout the day, going
forward without giving thought to anything else,
and who lay on the ground and watched the stars
at night. I would like to thank everyone who held
my hand during that arduous trek.

SoHee Park

Words from the Creator

Volume 12

I started working on ***Goong*** around the time of the last World Cup. And now the next World Cup is here. It's been exactly four years. Wow... While I was working on Volume 12, many happy things and some upsetting things happened. But Volume 12 came out anyway, and you should totally congratulate me. I thought I wouldn't feel excited about a new book this far into the series, but I'm still excited to have another volume come out. Thanks to everyone who helped me and cheered me up.

SoHee Park

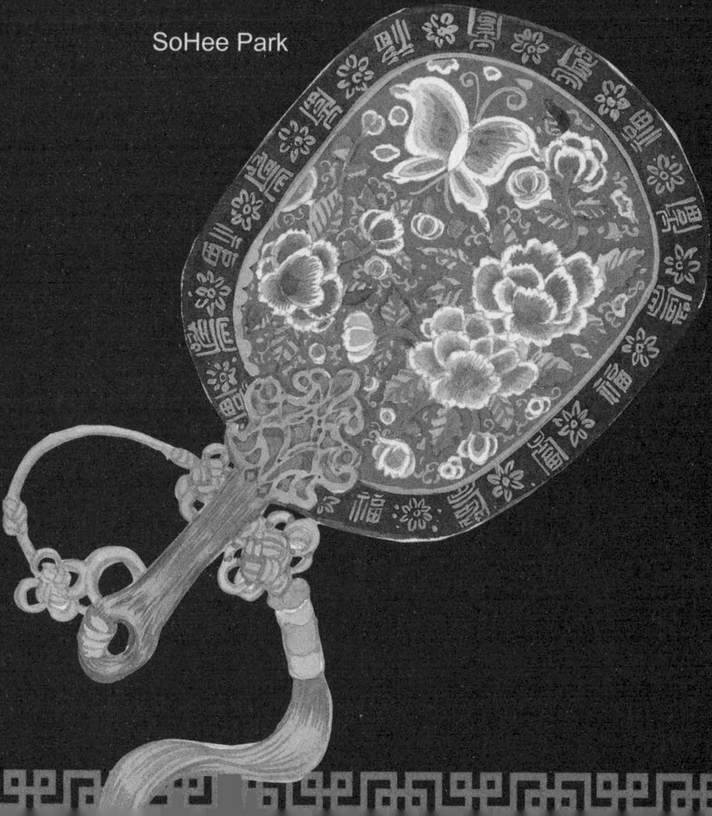

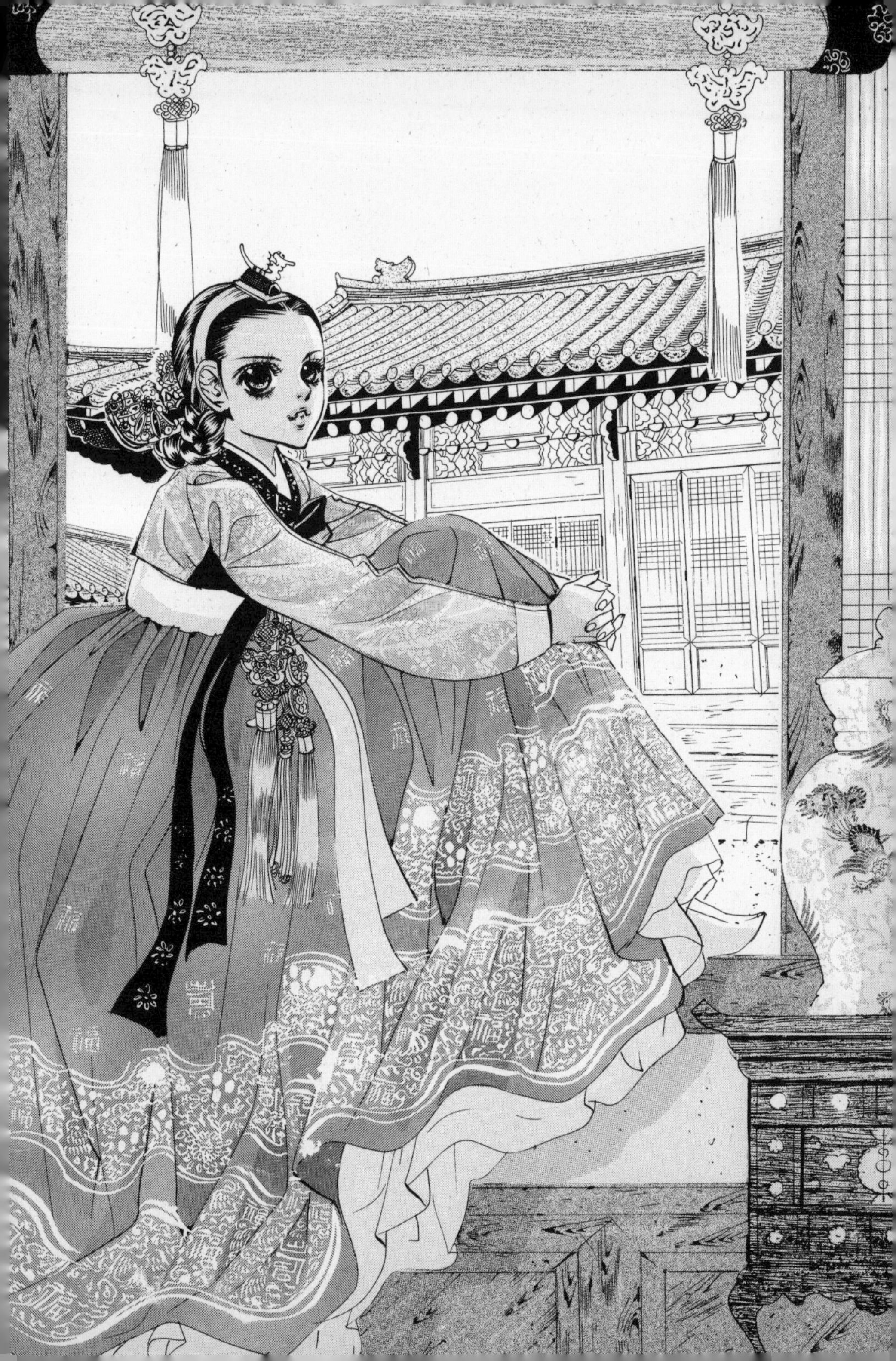

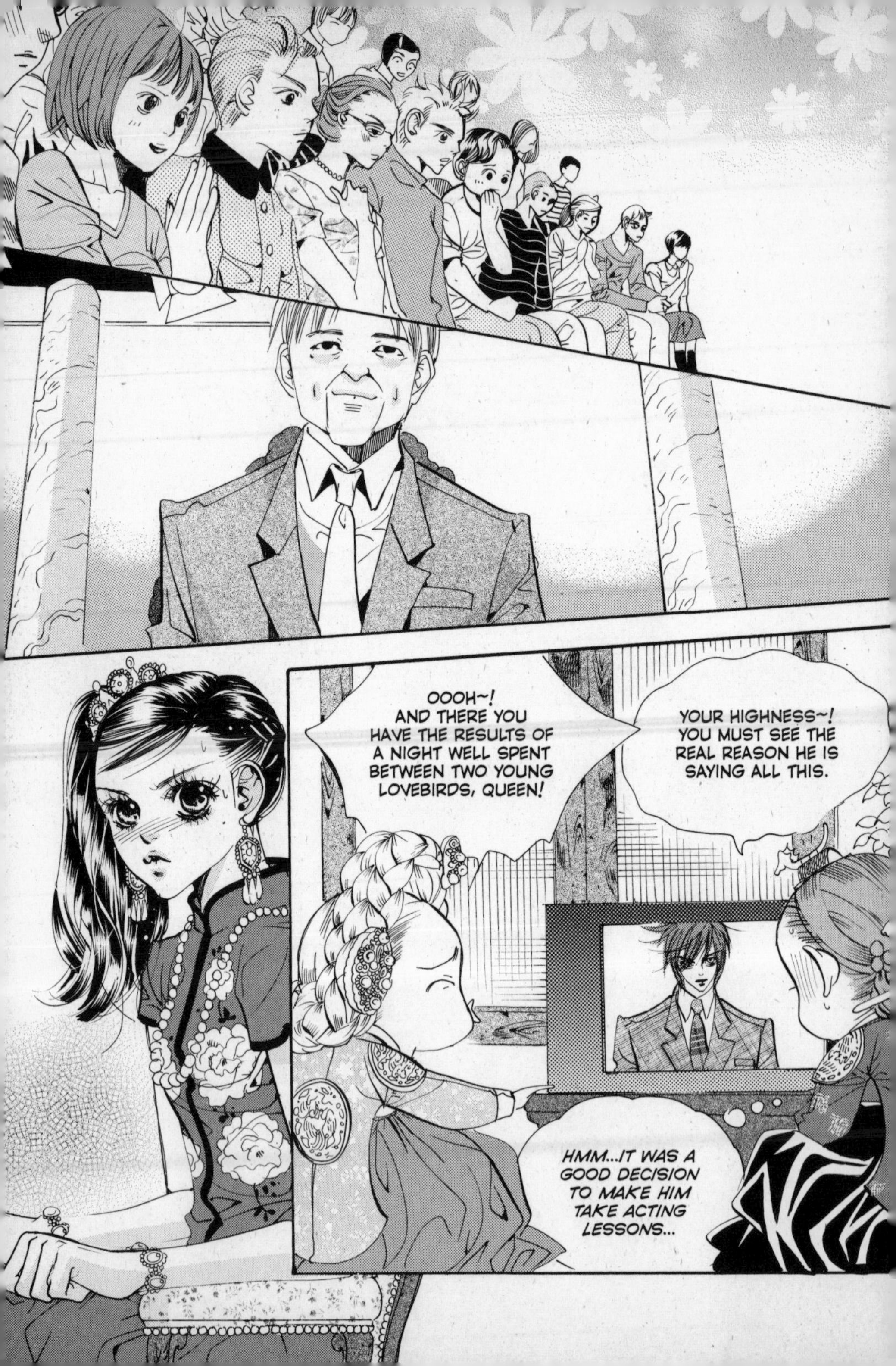
OOOH~! AND THERE YOU HAVE THE RESULTS OF A NIGHT WELL SPENT BETWEEN TWO YOUNG LOVEBIRDS, QUEEN!
YOUR HIGHNESS~! YOU MUST SEE THE REAL REASON HE IS SAYING ALL THIS.
HMM...IT WAS A GOOD DECISION TO MAKE HIM TAKE ACTING LESSONS...

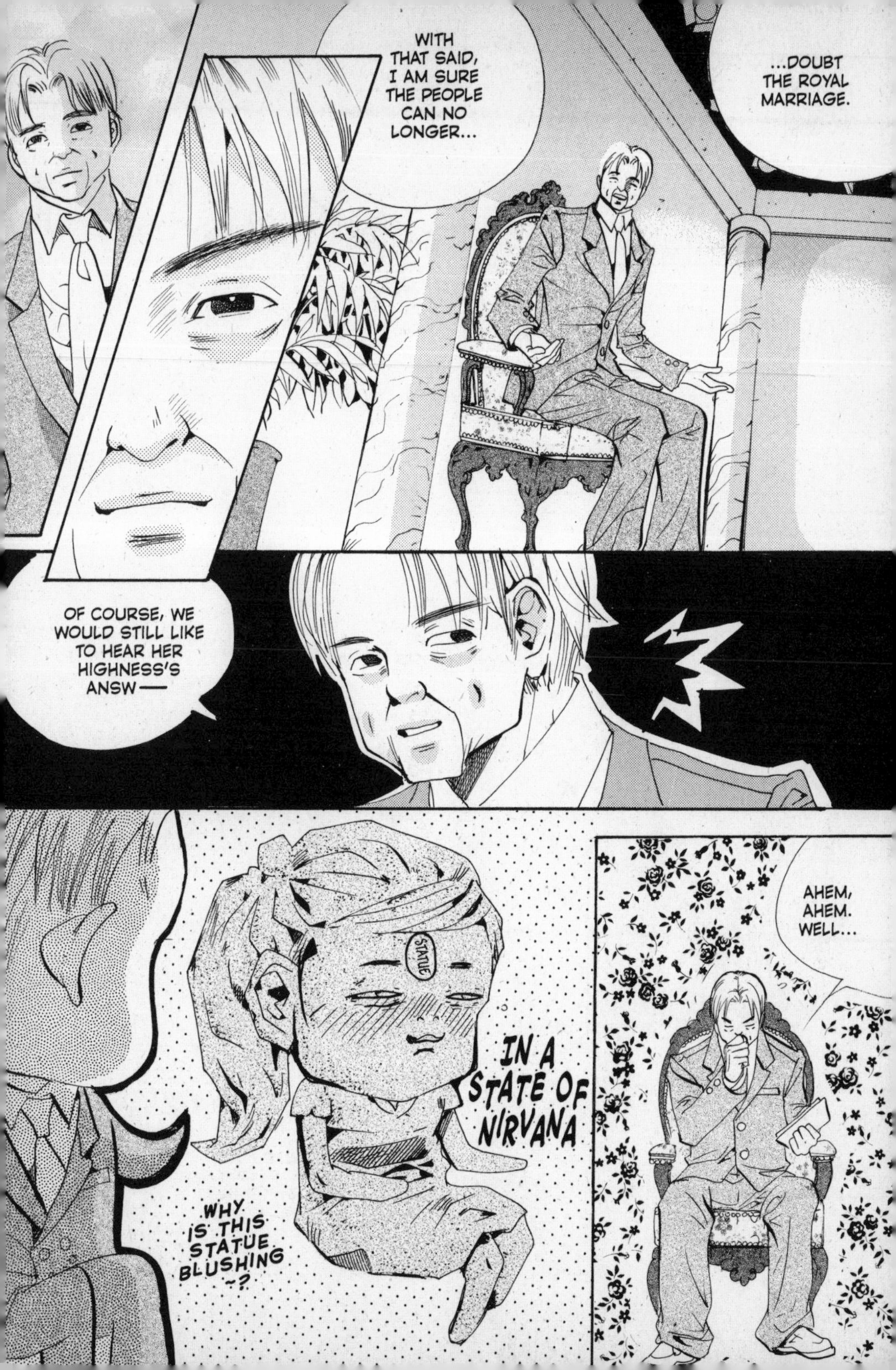
WITH THAT SAID, I AM SURE THE PEOPLE CAN NO LONGER...
...DOUBT THE ROYAL MARRIAGE.
OF COURSE, WE WOULD STILL LIKE TO HEAR HER HIGHNESS'S ANSW—
STATUE
IN A STATE OF NIRVANA
WHY IS THIS STATUE BLUSHING~?
AHEM, AHEM. WELL...

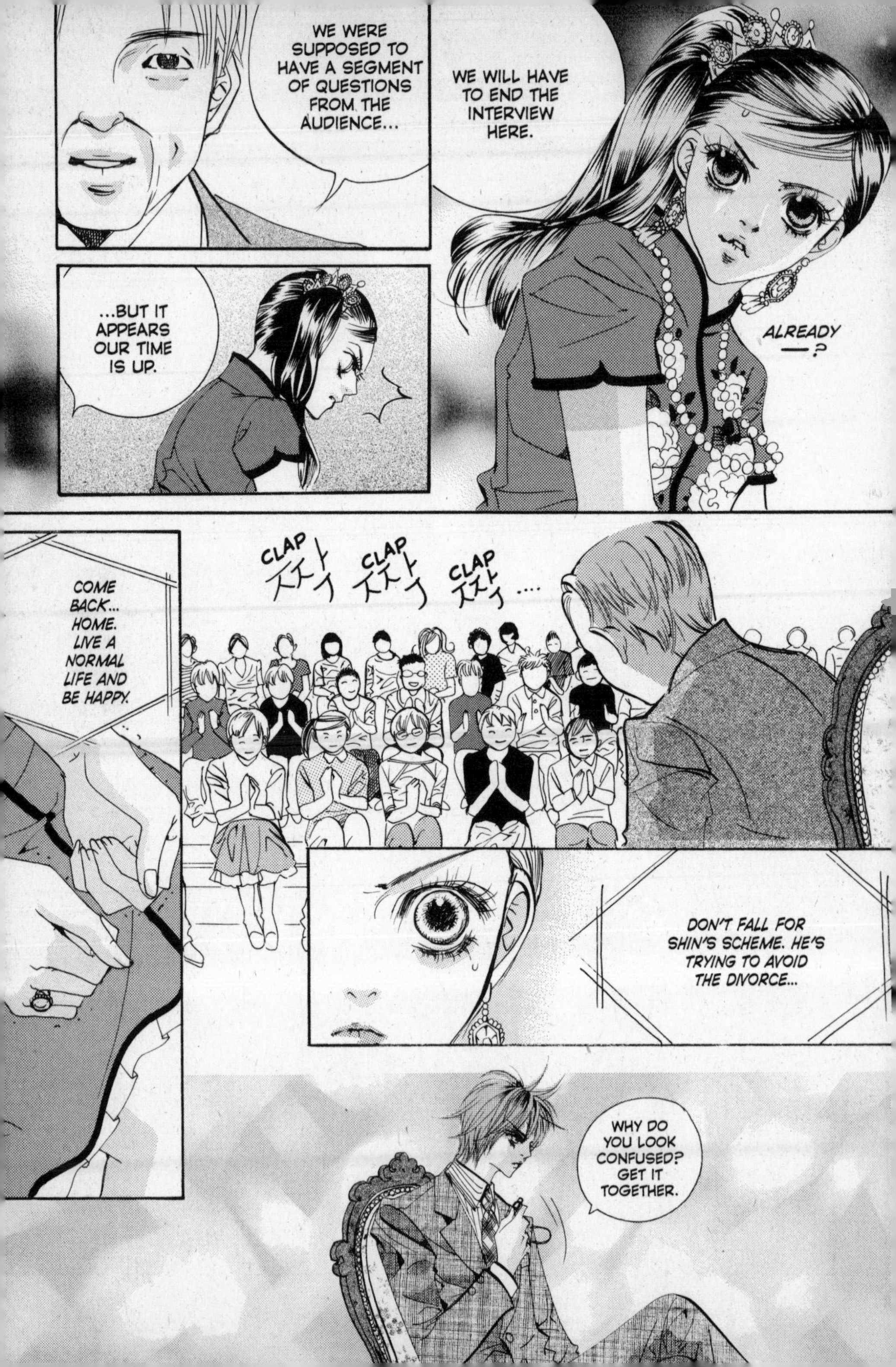
WE WERE SUPPOSED TO HAVE A SEGMENT OF QUESTIONS FROM THE AUDIENCE...
WE WILL HAVE TO END THE INTERVIEW HERE.
...BUT IT APPEARS OUR TIME IS UP.
ALREADY —?
COME BACK... HOME. LIVE A NORMAL LIFE AND BE HAPPY.
CLAP 짝 CLAP 짝 CLAP 짝....
DON'T FALL FOR SHIN'S SCHEME. HE'S TRYING TO AVOID THE DIVORCE...
WHY DO YOU LOOK CONFUSED? GET IT TOGETHER.

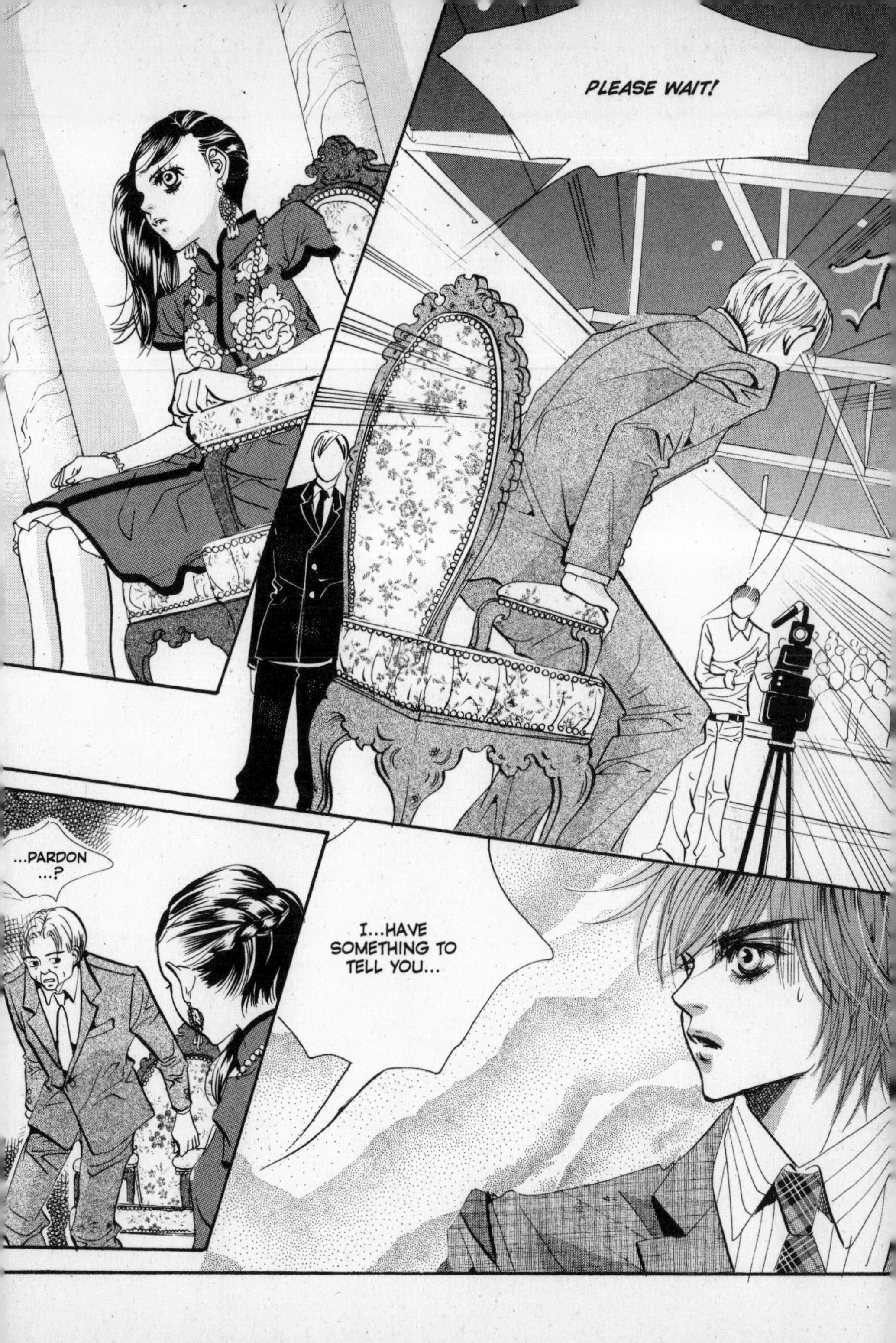
PLEASE WAIT!
...PARDON ...?
I...HAVE SOMETHING TO TELL YOU...

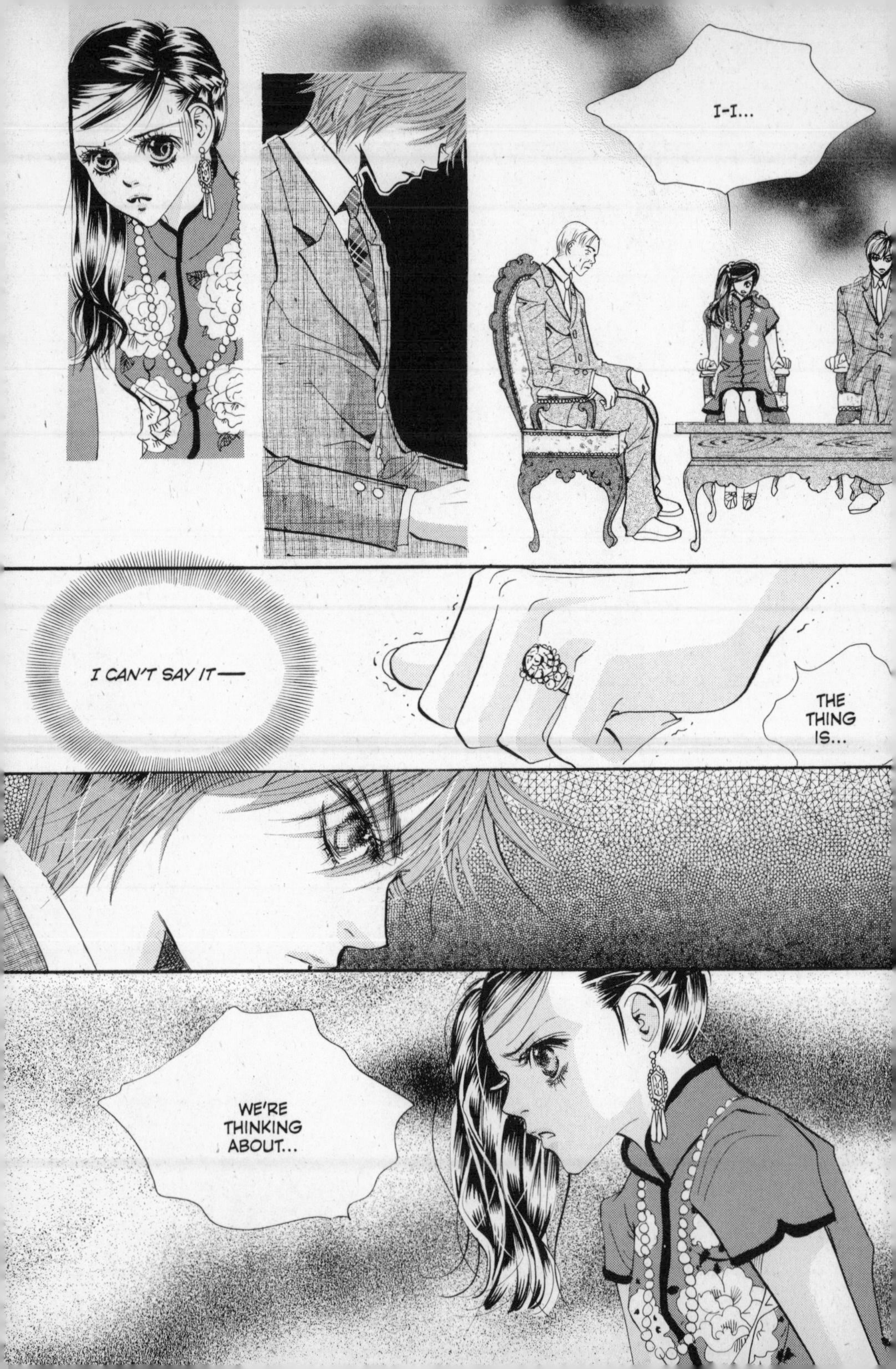

I-I...
I CAN'T SAY IT—
THE THING IS...
WE'RE THINKING ABOUT...

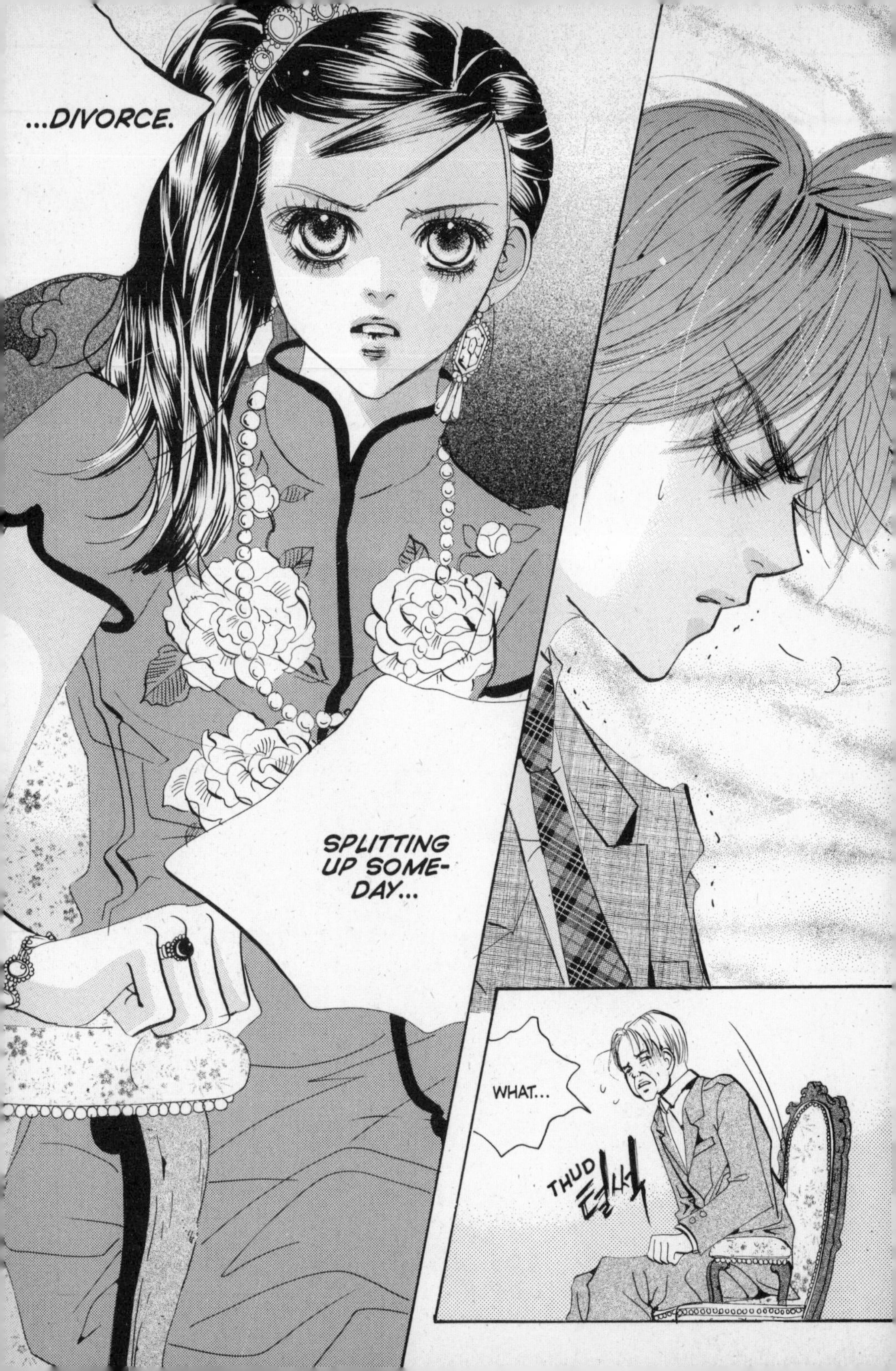
...DIVORCE.
SPLITTING UP SOME-DAY...
WHAT...
THUD

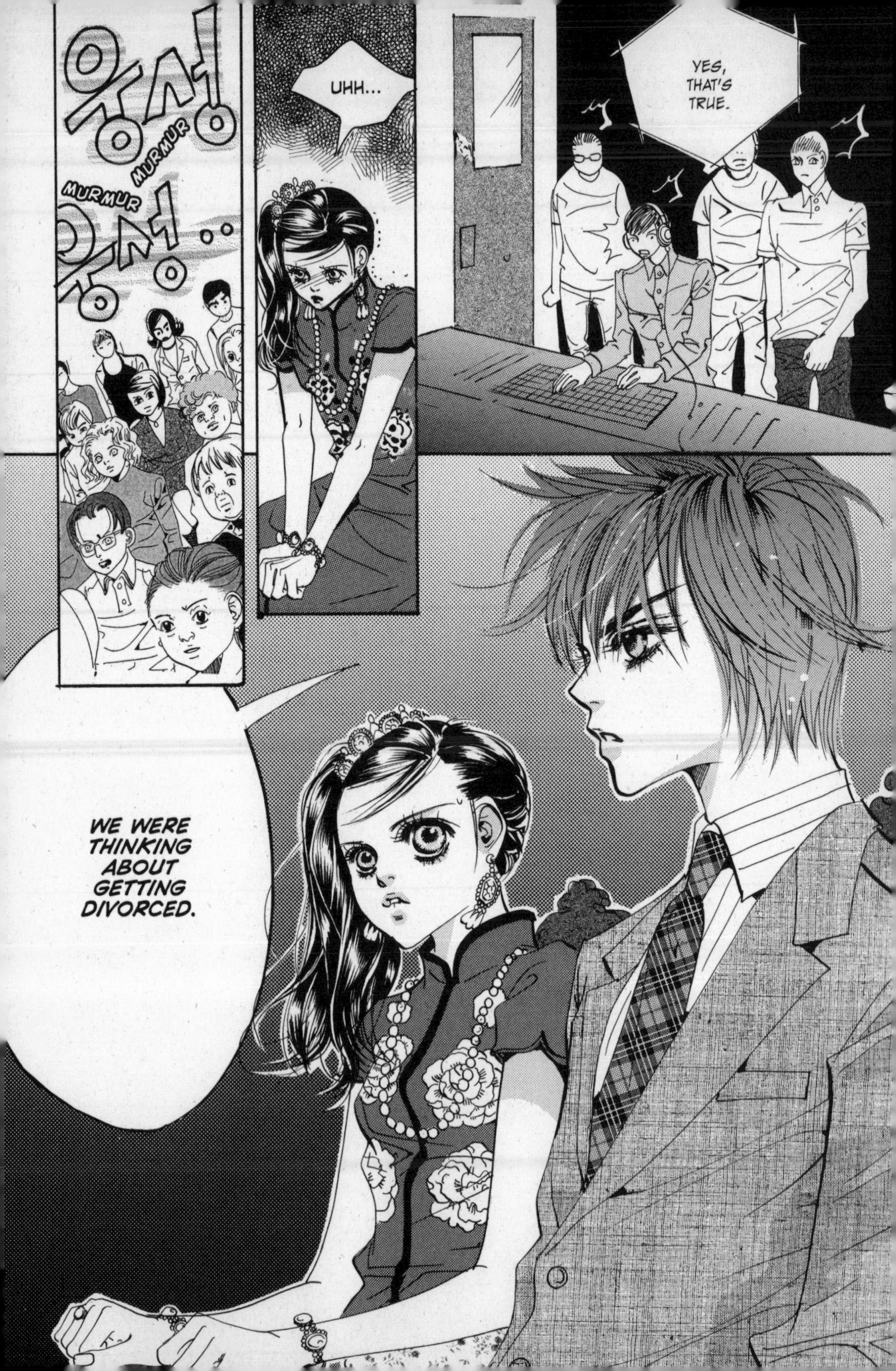

웅성
MURMUR
MURMUR
웅성..
UHH...
YES, THAT'S TRUE.
WE WERE THINKING ABOUT GETTING DIVORCED.

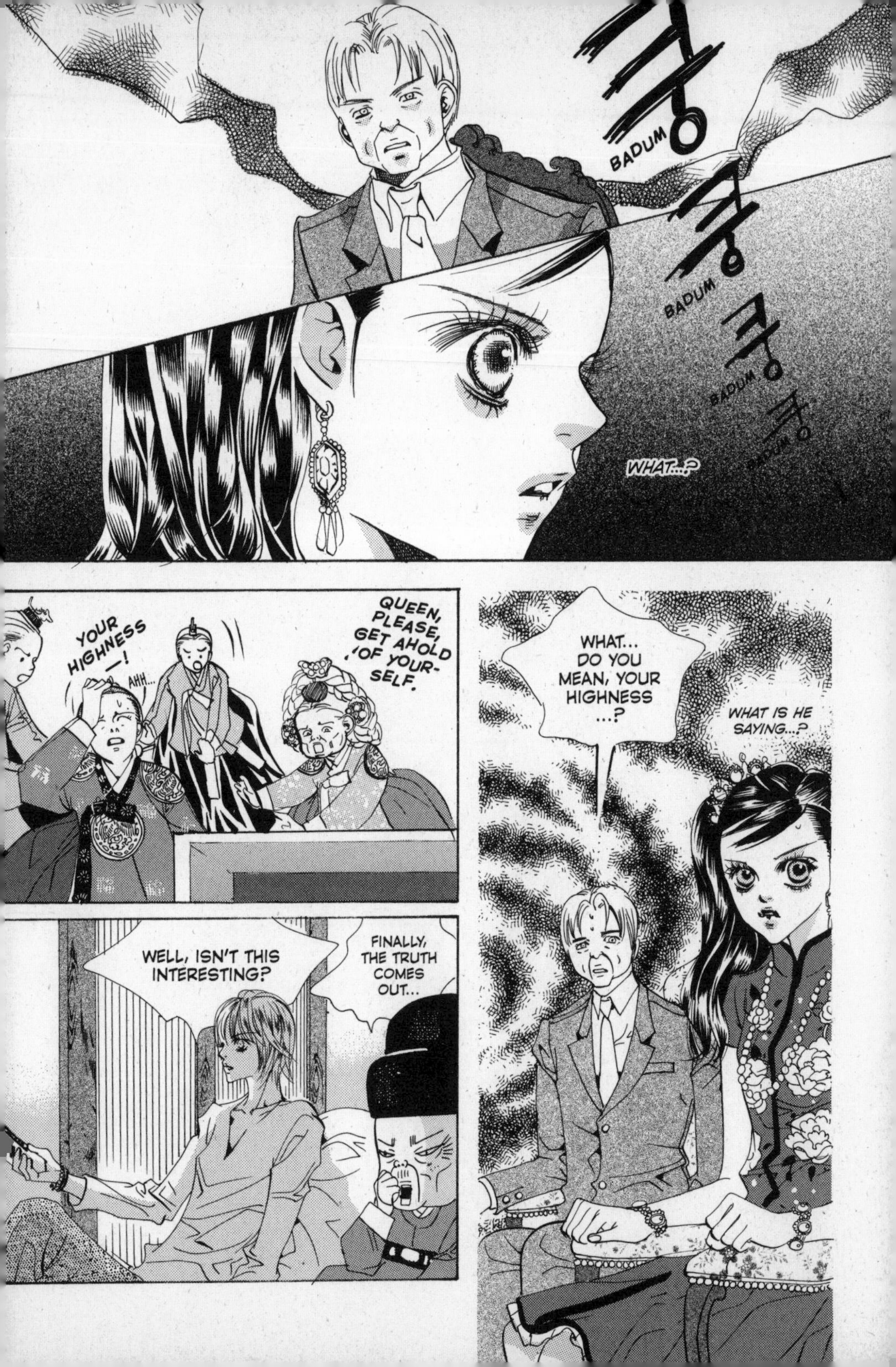

쿵
BADUM
쿵
BADUM
쿵
BADUM
쿵
BADUM
WHAT...?
YOUR HIGHNESS —!
AHH...
QUEEN, PLEASE, GET AHOLD OF YOURSELF.
WELL, ISN'T THIS INTERESTING?
FINALLY, THE TRUTH COMES OUT...
WHAT... DO YOU MEAN, YOUR HIGHNESS ...?
WHAT IS HE SAYING...?

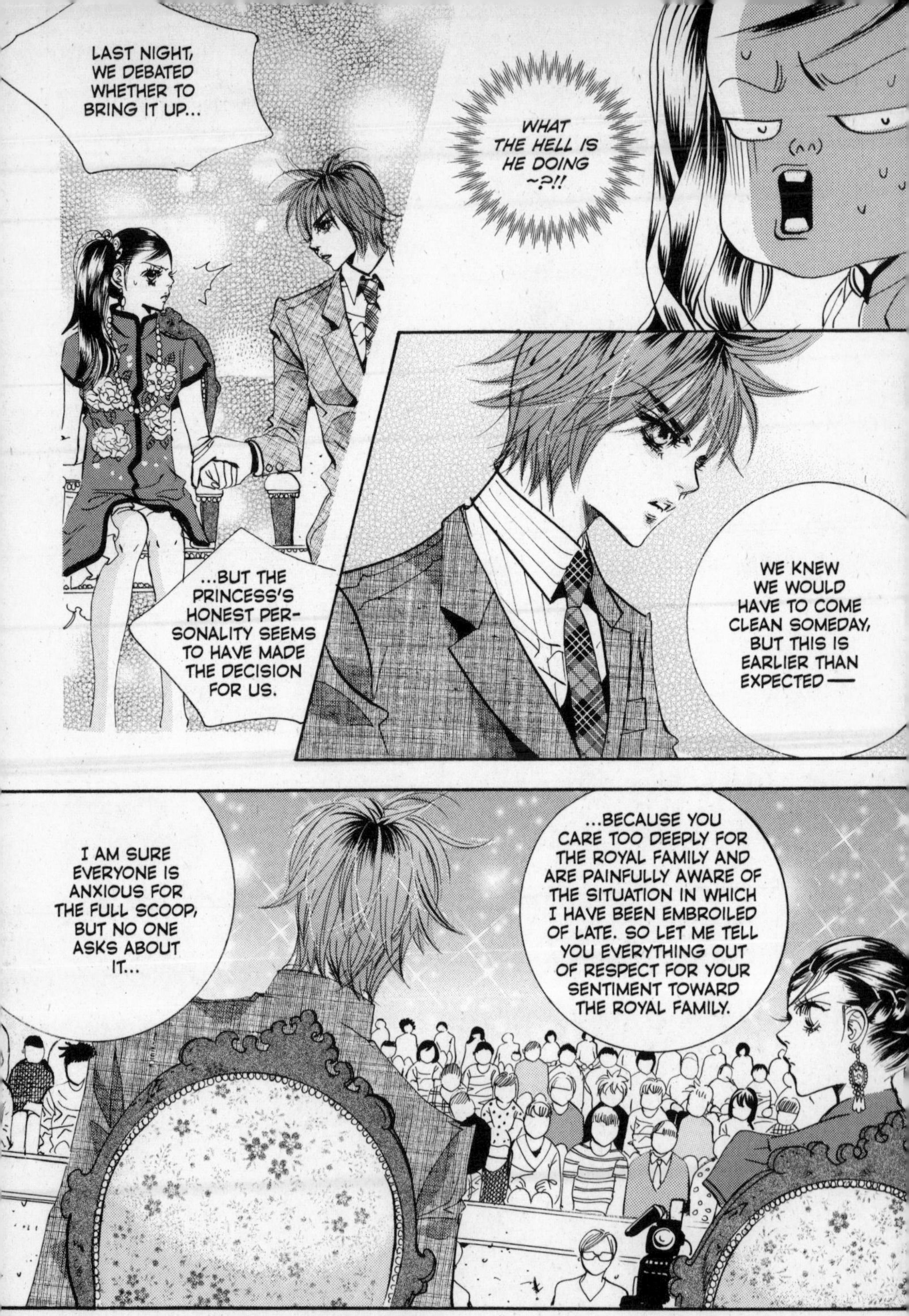
LAST NIGHT, WE DEBATED WHETHER TO BRING IT UP...
...BUT THE PRINCESS'S HONEST PER-SONALITY SEEMS TO HAVE MADE THE DECISION FOR US.
WHAT THE HELL IS HE DOING ~?!!
WE KNEW WE WOULD HAVE TO COME CLEAN SOMEDAY, BUT THIS IS EARLIER THAN EXPECTED—
I AM SURE EVERYONE IS ANXIOUS FOR THE FULL SCOOP, BUT NO ONE ASKS ABOUT IT...
...BECAUSE YOU CARE TOO DEEPLY FOR THE ROYAL FAMILY AND ARE PAINFULLY AWARE OF THE SITUATION IN WHICH I HAVE BEEN EMBROILED OF LATE. SO LET ME TELL YOU EVERYTHING OUT OF RESPECT FOR YOUR SENTIMENT TOWARD THE ROYAL FAMILY.

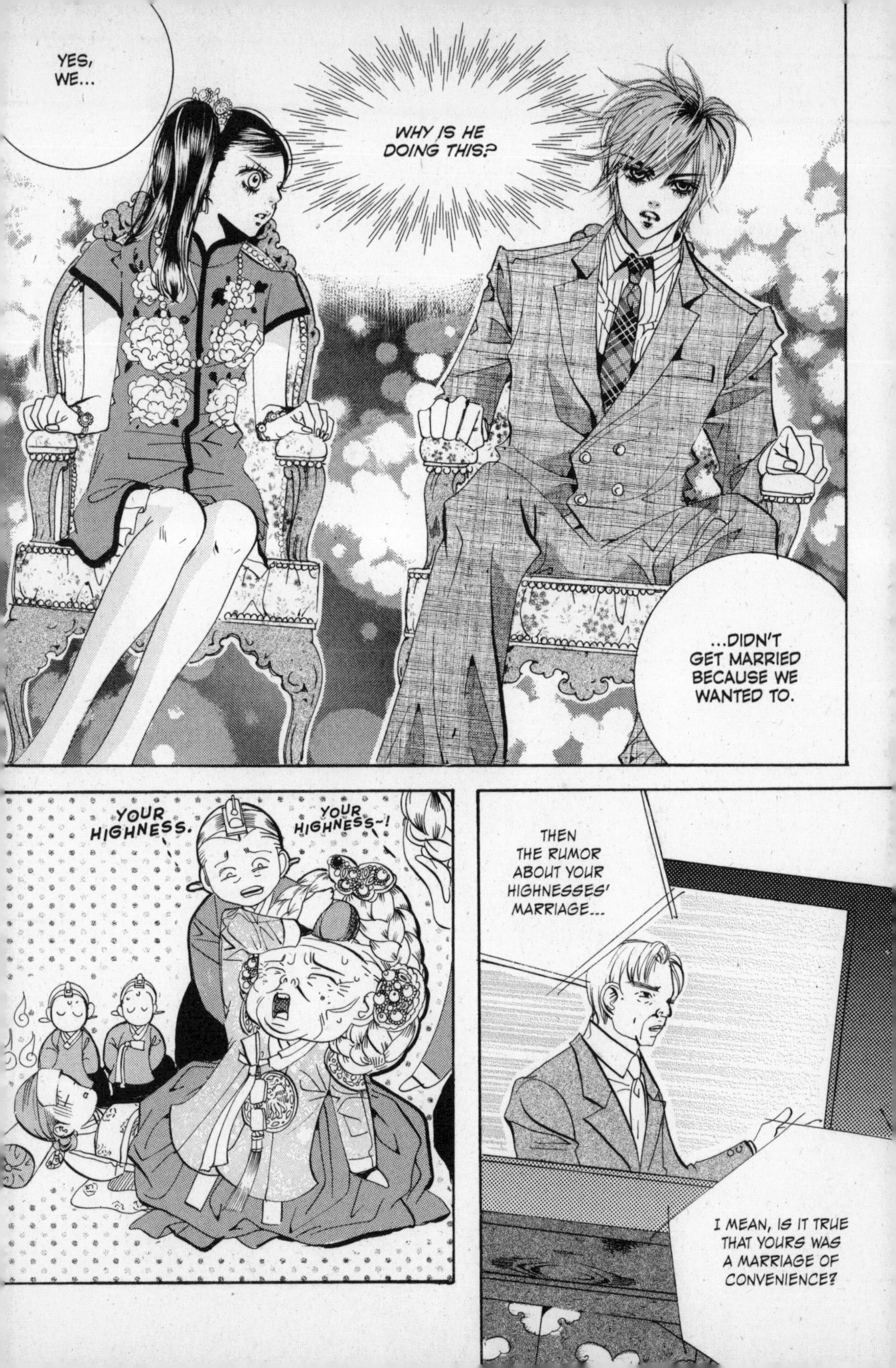
YES, WE...
WHY IS HE DOING THIS?
...DIDN'T GET MARRIED BECAUSE WE WANTED TO.
YOUR HIGHNESS.
YOUR HIGHNESS~!
THEN THE RUMOR ABOUT YOUR HIGHNESSES' MARRIAGE...
I MEAN, IS IT TRUE THAT YOURS WAS A MARRIAGE OF CONVENIENCE?

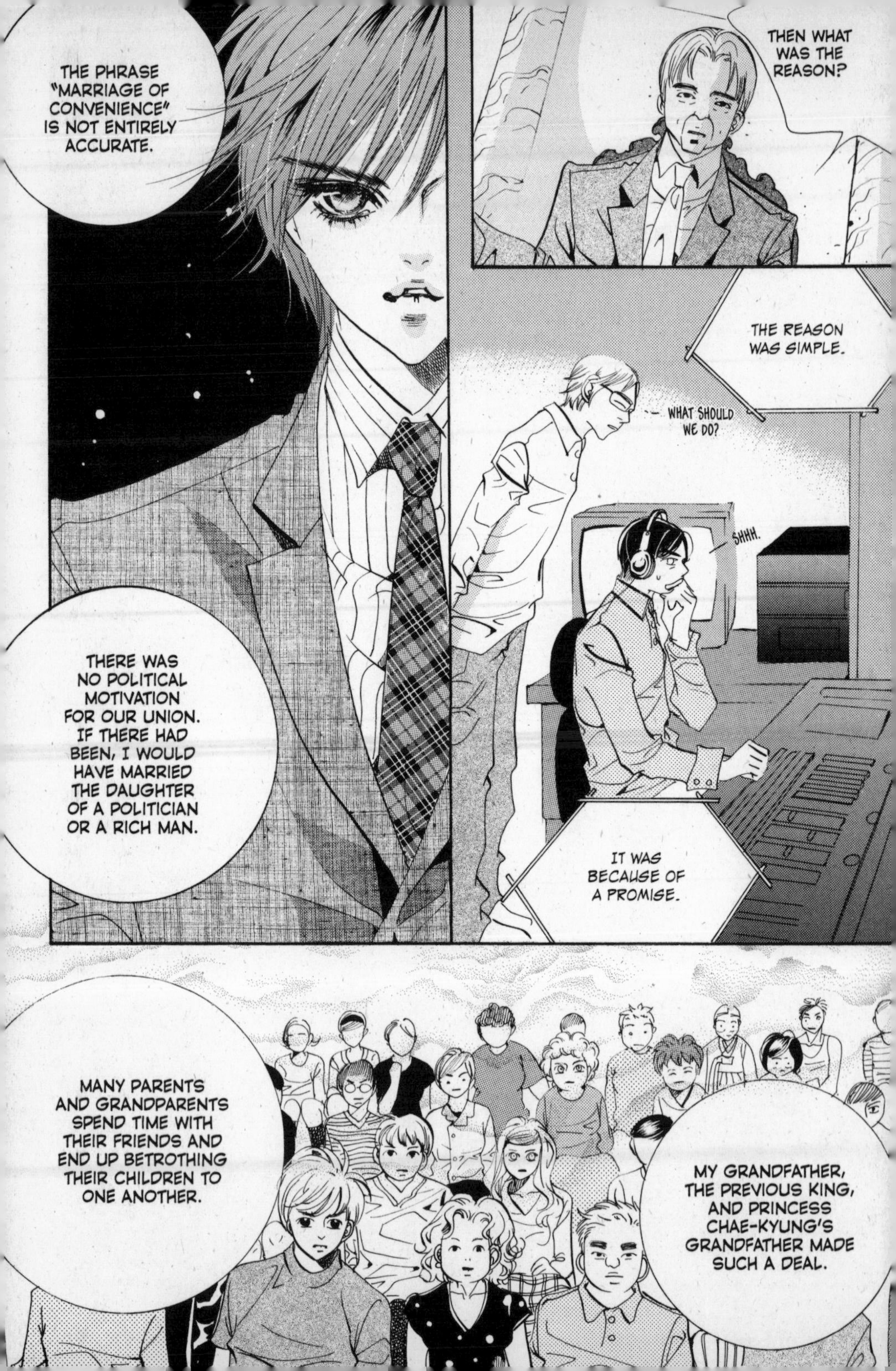
THE PHRASE "MARRIAGE OF CONVENIENCE" IS NOT ENTIRELY ACCURATE.
THERE WAS NO POLITICAL MOTIVATION FOR OUR UNION. IF THERE HAD BEEN, I WOULD HAVE MARRIED THE DAUGHTER OF A POLITICIAN OR A RICH MAN.
THEN WHAT WAS THE REASON?
THE REASON WAS SIMPLE.
-- WHAT SHOULD WE DO?
SHHH.
IT WAS BECAUSE OF A PROMISE.
MANY PARENTS AND GRANDPARENTS SPEND TIME WITH THEIR FRIENDS AND END UP BETROTHING THEIR CHILDREN TO ONE ANOTHER.
MY GRANDFATHER, THE PREVIOUS KING, AND PRINCESS CHAE-KYUNG'S GRANDFATHER MADE SUCH A DEAL.

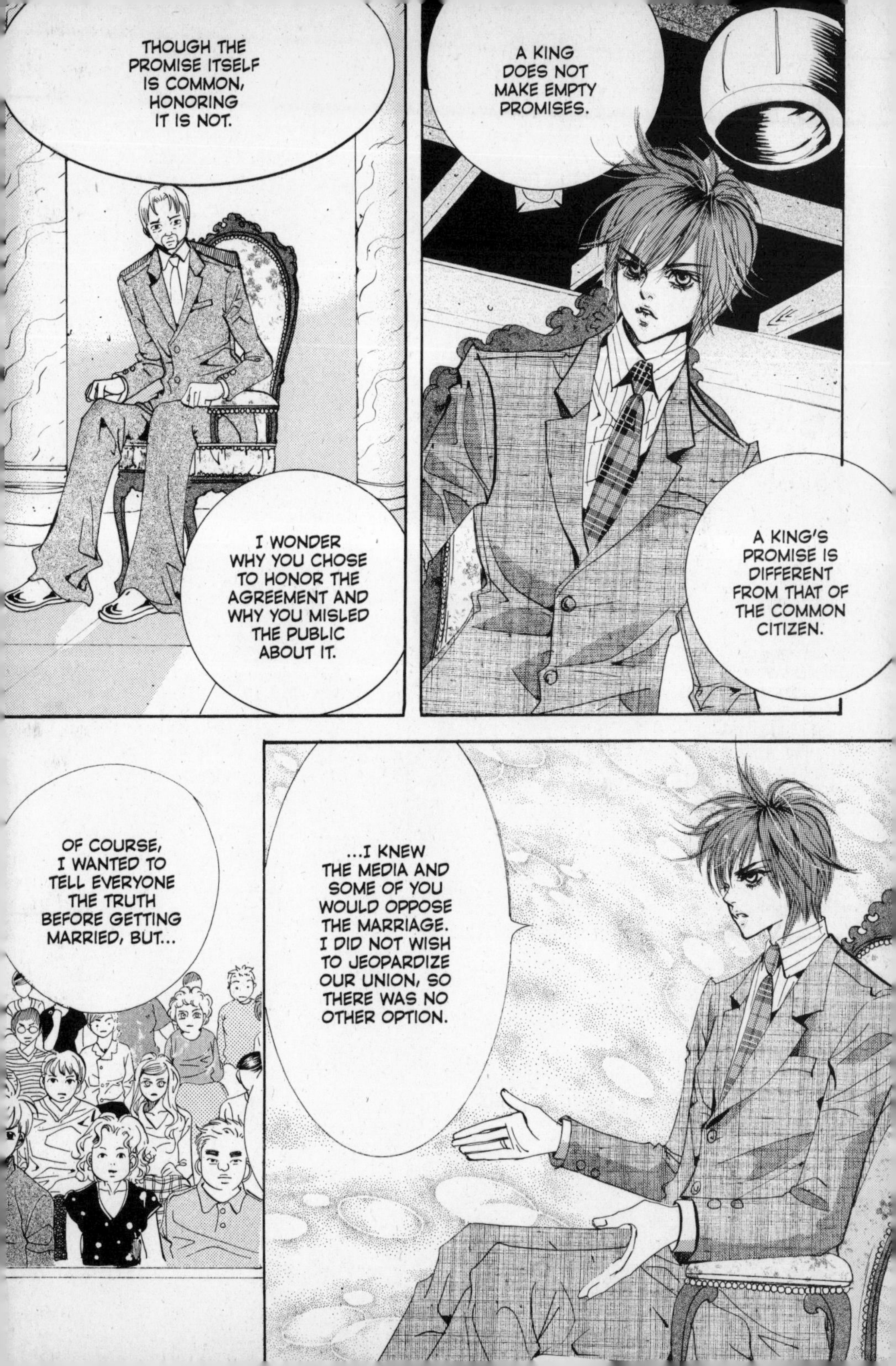
THOUGH THE PROMISE ITSELF IS COMMON, HONORING IT IS NOT.
I WONDER WHY YOU CHOSE TO HONOR THE AGREEMENT AND WHY YOU MISLED THE PUBLIC ABOUT IT.
A KING DOES NOT MAKE EMPTY PROMISES.
A KING'S PROMISE IS DIFFERENT FROM THAT OF THE COMMON CITIZEN.
OF COURSE, I WANTED TO TELL EVERYONE THE TRUTH BEFORE GETTING MARRIED, BUT...
...I KNEW THE MEDIA AND SOME OF YOU WOULD OPPOSE THE MARRIAGE. I DID NOT WISH TO JEOPARDIZE OUR UNION, SO THERE WAS NO OTHER OPTION.

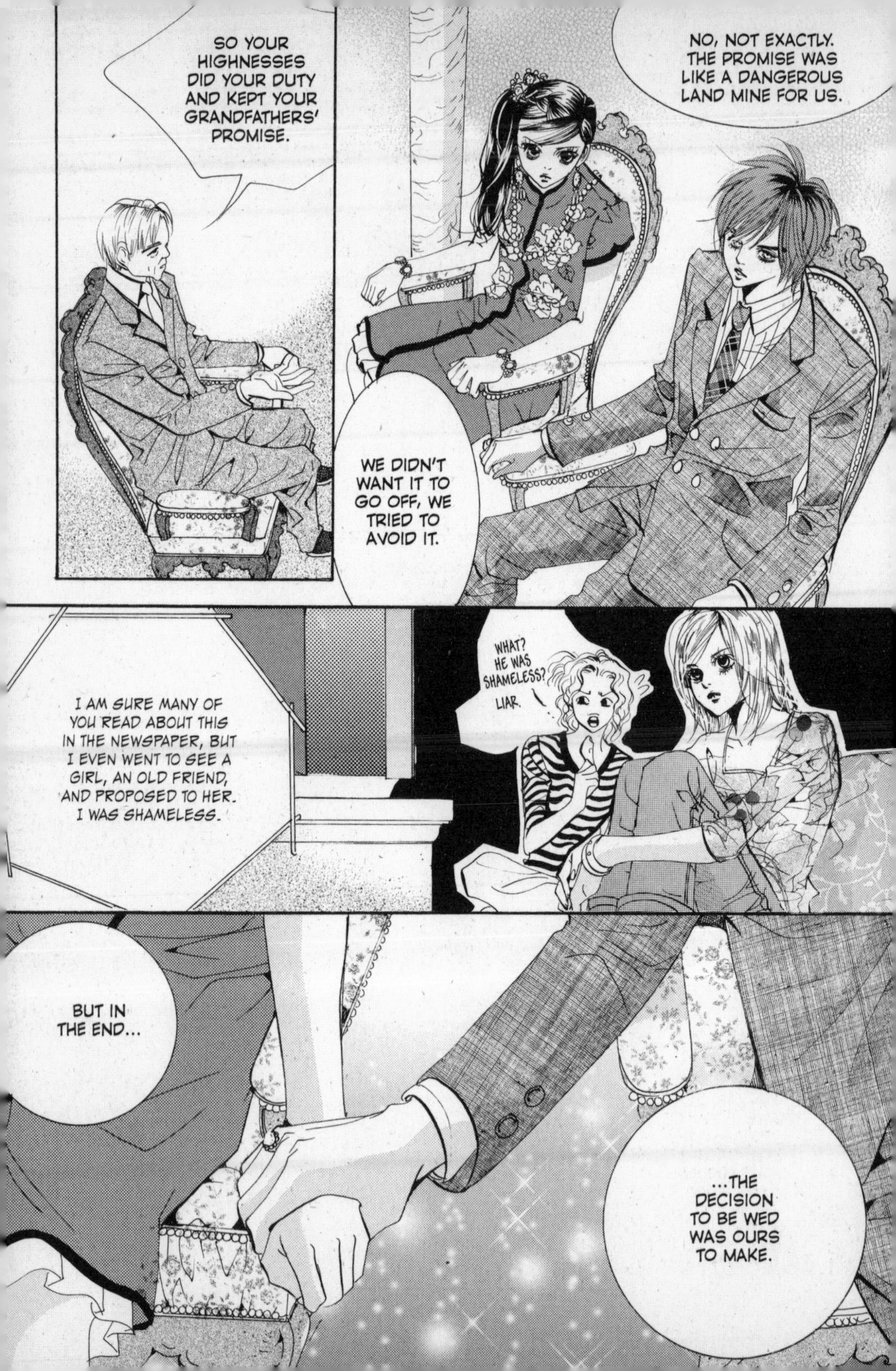
SO YOUR HIGHNESSES DID YOUR DUTY AND KEPT YOUR GRANDFATHERS' PROMISE.
NO, NOT EXACTLY. THE PROMISE WAS LIKE A DANGEROUS LAND MINE FOR US.
WE DIDN'T WANT IT TO GO OFF, WE TRIED TO AVOID IT.
I AM SURE MANY OF YOU READ ABOUT THIS IN THE NEWSPAPER, BUT I EVEN WENT TO SEE A GIRL, AN OLD FRIEND, AND PROPOSED TO HER. I WAS SHAMELESS.
WHAT? HE WAS SHAMELESS?
LIAR.
BUT IN THE END...
...THE DECISION TO BE WED WAS OURS TO MAKE.

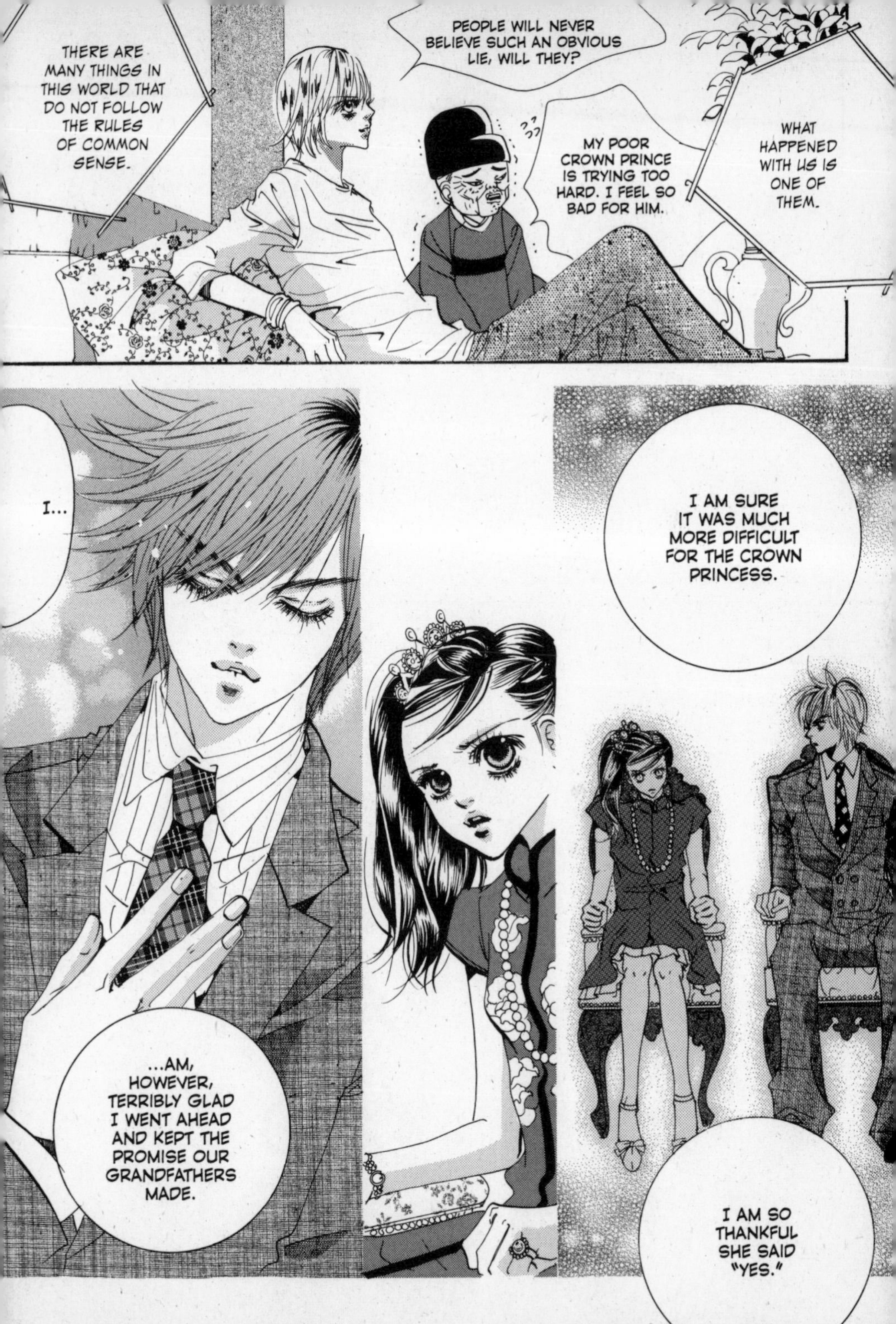
THERE ARE MANY THINGS IN THIS WORLD THAT DO NOT FOLLOW THE RULES OF COMMON SENSE.
PEOPLE WILL NEVER BELIEVE SUCH AN OBVIOUS LIE, WILL THEY?
MY POOR CROWN PRINCE IS TRYING TOO HARD. I FEEL SO BAD FOR HIM.
WHAT HAPPENED WITH US IS ONE OF THEM.
I...
...AM, HOWEVER, TERRIBLY GLAD I WENT AHEAD AND KEPT THE PROMISE OUR GRANDFATHERS MADE.
I AM SURE IT WAS MUCH MORE DIFFICULT FOR THE CROWN PRINCESS.
I AM SO THANKFUL SHE SAID "YES."

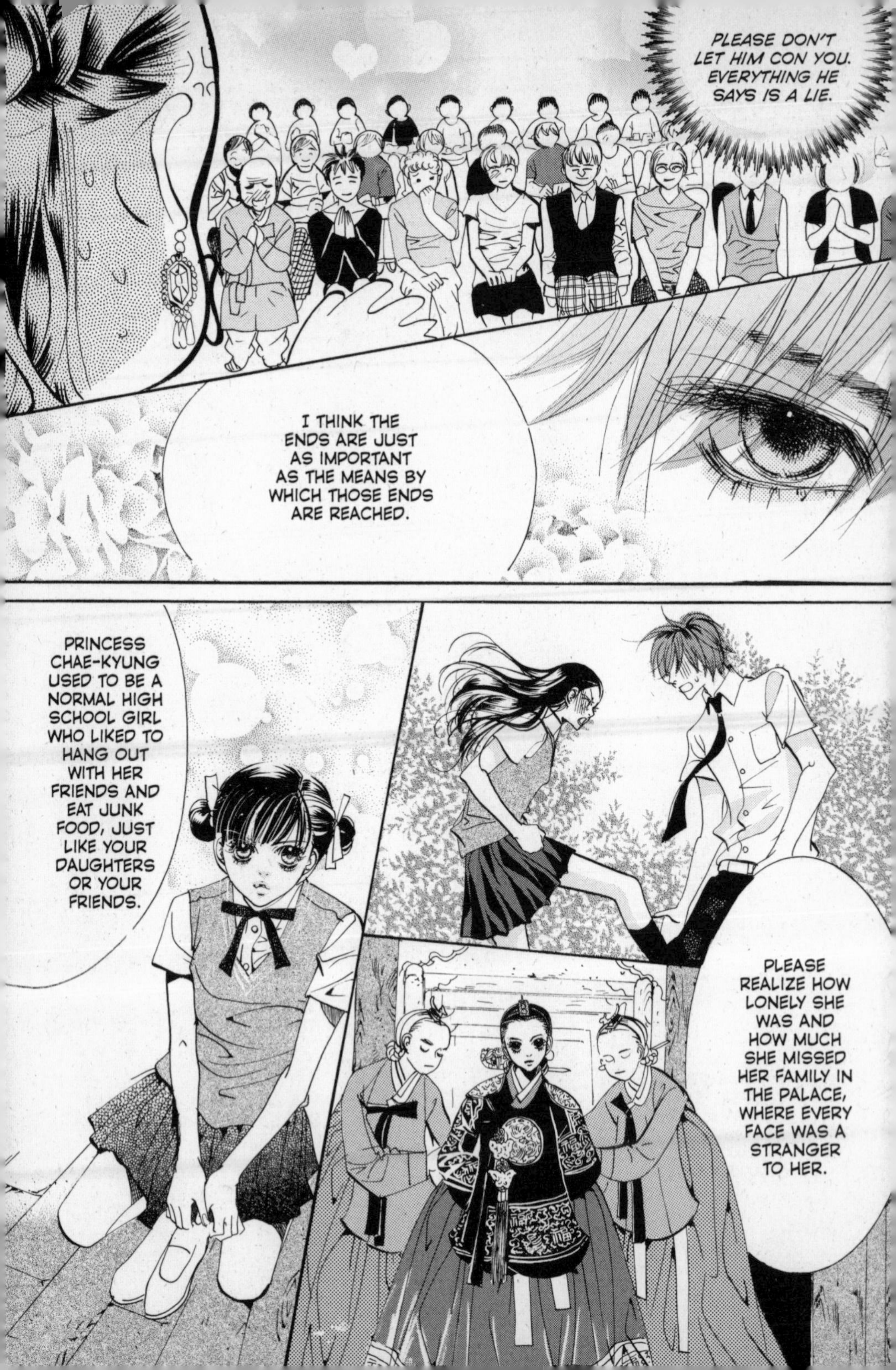

PLEASE DON'T LET HIM CON YOU. EVERYTHING HE SAYS IS A LIE.
I THINK THE ENDS ARE JUST AS IMPORTANT AS THE MEANS BY WHICH THOSE ENDS ARE REACHED.
PRINCESS CHAE-KYUNG USED TO BE A NORMAL HIGH SCHOOL GIRL WHO LIKED TO HANG OUT WITH HER FRIENDS AND EAT JUNK FOOD, JUST LIKE YOUR DAUGHTERS OR YOUR FRIENDS.
PLEASE REALIZE HOW LONELY SHE WAS AND HOW MUCH SHE MISSED HER FAMILY IN THE PALACE, WHERE EVERY FACE WAS A STRANGER TO HER.

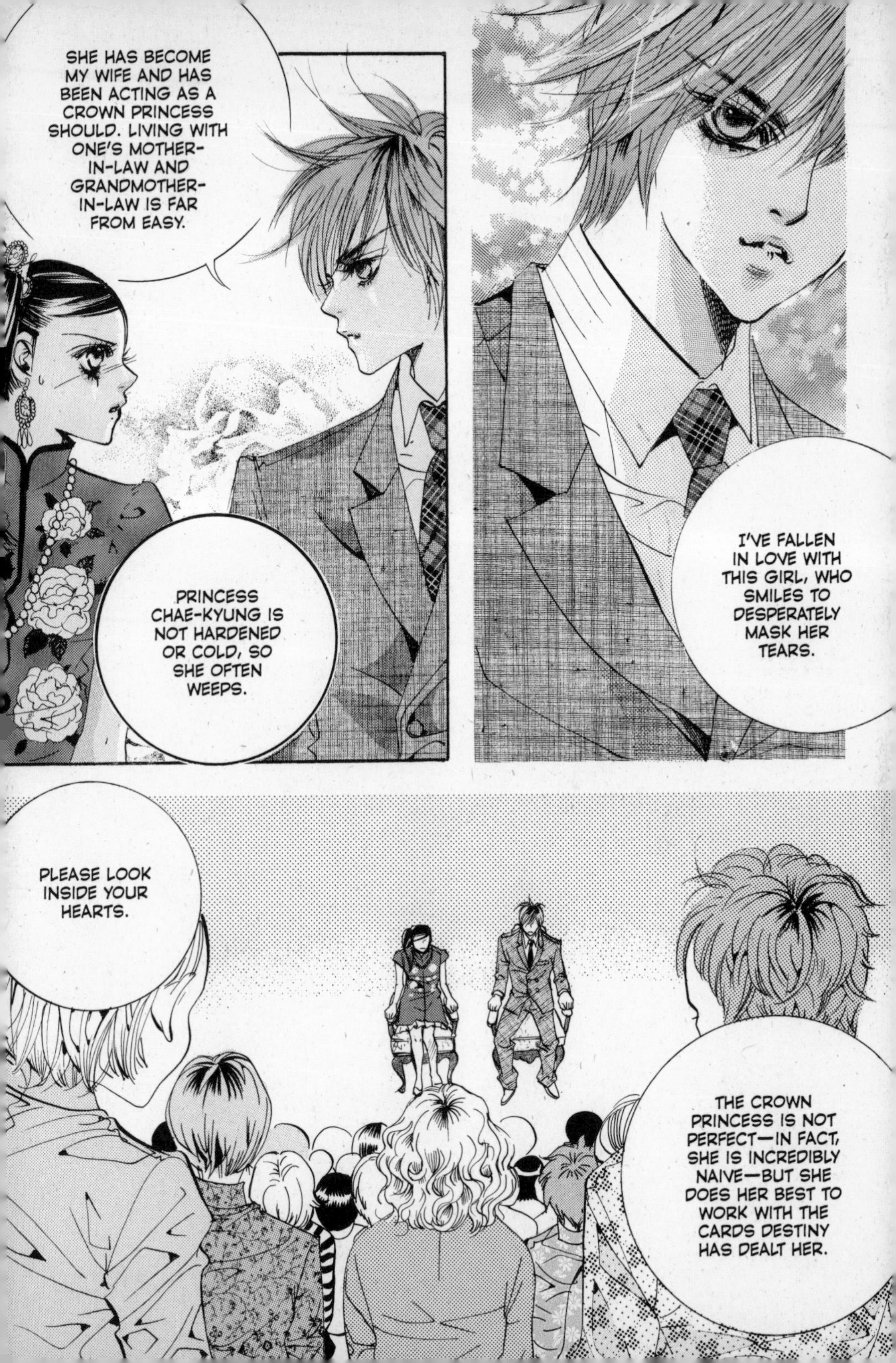
SHE HAS BECOME MY WIFE AND HAS BEEN ACTING AS A CROWN PRINCESS SHOULD. LIVING WITH ONE'S MOTHER-IN-LAW AND GRANDMOTHER-IN-LAW IS FAR FROM EASY.
PRINCESS CHAE-KYUNG IS NOT HARDENED OR COLD, SO SHE OFTEN WEEPS.
I'VE FALLEN IN LOVE WITH THIS GIRL, WHO SMILES TO DESPERATELY MASK HER TEARS.
PLEASE LOOK INSIDE YOUR HEARTS.
THE CROWN PRINCESS IS NOT PERFECT—IN FACT, SHE IS INCREDIBLY NAIVE—BUT SHE DOES HER BEST TO WORK WITH THE CARDS DESTINY HAS DEALT HER.

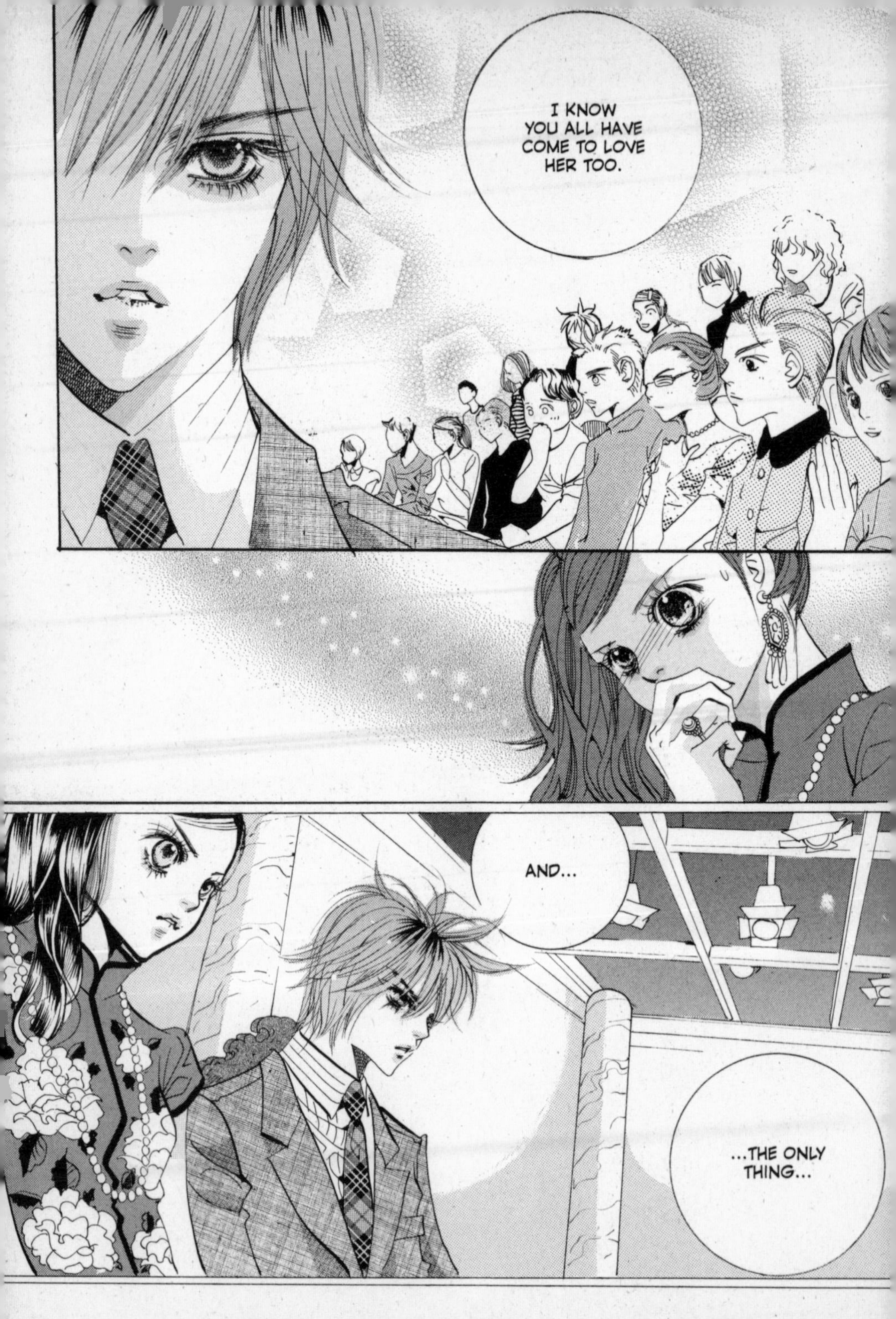
I KNOW YOU ALL HAVE COME TO LOVE HER TOO.
AND...
...THE ONLY THING...

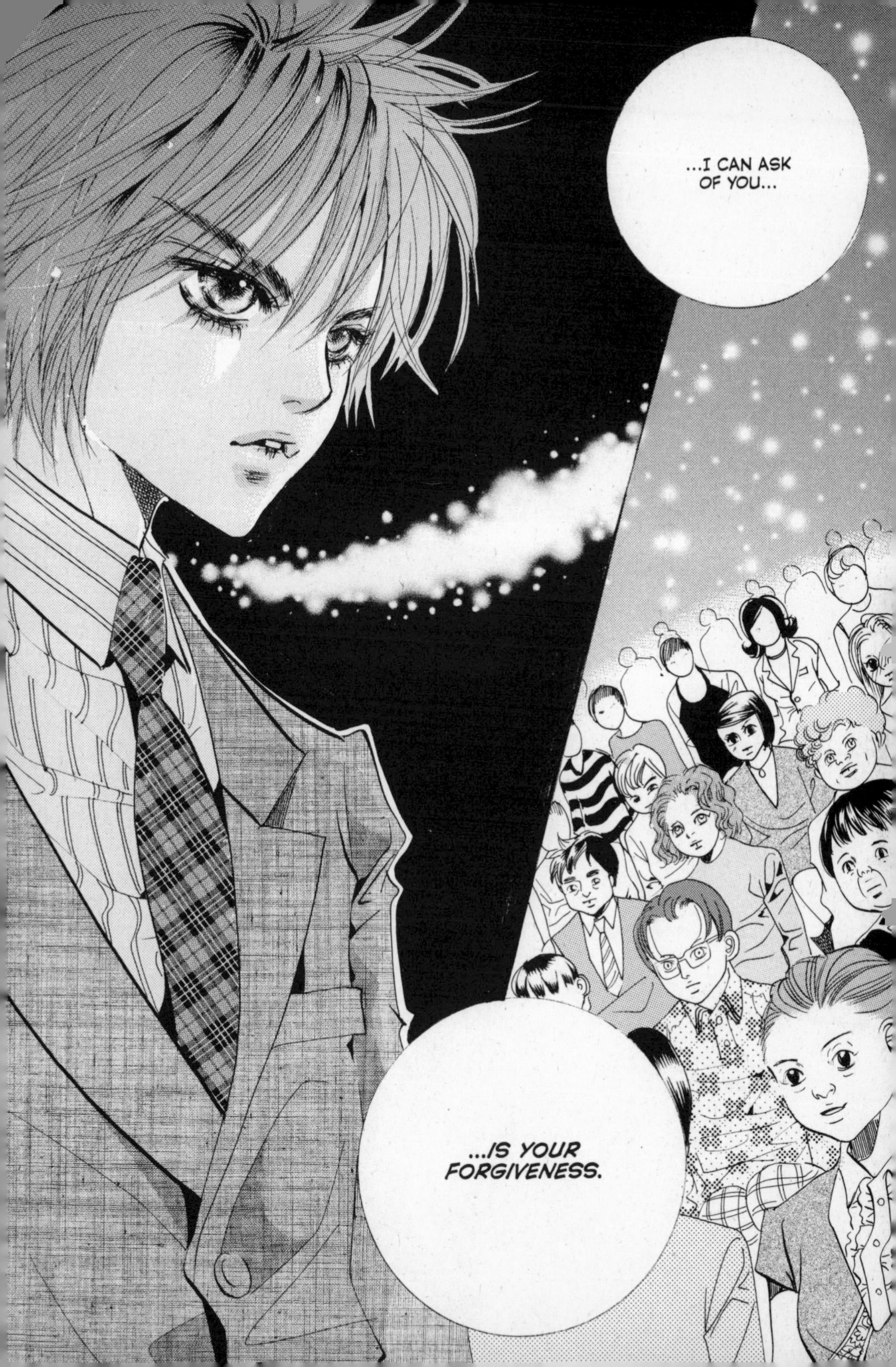
...I CAN ASK
OF YOU...
...IS YOUR
FORGIVENESS.

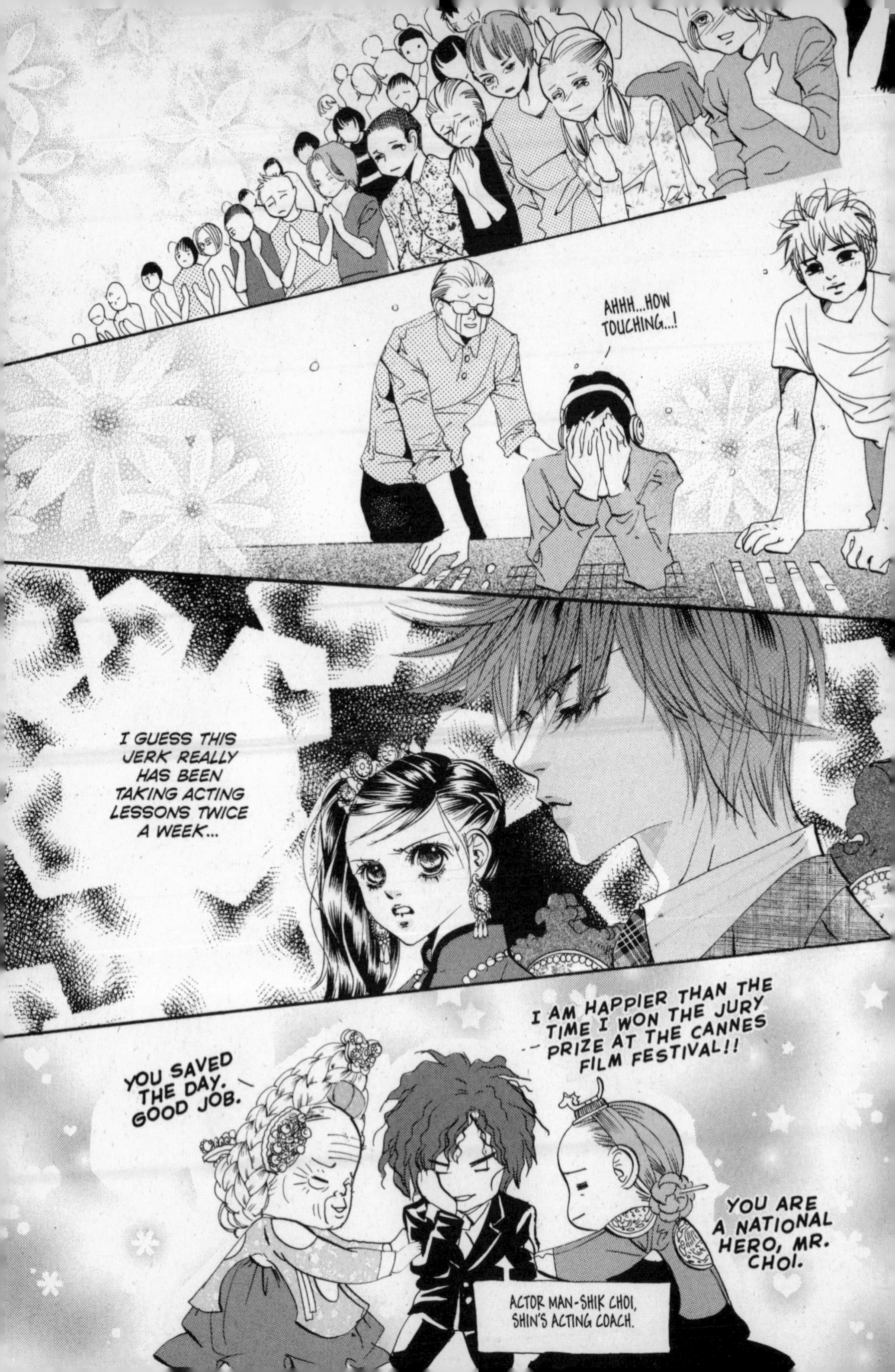
AHHH...HOW TOUCHING...!
I GUESS THIS JERK REALLY HAS BEEN TAKING ACTING LESSONS TWICE A WEEK...
YOU SAVED THE DAY. GOOD JOB.
I AM HAPPIER THAN THE TIME I WON THE JURY PRIZE AT THE CANNES FILM FESTIVAL!!
YOU ARE A NATIONAL HERO, MR. CHOI.
ACTOR MAN-SHIK CHOI, SHIN'S ACTING COACH.

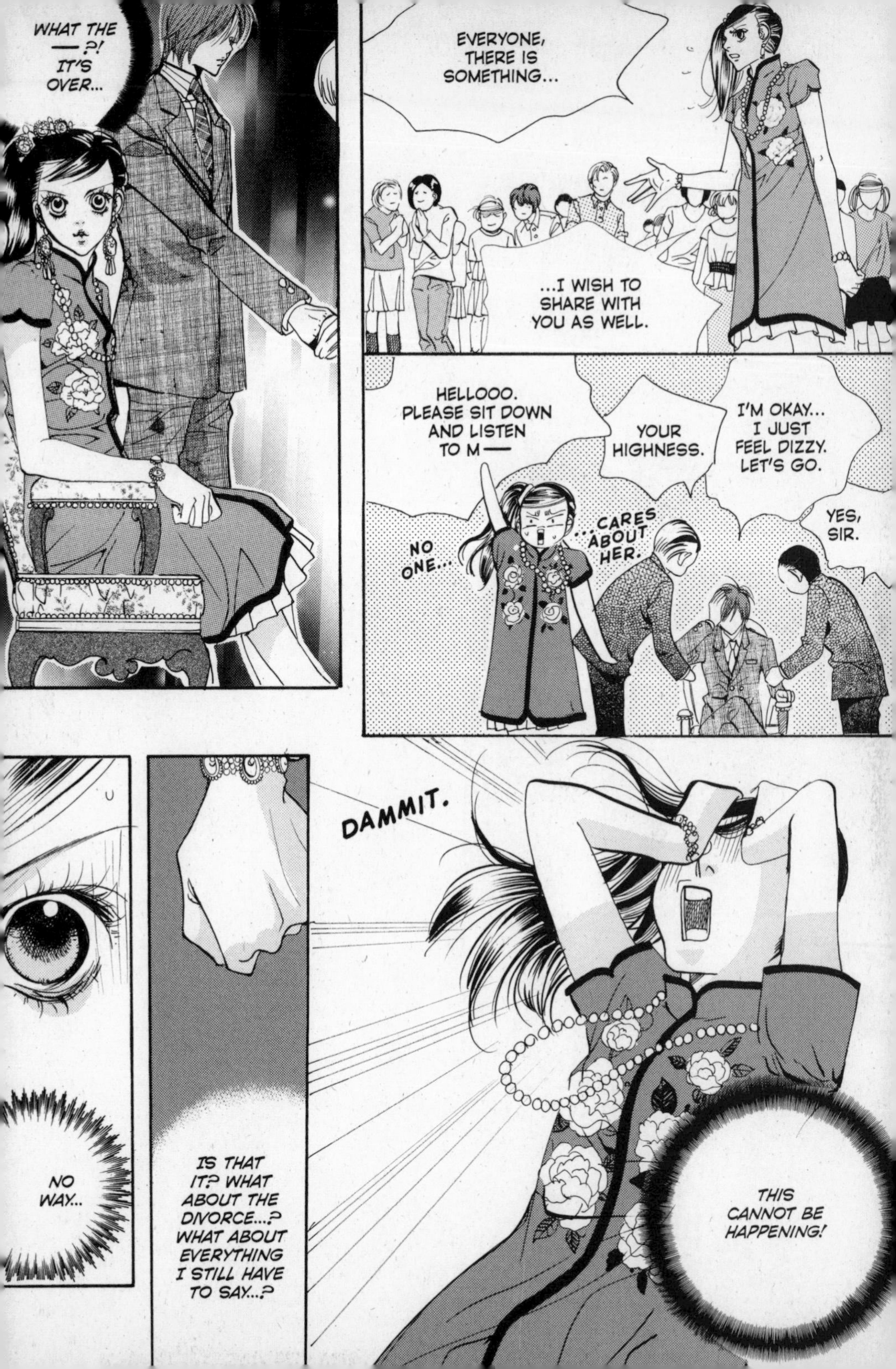
WHAT THE —?! IT'S OVER...
EVERYONE, THERE IS SOMETHING...
...I WISH TO SHARE WITH YOU AS WELL.
HELLOOO. PLEASE SIT DOWN AND LISTEN TO M—
YOUR HIGHNESS.
I'M OKAY... I JUST FEEL DIZZY. LET'S GO.
NO ONE...
...CARES ABOUT HER.
YES, SIR.
NO WAY...
IS THAT IT? WHAT ABOUT THE DIVORCE...? WHAT ABOUT EVERYTHING I STILL HAVE TO SAY...?
DAMMIT.
THIS CANNOT BE HAPPENING!

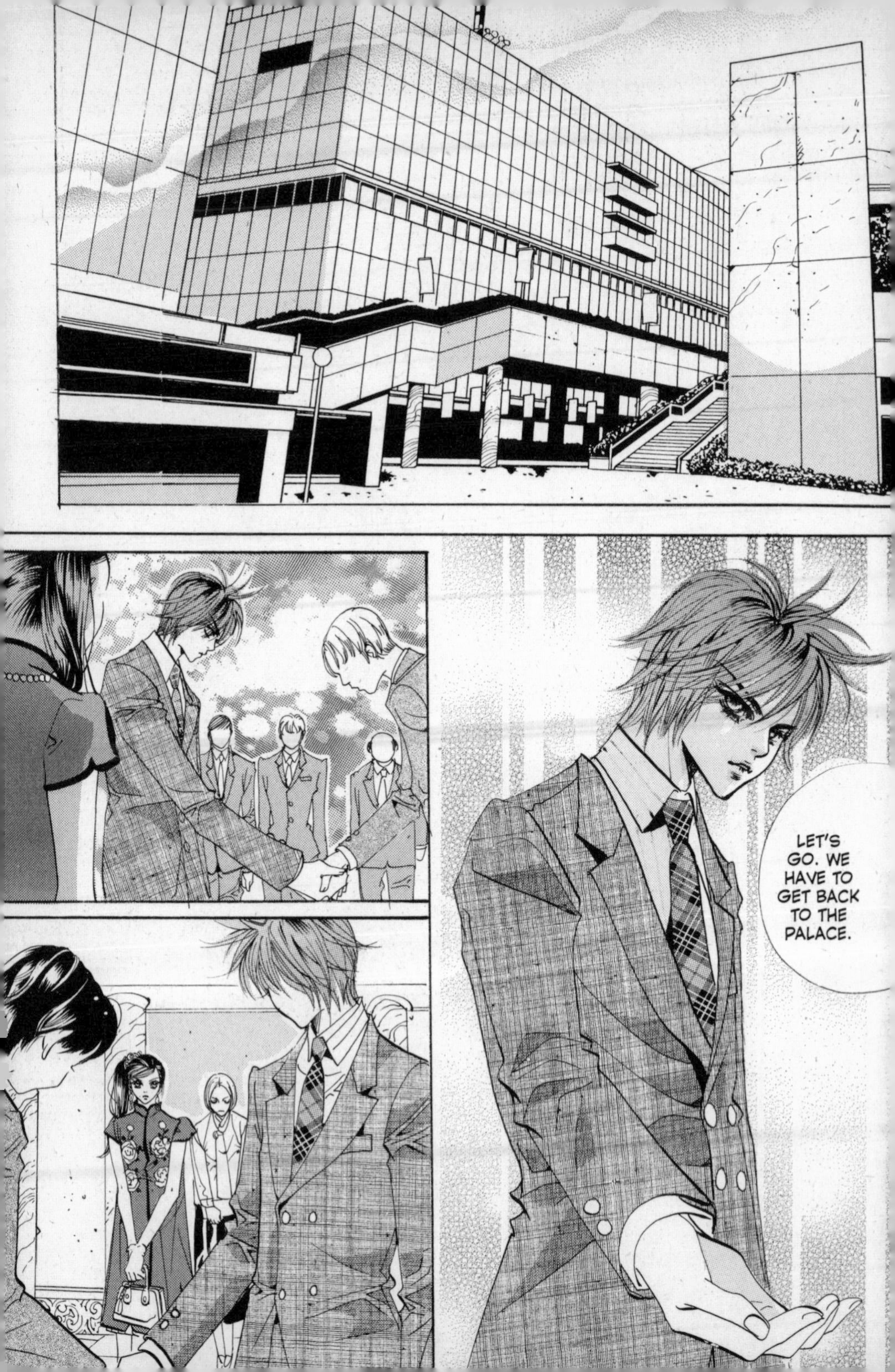
LET'S GO. WE HAVE TO GET BACK TO THE PALACE.

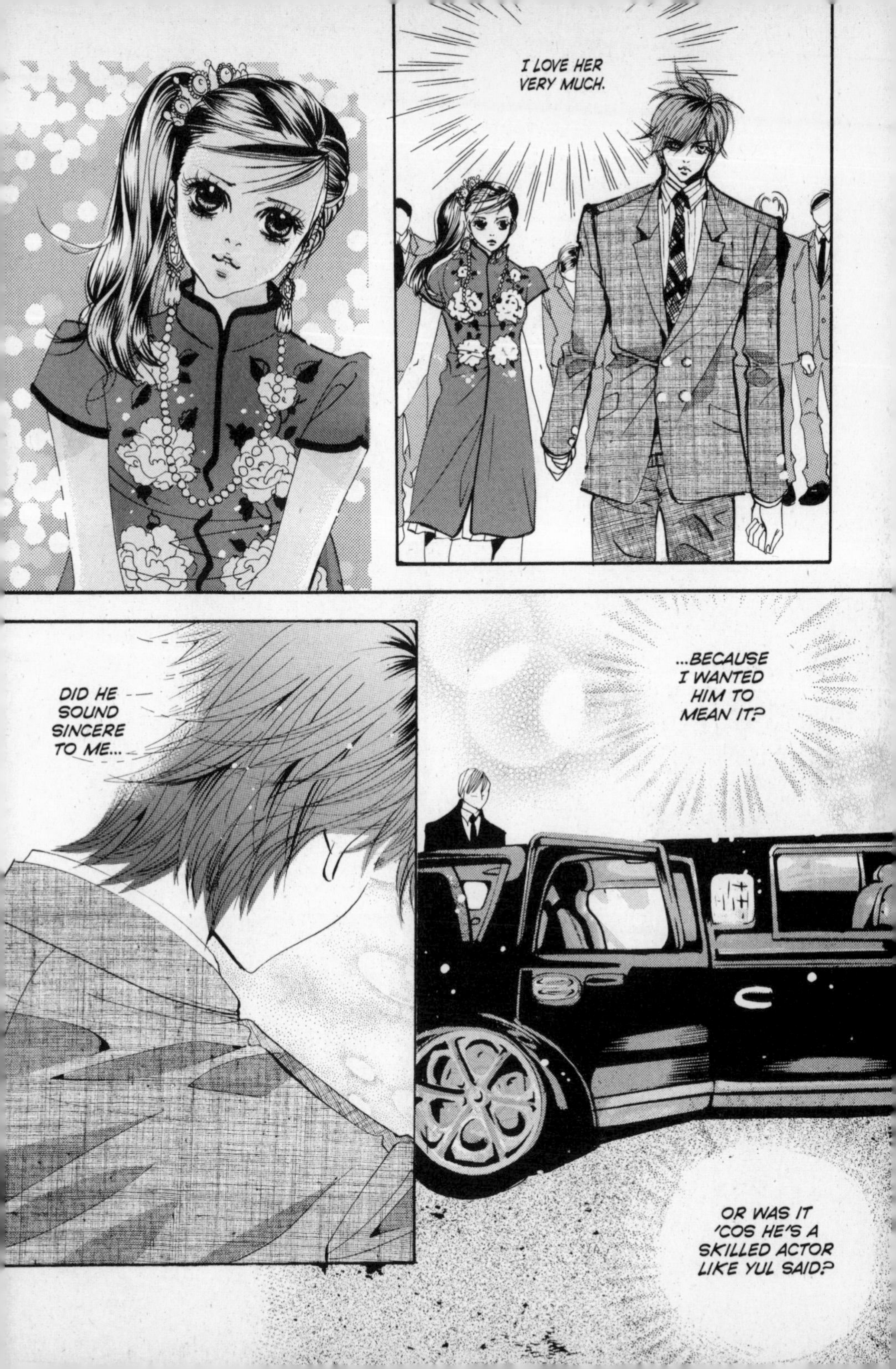
I LOVE HER VERY MUCH.
DID HE SOUND SINCERE TO ME...
...BECAUSE I WANTED HIM TO MEAN IT?
OR WAS IT 'COS HE'S A SKILLED ACTOR LIKE YUL SAID?

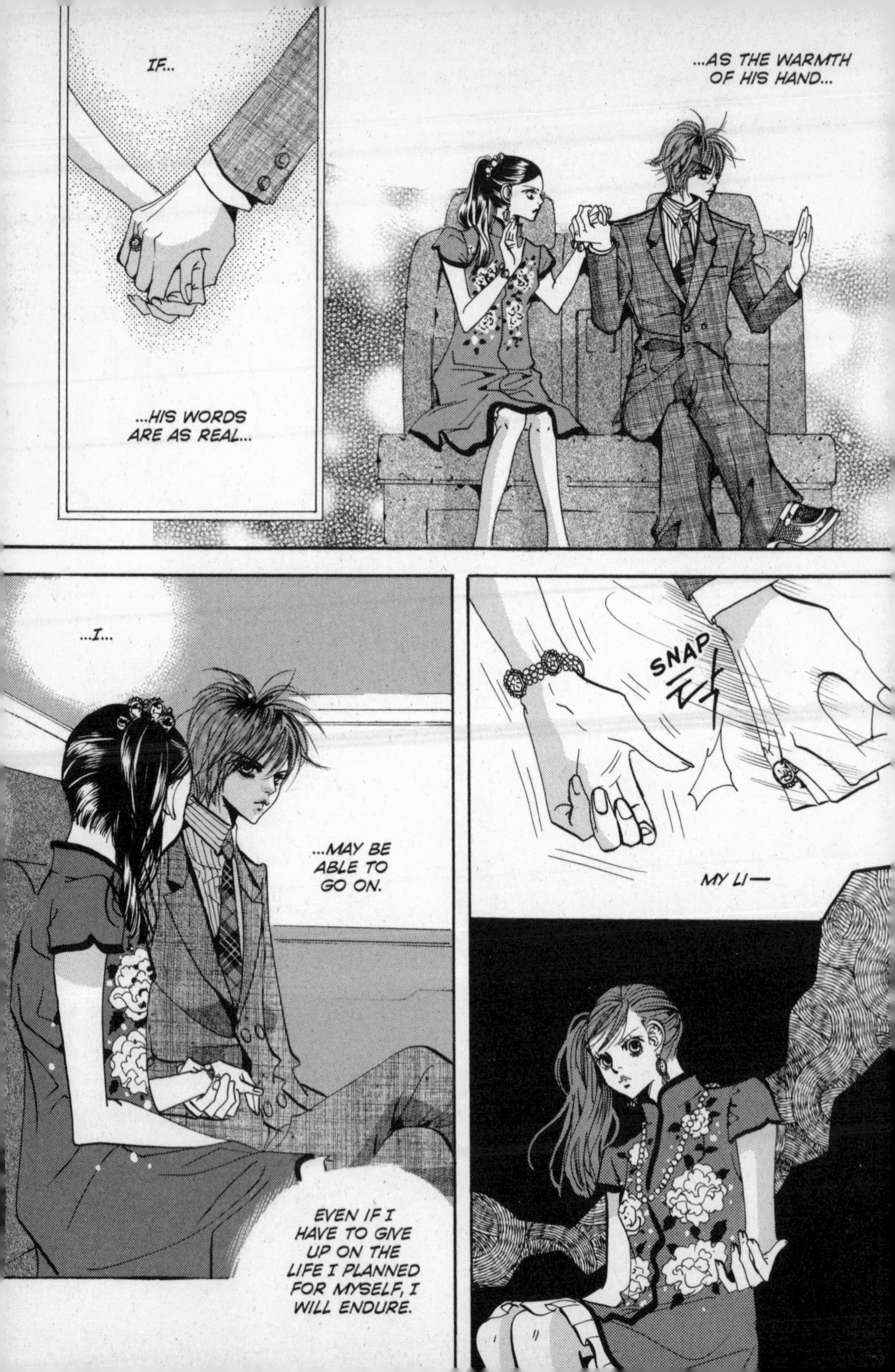
IF..
...HIS WORDS ARE AS REAL...
...AS THE WARMTH OF HIS HAND...
...I...
...MAY BE ABLE TO GO ON.
EVEN IF I HAVE TO GIVE UP ON THE LIFE I PLANNED FOR MYSELF, I WILL ENDURE.
SNAP
MY LI—

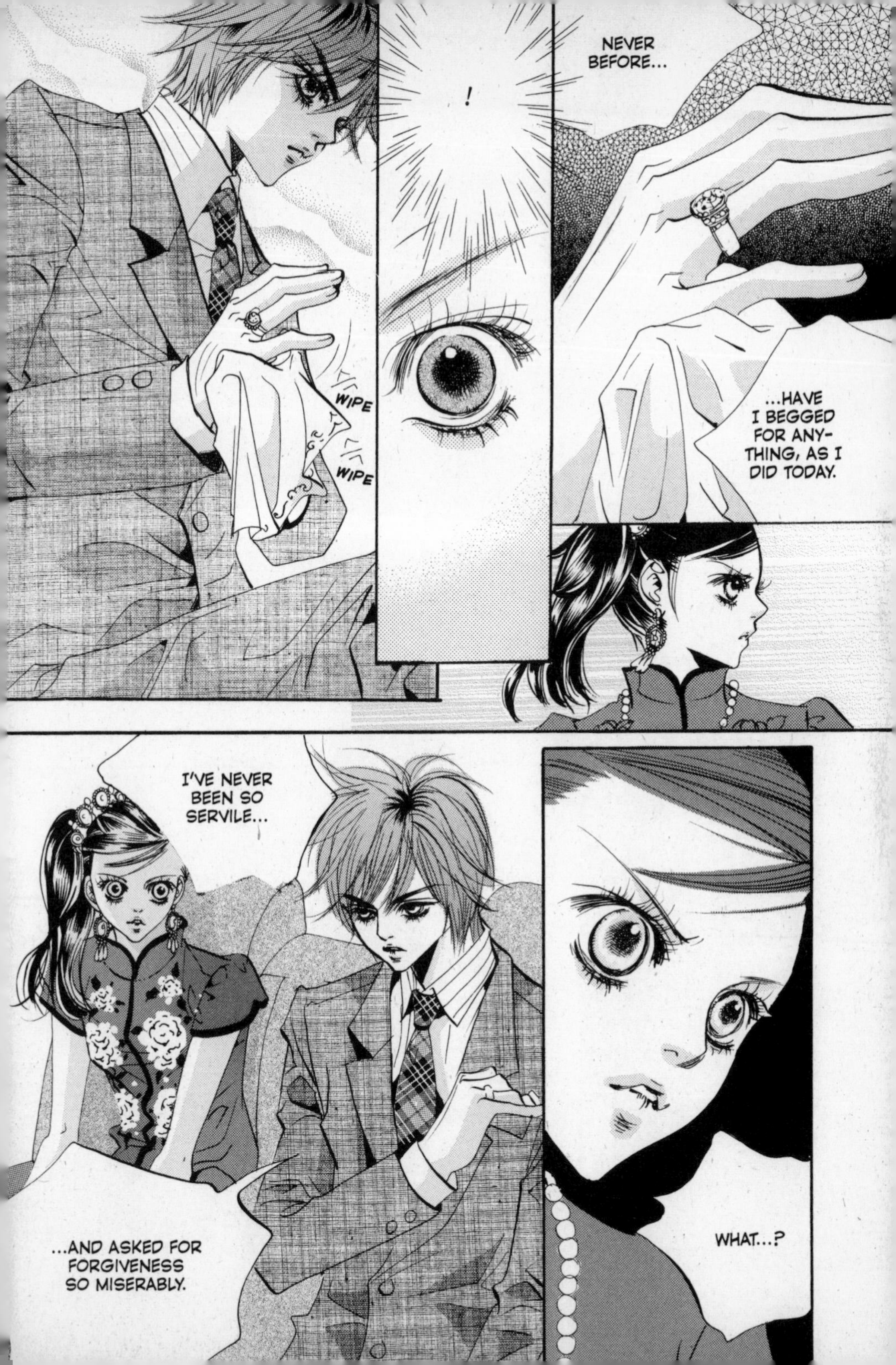
WIPE
WIPE
!
NEVER BEFORE...
...HAVE I BEGGED FOR ANY-THING, AS I DID TODAY.
I'VE NEVER BEEN SO SERVILE...
...AND ASKED FOR FORGIVENESS SO MISERABLY.
WHAT...?

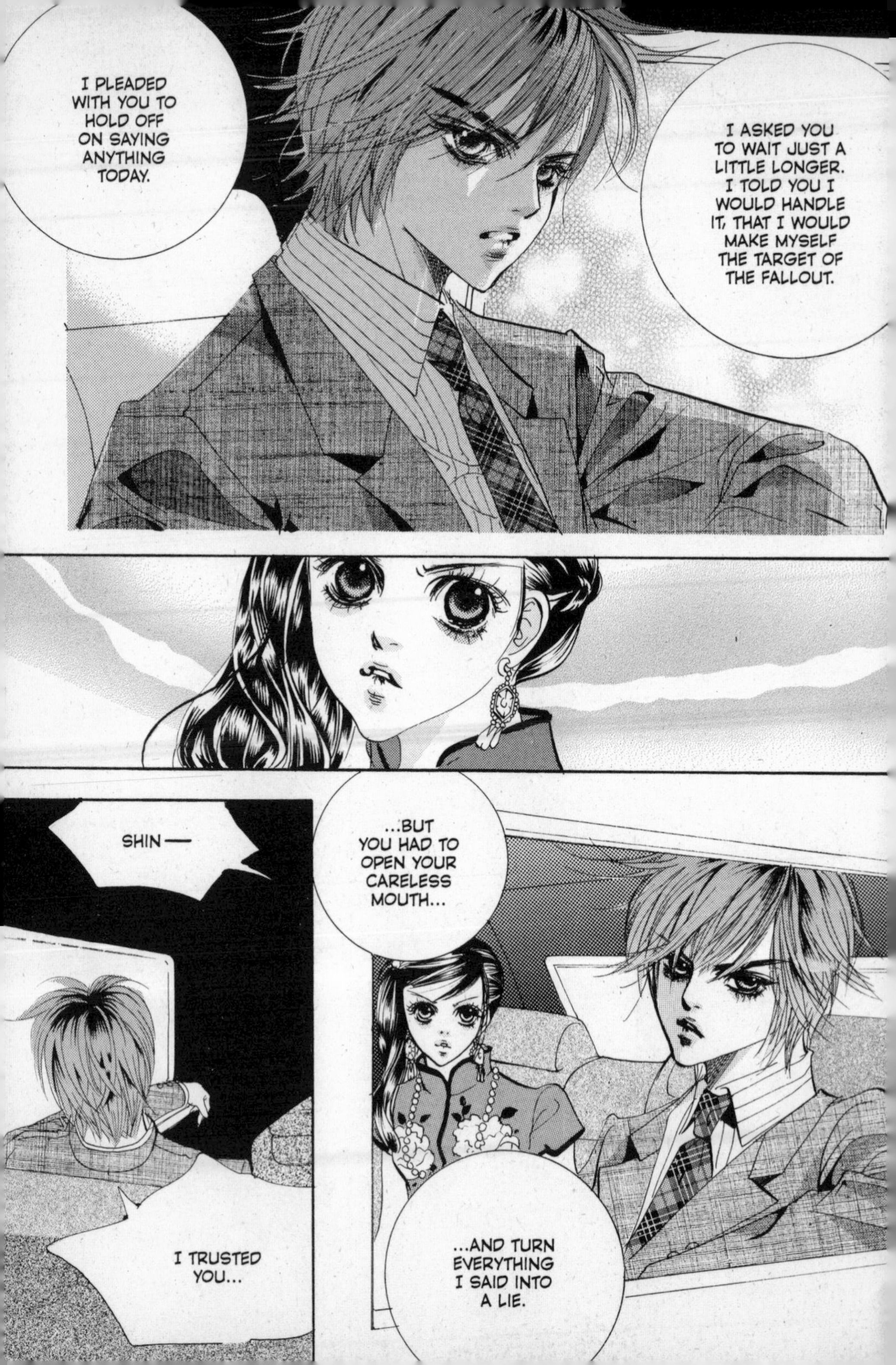
I PLEADED WITH YOU TO HOLD OFF ON SAYING ANYTHING TODAY.
I ASKED YOU TO WAIT JUST A LITTLE LONGER. I TOLD YOU I WOULD HANDLE IT, THAT I WOULD MAKE MYSELF THE TARGET OF THE FALLOUT.
SHIN—
...BUT YOU HAD TO OPEN YOUR CARELESS MOUTH...
I TRUSTED YOU...
...AND TURN EVERYTHING I SAID INTO A LIE.

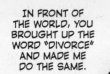

IN FRONT OF
THE WORLD, YOU
BROUGHT UP THE
WORD "DIVORCE"
AND MADE ME
DO THE SAME.

LISTEN TO
ME, SHIN...

I WON'T
STAND FOR THIS
ANYMORE.

I TRUSTED
AND RESPECTED
YOU, BUT YOU
WALKED ALL
OVER ME.

YOU
WANTED
A HUGE
PROBLEM,
NOW
YOU'VE
GOT IT.

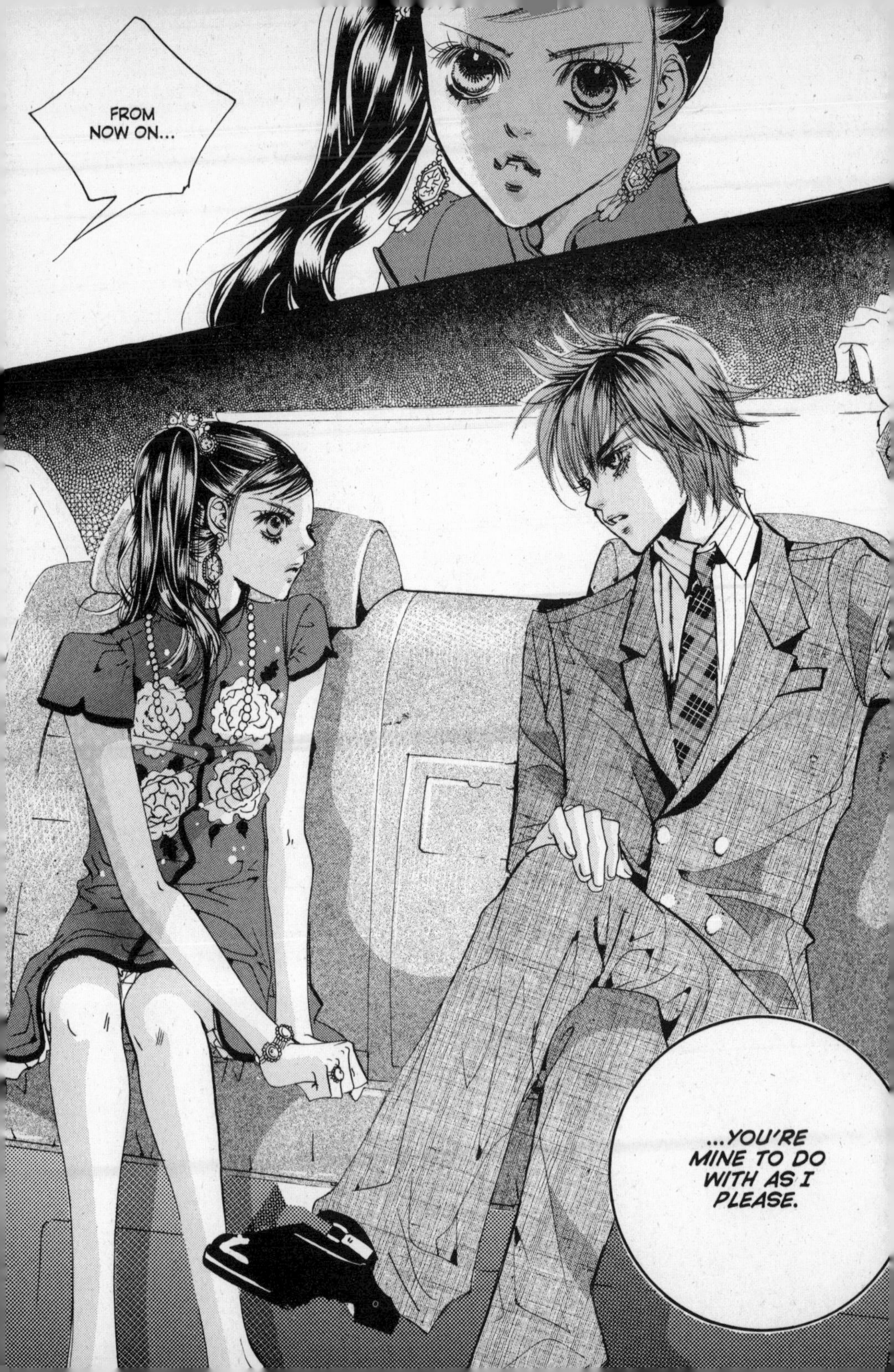
FROM NOW ON...
...YOU'RE MINE TO DO WITH AS I PLEASE.

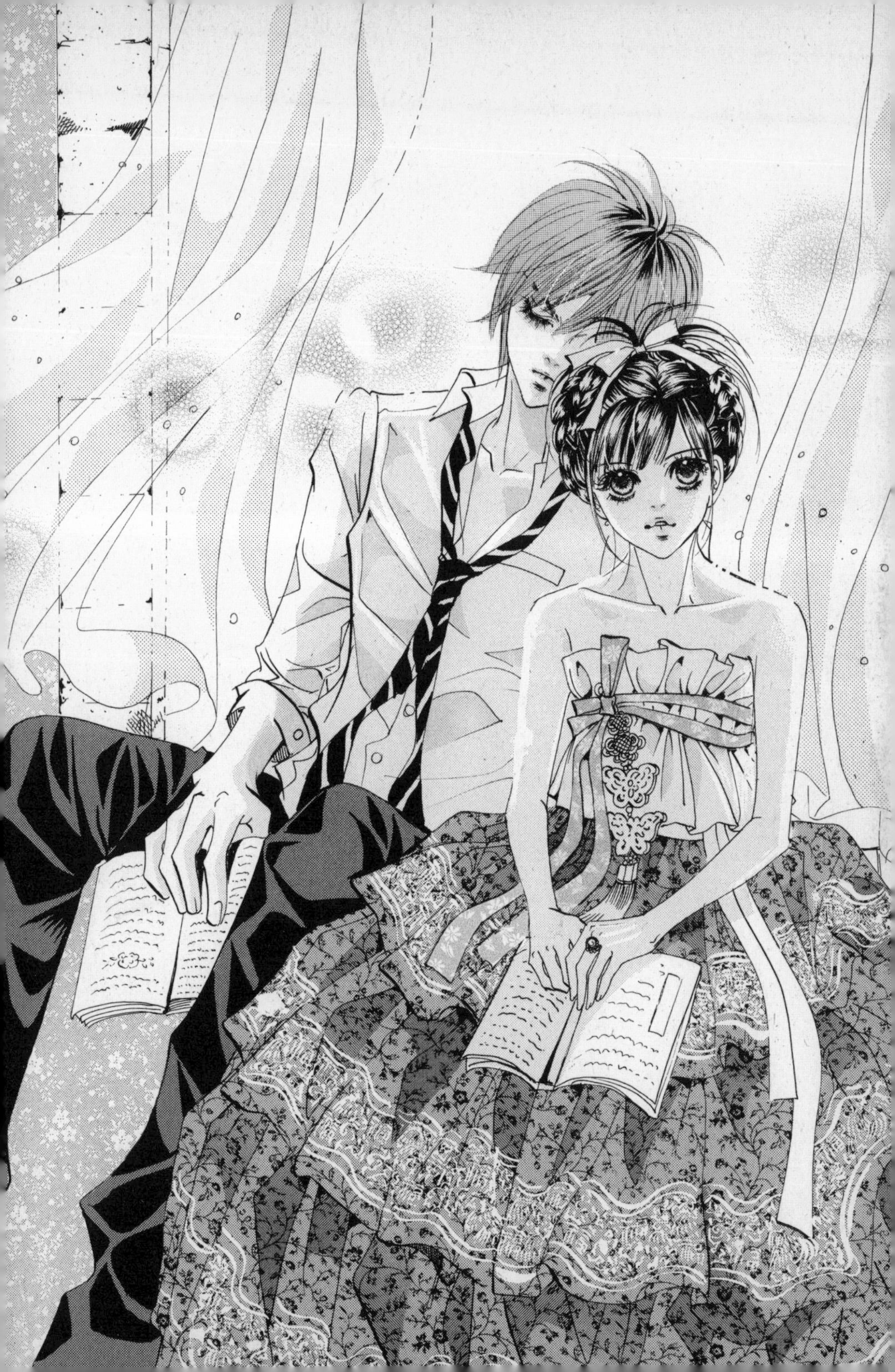

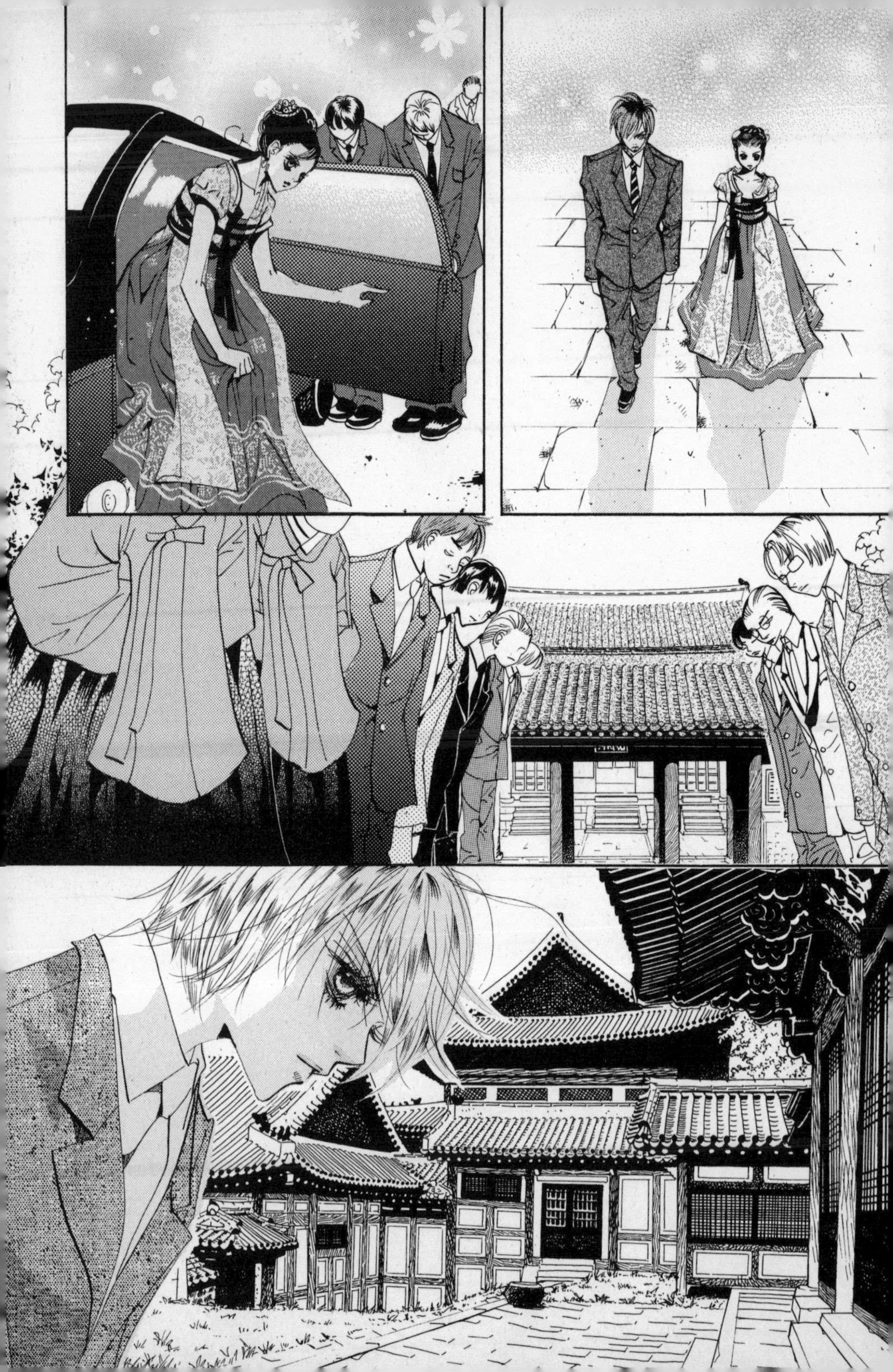

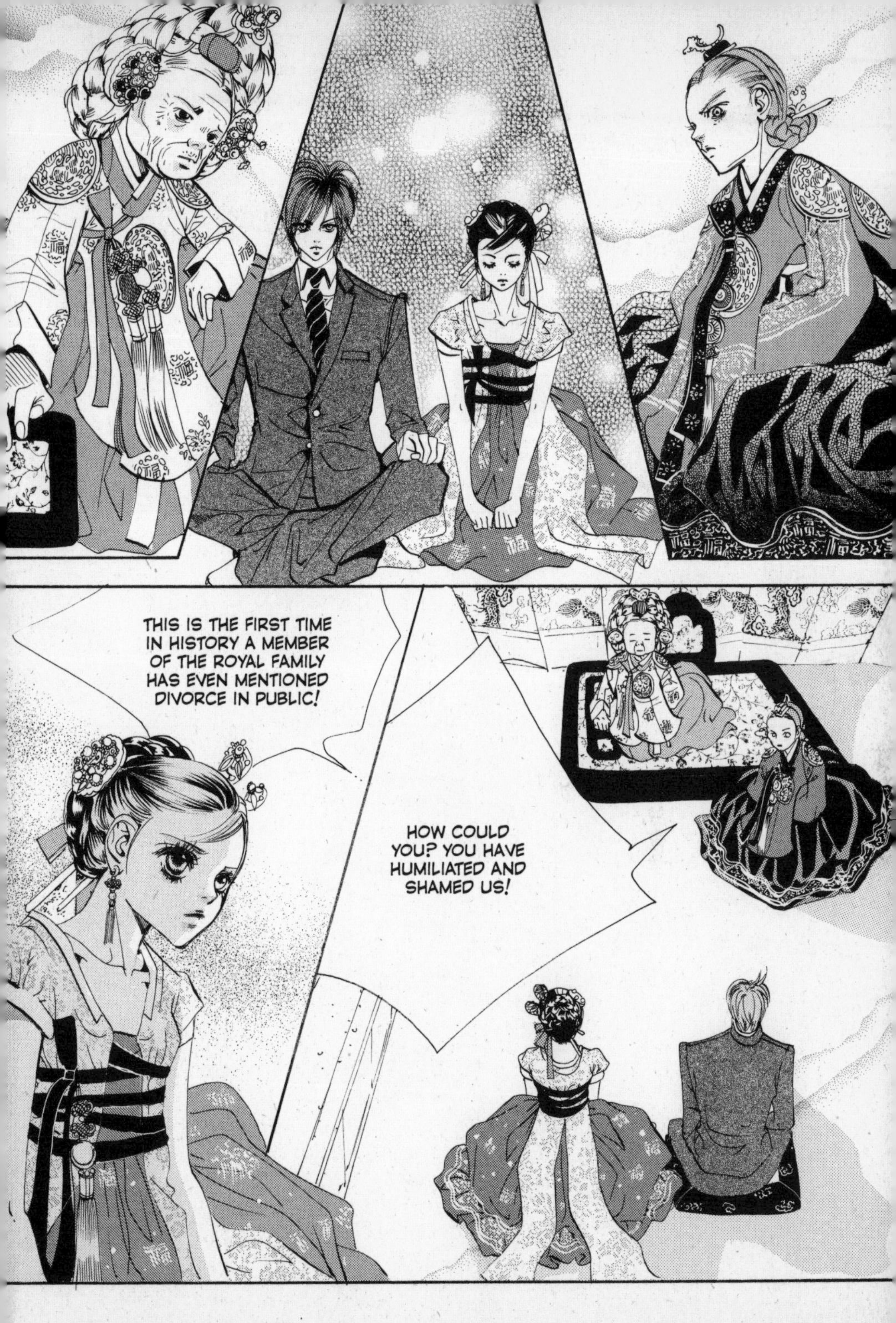
THIS IS THE FIRST TIME IN HISTORY A MEMBER OF THE ROYAL FAMILY HAS EVEN MENTIONED DIVORCE IN PUBLIC!
HOW COULD YOU? YOU HAVE HUMILIATED AND SHAMED US!

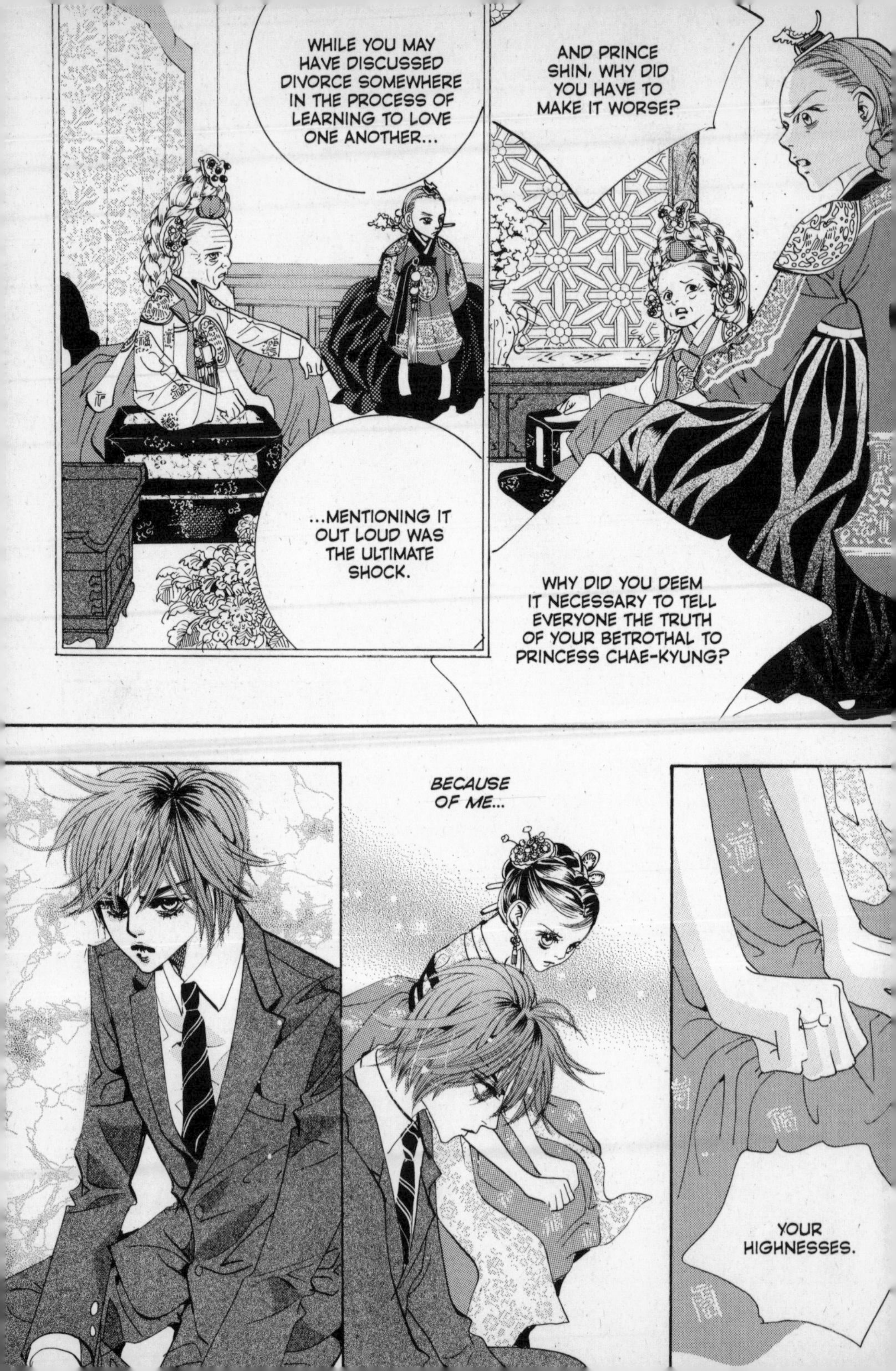
WHILE YOU MAY HAVE DISCUSSED DIVORCE SOMEWHERE IN THE PROCESS OF LEARNING TO LOVE ONE ANOTHER...
...MENTIONING IT OUT LOUD WAS THE ULTIMATE SHOCK.
AND PRINCE SHIN, WHY DID YOU HAVE TO MAKE IT WORSE?
WHY DID YOU DEEM IT NECESSARY TO TELL EVERYONE THE TRUTH OF YOUR BETROTHAL TO PRINCESS CHAE-KYUNG?
BECAUSE OF ME...
YOUR HIGHNESSES.

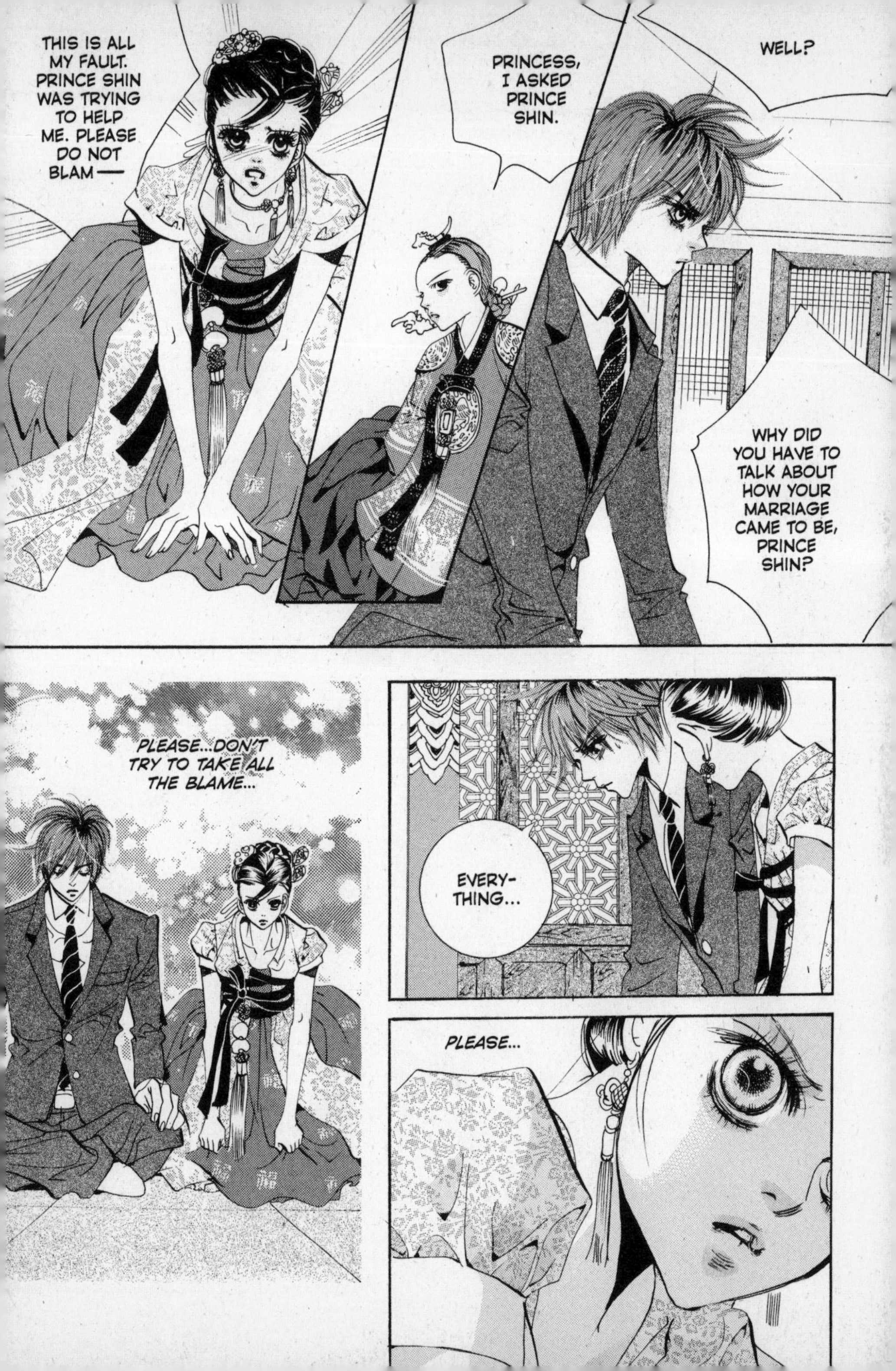
THIS IS ALL MY FAULT. PRINCE SHIN WAS TRYING TO HELP ME. PLEASE DO NOT BLAM—
PRINCESS, I ASKED PRINCE SHIN.
WELL?
WHY DID YOU HAVE TO TALK ABOUT HOW YOUR MARRIAGE CAME TO BE, PRINCE SHIN?
PLEASE...DON'T TRY TO TAKE ALL THE BLAME...
EVERY-THING...
PLEASE...

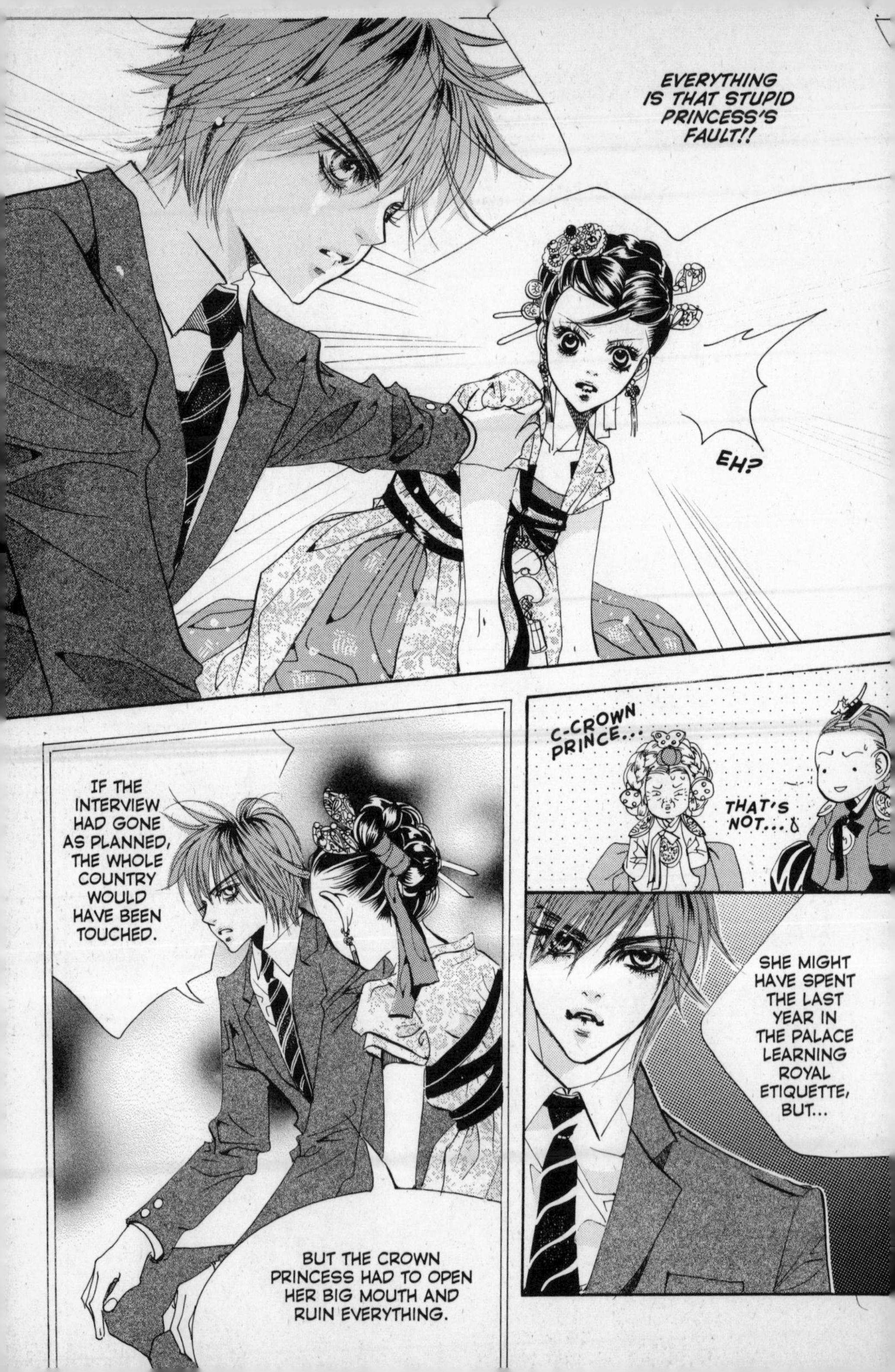
EVERYTHING IS THAT STUPID PRINCESS'S FAULT!!
EH?
IF THE INTERVIEW HAD GONE AS PLANNED, THE WHOLE COUNTRY WOULD HAVE BEEN TOUCHED.
BUT THE CROWN PRINCESS HAD TO OPEN HER BIG MOUTH AND RUIN EVERYTHING.
C-CROWN PRINCE...
THAT'S NOT...
SHE MIGHT HAVE SPENT THE LAST YEAR IN THE PALACE LEARNING ROYAL ETIQUETTE, BUT...

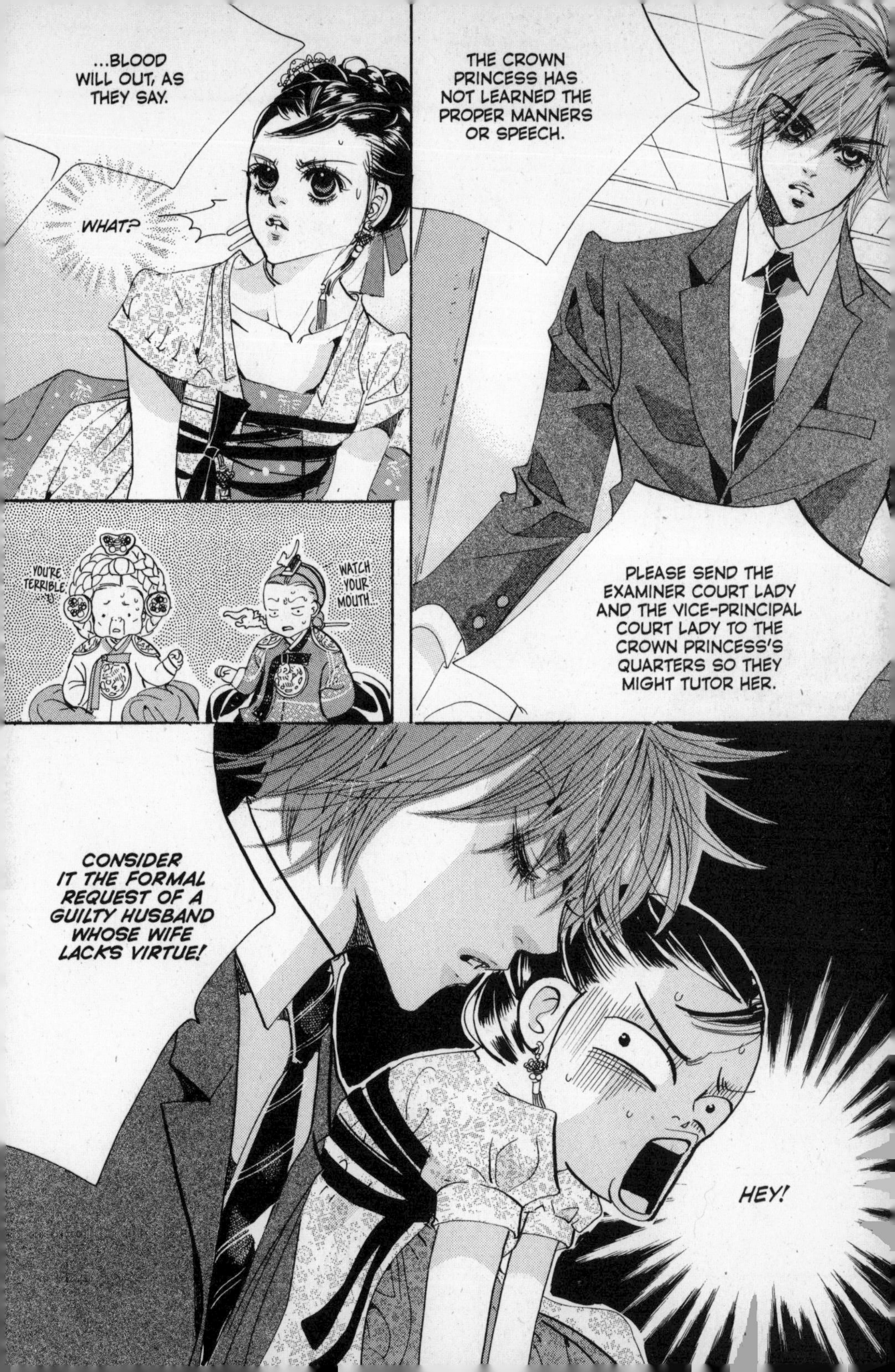
...BLOOD WILL OUT, AS THEY SAY.
WHAT?
THE CROWN PRINCESS HAS NOT LEARNED THE PROPER MANNERS OR SPEECH.
YOU'RE TERRIBLE.
WATCH YOUR MOUTH.
PLEASE SEND THE EXAMINER COURT LADY AND THE VICE-PRINCIPAL COURT LADY TO THE CROWN PRINCESS'S QUARTERS SO THEY MIGHT TUTOR HER.
CONSIDER IT THE FORMAL REQUEST OF A GUILTY HUSBAND WHOSE WIFE LACKS VIRTUE!
HEY!

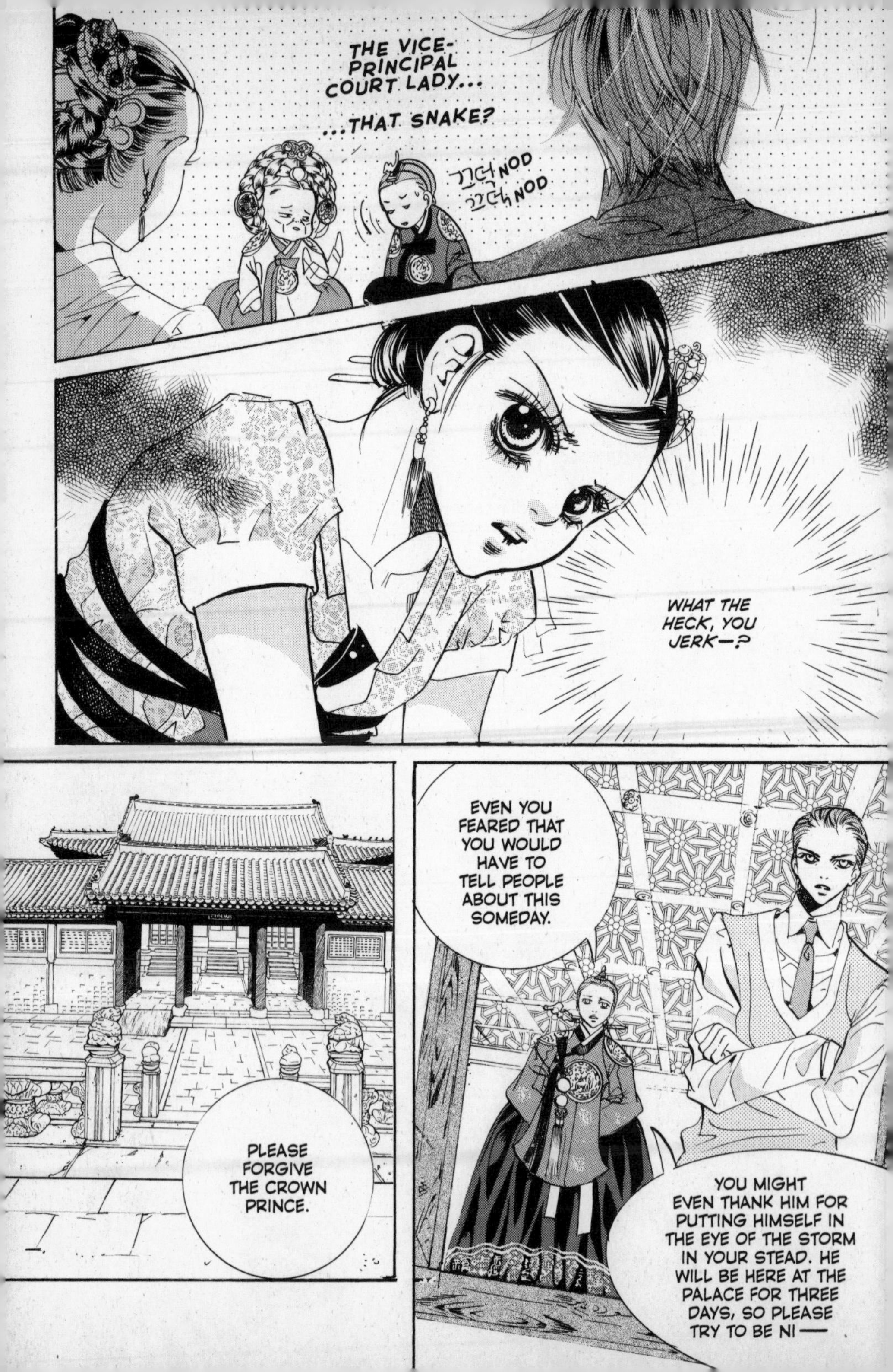
THE VICE-PRINCIPAL COURT LADY...
...THAT SNAKE?
끄덕 NOD
끄덕 NOD
WHAT THE HECK, YOU JERK—?
PLEASE FORGIVE THE CROWN PRINCE.
EVEN YOU FEARED THAT YOU WOULD HAVE TO TELL PEOPLE ABOUT THIS SOMEDAY.
YOU MIGHT EVEN THANK HIM FOR PUTTING HIMSELF IN THE EYE OF THE STORM IN YOUR STEAD. HE WILL BE HERE AT THE PALACE FOR THREE DAYS, SO PLEASE TRY TO BE NI—

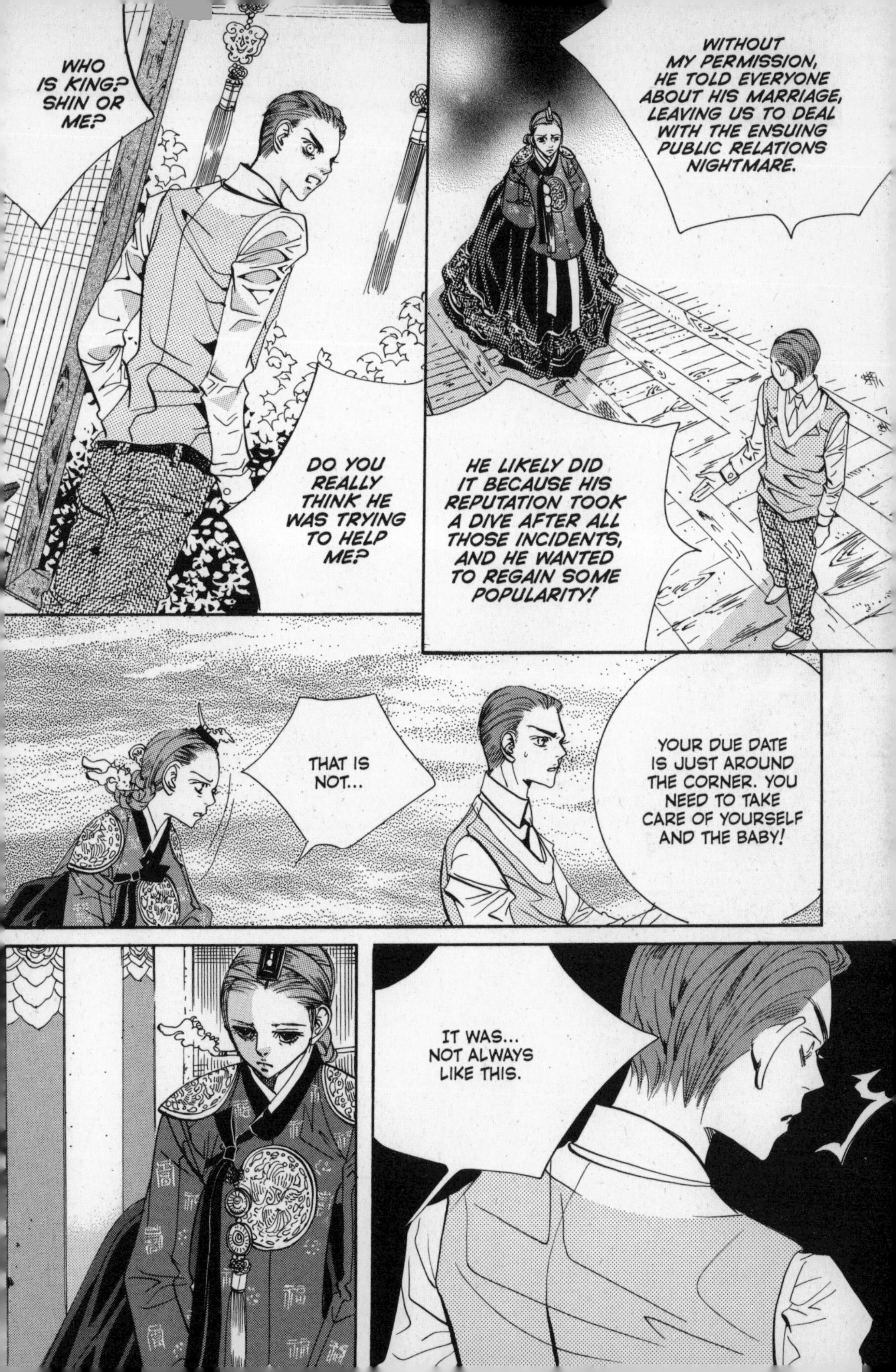
WHO IS KING? SHIN OR ME?
DO YOU REALLY THINK HE WAS TRYING TO HELP ME?
WITHOUT MY PERMISSION, HE TOLD EVERYONE ABOUT HIS MARRIAGE, LEAVING US TO DEAL WITH THE ENSUING PUBLIC RELATIONS NIGHTMARE.
HE LIKELY DID IT BECAUSE HIS REPUTATION TOOK A DIVE AFTER ALL THOSE INCIDENTS, AND HE WANTED TO REGAIN SOME POPULARITY!
THAT IS NOT...
YOUR DUE DATE IS JUST AROUND THE CORNER. YOU NEED TO TAKE CARE OF YOURSELF AND THE BABY!
IT WAS... NOT ALWAYS LIKE THIS.

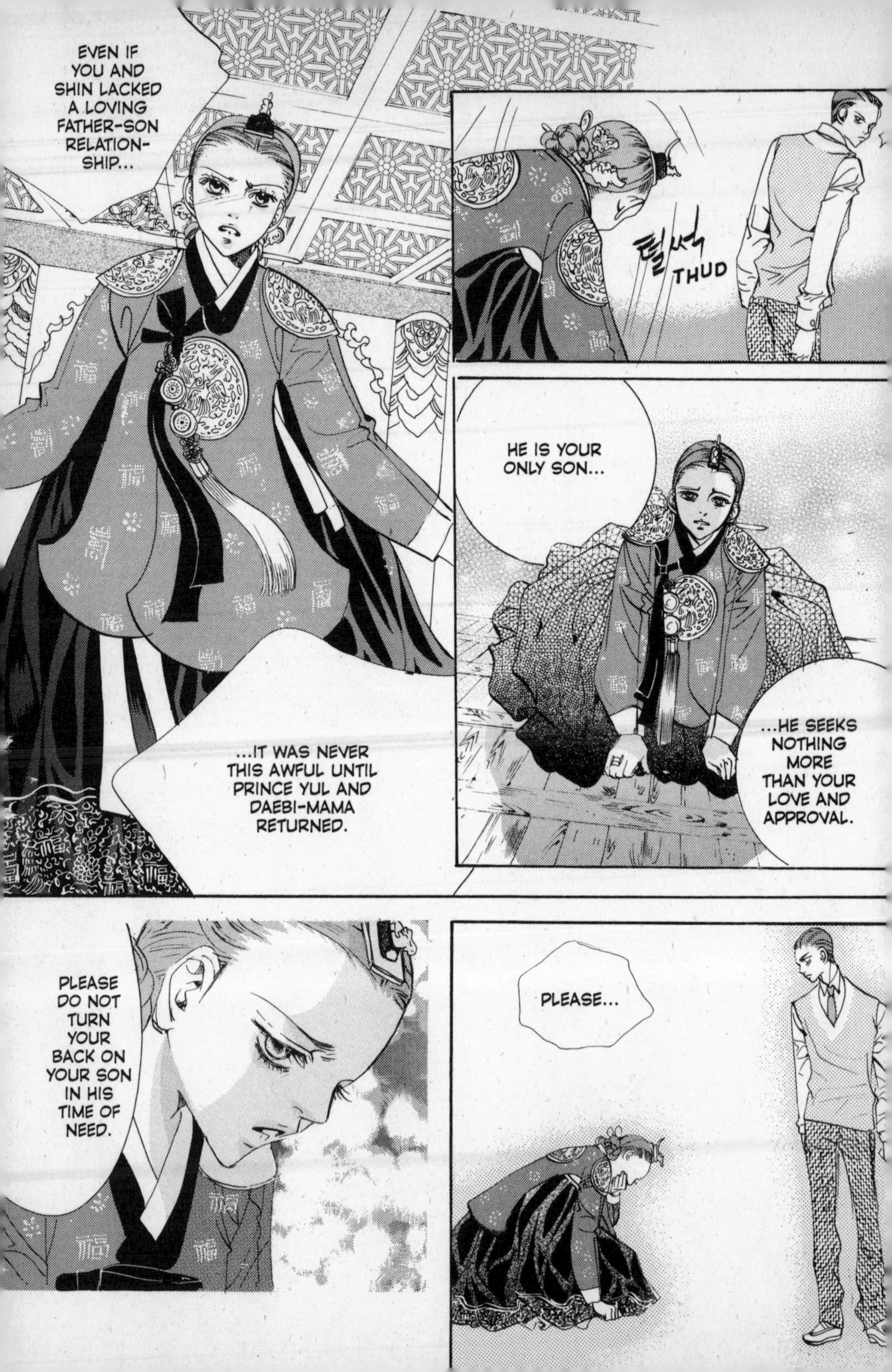
EVEN IF YOU AND SHIN LACKED A LOVING FATHER-SON RELATION-SHIP...
...IT WAS NEVER THIS AWFUL UNTIL PRINCE YUL AND DAEBI-MAMA RETURNED.
털썩
THUD
HE IS YOUR ONLY SON...
...HE SEEKS NOTHING MORE THAN YOUR LOVE AND APPROVAL.
PLEASE DO NOT TURN YOUR BACK ON YOUR SON IN HIS TIME OF NEED.
PLEASE...

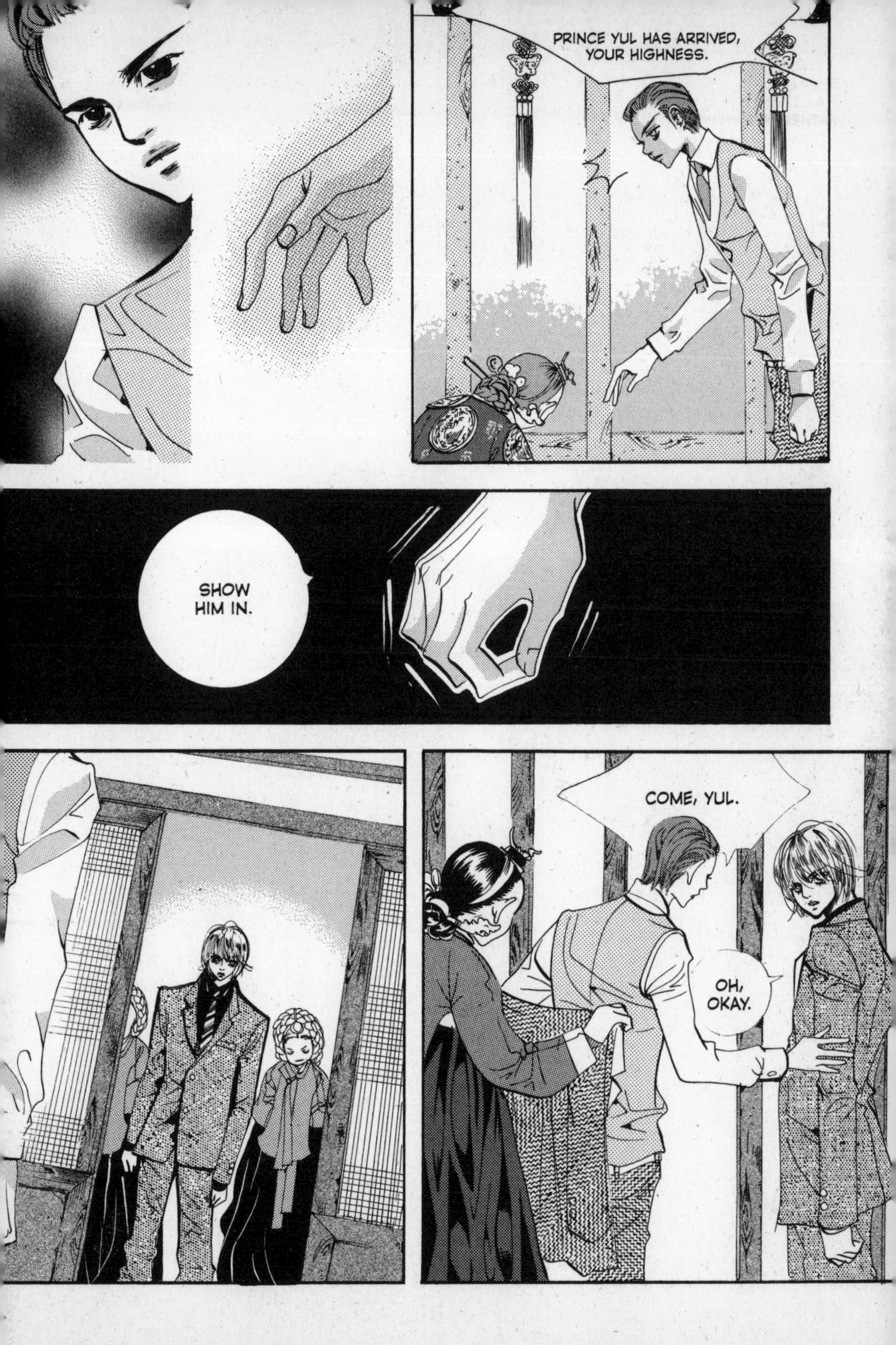
PRINCE YUL HAS ARRIVED, YOUR HIGHNESS.
SHOW HIM IN.
COME, YUL.
OH, OKAY.

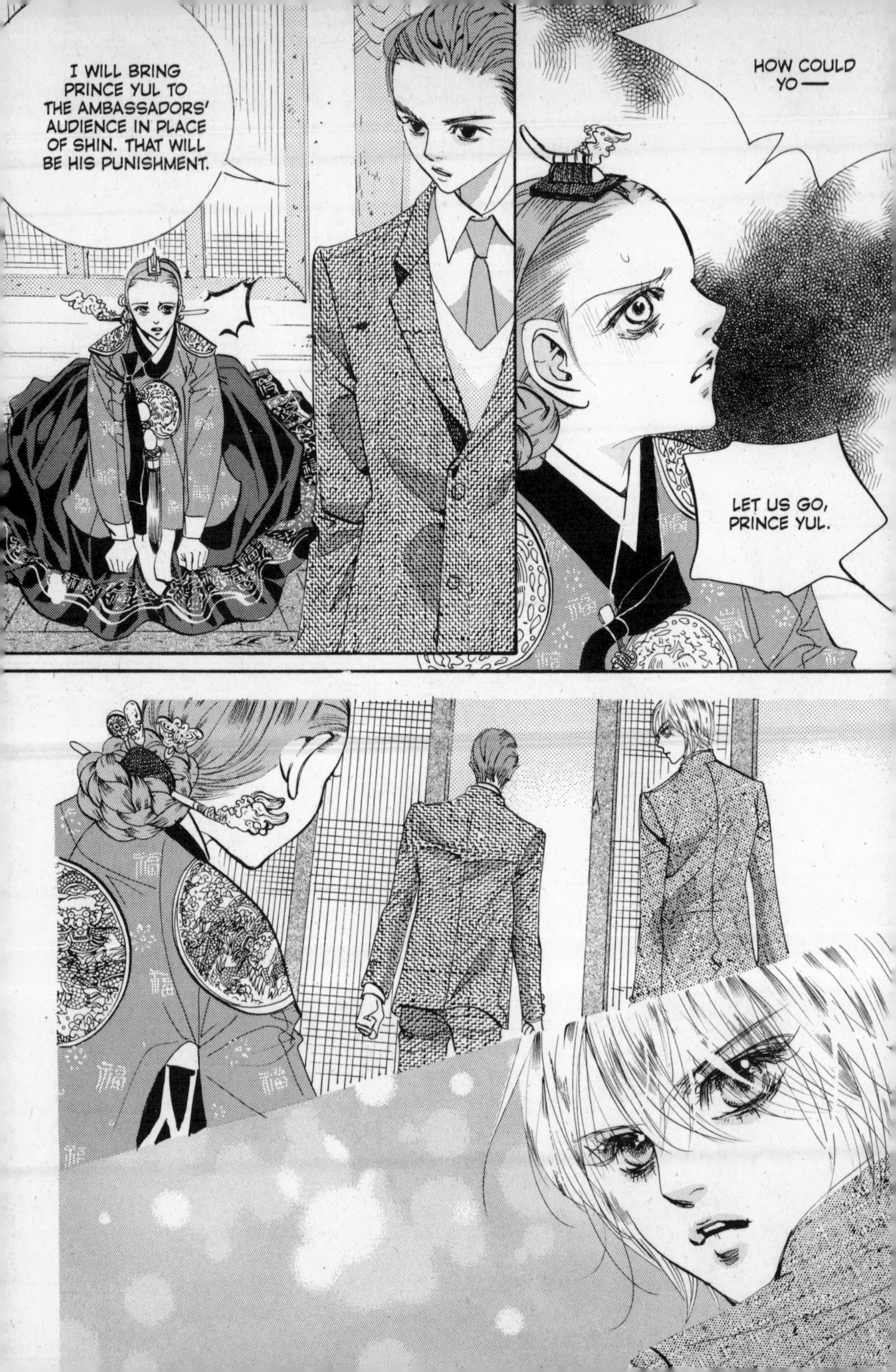
I WILL BRING PRINCE YUL TO THE AMBASSADORS' AUDIENCE IN PLACE OF SHIN. THAT WILL BE HIS PUNISHMENT.
HOW COULD YO—
LET US GO, PRINCE YUL.

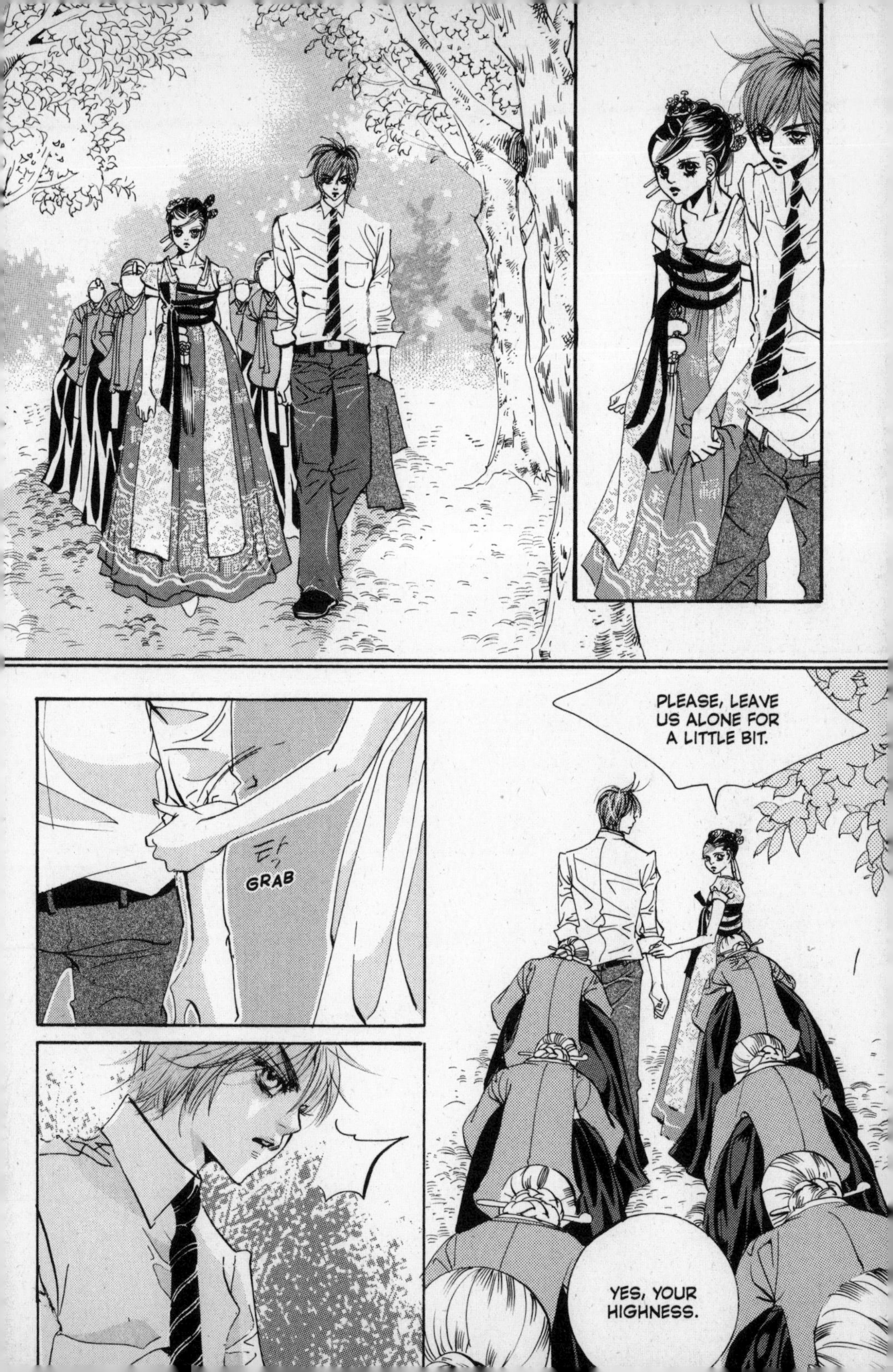
탁
GRAB
PLEASE, LEAVE US ALONE FOR A LITTLE BIT.
YES, YOUR HIGHNESS.

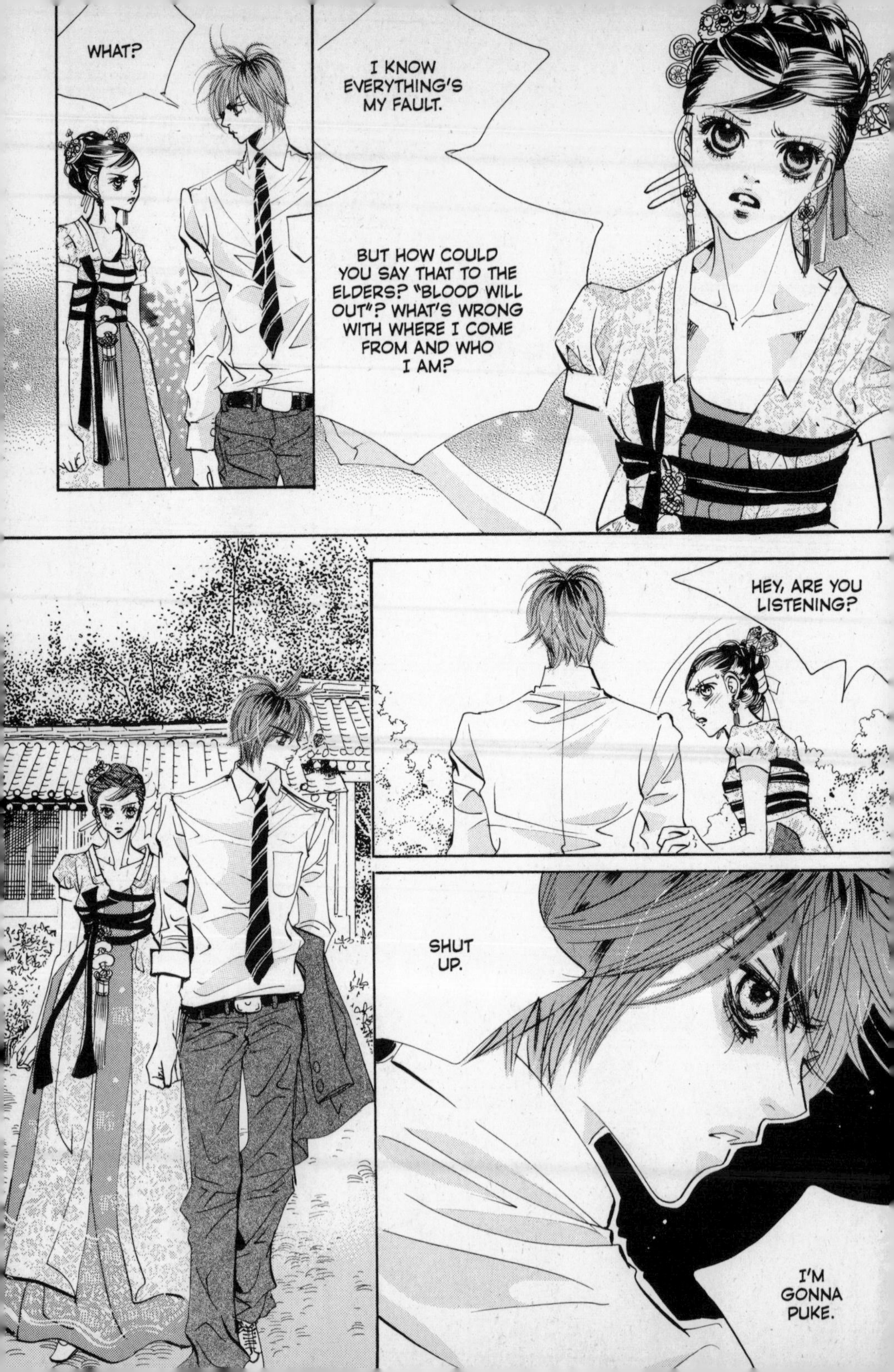
WHAT?
I KNOW EVERYTHING'S MY FAULT.
BUT HOW COULD YOU SAY THAT TO THE ELDERS? "BLOOD WILL OUT"? WHAT'S WRONG WITH WHERE I COME FROM AND WHO I AM?
HEY, ARE YOU LISTENING?
SHUT UP.
I'M GONNA PUKE.

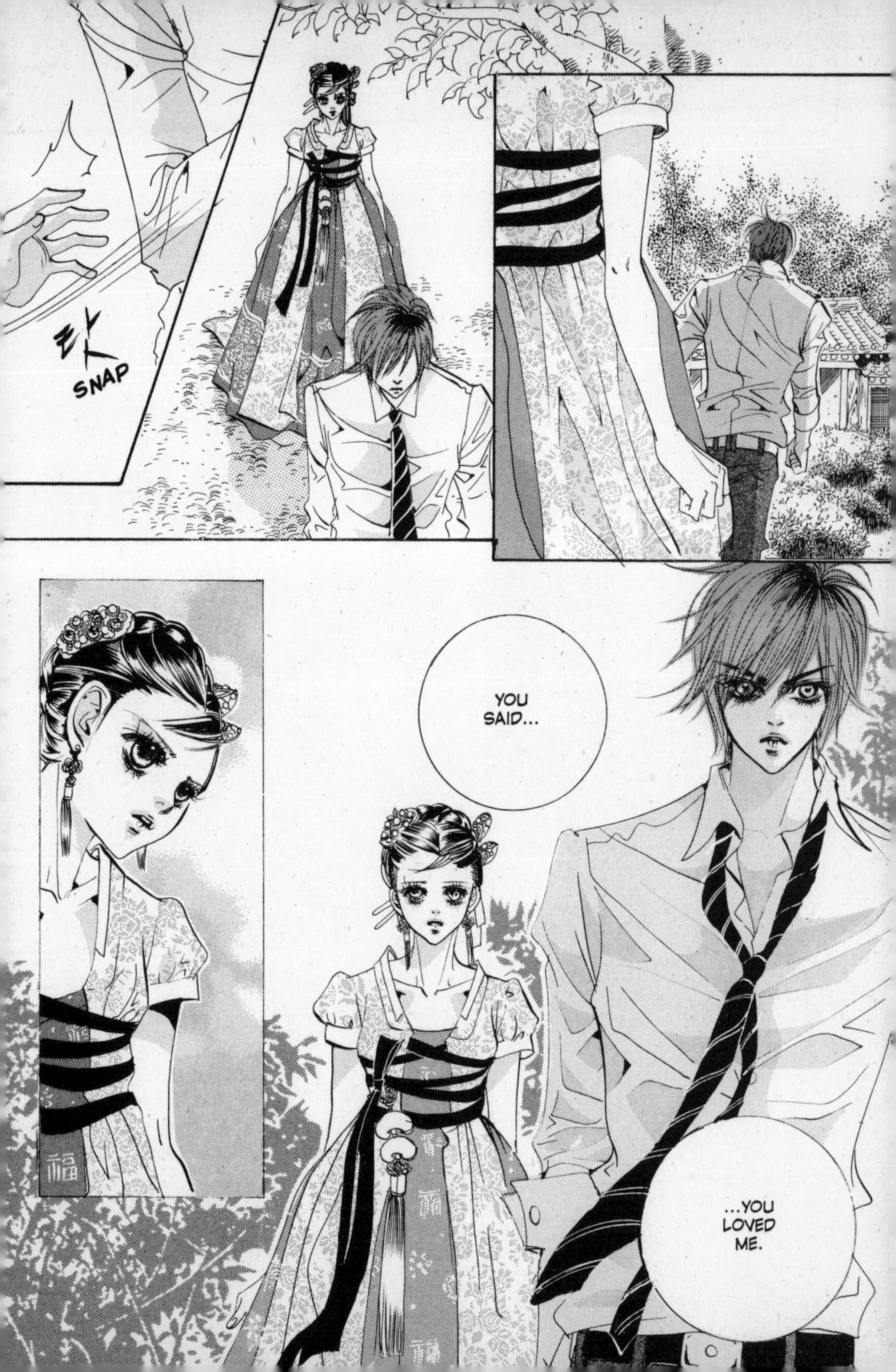
탁
SNAP
YOU SAID...
...YOU LOVED ME.

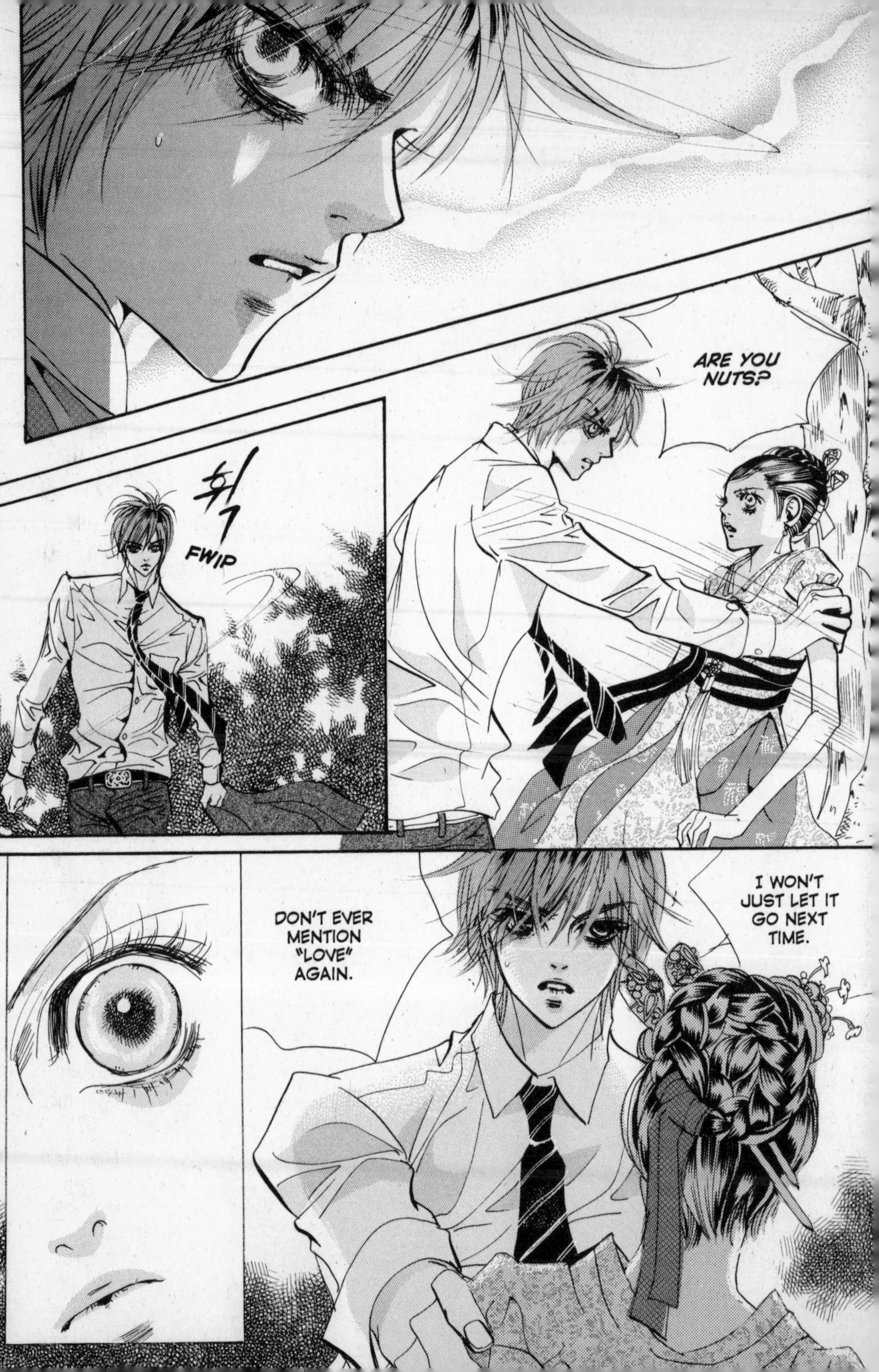
휙
FWIP
ARE YOU NUTS?
DON'T EVER MENTION "LOVE" AGAIN.
I WON'T JUST LET IT GO NEXT TIME.

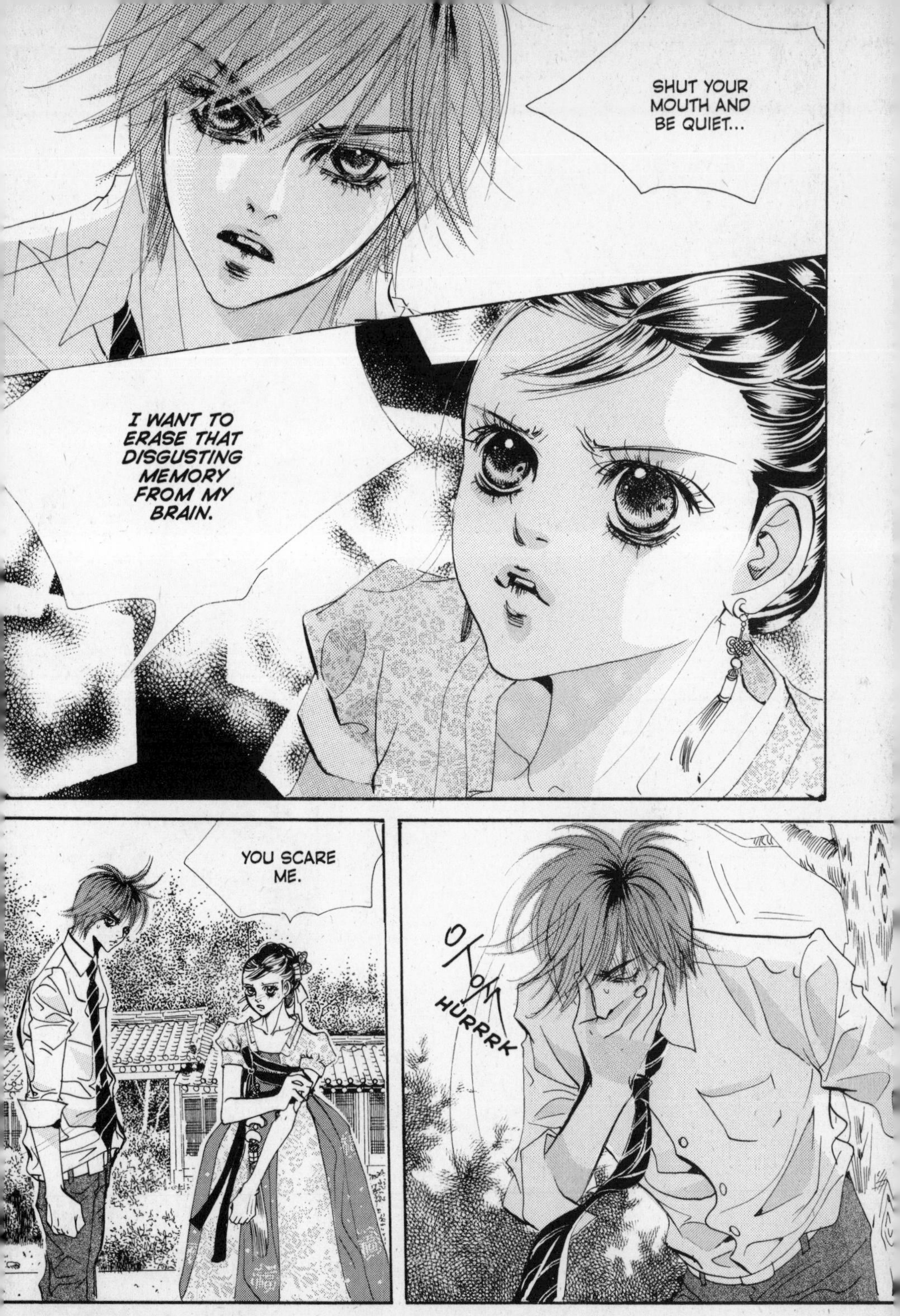
SHUT YOUR MOUTH AND BE QUIET...
I WANT TO ERASE THAT DISGUSTING MEMORY FROM MY BRAIN.
YOU SCARE ME.
HURRRK

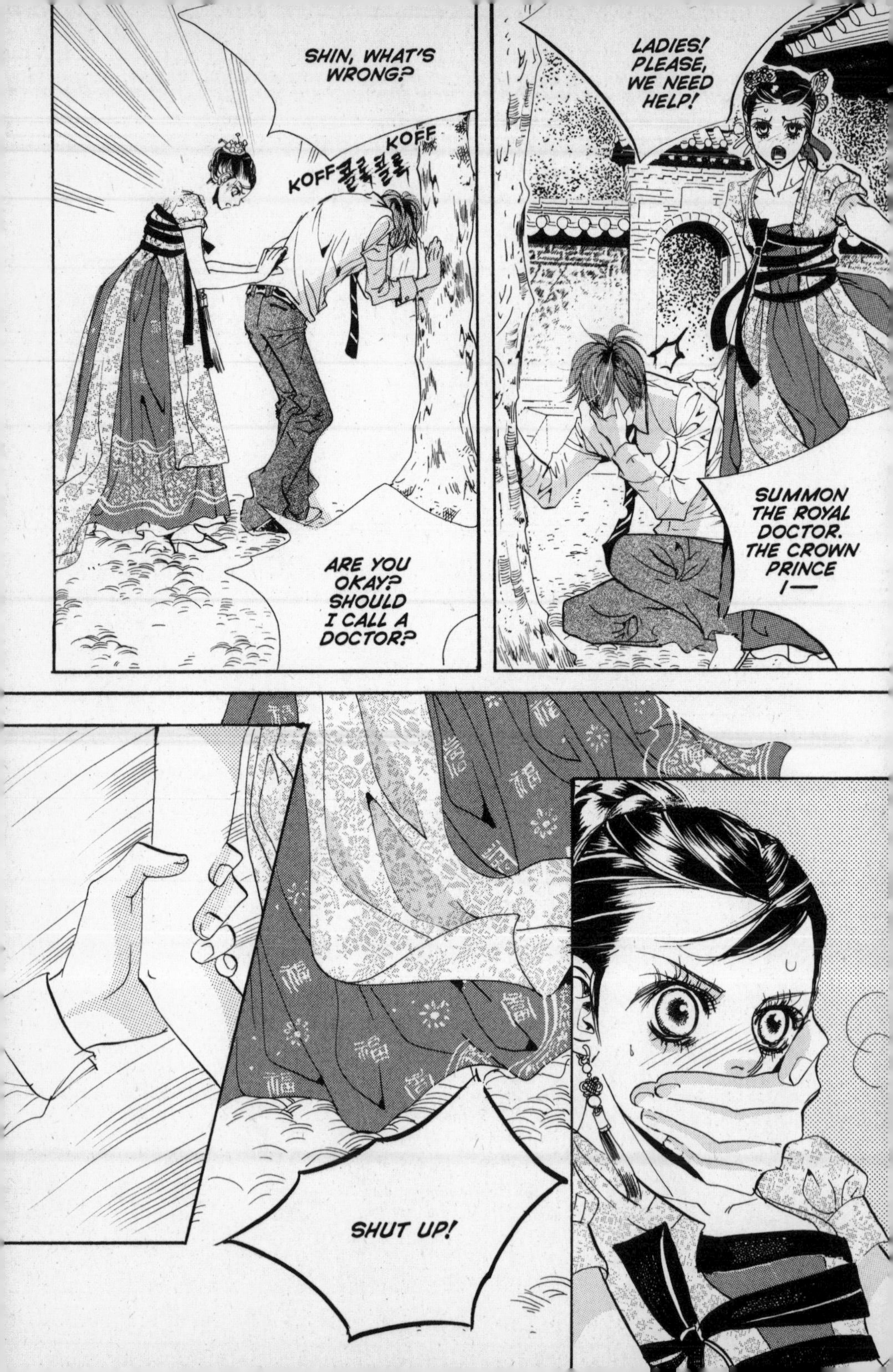
SHIN, WHAT'S WRONG?
KOFF 콜록콜록 KOFF
ARE YOU OKAY? SHOULD I CALL A DOCTOR?
LADIES! PLEASE, WE NEED HELP!
SUMMON THE ROYAL DOCTOR. THE CROWN PRINCE I—
SHUT UP!

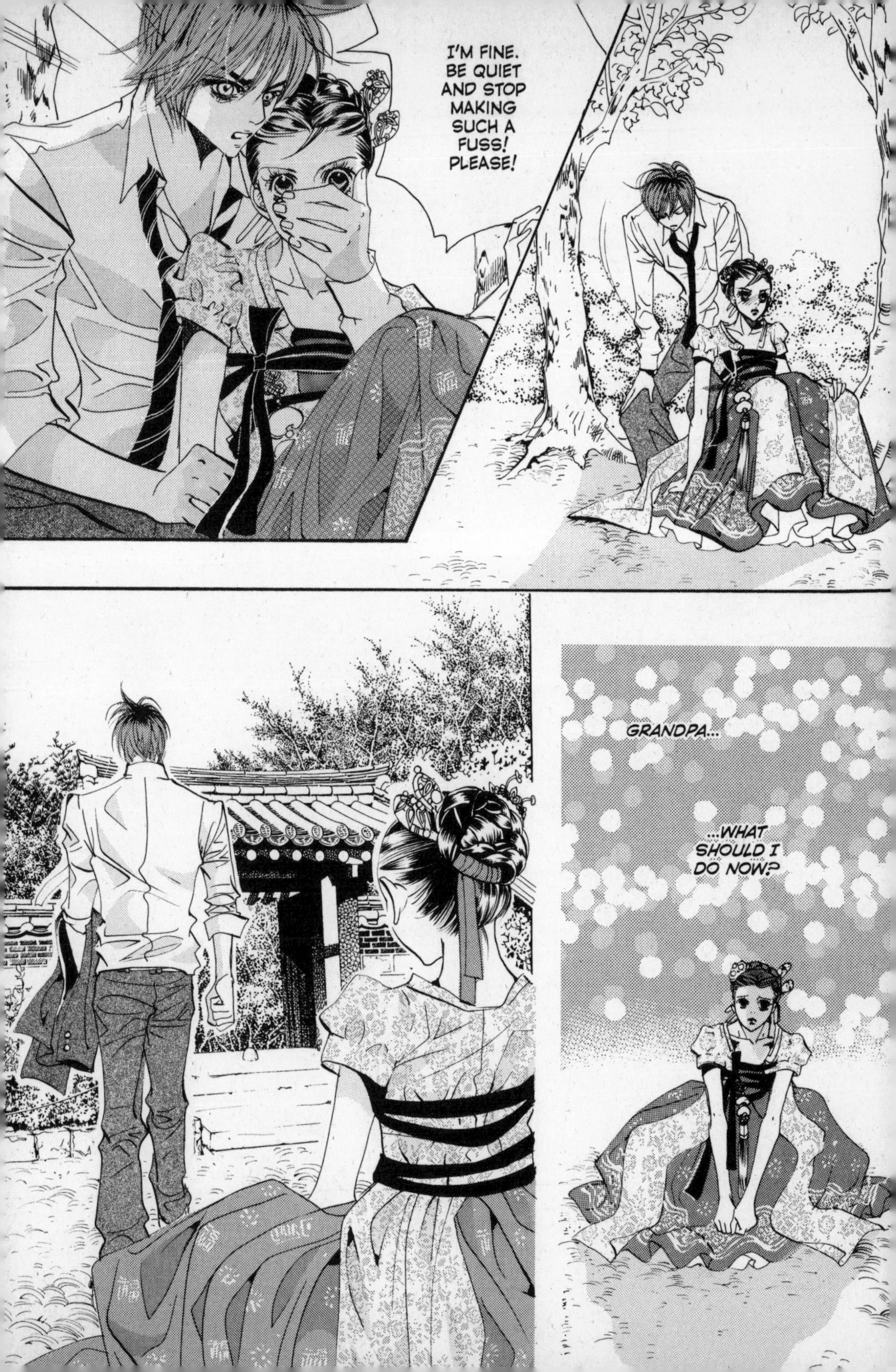
I'M FINE. BE QUIET AND STOP MAKING SUCH A FUSS! PLEASE!
GRANDPA...
...WHAT SHOULD I DO NOW?

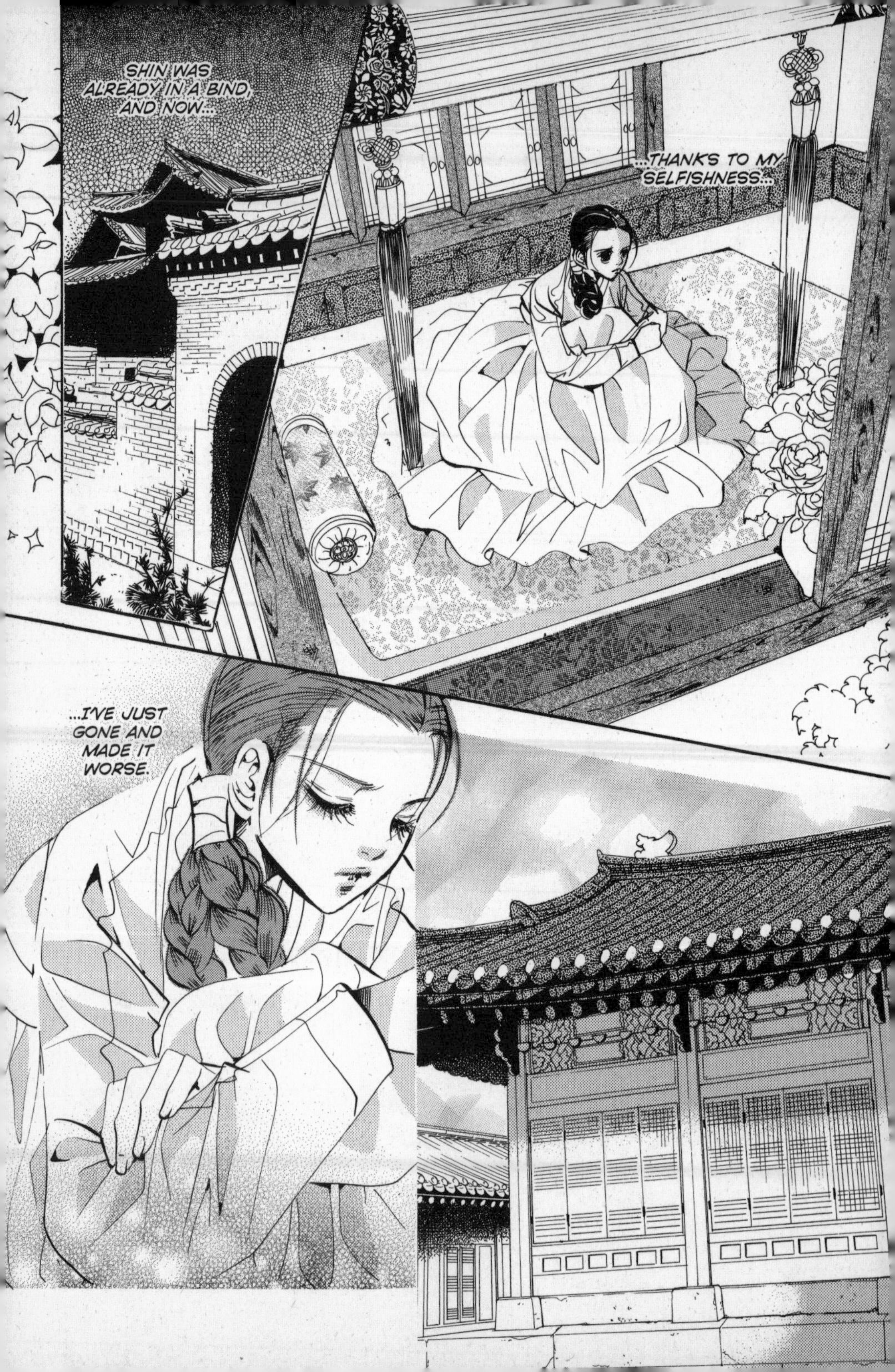
SHIN WAS ALREADY IN A BIND, AND NOW...
...THANKS TO MY SELFISHNESS...
...I'VE JUST GONE AND MADE IT WORSE.

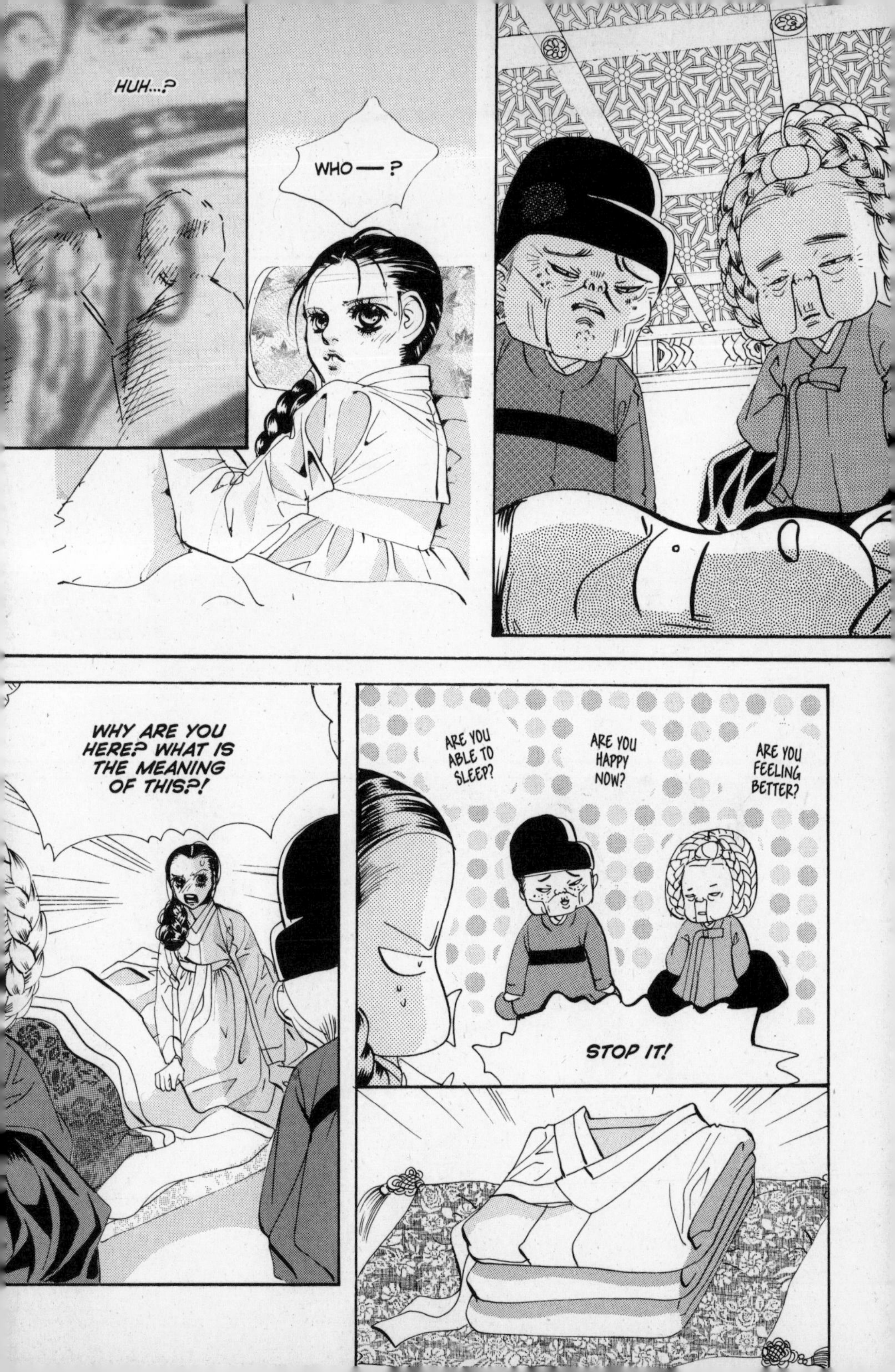
HUH...?
WHO—?
WHY ARE YOU HERE? WHAT IS THE MEANING OF THIS?!
ARE YOU ABLE TO SLEEP?
ARE YOU HAPPY NOW?
ARE YOU FEELING BETTER?
STOP IT!

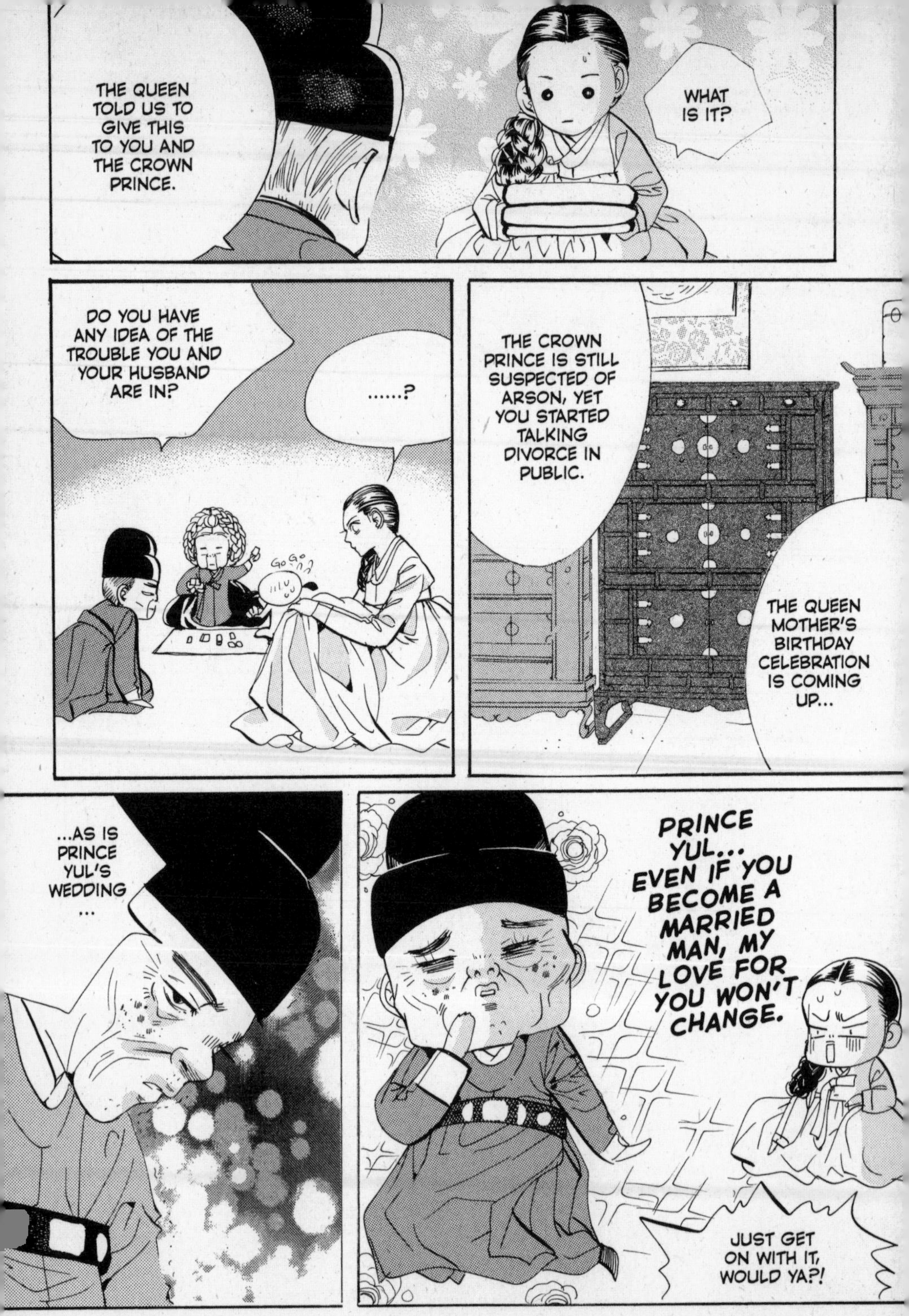
THE QUEEN TOLD US TO GIVE THIS TO YOU AND THE CROWN PRINCE.
WHAT IS IT?
DO YOU HAVE ANY IDEA OF THE TROUBLE YOU AND YOUR HUSBAND ARE IN?
......?
THE CROWN PRINCE IS STILL SUSPECTED OF ARSON, YET YOU STARTED TALKING DIVORCE IN PUBLIC.
THE QUEEN MOTHER'S BIRTHDAY CELEBRATION IS COMING UP...
...AS IS PRINCE YUL'S WEDDING ...
PRINCE YUL... EVEN IF YOU BECOME A MARRIED MAN, MY LOVE FOR YOU WON'T CHANGE.
JUST GET ON WITH IT, WOULD YA?!

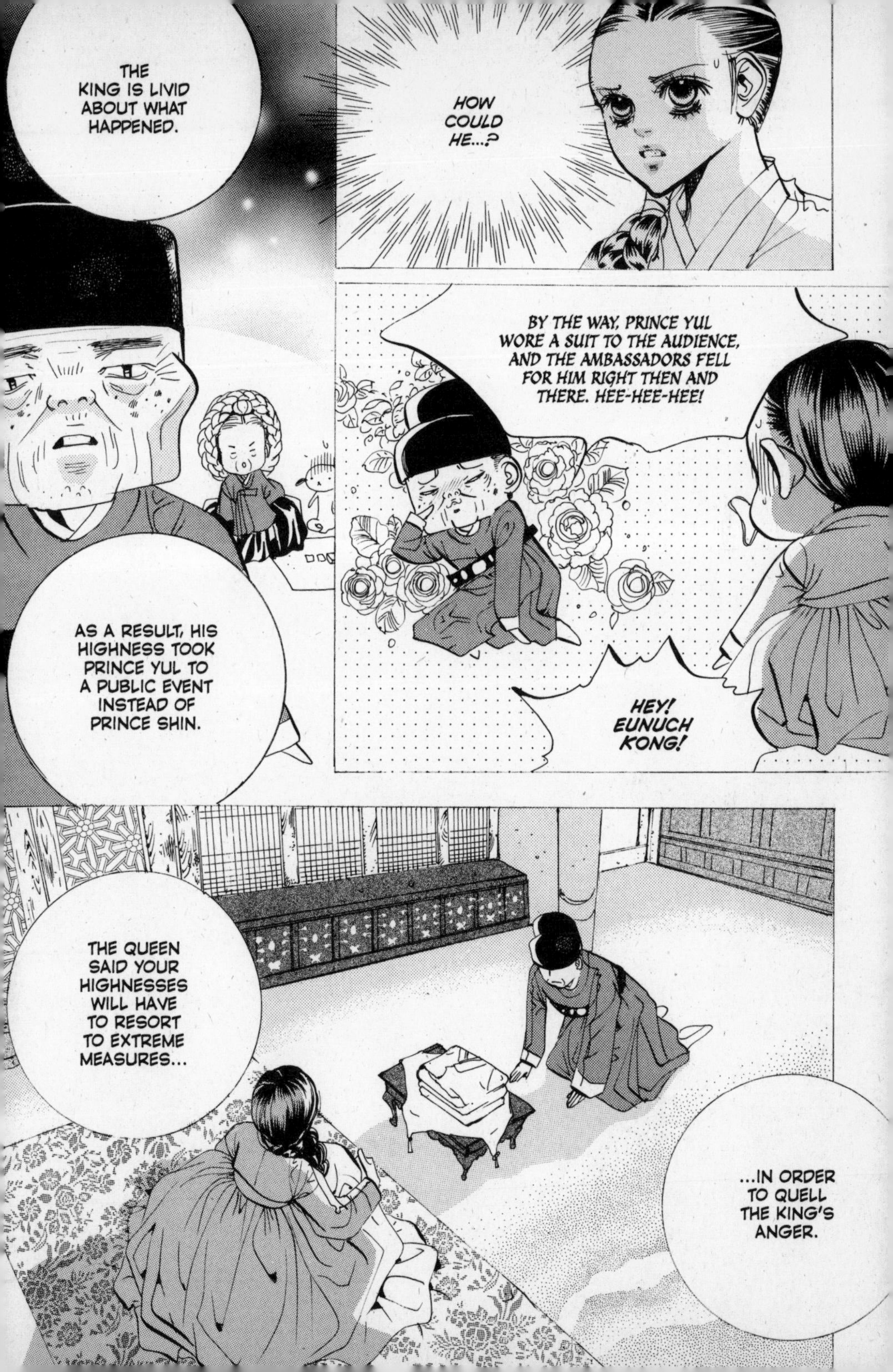
THE KING IS LIVID ABOUT WHAT HAPPENED.
AS A RESULT, HIS HIGHNESS TOOK PRINCE YUL TO A PUBLIC EVENT INSTEAD OF PRINCE SHIN.
HOW COULD HE...?
BY THE WAY, PRINCE YUL WORE A SUIT TO THE AUDIENCE, AND THE AMBASSADORS FELL FOR HIM RIGHT THEN AND THERE. HEE-HEE-HEE!
HEY! EUNUCH KONG!
THE QUEEN SAID YOUR HIGHNESSES WILL HAVE TO RESORT TO EXTREME MEASURES...
...IN ORDER TO QUELL THE KING'S ANGER.

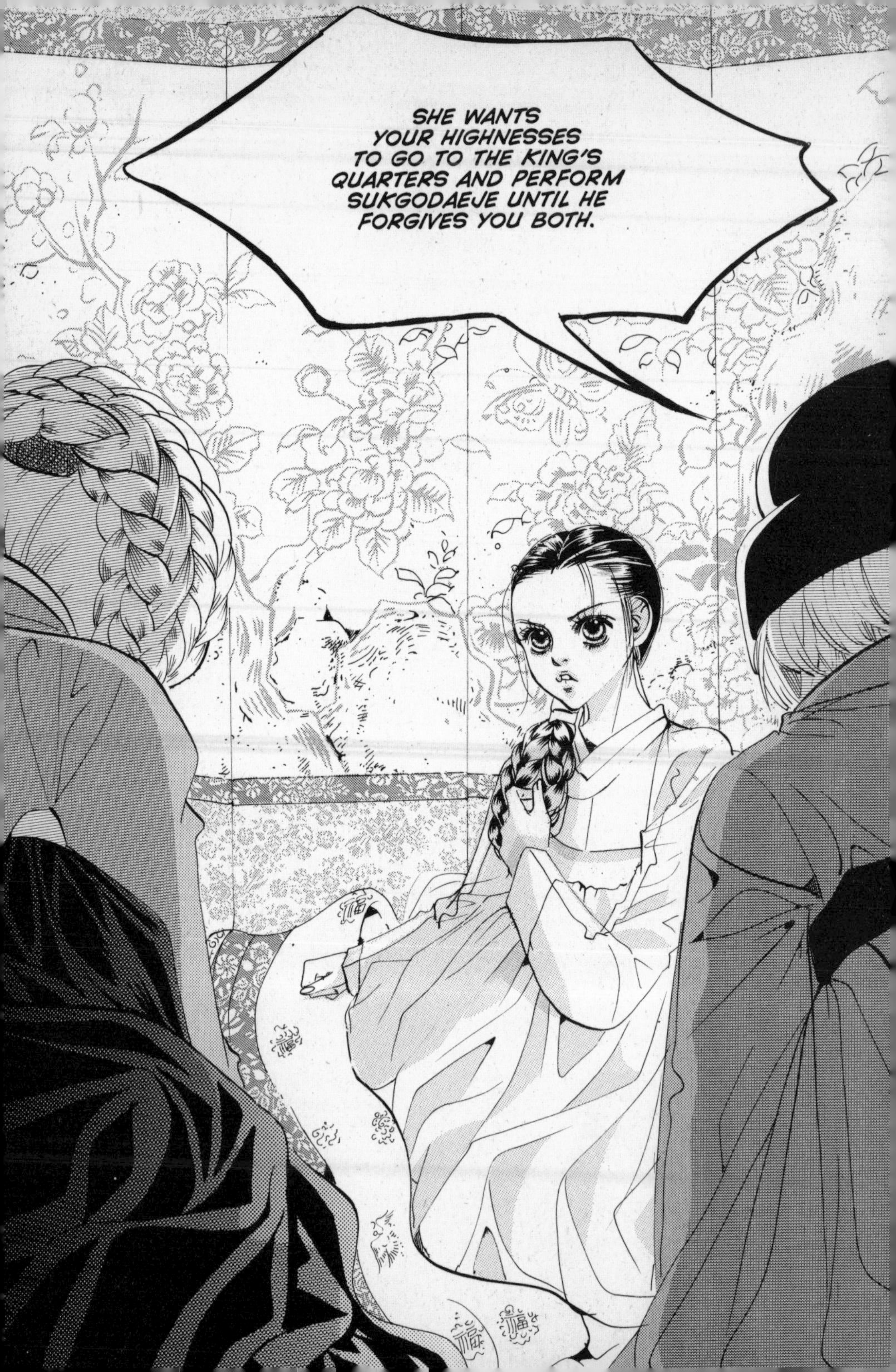
SHE WANTS YOUR HIGHNESSES TO GO TO THE KING'S QUARTERS AND PERFORM SUKGODAEJE UNTIL HE FORGIVES YOU BOTH.

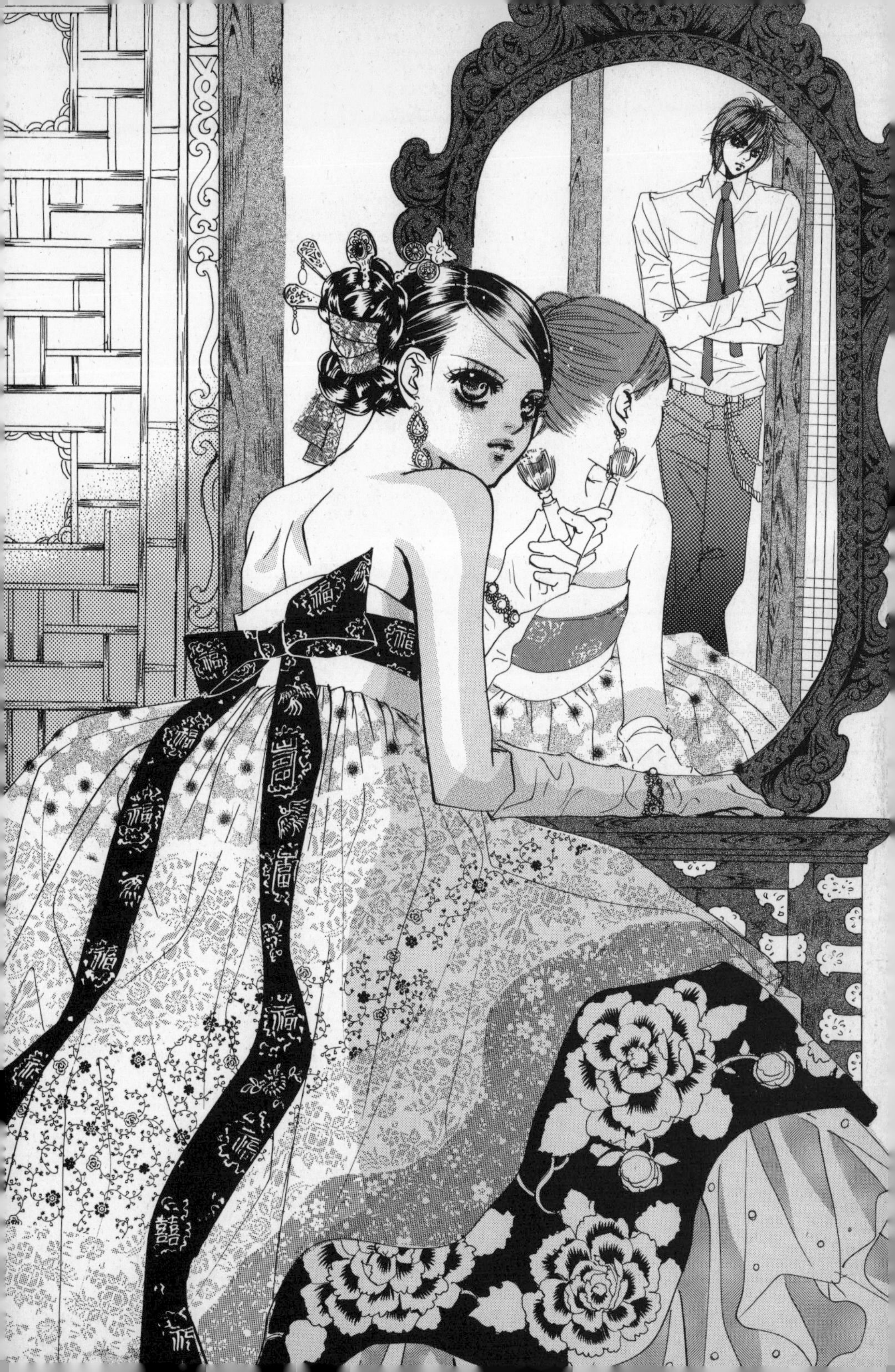

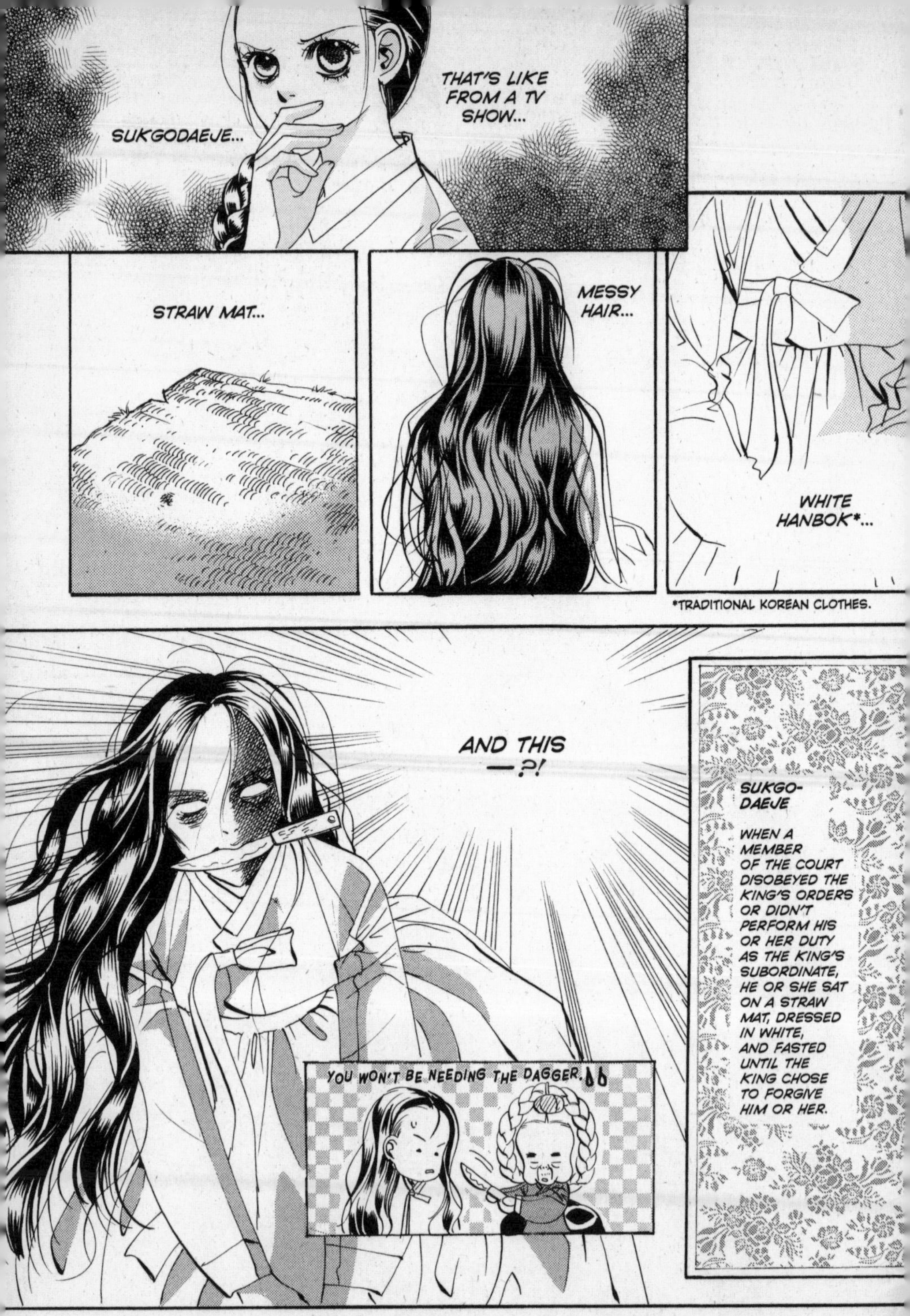
SUKGODAEJE...
THAT'S LIKE FROM A TV SHOW...
STRAW MAT...
MESSY HAIR...
WHITE HANBOK*...
*TRADITIONAL KOREAN CLOTHES.
AND THIS —?!
YOU WON'T BE NEEDING THE DAGGER.
SUKGO-DAEJE
WHEN A MEMBER OF THE COURT DISOBEYED THE KING'S ORDERS OR DIDN'T PERFORM HIS OR HER DUTY AS THE KING'S SUBORDINATE, HE OR SHE SAT ON A STRAW MAT, DRESSED IN WHITE, AND FASTED UNTIL THE KING CHOSE TO FORGIVE HIM OR HER.

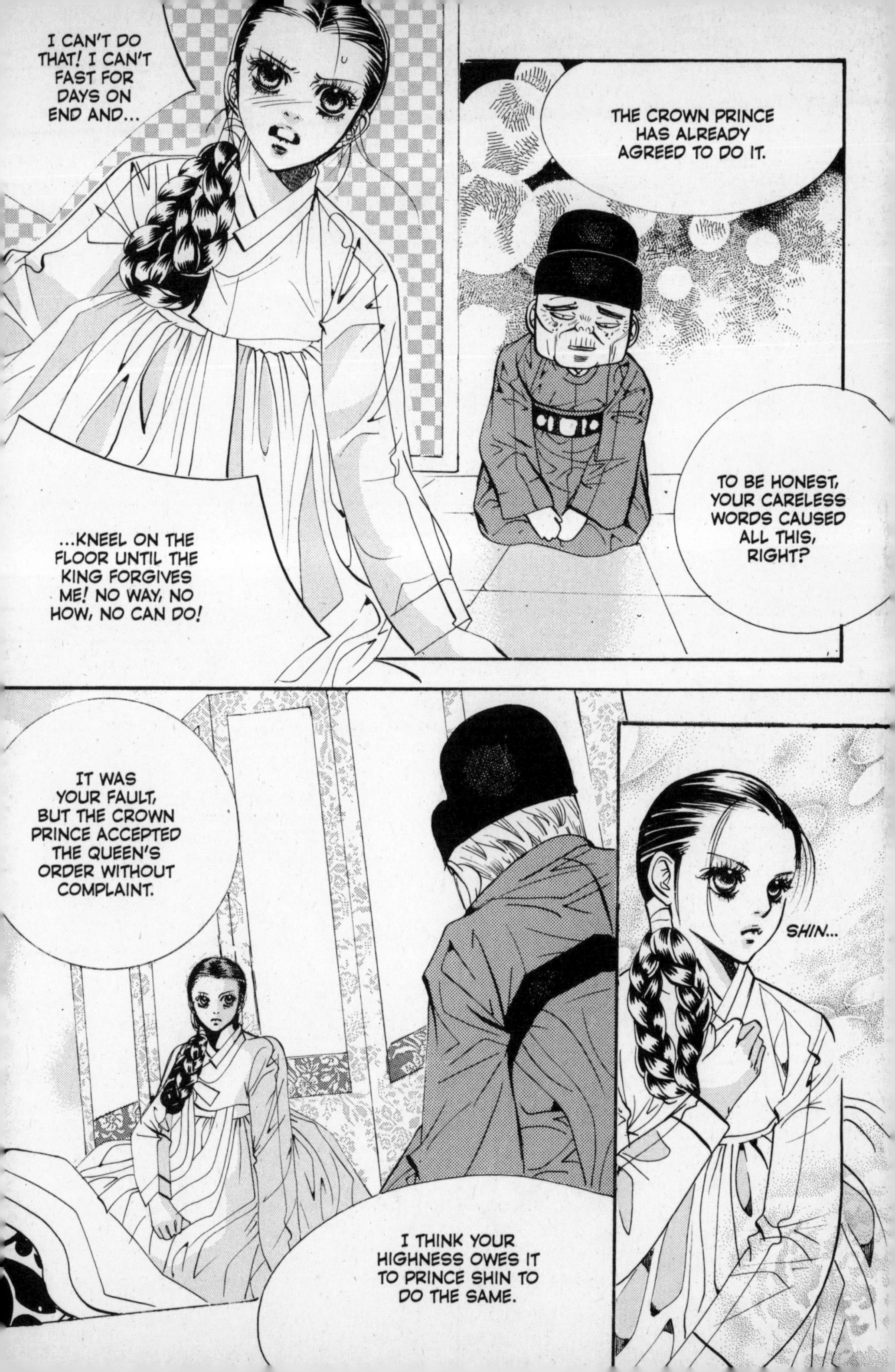
I CAN'T DO THAT! I CAN'T FAST FOR DAYS ON END AND...
...KNEEL ON THE FLOOR UNTIL THE KING FORGIVES ME! NO WAY, NO HOW, NO CAN DO!
THE CROWN PRINCE HAS ALREADY AGREED TO DO IT.
TO BE HONEST, YOUR CARELESS WORDS CAUSED ALL THIS, RIGHT?
IT WAS YOUR FAULT, BUT THE CROWN PRINCE ACCEPTED THE QUEEN'S ORDER WITHOUT COMPLAINT.
I THINK YOUR HIGHNESS OWES IT TO PRINCE SHIN TO DO THE SAME.
SHIN...

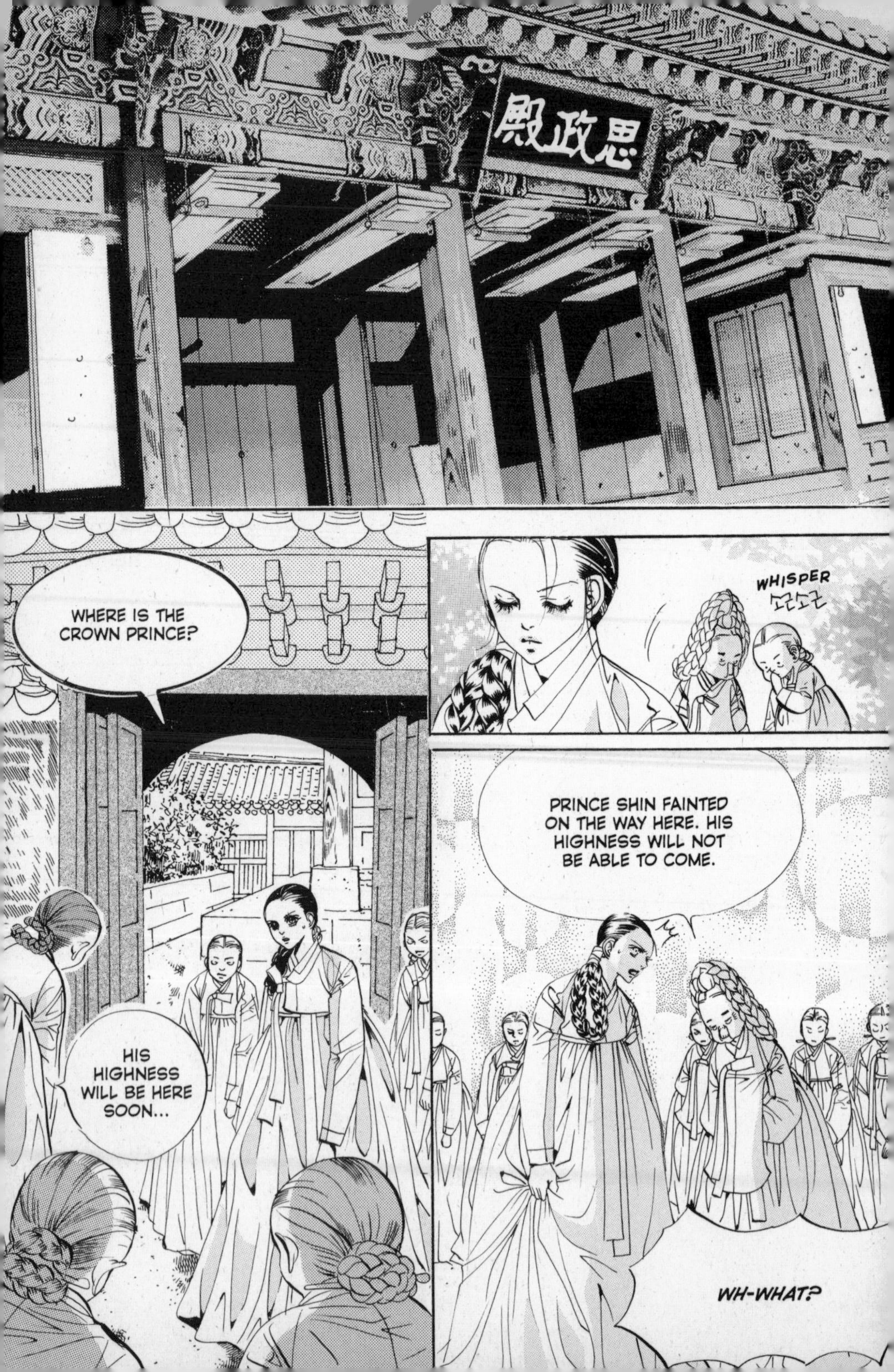
思政殿
WHERE IS THE CROWN PRINCE?
HIS HIGHNESS WILL BE HERE SOON...
WHISPER
소곤소곤
PRINCE SHIN FAINTED ON THE WAY HERE. HIS HIGHNESS WILL NOT BE ABLE TO COME.
WH-WHAT?

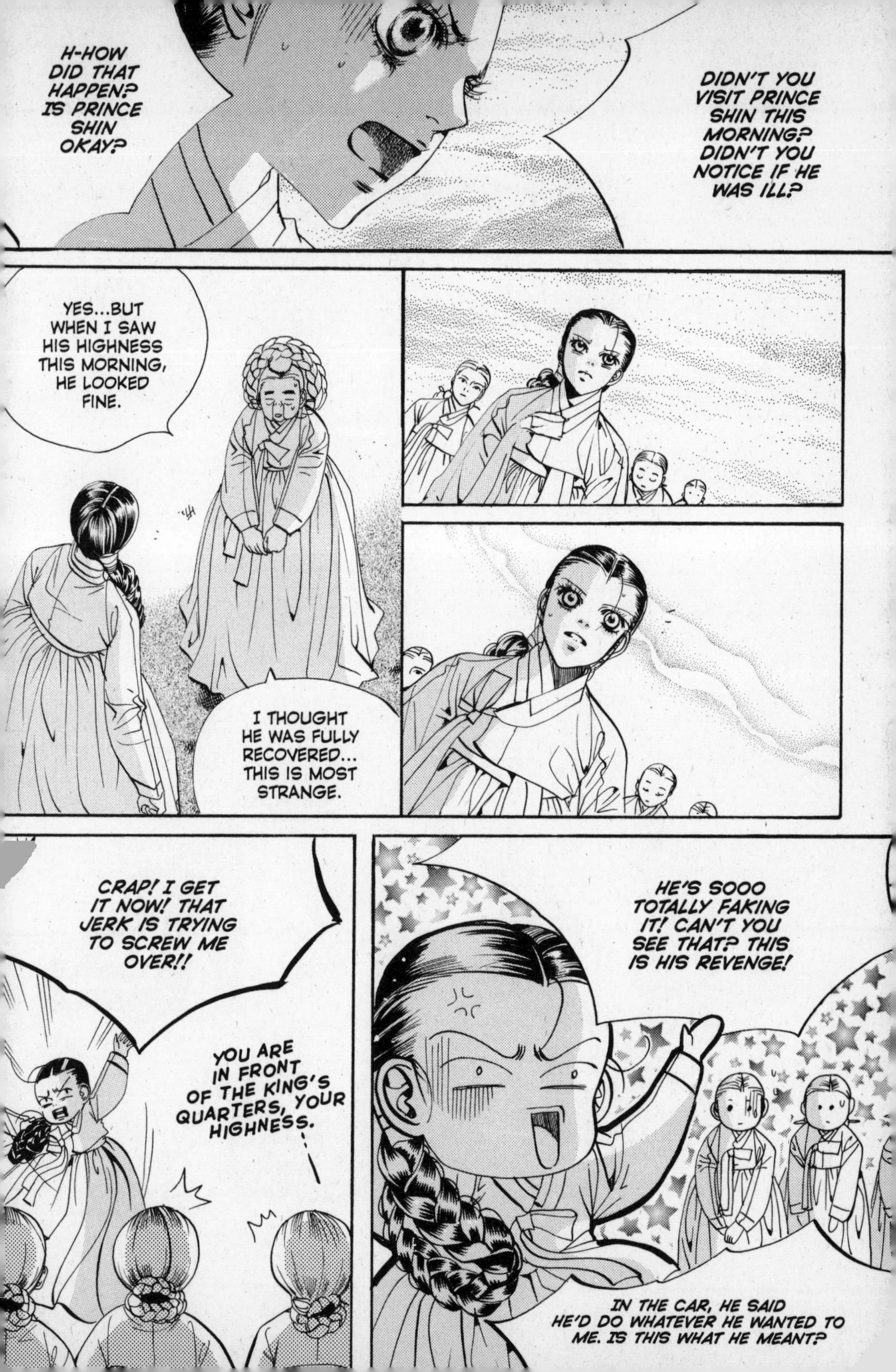

H-HOW DID THAT HAPPEN? IS PRINCE SHIN OKAY?
DIDN'T YOU VISIT PRINCE SHIN THIS MORNING? DIDN'T YOU NOTICE IF HE WAS ILL?
YES...BUT WHEN I SAW HIS HIGHNESS THIS MORNING, HE LOOKED FINE.
I THOUGHT HE WAS FULLY RECOVERED... THIS IS MOST STRANGE.
CRAP! I GET IT NOW! THAT JERK IS TRYING TO SCREW ME OVER!!
YOU ARE IN FRONT OF THE KING'S QUARTERS, YOUR HIGHNESS.
HE'S SOOO TOTALLY FAKING IT! CAN'T YOU SEE THAT? THIS IS HIS REVENGE!
IN THE CAR, HE SAID HE'D DO WHATEVER HE WANTED TO ME. IS THIS WHAT HE MEANT?

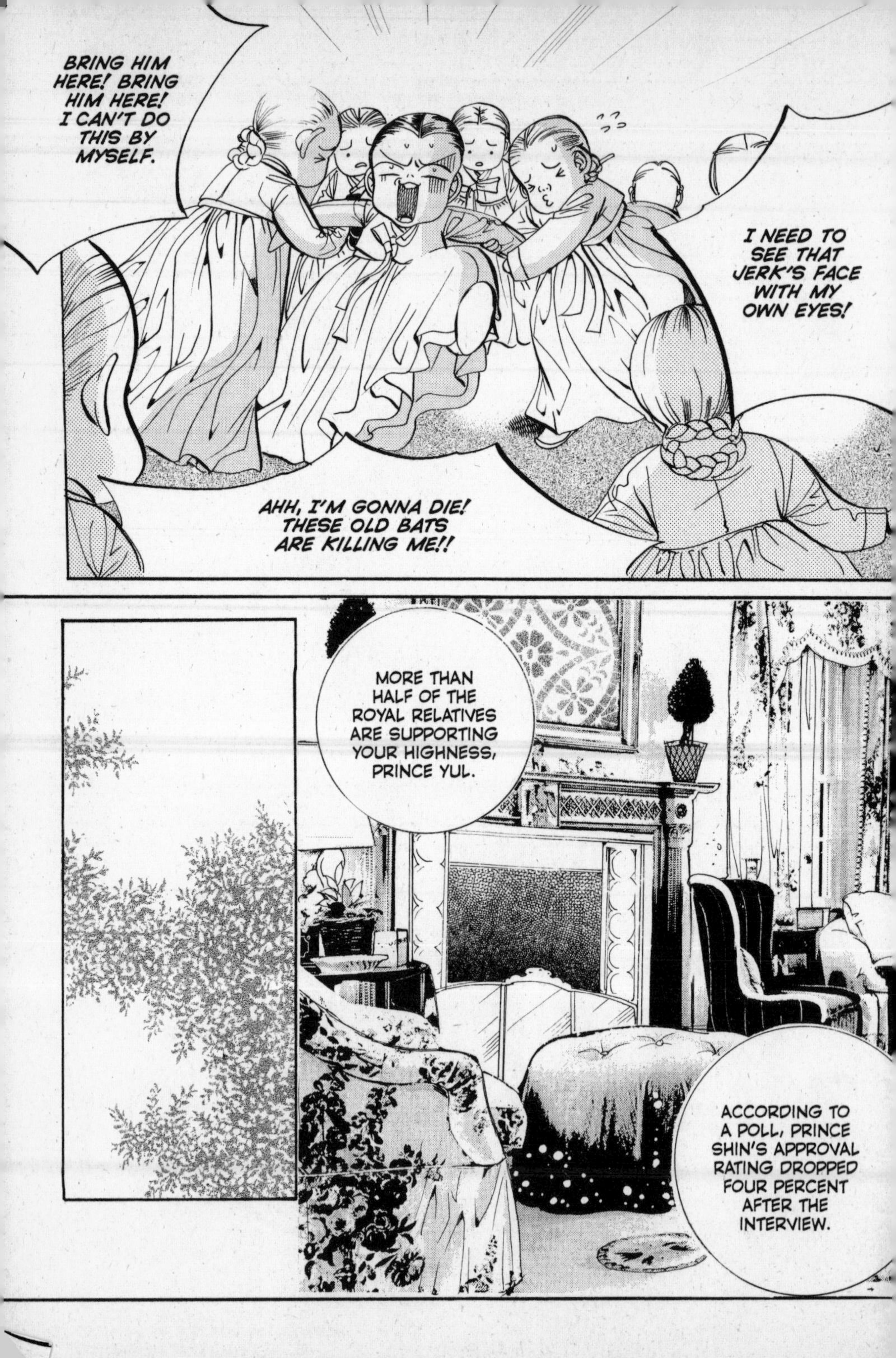
BRING HIM HERE! BRING HIM HERE! I CAN'T DO THIS BY MYSELF.
I NEED TO SEE THAT JERK'S FACE WITH MY OWN EYES!
AHH, I'M GONNA DIE! THESE OLD BATS ARE KILLING ME!!
MORE THAN HALF OF THE ROYAL RELATIVES ARE SUPPORTING YOUR HIGHNESS, PRINCE YUL.
ACCORDING TO A POLL, PRINCE SHIN'S APPROVAL RATING DROPPED FOUR PERCENT AFTER THE INTERVIEW.

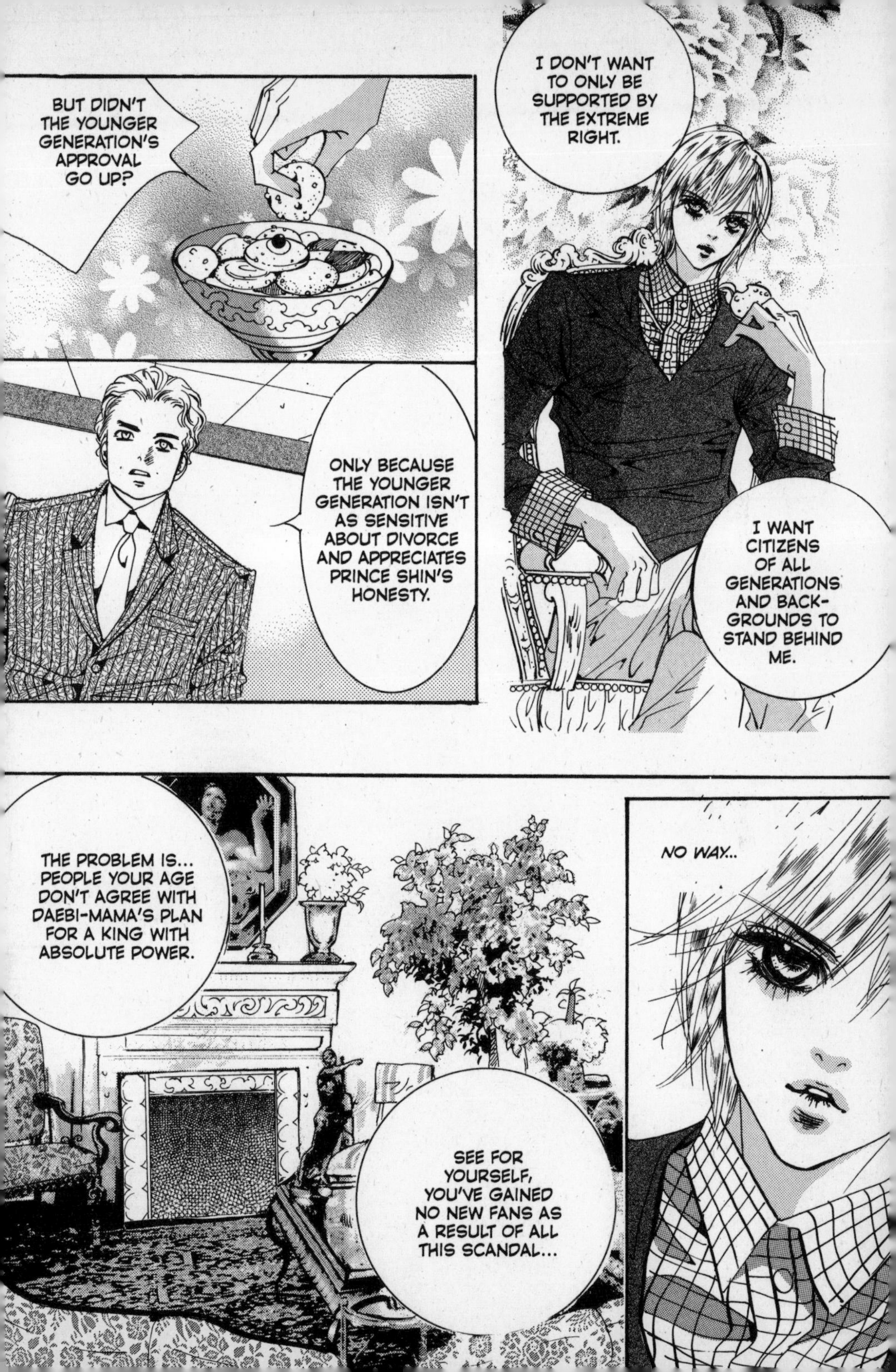
BUT DIDN'T THE YOUNGER GENERATION'S APPROVAL GO UP?
ONLY BECAUSE THE YOUNGER GENERATION ISN'T AS SENSITIVE ABOUT DIVORCE AND APPRECIATES PRINCE SHIN'S HONESTY.
I DON'T WANT TO ONLY BE SUPPORTED BY THE EXTREME RIGHT.
I WANT CITIZENS OF ALL GENERATIONS AND BACK-GROUNDS TO STAND BEHIND ME.
THE PROBLEM IS... PEOPLE YOUR AGE DON'T AGREE WITH DAEBI-MAMA'S PLAN FOR A KING WITH ABSOLUTE POWER.
SEE FOR YOURSELF, YOU'VE GAINED NO NEW FANS AS A RESULT OF ALL THIS SCANDAL...
NO WAY...

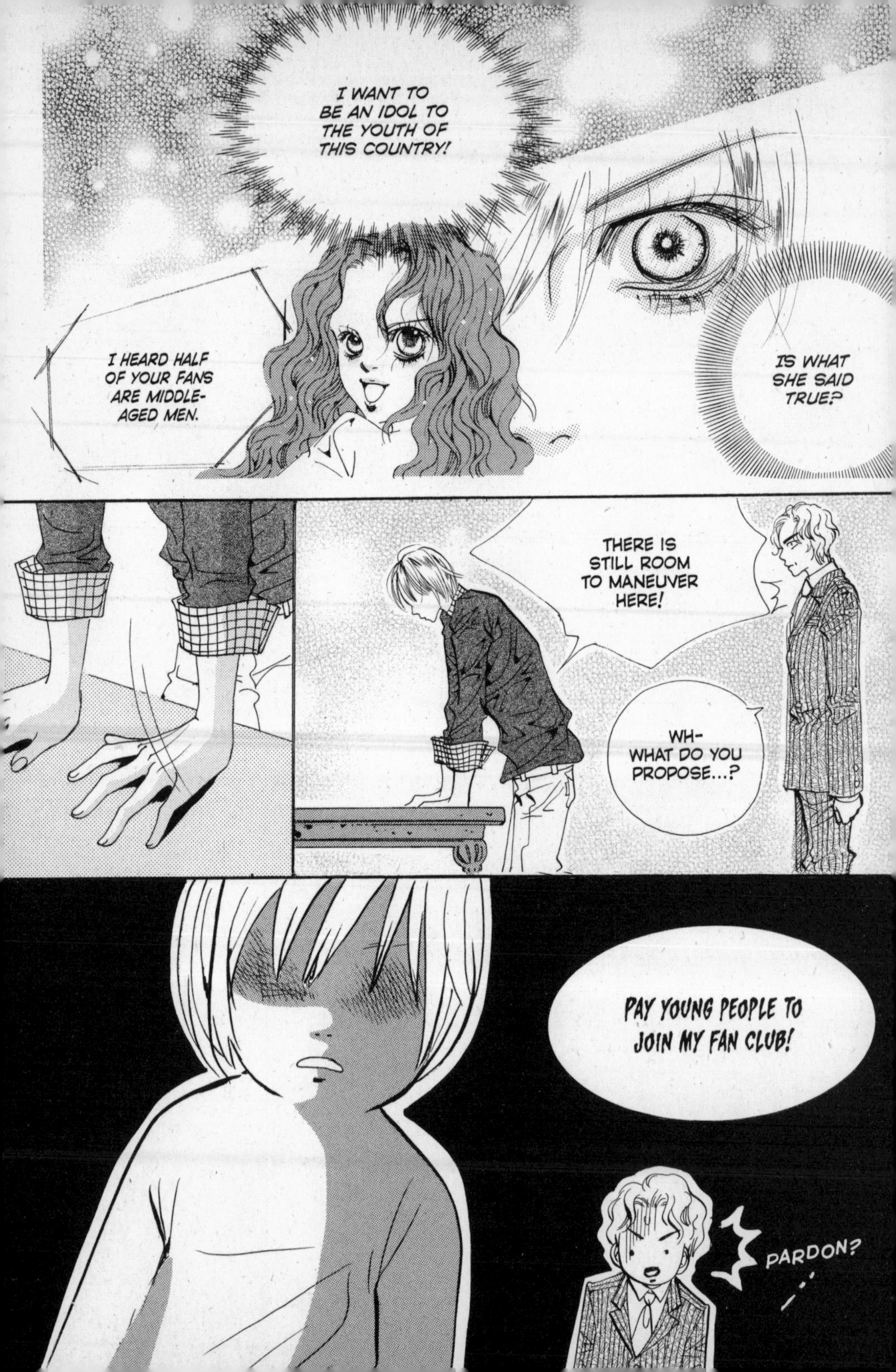
I WANT TO BE AN IDOL TO THE YOUTH OF THIS COUNTRY!
I HEARD HALF OF YOUR FANS ARE MIDDLE-AGED MEN.
IS WHAT SHE SAID TRUE?
THERE IS STILL ROOM TO MANEUVER HERE!
WH- WHAT DO YOU PROPOSE...?
PAY YOUNG PEOPLE TO JOIN MY FAN CLUB!
PARDON?

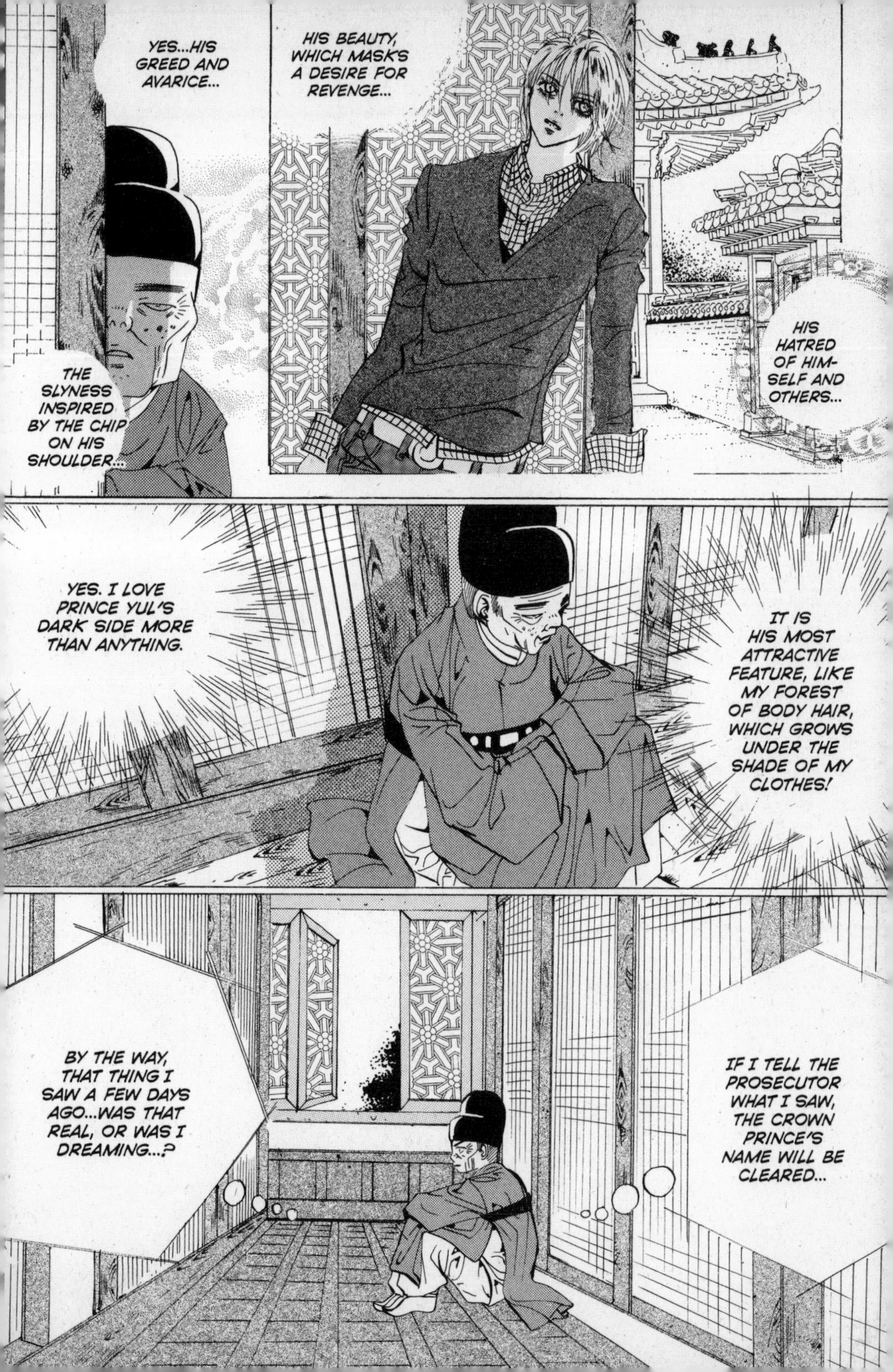
YES...HIS GREED AND AVARICE...
THE SLYNESS INSPIRED BY THE CHIP ON HIS SHOULDER...
HIS BEAUTY, WHICH MASKS A DESIRE FOR REVENGE...
HIS HATRED OF HIM-SELF AND OTHERS...
YES. I LOVE PRINCE YUL'S DARK SIDE MORE THAN ANYTHING.
IT IS HIS MOST ATTRACTIVE FEATURE, LIKE MY FOREST OF BODY HAIR, WHICH GROWS UNDER THE SHADE OF MY CLOTHES!
BY THE WAY, THAT THING I SAW A FEW DAYS AGO...WAS THAT REAL, OR WAS I DREAMING...?
IF I TELL THE PROSECUTOR WHAT I SAW, THE CROWN PRINCE'S NAME WILL BE CLEARED...

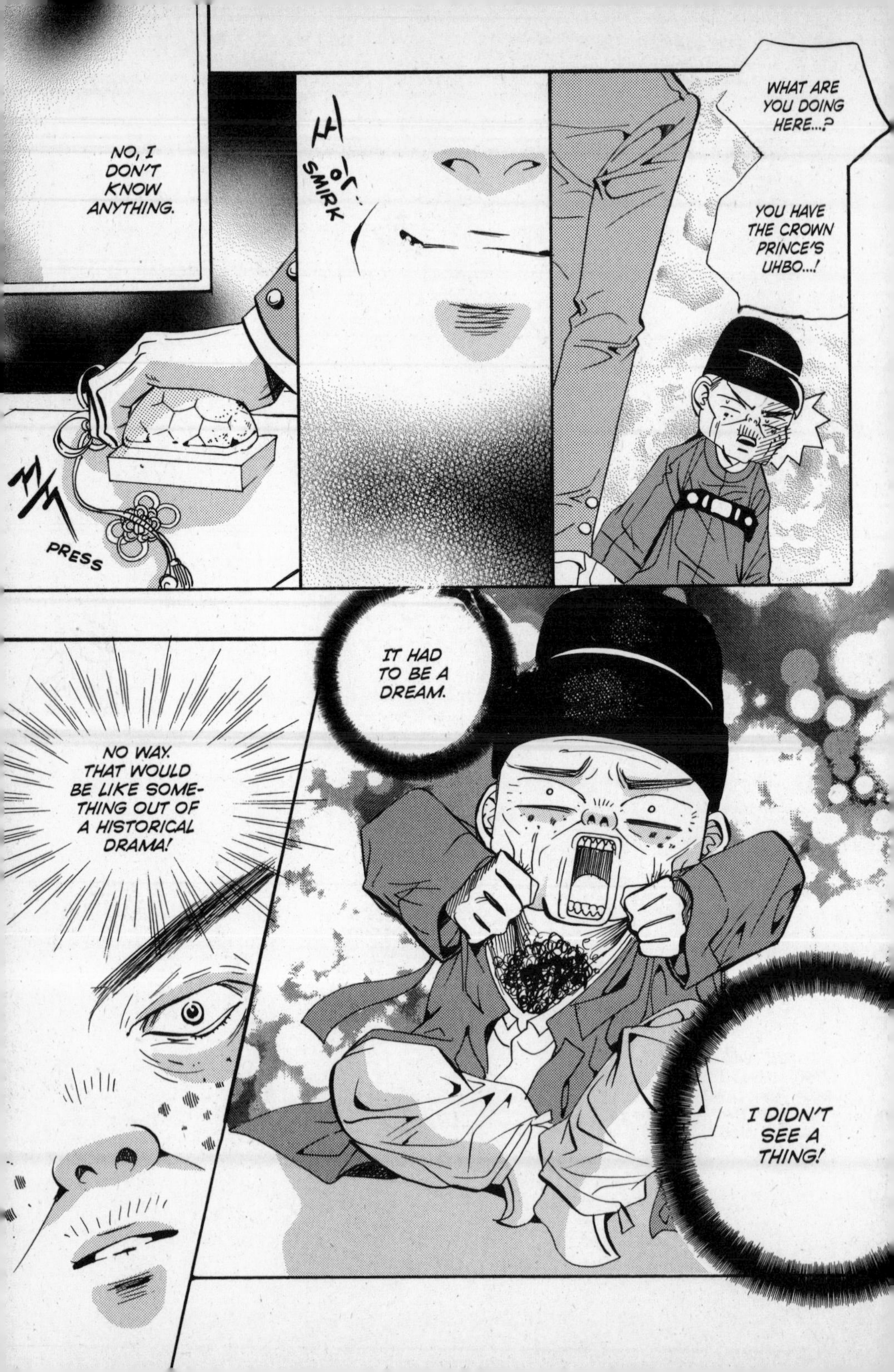
NO, I DON'T KNOW ANYTHING.
PRESS
SMIRK
WHAT ARE YOU DOING HERE...?
YOU HAVE THE CROWN PRINCE'S UHBO...!
NO WAY. THAT WOULD BE LIKE SOME-THING OUT OF A HISTORICAL DRAMA!
IT HAD TO BE A DREAM.
I DIDN'T SEE A THING!

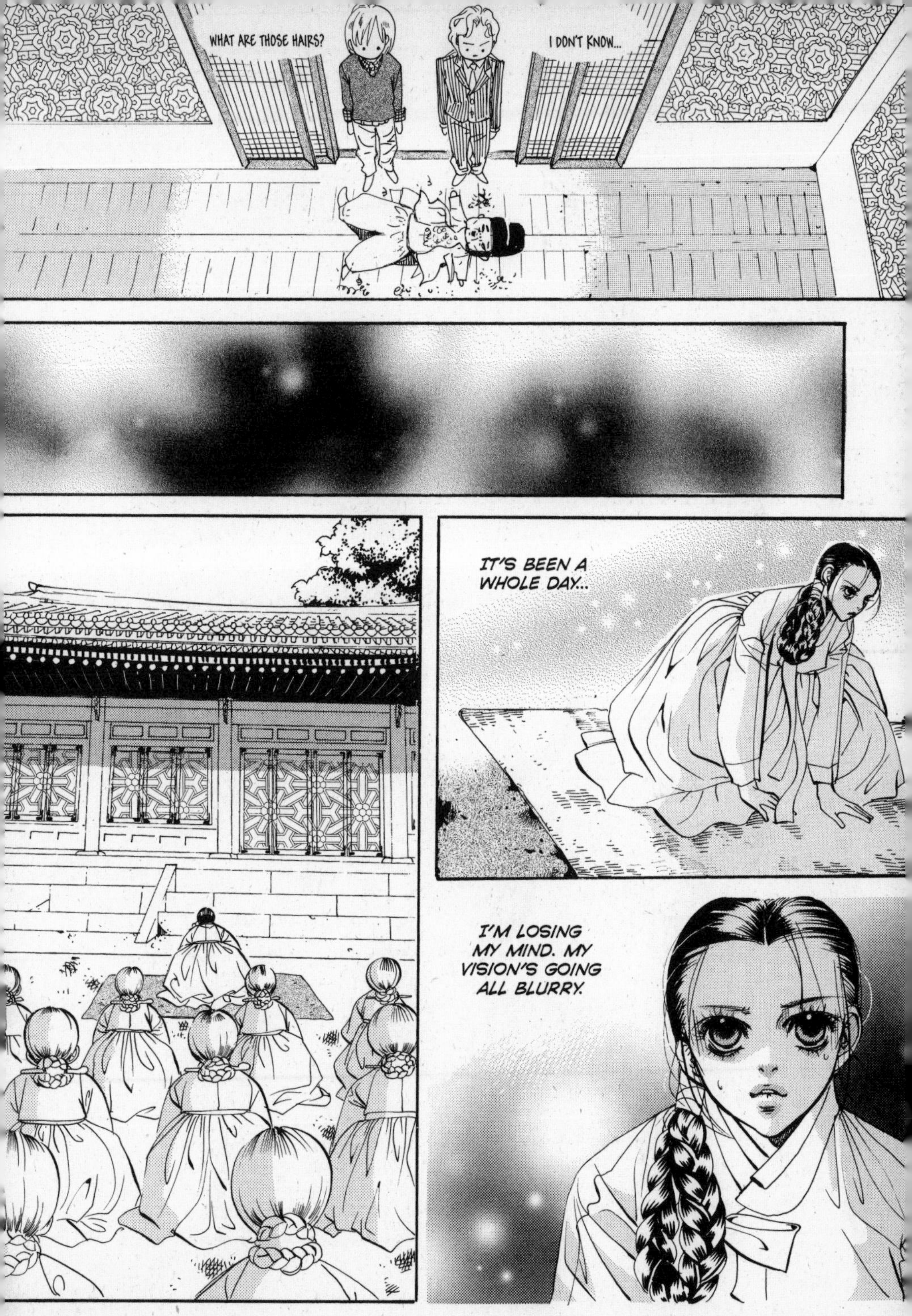

WHAT ARE THOSE HAIRS?
I DON'T KNOW...
IT'S BEEN A WHOLE DAY...
I'M LOSING MY MIND. MY VISION'S GOING ALL BLURRY.

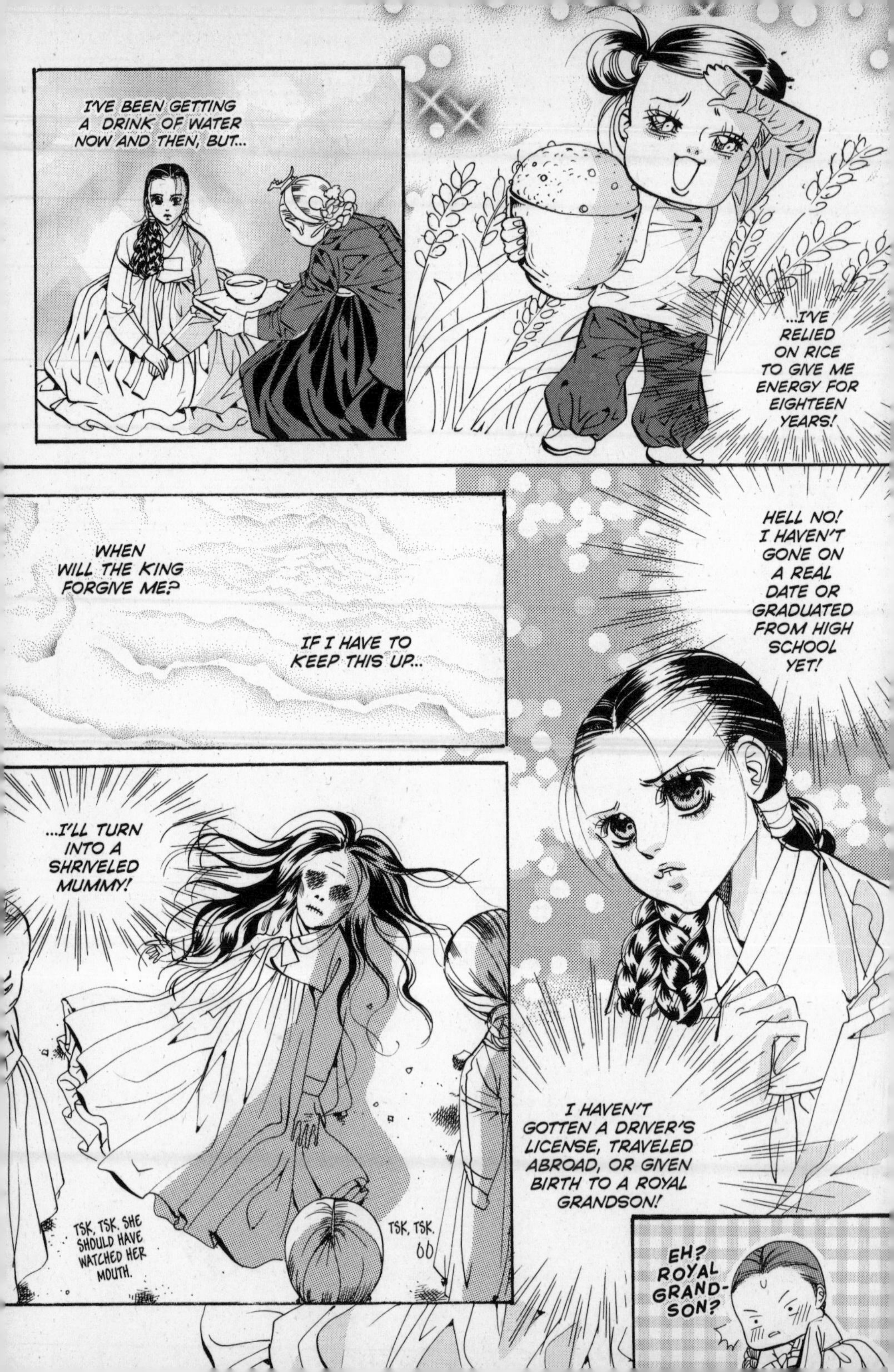
I'VE BEEN GETTING A DRINK OF WATER NOW AND THEN, BUT...
...I'VE RELIED ON RICE TO GIVE ME ENERGY FOR EIGHTEEN YEARS!
WHEN WILL THE KING FORGIVE ME?
IF I HAVE TO KEEP THIS UP...
...I'LL TURN INTO A SHRIVELED MUMMY!
TSK, TSK. SHE SHOULD HAVE WATCHED HER MOUTH.
TSK, TSK.
HELL NO! I HAVEN'T GONE ON A REAL DATE OR GRADUATED FROM HIGH SCHOOL YET!
I HAVEN'T GOTTEN A DRIVER'S LICENSE, TRAVELED ABROAD, OR GIVEN BIRTH TO A ROYAL GRANDSON!
EH? ROYAL GRAND-SON?

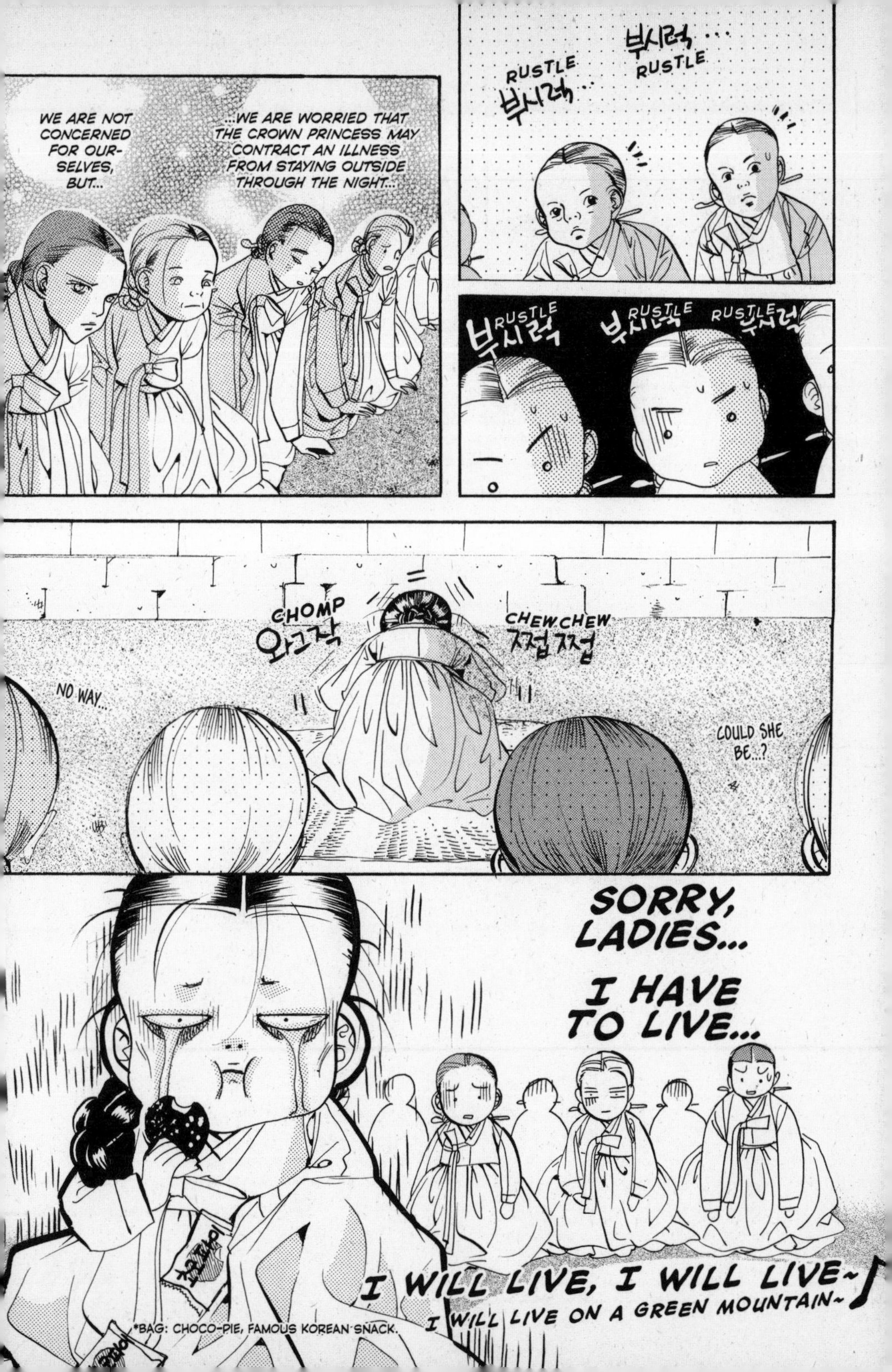
WE ARE NOT CONCERNED FOR OUR-SELVES, BUT...
...WE ARE WORRIED THAT THE CROWN PRINCESS MAY CONTRACT AN ILLNESS FROM STAYING OUTSIDE THROUGH THE NIGHT...
RUSTLE
부시럭...
부시럭...
RUSTLE
RUSTLE 부시럭
RUSTLE 부시럭
RUSTLE 부시럭
CHOMP 와그작
CHEW CHEW 자접자접
NO WAY...
COULD SHE BE...?
SORRY, LADIES...
I HAVE TO LIVE...
I WILL LIVE, I WILL LIVE~
I WILL LIVE ON A GREEN MOUNTAIN~
*BAG: CHOCO-PIE, FAMOUS KOREAN SNACK.

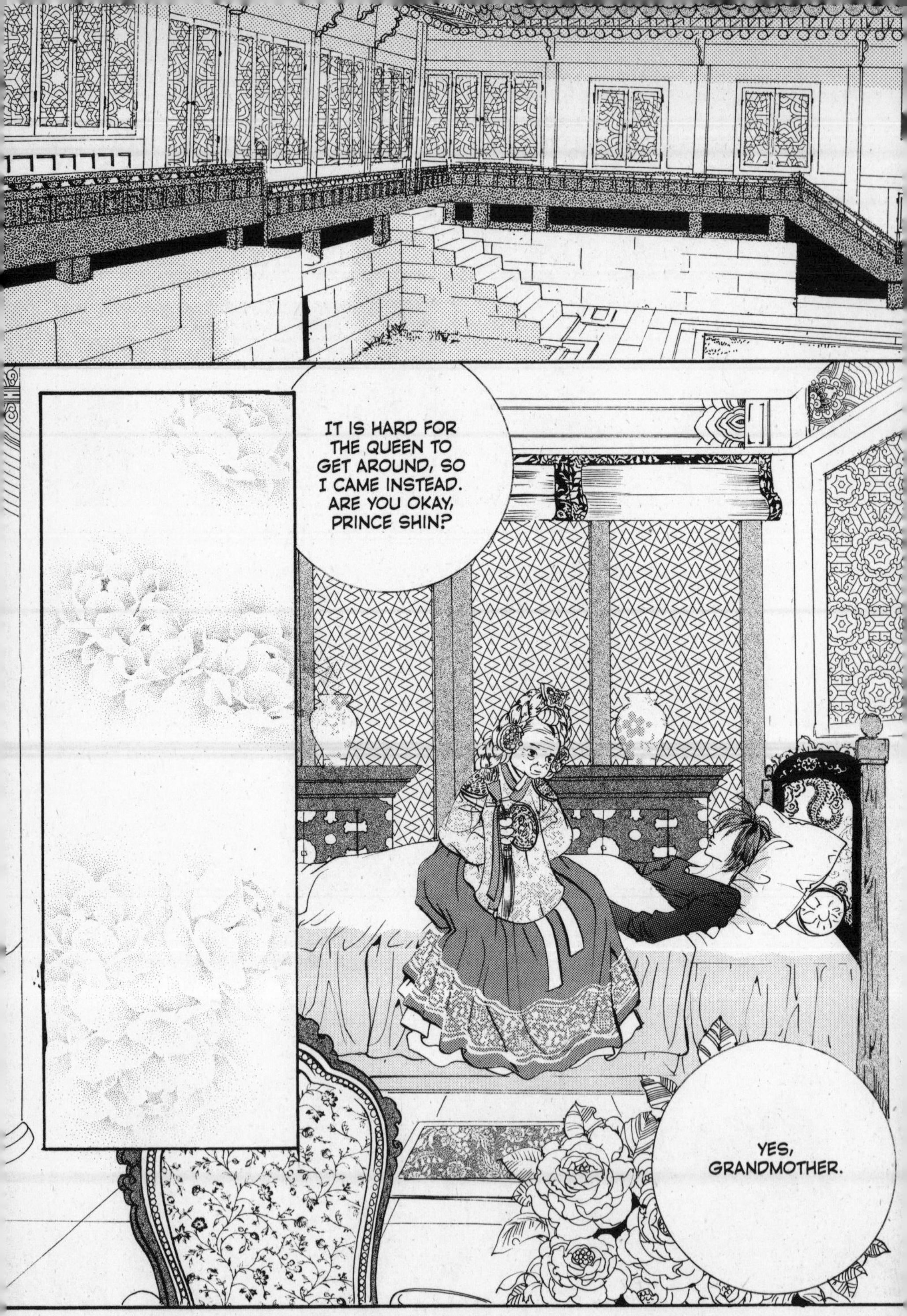
IT IS HARD FOR THE QUEEN TO GET AROUND, SO I CAME INSTEAD. ARE YOU OKAY, PRINCE SHIN?
YES, GRANDMOTHER.

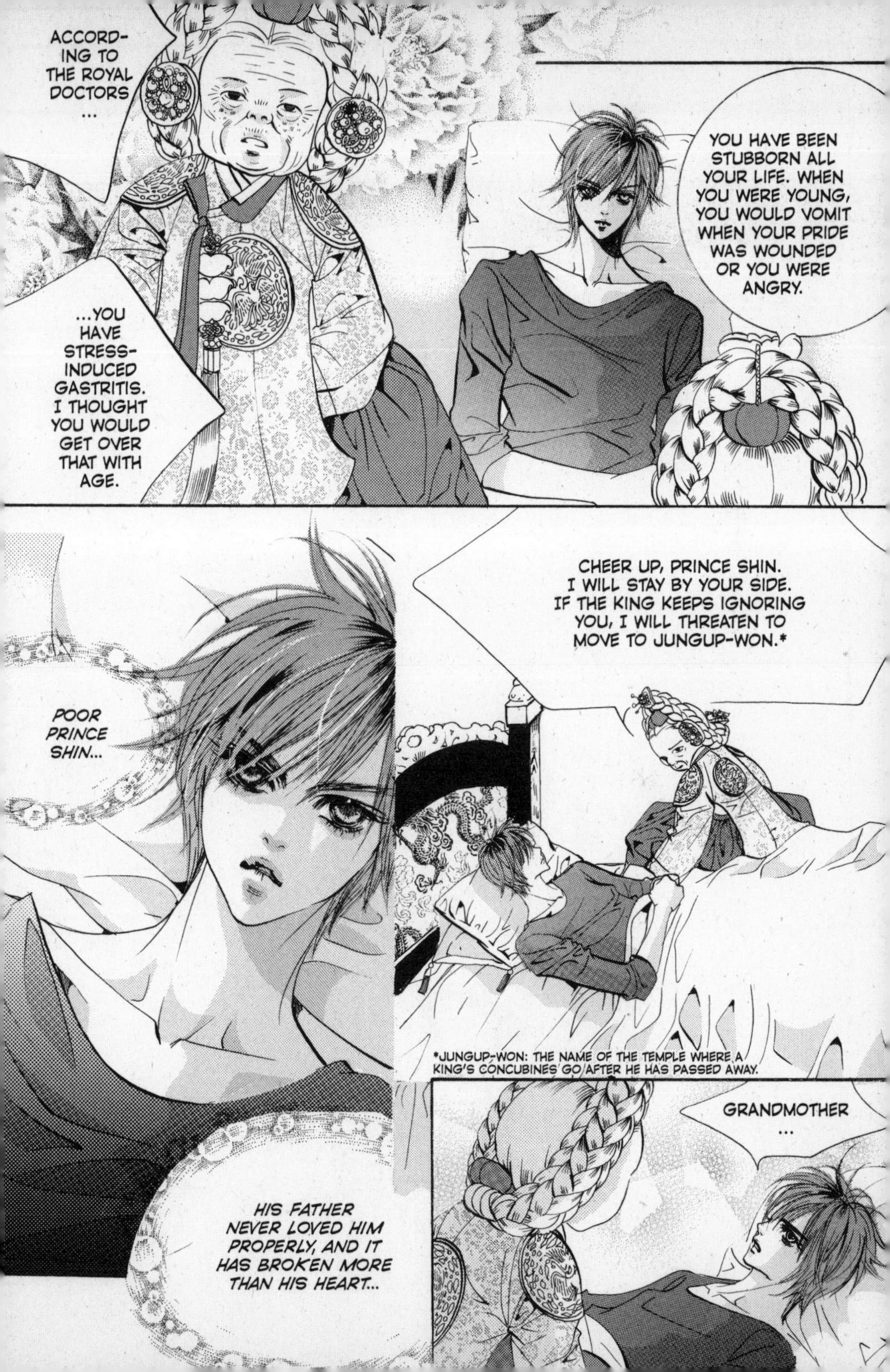
ACCORD-ING TO THE ROYAL DOCTORS ...
...YOU HAVE STRESS-INDUCED GASTRITIS. I THOUGHT YOU WOULD GET OVER THAT WITH AGE.
YOU HAVE BEEN STUBBORN ALL YOUR LIFE. WHEN YOU WERE YOUNG, YOU WOULD VOMIT WHEN YOUR PRIDE WAS WOUNDED OR YOU WERE ANGRY.
POOR PRINCE SHIN...
HIS FATHER NEVER LOVED HIM PROPERLY, AND IT HAS BROKEN MORE THAN HIS HEART...
CHEER UP, PRINCE SHIN. I WILL STAY BY YOUR SIDE. IF THE KING KEEPS IGNORING YOU, I WILL THREATEN TO MOVE TO JUNGUP-WON.*
*JUNGUP-WON: THE NAME OF THE TEMPLE WHERE A KING'S CONCUBINES GO AFTER HE HAS PASSED AWAY.
GRANDMOTHER ...

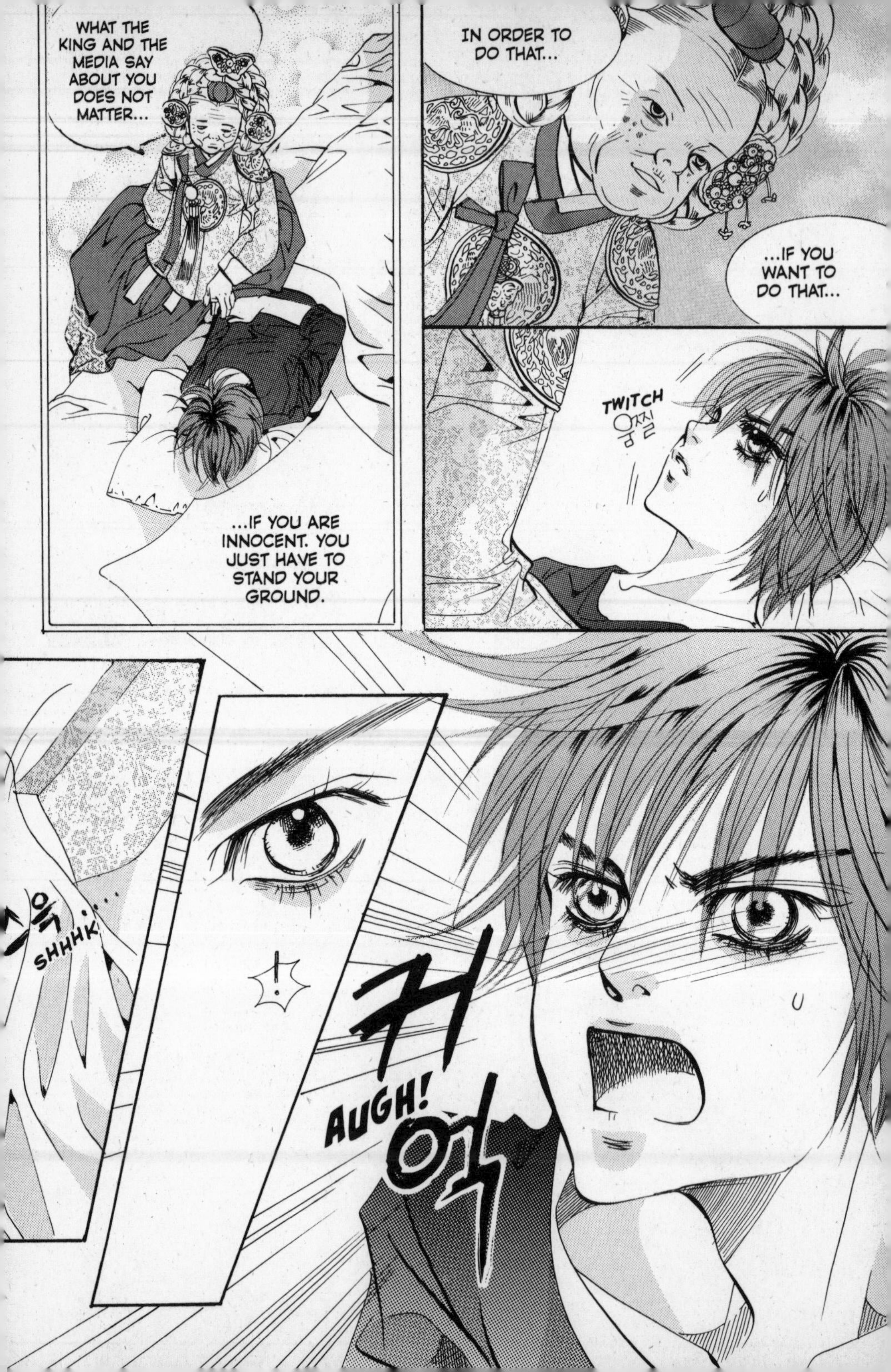
WHAT THE KING AND THE MEDIA SAY ABOUT YOU DOES NOT MATTER...
...IF YOU ARE INNOCENT. YOU JUST HAVE TO STAND YOUR GROUND.
IN ORDER TO DO THAT...
...IF YOU WANT TO DO THAT...
TWITCH
움찔
SHHHK
!
AUGH!

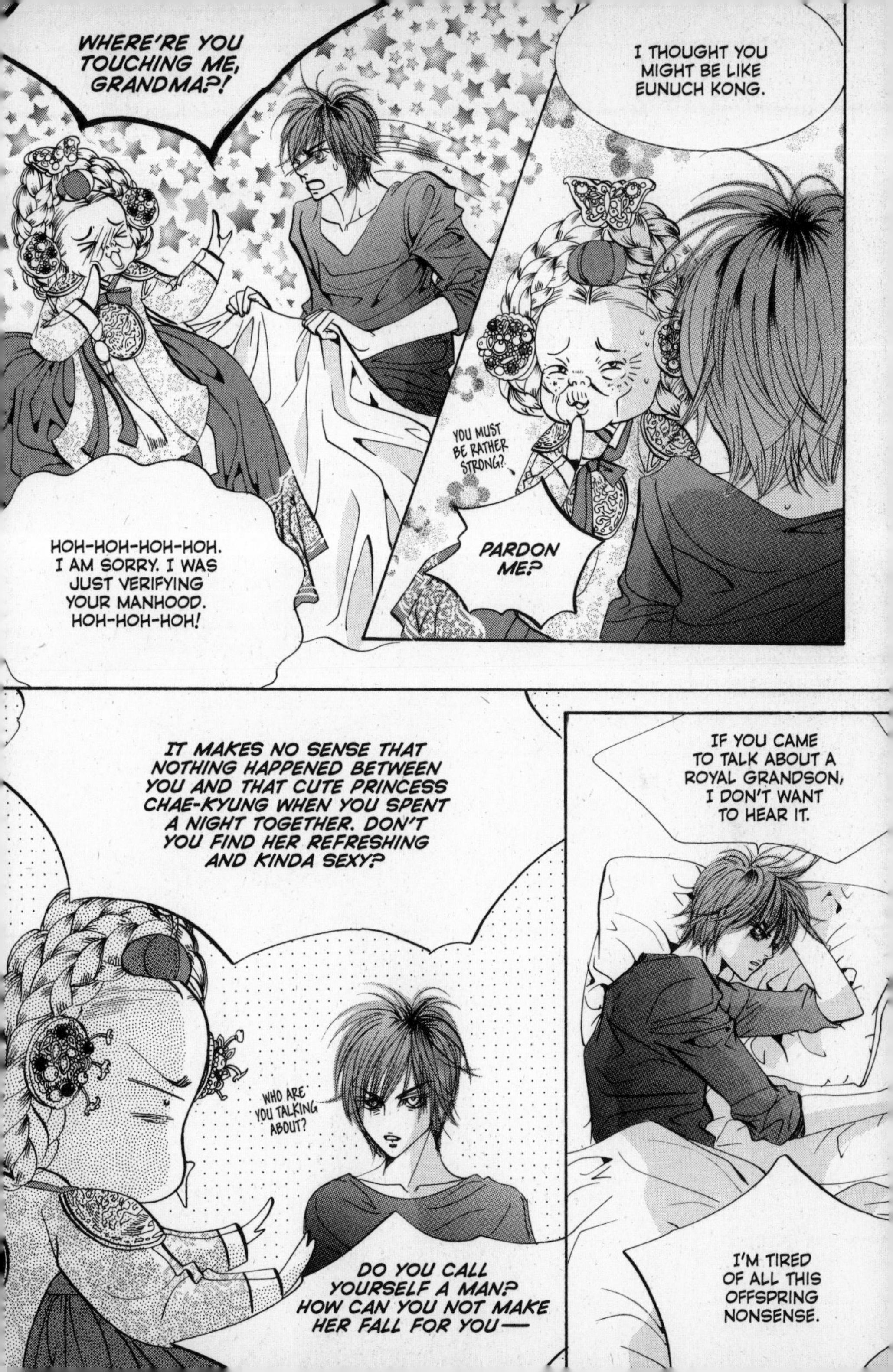

WHERE'RE YOU TOUCHING ME, GRANDMA?!
HOH-HOH-HOH-HOH. I AM SORRY. I WAS JUST VERIFYING YOUR MANHOOD. HOH-HOH-HOH!
I THOUGHT YOU MIGHT BE LIKE EUNUCH KONG.
YOU MUST BE RATHER STRONG?
PARDON ME?
IT MAKES NO SENSE THAT NOTHING HAPPENED BETWEEN YOU AND THAT CUTE PRINCESS CHAE-KYUNG WHEN YOU SPENT A NIGHT TOGETHER. DON'T YOU FIND HER REFRESHING AND KINDA SEXY?
WHO ARE YOU TALKING ABOUT?
DO YOU CALL YOURSELF A MAN? HOW CAN YOU NOT MAKE HER FALL FOR YOU—
IF YOU CAME TO TALK ABOUT A ROYAL GRANDSON, I DON'T WANT TO HEAR IT.
I'M TIRED OF ALL THIS OFFSPRING NONSENSE.

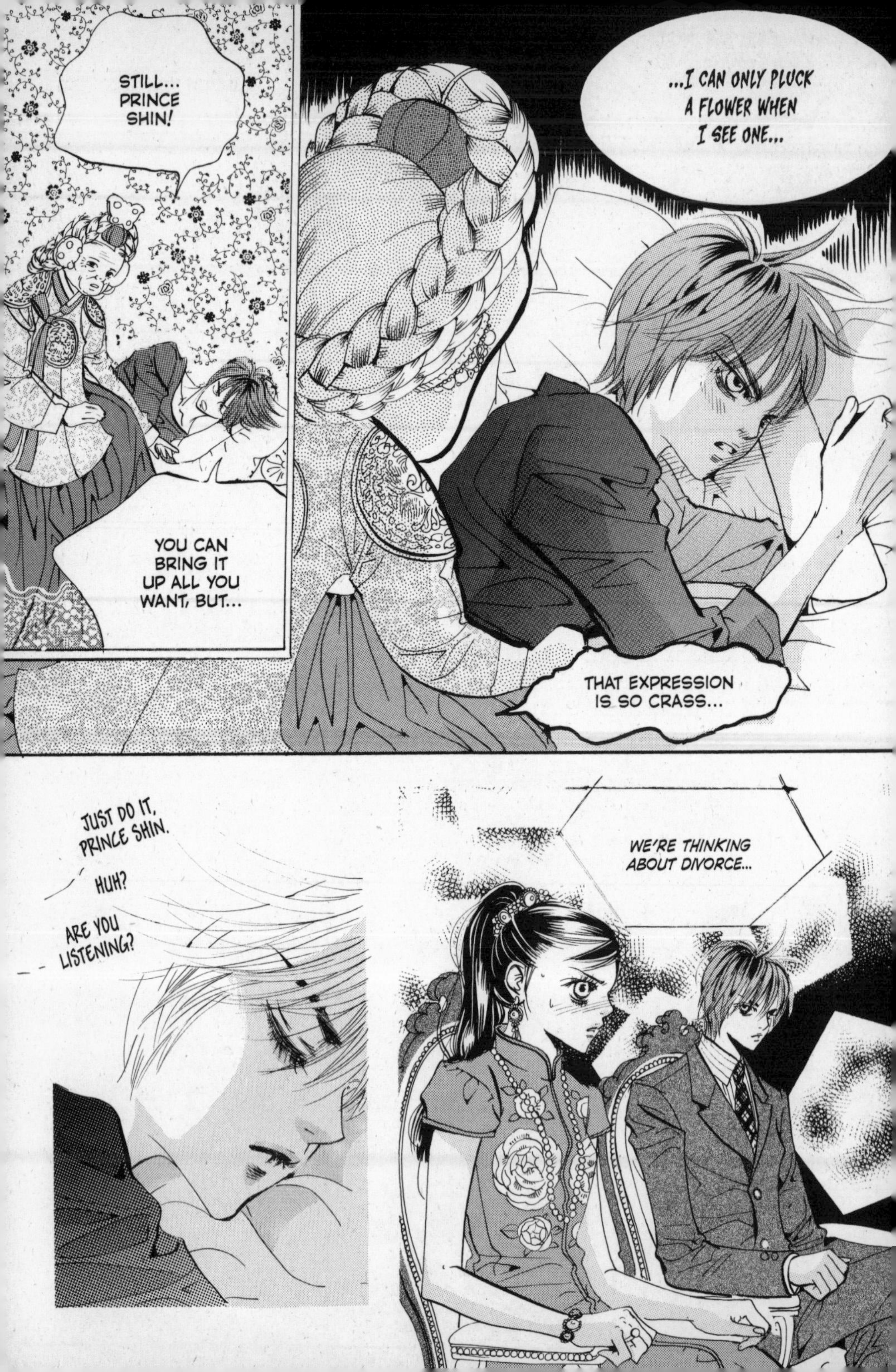
STILL... PRINCE SHIN!
YOU CAN BRING IT UP ALL YOU WANT, BUT...
...I CAN ONLY PLUCK A FLOWER WHEN I SEE ONE...
THAT EXPRESSION IS SO CRASS...
JUST DO IT, PRINCE SHIN.
HUH?
ARE YOU LISTENING?
WE'RE THINKING ABOUT DIVORCE...

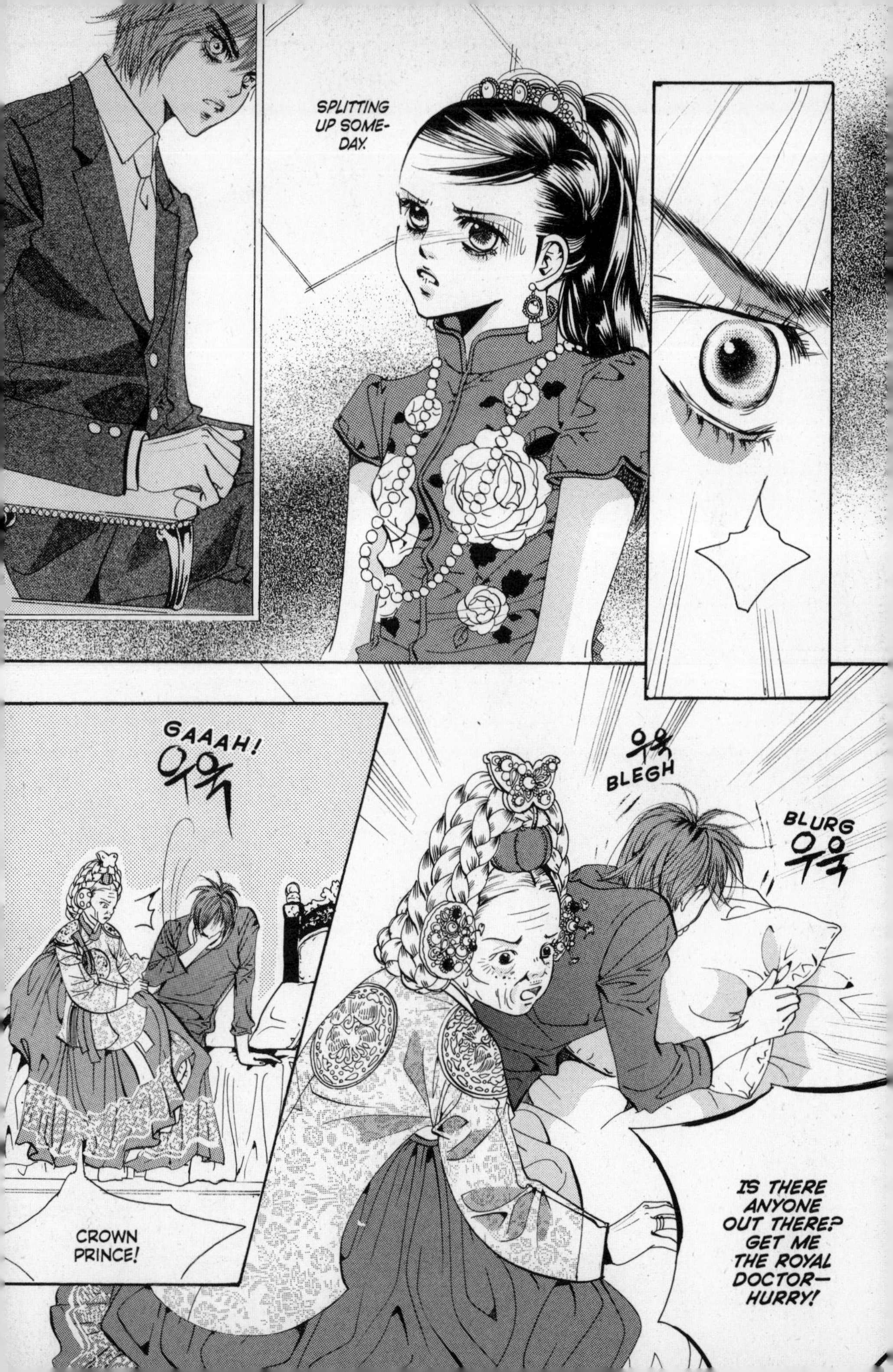
SPLITTING UP SOME-DAY.
GAAAH!
CROWN PRINCE!
BLEGH
BLURG
IS THERE ANYONE OUT THERE? GET ME THE ROYAL DOCTOR—HURRY!

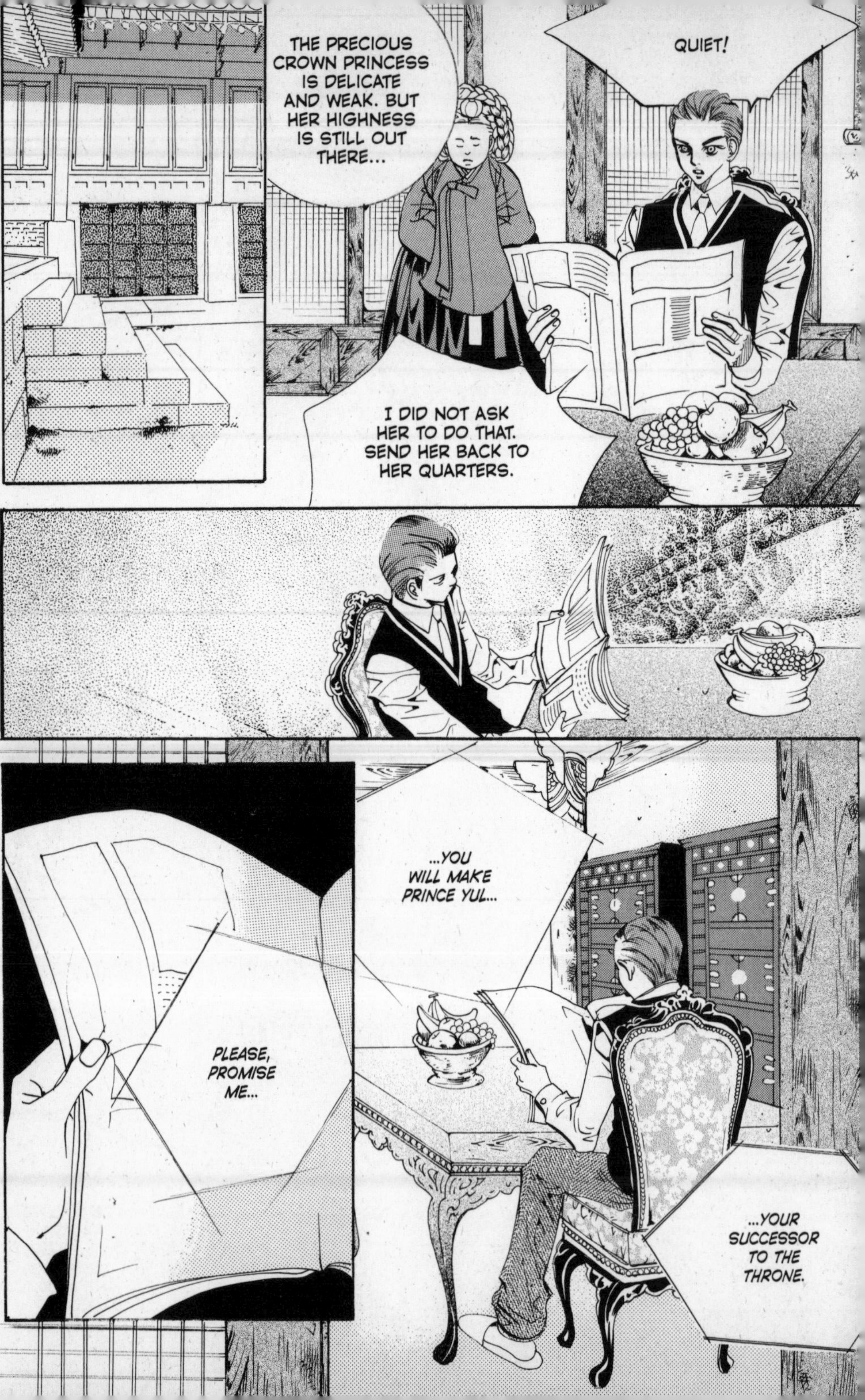
THE PRECIOUS CROWN PRINCESS IS DELICATE AND WEAK. BUT HER HIGHNESS IS STILL OUT THERE...
QUIET!
I DID NOT ASK HER TO DO THAT. SEND HER BACK TO HER QUARTERS.
...YOU WILL MAKE PRINCE YUL...
PLEASE, PROMISE ME...
...YOUR SUCCESSOR TO THE THRONE.

HIS END WAS NEAR...

CAN YOU PROMISE ME THAT?

HE LOOKED DESPERATE...

...WHEN MY OLDER BROTHER, WHO NEVER SEEMED TO DESIRE POWER, SUDDENLY ASKED THIS FAVOR OF ME.

YES...

...SO I SAID WHAT HE WANTED TO HEAR.

...I PROMISE YOU, BIG BROTHER.

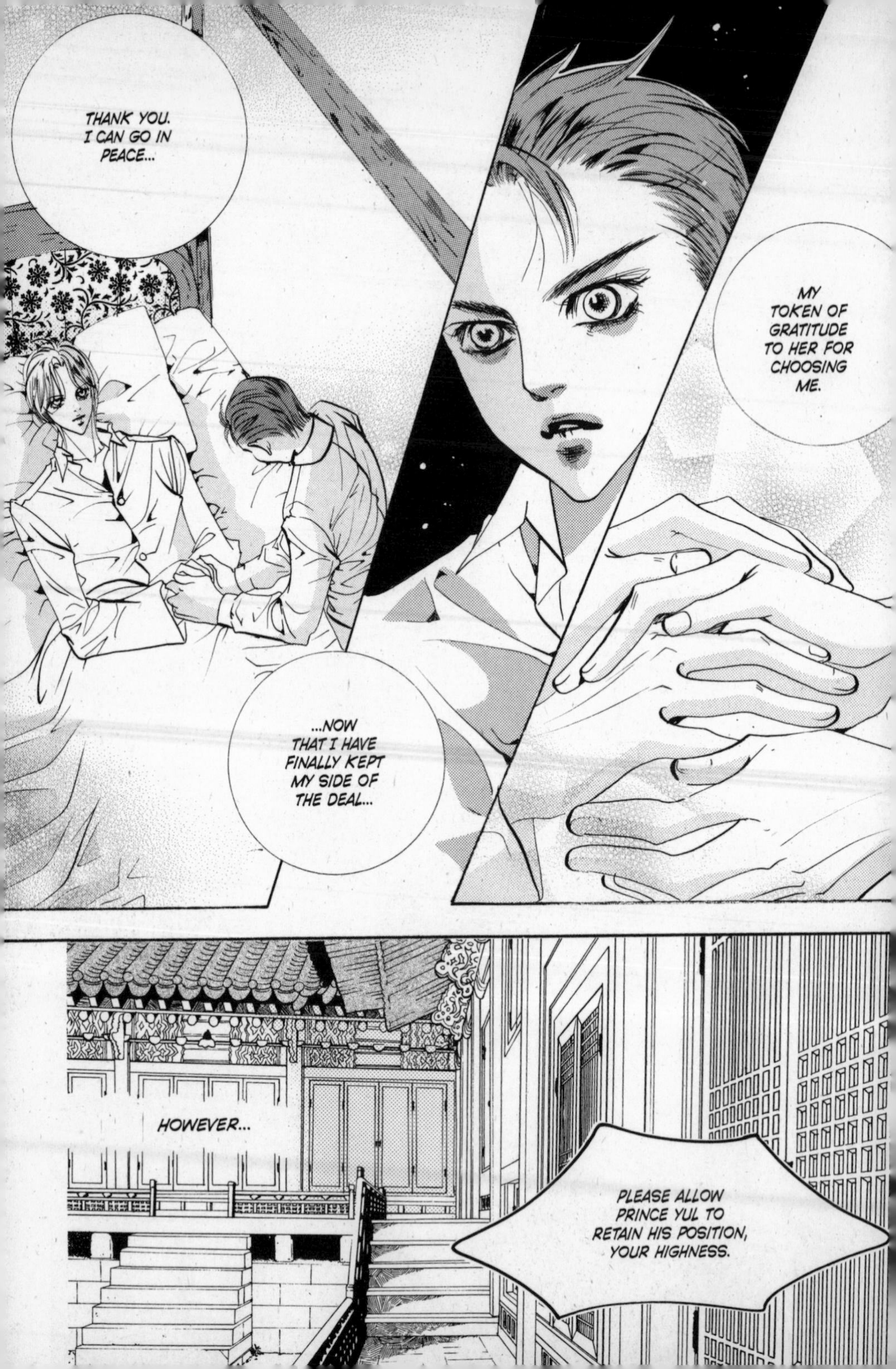
THANK YOU. I CAN GO IN PEACE...
...NOW THAT I HAVE FINALLY KEPT MY SIDE OF THE DEAL...
MY TOKEN OF GRATITUDE TO HER FOR CHOOSING ME.
HOWEVER...
PLEASE ALLOW PRINCE YUL TO RETAIN HIS POSITION, YOUR HIGHNESS.

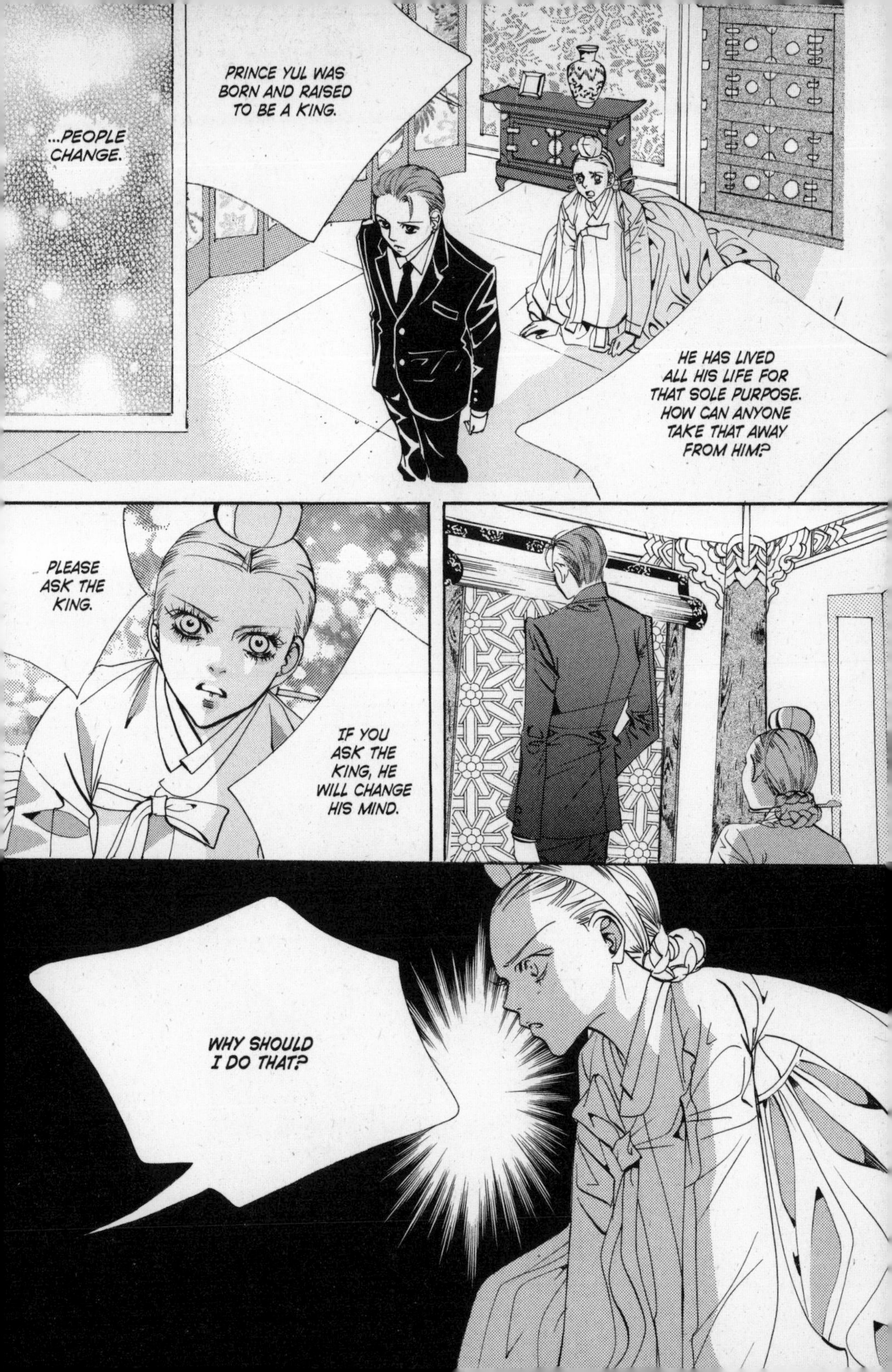
...PEOPLE CHANGE.
PRINCE YUL WAS BORN AND RAISED TO BE A KING.
HE HAS LIVED ALL HIS LIFE FOR THAT SOLE PURPOSE. HOW CAN ANYONE TAKE THAT AWAY FROM HIM?
PLEASE ASK THE KING.
IF YOU ASK THE KING, HE WILL CHANGE HIS MIND.
WHY SHOULD I DO THAT?

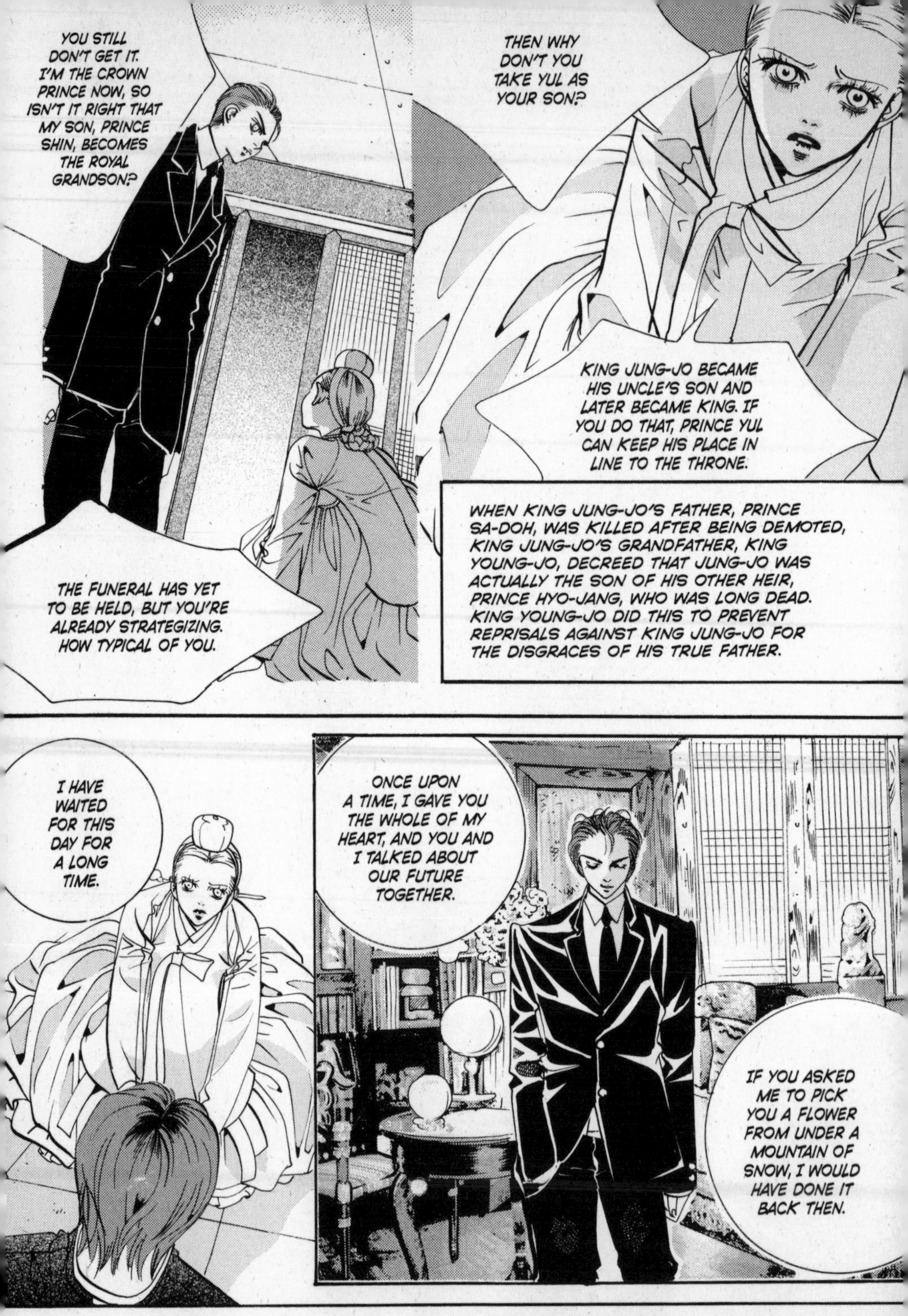
YOU STILL DON'T GET IT. I'M THE CROWN PRINCE NOW, SO ISN'T IT RIGHT THAT MY SON, PRINCE SHIN, BECOMES THE ROYAL GRANDSON?
THE FUNERAL HAS YET TO BE HELD, BUT YOU'RE ALREADY STRATEGIZING. HOW TYPICAL OF YOU.
THEN WHY DON'T YOU TAKE YUL AS YOUR SON?
KING JUNG-JO BECAME HIS UNCLE'S SON AND LATER BECAME KING. IF YOU DO THAT, PRINCE YUL CAN KEEP HIS PLACE IN LINE TO THE THRONE.
WHEN KING JUNG-JO'S FATHER, PRINCE SA-DOH, WAS KILLED AFTER BEING DEMOTED, KING JUNG-JO'S GRANDFATHER, KING YOUNG-JO, DECREED THAT JUNG-JO WAS ACTUALLY THE SON OF HIS OTHER HEIR, PRINCE HYO-JANG, WHO WAS LONG DEAD. KING YOUNG-JO DID THIS TO PREVENT REPRISALS AGAINST KING JUNG-JO FOR THE DISGRACES OF HIS TRUE FATHER.
I HAVE WAITED FOR THIS DAY FOR A LONG TIME.
ONCE UPON A TIME, I GAVE YOU THE WHOLE OF MY HEART, AND YOU AND I TALKED ABOUT OUR FUTURE TOGETHER.
IF YOU ASKED ME TO PICK YOU A FLOWER FROM UNDER A MOUNTAIN OF SNOW, I WOULD HAVE DONE IT BACK THEN.

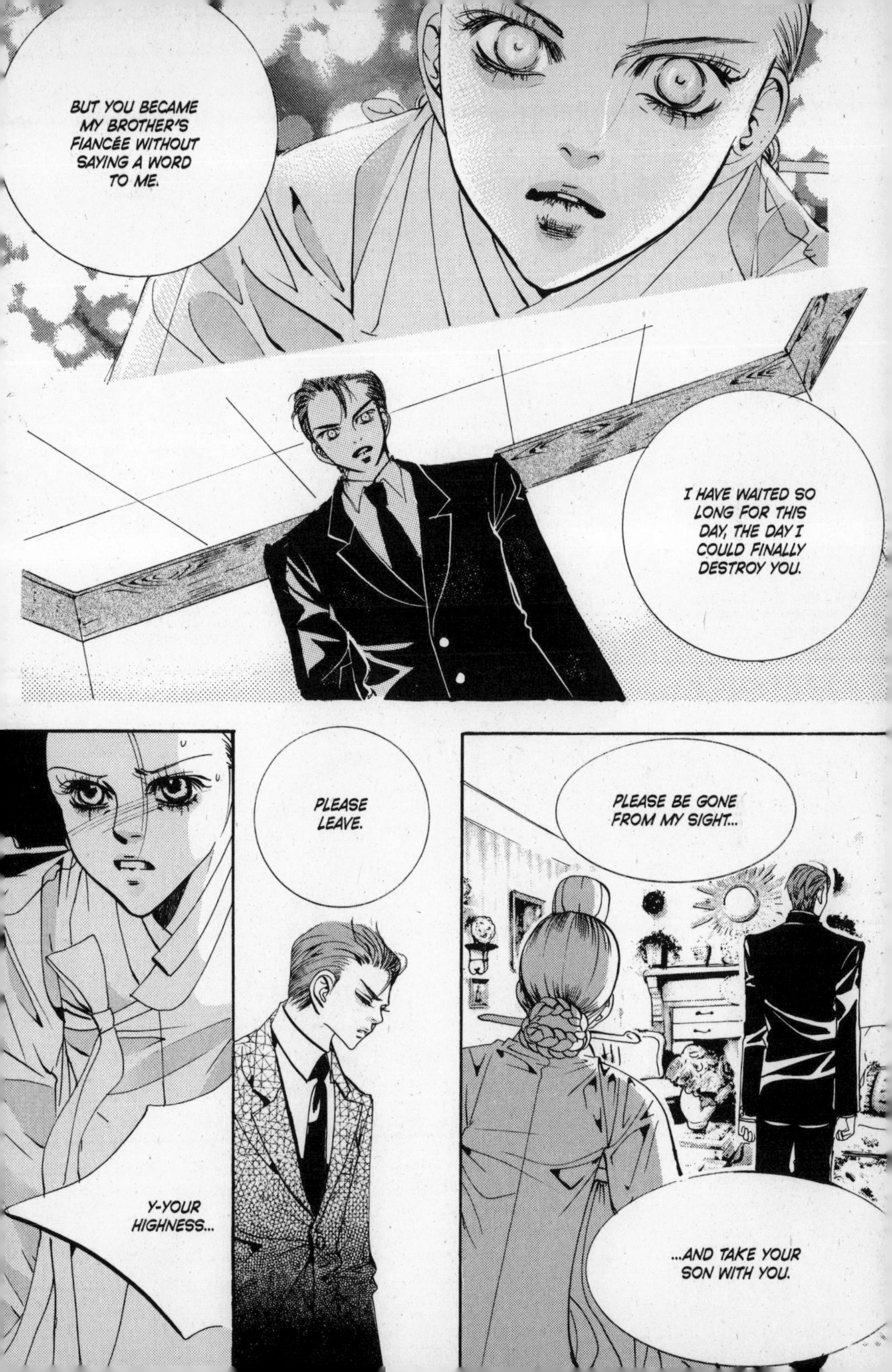
BUT YOU BECAME MY BROTHER'S FIANCÉE WITHOUT SAYING A WORD TO ME.
I HAVE WAITED SO LONG FOR THIS DAY, THE DAY I COULD FINALLY DESTROY YOU.
Y-YOUR HIGHNESS...
PLEASE LEAVE.
PLEASE BE GONE FROM MY SIGHT...
...AND TAKE YOUR SON WITH YOU.

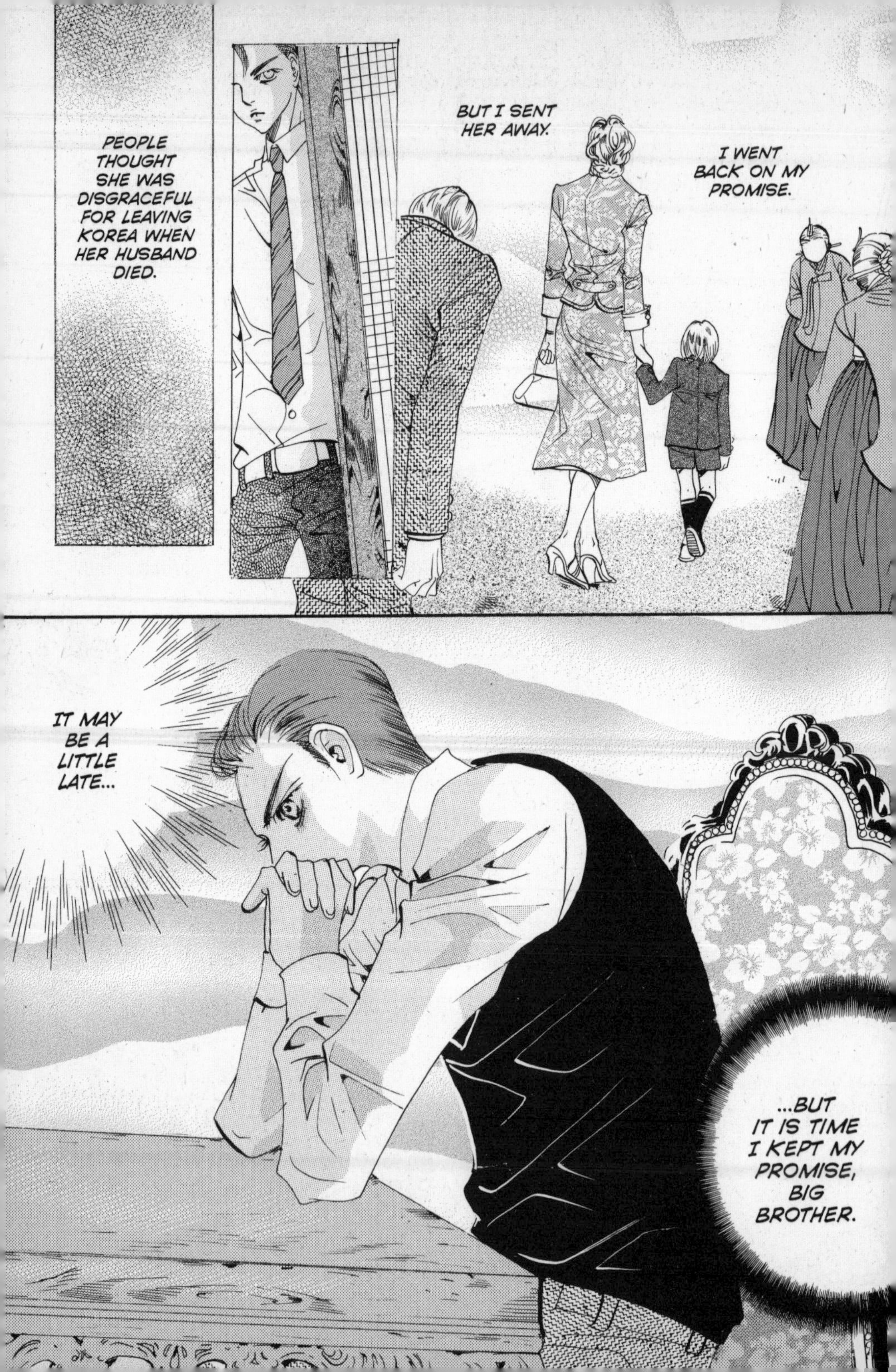
PEOPLE THOUGHT SHE WAS DISGRACEFUL FOR LEAVING KOREA WHEN HER HUSBAND DIED.
BUT I SENT HER AWAY.
I WENT BACK ON MY PROMISE.
IT MAY BE A LITTLE LATE...
...BUT IT IS TIME I KEPT MY PROMISE, BIG BROTHER.

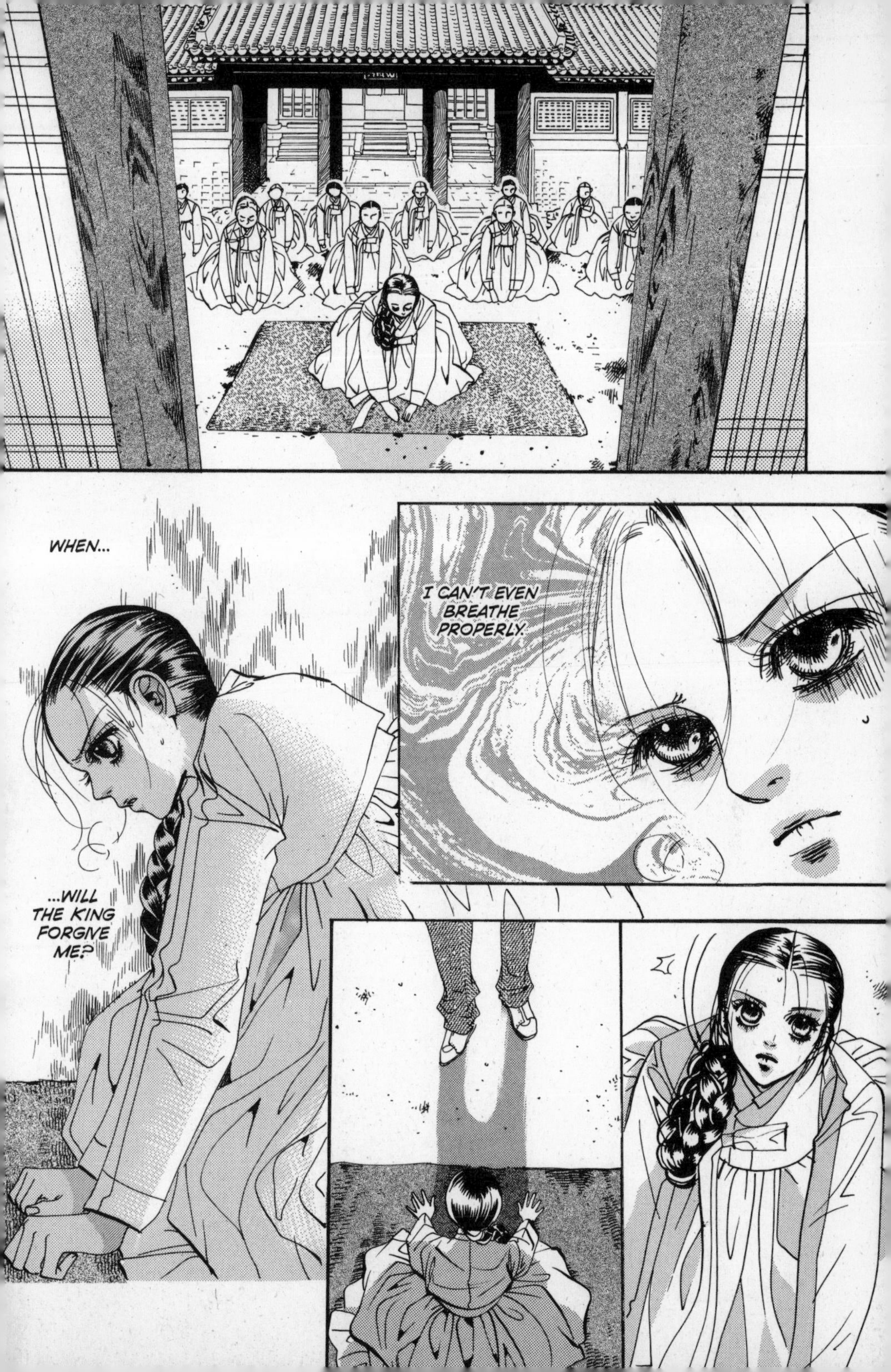
WHEN...
...WILL THE KING FORGIVE ME?
I CAN'T EVEN BREATHE PROPERLY.

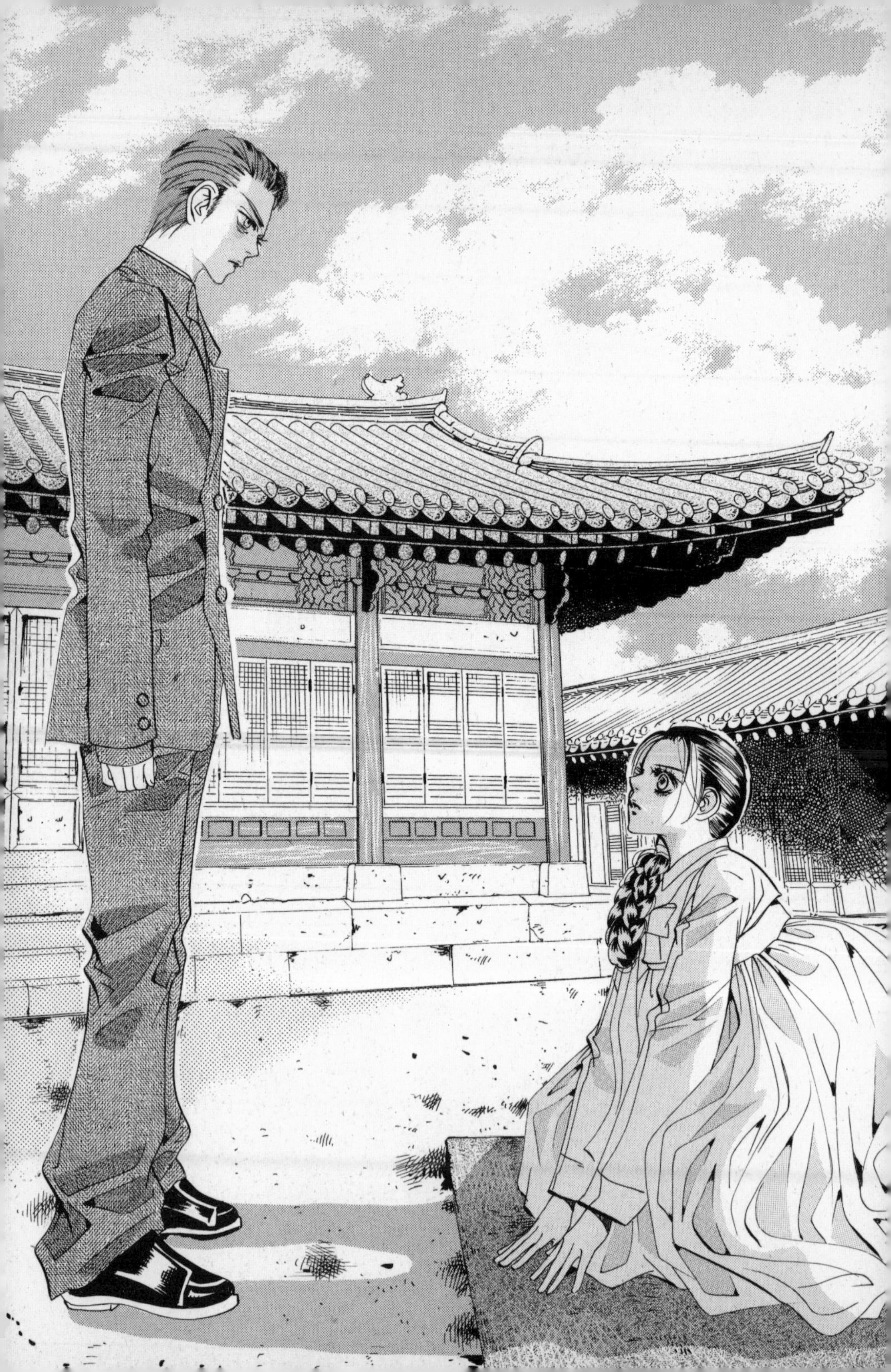

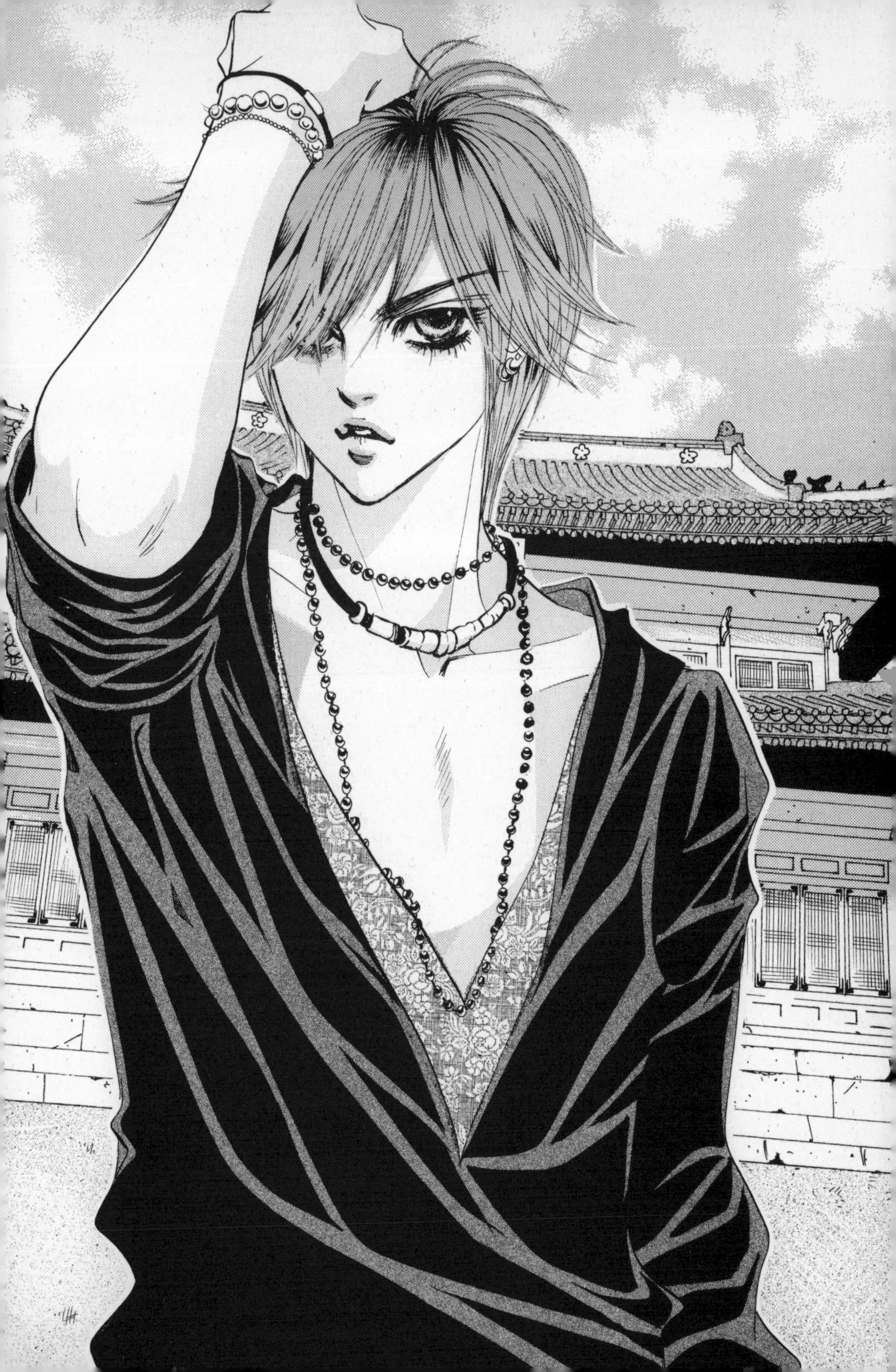

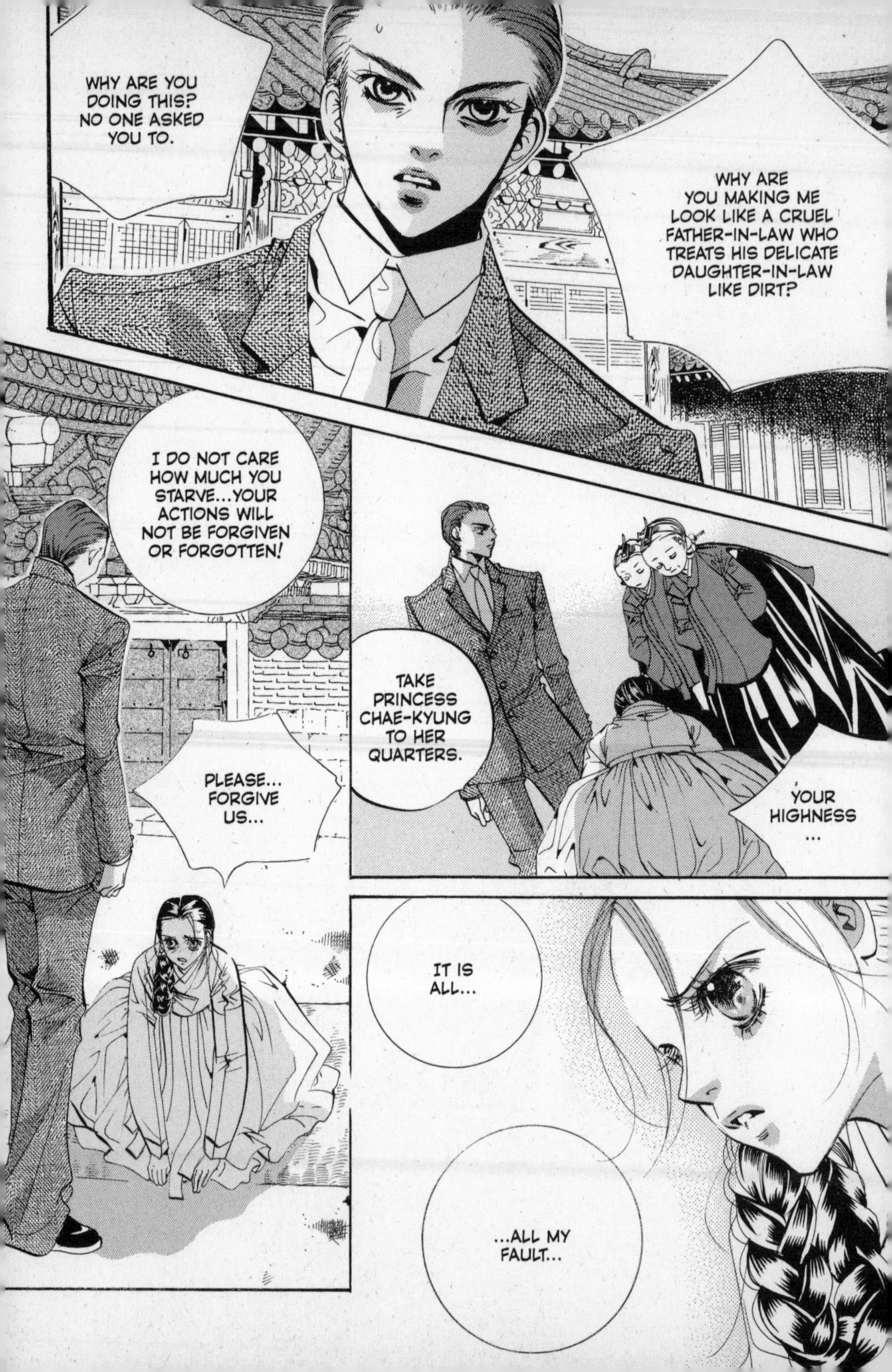
WHY ARE YOU DOING THIS? NO ONE ASKED YOU TO.
WHY ARE YOU MAKING ME LOOK LIKE A CRUEL FATHER-IN-LAW WHO TREATS HIS DELICATE DAUGHTER-IN-LAW LIKE DIRT?
I DO NOT CARE HOW MUCH YOU STARVE...YOUR ACTIONS WILL NOT BE FORGIVEN OR FORGOTTEN!
PLEASE... FORGIVE US...
TAKE PRINCESS CHAE-KYUNG TO HER QUARTERS.
YOUR HIGHNESS ...
IT IS ALL...
...ALL MY FAULT...

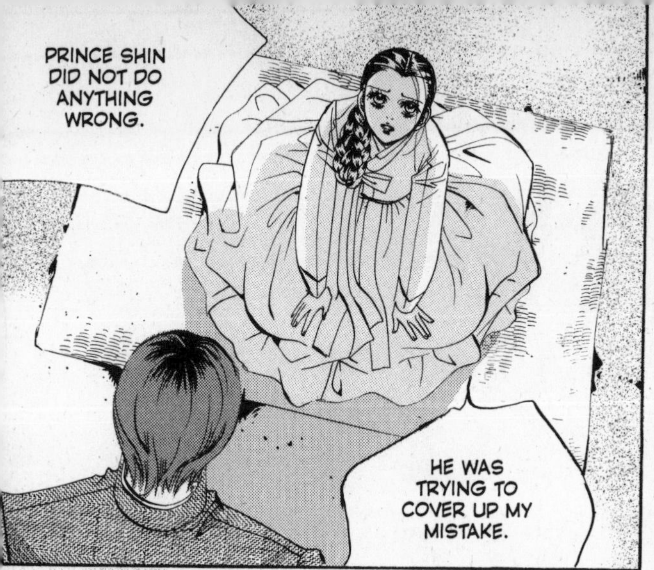
PRINCE SHIN DID NOT DO ANYTHING WRONG.
HE WAS TRYING TO COVER UP MY MISTAKE.
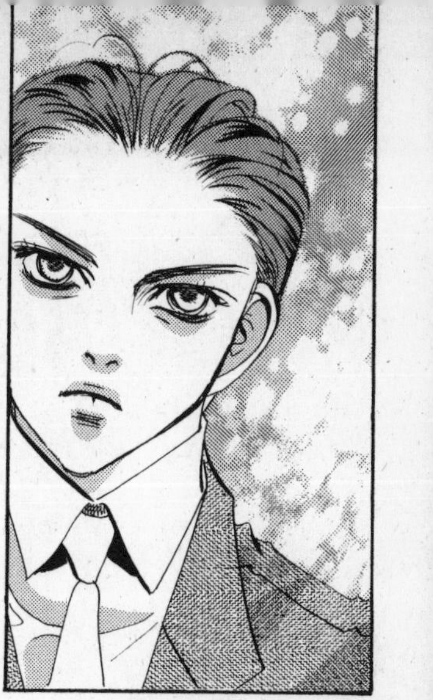
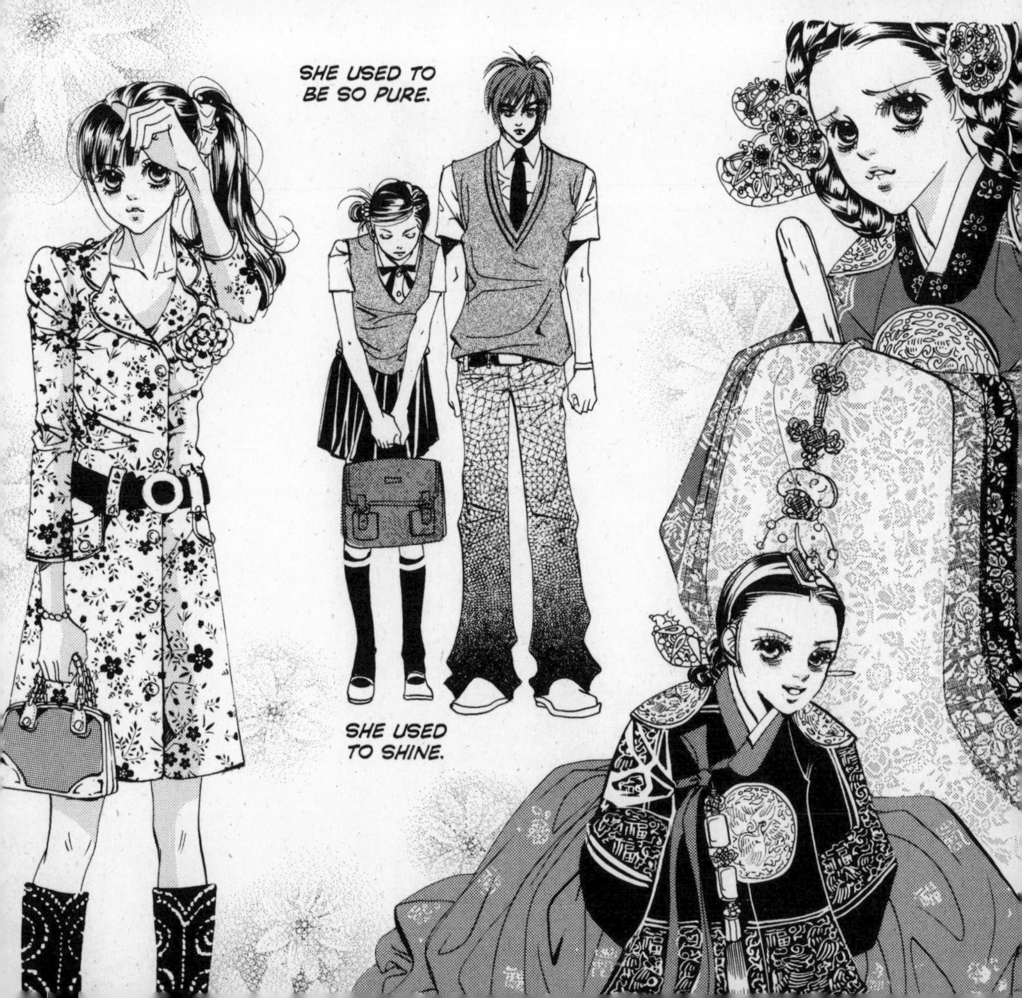
SHE USED TO BE SO PURE.
SHE USED TO SHINE.

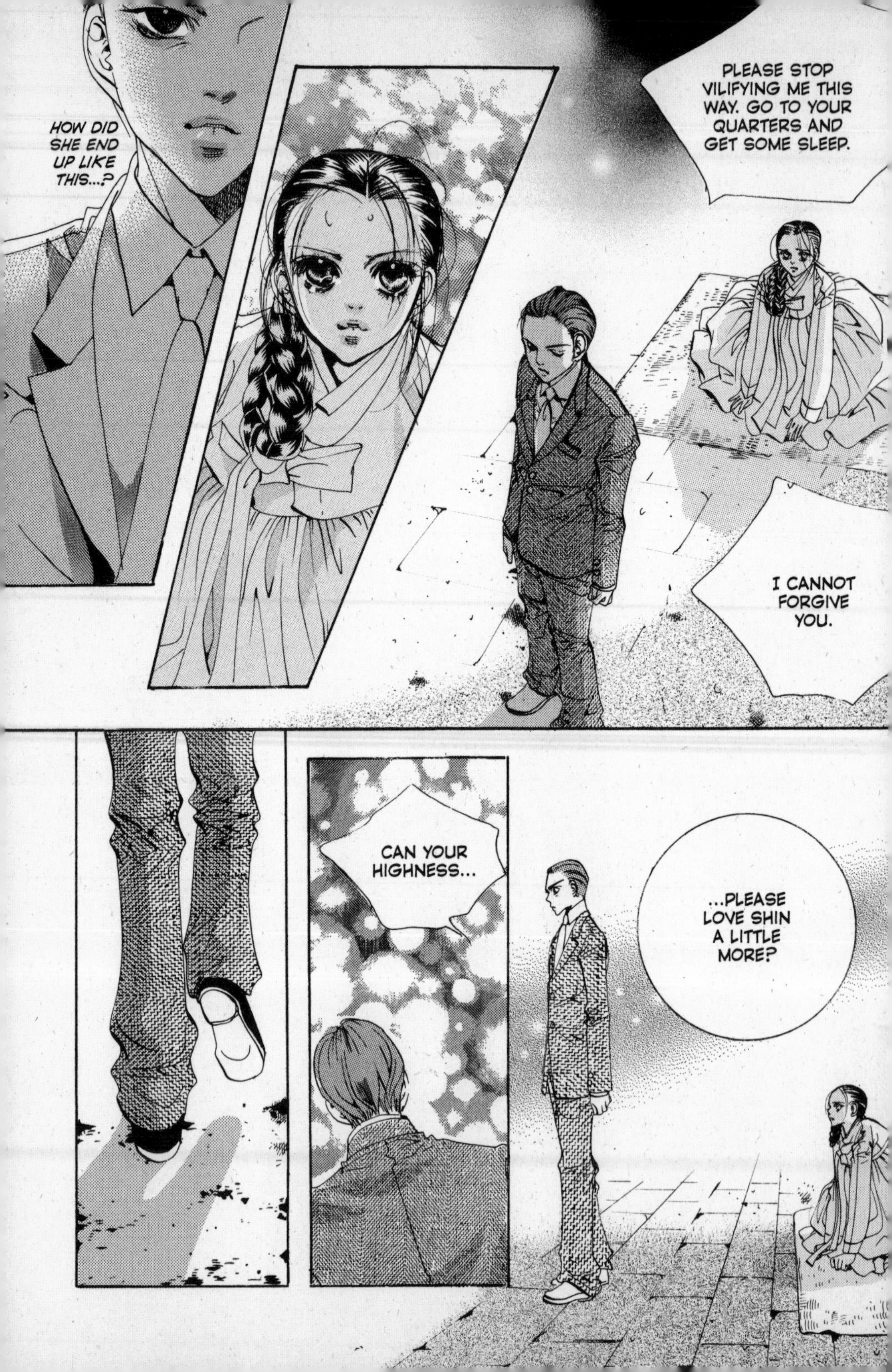
HOW DID SHE END UP LIKE THIS...?
PLEASE STOP VILIFYING ME THIS WAY. GO TO YOUR QUARTERS AND GET SOME SLEEP.
I CANNOT FORGIVE YOU.
CAN YOUR HIGHNESS...
...PLEASE LOVE SHIN A LITTLE MORE?

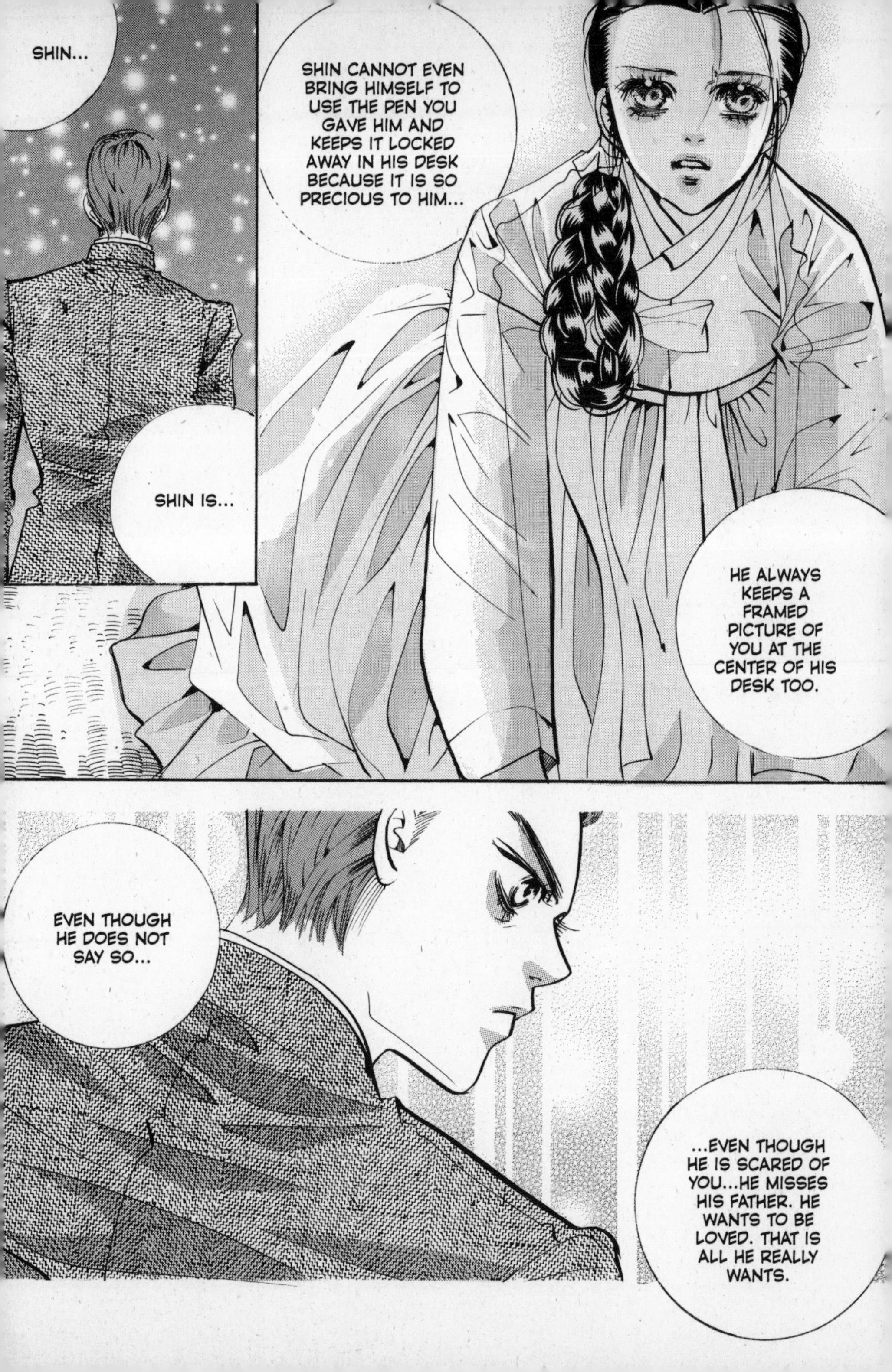
SHIN...
SHIN IS...
SHIN CANNOT EVEN BRING HIMSELF TO USE THE PEN YOU GAVE HIM AND KEEPS IT LOCKED AWAY IN HIS DESK BECAUSE IT IS SO PRECIOUS TO HIM...
HE ALWAYS KEEPS A FRAMED PICTURE OF YOU AT THE CENTER OF HIS DESK TOO.
EVEN THOUGH HE DOES NOT SAY SO...
...EVEN THOUGH HE IS SCARED OF YOU...HE MISSES HIS FATHER. HE WANTS TO BE LOVED. THAT IS ALL HE REALLY WANTS.

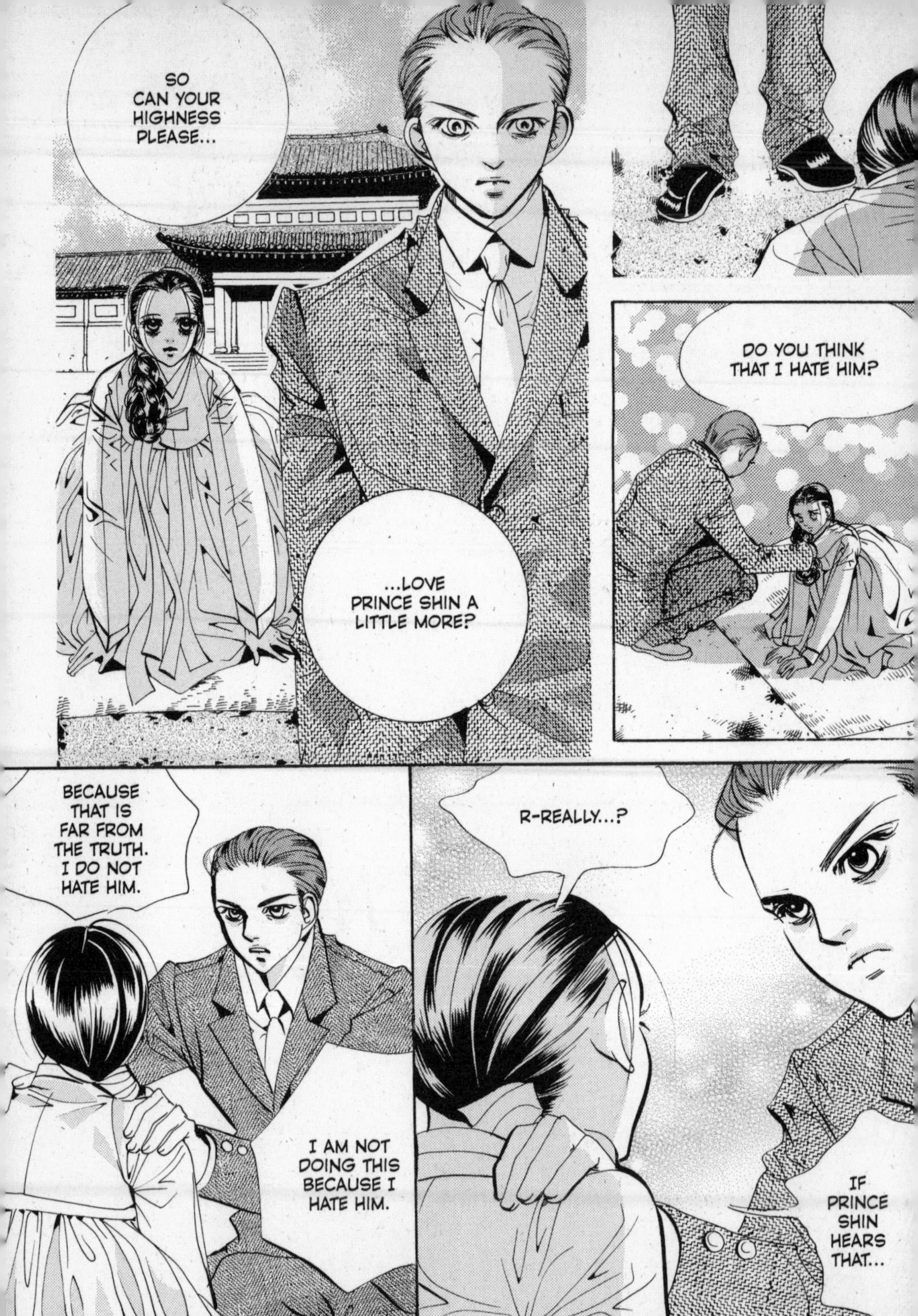
SO CAN YOUR HIGHNESS PLEASE...
...LOVE PRINCE SHIN A LITTLE MORE?
DO YOU THINK THAT I HATE HIM?
BECAUSE THAT IS FAR FROM THE TRUTH. I DO NOT HATE HIM.
I AM NOT DOING THIS BECAUSE I HATE HIM.
R-REALLY...?
IF PRINCE SHIN HEARS THAT...

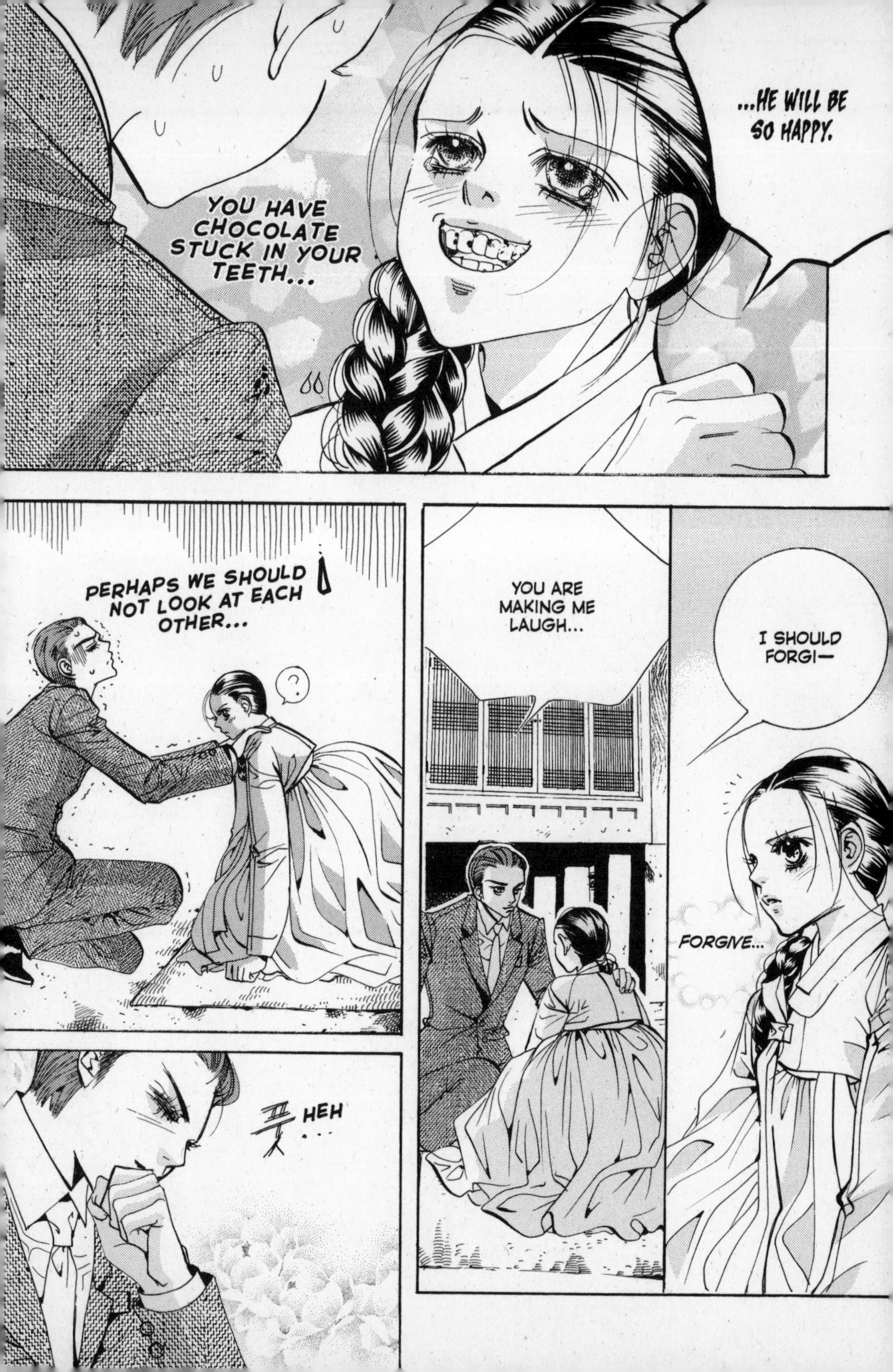
YOU HAVE CHOCOLATE STUCK IN YOUR TEETH...
...HE WILL BE SO HAPPY.
PERHAPS WE SHOULD NOT LOOK AT EACH OTHER...
?
HEH...
YOU ARE MAKING ME LAUGH...
I SHOULD FORGI—
FORGIVE...

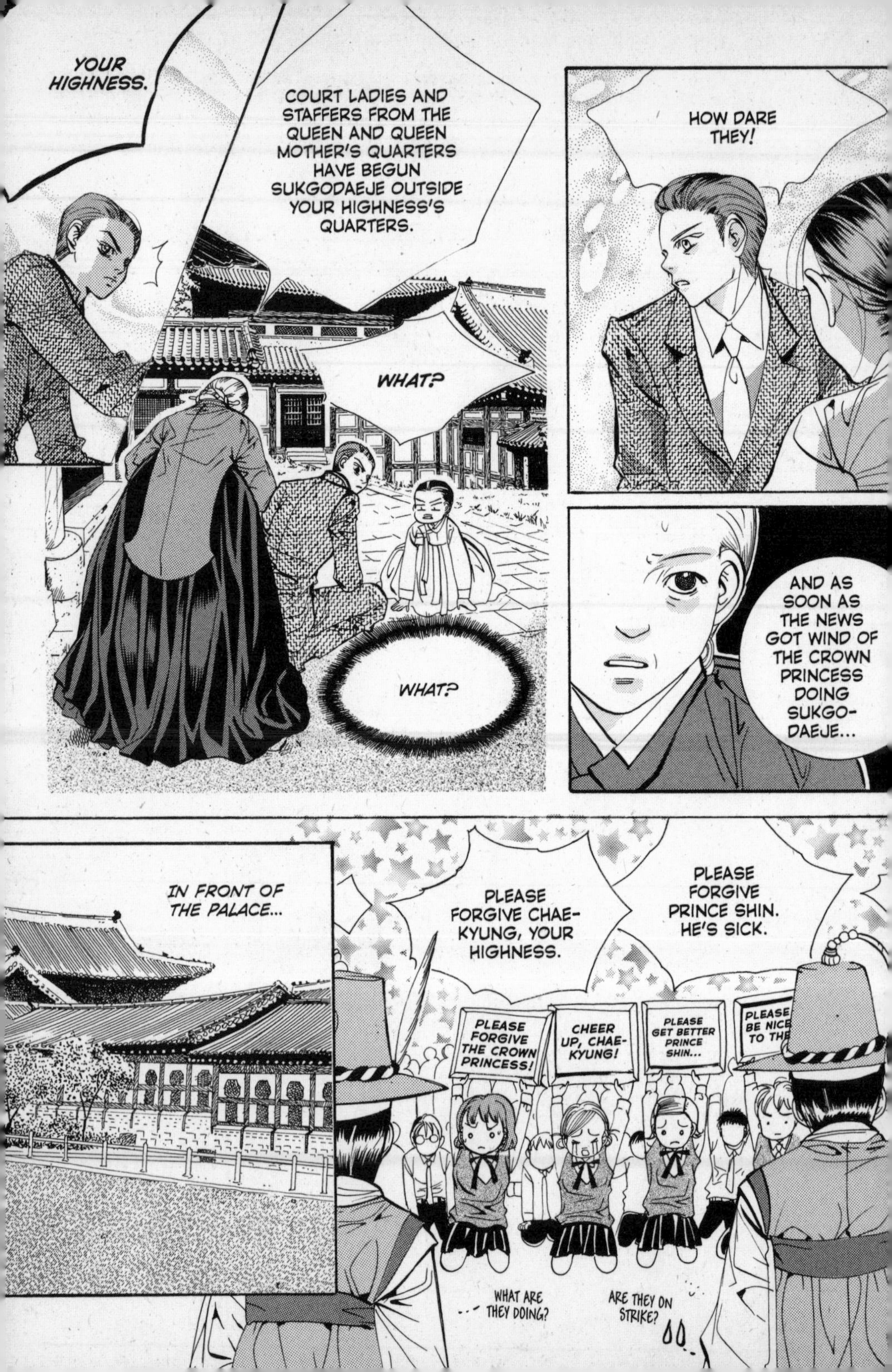

YOUR HIGHNESS.
COURT LADIES AND STAFFERS FROM THE QUEEN AND QUEEN MOTHER'S QUARTERS HAVE BEGUN SUKGODAEJE OUTSIDE YOUR HIGHNESS'S QUARTERS.
WHAT?
WHAT?
HOW DARE THEY!
AND AS SOON AS THE NEWS GOT WIND OF THE CROWN PRINCESS DOING SUKGO-DAEJE...
IN FRONT OF THE PALACE...
PLEASE FORGIVE CHAE-KYUNG, YOUR HIGHNESS.
PLEASE FORGIVE PRINCE SHIN. HE'S SICK.
PLEASE FORGIVE THE CROWN PRINCESS!
CHEER UP, CHAE-KYUNG!
PLEASE GET BETTER PRINCE SHIN...
PLEASE BE NICE TO THE
WHAT ARE THEY DOING?
ARE THEY ON STRIKE?

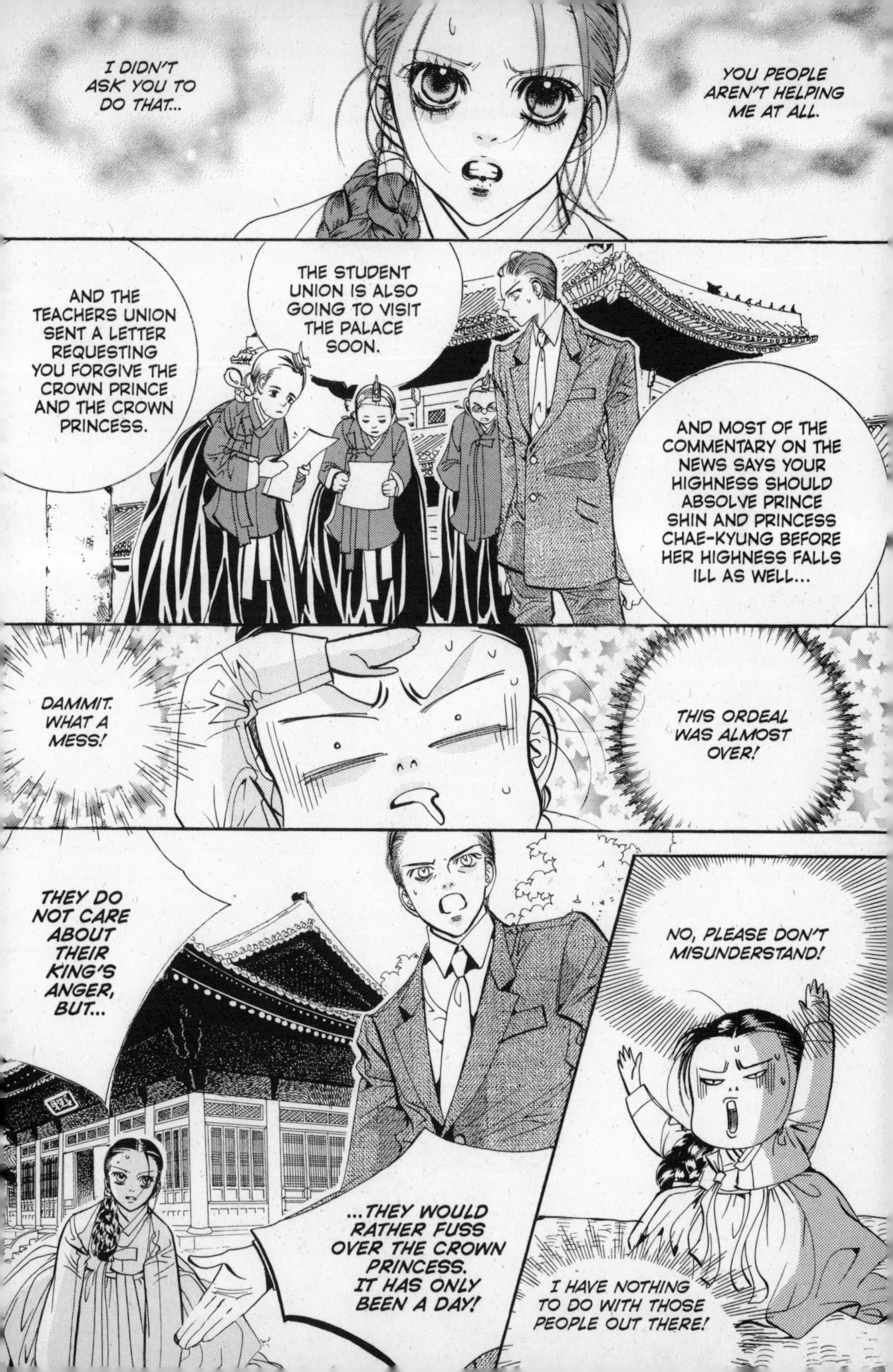
I DIDN'T ASK YOU TO DO THAT...
YOU PEOPLE AREN'T HELPING ME AT ALL.
AND THE TEACHERS UNION SENT A LETTER REQUESTING YOU FORGIVE THE CROWN PRINCE AND THE CROWN PRINCESS.
THE STUDENT UNION IS ALSO GOING TO VISIT THE PALACE SOON.
AND MOST OF THE COMMENTARY ON THE NEWS SAYS YOUR HIGHNESS SHOULD ABSOLVE PRINCE SHIN AND PRINCESS CHAE-KYUNG BEFORE HER HIGHNESS FALLS ILL AS WELL...
DAMMIT. WHAT A MESS!
THIS ORDEAL WAS ALMOST OVER!
THEY DO NOT CARE ABOUT THEIR KING'S ANGER, BUT...
...THEY WOULD RATHER FUSS OVER THE CROWN PRINCESS. IT HAS ONLY BEEN A DAY!
NO, PLEASE DON'T MISUNDERSTAND!
I HAVE NOTHING TO DO WITH THOSE PEOPLE OUT THERE!

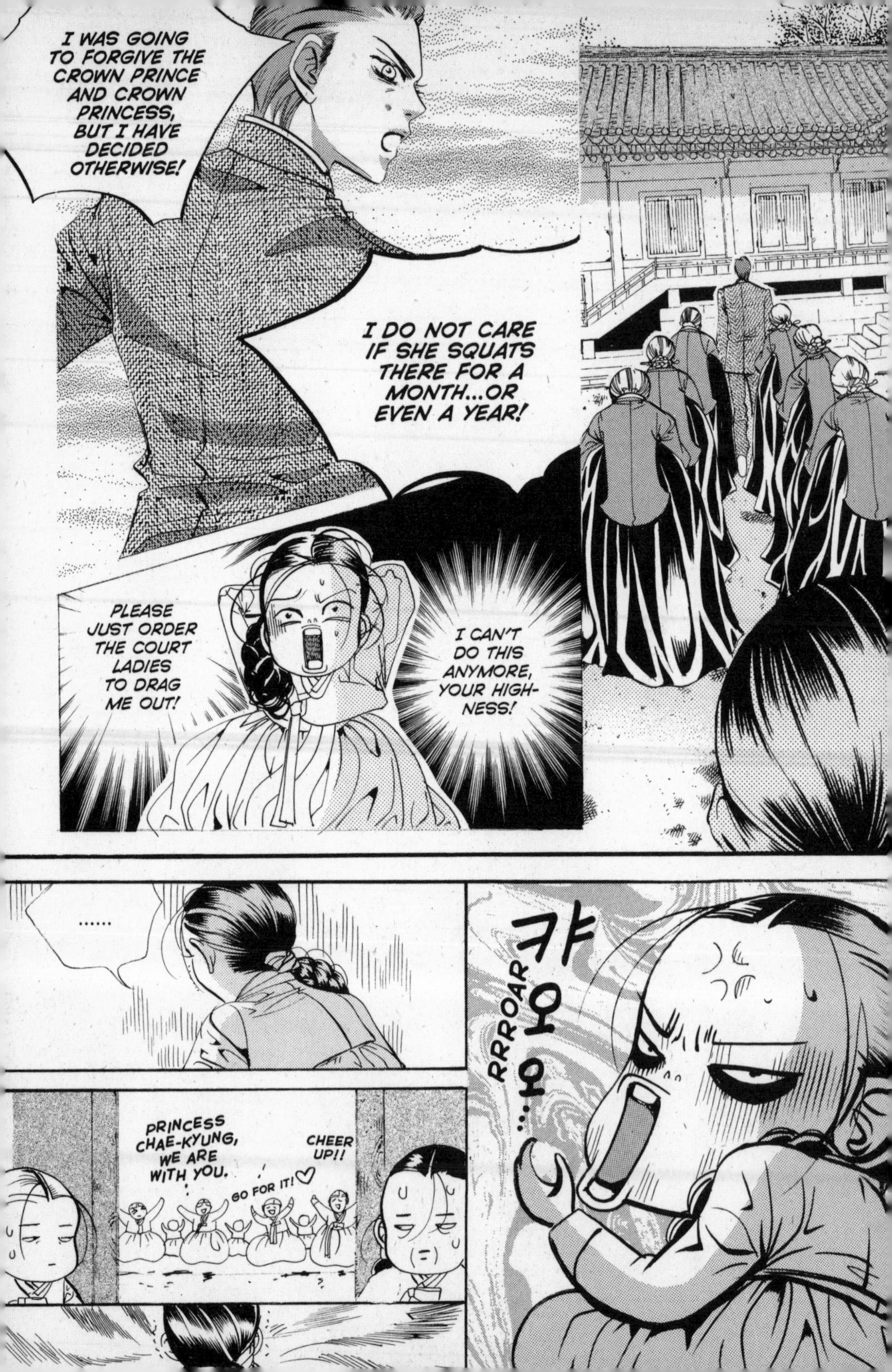
I WAS GOING TO FORGIVE THE CROWN PRINCE AND CROWN PRINCESS, BUT I HAVE DECIDED OTHERWISE!
I DO NOT CARE IF SHE SQUATS THERE FOR A MONTH...OR EVEN A YEAR!
PLEASE JUST ORDER THE COURT LADIES TO DRAG ME OUT!
I CAN'T DO THIS ANYMORE, YOUR HIGH-NESS!
......
PRINCESS CHAE-KYUNG, WE ARE WITH YOU.
GO FOR IT! ♡
CHEER UP!!
캬오오...
RRROAR

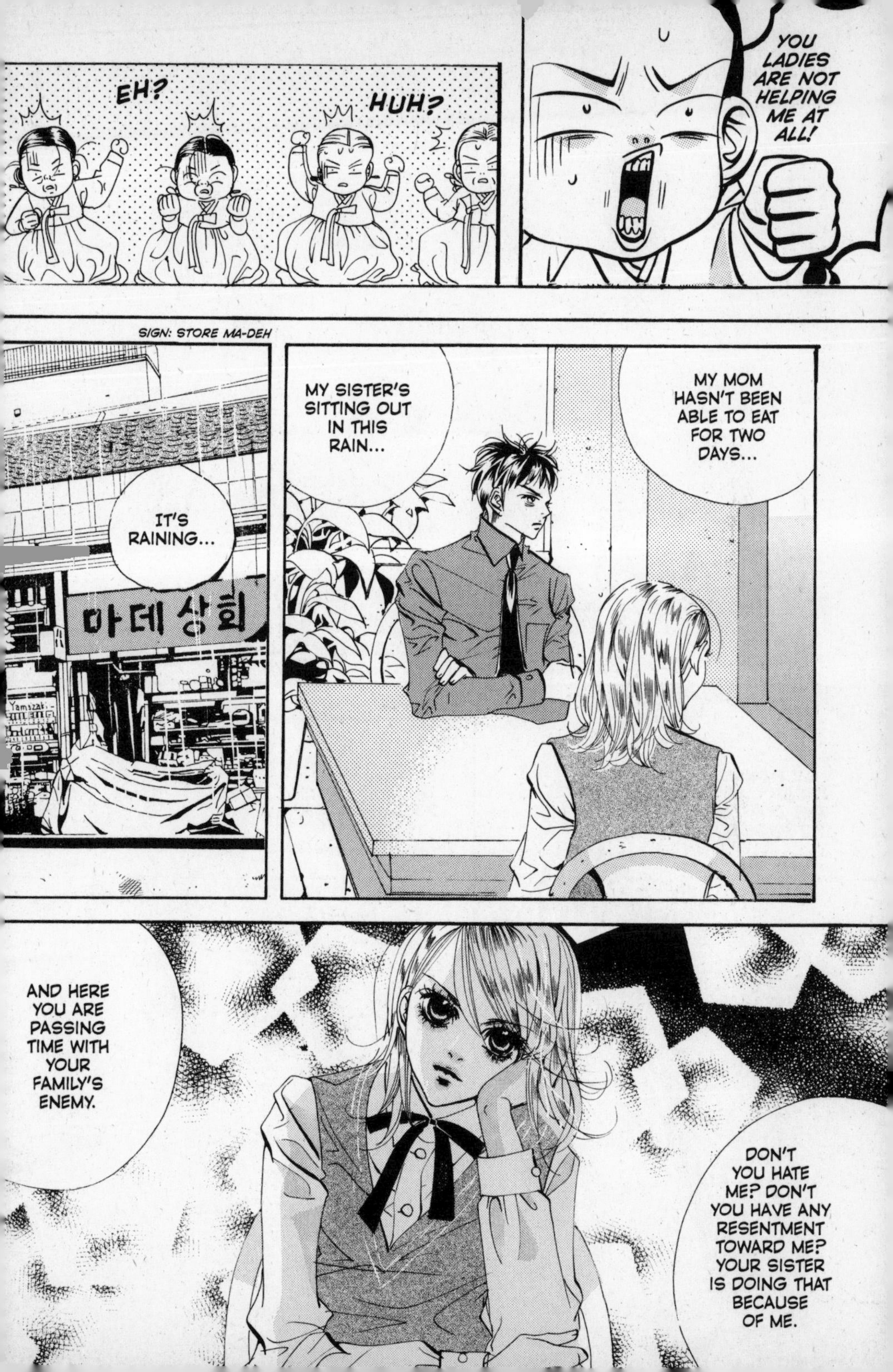
EH?
HUH?
YOU LADIES ARE NOT HELPING ME AT ALL!
SIGN: STORE MA-DEH
마데상회
IT'S RAINING...
MY SISTER'S SITTING OUT IN THIS RAIN...
MY MOM HASN'T BEEN ABLE TO EAT FOR TWO DAYS...
AND HERE YOU ARE PASSING TIME WITH YOUR FAMILY'S ENEMY.
DON'T YOU HATE ME? DON'T YOU HAVE ANY RESENTMENT TOWARD ME? YOUR SISTER IS DOING THAT BECAUSE OF ME.

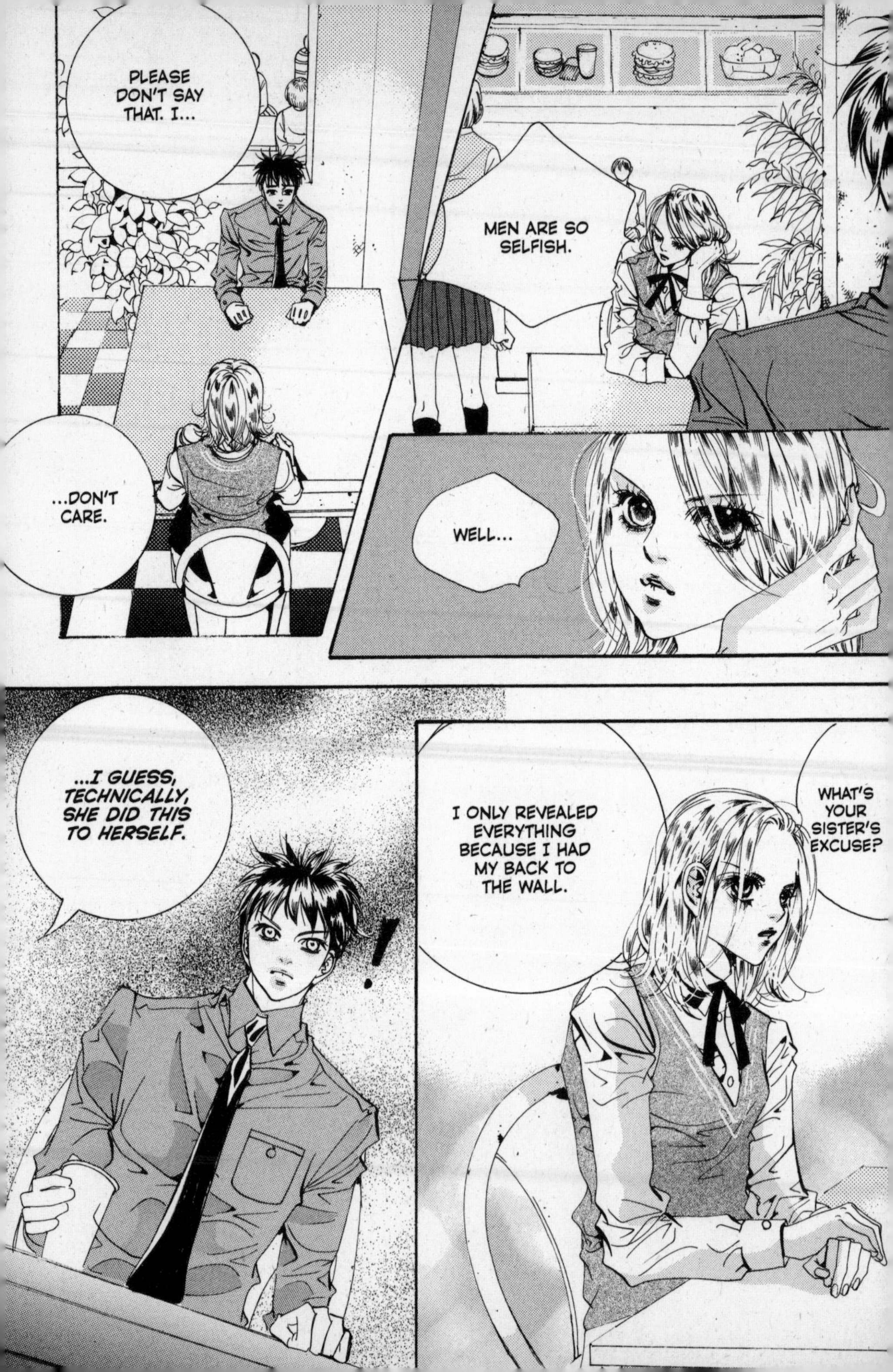
PLEASE DON'T SAY THAT. I...
...DON'T CARE.
MEN ARE SO SELFISH.
WELL...
...I GUESS, TECHNICALLY, SHE DID THIS TO HERSELF.
!
I ONLY REVEALED EVERYTHING BECAUSE I HAD MY BACK TO THE WALL.
WHAT'S YOUR SISTER'S EXCUSE?

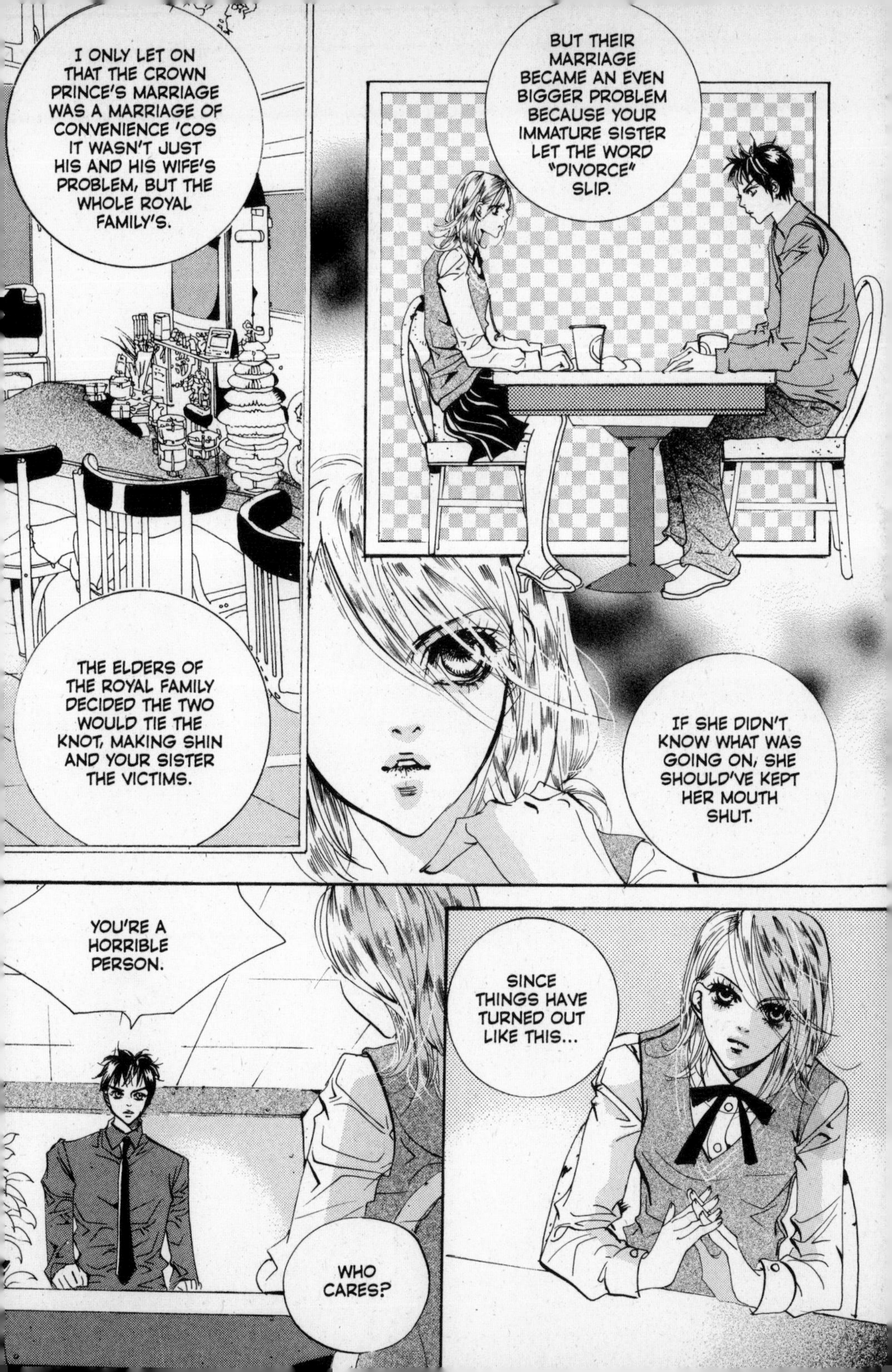
I ONLY LET ON THAT THE CROWN PRINCE'S MARRIAGE WAS A MARRIAGE OF CONVENIENCE 'COS IT WASN'T JUST HIS AND HIS WIFE'S PROBLEM, BUT THE WHOLE ROYAL FAMILY'S.
BUT THEIR MARRIAGE BECAME AN EVEN BIGGER PROBLEM BECAUSE YOUR IMMATURE SISTER LET THE WORD "DIVORCE" SLIP.
THE ELDERS OF THE ROYAL FAMILY DECIDED THE TWO WOULD TIE THE KNOT, MAKING SHIN AND YOUR SISTER THE VICTIMS.
IF SHE DIDN'T KNOW WHAT WAS GOING ON, SHE SHOULD'VE KEPT HER MOUTH SHUT.
YOU'RE A HORRIBLE PERSON.
WHO CARES?
SINCE THINGS HAVE TURNED OUT LIKE THIS...

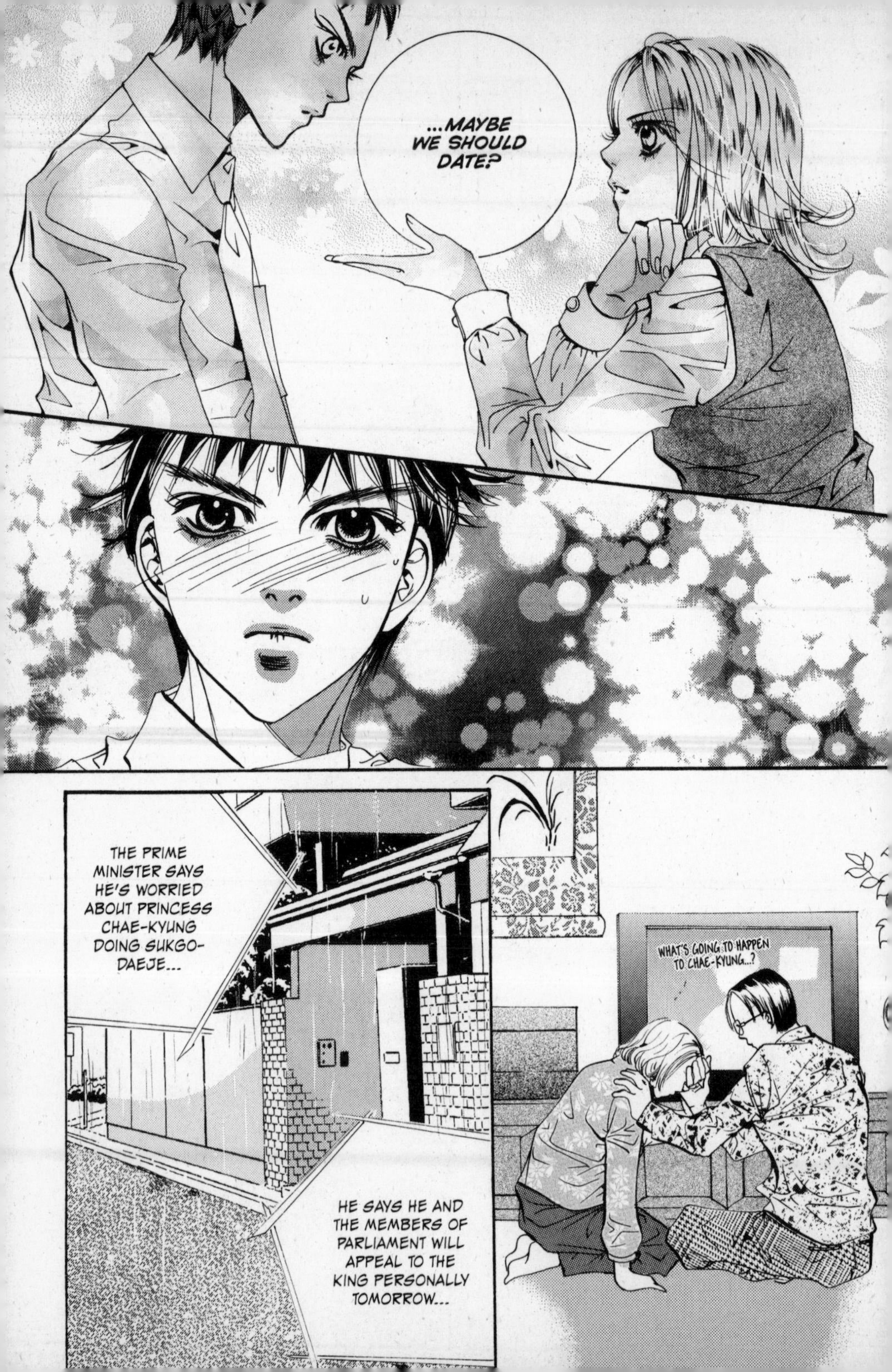
...MAYBE WE SHOULD DATE?
THE PRIME MINISTER SAYS HE'S WORRIED ABOUT PRINCESS CHAE-KYUNG DOING SUKGO-DAEJE...
HE SAYS HE AND THE MEMBERS OF PARLIAMENT WILL APPEAL TO THE KING PERSONALLY TOMORROW...
WHAT'S GOING TO HAPPEN TO CHAE-KYUNG...?

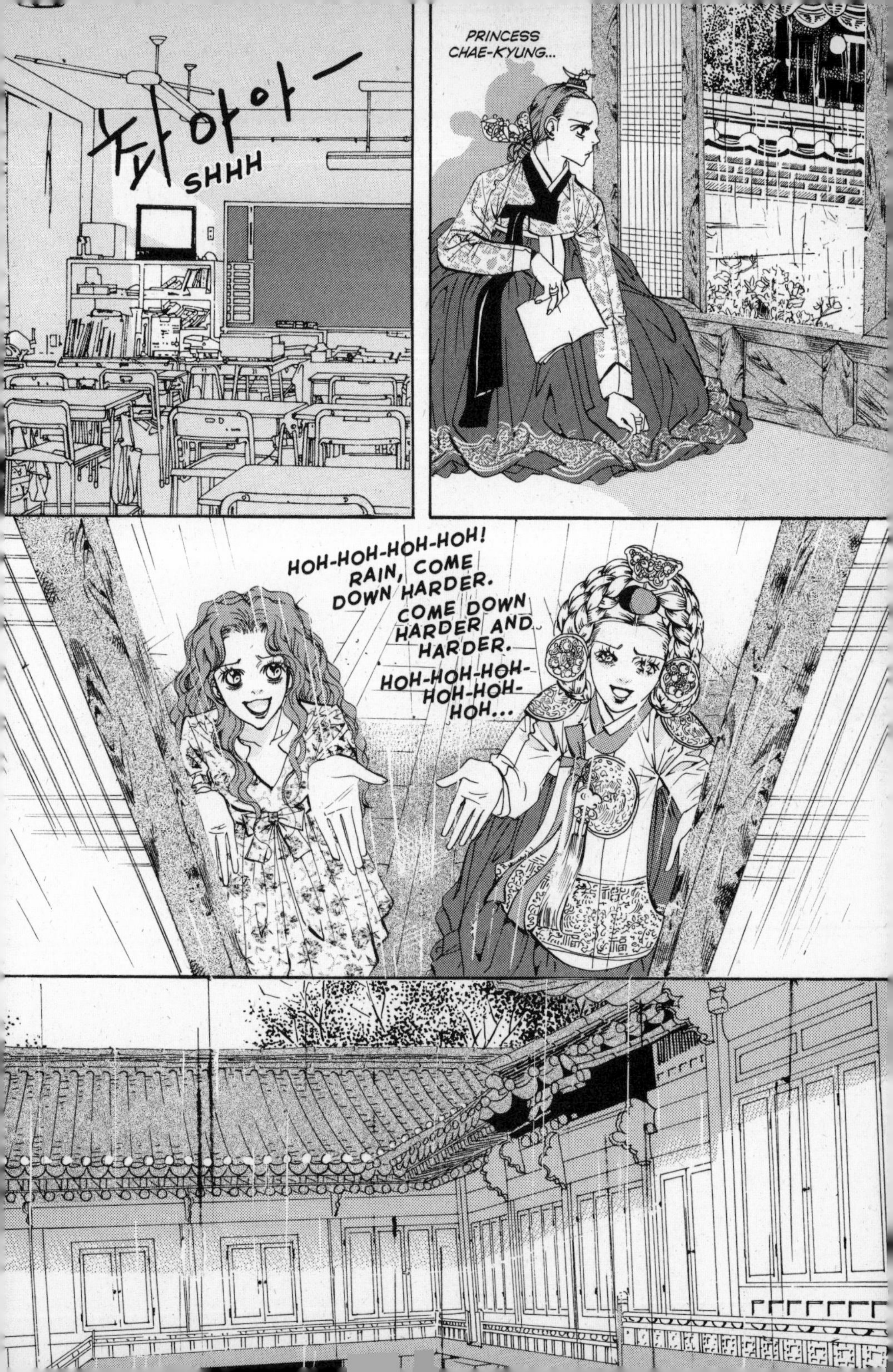

쏴아아ㅡ
SHHH
PRINCESS CHAE-KYUNG...
HOH-HOH-HOH-HOH! RAIN, COME DOWN HARDER.
COME DOWN HARDER AND HARDER.
HOH-HOH-HOH-HOH-HOH-HOH...

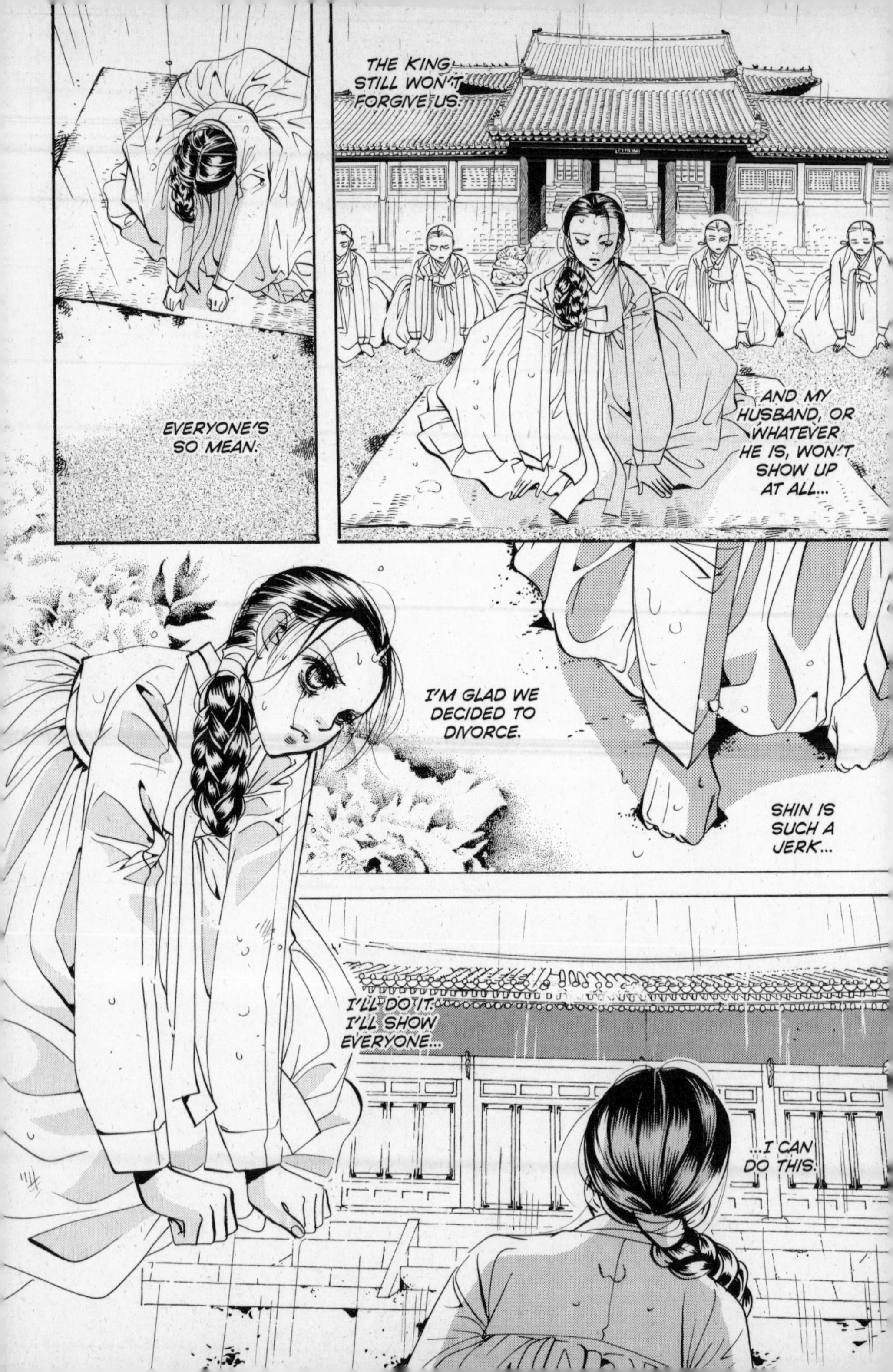
EVERYONE'S SO MEAN.
THE KING STILL WON'T FORGIVE US.
AND MY HUSBAND, OR WHATEVER HE IS, WON'T SHOW UP AT ALL...
I'M GLAD WE DECIDED TO DIVORCE.
SHIN IS SUCH A JERK...
I'LL DO IT. I'LL SHOW EVERYONE...
...I CAN DO THIS.

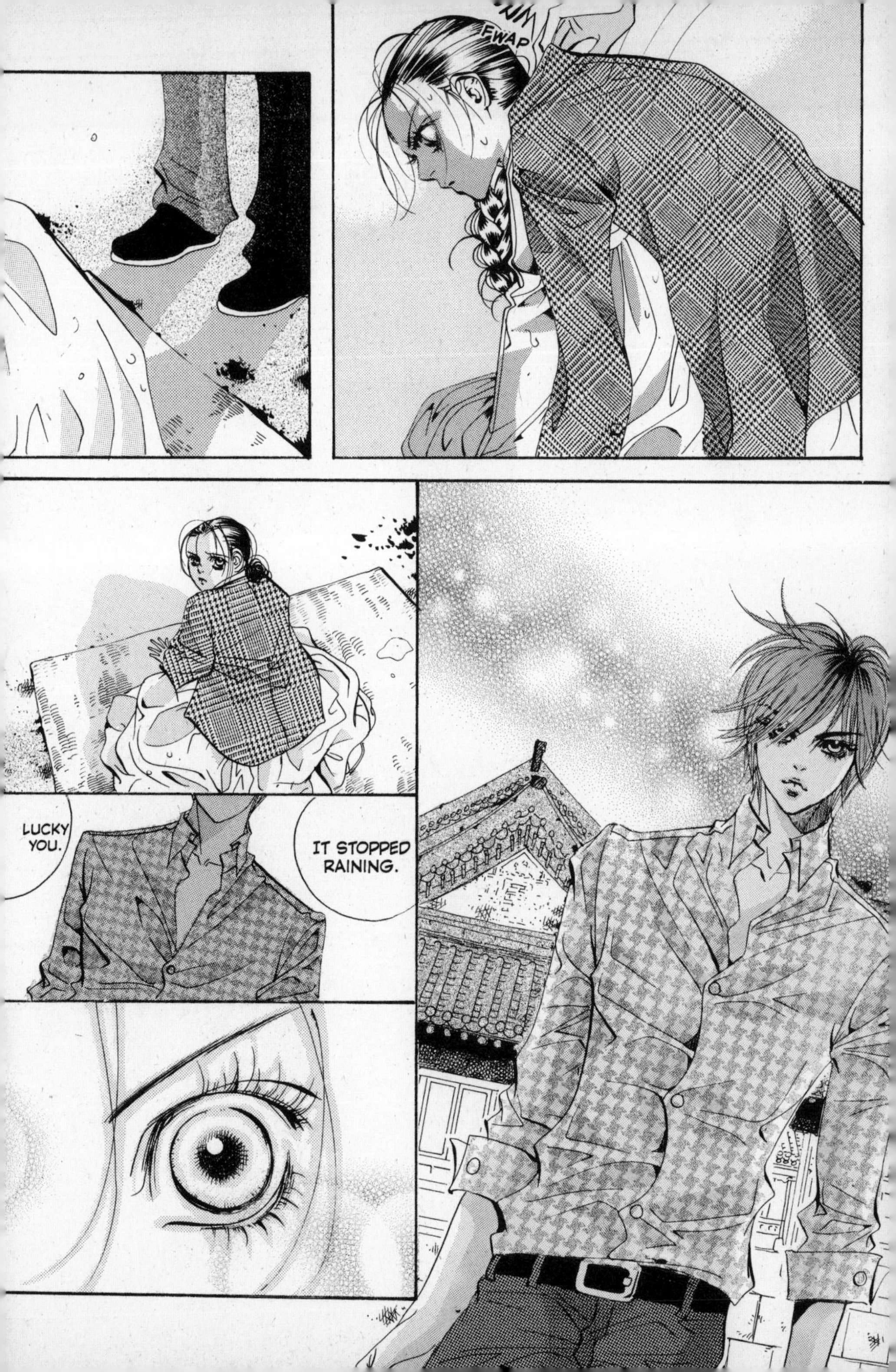
FWAP
LUCKY YOU.
IT STOPPED RAINING.

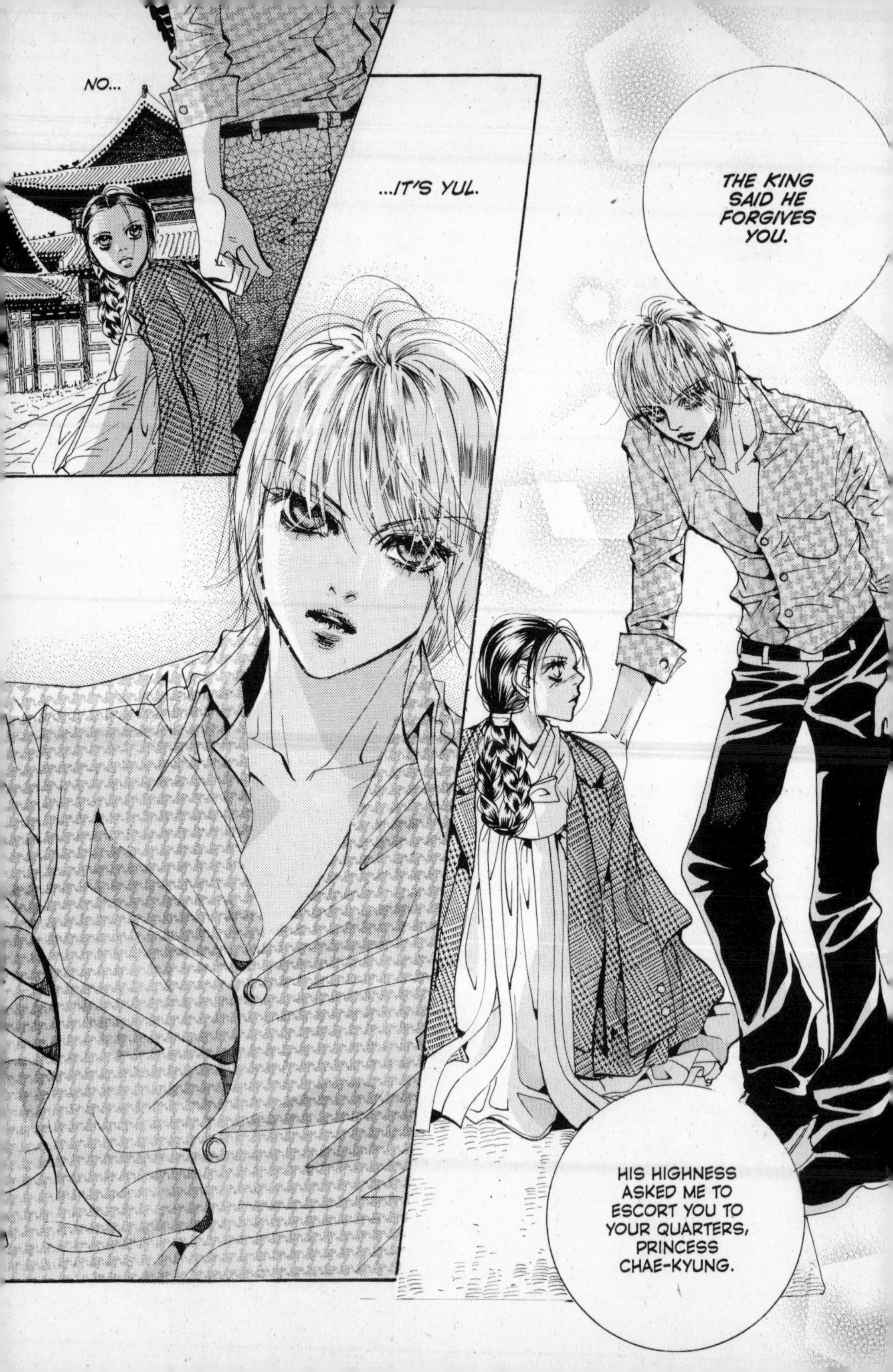
NO...
...IT'S YUL.
THE KING SAID HE FORGIVES YOU.
HIS HIGHNESS ASKED ME TO ESCORT YOU TO YOUR QUARTERS, PRINCESS CHAE-KYUNG.

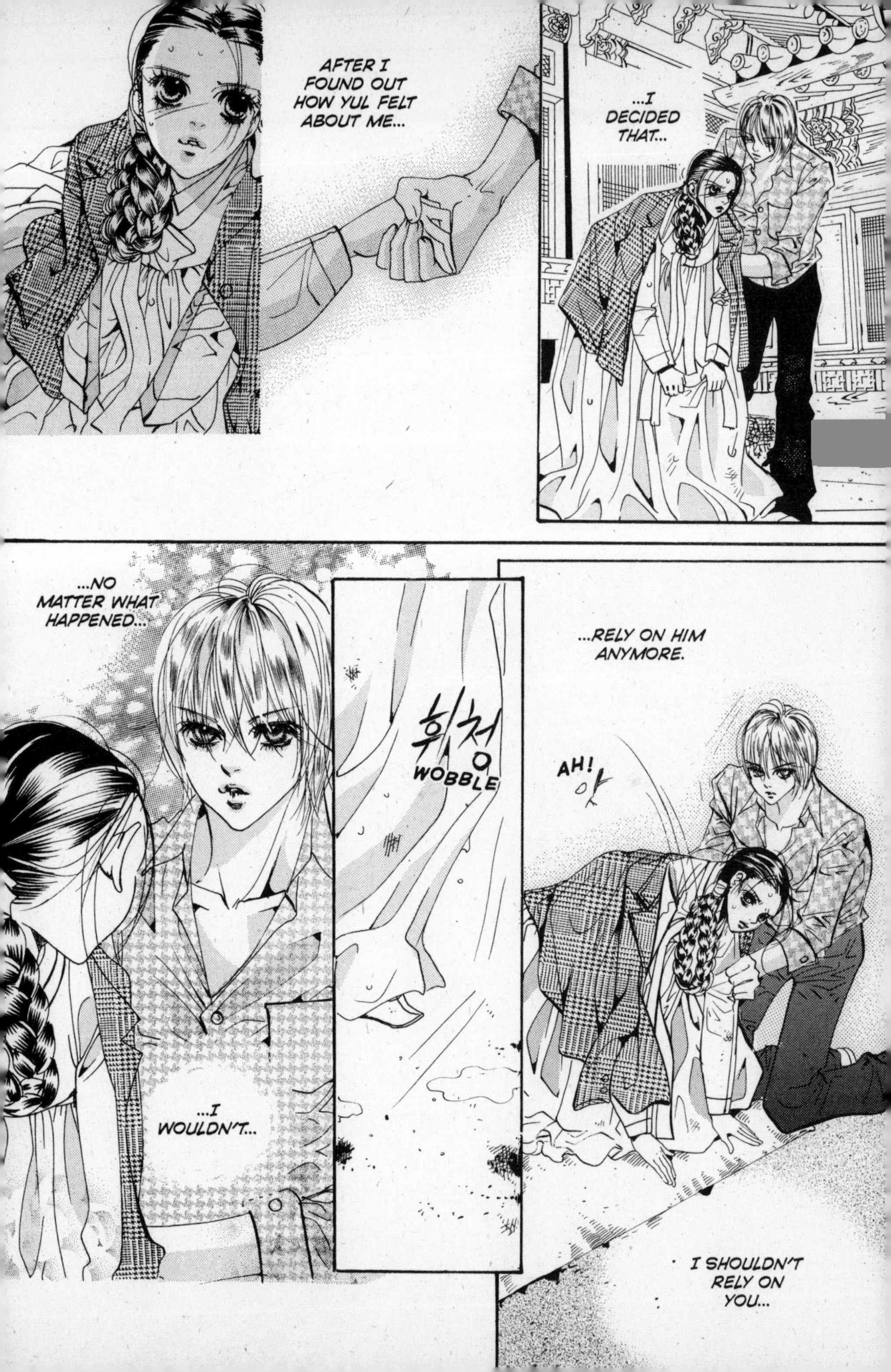
AFTER I FOUND OUT HOW YUL FELT ABOUT ME...
...I DECIDED THAT...
...NO MATTER WHAT HAPPENED...
...I WOULDN'T...
휘청
WOBBLE
...RELY ON HIM ANYMORE.
AH! 아
I SHOULDN'T RELY ON YOU...

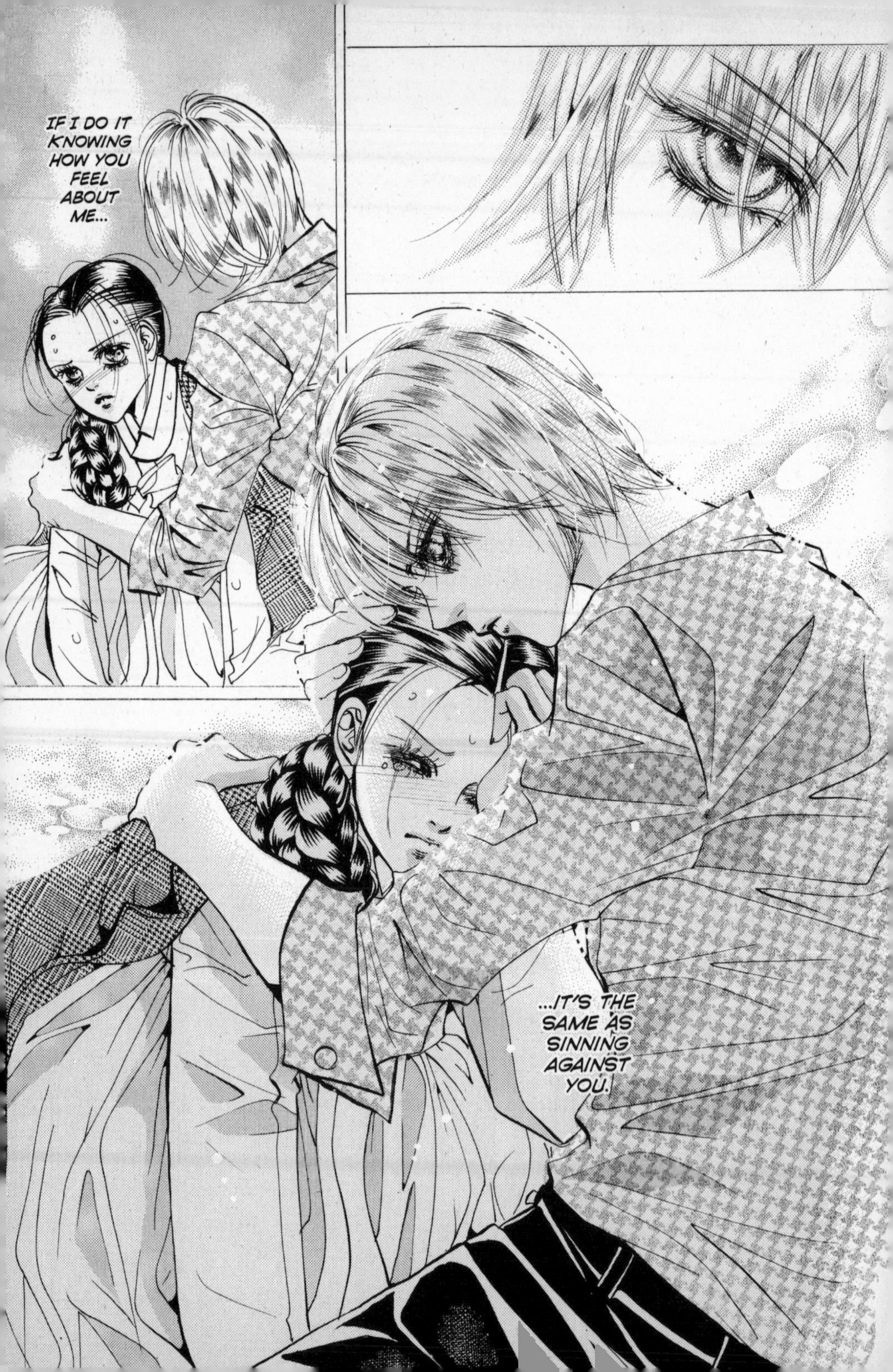
IF I DO IT KNOWING HOW YOU FEEL ABOUT ME...
...IT'S THE SAME AS SINNING AGAINST YOU.

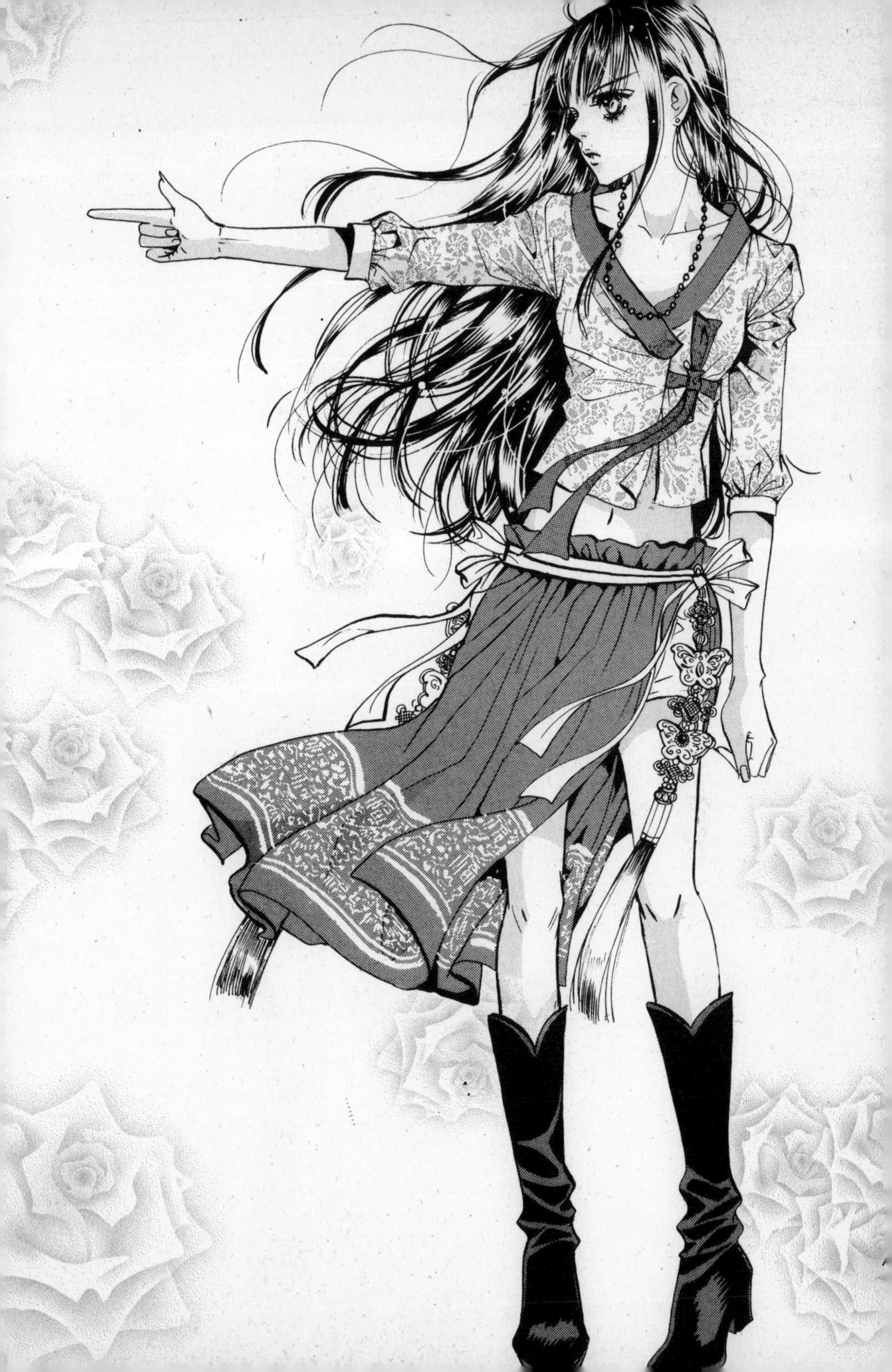

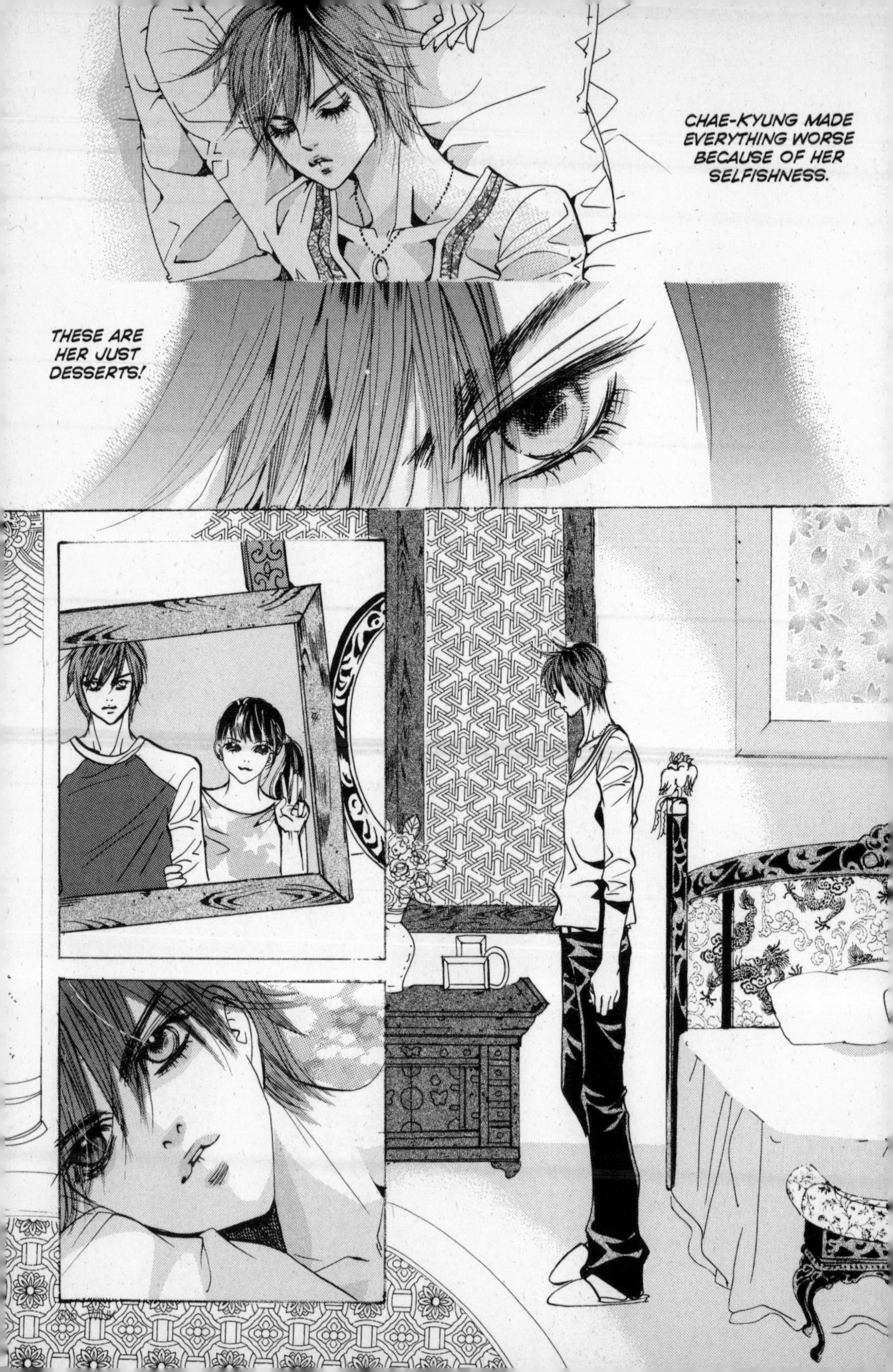
CHAE-KYUNG MADE EVERYTHING WORSE BECAUSE OF HER SELFISHNESS.
THESE ARE HER JUST DESSERTS!

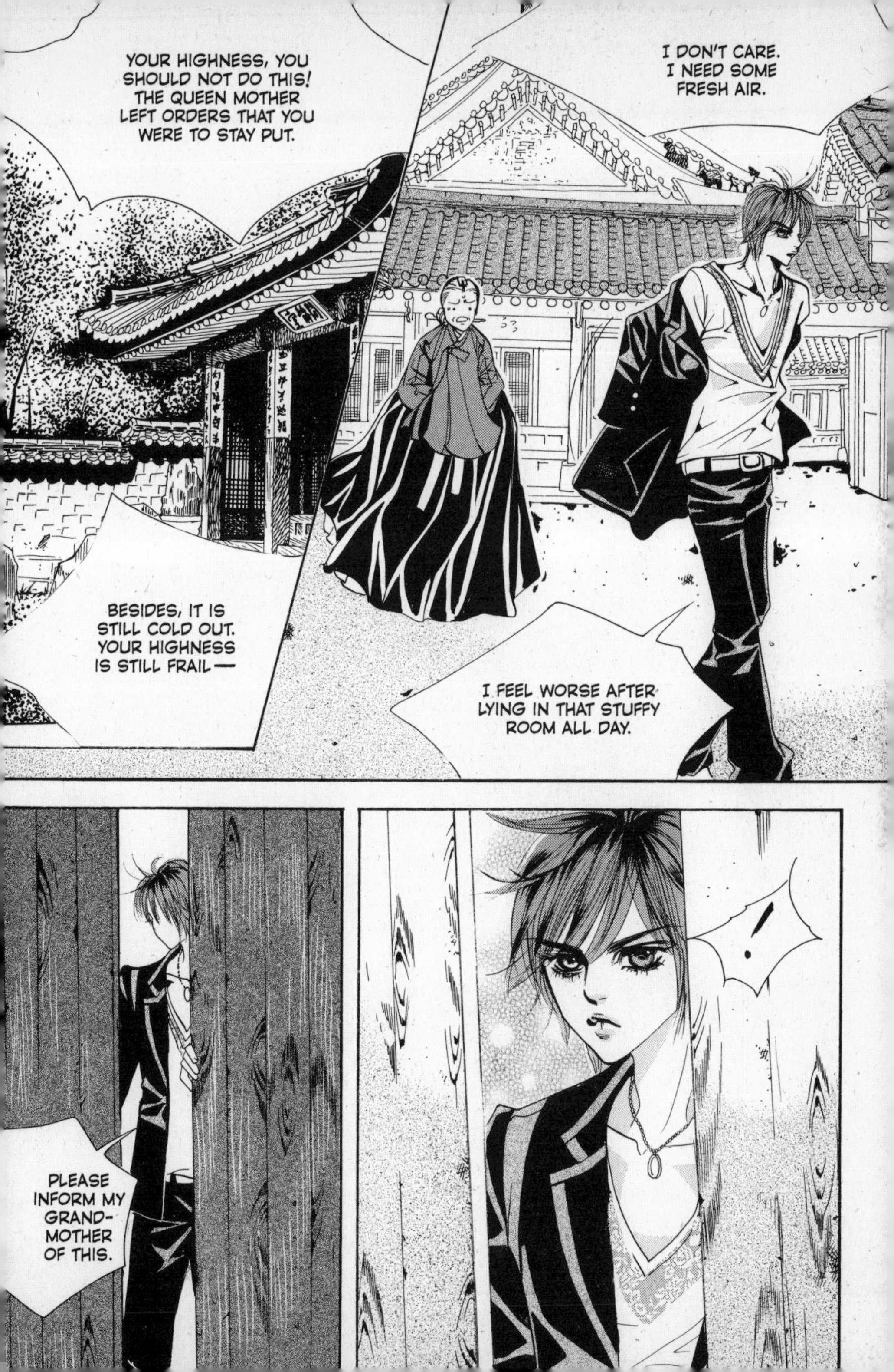
YOUR HIGHNESS, YOU SHOULD NOT DO THIS! THE QUEEN MOTHER LEFT ORDERS THAT YOU WERE TO STAY PUT.
BESIDES, IT IS STILL COLD OUT. YOUR HIGHNESS IS STILL FRAIL—
I DON'T CARE. I NEED SOME FRESH AIR.
I FEEL WORSE AFTER LYING IN THAT STUFFY ROOM ALL DAY.
PLEASE INFORM MY GRAND-MOTHER OF THIS.
!

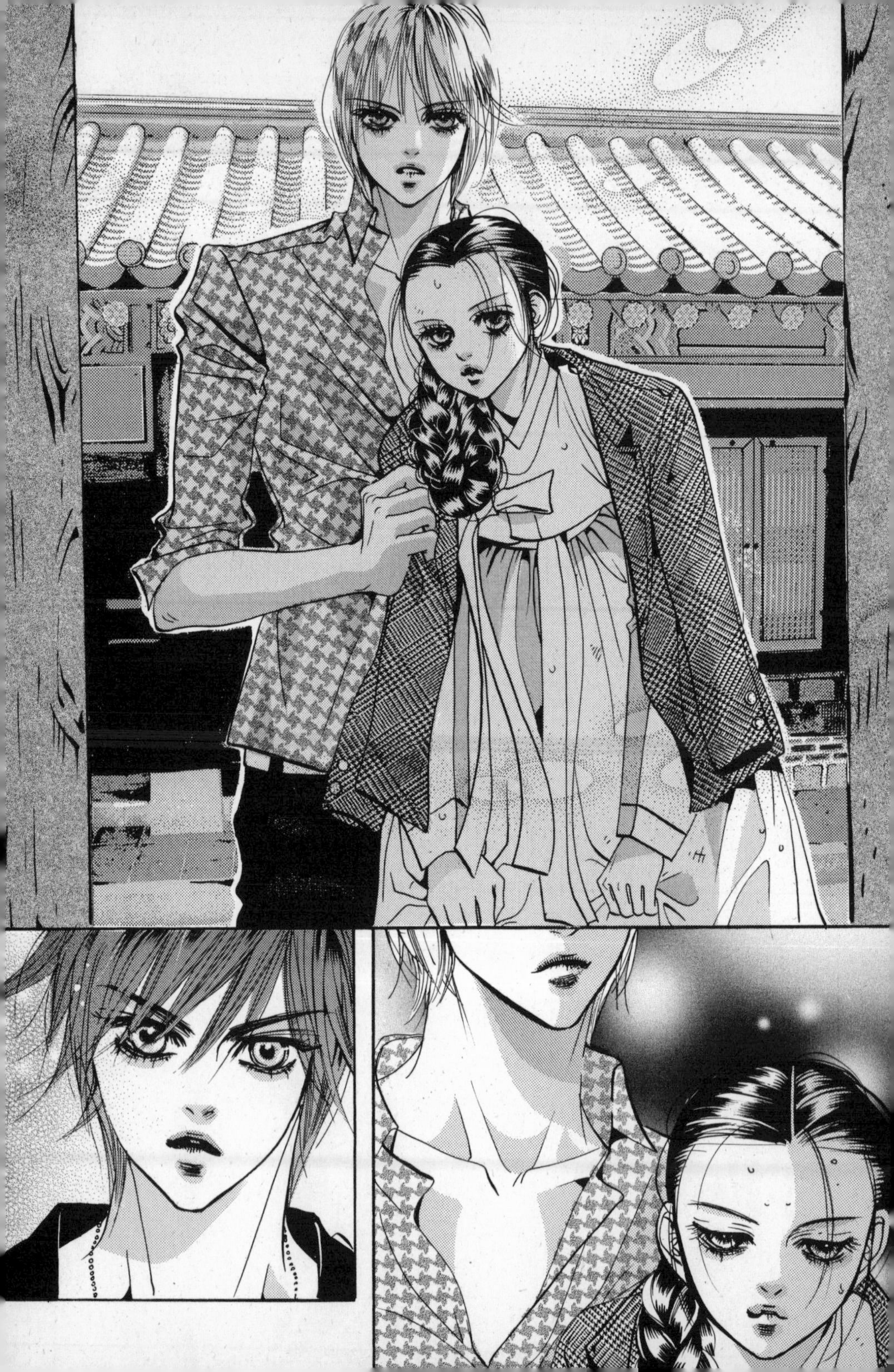

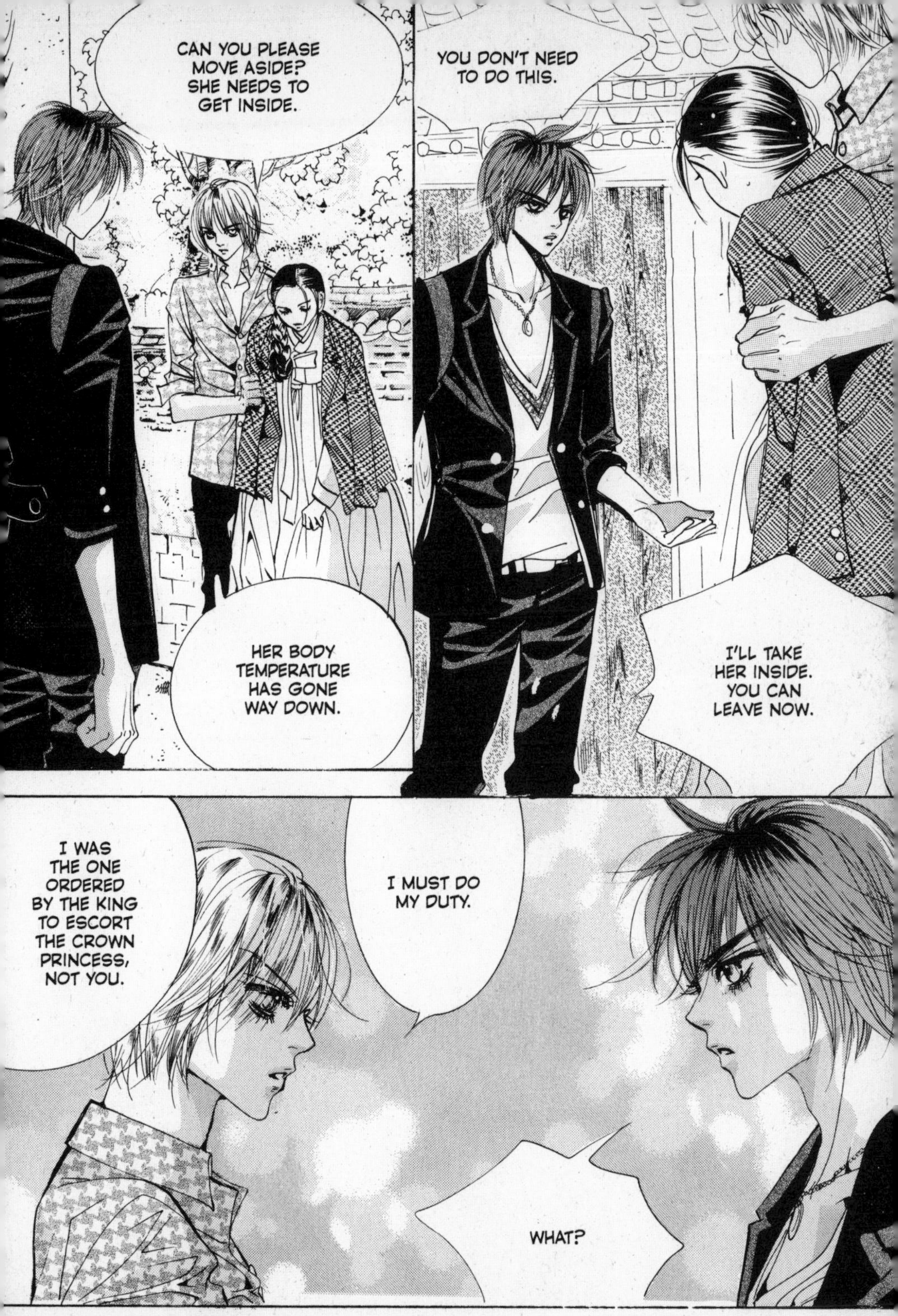
CAN YOU PLEASE MOVE ASIDE? SHE NEEDS TO GET INSIDE.
HER BODY TEMPERATURE HAS GONE WAY DOWN.
YOU DON'T NEED TO DO THIS.
I'LL TAKE HER INSIDE. YOU CAN LEAVE NOW.
I WAS THE ONE ORDERED BY THE KING TO ESCORT THE CROWN PRINCESS, NOT YOU.
I MUST DO MY DUTY.
WHAT?

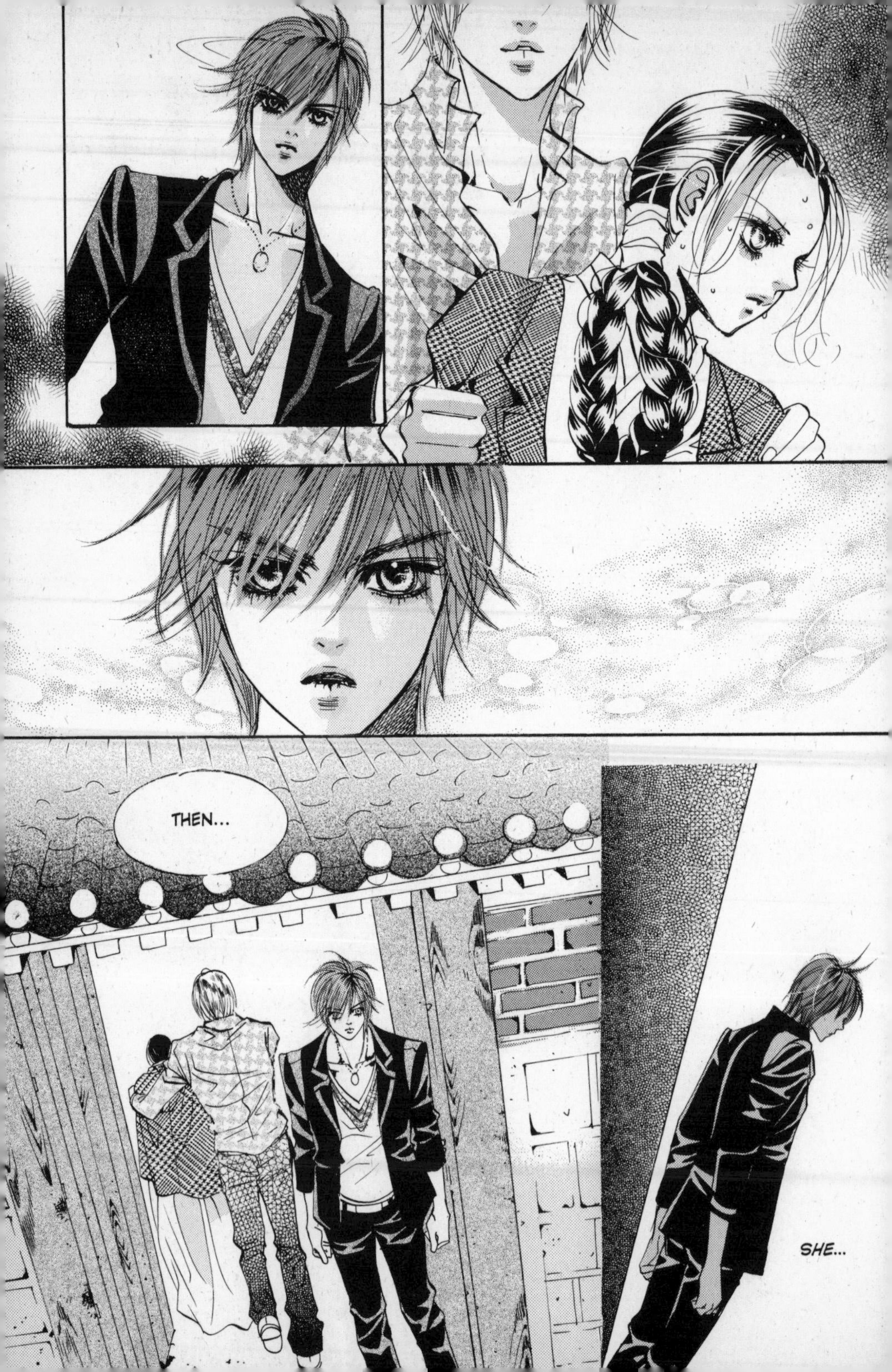
THEN...
SHE...

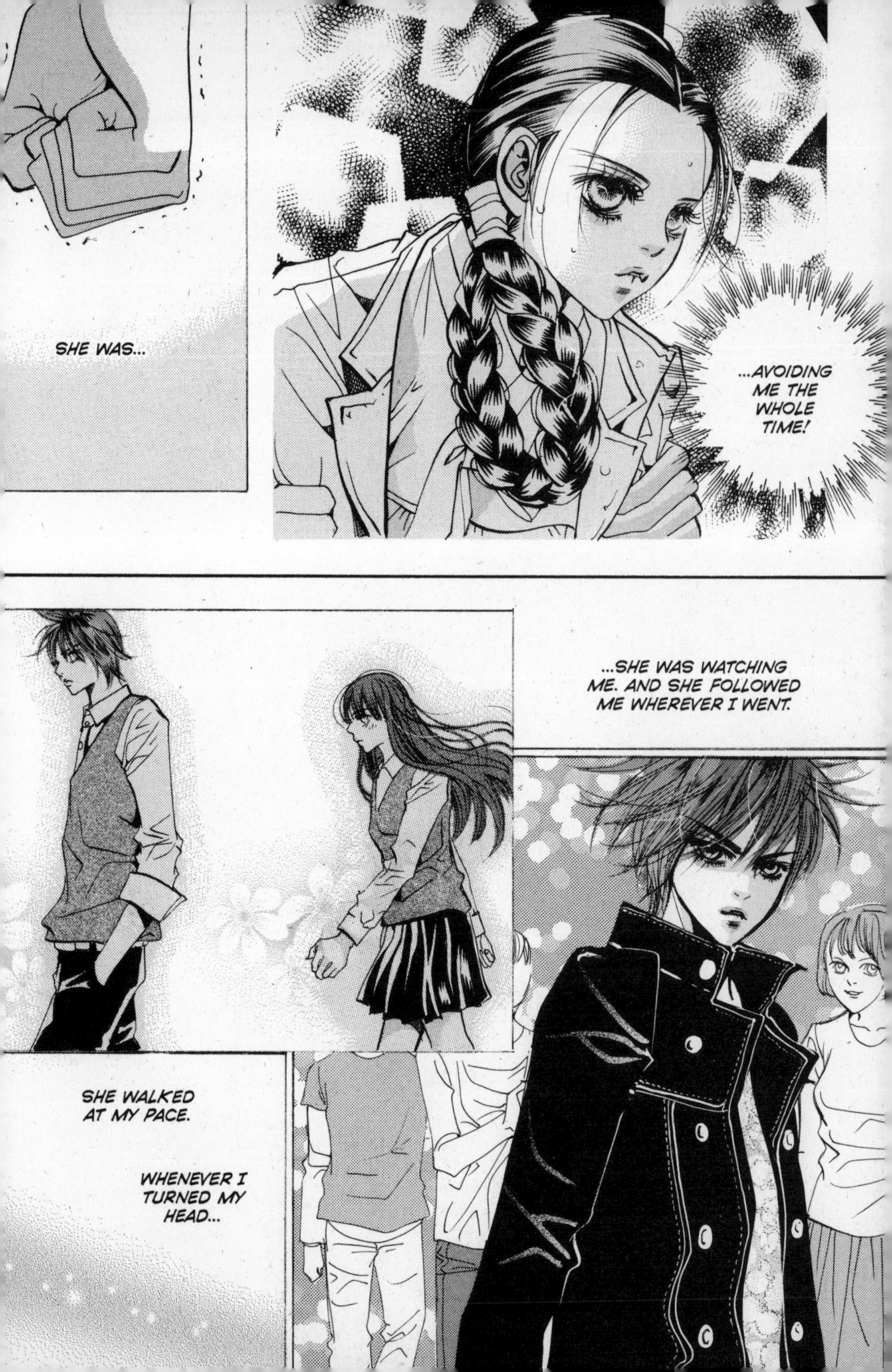
SHE WAS...
...AVOIDING ME THE WHOLE TIME!
...SHE WAS WATCHING ME. AND SHE FOLLOWED ME WHEREVER I WENT.
SHE WALKED AT MY PACE.
WHENEVER I TURNED MY HEAD...

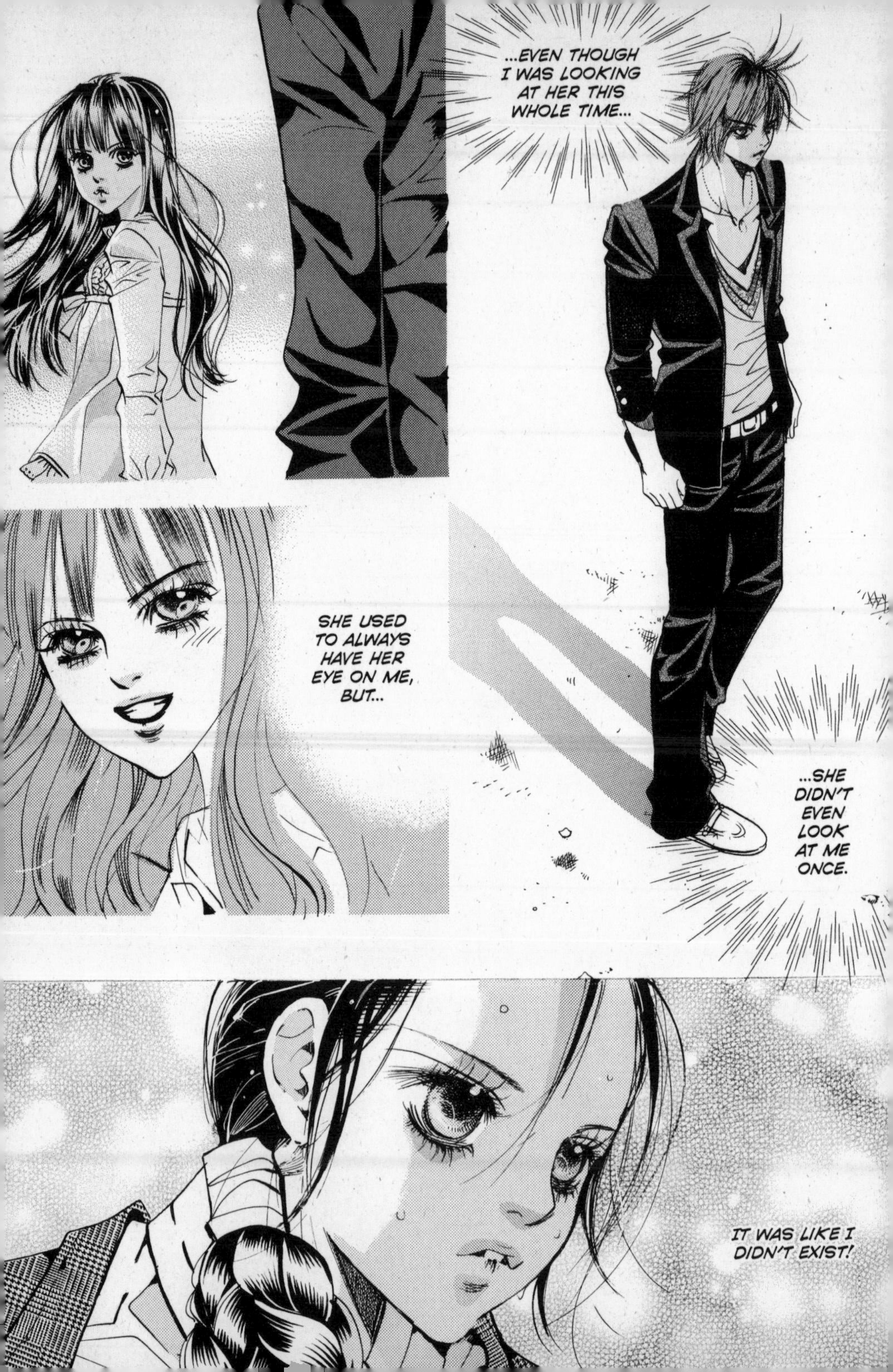
...EVEN THOUGH I WAS LOOKING AT HER THIS WHOLE TIME...
SHE USED TO ALWAYS HAVE HER EYE ON ME, BUT...
...SHE DIDN'T EVEN LOOK AT ME ONCE.
IT WAS LIKE I DIDN'T EXIST!

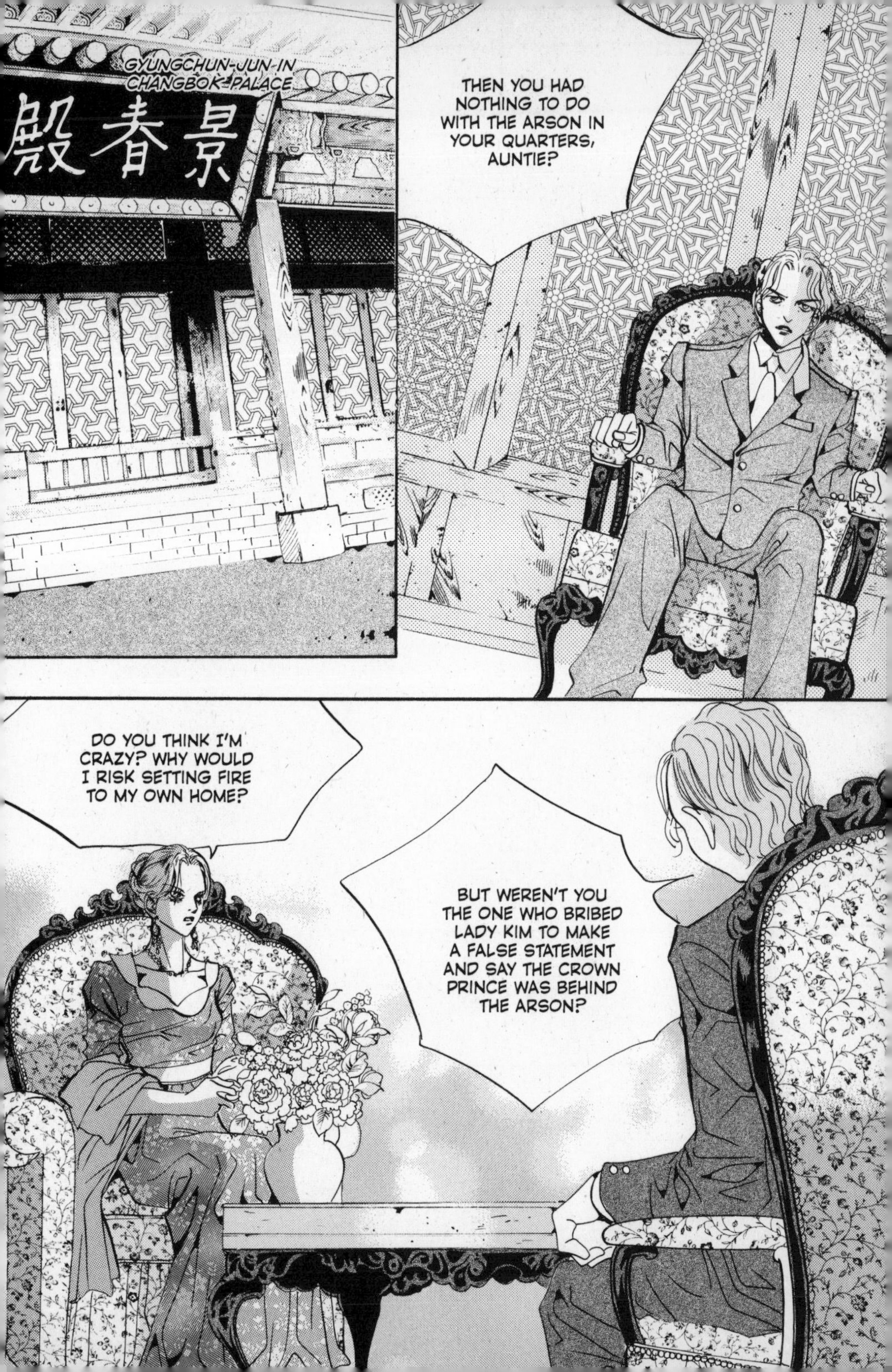
GYUNGCHUN-JUN IN CHANGBOK-PALACE
殿春景
THEN YOU HAD NOTHING TO DO WITH THE ARSON IN YOUR QUARTERS, AUNTIE?
DO YOU THINK I'M CRAZY? WHY WOULD I RISK SETTING FIRE TO MY OWN HOME?
BUT WEREN'T YOU THE ONE WHO BRIBED LADY KIM TO MAKE A FALSE STATEMENT AND SAY THE CROWN PRINCE WAS BEHIND THE ARSON?

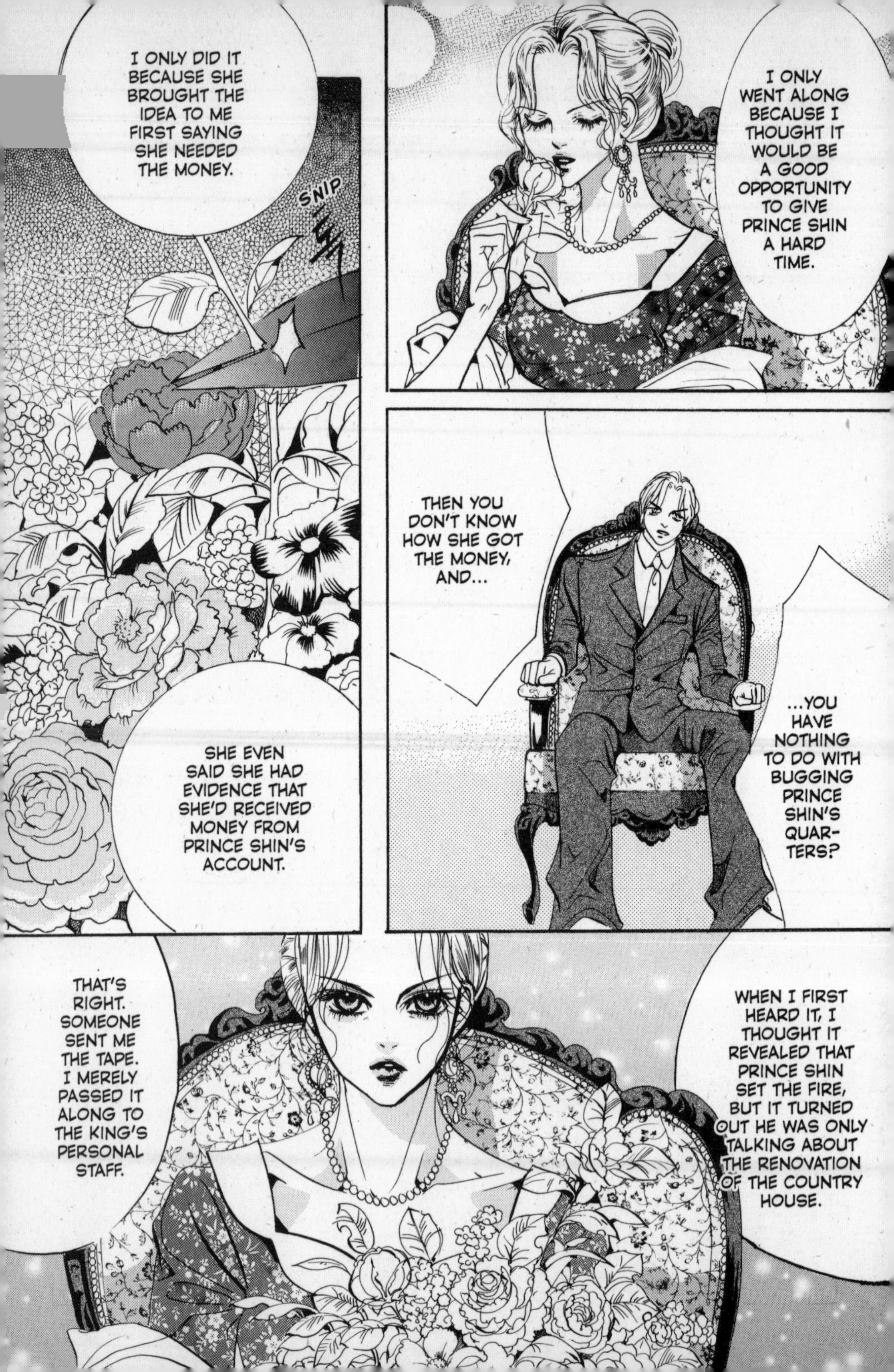
I ONLY DID IT BECAUSE SHE BROUGHT THE IDEA TO ME FIRST SAYING SHE NEEDED THE MONEY.
SNIP
SHE EVEN SAID SHE HAD EVIDENCE THAT SHE'D RECEIVED MONEY FROM PRINCE SHIN'S ACCOUNT.
I ONLY WENT ALONG BECAUSE I THOUGHT IT WOULD BE A GOOD OPPORTUNITY TO GIVE PRINCE SHIN A HARD TIME.
THEN YOU DON'T KNOW HOW SHE GOT THE MONEY, AND...
...YOU HAVE NOTHING TO DO WITH BUGGING PRINCE SHIN'S QUAR-TERS?
THAT'S RIGHT. SOMEONE SENT ME THE TAPE. I MERELY PASSED IT ALONG TO THE KING'S PERSONAL STAFF.
WHEN I FIRST HEARD IT, I THOUGHT IT REVEALED THAT PRINCE SHIN SET THE FIRE, BUT IT TURNED OUT HE WAS ONLY TALKING ABOUT THE RENOVATION OF THE COUNTRY HOUSE.

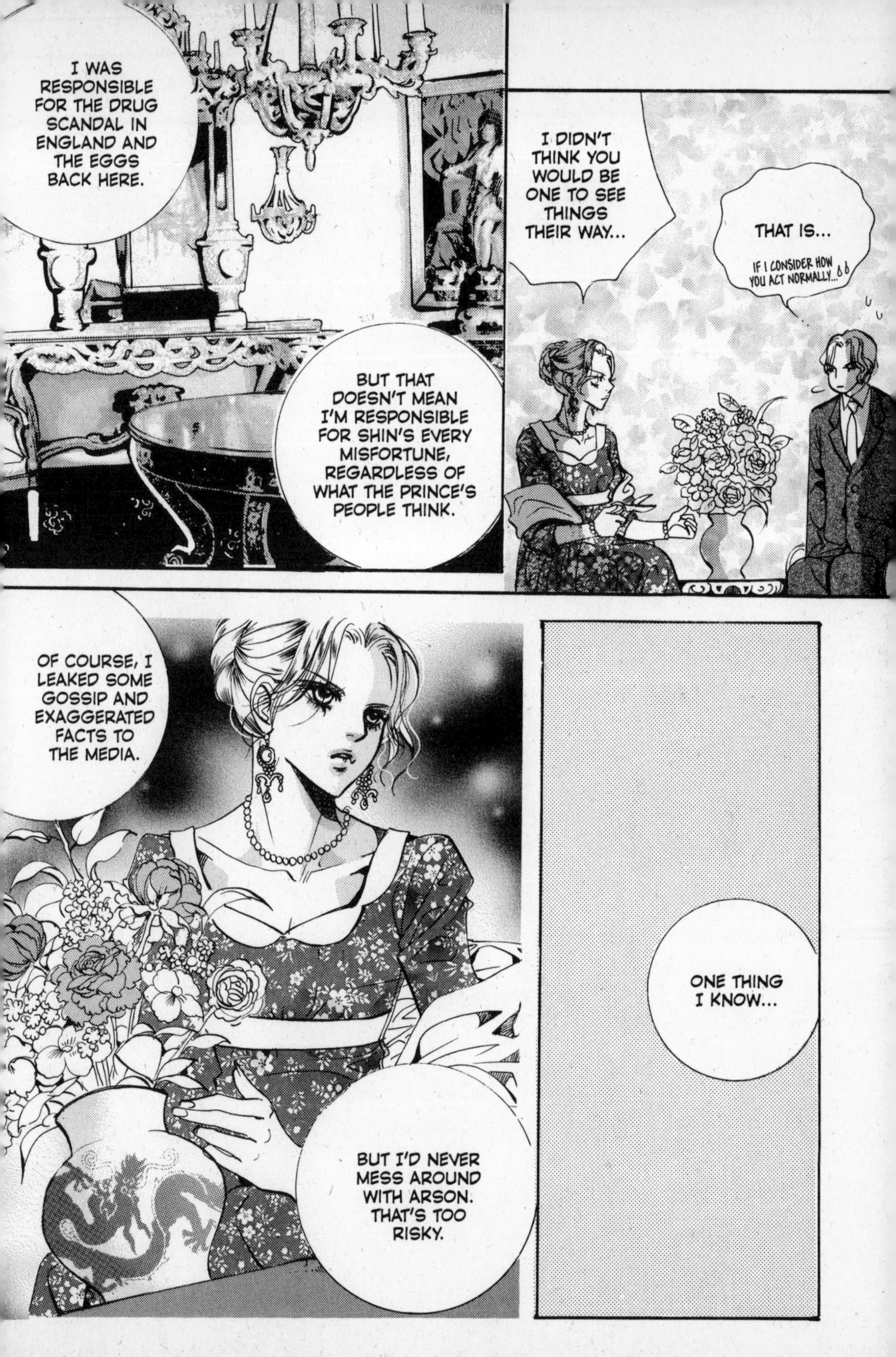
I WAS RESPONSIBLE FOR THE DRUG SCANDAL IN ENGLAND AND THE EGGS BACK HERE.
BUT THAT DOESN'T MEAN I'M RESPONSIBLE FOR SHIN'S EVERY MISFORTUNE, REGARDLESS OF WHAT THE PRINCE'S PEOPLE THINK.
I DIDN'T THINK YOU WOULD BE ONE TO SEE THINGS THEIR WAY...
THAT IS...
IF I CONSIDER HOW YOU ACT NORMALLY...
OF COURSE, I LEAKED SOME GOSSIP AND EXAGGERATED FACTS TO THE MEDIA.
BUT I'D NEVER MESS AROUND WITH ARSON. THAT'S TOO RISKY.
ONE THING I KNOW...

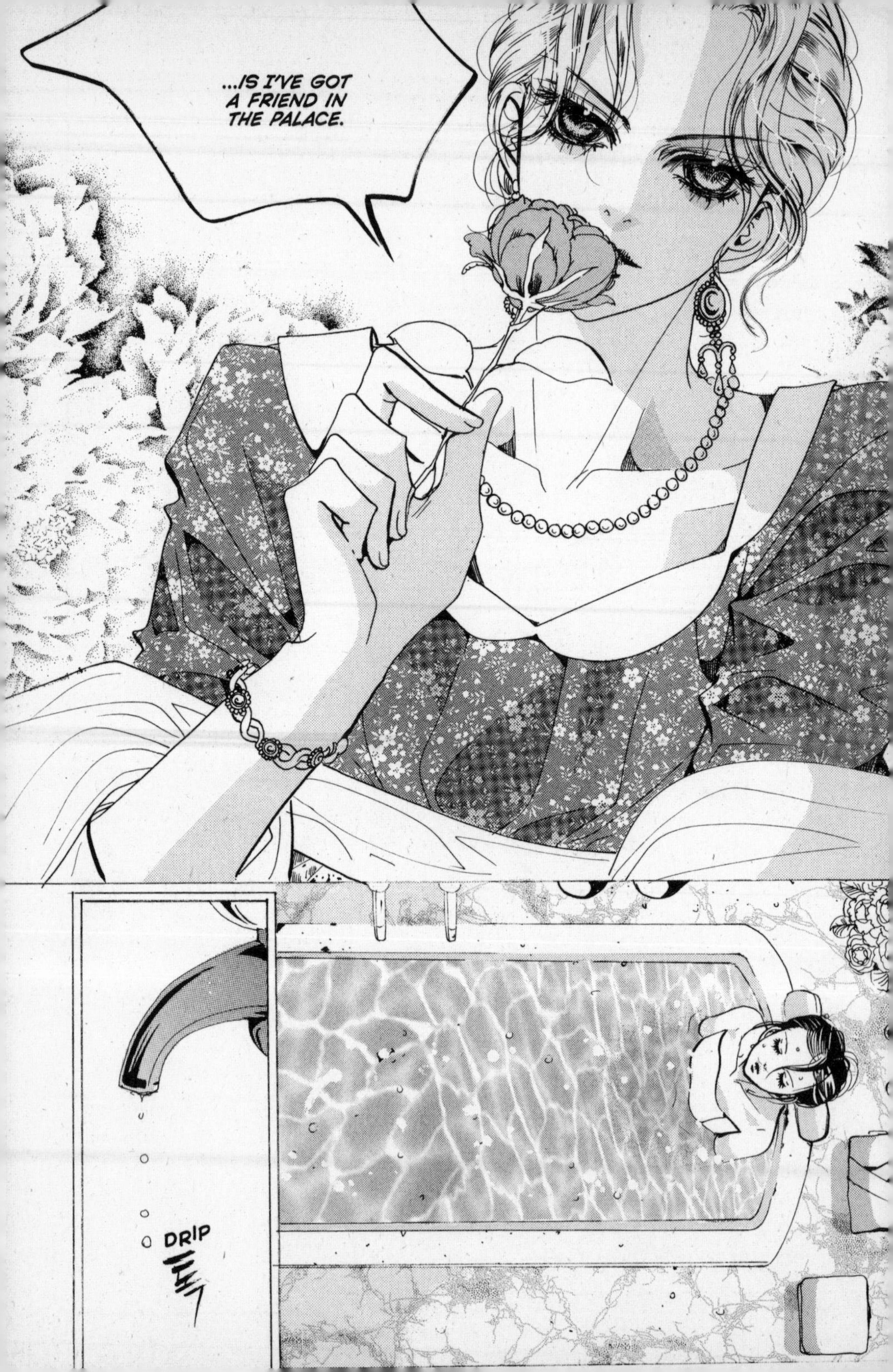
...IS I'VE GOT A FRIEND IN THE PALACE.
DRIP

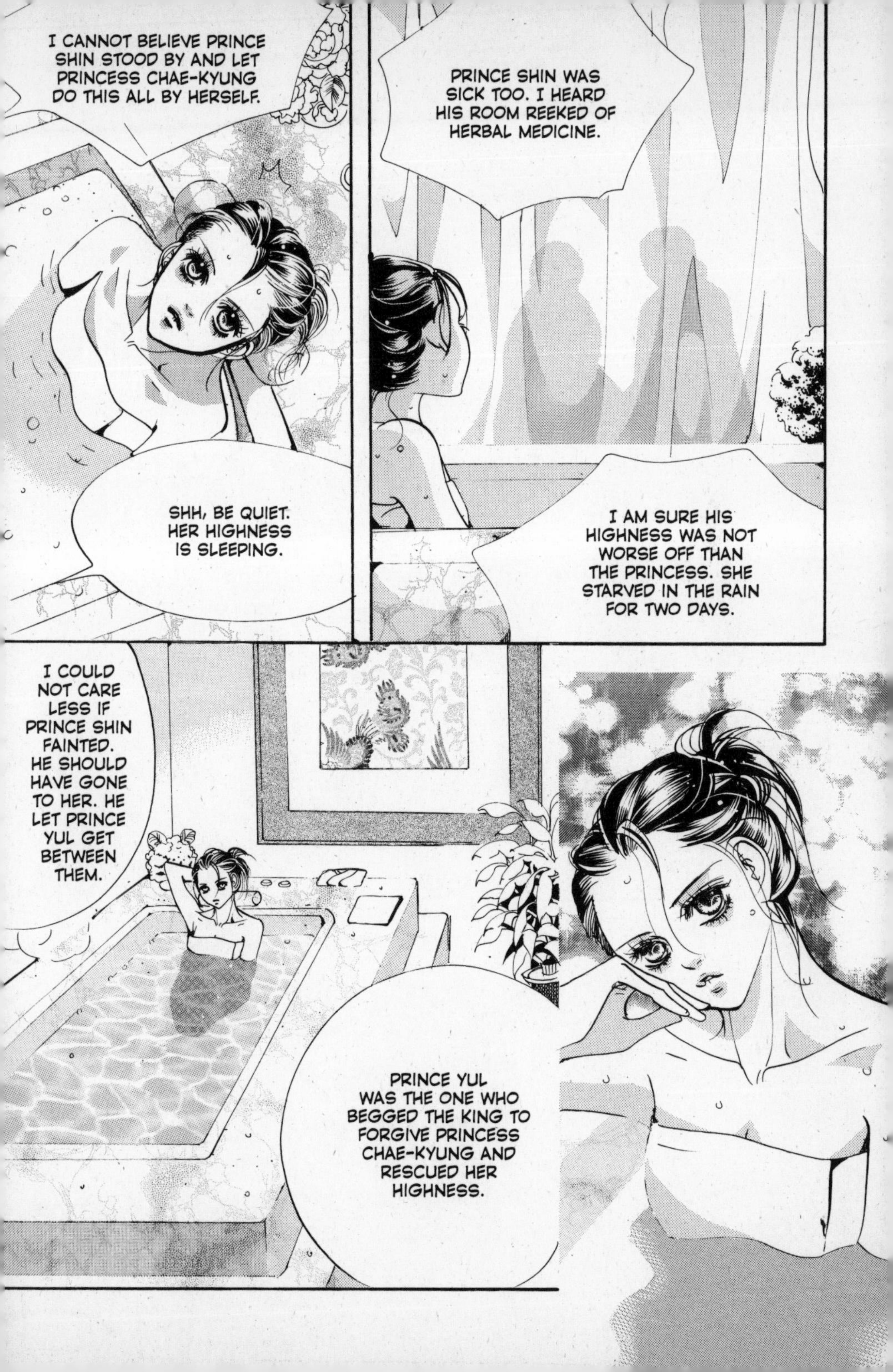
I CANNOT BELIEVE PRINCE SHIN STOOD BY AND LET PRINCESS CHAE-KYUNG DO THIS ALL BY HERSELF.
SHH, BE QUIET. HER HIGHNESS IS SLEEPING.
PRINCE SHIN WAS SICK TOO. I HEARD HIS ROOM REEKED OF HERBAL MEDICINE.
I AM SURE HIS HIGHNESS WAS NOT WORSE OFF THAN THE PRINCESS. SHE STARVED IN THE RAIN FOR TWO DAYS.
I COULD NOT CARE LESS IF PRINCE SHIN FAINTED. HE SHOULD HAVE GONE TO HER. HE LET PRINCE YUL GET BETWEEN THEM.
PRINCE YUL WAS THE ONE WHO BEGGED THE KING TO FORGIVE PRINCESS CHAE-KYUNG AND RESCUED HER HIGHNESS.

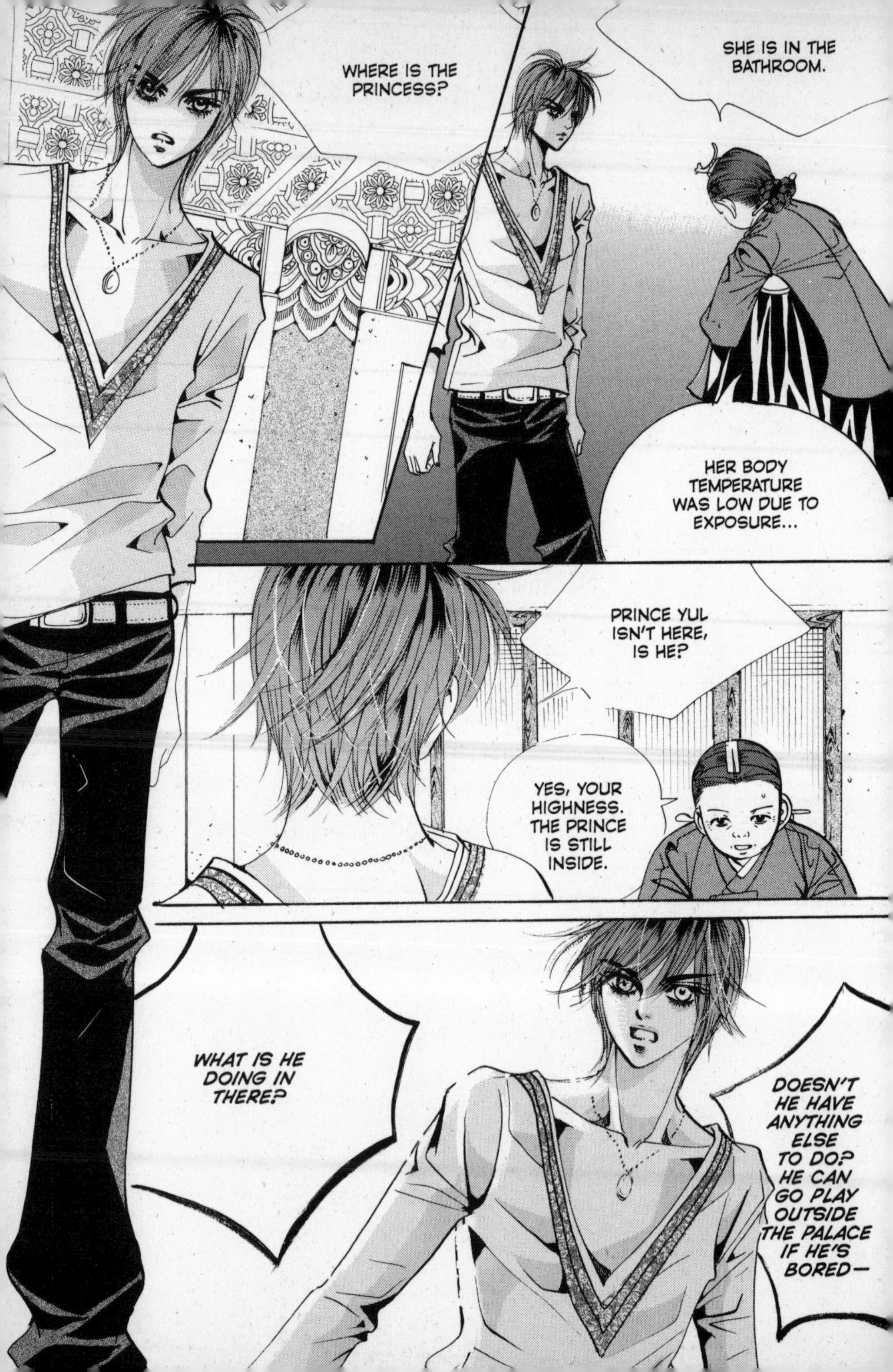
WHERE IS THE PRINCESS?
SHE IS IN THE BATHROOM.
HER BODY TEMPERATURE WAS LOW DUE TO EXPOSURE...
PRINCE YUL ISN'T HERE, IS HE?
YES, YOUR HIGHNESS. THE PRINCE IS STILL INSIDE.
WHAT IS HE DOING IN THERE?
DOESN'T HE HAVE ANYTHING ELSE TO DO? HE CAN GO PLAY OUTSIDE THE PALACE IF HE'S BORED—

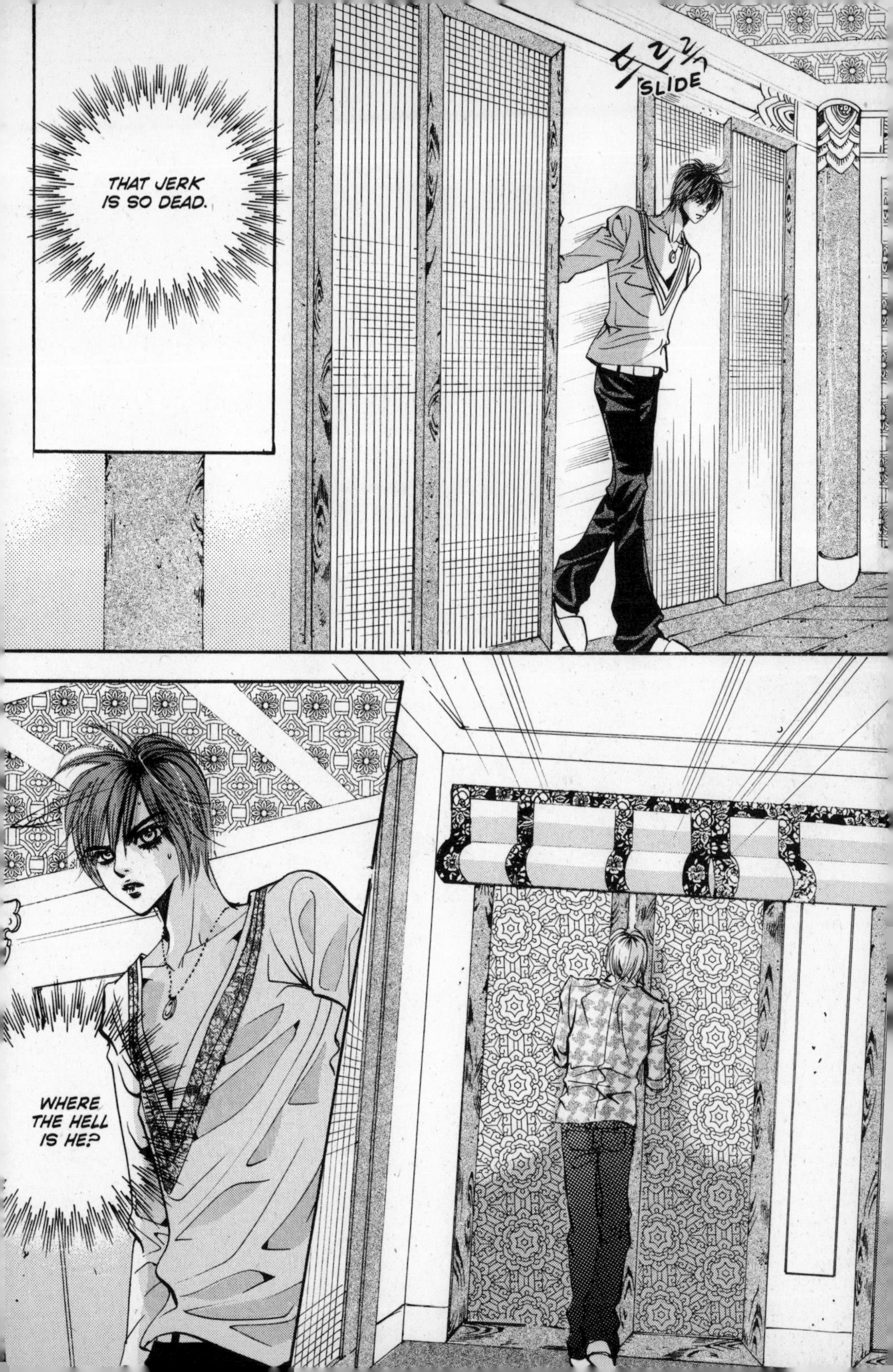
THAT JERK IS SO DEAD.
SLIDE
WHERE THE HELL IS HE?

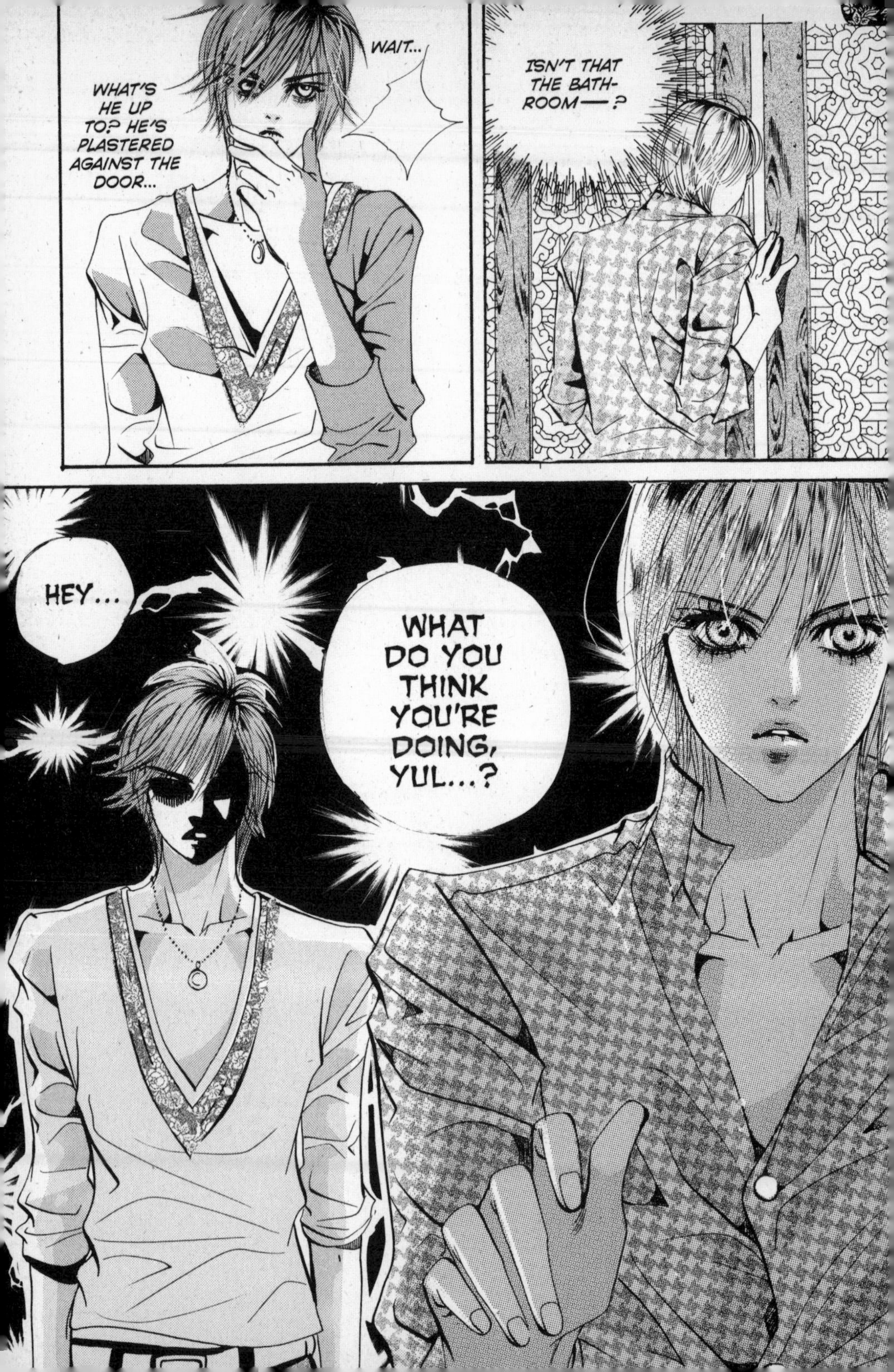
WHAT'S HE UP TO? HE'S PLASTERED AGAINST THE DOOR...
WAIT...
ISN'T THAT THE BATH-ROOM—?
HEY...
WHAT DO YOU THINK YOU'RE DOING, YUL...?

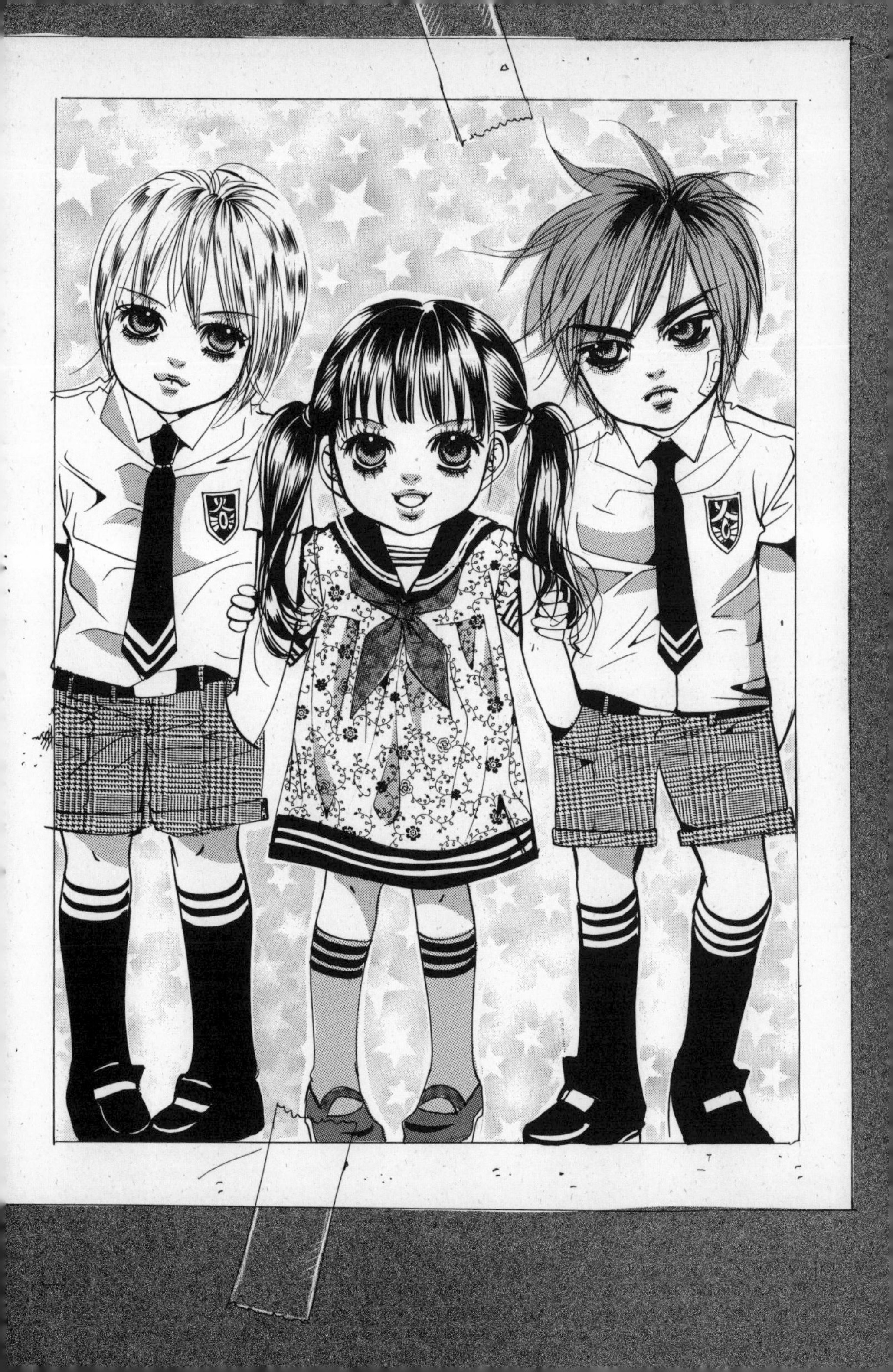

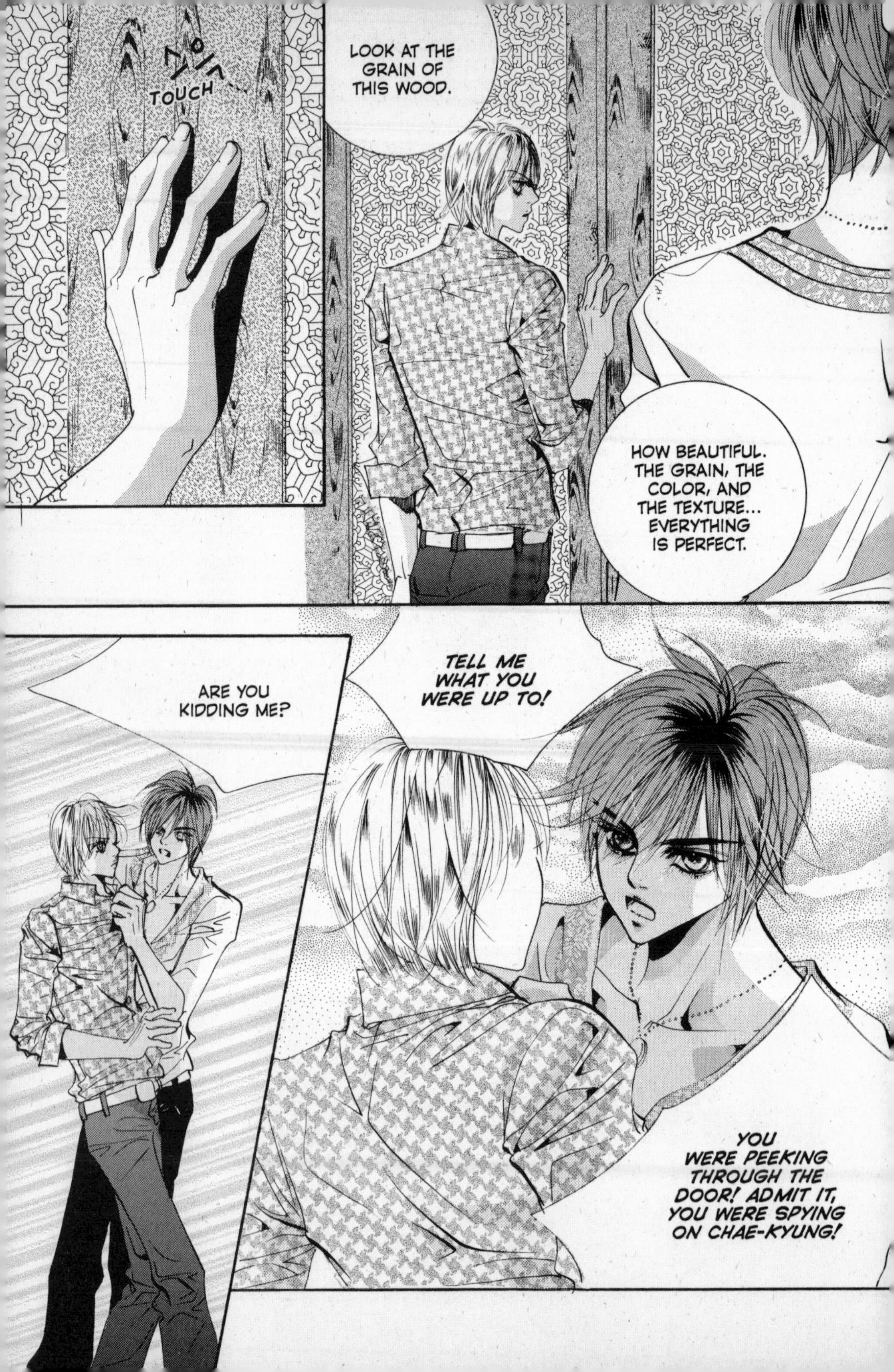

TOUCH
LOOK AT THE GRAIN OF THIS WOOD.
HOW BEAUTIFUL. THE GRAIN, THE COLOR, AND THE TEXTURE... EVERYTHING IS PERFECT.
ARE YOU KIDDING ME?
TELL ME WHAT YOU WERE UP TO!
YOU WERE PEEKING THROUGH THE DOOR! ADMIT IT, YOU WERE SPYING ON CHAE-KYUNG!

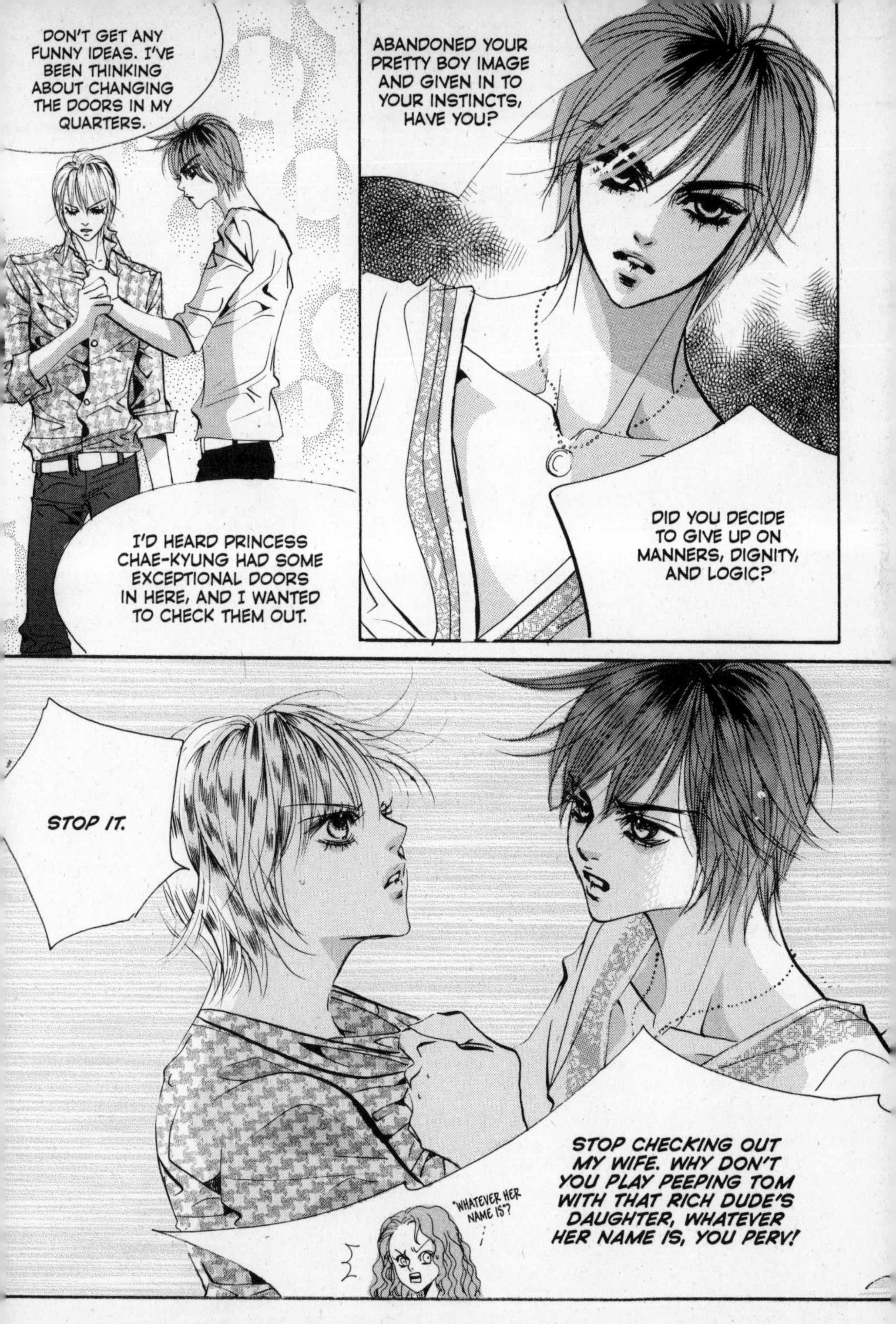
DON'T GET ANY FUNNY IDEAS. I'VE BEEN THINKING ABOUT CHANGING THE DOORS IN MY QUARTERS.
I'D HEARD PRINCESS CHAE-KYUNG HAD SOME EXCEPTIONAL DOORS IN HERE, AND I WANTED TO CHECK THEM OUT.
ABANDONED YOUR PRETTY BOY IMAGE AND GIVEN IN TO YOUR INSTINCTS, HAVE YOU?
DID YOU DECIDE TO GIVE UP ON MANNERS, DIGNITY, AND LOGIC?
STOP IT.
STOP CHECKING OUT MY WIFE. WHY DON'T YOU PLAY PEEPING TOM WITH THAT RICH DUDE'S DAUGHTER, WHATEVER HER NAME IS, YOU PERV!
"WHATEVER HER NAME IS"?

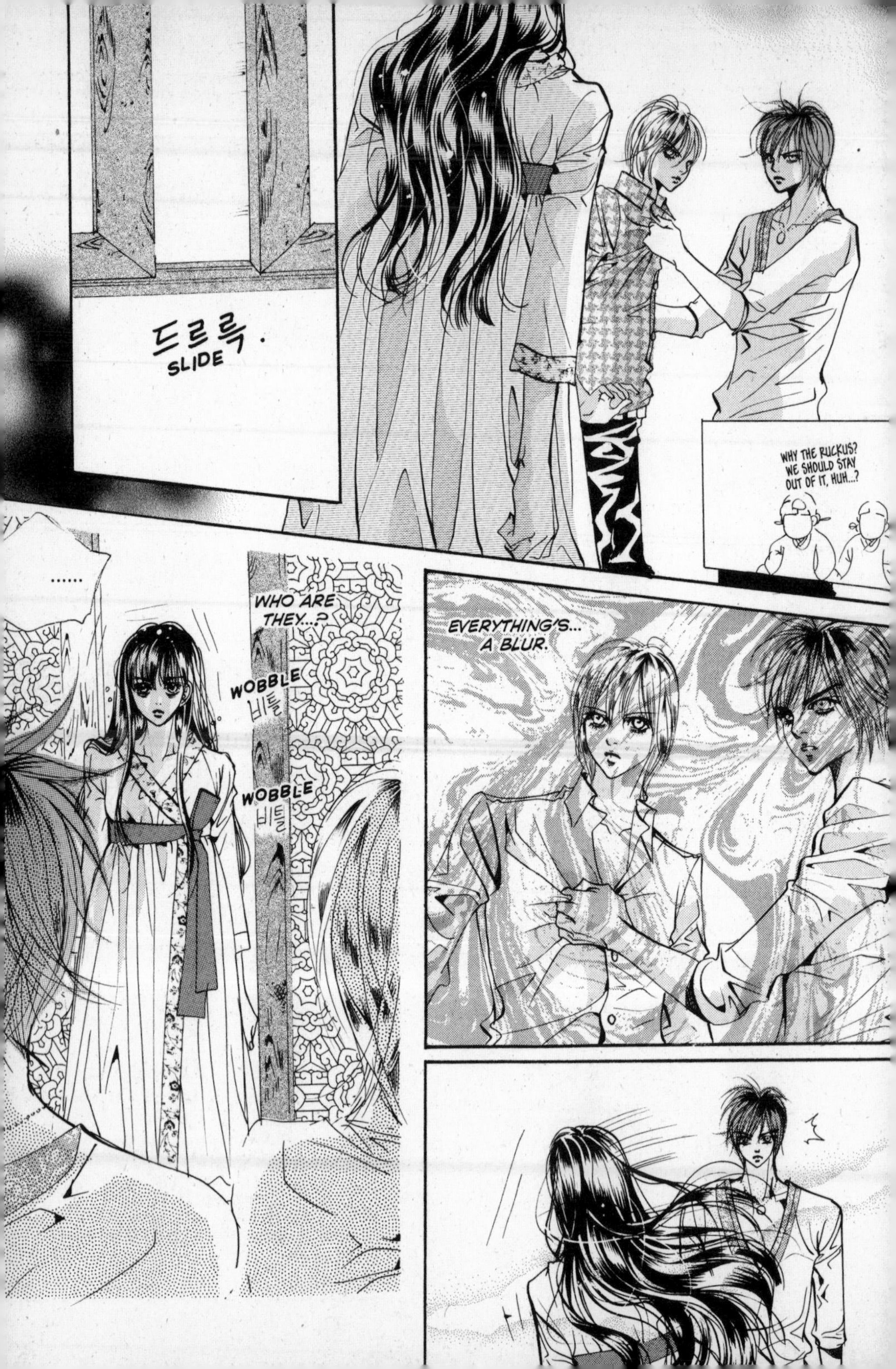

드르륵.
SLIDE
WHY THE RUCKUS? WE SHOULD STAY OUT OF IT, HUH...?
......
WHO ARE THEY...?
WOBBLE
비틀
WOBBLE
비틀
EVERYTHING'S... A BLUR.

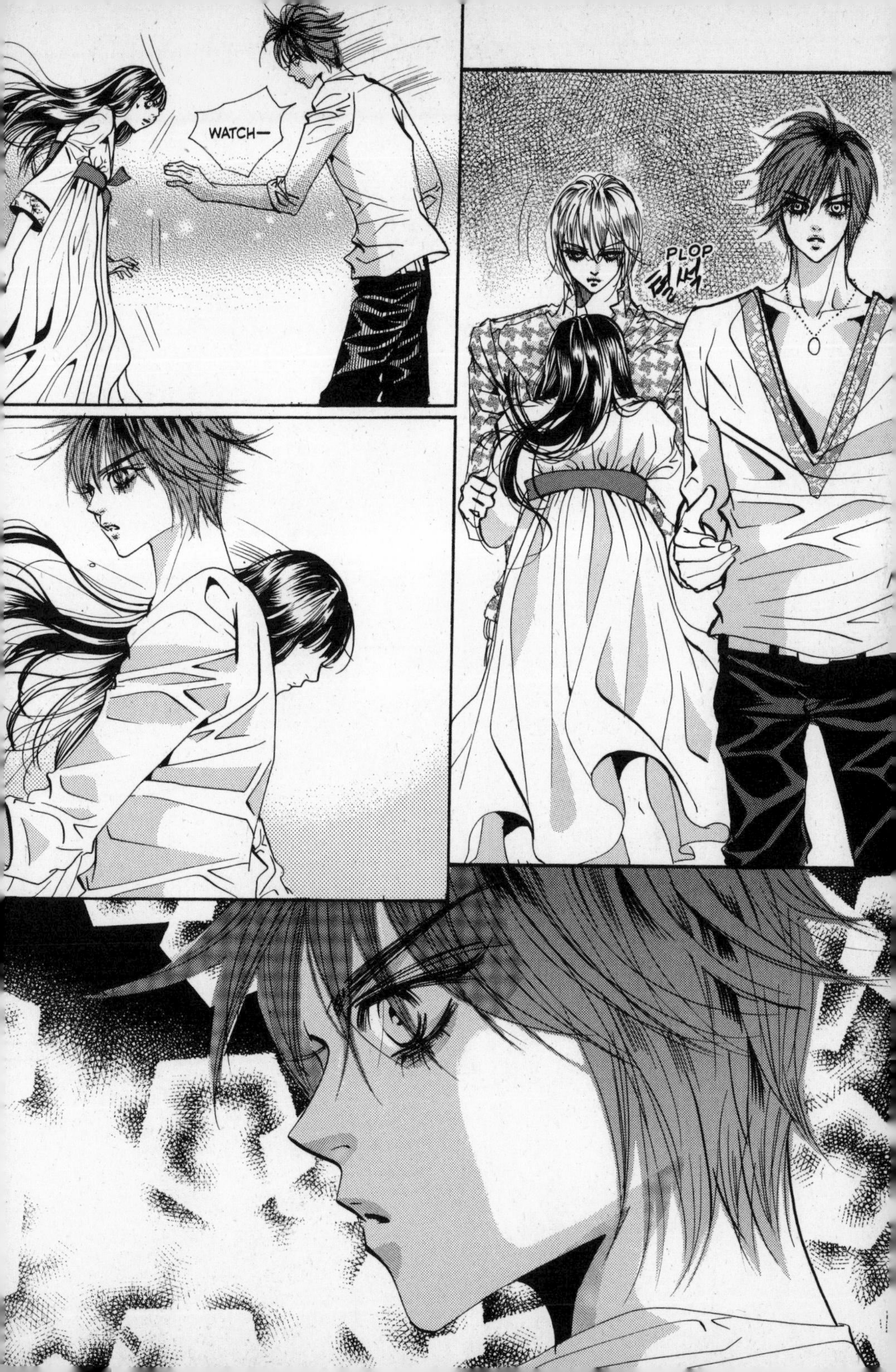
WATCH—
PLOP
털썩

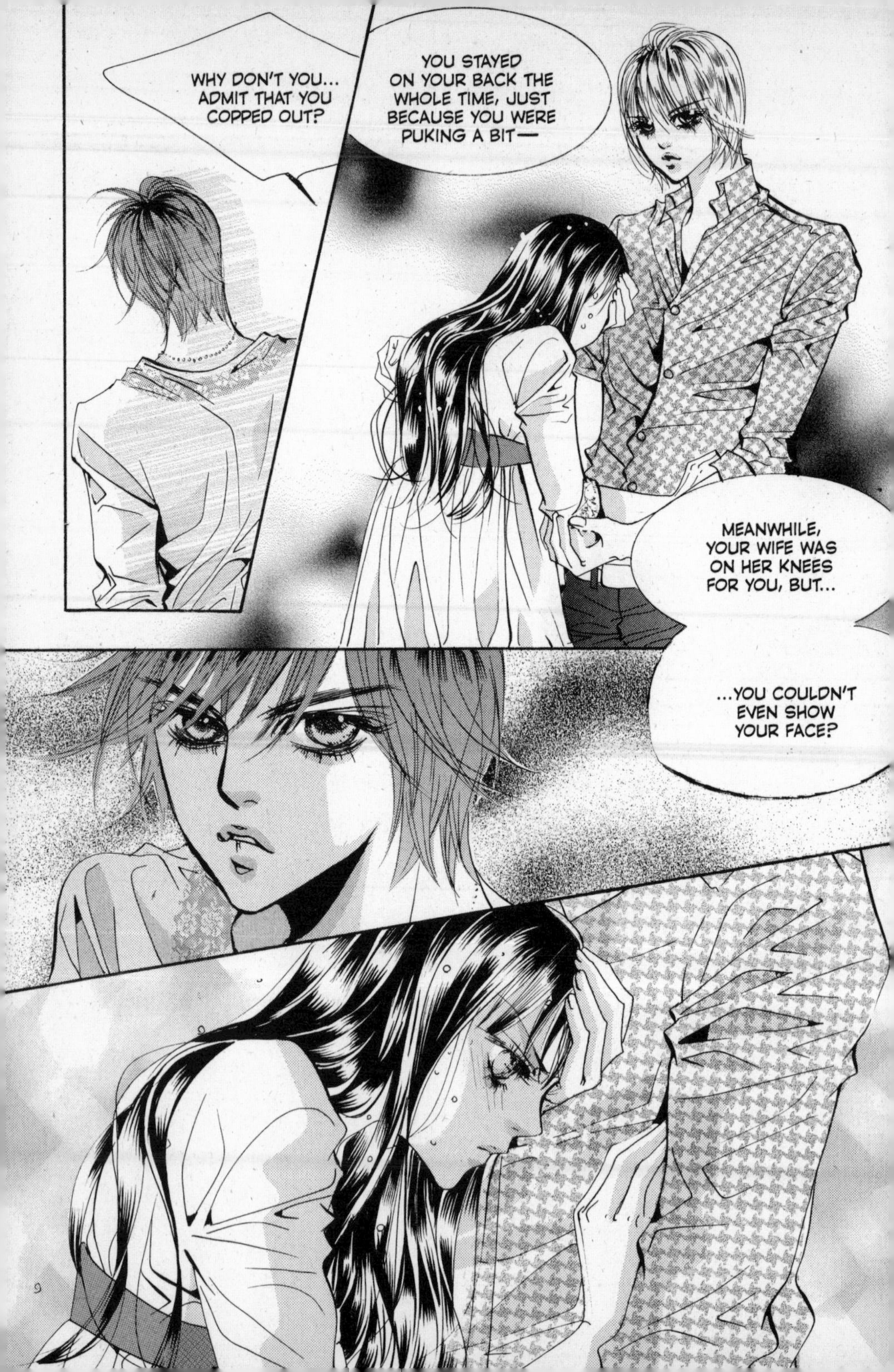
WHY DON'T YOU... ADMIT THAT YOU COPPED OUT?
YOU STAYED ON YOUR BACK THE WHOLE TIME, JUST BECAUSE YOU WERE PUKING A BIT—
MEANWHILE, YOUR WIFE WAS ON HER KNEES FOR YOU, BUT...
...YOU COULDN'T EVEN SHOW YOUR FACE?

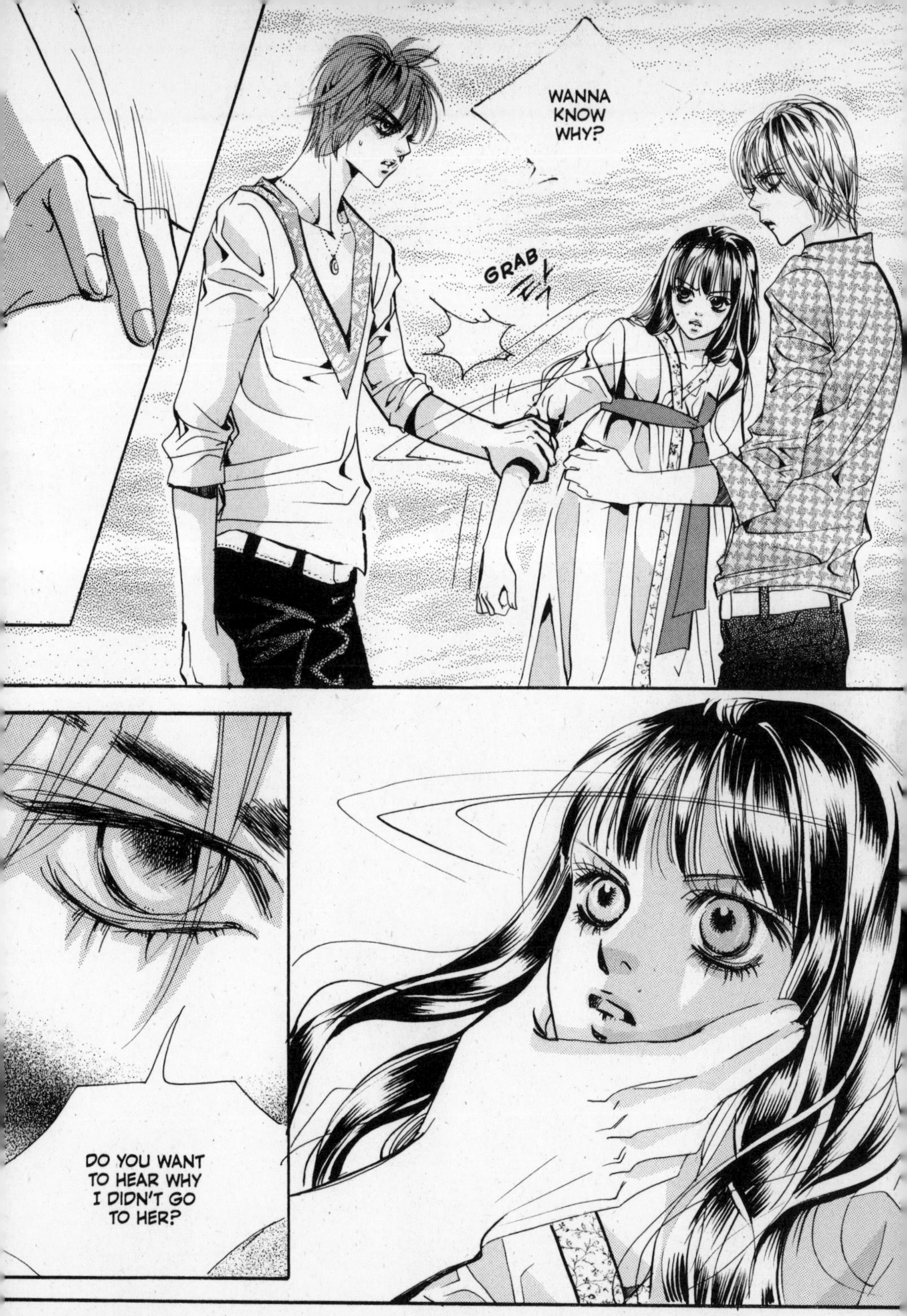
WANNA KNOW WHY?
GRAB
DO YOU WANT TO HEAR WHY I DIDN'T GO TO HER?

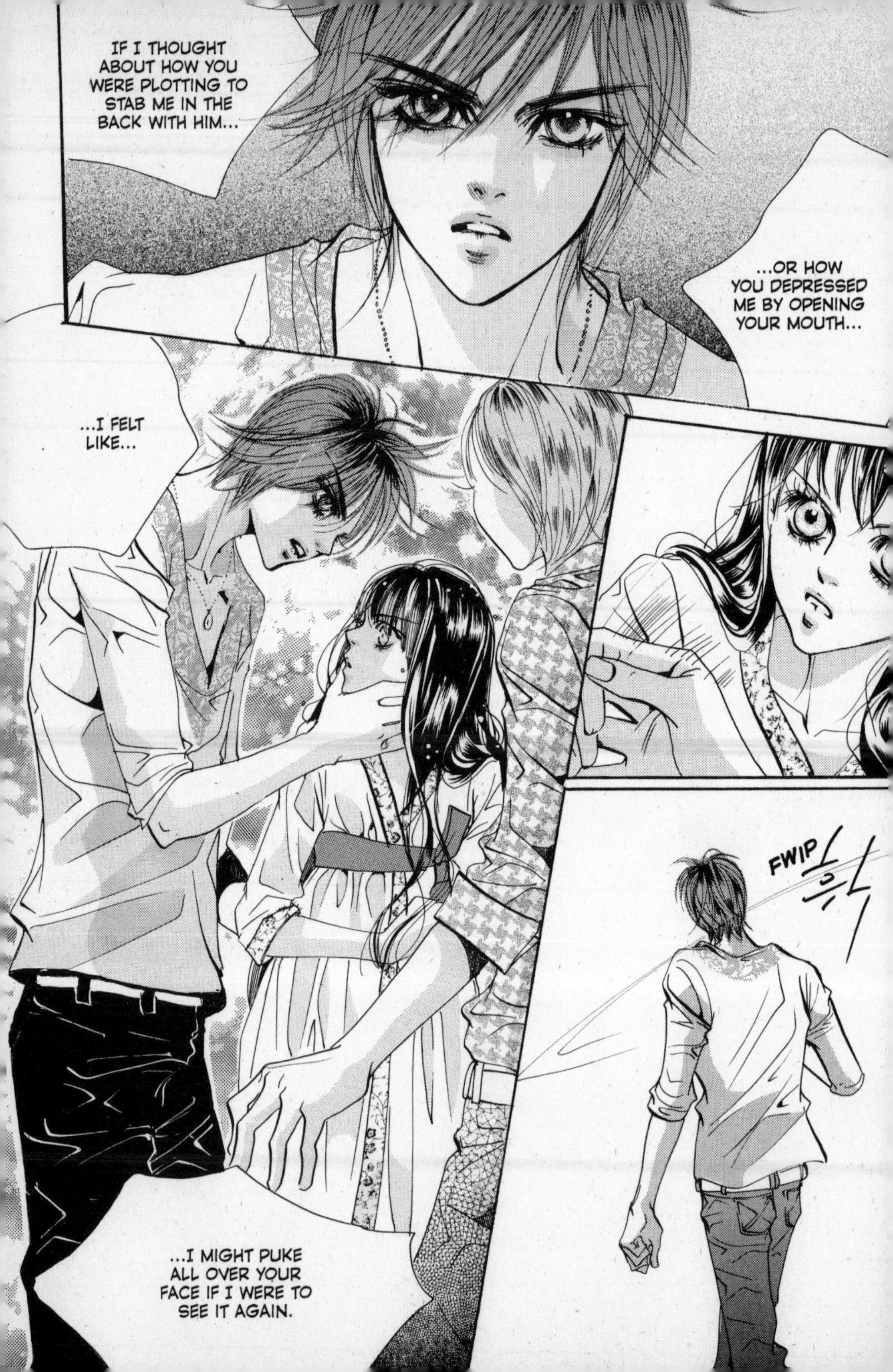
IF I THOUGHT ABOUT HOW YOU WERE PLOTTING TO STAB ME IN THE BACK WITH HIM...
...OR HOW YOU DEPRESSED ME BY OPENING YOUR MOUTH...
...I FELT LIKE...
...I MIGHT PUKE ALL OVER YOUR FACE IF I WERE TO SEE IT AGAIN.
FWIP

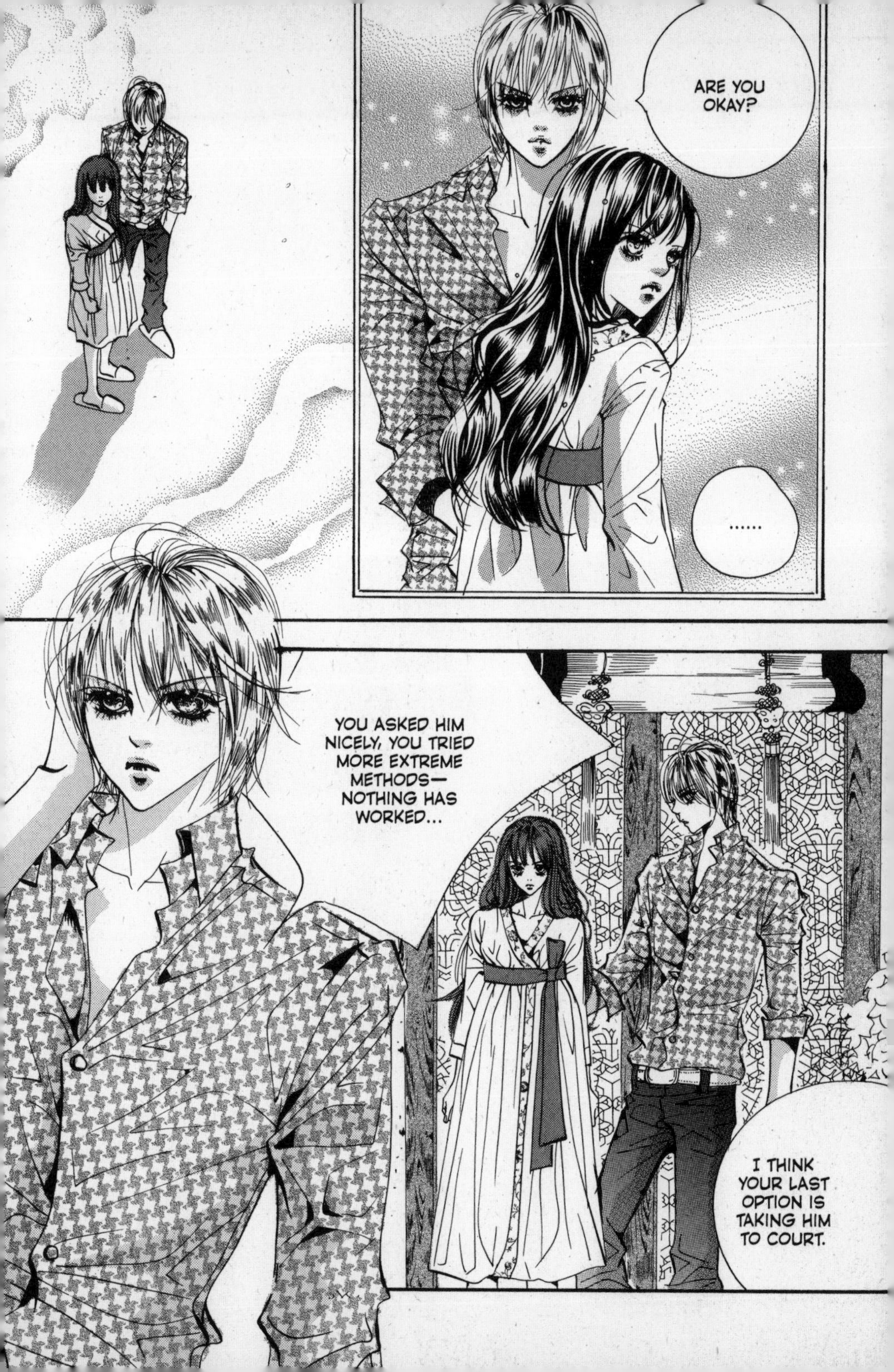
ARE YOU OKAY?
......
YOU ASKED HIM NICELY, YOU TRIED MORE EXTREME METHODS— NOTHING HAS WORKED...
I THINK YOUR LAST OPTION IS TAKING HIM TO COURT.

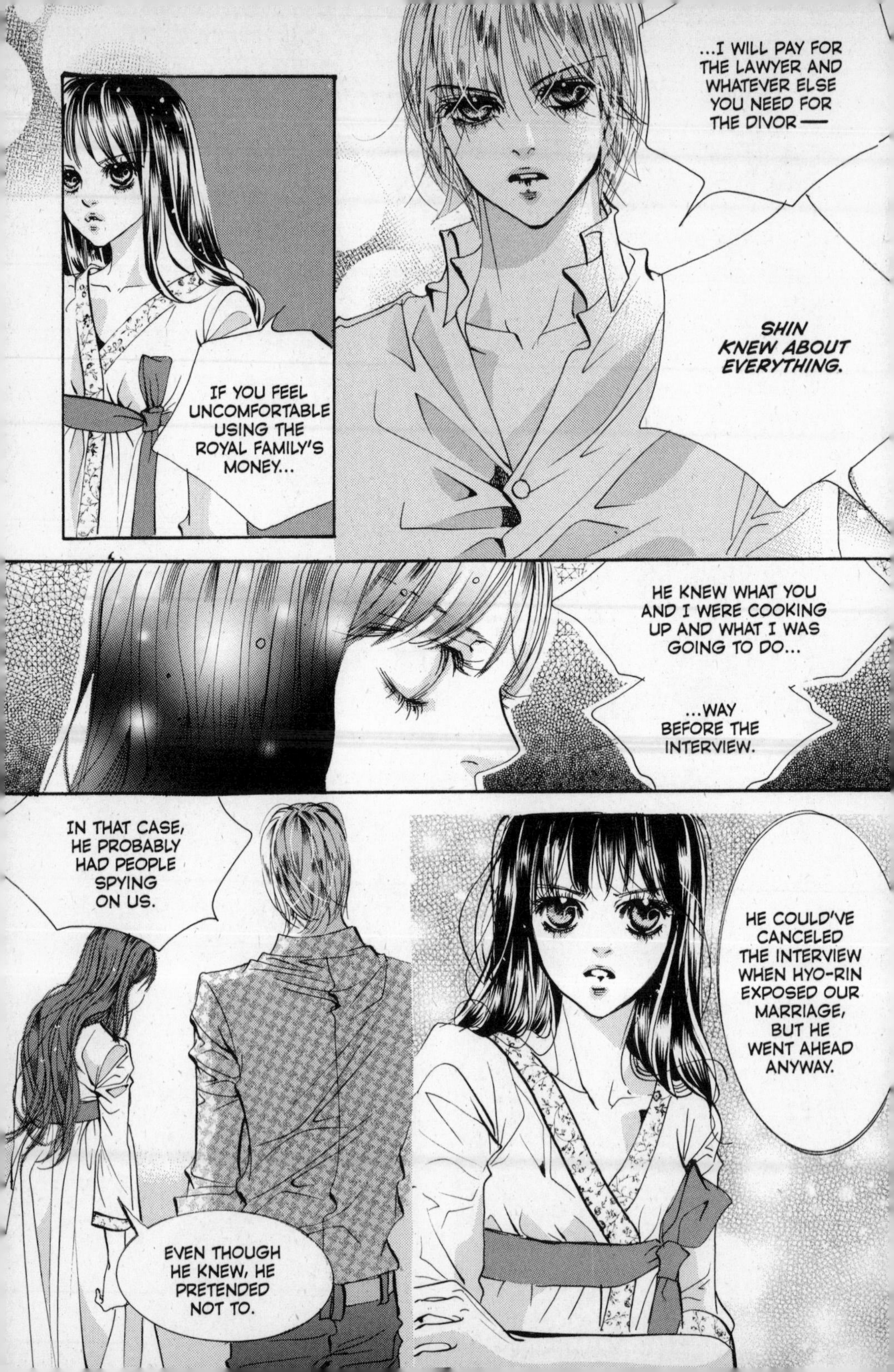
IF YOU FEEL UNCOMFORTABLE USING THE ROYAL FAMILY'S MONEY...
...I WILL PAY FOR THE LAWYER AND WHATEVER ELSE YOU NEED FOR THE DIVOR—
SHIN KNEW ABOUT EVERYTHING.
HE KNEW WHAT YOU AND I WERE COOKING UP AND WHAT I WAS GOING TO DO...
...WAY BEFORE THE INTERVIEW.
IN THAT CASE, HE PROBABLY HAD PEOPLE SPYING ON US.
EVEN THOUGH HE KNEW, HE PRETENDED NOT TO.
HE COULD'VE CANCELED THE INTERVIEW WHEN HYO-RIN EXPOSED OUR MARRIAGE, BUT HE WENT AHEAD ANYWAY.

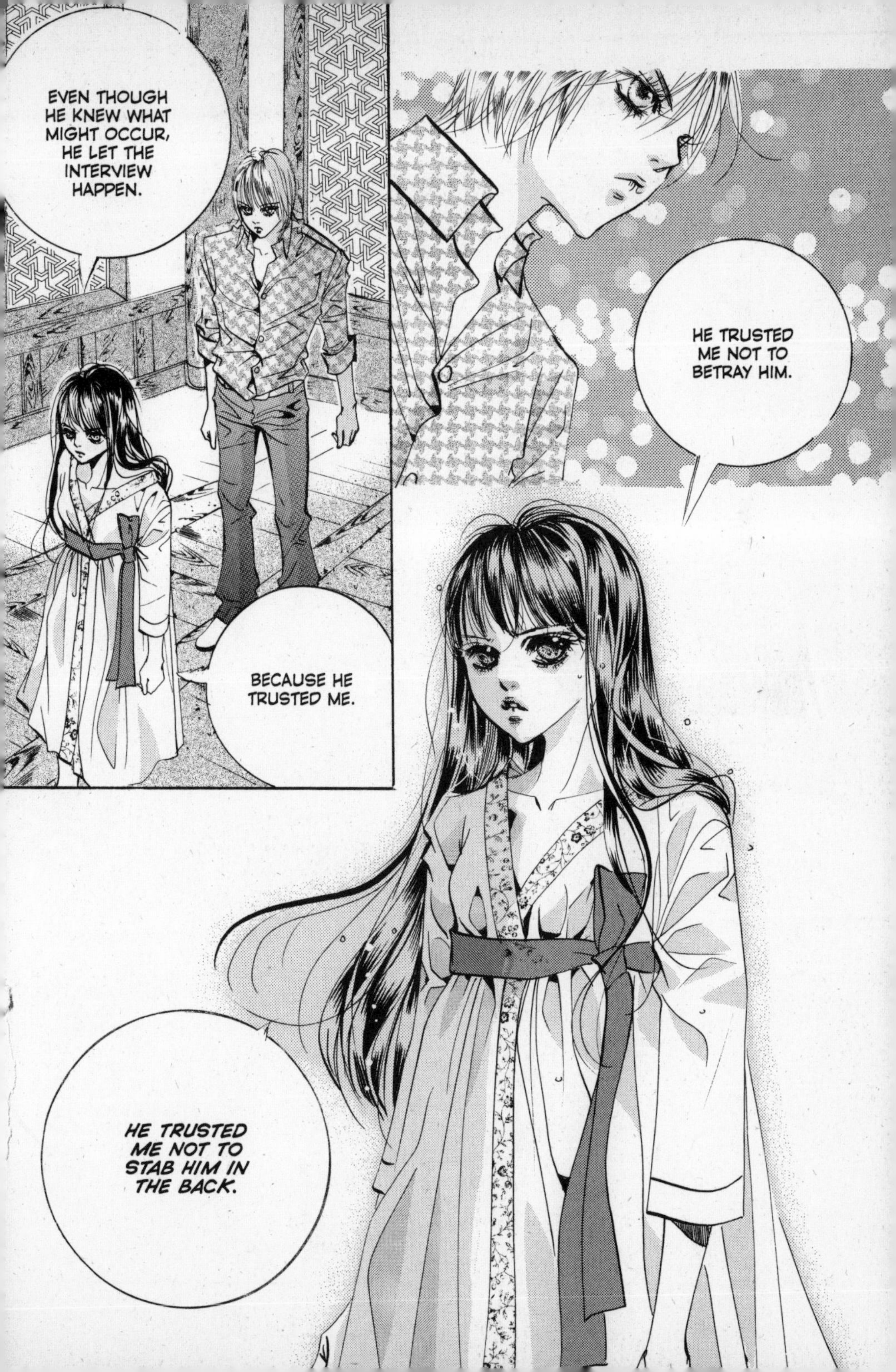
EVEN THOUGH HE KNEW WHAT MIGHT OCCUR, HE LET THE INTERVIEW HAPPEN.
BECAUSE HE TRUSTED ME.
HE TRUSTED ME NOT TO BETRAY HIM.
HE TRUSTED ME NOT TO STAB HIM IN THE BACK.

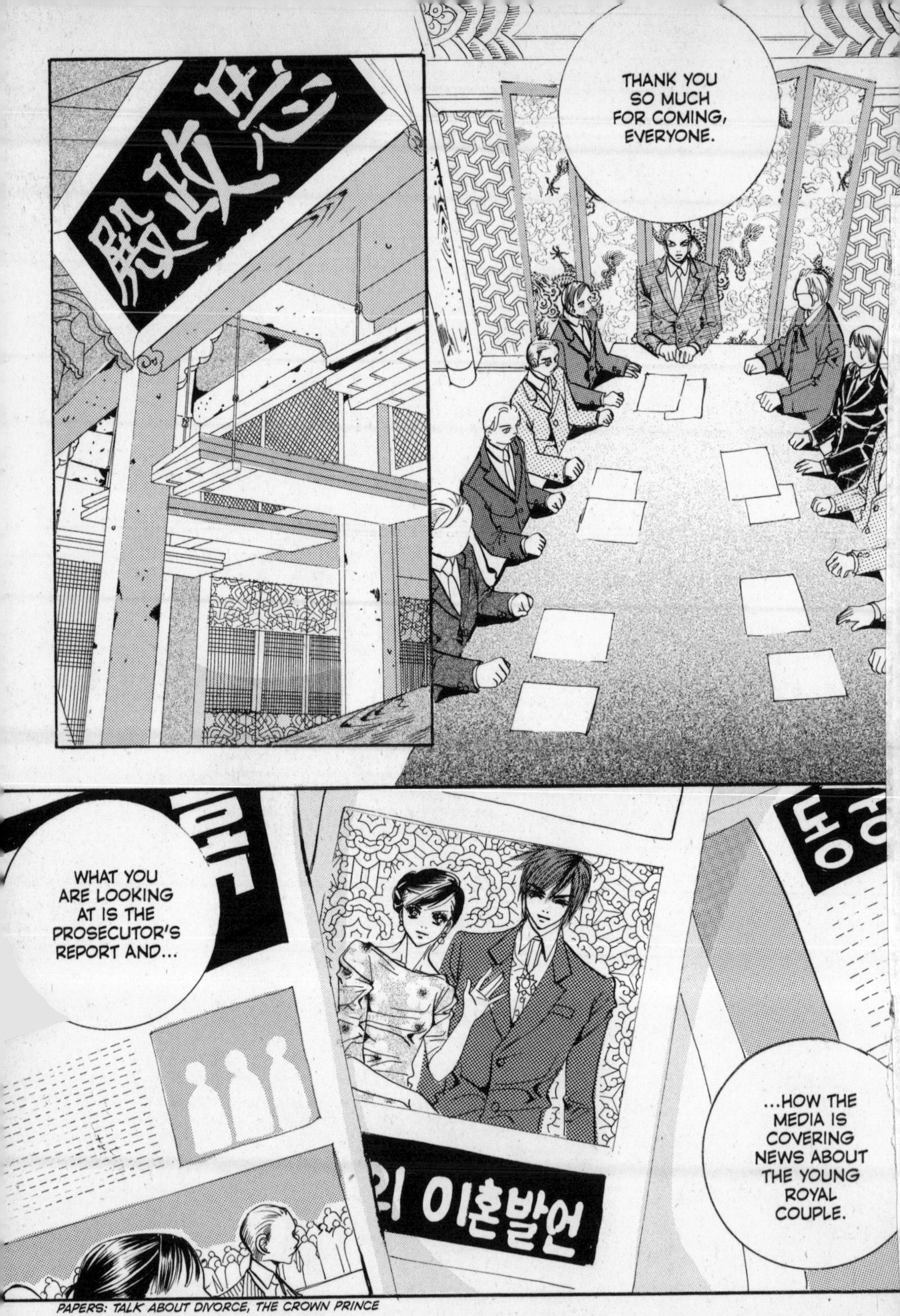
THANK YOU SO MUCH FOR COMING, EVERYONE.
WHAT YOU ARE LOOKING AT IS THE PROSECUTOR'S REPORT AND...
이혼발언
...HOW THE MEDIA IS COVERING NEWS ABOUT THE YOUNG ROYAL COUPLE.

PAPERS: TALK ABOUT DIVORCE, THE CROWN PRINCE

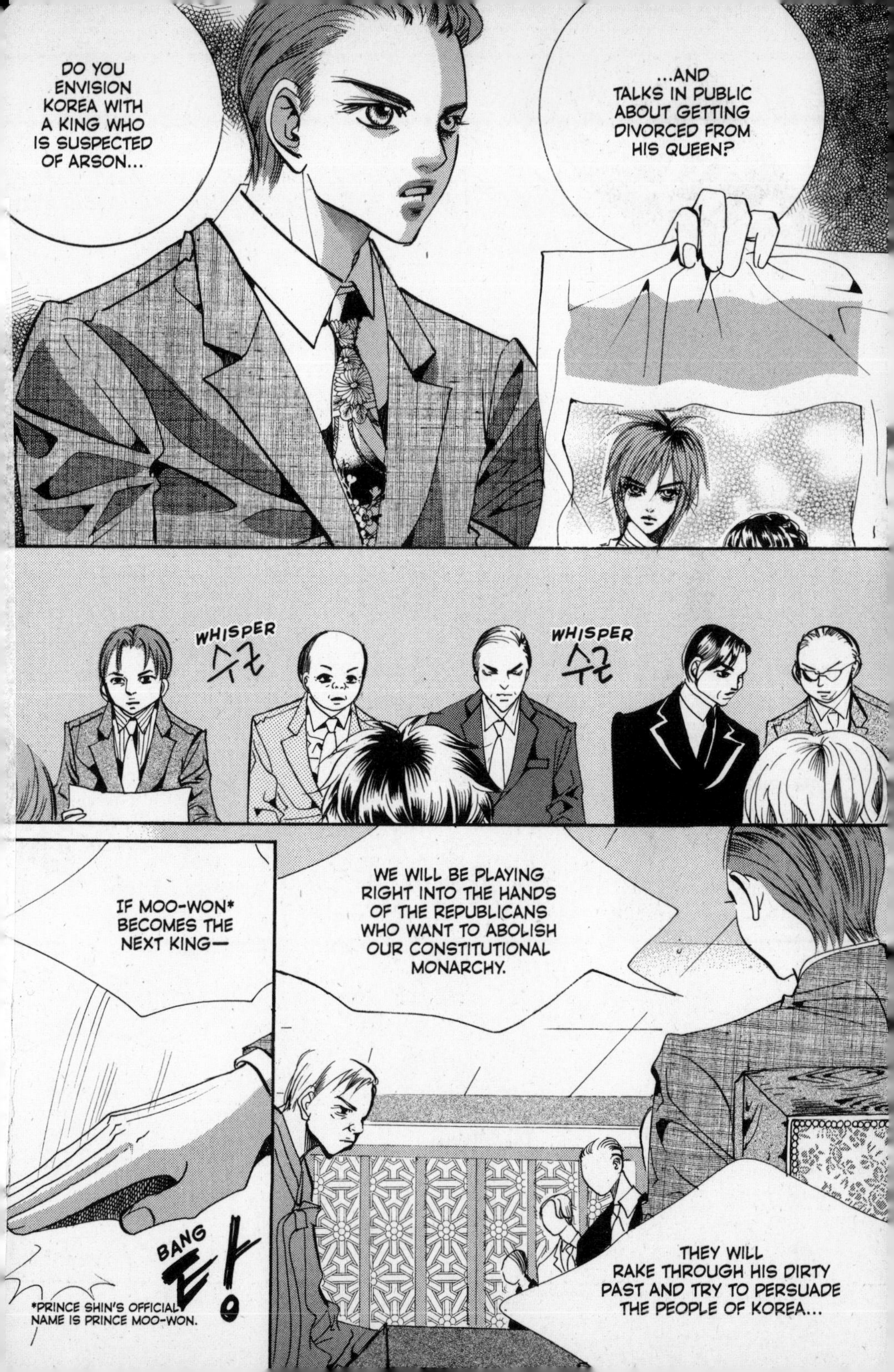
DO YOU ENVISION KOREA WITH A KING WHO IS SUSPECTED OF ARSON...
...AND TALKS IN PUBLIC ABOUT GETTING DIVORCED FROM HIS QUEEN?
WHISPER
수군
WHISPER
수군
IF MOO-WON* BECOMES THE NEXT KING—
WE WILL BE PLAYING RIGHT INTO THE HANDS OF THE REPUBLICANS WHO WANT TO ABOLISH OUR CONSTITUTIONAL MONARCHY.
BANG
탁
THEY WILL RAKE THROUGH HIS DIRTY PAST AND TRY TO PERSUADE THE PEOPLE OF KOREA...
*PRINCE SHIN'S OFFICIAL NAME IS PRINCE MOO-WON.

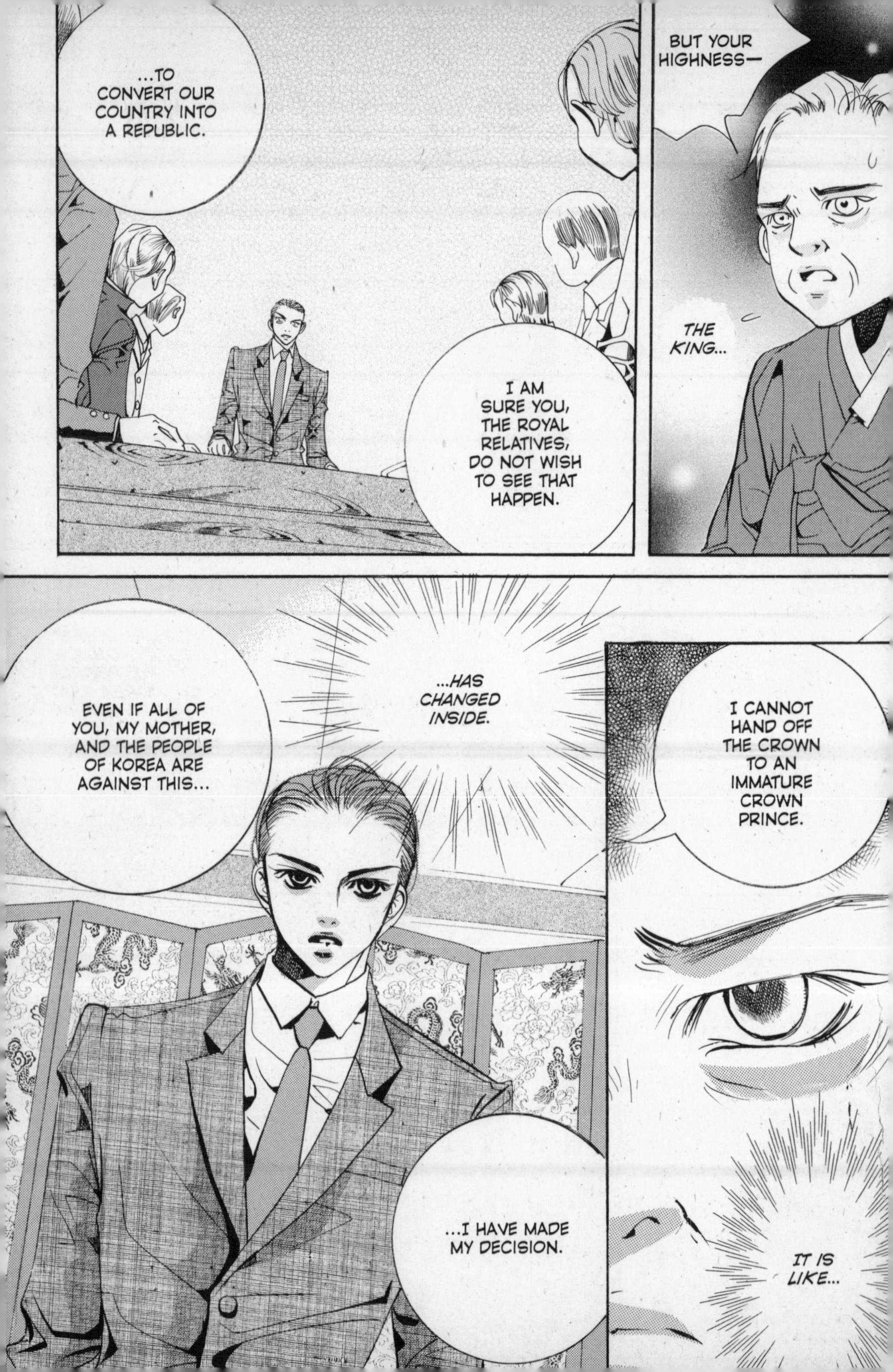
...TO CONVERT OUR COUNTRY INTO A REPUBLIC.
I AM SURE YOU, THE ROYAL RELATIVES, DO NOT WISH TO SEE THAT HAPPEN.
BUT YOUR HIGHNESS—
THE KING...
EVEN IF ALL OF YOU, MY MOTHER, AND THE PEOPLE OF KOREA ARE AGAINST THIS...
...I HAVE MADE MY DECISION.
...HAS CHANGED INSIDE.
I CANNOT HAND OFF THE CROWN TO AN IMMATURE CROWN PRINCE.
IT IS LIKE...

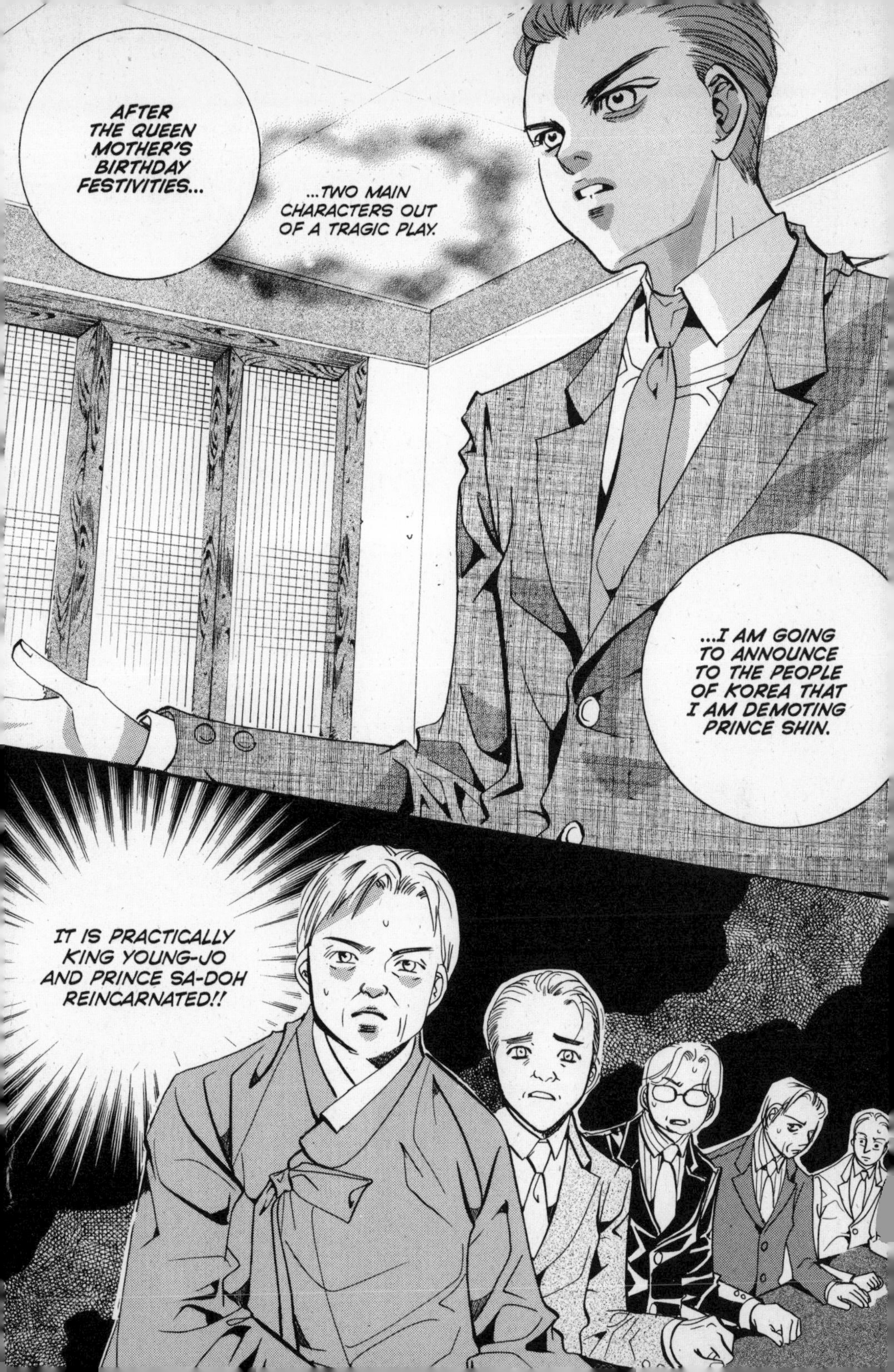
AFTER THE QUEEN MOTHER'S BIRTHDAY FESTIVITIES...
...TWO MAIN CHARACTERS OUT OF A TRAGIC PLAY.
...I AM GOING TO ANNOUNCE TO THE PEOPLE OF KOREA THAT I AM DEMOTING PRINCE SHIN.
IT IS PRACTICALLY KING YOUNG-JO AND PRINCE SA-DOH REINCARNATED!!

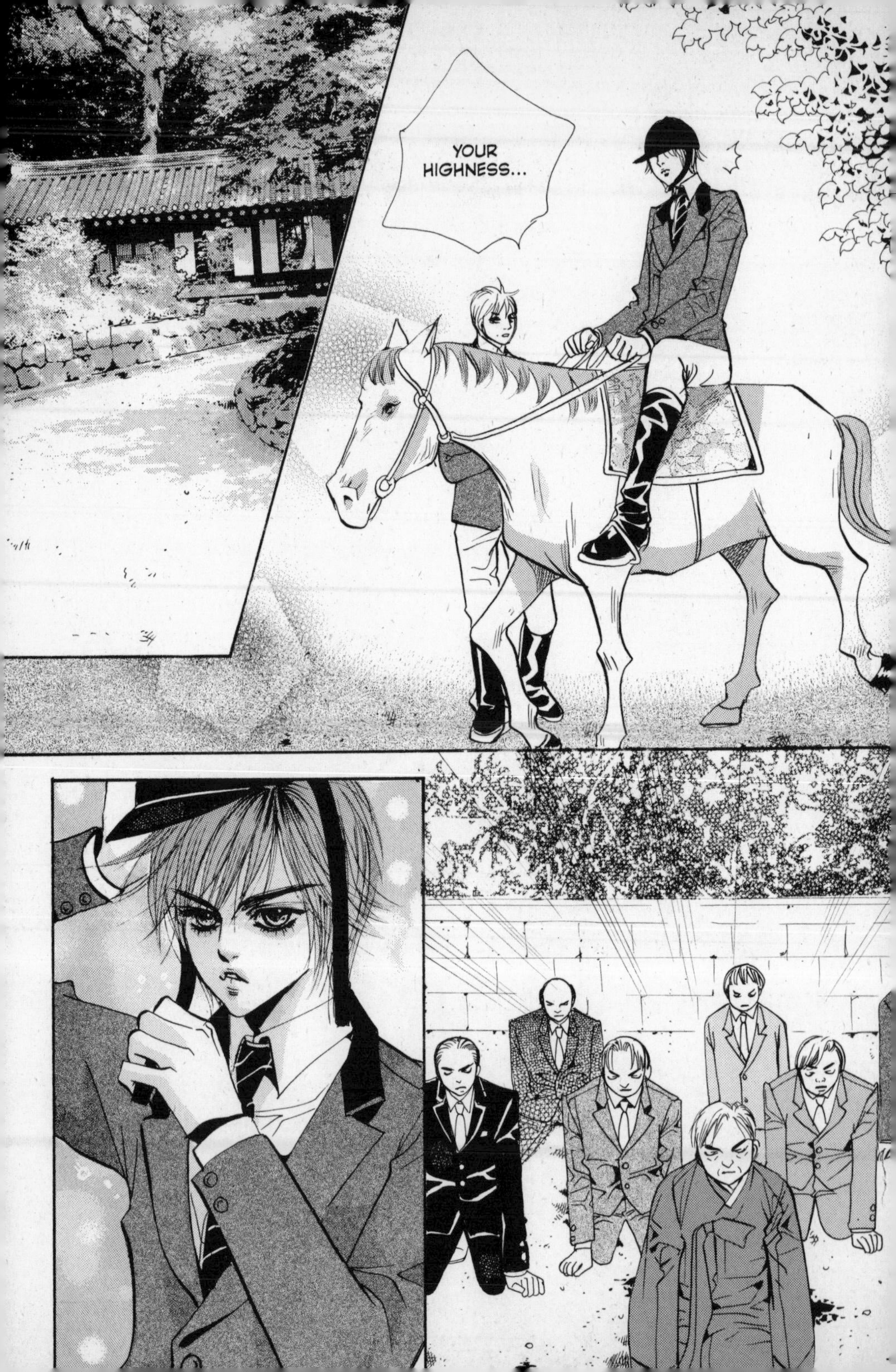
YOUR HIGHNESS...

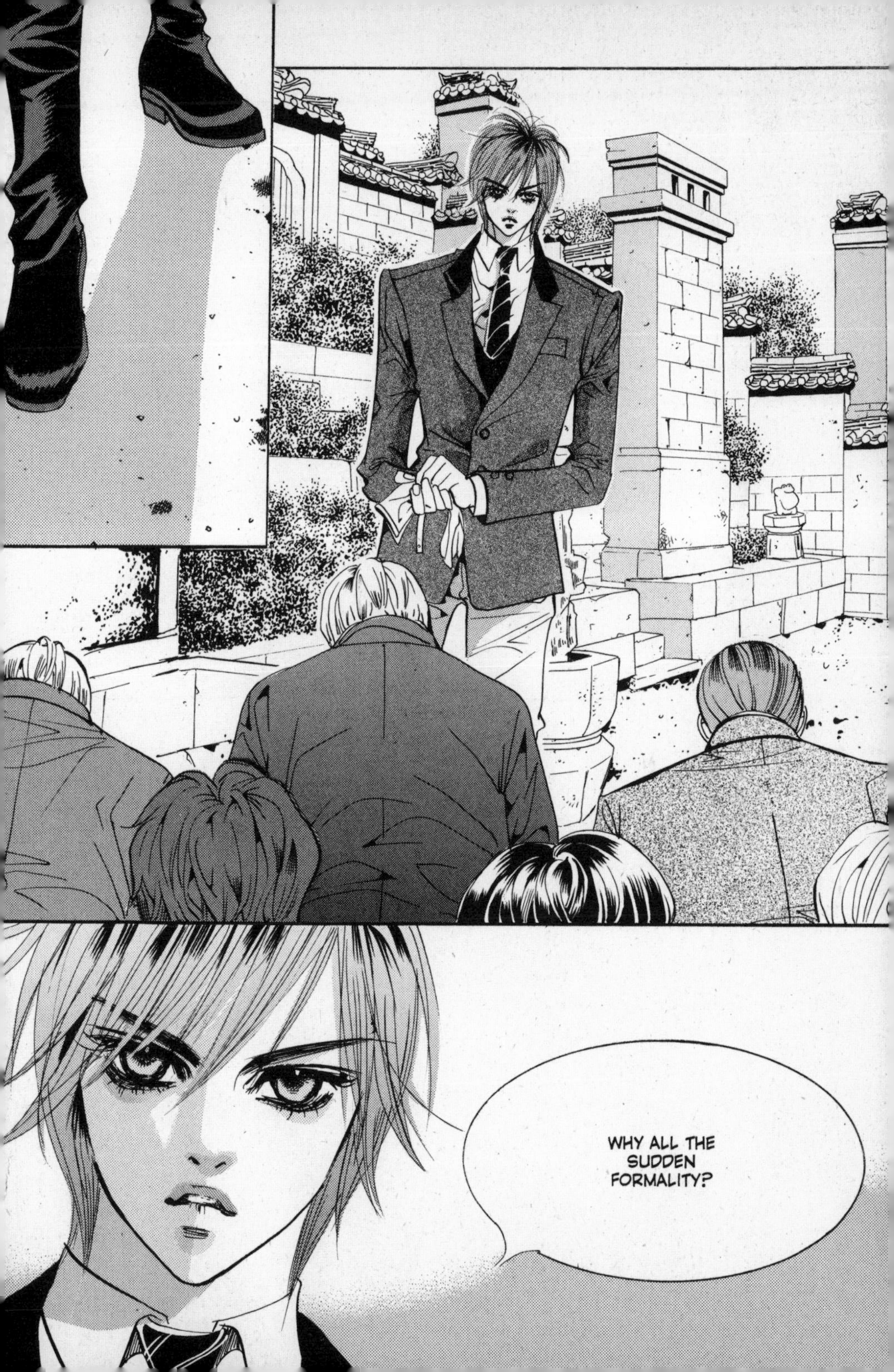
WHY ALL THE SUDDEN FORMALITY?

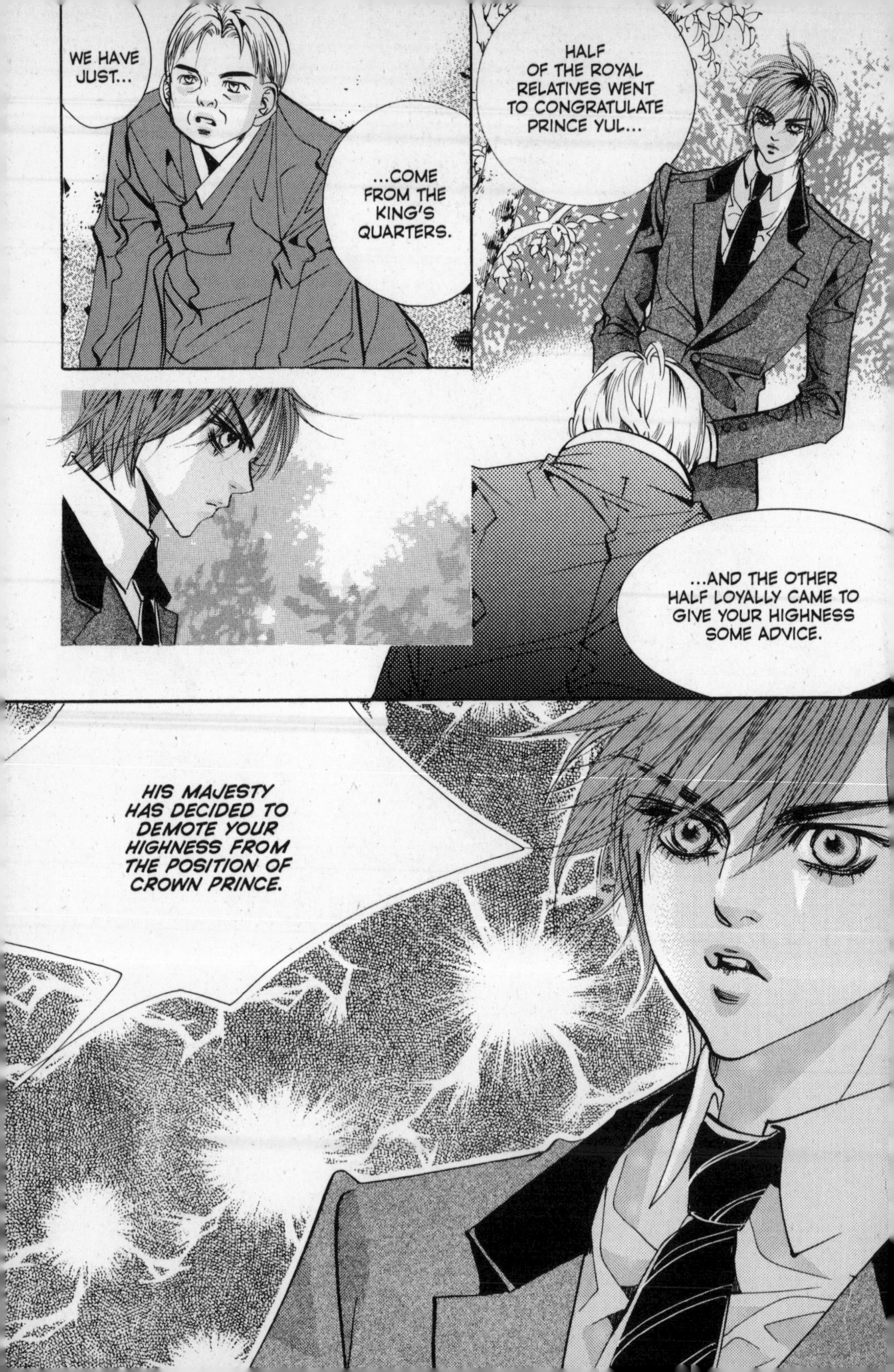
WE HAVE JUST...
...COME FROM THE KING'S QUARTERS.
HALF OF THE ROYAL RELATIVES WENT TO CONGRATULATE PRINCE YUL...
...AND THE OTHER HALF LOYALLY CAME TO GIVE YOUR HIGHNESS SOME ADVICE.
HIS MAJESTY HAS DECIDED TO DEMOTE YOUR HIGHNESS FROM THE POSITION OF CROWN PRINCE.

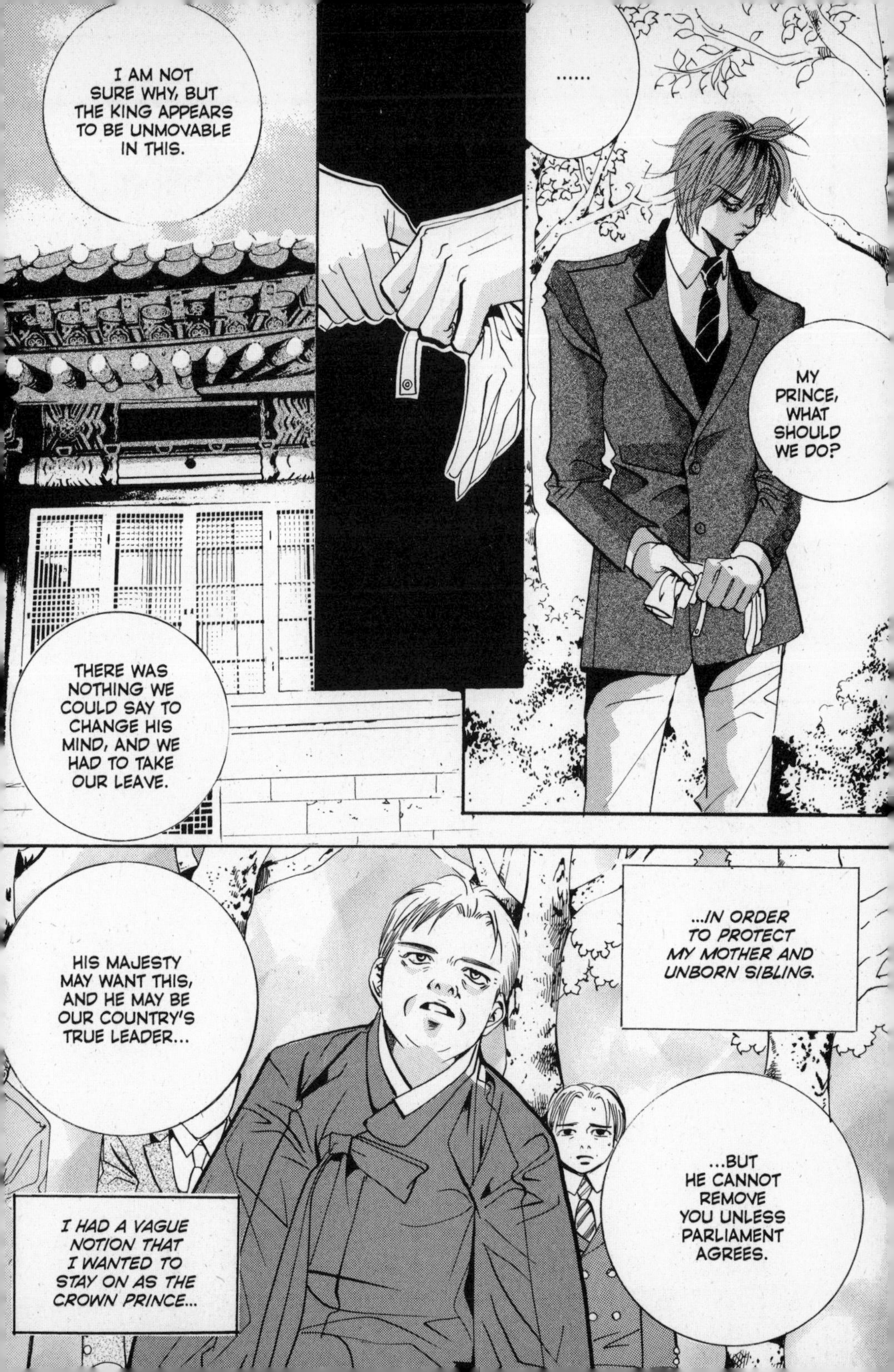
I AM NOT SURE WHY, BUT THE KING APPEARS TO BE UNMOVABLE IN THIS.
THERE WAS NOTHING WE COULD SAY TO CHANGE HIS MIND, AND WE HAD TO TAKE OUR LEAVE.
......
MY PRINCE, WHAT SHOULD WE DO?
HIS MAJESTY MAY WANT THIS, AND HE MAY BE OUR COUNTRY'S TRUE LEADER...
...BUT HE CANNOT REMOVE YOU UNLESS PARLIAMENT AGREES.
I HAD A VAGUE NOTION THAT I WANTED TO STAY ON AS THE CROWN PRINCE...
...IN ORDER TO PROTECT MY MOTHER AND UNBORN SIBLING.

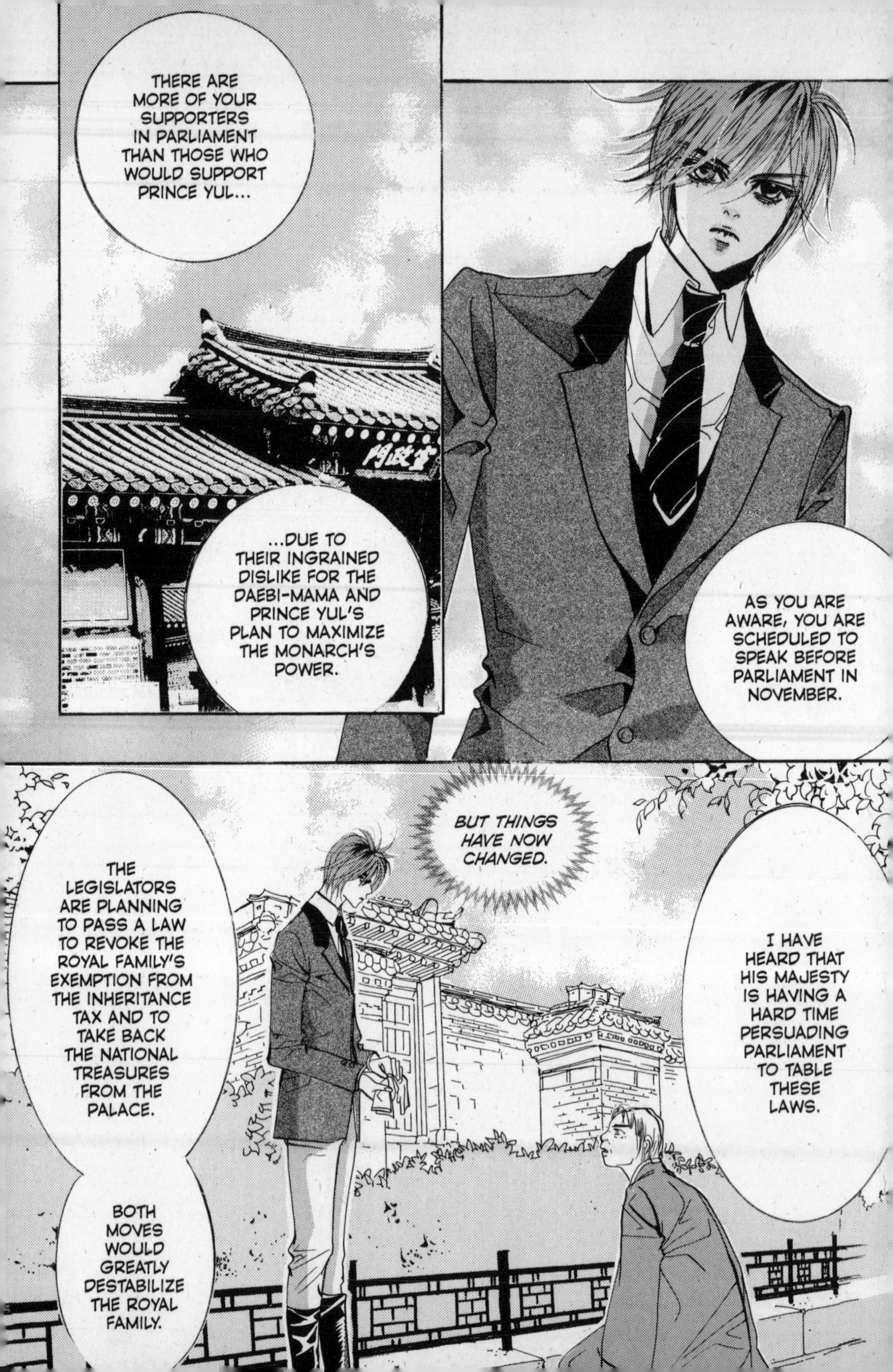
THERE ARE MORE OF YOUR SUPPORTERS IN PARLIAMENT THAN THOSE WHO WOULD SUPPORT PRINCE YUL...
...DUE TO THEIR INGRAINED DISLIKE FOR THE DAEBI-MAMA AND PRINCE YUL'S PLAN TO MAXIMIZE THE MONARCH'S POWER.
AS YOU ARE AWARE, YOU ARE SCHEDULED TO SPEAK BEFORE PARLIAMENT IN NOVEMBER.
THE LEGISLATORS ARE PLANNING TO PASS A LAW TO REVOKE THE ROYAL FAMILY'S EXEMPTION FROM THE INHERITANCE TAX AND TO TAKE BACK THE NATIONAL TREASURES FROM THE PALACE.
BOTH MOVES WOULD GREATLY DESTABILIZE THE ROYAL FAMILY.
BUT THINGS HAVE NOW CHANGED.
I HAVE HEARD THAT HIS MAJESTY IS HAVING A HARD TIME PERSUADING PARLIAMENT TO TABLE THESE LAWS.

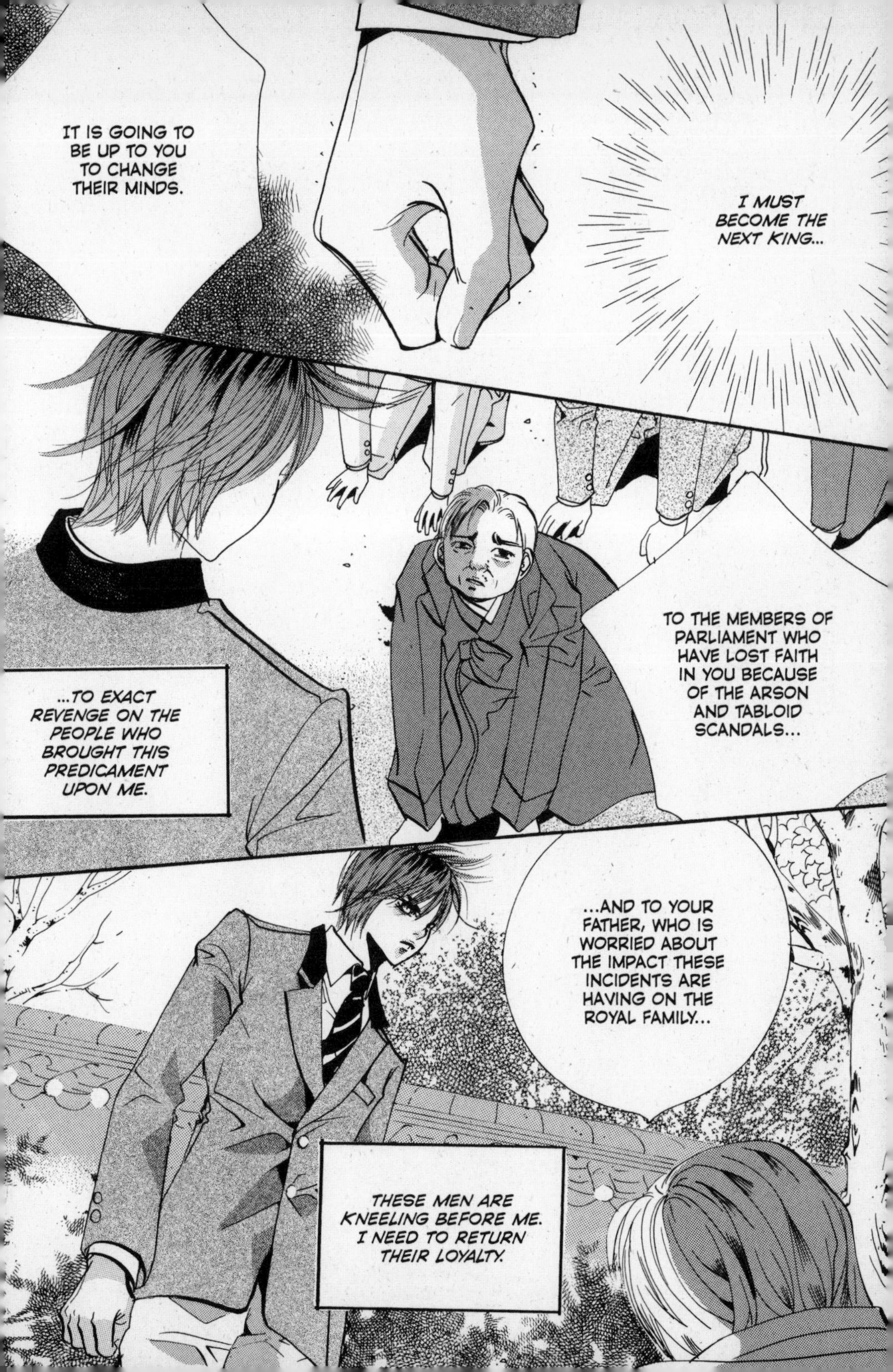
IT IS GOING TO BE UP TO YOU TO CHANGE THEIR MINDS.
I MUST BECOME THE NEXT KING...
...TO EXACT REVENGE ON THE PEOPLE WHO BROUGHT THIS PREDICAMENT UPON ME.
TO THE MEMBERS OF PARLIAMENT WHO HAVE LOST FAITH IN YOU BECAUSE OF THE ARSON AND TABLOID SCANDALS...
...AND TO YOUR FATHER, WHO IS WORRIED ABOUT THE IMPACT THESE INCIDENTS ARE HAVING ON THE ROYAL FAMILY...
THESE MEN ARE KNEELING BEFORE ME. I NEED TO RETURN THEIR LOYALTY.

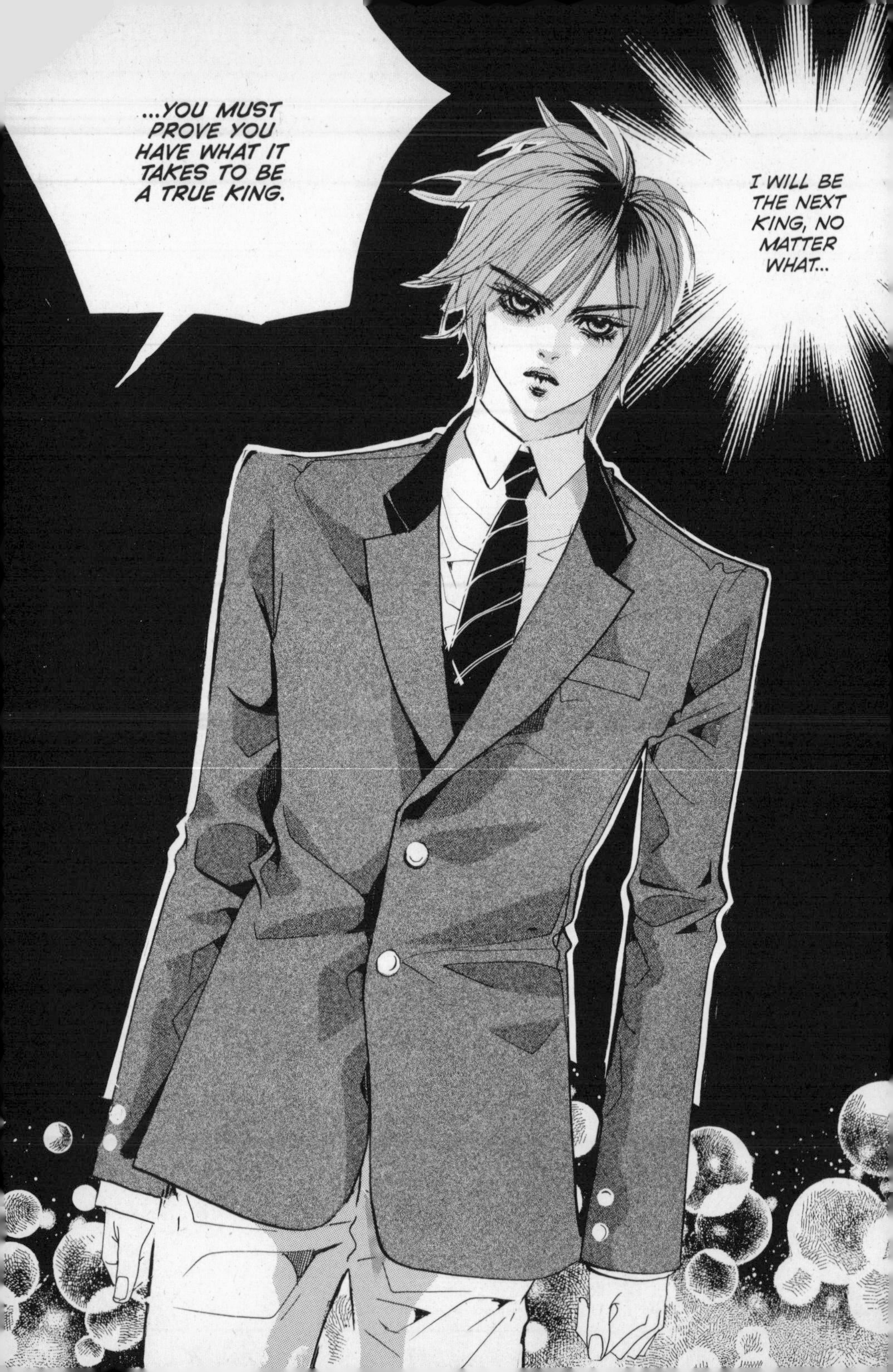
...YOU MUST PROVE YOU HAVE WHAT IT TAKES TO BE A TRUE KING.
I WILL BE THE NEXT KING, NO MATTER WHAT...

WHEN YOU GO TO GYEONGBOK-GOONG NOW, THERE AREN'T MANY BUILDINGS LEFT. THERE ARE MANY EMPTY PARCELS OF LAND.

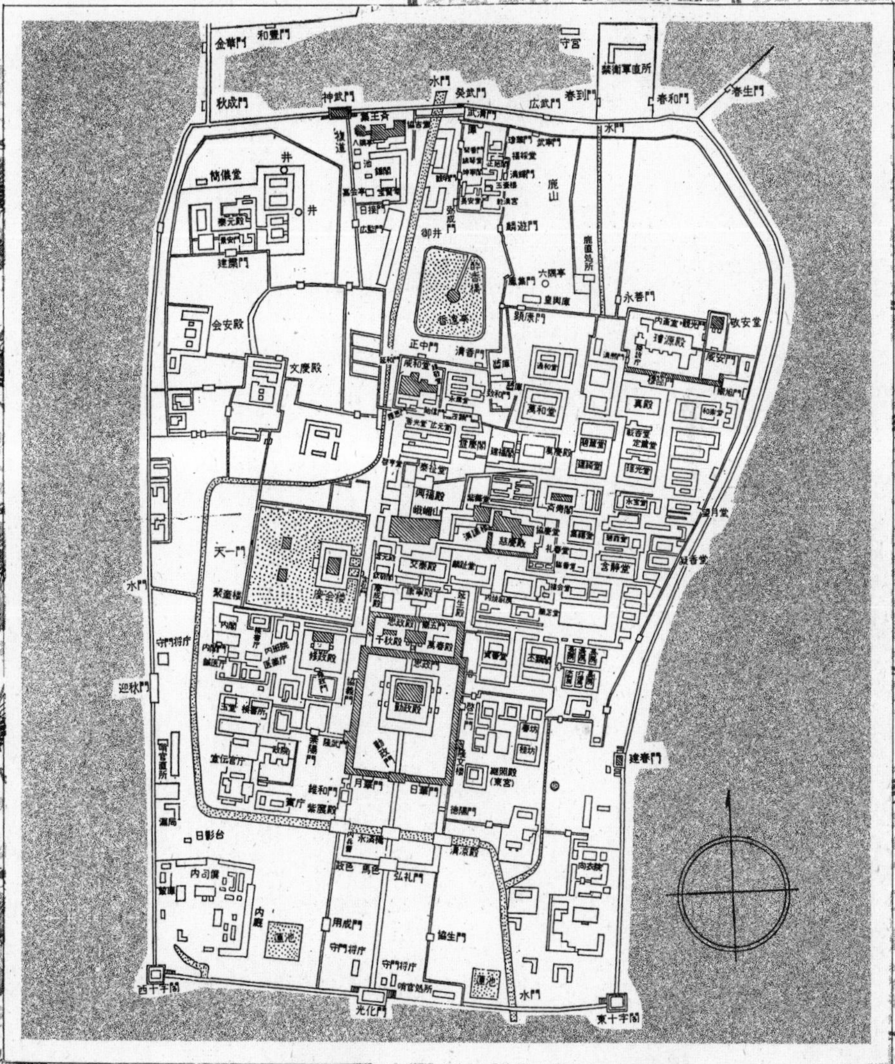

金華門
和豊門
守宮
禁衛軍直所
水門
神武門
癸武門
広武門
春到門
春和門
春生門
秋成門
武清門
鹿山
香遠亭
永善門
正中門
文慶殿
会安殿
天一門
水門
慶会楼
康寧殿
交泰殿
慈慶殿
勤政殿
建春門
迎秋門
日影台
永済橋
弘礼門
用成門
協生門
西十字閣
光化門
東十字閣

*AT ONE TIME, THERE WERE MORE THAN SEVEN THOUSAND BUILDINGS, AS YOU CAN SEE IN THE ABOVE PICTURE. THE CIRCUMFERENCE OF THE PALACE WAS 1,813 STEPS. IF SO MANY BUILDINGS HAD NOT BEEN DAMAGED BY FIRE OR RELOCATED AT THE END OF THE CHOSUN DYNASTY, GYEONGBOK-GOONG WOULD BE EVEN MORE AMAZING NOW, WOULDN'T IT? OF COURSE, I DRAW **GOONG** BASED ON THE PALACE BEFORE ANY CHANGE OR DAMAGE HAD OCCURRED. IN ACTUALITY, THERE WOULD NOT HAVE BEEN SO MANY TALL BUILDINGS AROUND THE PALACE BECAUSE PEOPLE WOULD HAVE BEEN ABLE TO PEEP INTO THE PRIVATE LIVES OF THE ROYAL FAMILY.*

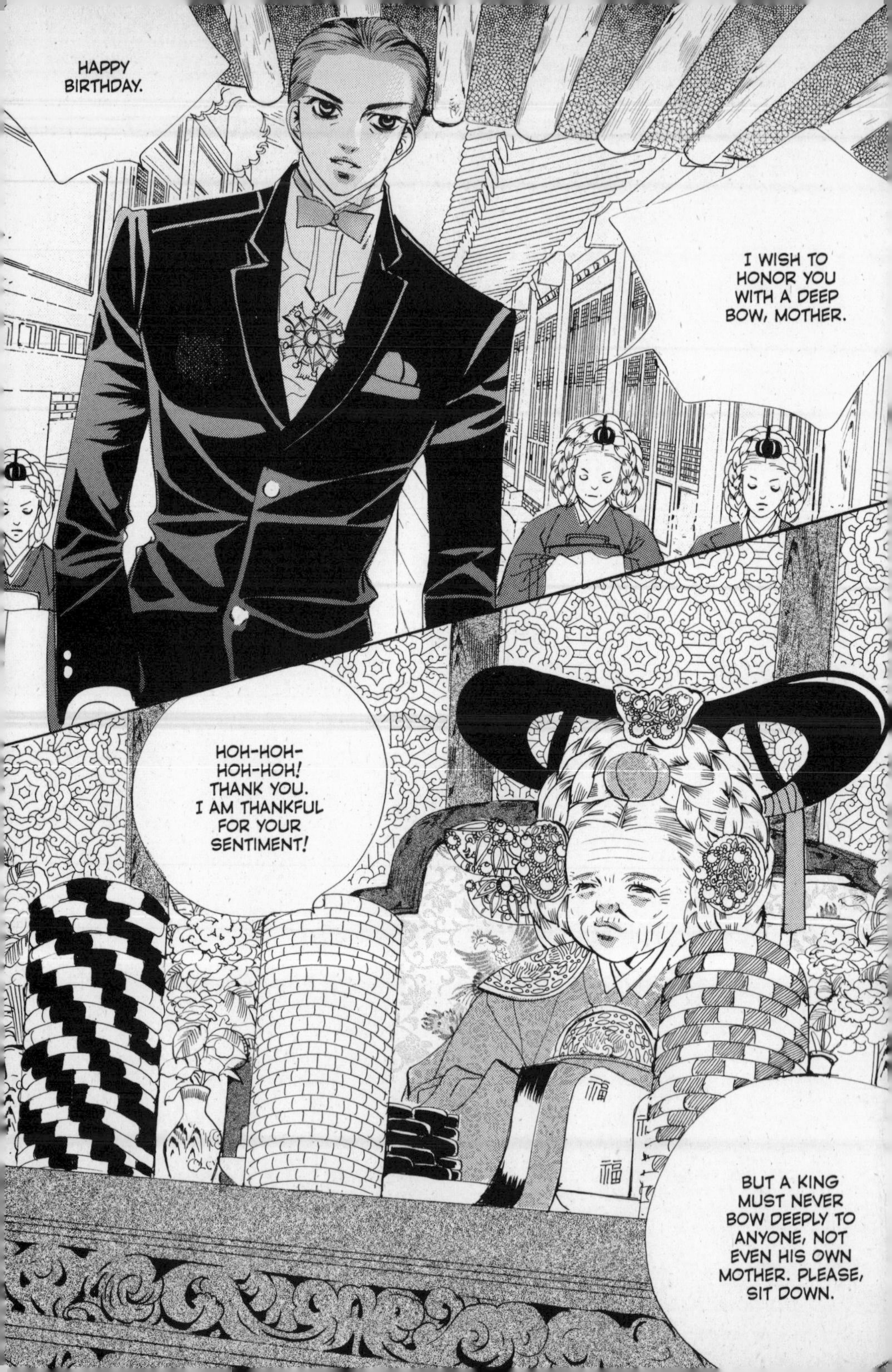
HAPPY BIRTHDAY.
I WISH TO HONOR YOU WITH A DEEP BOW, MOTHER.
HOH-HOH-HOH-HOH! THANK YOU. I AM THANKFUL FOR YOUR SENTIMENT!
BUT A KING MUST NEVER BOW DEEPLY TO ANYONE, NOT EVEN HIS OWN MOTHER. PLEASE, SIT DOWN.

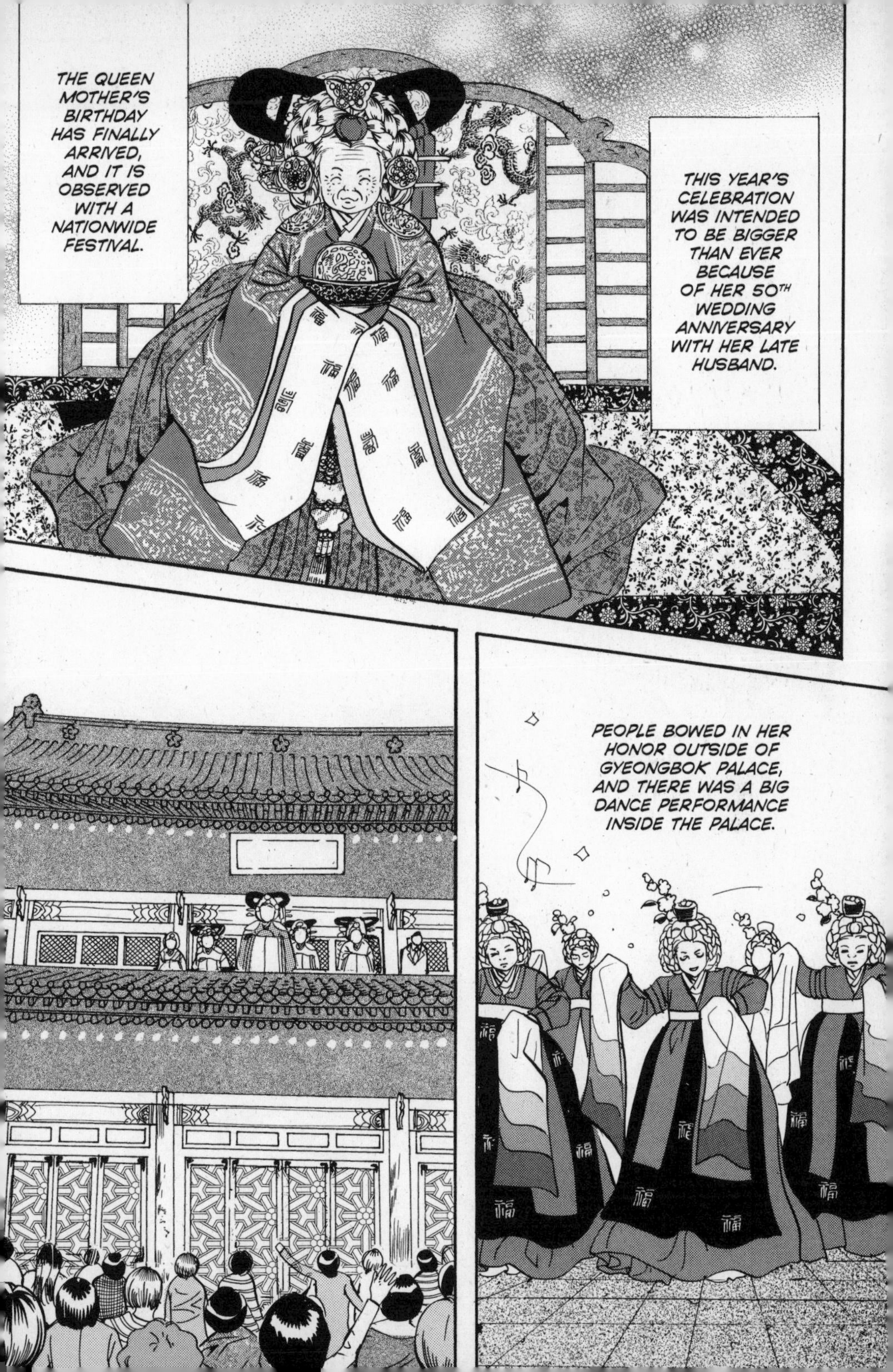
THE QUEEN MOTHER'S BIRTHDAY HAS FINALLY ARRIVED, AND IT IS OBSERVED WITH A NATIONWIDE FESTIVAL.
THIS YEAR'S CELEBRATION WAS INTENDED TO BE BIGGER THAN EVER BECAUSE OF HER 50TH WEDDING ANNIVERSARY WITH HER LATE HUSBAND.
PEOPLE BOWED IN HER HONOR OUTSIDE OF GYEONGBOK PALACE, AND THERE WAS A BIG DANCE PERFORMANCE INSIDE THE PALACE.

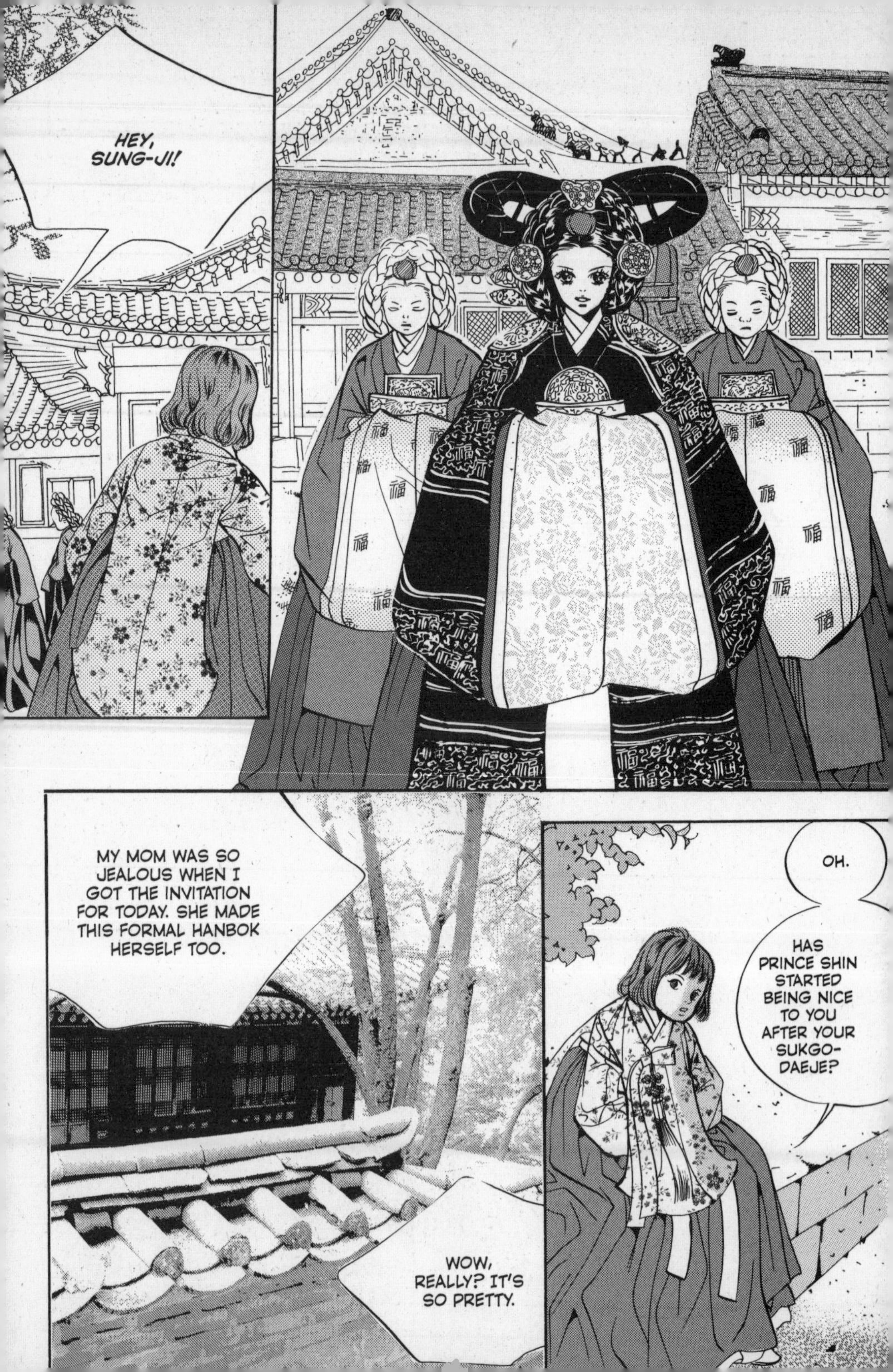

HEY, SUNG-JI!
MY MOM WAS SO JEALOUS WHEN I GOT THE INVITATION FOR TODAY. SHE MADE THIS FORMAL HANBOK HERSELF TOO.
WOW, REALLY? IT'S SO PRETTY.
OH.
HAS PRINCE SHIN STARTED BEING NICE TO YOU AFTER YOUR SUKGO-DAEJE?

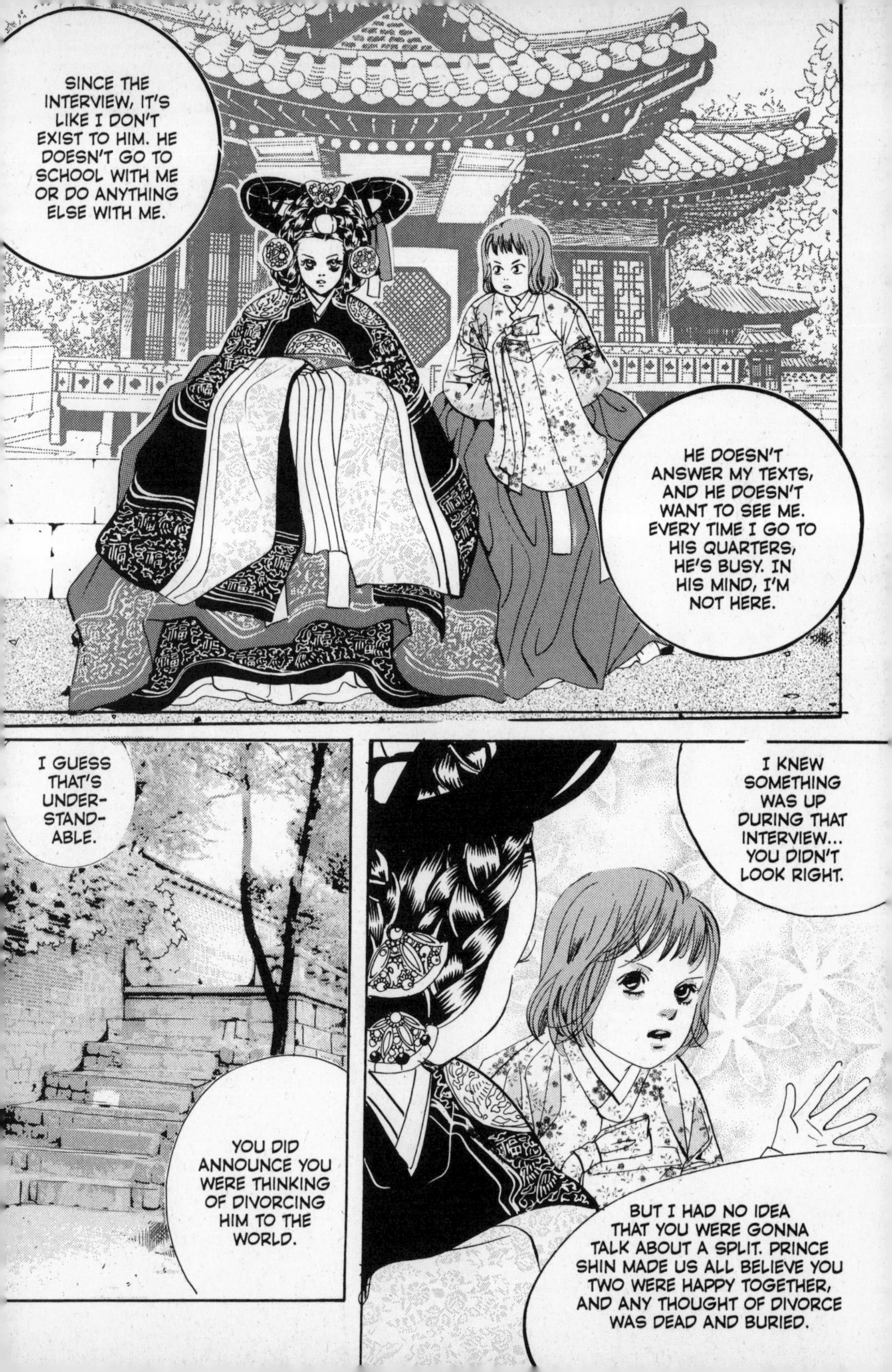
SINCE THE INTERVIEW, IT'S LIKE I DON'T EXIST TO HIM. HE DOESN'T GO TO SCHOOL WITH ME OR DO ANYTHING ELSE WITH ME.
HE DOESN'T ANSWER MY TEXTS, AND HE DOESN'T WANT TO SEE ME. EVERY TIME I GO TO HIS QUARTERS, HE'S BUSY. IN HIS MIND, I'M NOT HERE.
I GUESS THAT'S UNDER-STAND-ABLE.
YOU DID ANNOUNCE YOU WERE THINKING OF DIVORCING HIM TO THE WORLD.
I KNEW SOMETHING WAS UP DURING THAT INTERVIEW... YOU DIDN'T LOOK RIGHT.
BUT I HAD NO IDEA THAT YOU WERE GONNA TALK ABOUT A SPLIT. PRINCE SHIN MADE US ALL BELIEVE YOU TWO WERE HAPPY TOGETHER, AND ANY THOUGHT OF DIVORCE WAS DEAD AND BURIED.

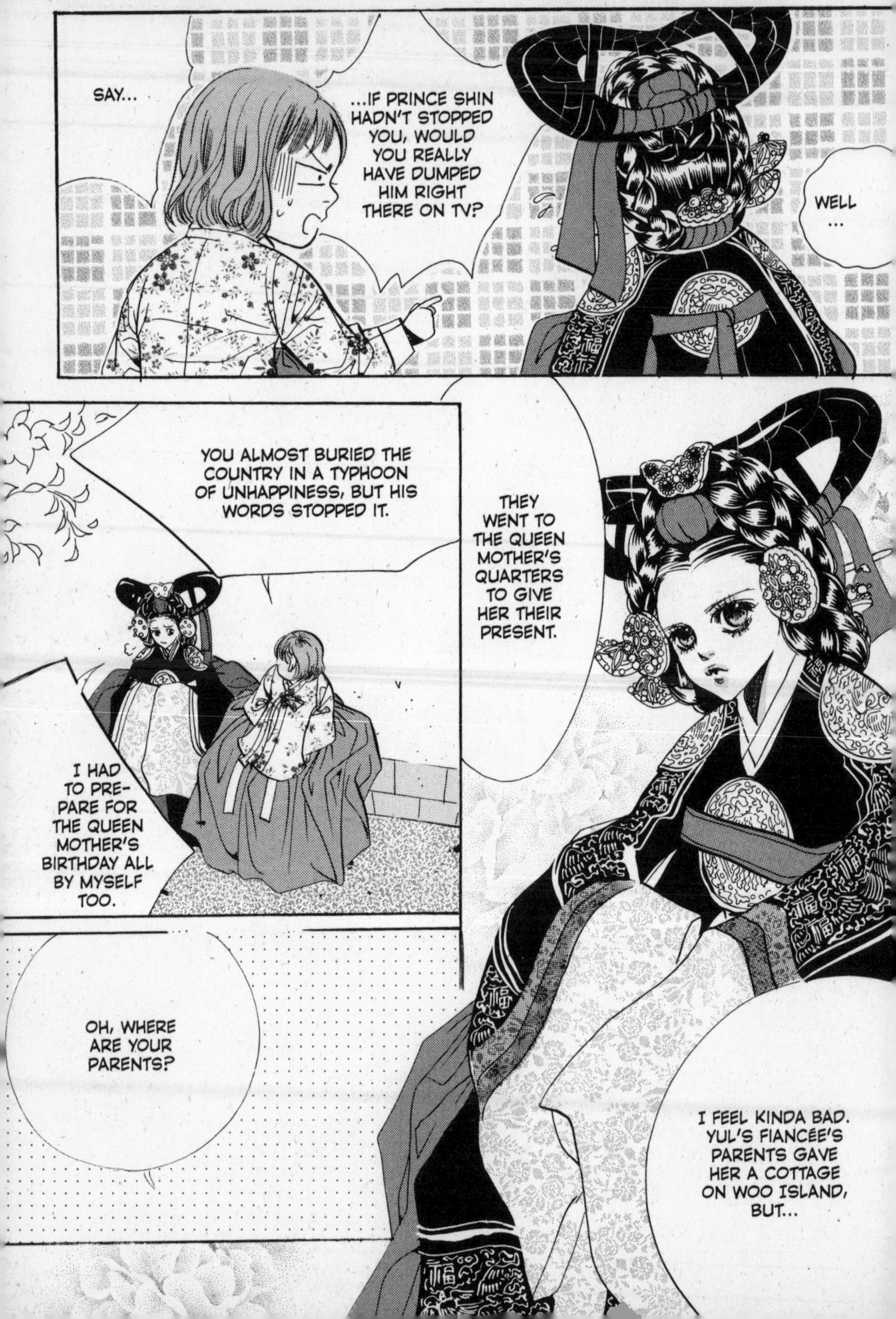
SAY...
...IF PRINCE SHIN HADN'T STOPPED YOU, WOULD YOU REALLY HAVE DUMPED HIM RIGHT THERE ON TV?
WELL ...
YOU ALMOST BURIED THE COUNTRY IN A TYPHOON OF UNHAPPINESS, BUT HIS WORDS STOPPED IT.
I HAD TO PRE-PARE FOR THE QUEEN MOTHER'S BIRTHDAY ALL BY MYSELF TOO.
OH, WHERE ARE YOUR PARENTS?
THEY WENT TO THE QUEEN MOTHER'S QUARTERS TO GIVE HER THEIR PRESENT.
I FEEL KINDA BAD. YUL'S FIANCÉE'S PARENTS GAVE HER A COTTAGE ON WOO ISLAND, BUT...

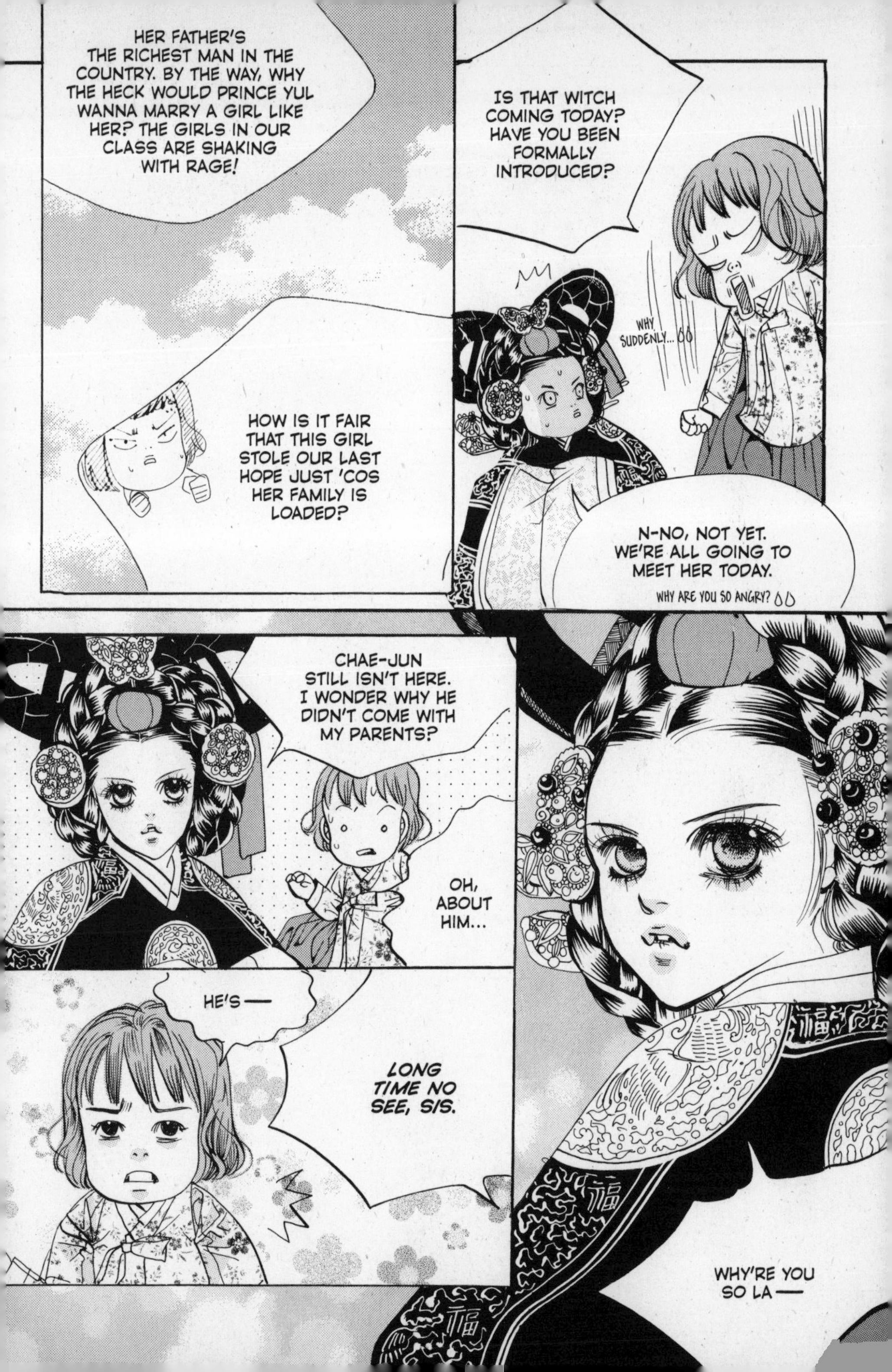
HER FATHER'S THE RICHEST MAN IN THE COUNTRY. BY THE WAY, WHY THE HECK WOULD PRINCE YUL WANNA MARRY A GIRL LIKE HER? THE GIRLS IN OUR CLASS ARE SHAKING WITH RAGE!
HOW IS IT FAIR THAT THIS GIRL STOLE OUR LAST HOPE JUST 'COS HER FAMILY IS LOADED?
IS THAT WITCH COMING TODAY? HAVE YOU BEEN FORMALLY INTRODUCED?
WHY SUDDENLY...
N-NO, NOT YET. WE'RE ALL GOING TO MEET HER TODAY.
WHY ARE YOU SO ANGRY?
CHAE-JUN STILL ISN'T HERE. I WONDER WHY HE DIDN'T COME WITH MY PARENTS?
OH, ABOUT HIM...
HE'S—
LONG TIME NO SEE, SIS.
WHY'RE YOU SO LA—

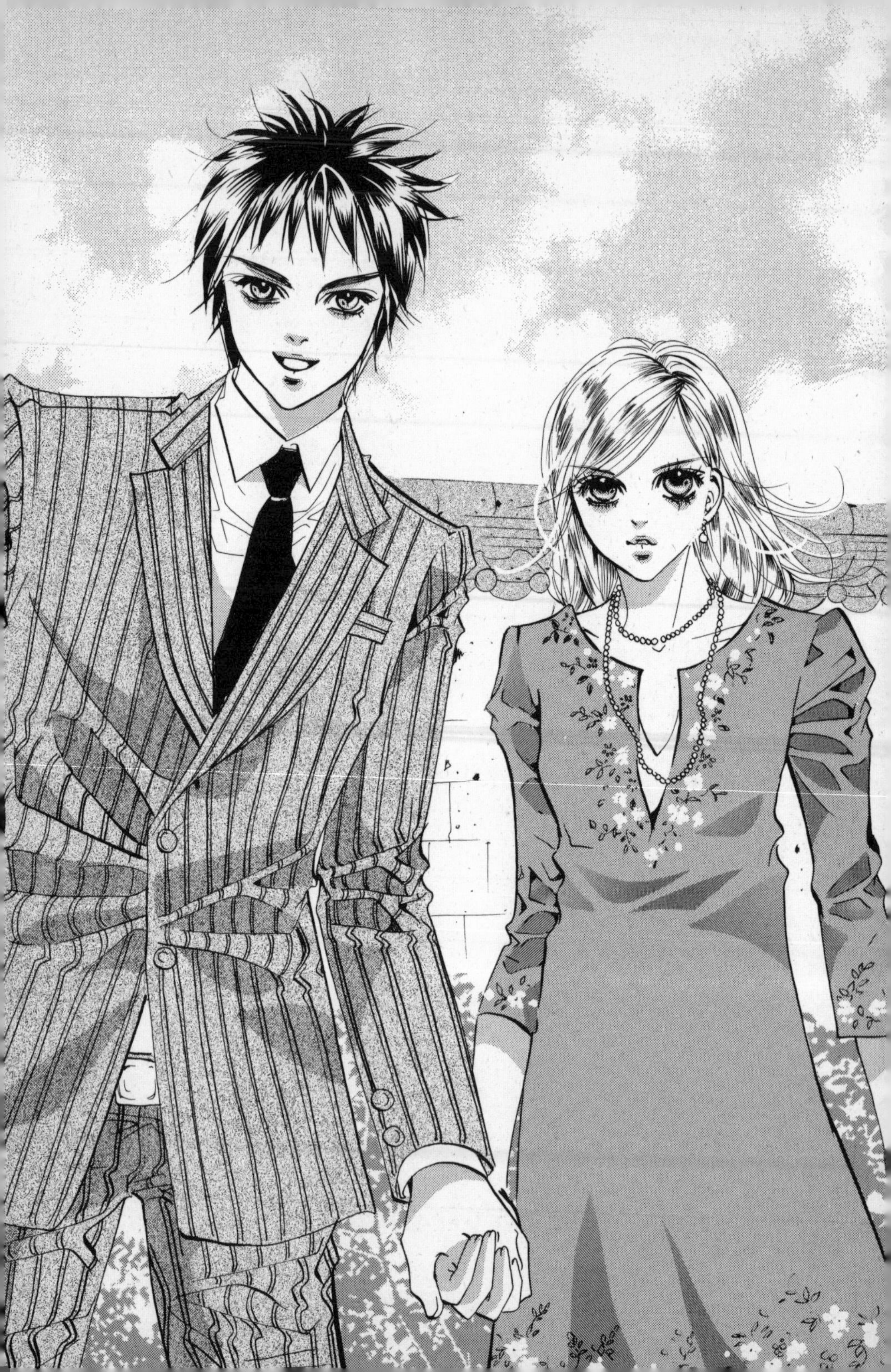

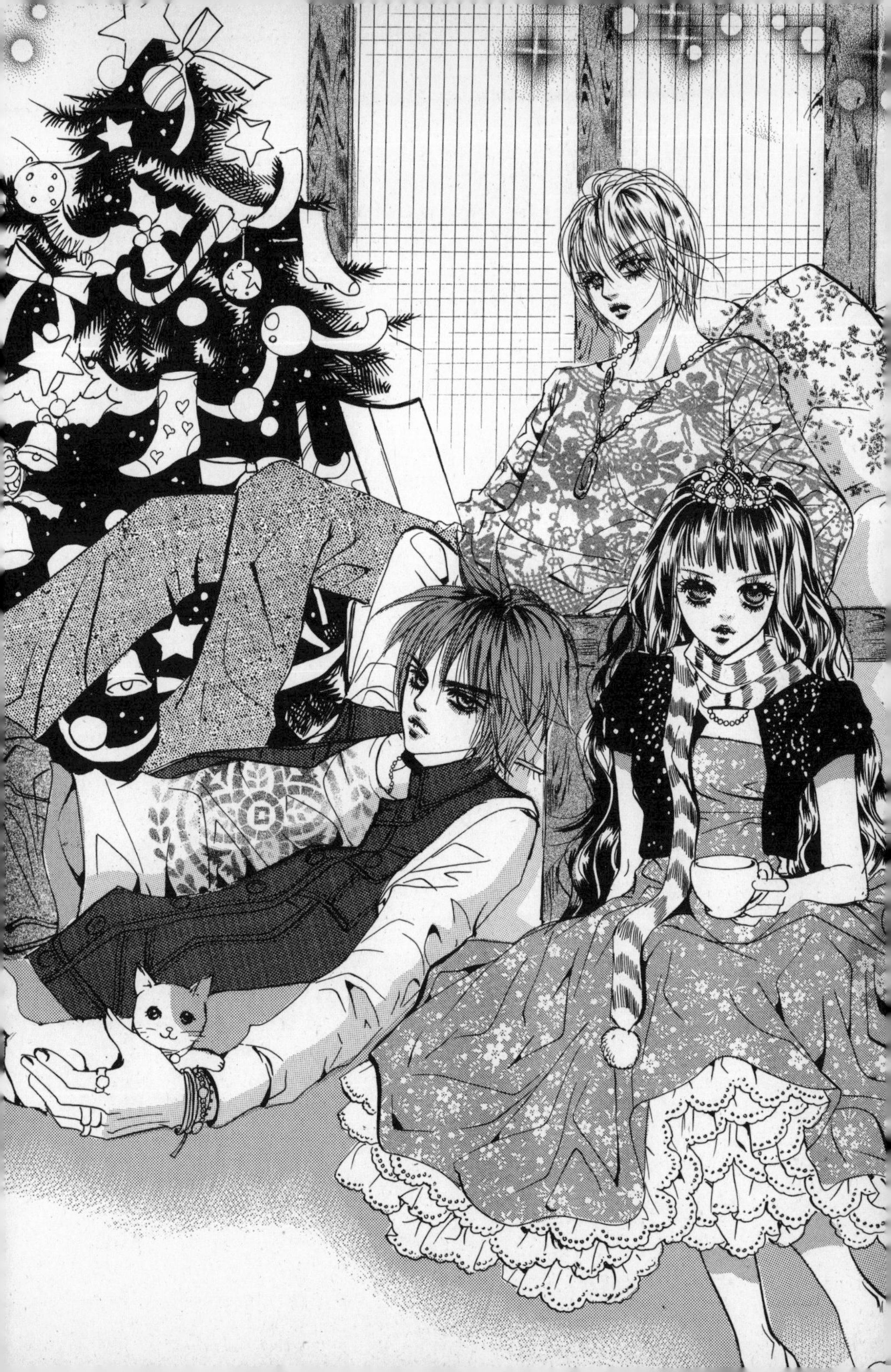

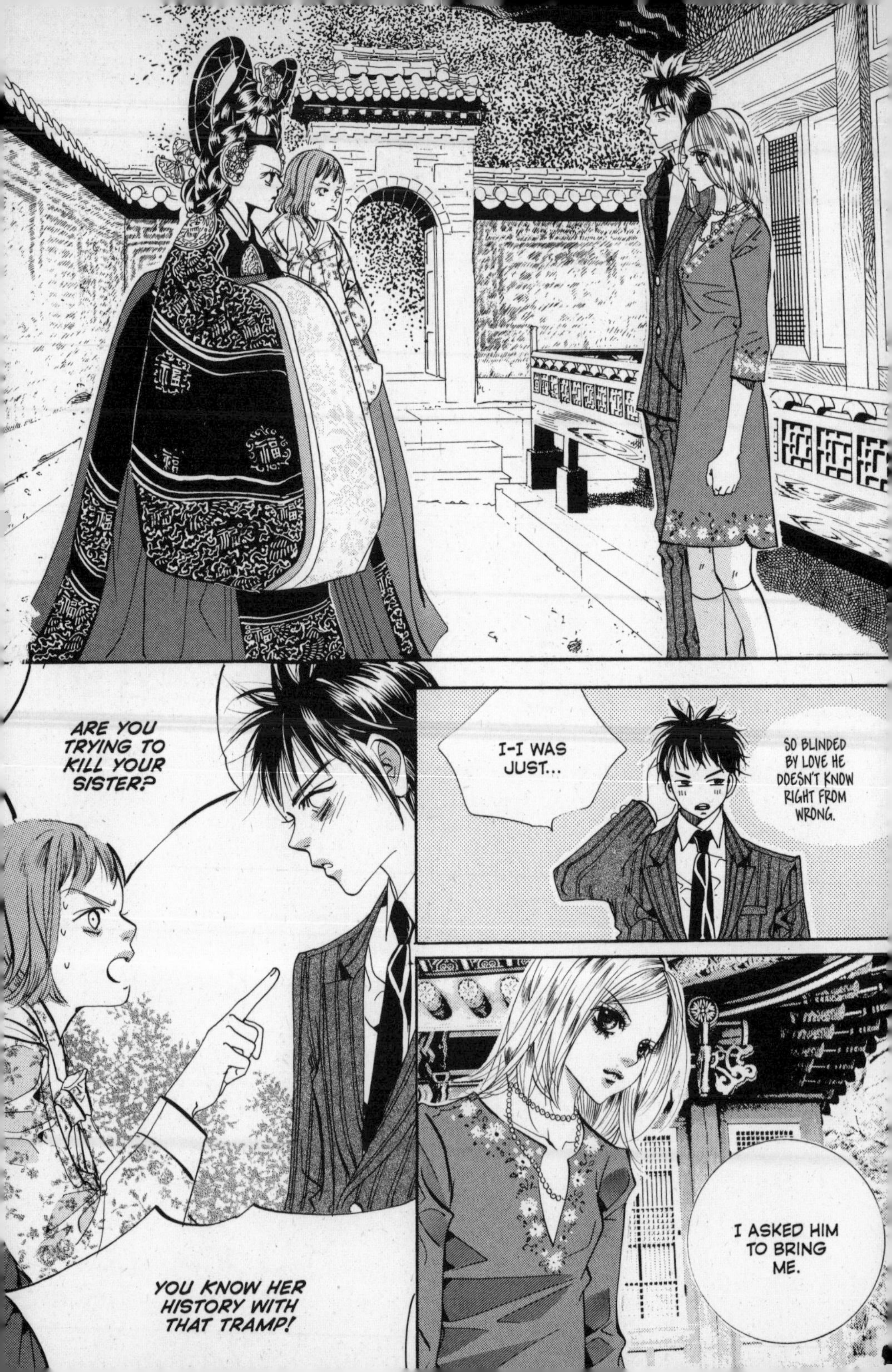
ARE YOU TRYING TO KILL YOUR SISTER?
YOU KNOW HER HISTORY WITH THAT TRAMP!
I-I WAS JUST...
SO BLINDED BY LOVE HE DOESN'T KNOW RIGHT FROM WRONG.
I ASKED HIM TO BRING ME.

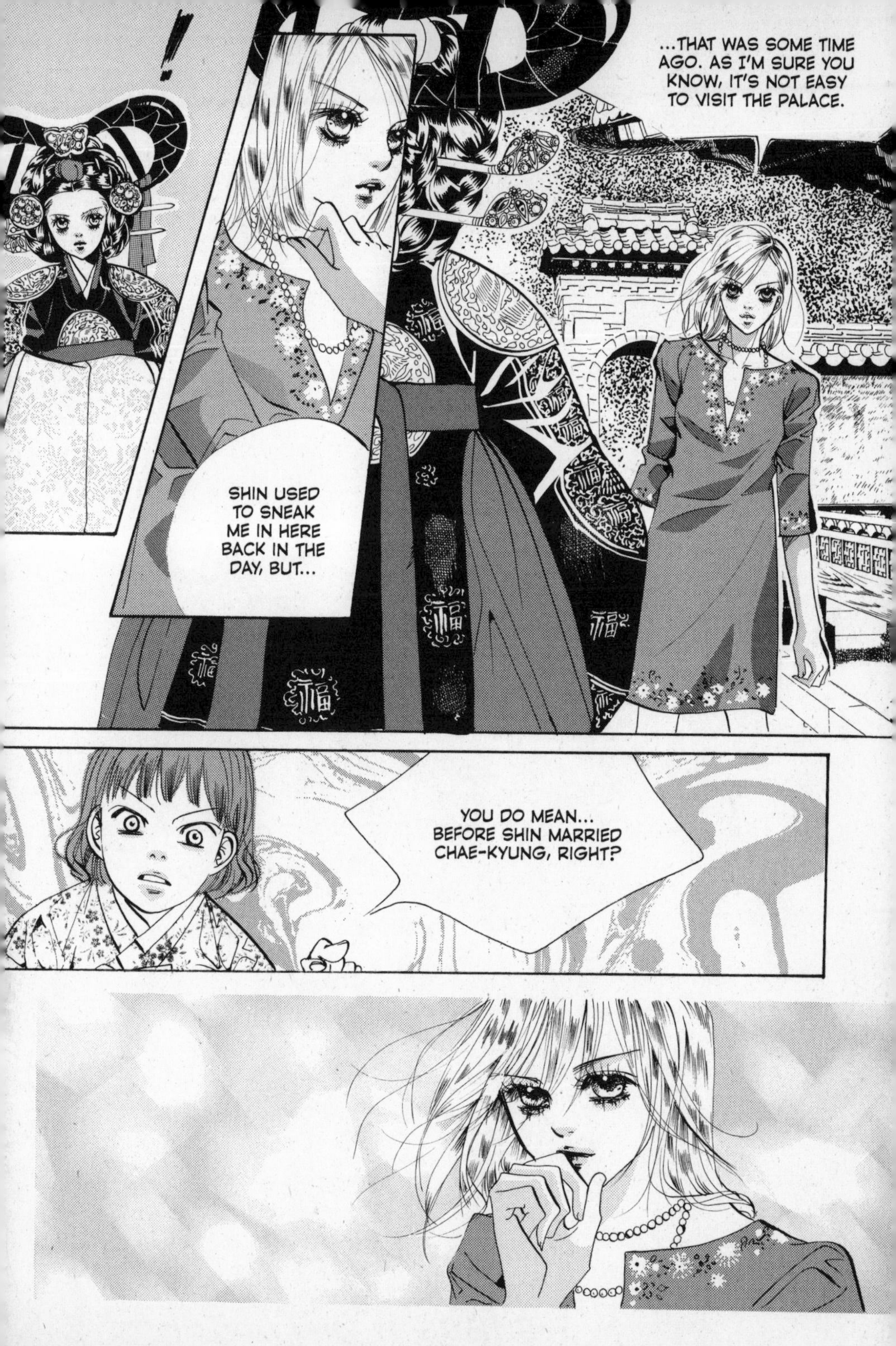
!
SHIN USED TO SNEAK ME IN HERE BACK IN THE DAY, BUT...
...THAT WAS SOME TIME AGO. AS I'M SURE YOU KNOW, IT'S NOT EASY TO VISIT THE PALACE.
YOU DO MEAN... BEFORE SHIN MARRIED CHAE-KYUNG, RIGHT?

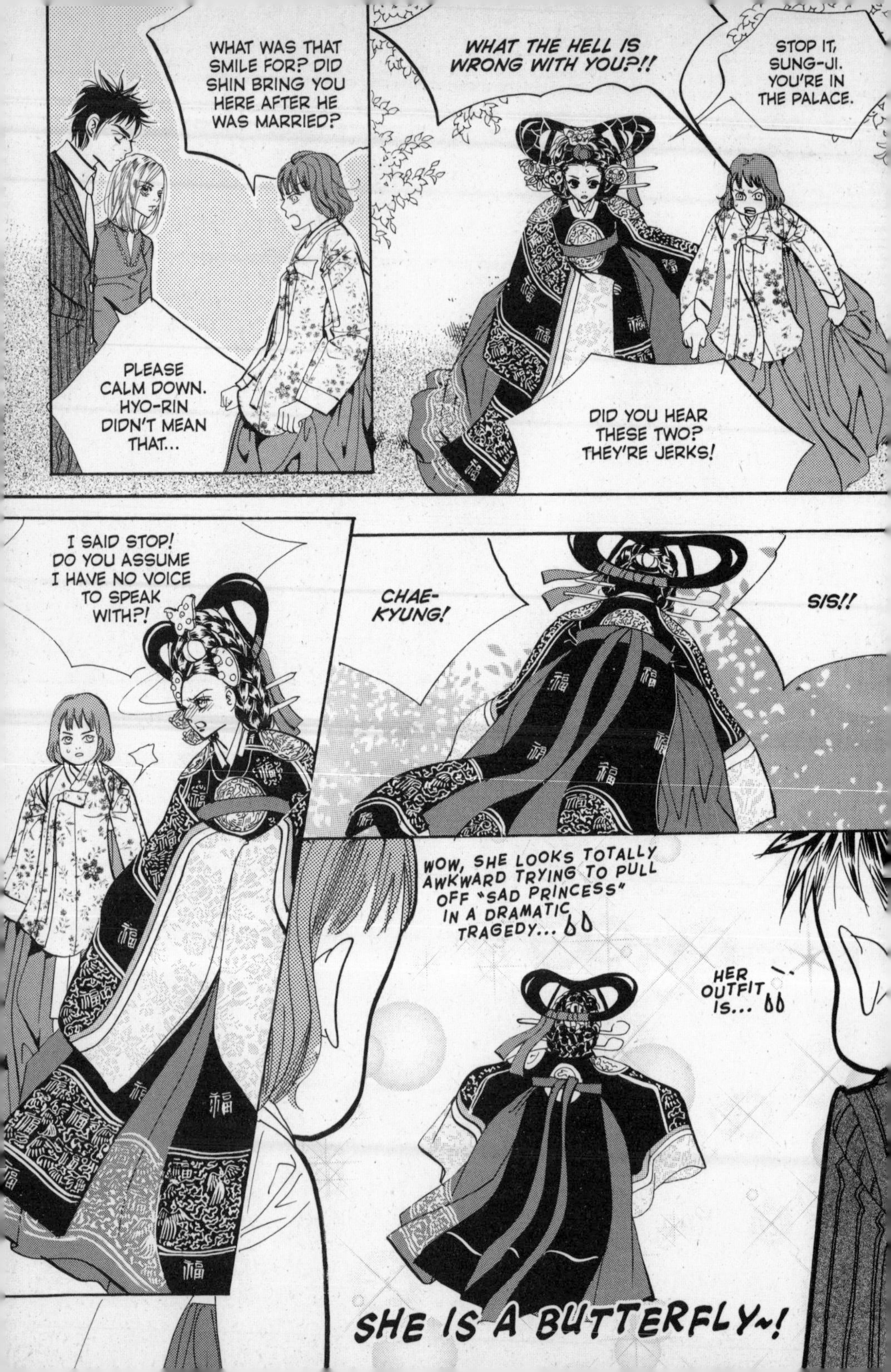
WHAT WAS THAT SMILE FOR? DID SHIN BRING YOU HERE AFTER HE WAS MARRIED?
PLEASE CALM DOWN. HYO-RIN DIDN'T MEAN THAT...
WHAT THE HELL IS WRONG WITH YOU?!!
STOP IT, SUNG-JI. YOU'RE IN THE PALACE.
DID YOU HEAR THESE TWO? THEY'RE JERKS!
I SAID STOP! DO YOU ASSUME I HAVE NO VOICE TO SPEAK WITH?!
CHAE-KYUNG!
SIS!!
WOW, SHE LOOKS TOTALLY AWKWARD TRYING TO PULL OFF "SAD PRINCESS" IN A DRAMATIC TRAGEDY...
HER OUTFIT IS...
SHE IS A BUTTERFLY~!

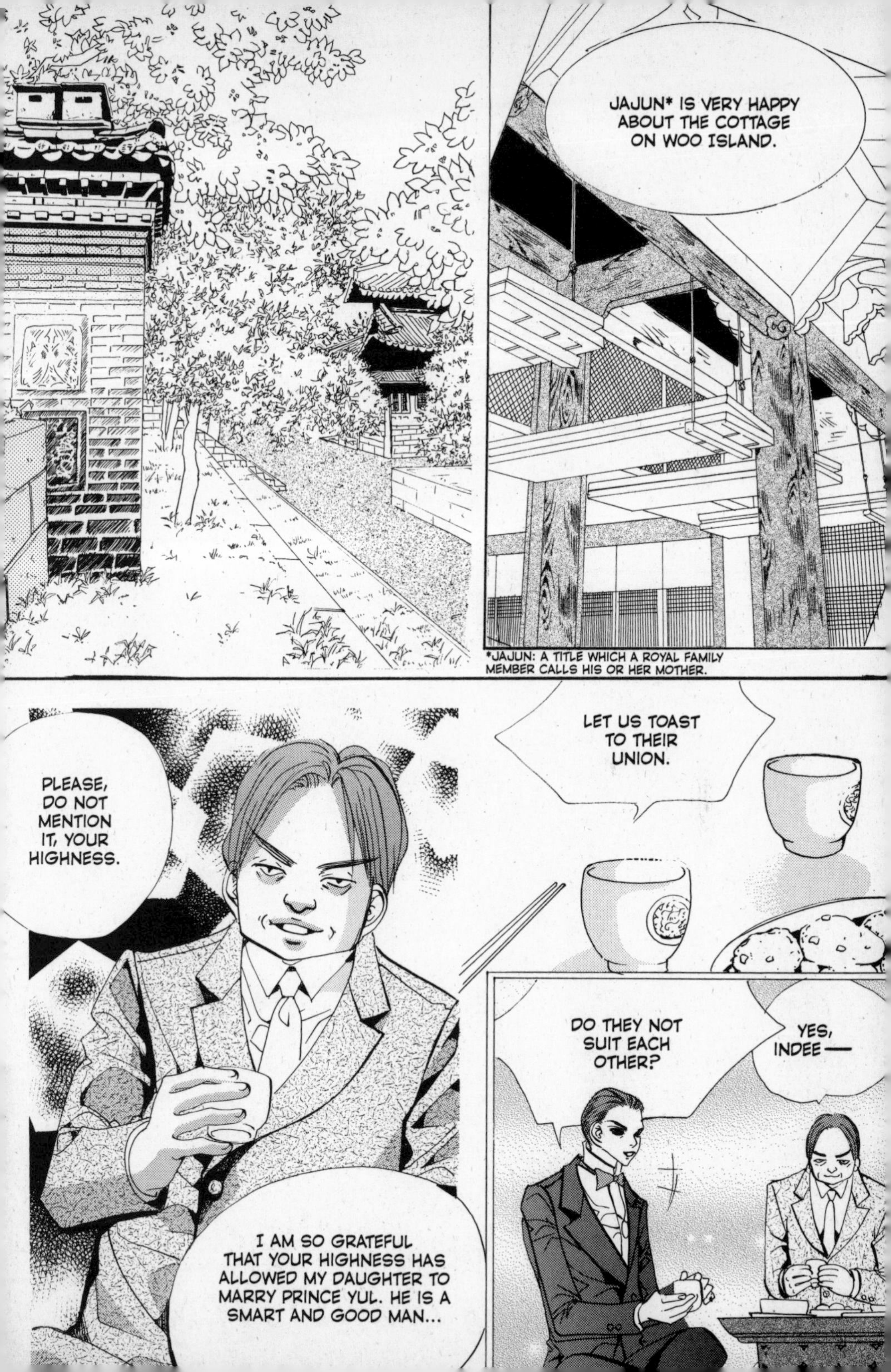
JAJUN* IS VERY HAPPY ABOUT THE COTTAGE ON WOO ISLAND.
PLEASE, DO NOT MENTION IT, YOUR HIGHNESS.
I AM SO GRATEFUL THAT YOUR HIGHNESS HAS ALLOWED MY DAUGHTER TO MARRY PRINCE YUL. HE IS A SMART AND GOOD MAN...
LET US TOAST TO THEIR UNION.
DO THEY NOT SUIT EACH OTHER?
YES, INDEE—

*JAJUN: A TITLE WHICH A ROYAL FAMILY MEMBER CALLS HIS OR HER MOTHER.

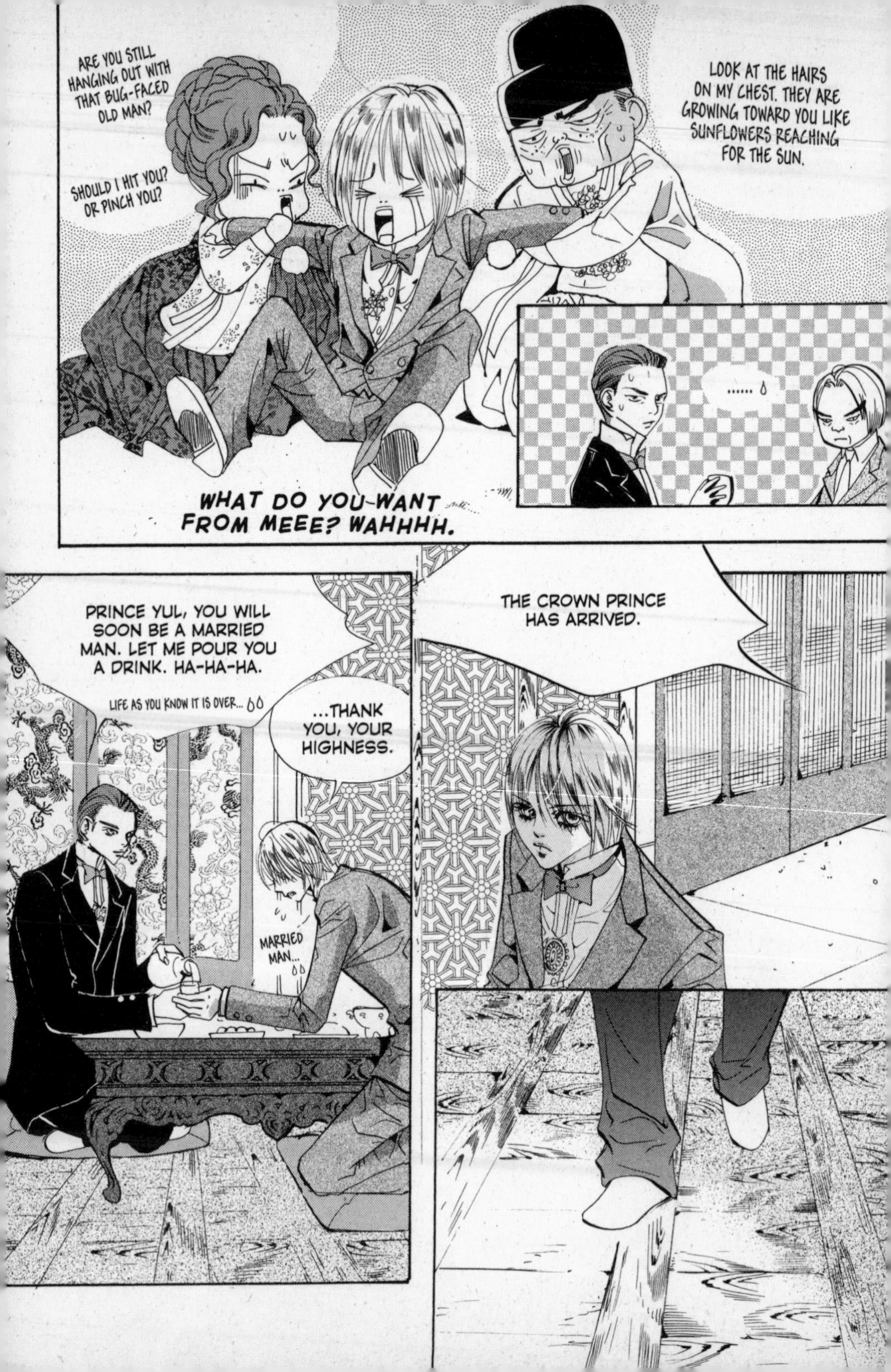
ARE YOU STILL HANGING OUT WITH THAT BUG-FACED OLD MAN?
SHOULD I HIT YOU? OR PINCH YOU?
LOOK AT THE HAIRS ON MY CHEST. THEY ARE GROWING TOWARD YOU LIKE SUNFLOWERS REACHING FOR THE SUN.
WHAT DO YOU-WANT FROM MEEE? WAHHHH.
......
PRINCE YUL, YOU WILL SOON BE A MARRIED MAN. LET ME POUR YOU A DRINK. HA-HA-HA.
LIFE AS YOU KNOW IT IS OVER...
...THANK YOU, YOUR HIGHNESS.
MARRIED MAN...
THE CROWN PRINCE HAS ARRIVED.

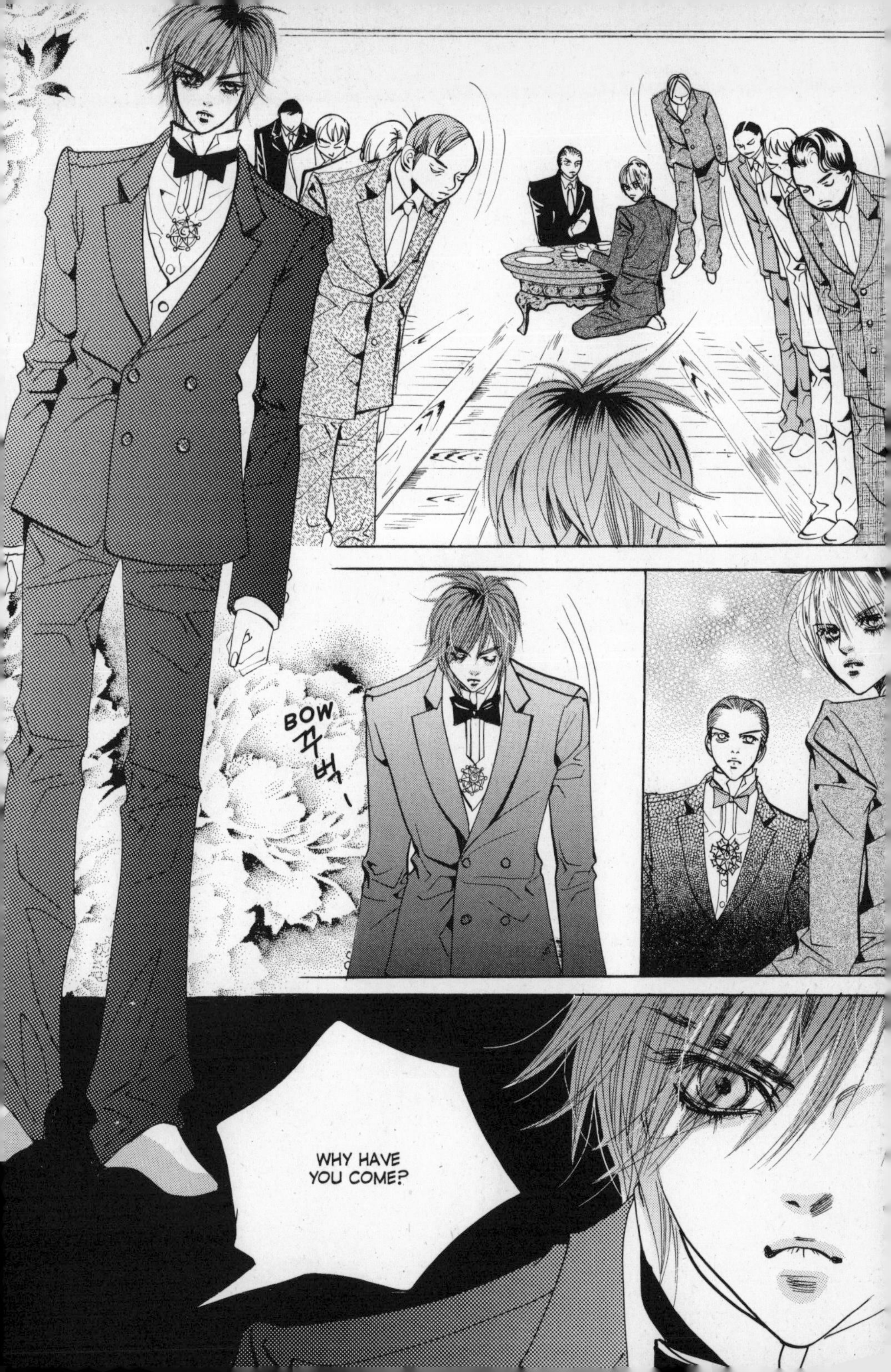
BOW
꾸벅
WHY HAVE YOU COME?

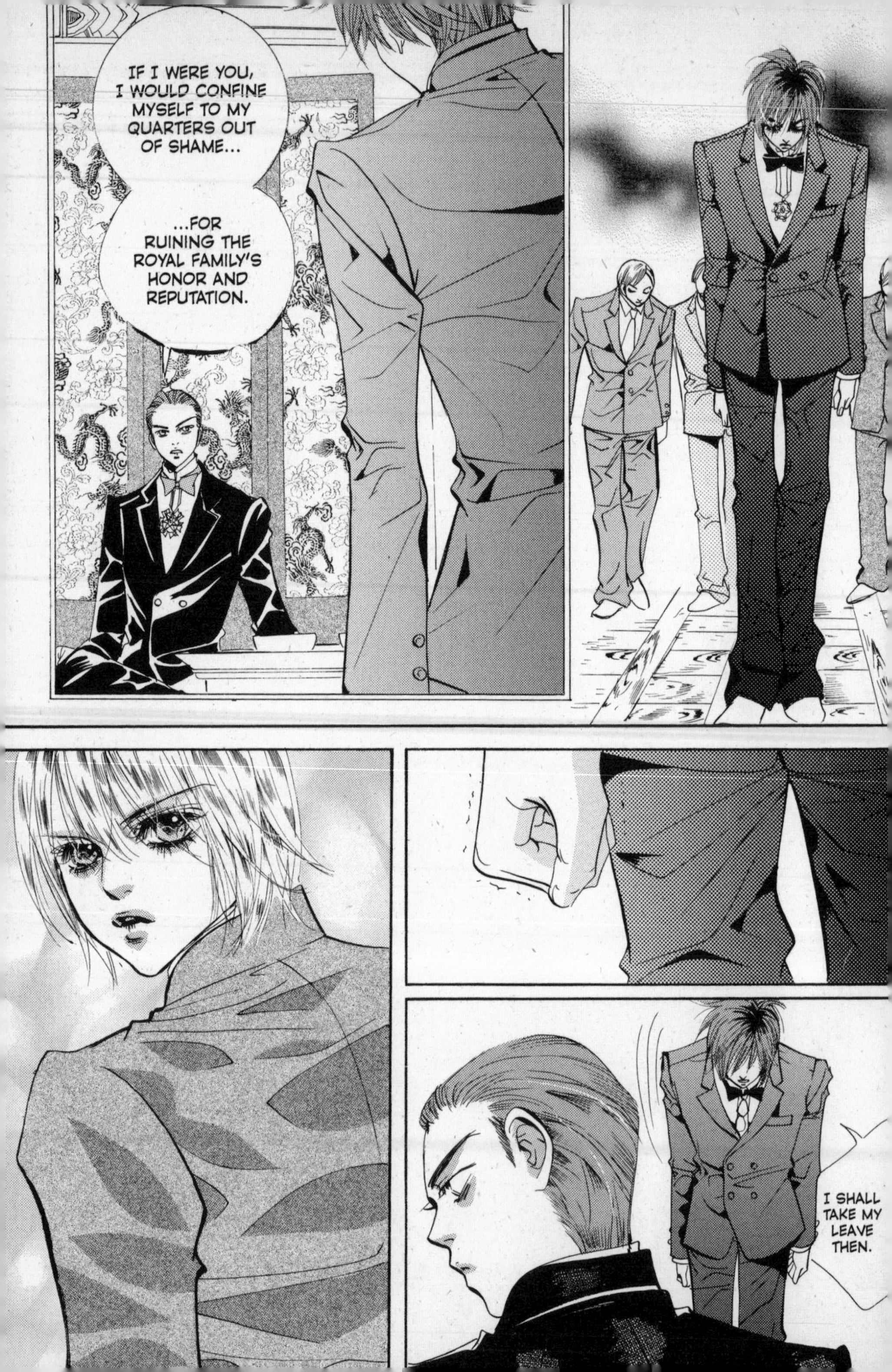
IF I WERE YOU, I WOULD CONFINE MYSELF TO MY QUARTERS OUT OF SHAME...
...FOR RUINING THE ROYAL FAMILY'S HONOR AND REPUTATION.
I SHALL TAKE MY LEAVE THEN.

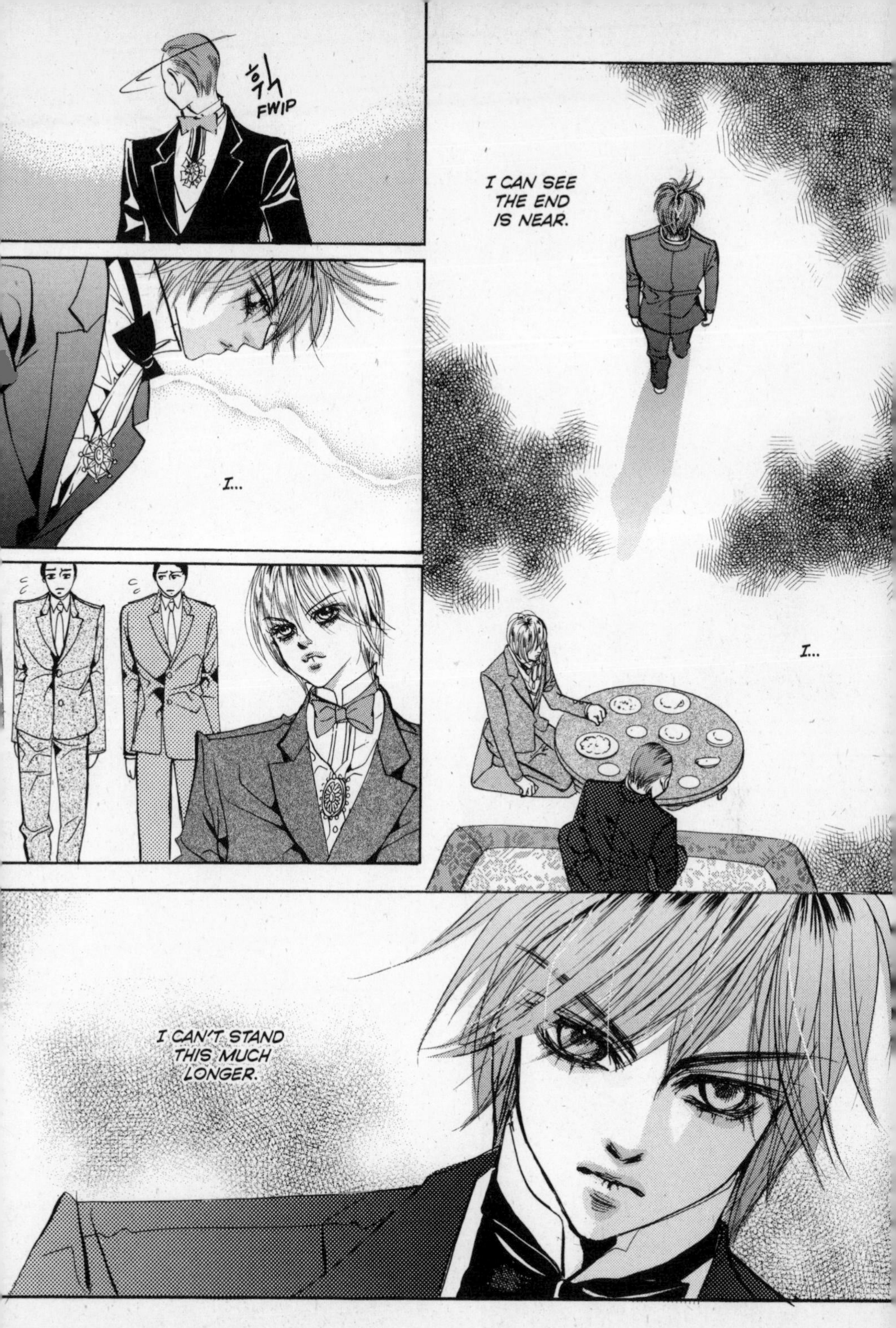
휙
FWIP
I...
I CAN SEE THE END IS NEAR.
I...
I CAN'T STAND THIS MUCH LONGER.

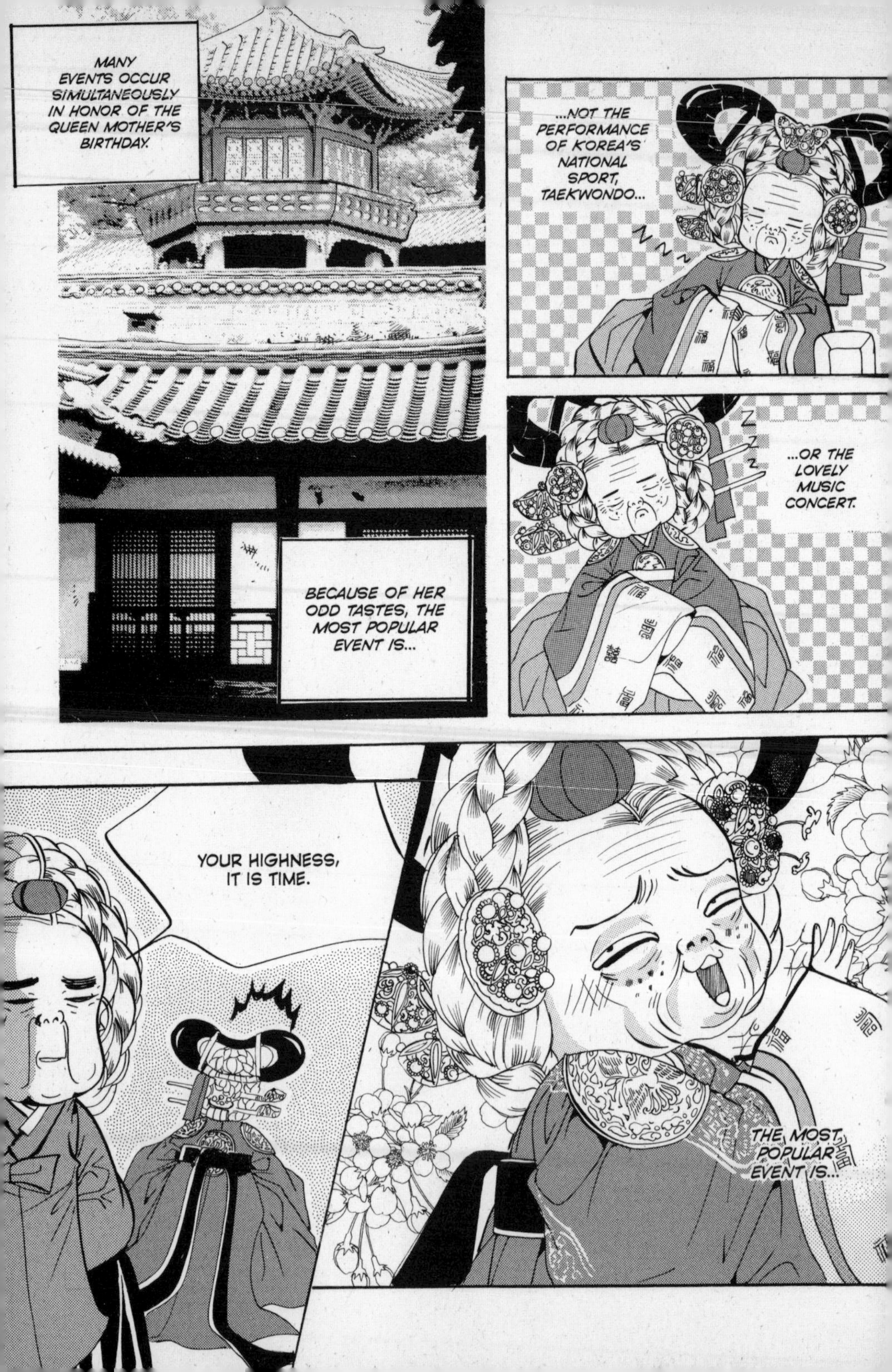
MANY EVENTS OCCUR SIMULTANEOUSLY IN HONOR OF THE QUEEN MOTHER'S BIRTHDAY.
BECAUSE OF HER ODD TASTES, THE MOST POPULAR EVENT IS...
...NOT THE PERFORMANCE OF KOREA'S NATIONAL SPORT, TAEKWONDO...
...OR THE LOVELY MUSIC CONCERT.
YOUR HIGHNESS, IT IS TIME.
THE MOST POPULAR EVENT IS...

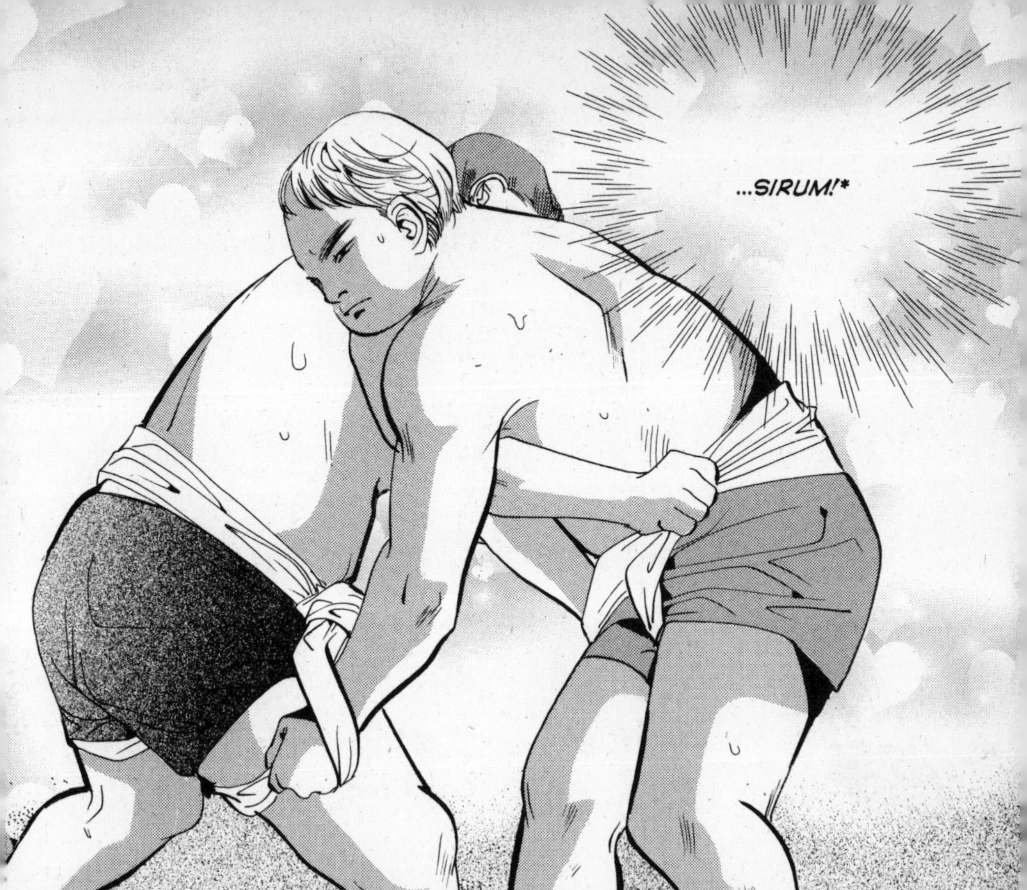
...SIRUM!*

*SIRUM = TRADITIONAL KOREAN WRESTLING

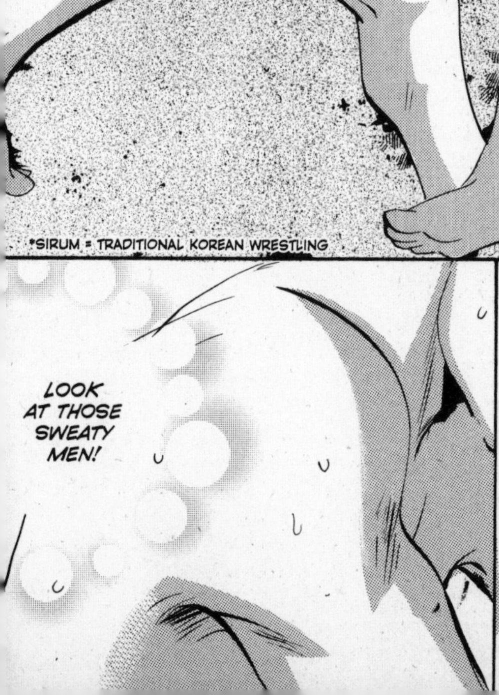
LOOK AT THOSE SWEATY MEN!

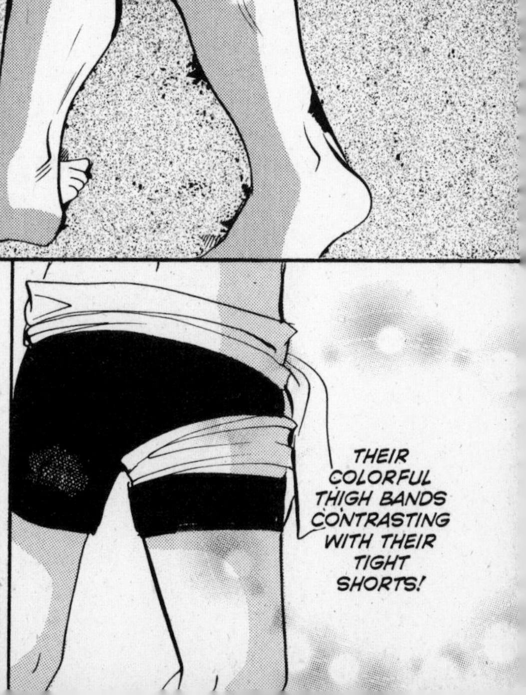
THEIR COLORFUL THIGH BANDS CONTRASTING WITH THEIR TIGHT SHORTS!

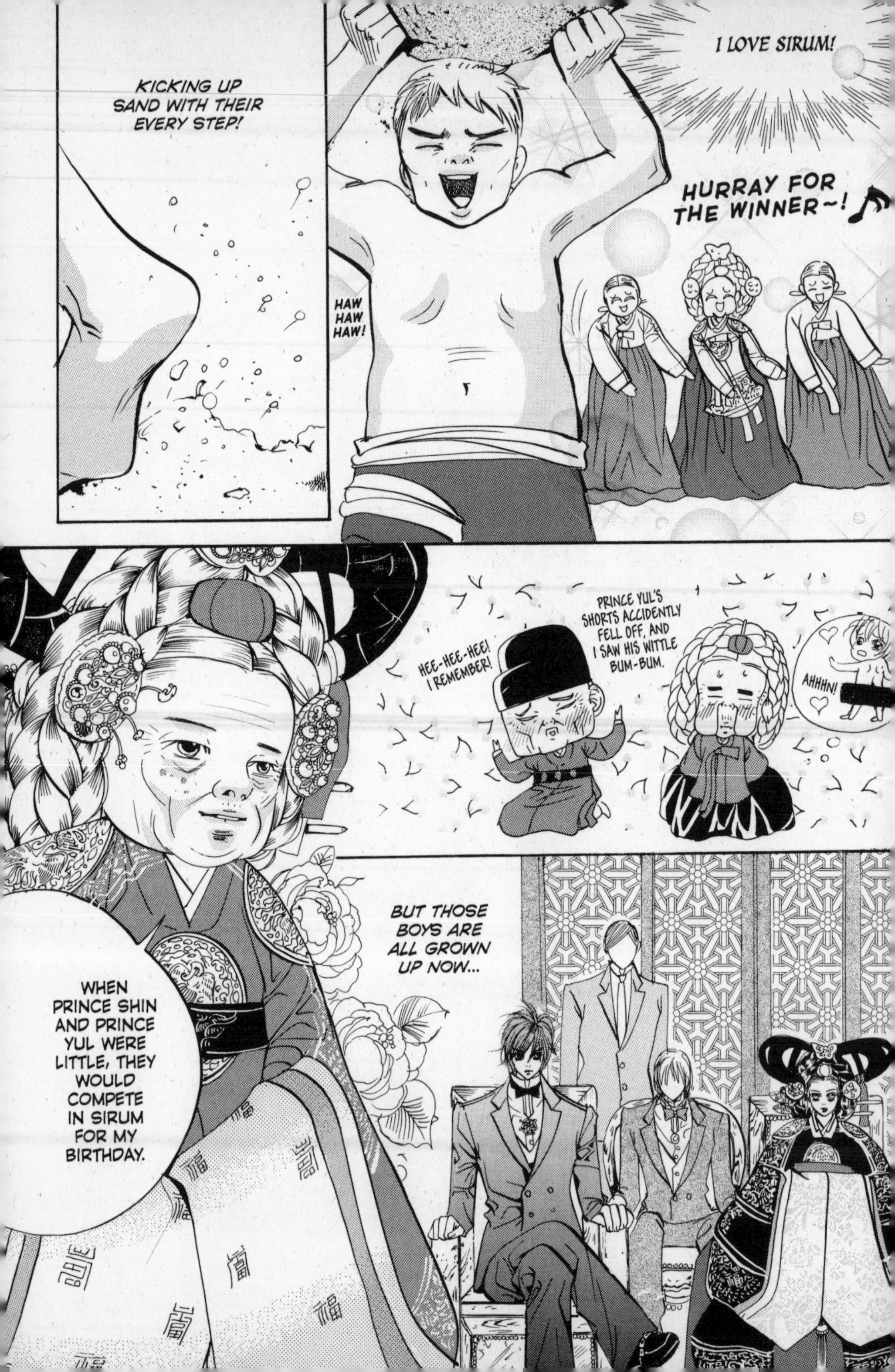
KICKING UP SAND WITH THEIR EVERY STEP!
HAW HAW HAW!
I LOVE SIRUM!
HURRAY FOR THE WINNER~!
WHEN PRINCE SHIN AND PRINCE YUL WERE LITTLE, THEY WOULD COMPETE IN SIRUM FOR MY BIRTHDAY.
HEE-HEE-HEE! I REMEMBER!
PRINCE YUL'S SHORTS ACCIDENTLY FELL OFF, AND I SAW HIS WITTLE BUM-BUM.
AHHHN!
BUT THOSE BOYS ARE ALL GROWN UP NOW...

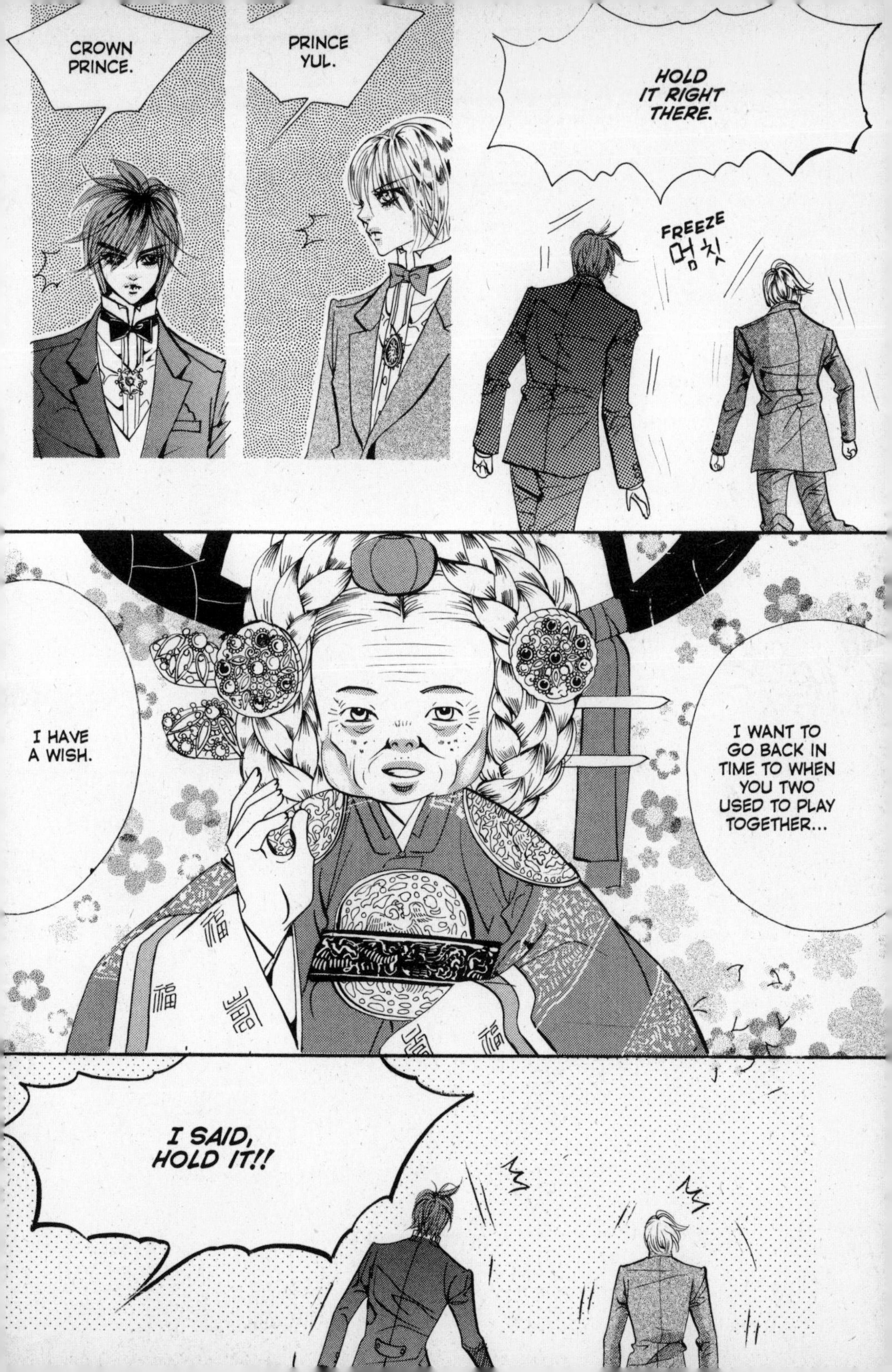
CROWN PRINCE.
PRINCE YUL.
HOLD IT RIGHT THERE.
FREEZE
멈칫
I HAVE A WISH.
I WANT TO GO BACK IN TIME TO WHEN YOU TWO USED TO PLAY TOGETHER...
I SAID, HOLD IT!!

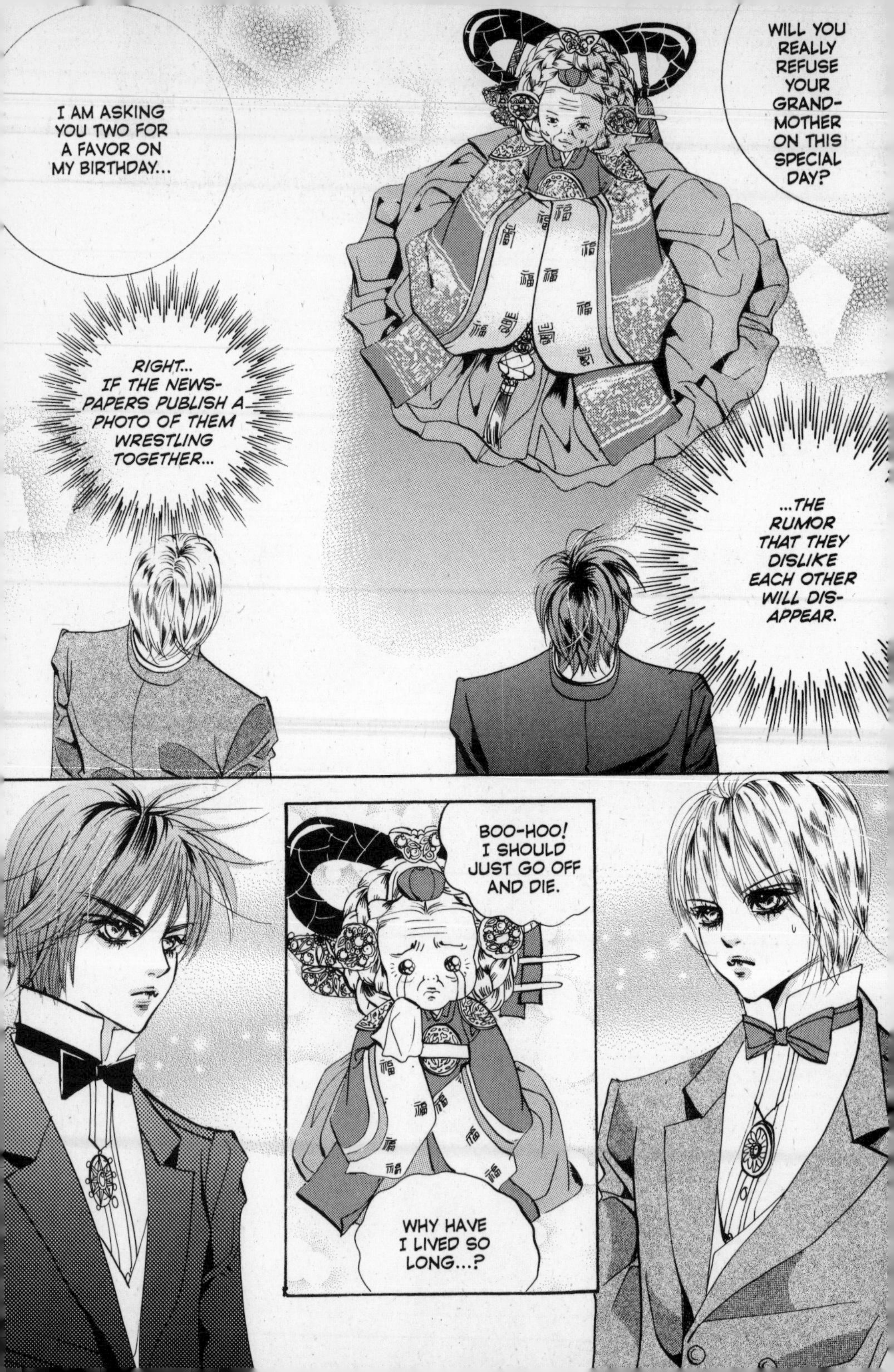
I AM ASKING YOU TWO FOR A FAVOR ON MY BIRTHDAY...
WILL YOU REALLY REFUSE YOUR GRAND-MOTHER ON THIS SPECIAL DAY?
RIGHT... IF THE NEWS-PAPERS PUBLISH A PHOTO OF THEM WRESTLING TOGETHER...
...THE RUMOR THAT THEY DISLIKE EACH OTHER WILL DIS-APPEAR.
BOO-HOO! I SHOULD JUST GO OFF AND DIE.
WHY HAVE I LIVED SO LONG...?

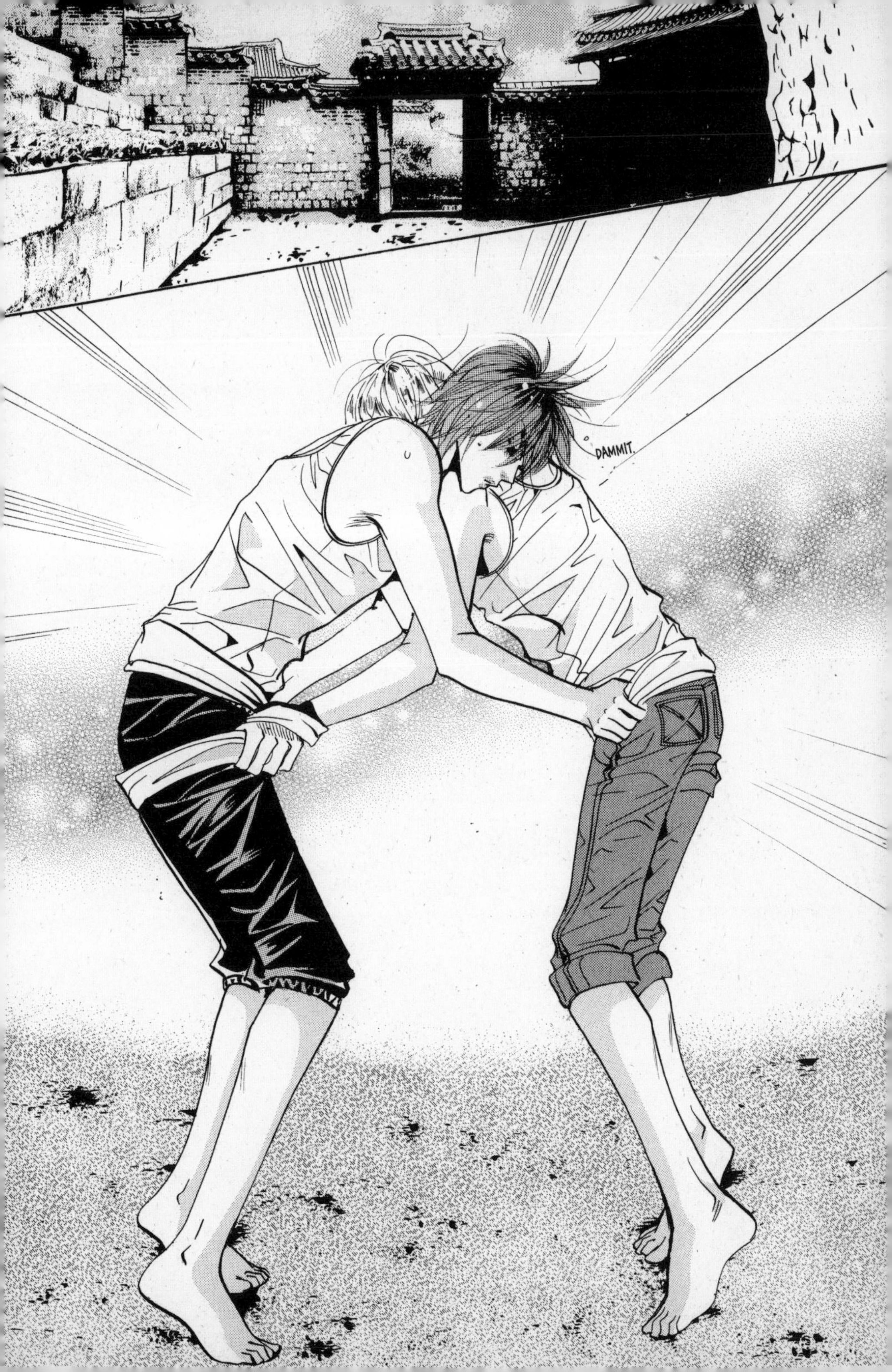
DAMMIT.

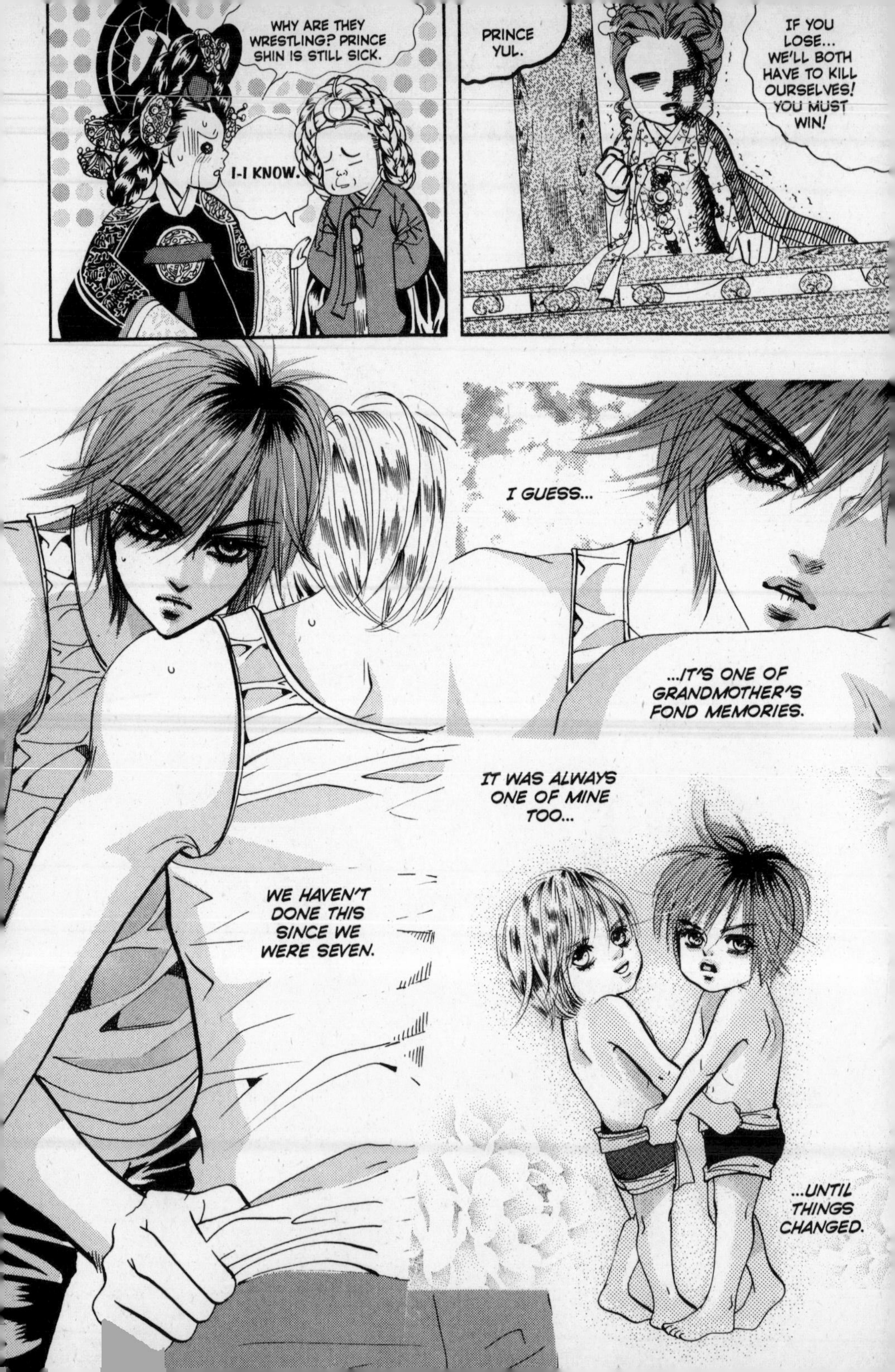
WHY ARE THEY WRESTLING? PRINCE SHIN IS STILL SICK.
I-I KNOW.
PRINCE YUL.
IF YOU LOSE... WE'LL BOTH HAVE TO KILL OURSELVES! YOU MUST WIN!
WE HAVEN'T DONE THIS SINCE WE WERE SEVEN.
I GUESS...
...IT'S ONE OF GRANDMOTHER'S FOND MEMORIES.
IT WAS ALWAYS ONE OF MINE TOO...
...UNTIL THINGS CHANGED.

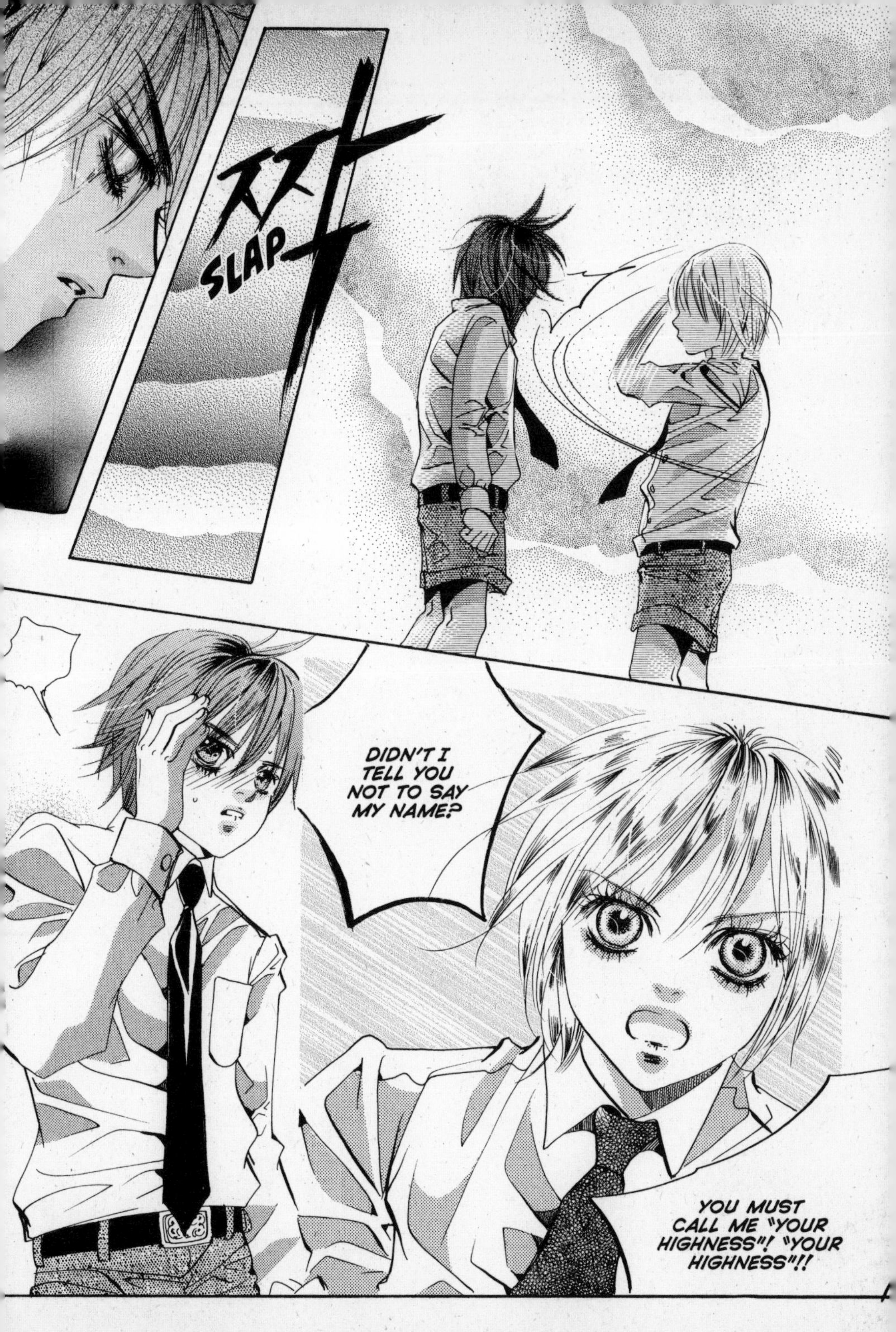
SLAP
DIDN'T I TELL YOU NOT TO SAY MY NAME?
YOU MUST CALL ME "YOUR HIGHNESS"! "YOUR HIGHNESS"!!

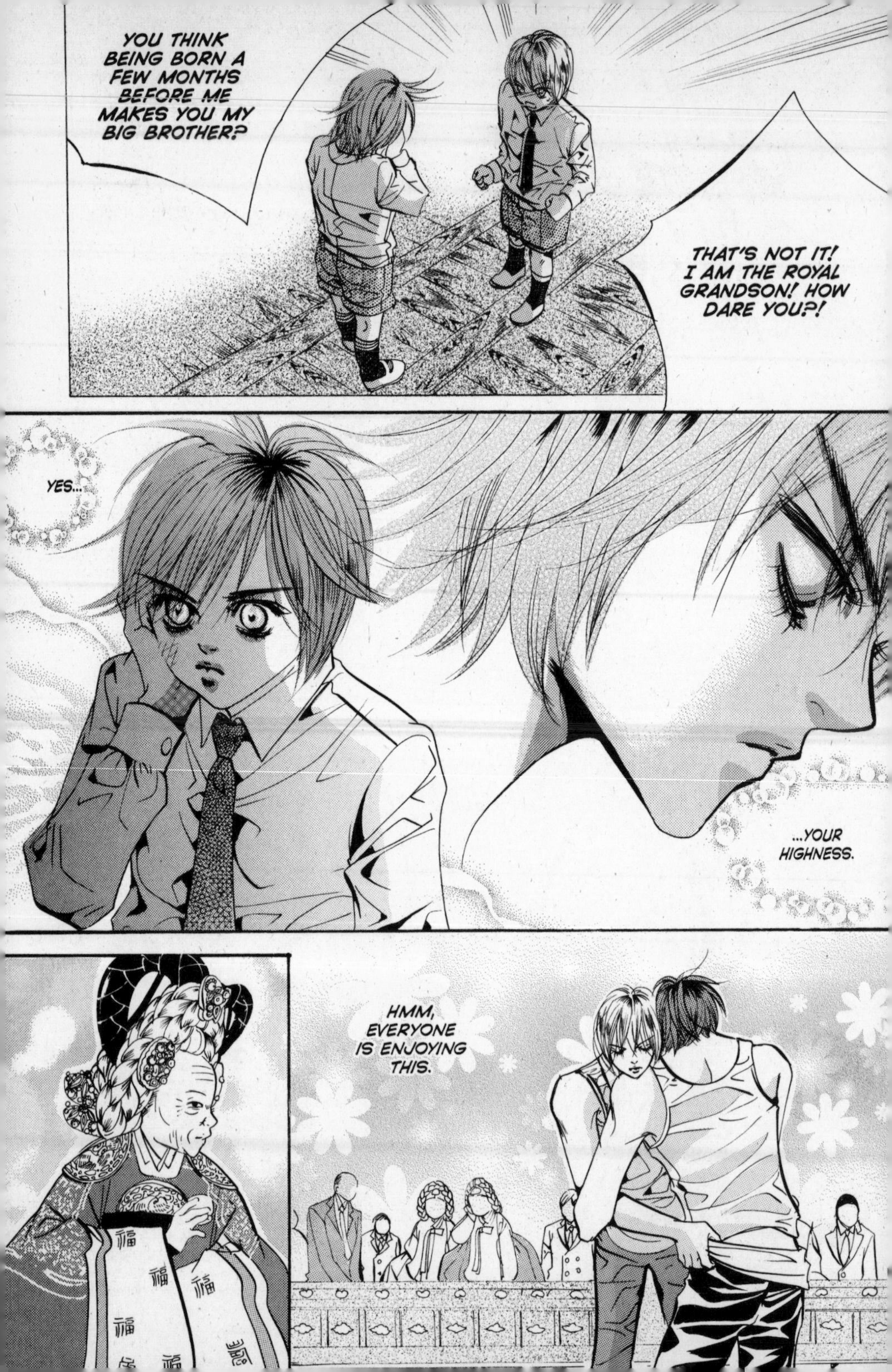
YOU THINK BEING BORN A FEW MONTHS BEFORE ME MAKES YOU MY BIG BROTHER?
THAT'S NOT IT! I AM THE ROYAL GRANDSON! HOW DARE YOU?!
YES...
...YOUR HIGHNESS.
HMM, EVERYONE IS ENJOYING THIS.

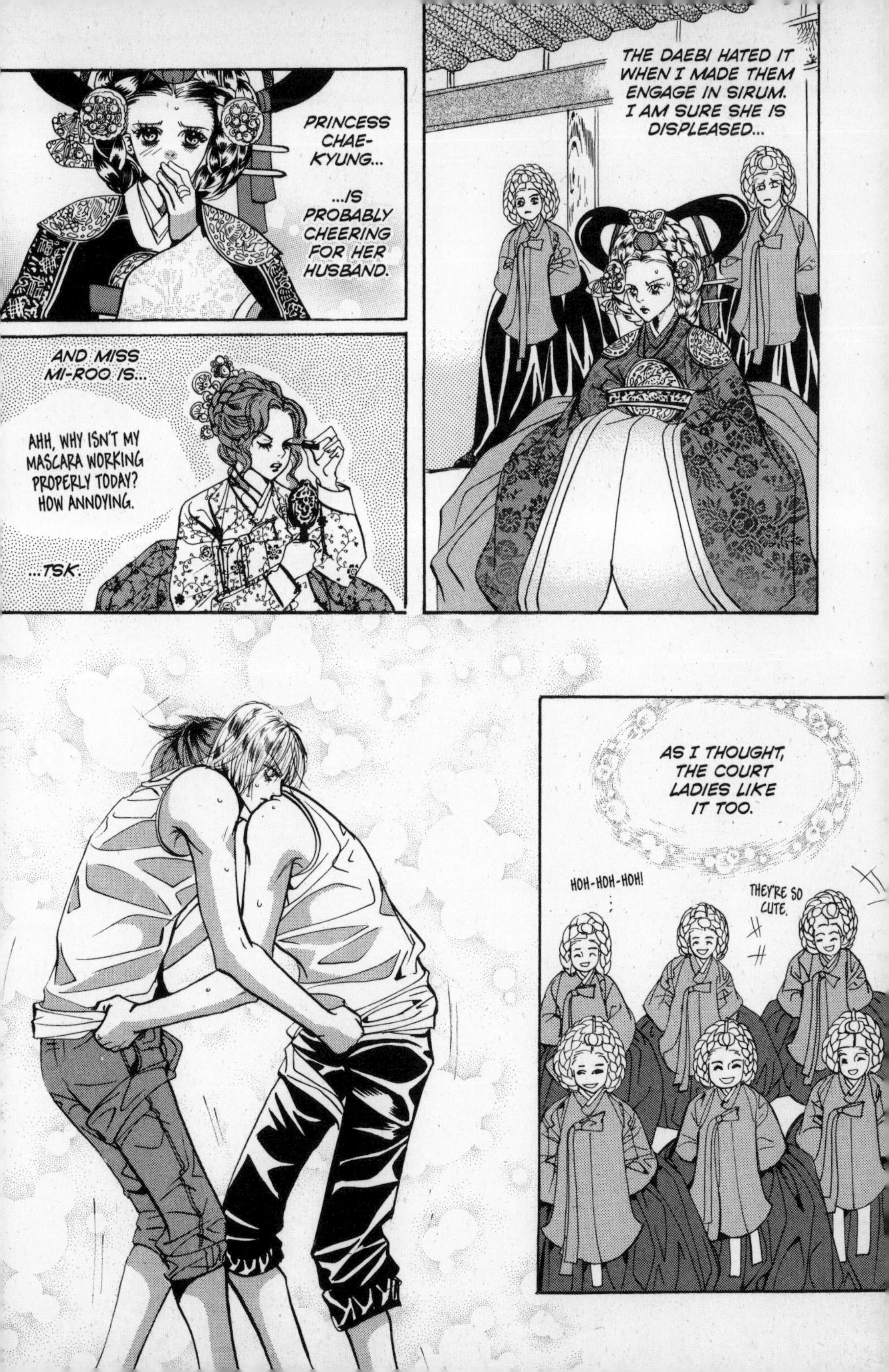
PRINCESS CHAE-KYUNG...
...IS PROBABLY CHEERING FOR HER HUSBAND.
AND MISS MI-ROO IS...
AHH, WHY ISN'T MY MASCARA WORKING PROPERLY TODAY? HOW ANNOYING.
...TSK.
THE DAEBI HATED IT WHEN I MADE THEM ENGAGE IN SIRUM. I AM SURE SHE IS DISPLEASED...
AS I THOUGHT, THE COURT LADIES LIKE IT TOO.
HOH-HOH-HOH!
THEY'RE SO CUTE.

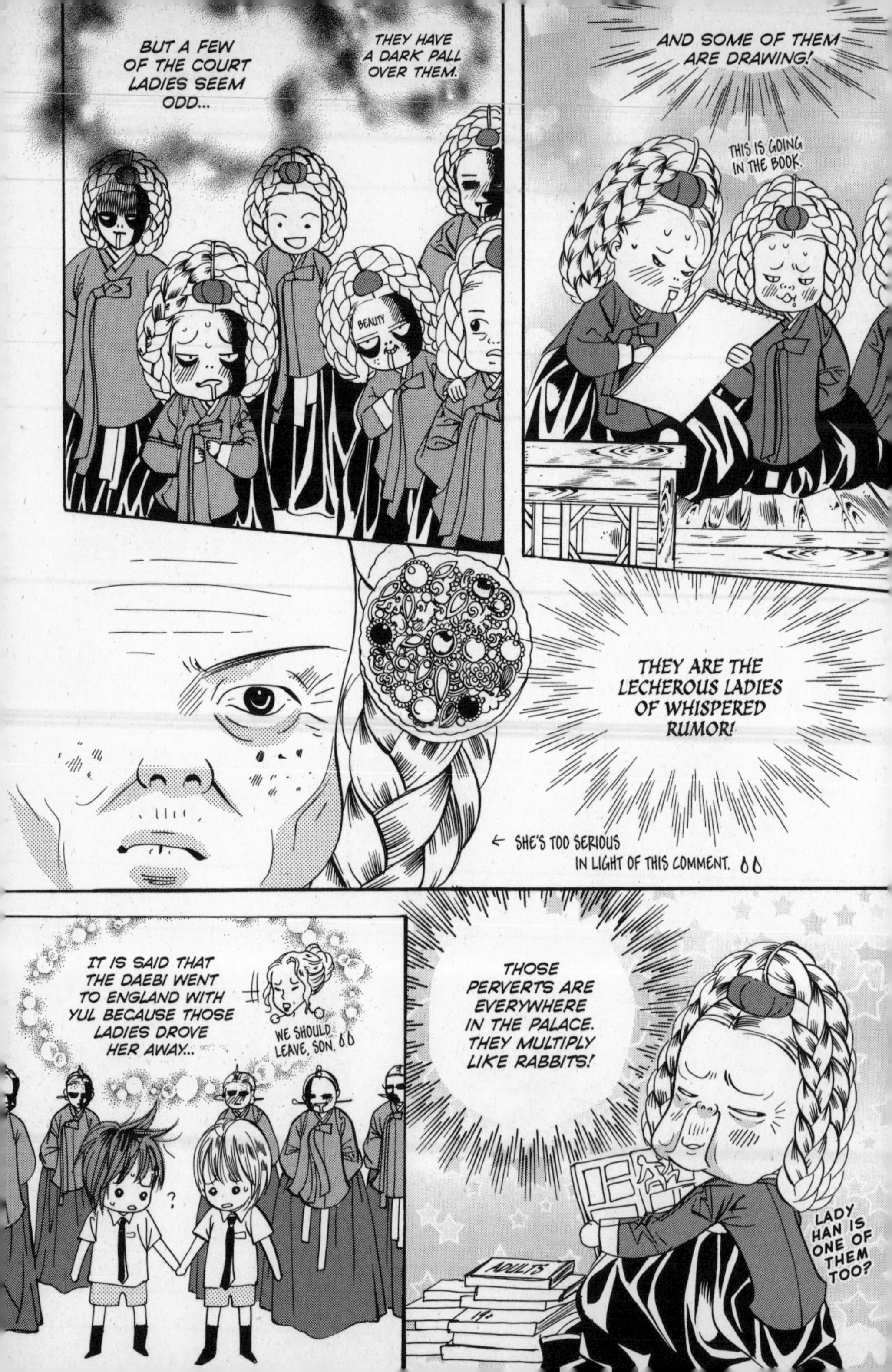
BUT A FEW OF THE COURT LADIES SEEM ODD...
THEY HAVE A DARK PALL OVER THEM.
BEAUTY
AND SOME OF THEM ARE DRAWING!
THIS IS GOING IN THE BOOK.
THEY ARE THE LECHEROUS LADIES OF WHISPERED RUMOR!
← SHE'S TOO SERIOUS IN LIGHT OF THIS COMMENT.
IT IS SAID THAT THE DAEBI WENT TO ENGLAND WITH YUL BECAUSE THOSE LADIES DROVE HER AWAY...
WE SHOULD LEAVE, SON.
?
THOSE PERVERTS ARE EVERYWHERE IN THE PALACE. THEY MULTIPLY LIKE RABBITS!
LADY HAN IS ONE OF THEM TOO?
ADULTS
19+

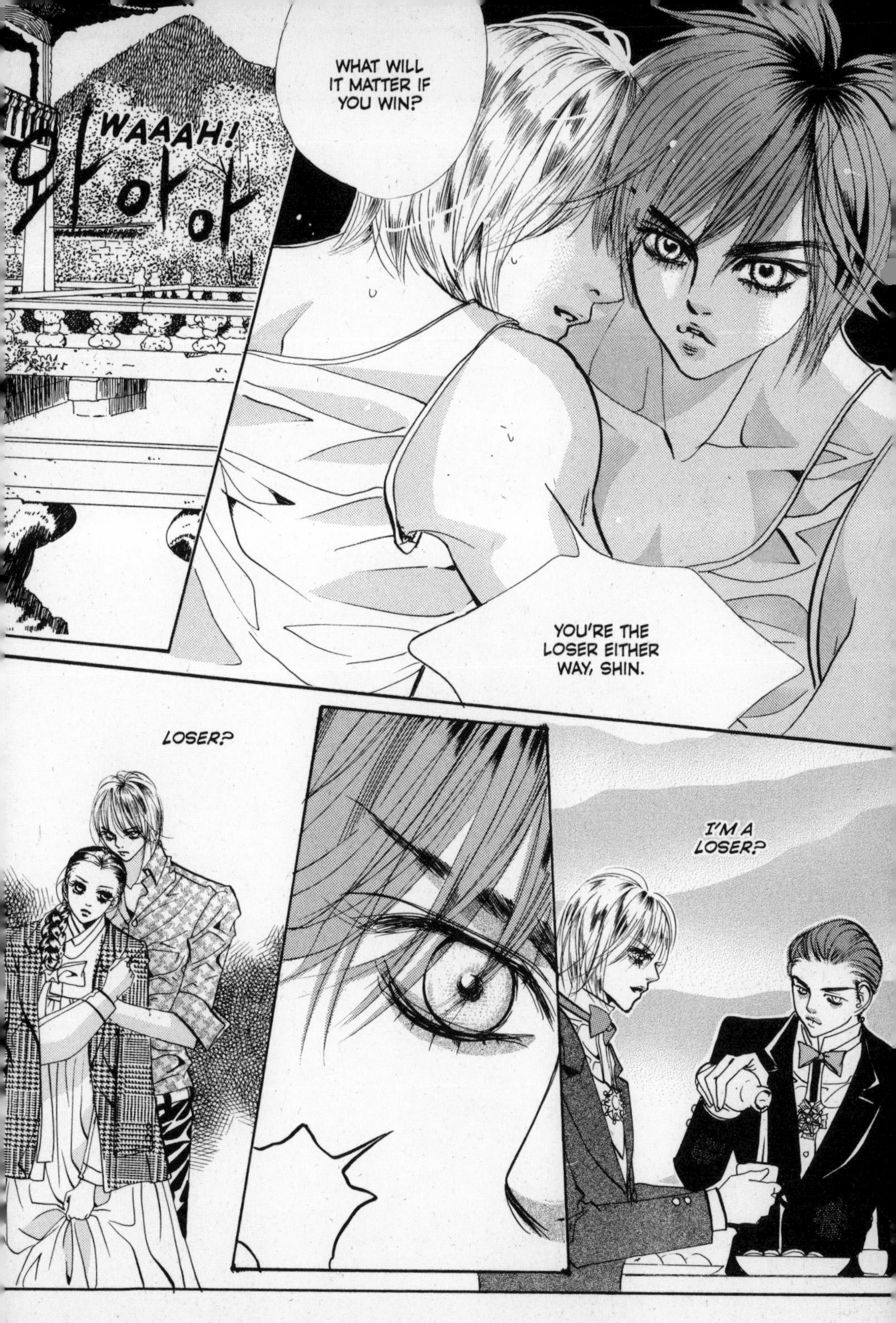
WAAAH!
와아아아
WHAT WILL IT MATTER IF YOU WIN?
YOU'RE THE LOSER EITHER WAY, SHIN.
LOSER?
I'M A LOSER?

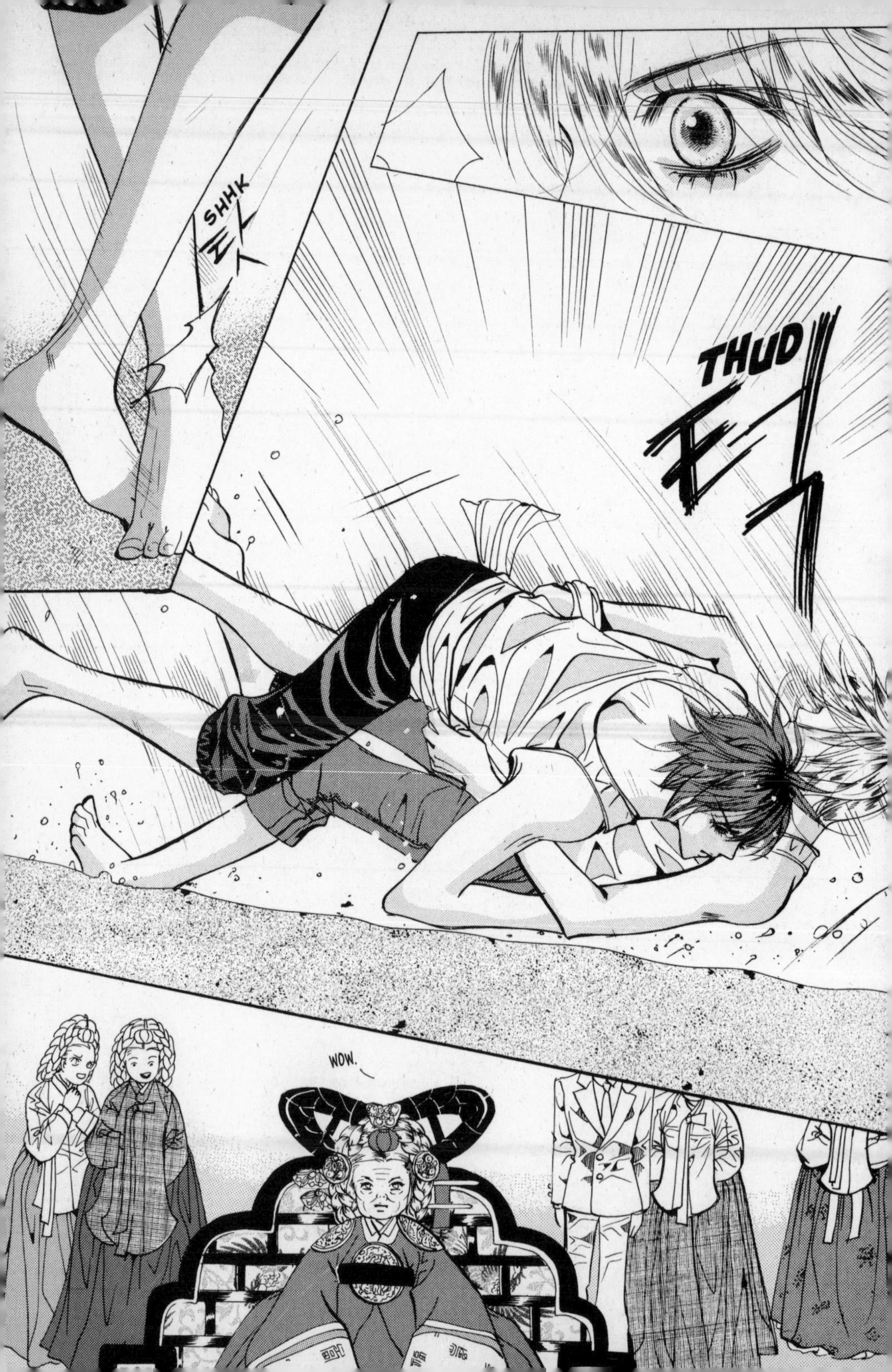
SHHK
THUD
WOW.

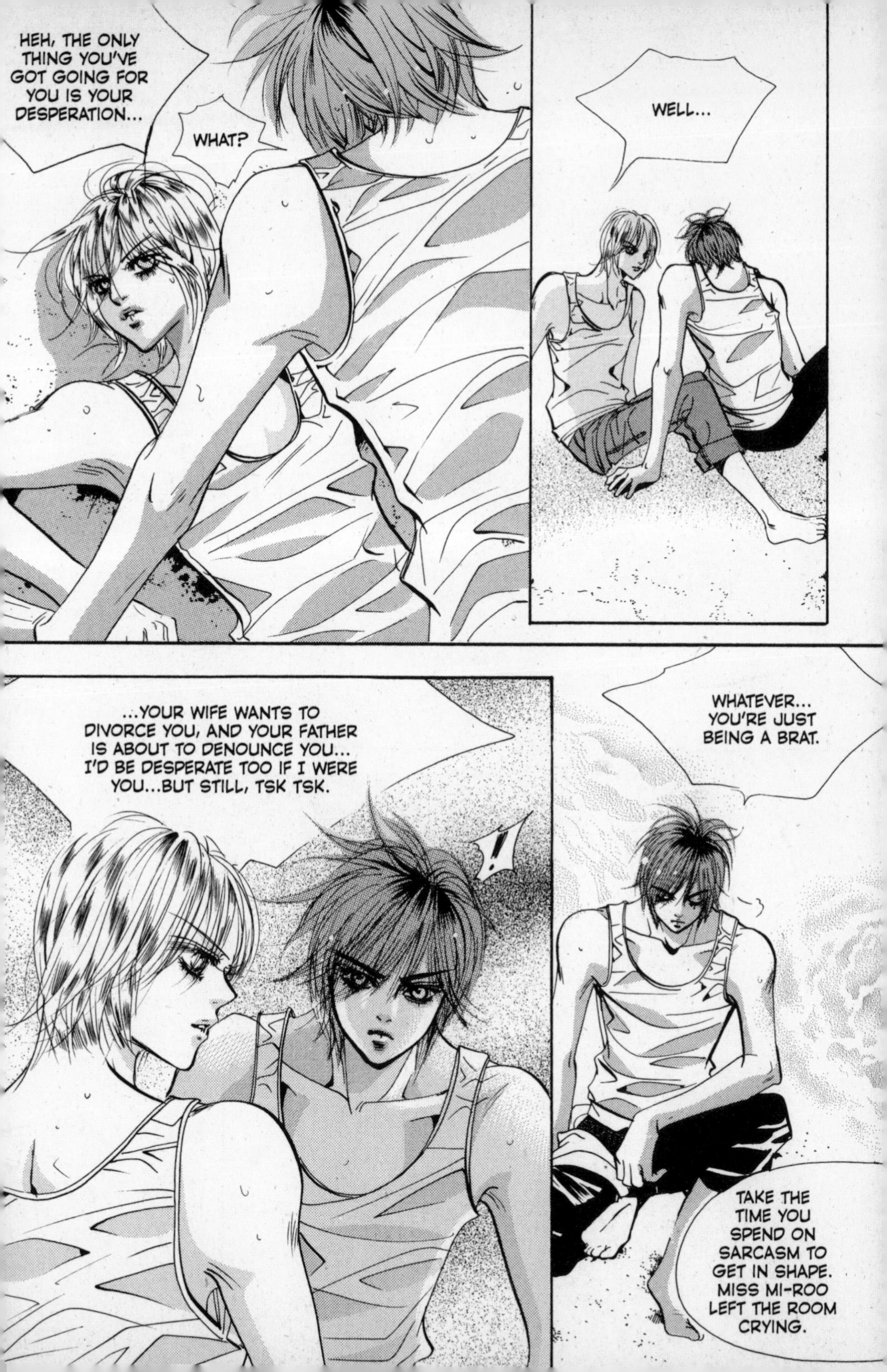
HEH, THE ONLY THING YOU'VE GOT GOING FOR YOU IS YOUR DESPERATION...
WHAT?
WELL...
...YOUR WIFE WANTS TO DIVORCE YOU, AND YOUR FATHER IS ABOUT TO DENOUNCE YOU... I'D BE DESPERATE TOO IF I WERE YOU...BUT STILL, TSK TSK.
!
WHATEVER... YOU'RE JUST BEING A BRAT.
TAKE THE TIME YOU SPEND ON SARCASM TO GET IN SHAPE. MISS MI-ROO LEFT THE ROOM CRYING.

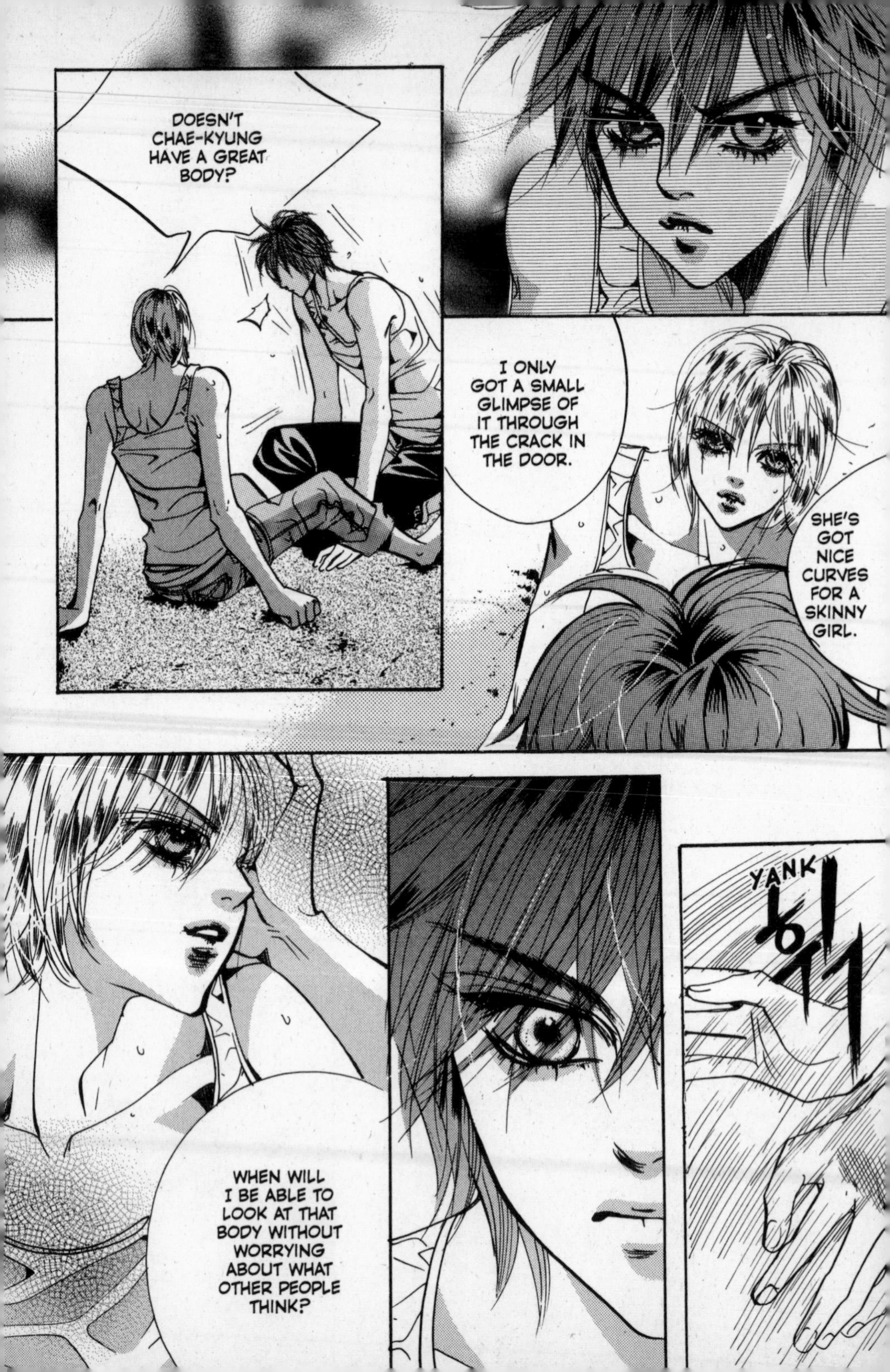
DOESN'T CHAE-KYUNG HAVE A GREAT BODY?
I ONLY GOT A SMALL GLIMPSE OF IT THROUGH THE CRACK IN THE DOOR.
SHE'S GOT NICE CURVES FOR A SKINNY GIRL.
WHEN WILL I BE ABLE TO LOOK AT THAT BODY WITHOUT WORRYING ABOUT WHAT OTHER PEOPLE THINK?
YANK

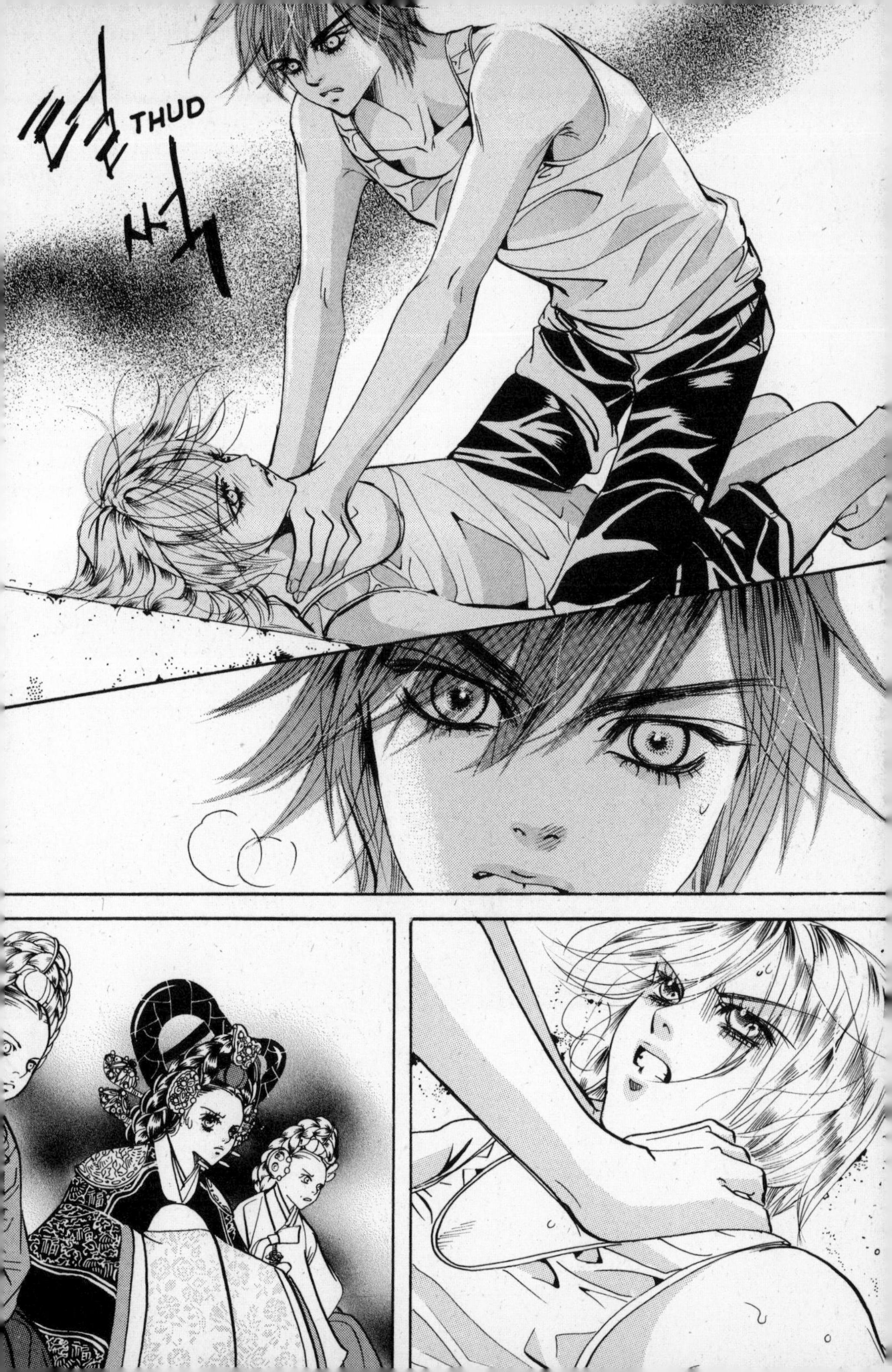
털썩
THUD

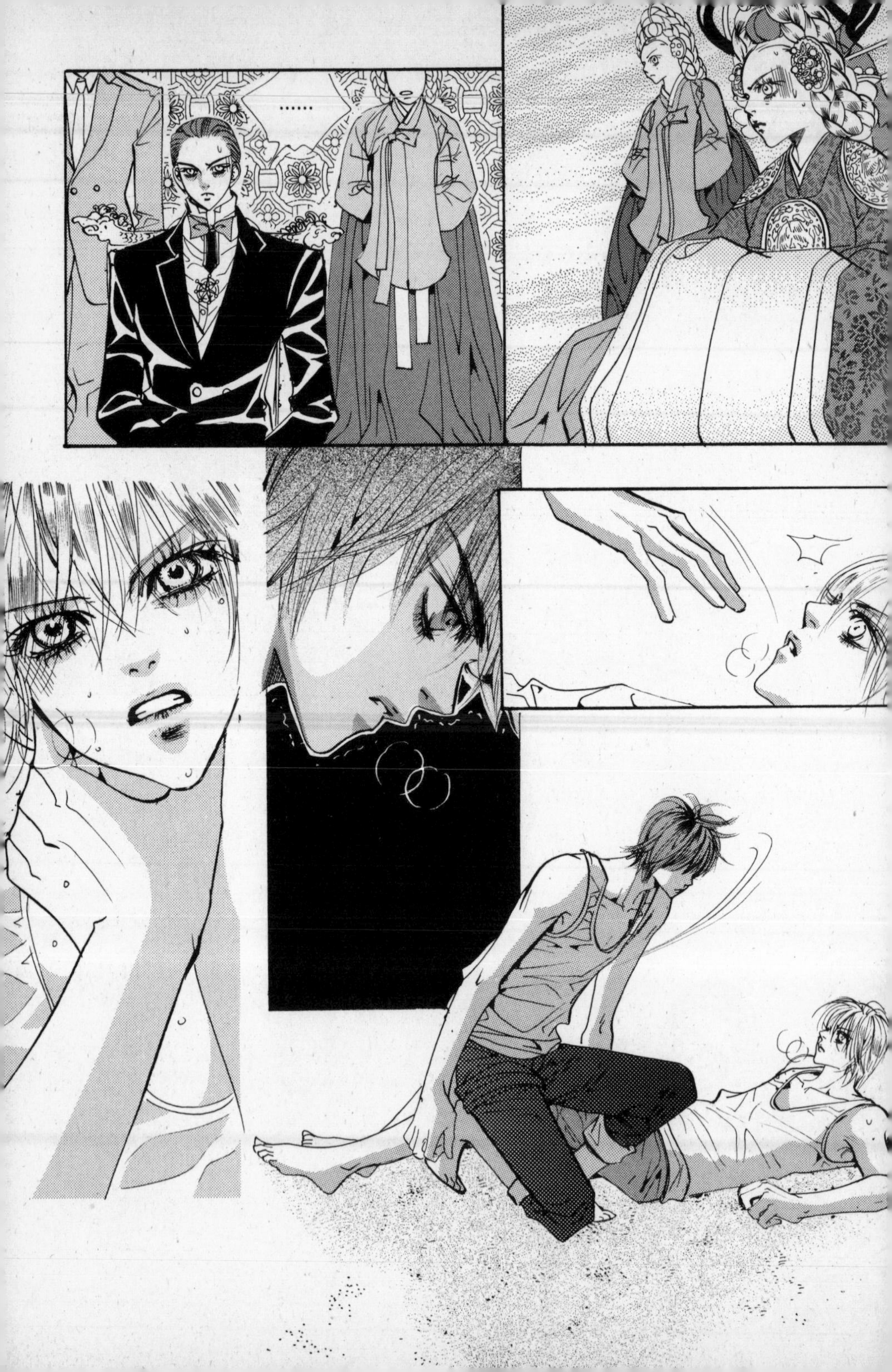
......

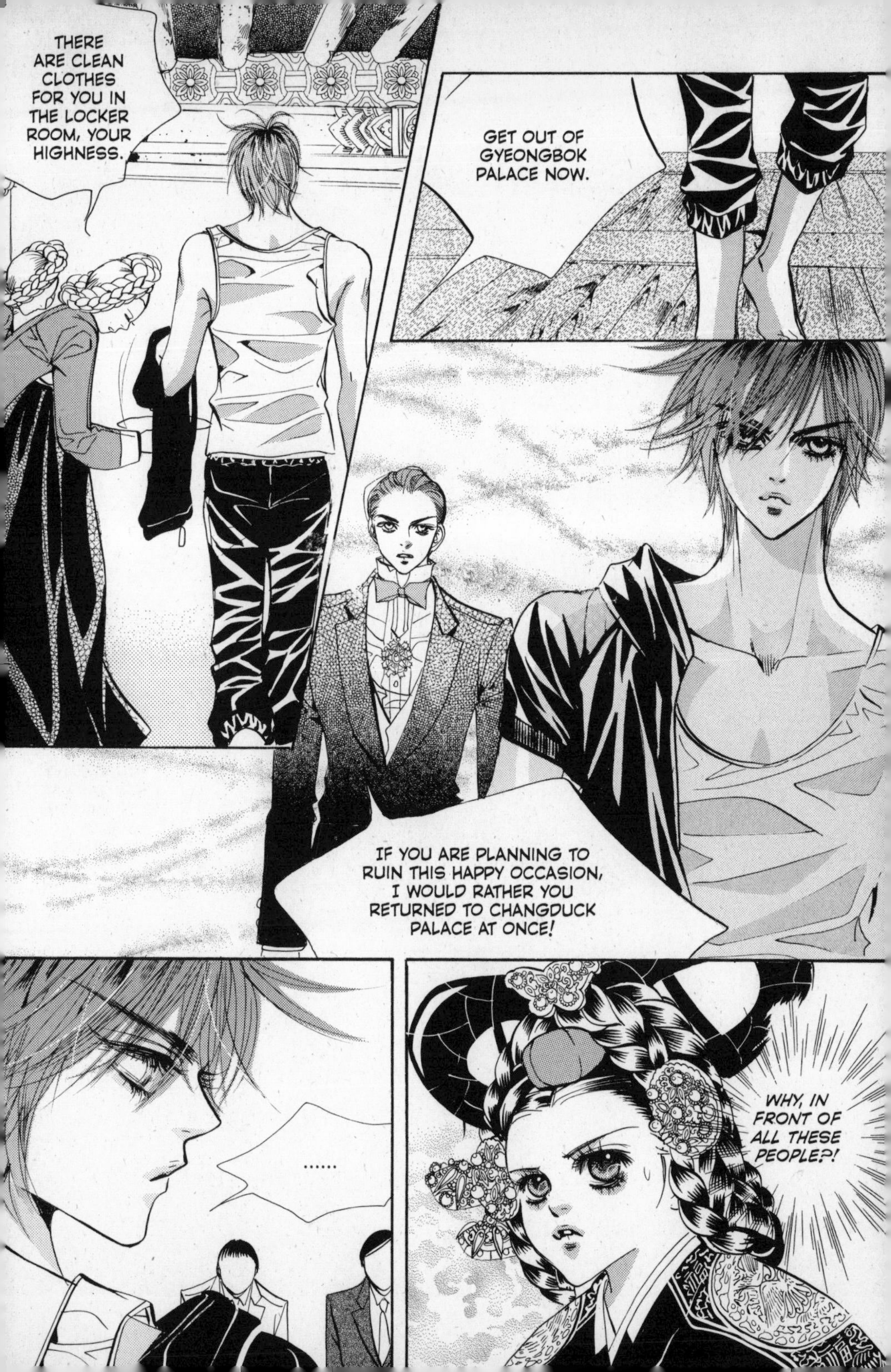
THERE ARE CLEAN CLOTHES FOR YOU IN THE LOCKER ROOM, YOUR HIGHNESS.
GET OUT OF GYEONGBOK PALACE NOW.
IF YOU ARE PLANNING TO RUIN THIS HAPPY OCCASION, I WOULD RATHER YOU RETURNED TO CHANGDUCK PALACE AT ONCE!
......
WHY, IN FRONT OF ALL THESE PEOPLE?!

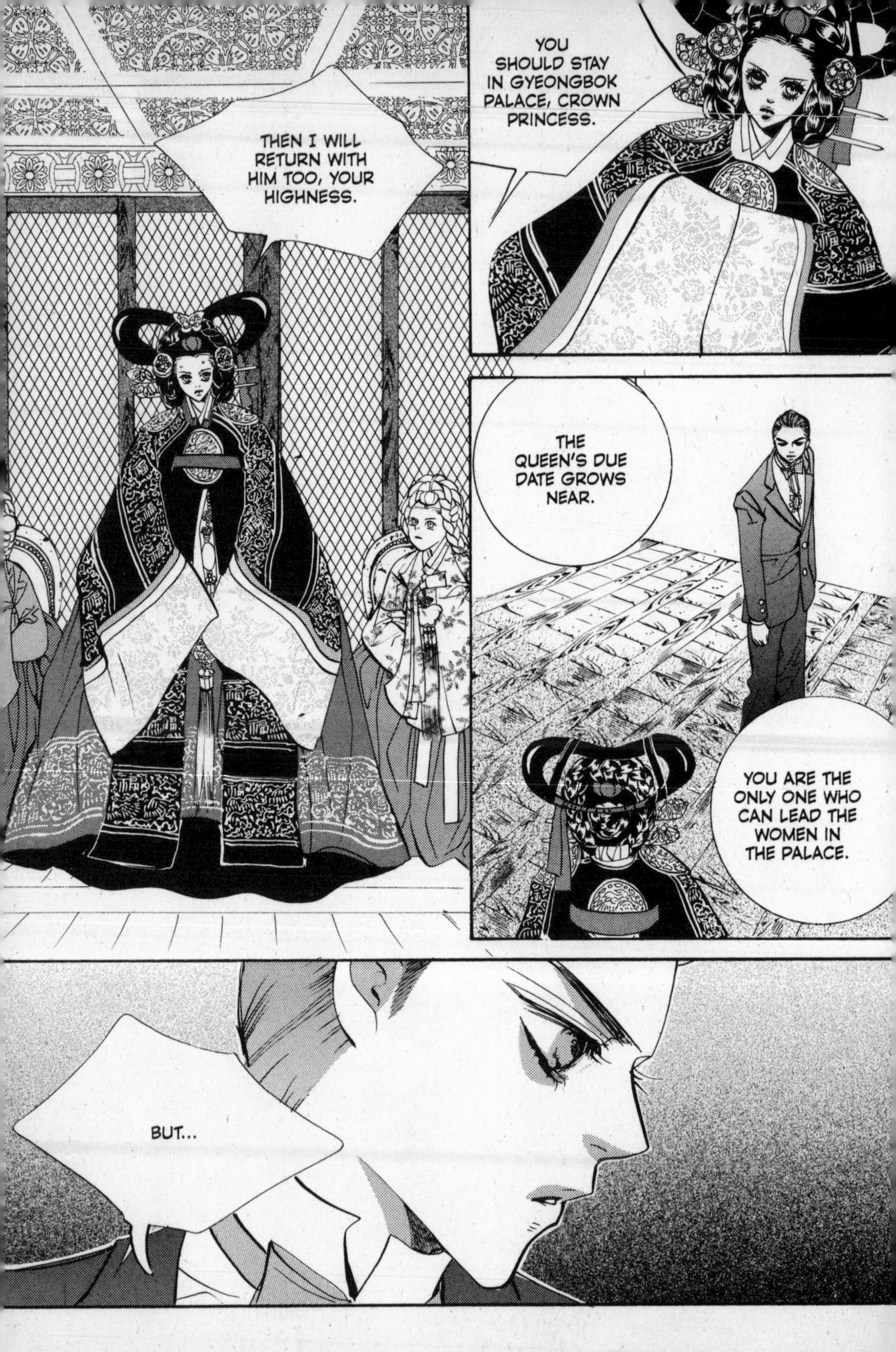
THEN I WILL RETURN WITH HIM TOO, YOUR HIGHNESS.
YOU SHOULD STAY IN GYEONGBOK PALACE, CROWN PRINCESS.
THE QUEEN'S DUE DATE GROWS NEAR.
YOU ARE THE ONLY ONE WHO CAN LEAD THE WOMEN IN THE PALACE.
BUT...

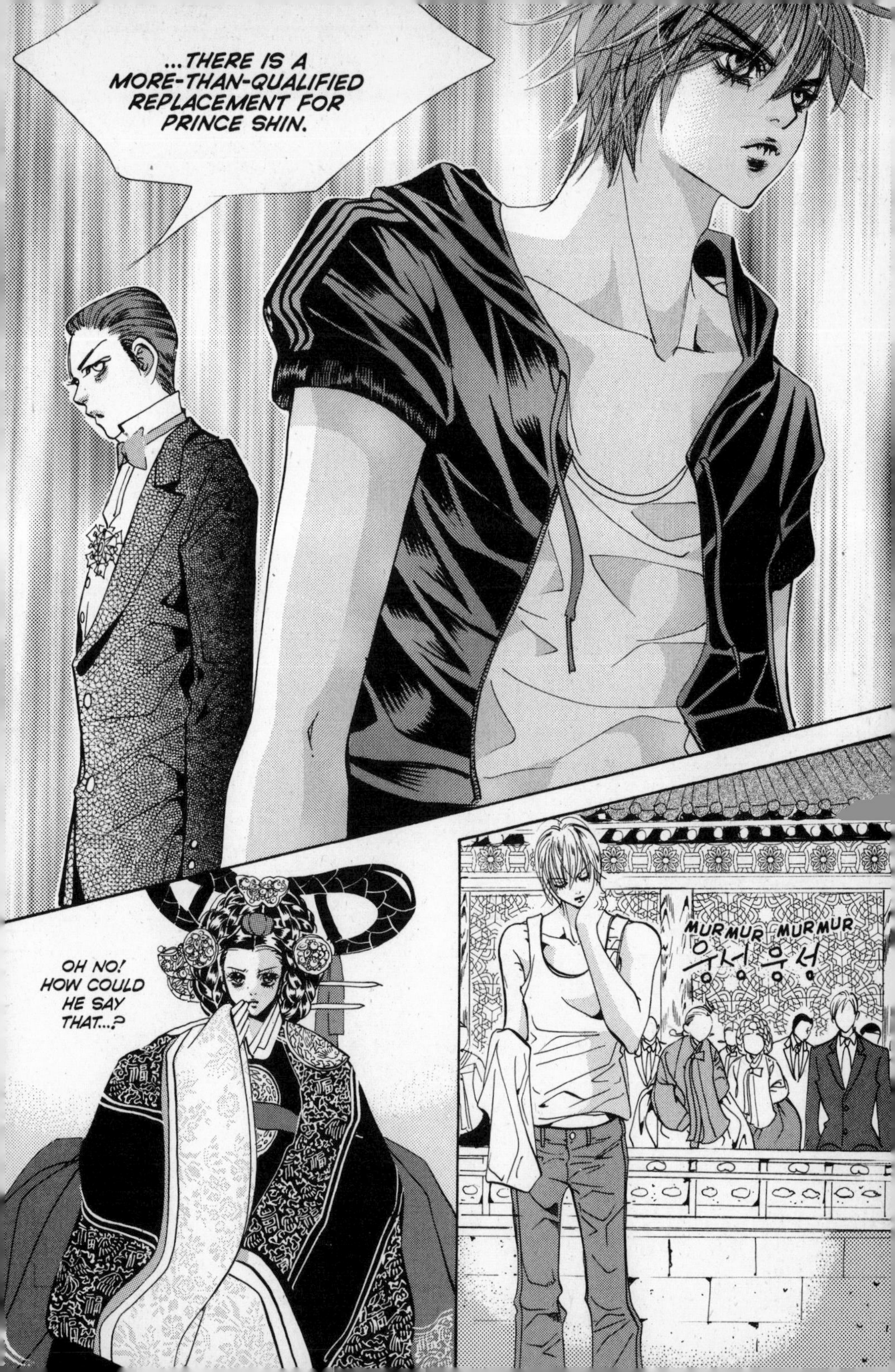
...THERE IS A MORE-THAN-QUALIFIED REPLACEMENT FOR PRINCE SHIN.
OH NO! HOW COULD HE SAY THAT...?
MURMUR MURMUR
웅성웅성

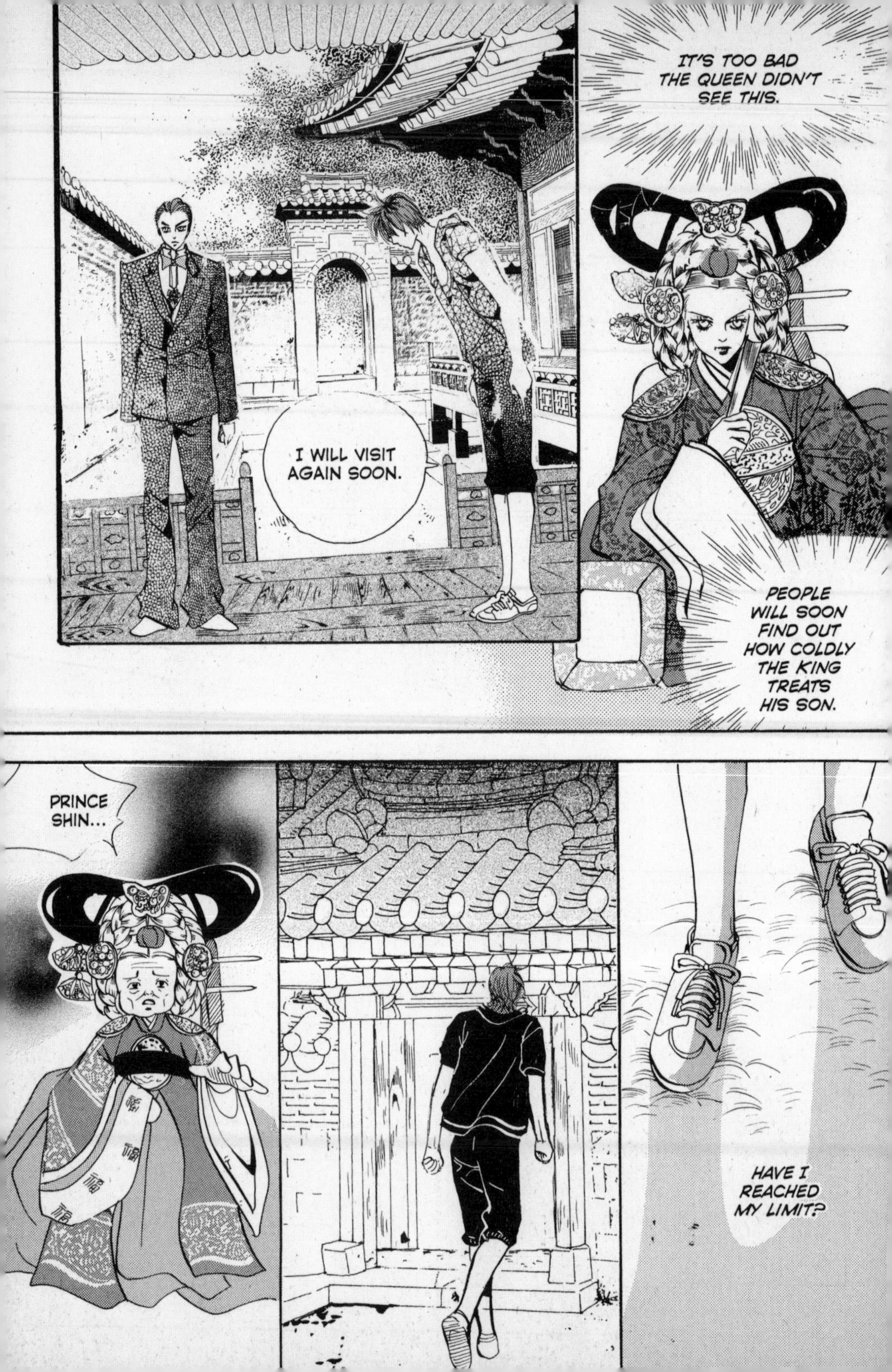
I WILL VISIT AGAIN SOON.
IT'S TOO BAD THE QUEEN DIDN'T SEE THIS.
PEOPLE WILL SOON FIND OUT HOW COLDLY THE KING TREATS HIS SON.
PRINCE SHIN...
HAVE I REACHED MY LIMIT?

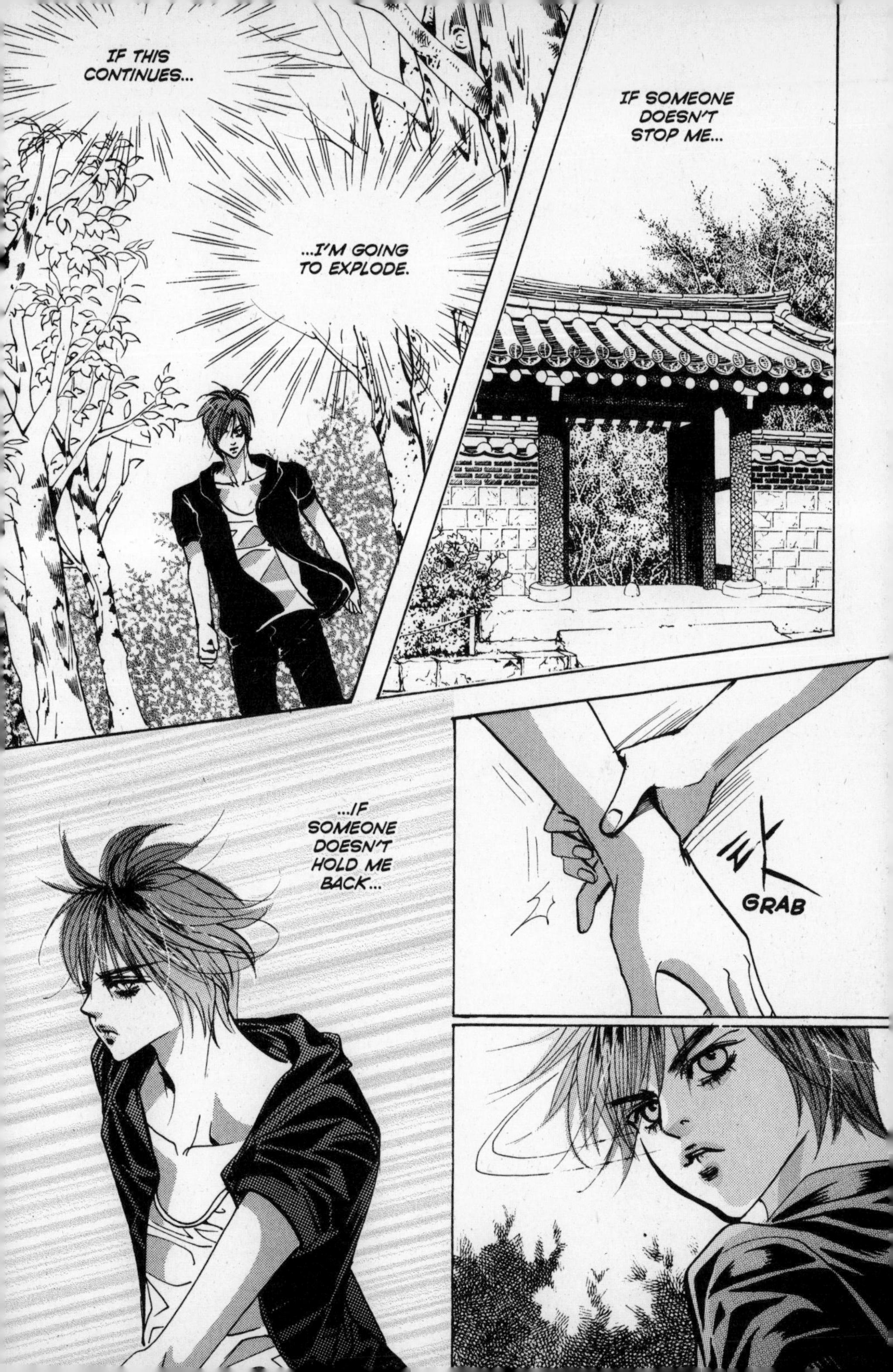
IF THIS CONTINUES...
...I'M GOING TO EXPLODE.
IF SOMEONE DOESN'T STOP ME...
...IF SOMEONE DOESN'T HOLD ME BACK...
GRAB

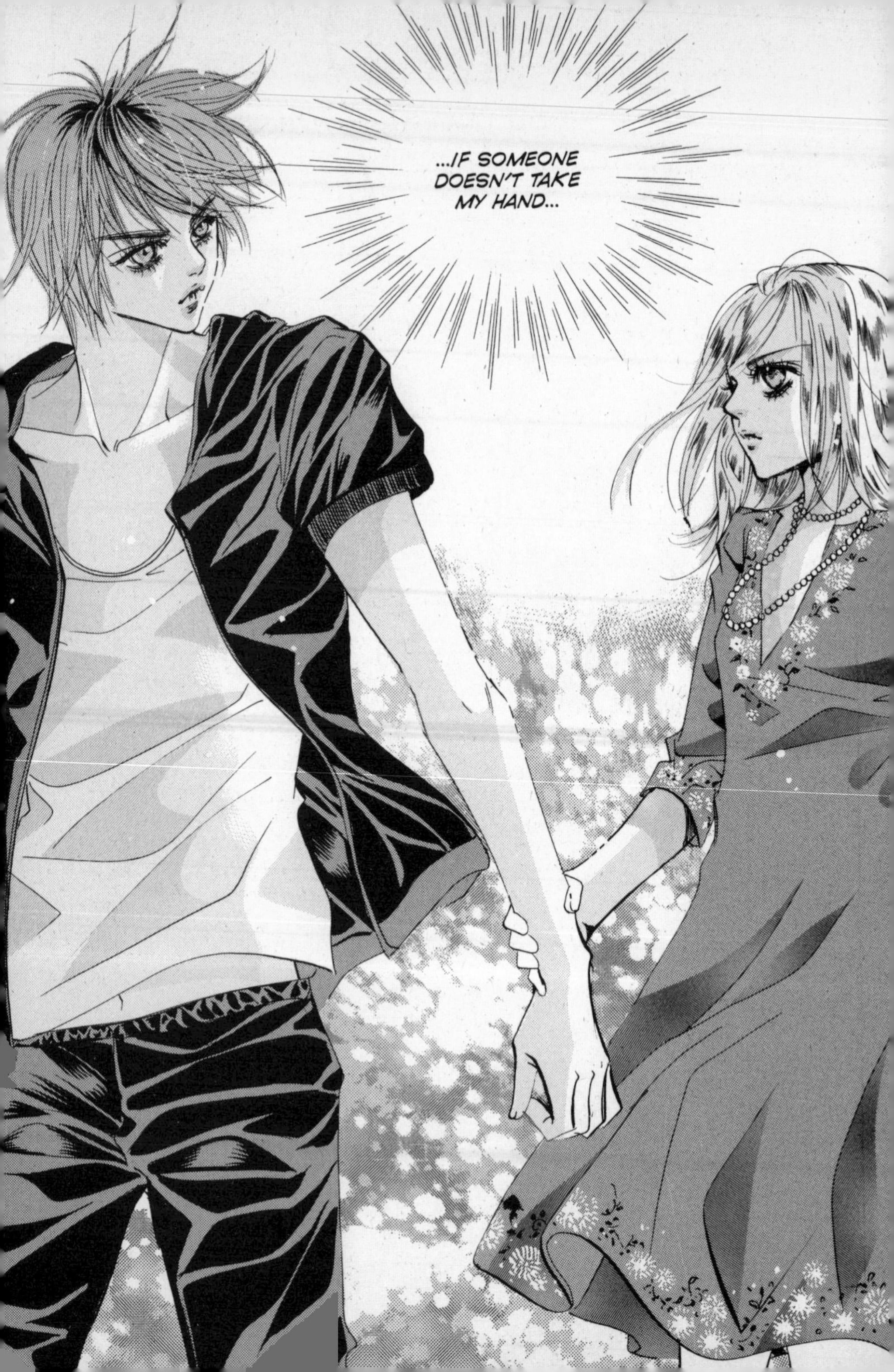
...IF SOMEONE DOESN'T TAKE MY HAND...

THE SECRET OF PAGE 173.

— BEAUTY PARK'S OWN SECRET DESIRES —

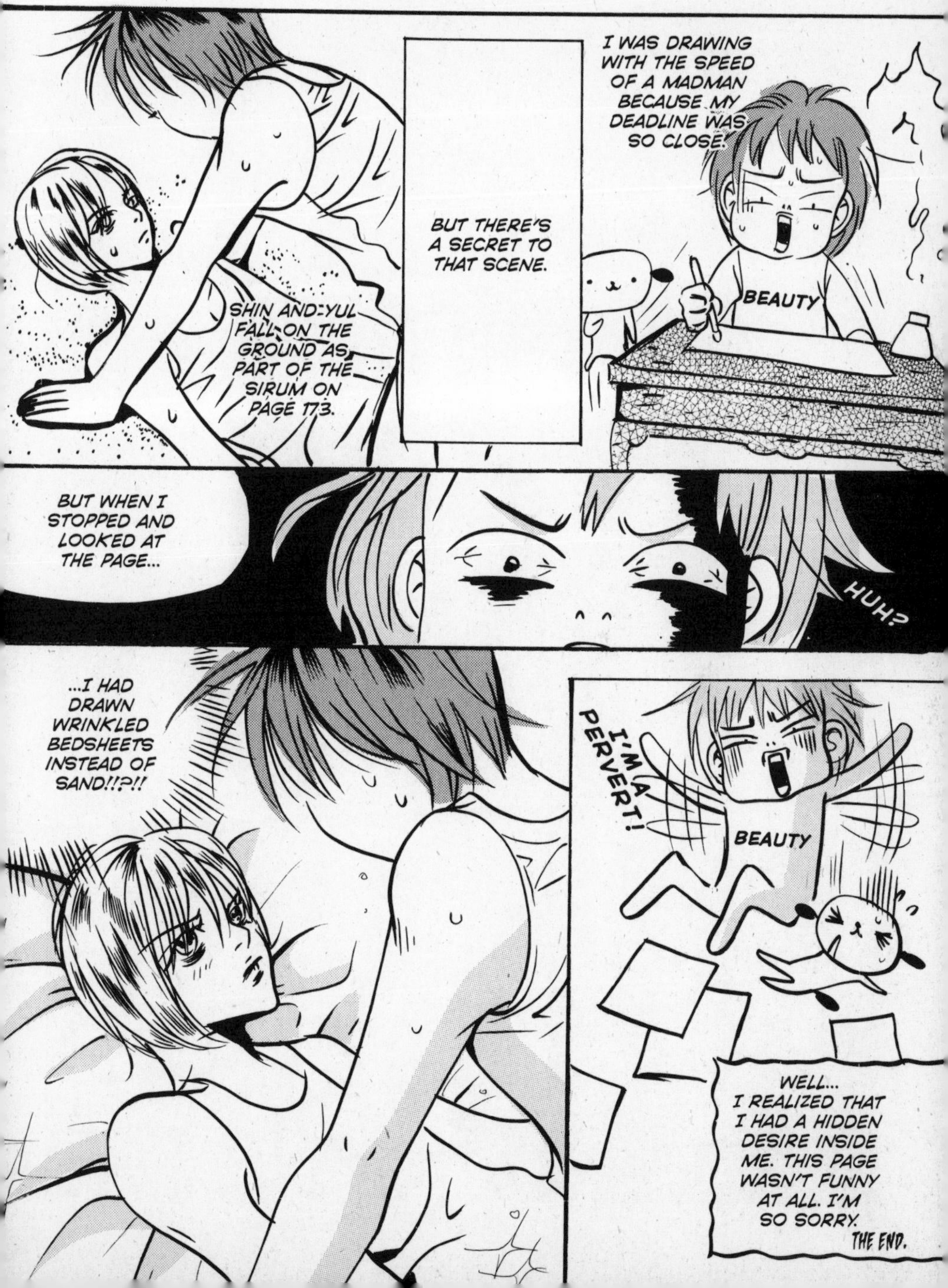

SHIN AND YUL FALL ON THE GROUND AS PART OF THE SIRUM ON PAGE 173.
BUT THERE'S A SECRET TO THAT SCENE.
I WAS DRAWING WITH THE SPEED OF A MADMAN BECAUSE MY DEADLINE WAS SO CLOSE.
BEAUTY
BUT WHEN I STOPPED AND LOOKED AT THE PAGE...
HUH?
...I HAD DRAWN WRINKLED BEDSHEETS INSTEAD OF SAND!!?!!
I'M A PERVERT!
BEAUTY
WELL... I REALIZED THAT I HAD A HIDDEN DESIRE INSIDE ME. THIS PAGE WASN'T FUNNY AT ALL. I'M SO SORRY.
THE END.

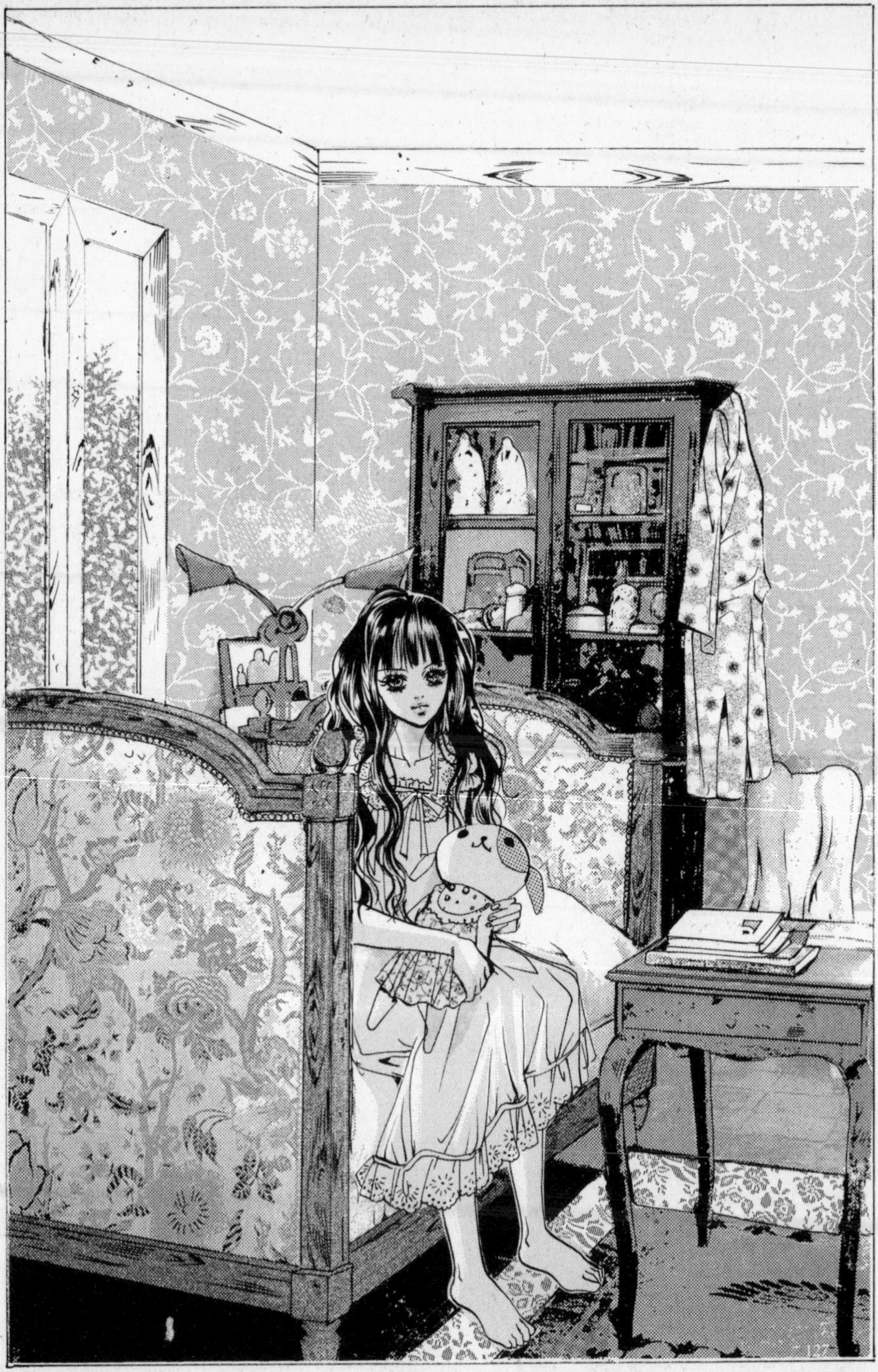

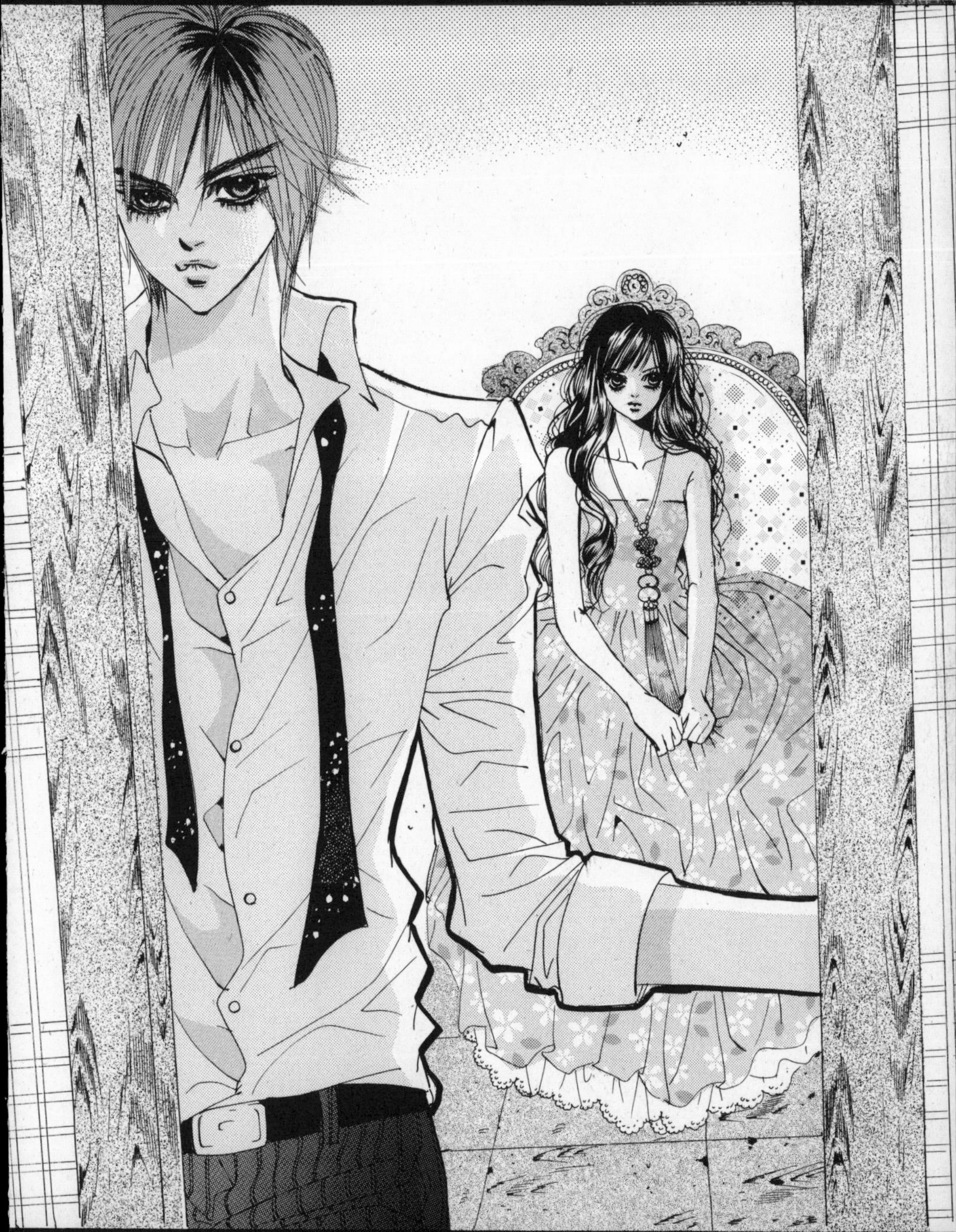

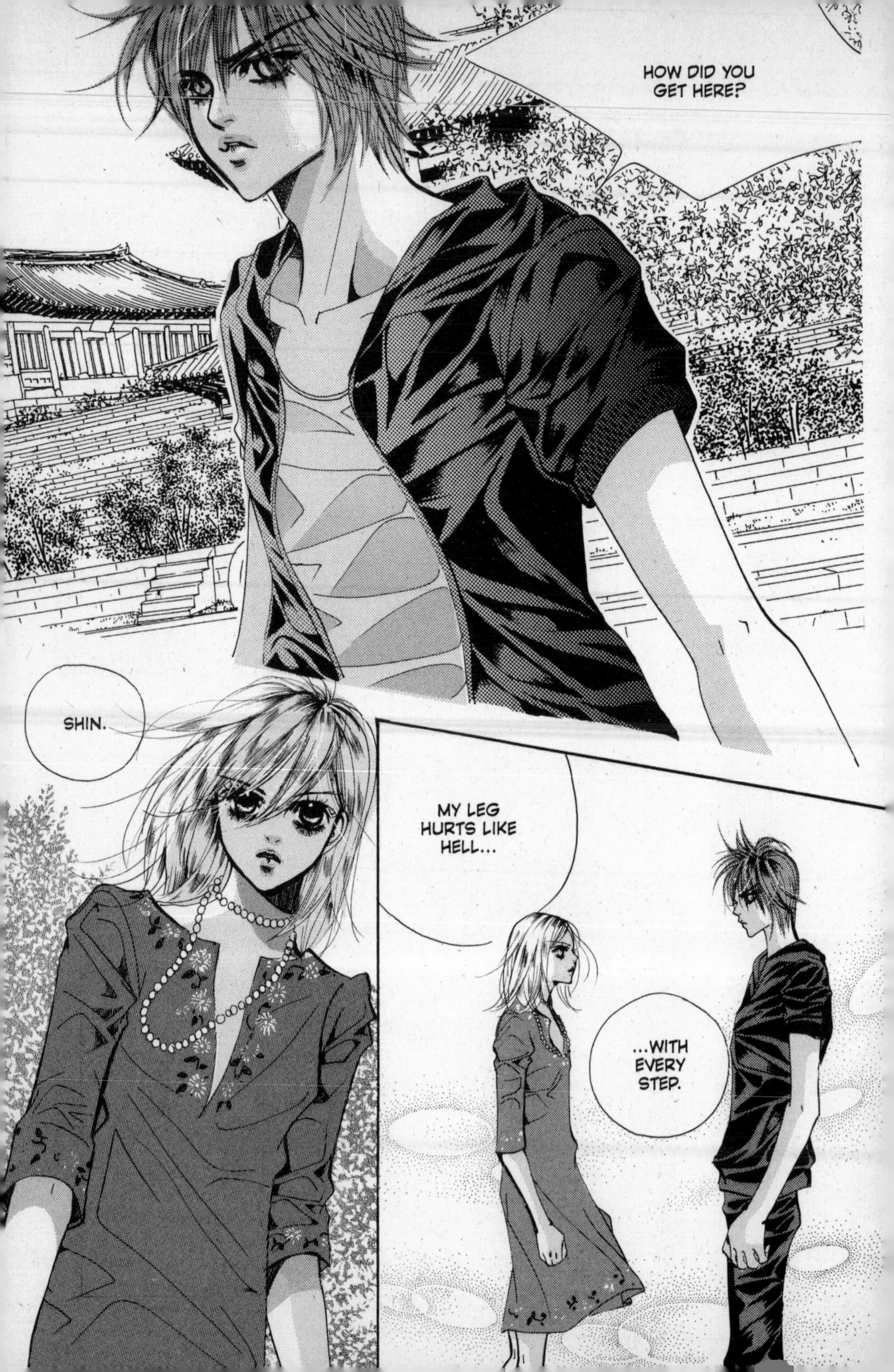
HOW DID YOU GET HERE?
SHIN.
MY LEG HURTS LIKE HELL...
...WITH EVERY STEP.

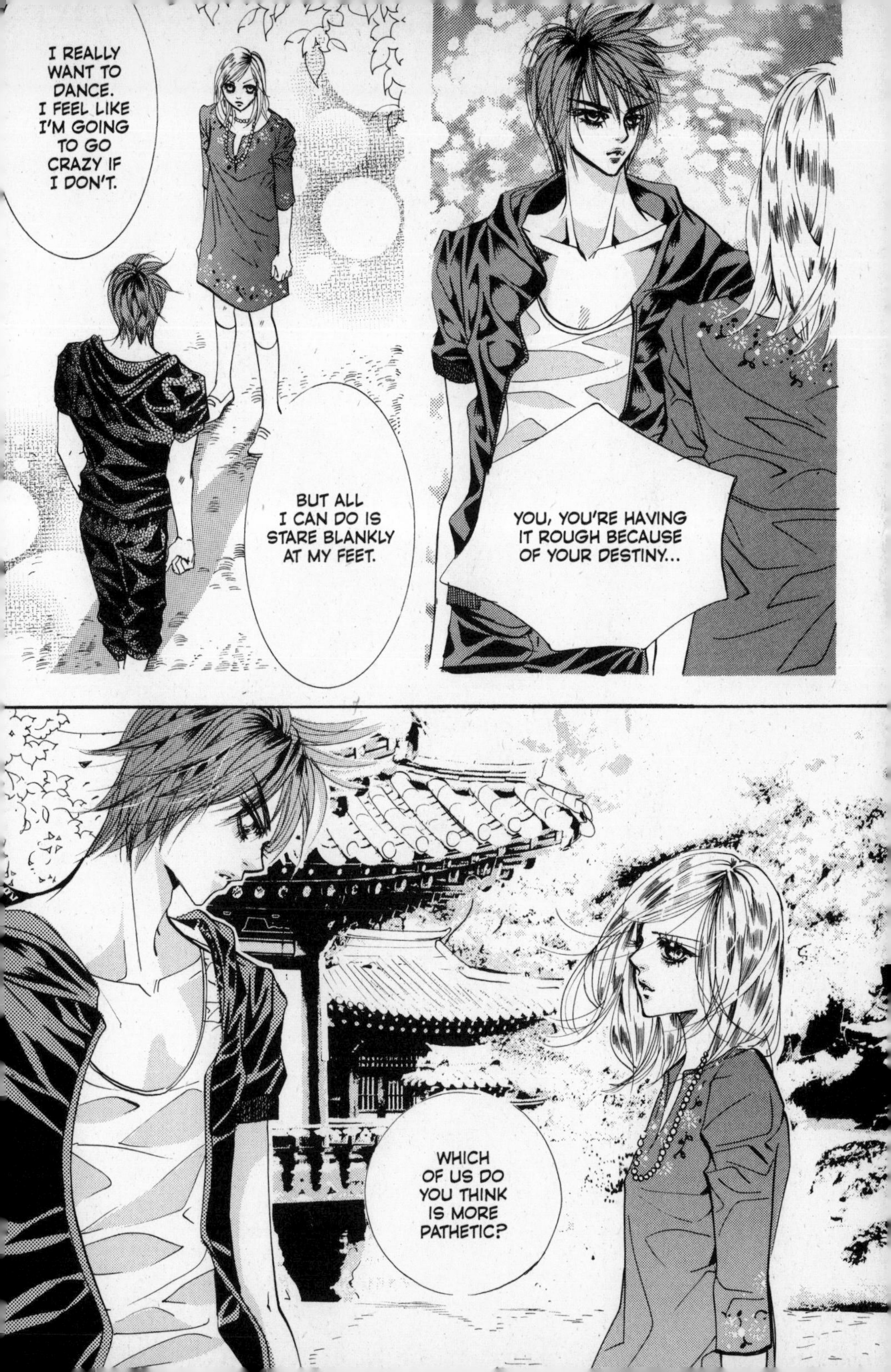
I REALLY WANT TO DANCE. I FEEL LIKE I'M GOING TO GO CRAZY IF I DON'T.
BUT ALL I CAN DO IS STARE BLANKLY AT MY FEET.
YOU, YOU'RE HAVING IT ROUGH BECAUSE OF YOUR DESTINY...
WHICH OF US DO YOU THINK IS MORE PATHETIC?

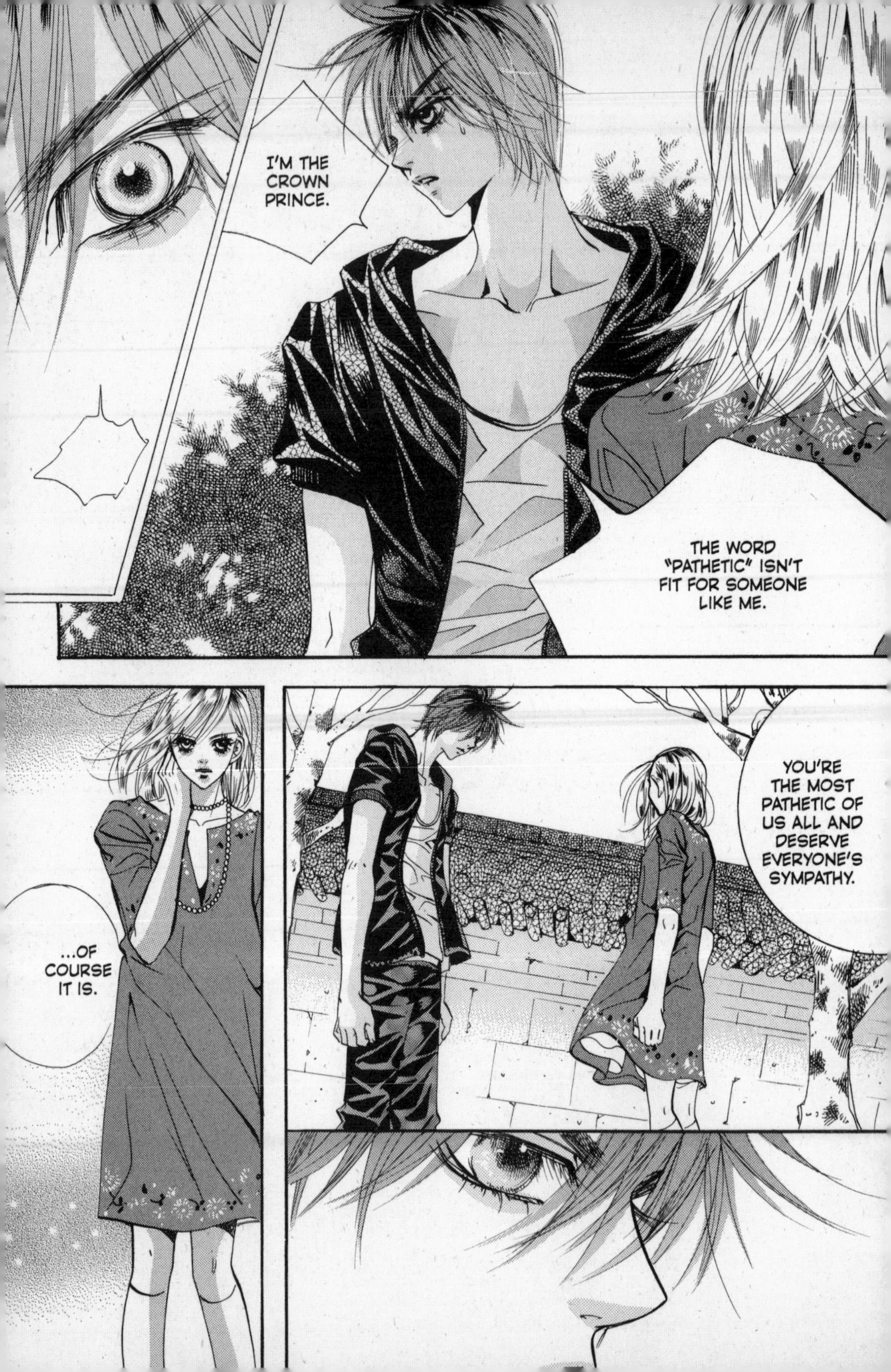
I'M THE CROWN PRINCE.
THE WORD "PATHETIC" ISN'T FIT FOR SOMEONE LIKE ME.
...OF COURSE IT IS.
YOU'RE THE MOST PATHETIC OF US ALL AND DESERVE EVERYONE'S SYMPATHY.

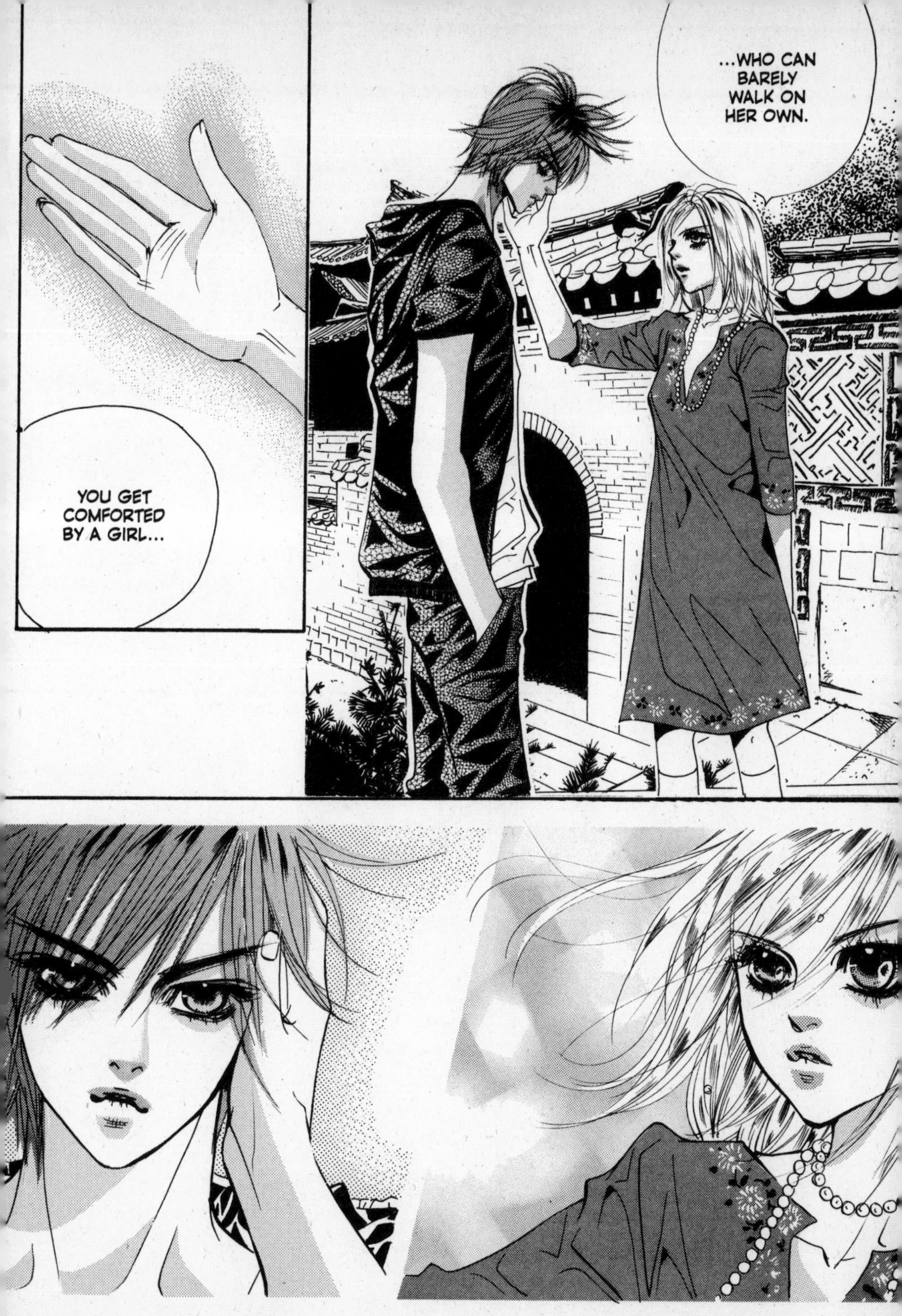
YOU GET COMFORTED BY A GIRL...
...WHO CAN BARELY WALK ON HER OWN.

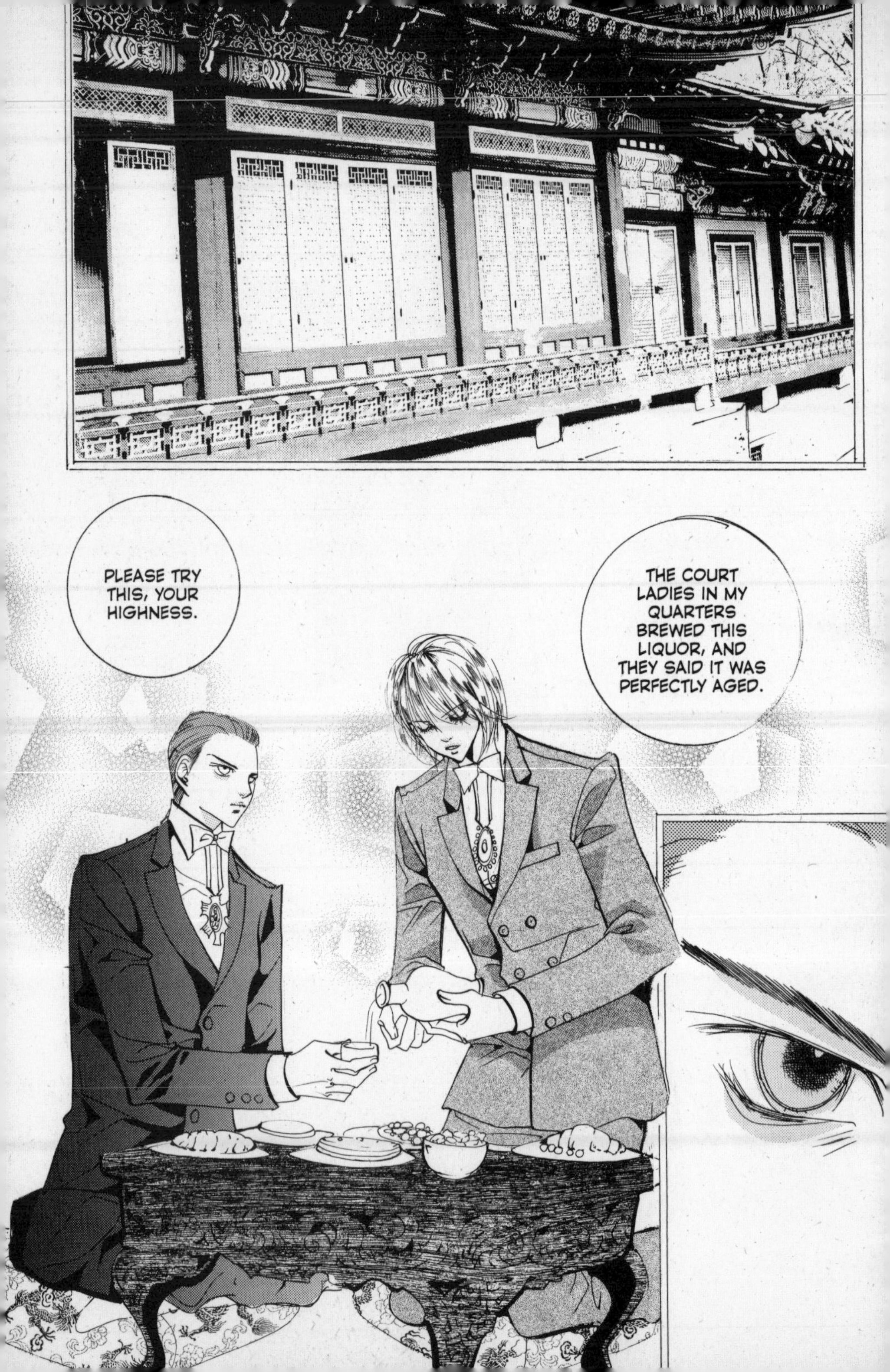
PLEASE TRY THIS, YOUR HIGHNESS.
THE COURT LADIES IN MY QUARTERS BREWED THIS LIQUOR, AND THEY SAID IT WAS PERFECTLY AGED.

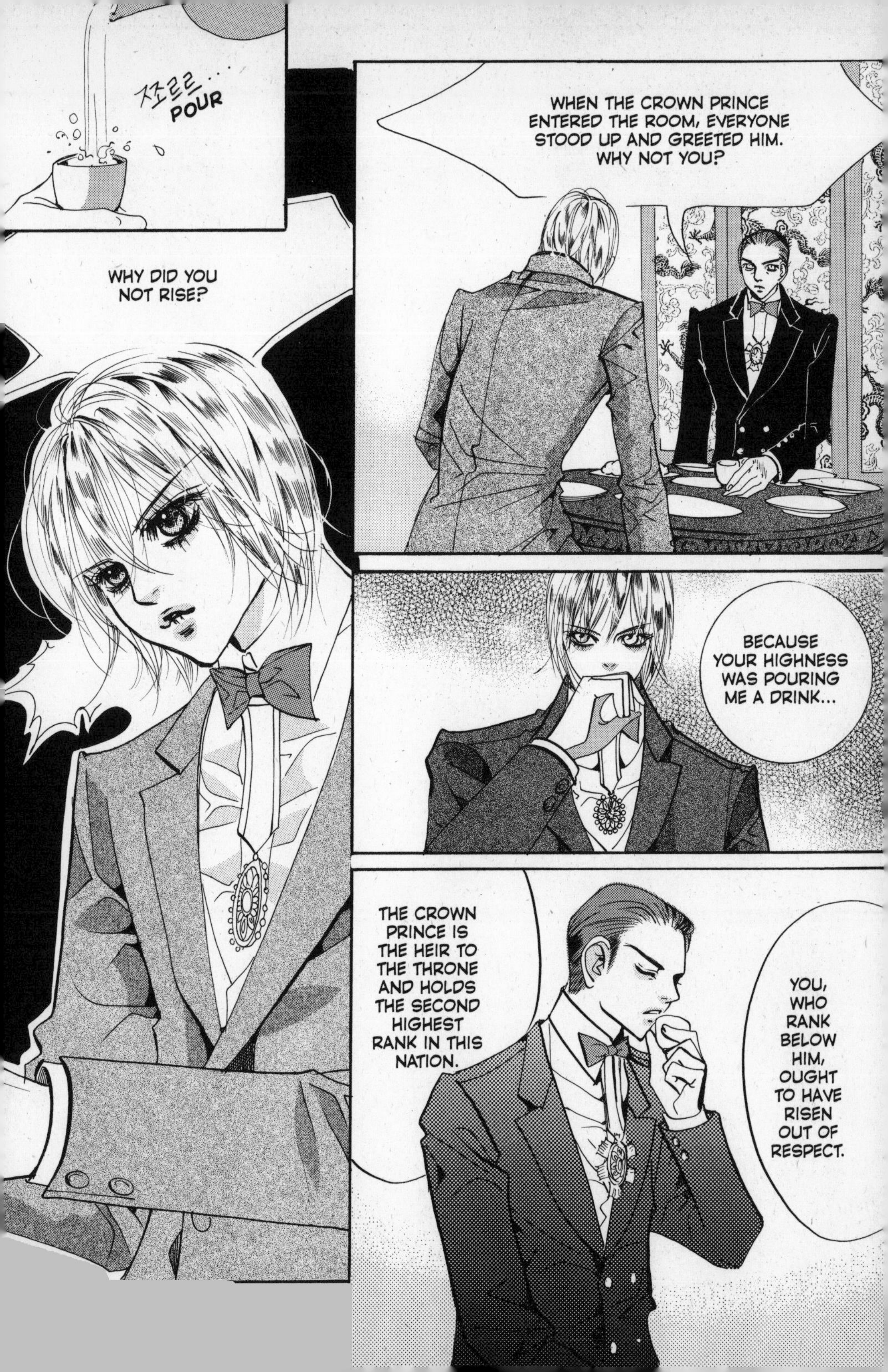

조르르...
POUR
WHY DID YOU NOT RISE?
WHEN THE CROWN PRINCE ENTERED THE ROOM, EVERYONE STOOD UP AND GREETED HIM. WHY NOT YOU?
BECAUSE YOUR HIGHNESS WAS POURING ME A DRINK...
THE CROWN PRINCE IS THE HEIR TO THE THRONE AND HOLDS THE SECOND HIGHEST RANK IN THIS NATION.
YOU, WHO RANK BELOW HIM, OUGHT TO HAVE RISEN OUT OF RESPECT.

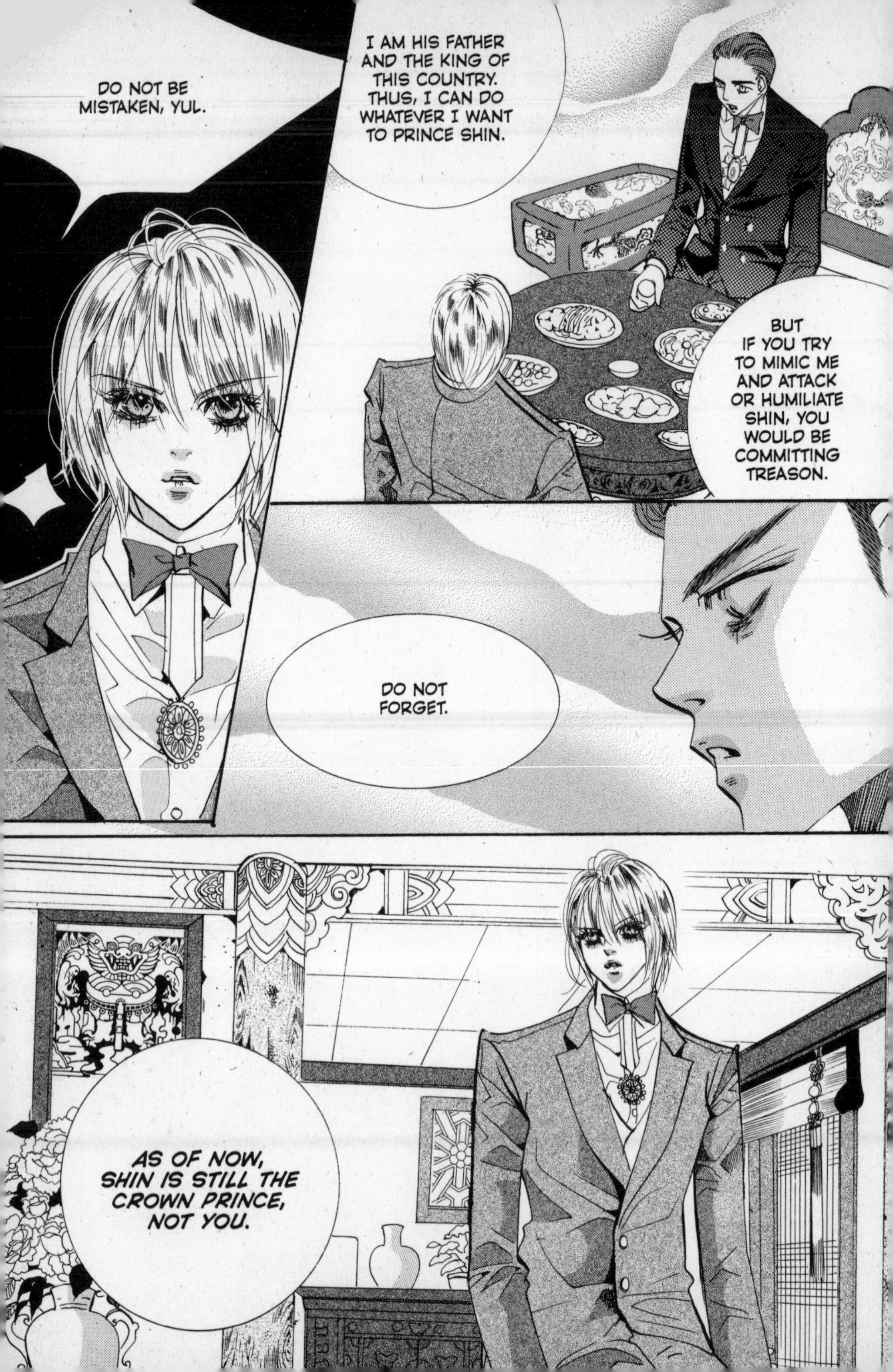
DO NOT BE MISTAKEN, YUL.
I AM HIS FATHER AND THE KING OF THIS COUNTRY. THUS, I CAN DO WHATEVER I WANT TO PRINCE SHIN.
BUT IF YOU TRY TO MIMIC ME AND ATTACK OR HUMILIATE SHIN, YOU WOULD BE COMMITTING TREASON.
DO NOT FORGET.
AS OF NOW, SHIN IS STILL THE CROWN PRINCE, NOT YOU.

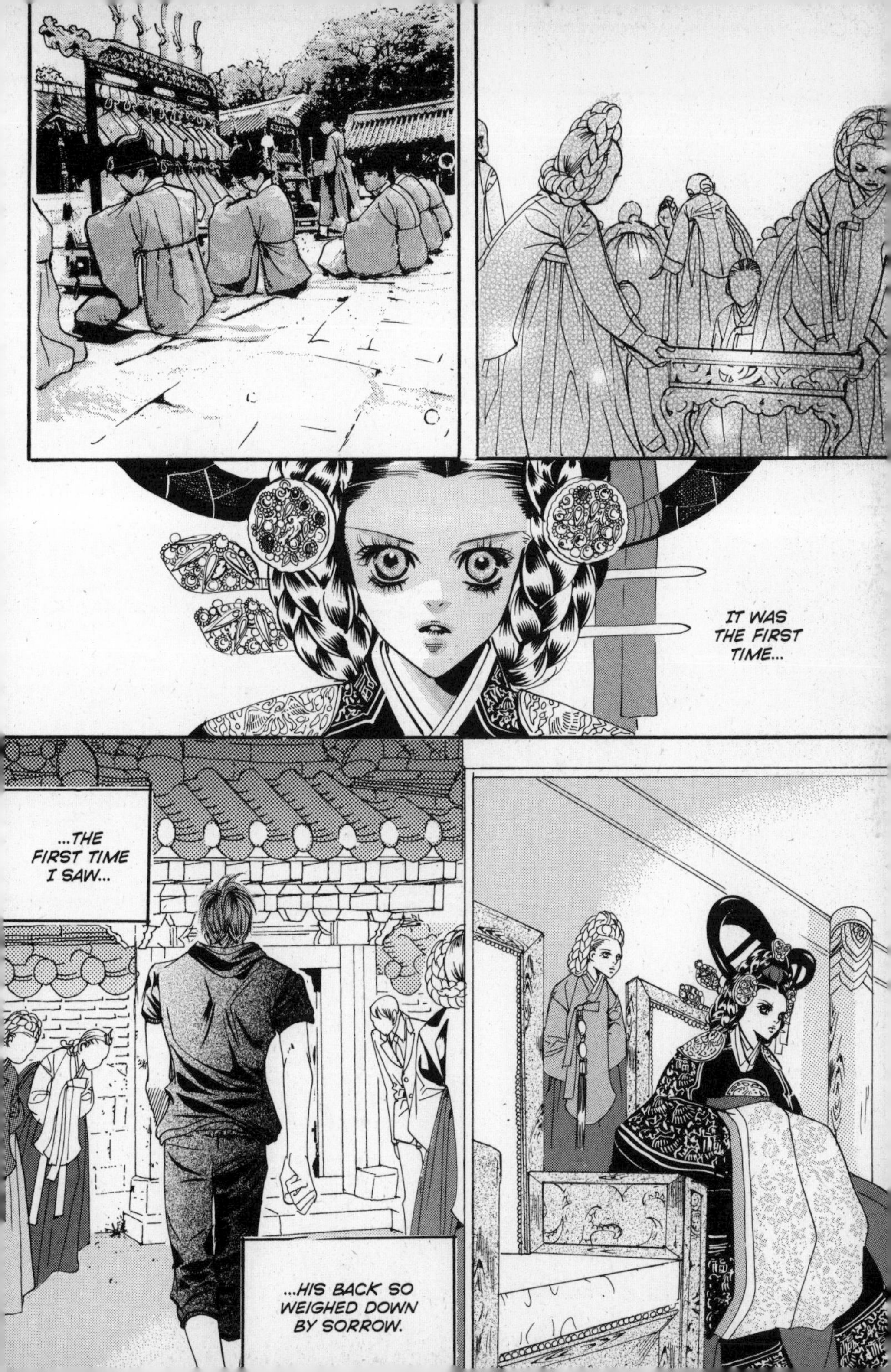
IT WAS THE FIRST TIME...
...THE FIRST TIME I SAW...
...HIS BACK SO WEIGHED DOWN BY SORROW.

SHIN WAS DISGRACED...

...AND YET EVERYONE JUST KEEPS LAUGHING AS IF NOTHING HAPPENED?

HOW COULD EVERYONE BE SO MEAN?

EVERYONE IS FRIGHTENED OF HIS MAJESTY.

THEY DON'T CARE WHAT HAPPENS TO SHIN. THEY ONLY WORRY ABOUT FALLING OUT OF FAVOR WITH HIS FATHER.

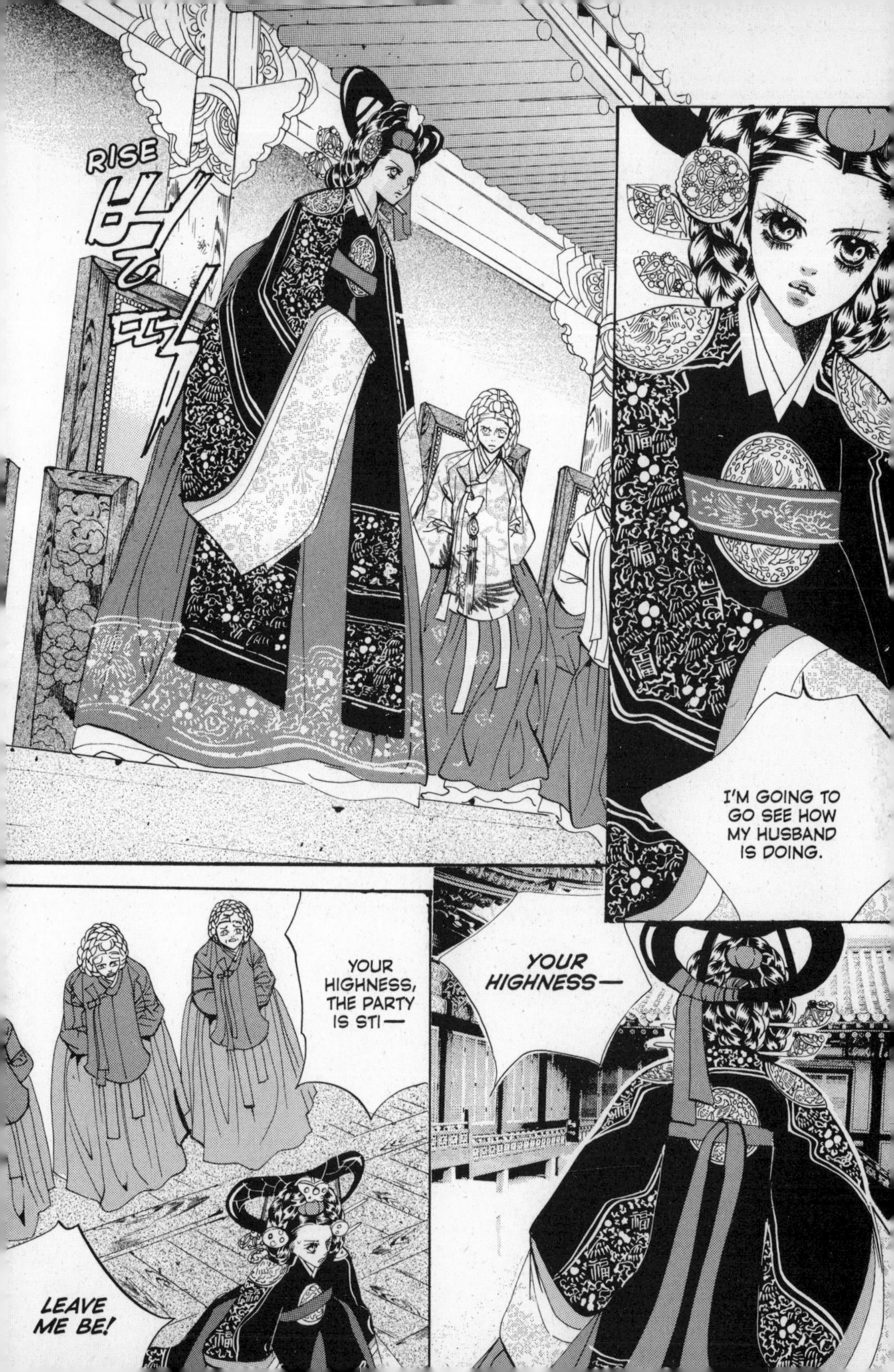
RISE
벌떡
I'M GOING TO GO SEE HOW MY HUSBAND IS DOING.
YOUR HIGHNESS, THE PARTY IS STI—
LEAVE ME BE!
YOUR HIGHNESS—

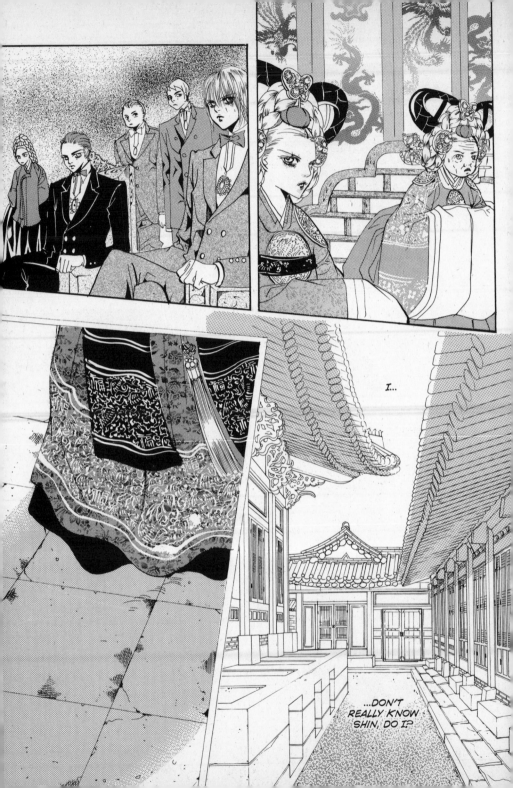

I...

...DON'T
REALLY KNOW
SHIN, DO I?

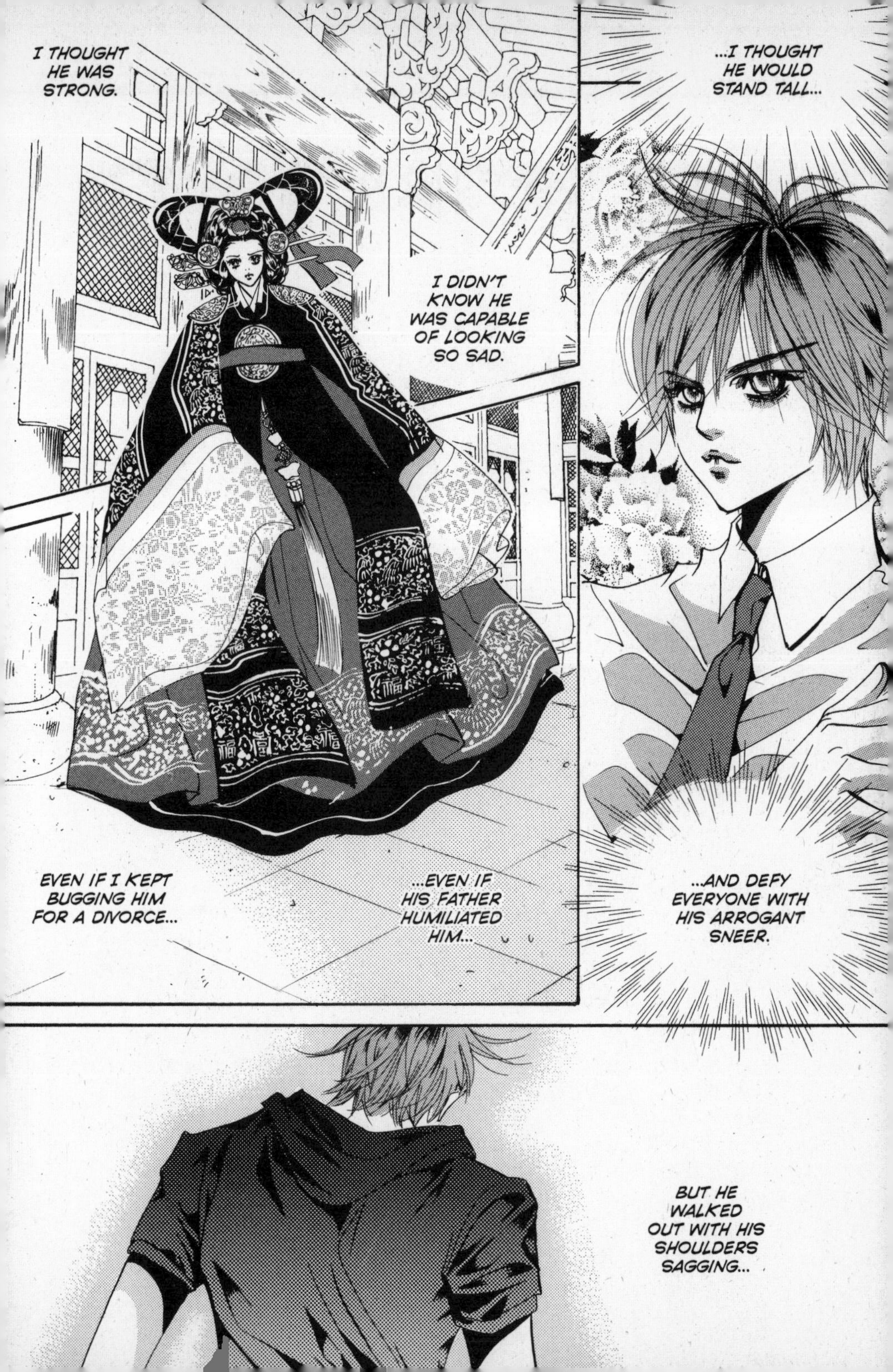
I THOUGHT HE WAS STRONG.
I DIDN'T KNOW HE WAS CAPABLE OF LOOKING SO SAD.
EVEN IF I KEPT BUGGING HIM FOR A DIVORCE...
...EVEN IF HIS FATHER HUMILIATED HIM...
...I THOUGHT HE WOULD STAND TALL...
...AND DEFY EVERYONE WITH HIS ARROGANT SNEER.
BUT HE WALKED OUT WITH HIS SHOULDERS SAGGING...

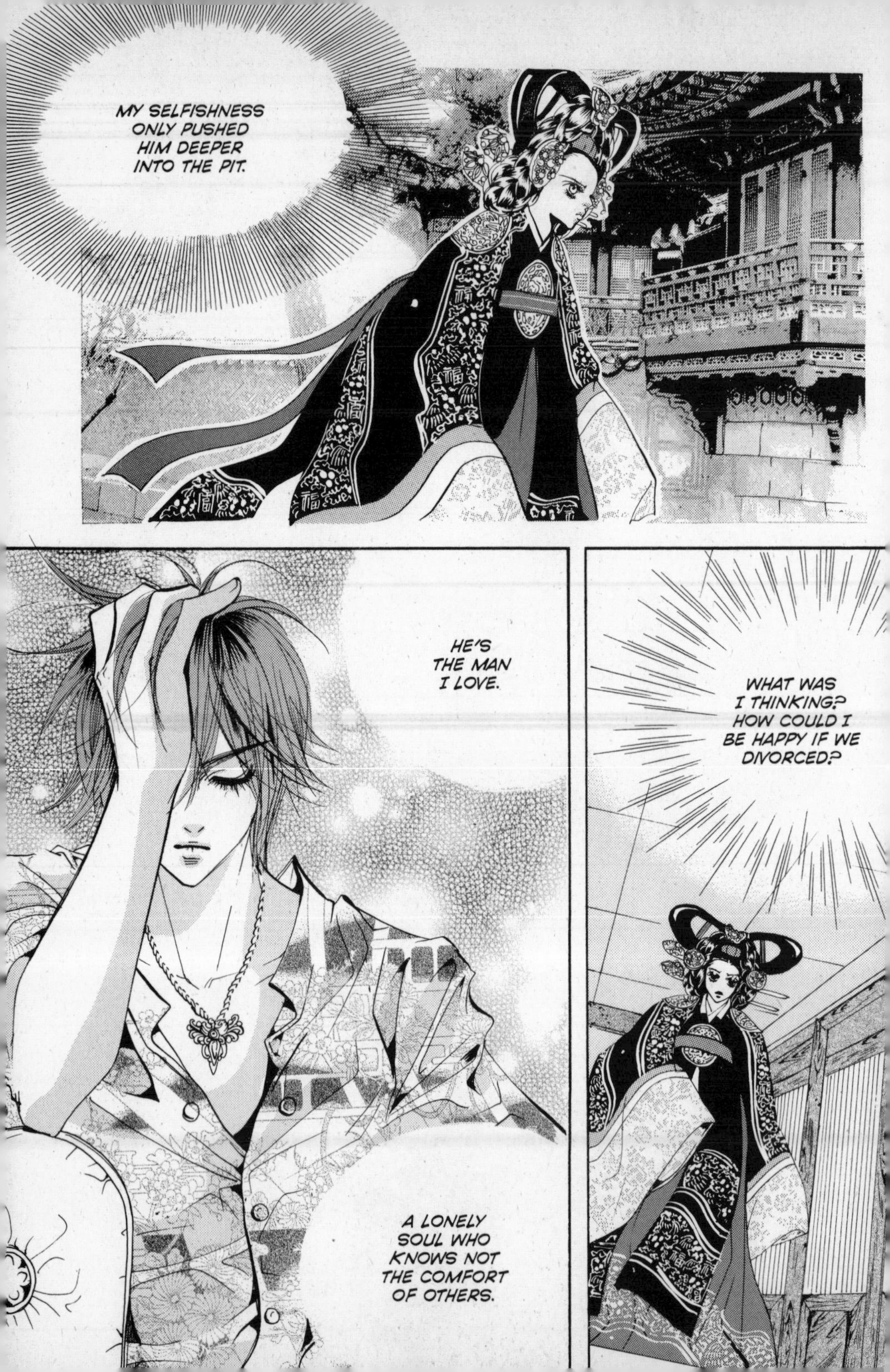
MY SELFISHNESS ONLY PUSHED HIM DEEPER INTO THE PIT.
HE'S THE MAN I LOVE.
A LONELY SOUL WHO KNOWS NOT THE COMFORT OF OTHERS.
WHAT WAS I THINKING? HOW COULD I BE HAPPY IF WE DIVORCED?

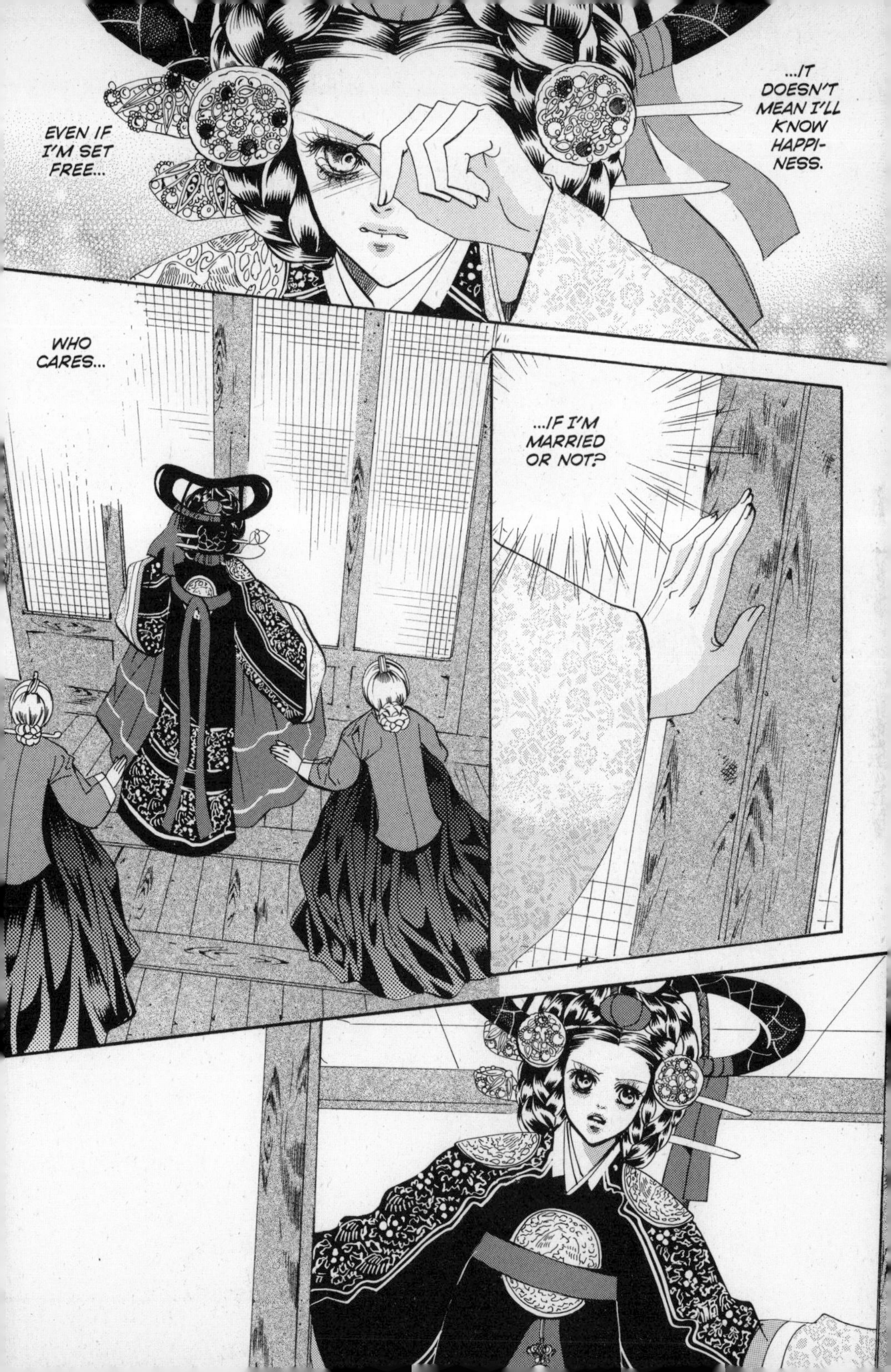
EVEN IF I'M SET FREE...
...IT DOESN'T MEAN I'LL KNOW HAPPI-NESS.
WHO CARES...
...IF I'M MARRIED OR NOT?

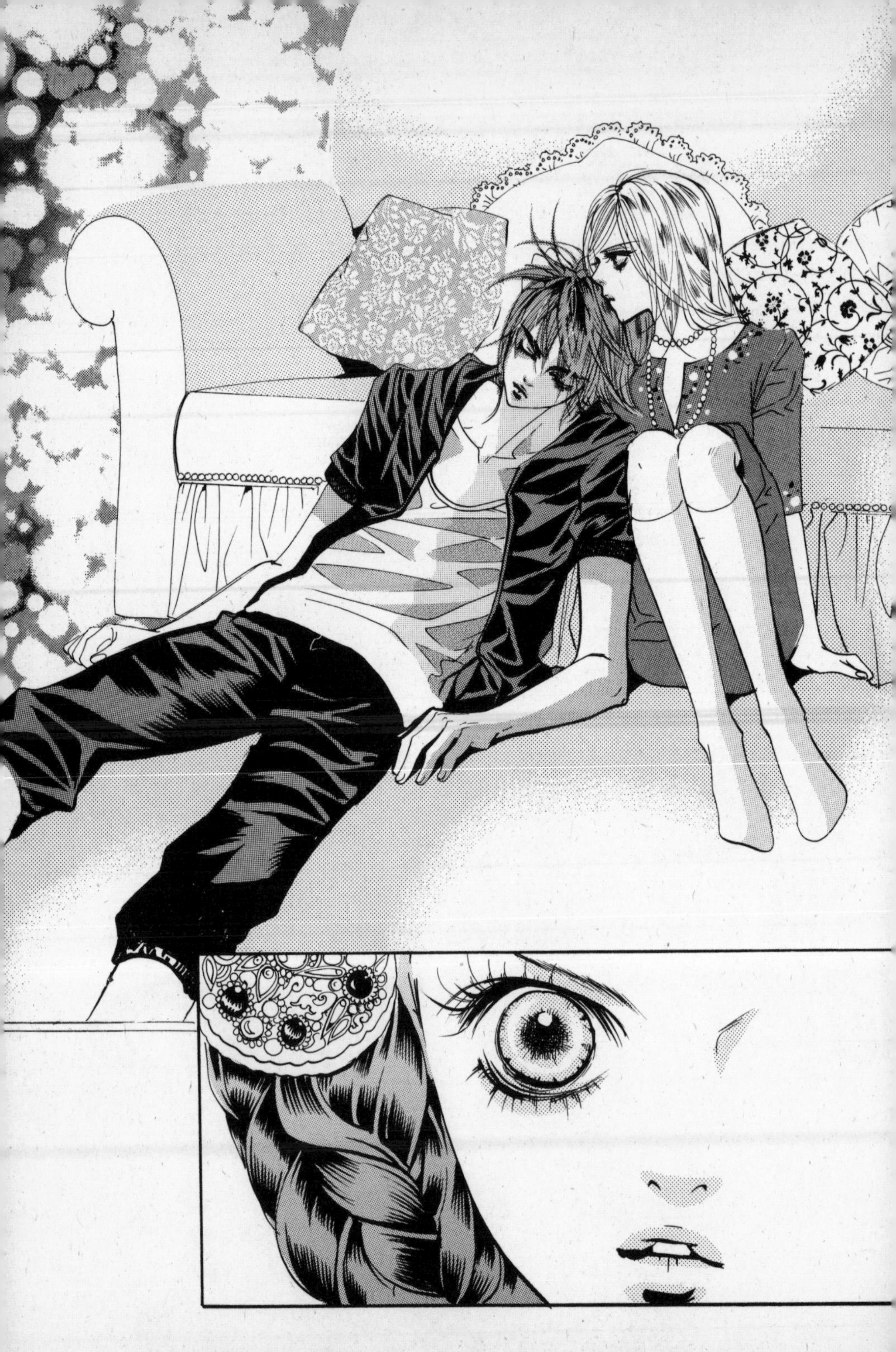

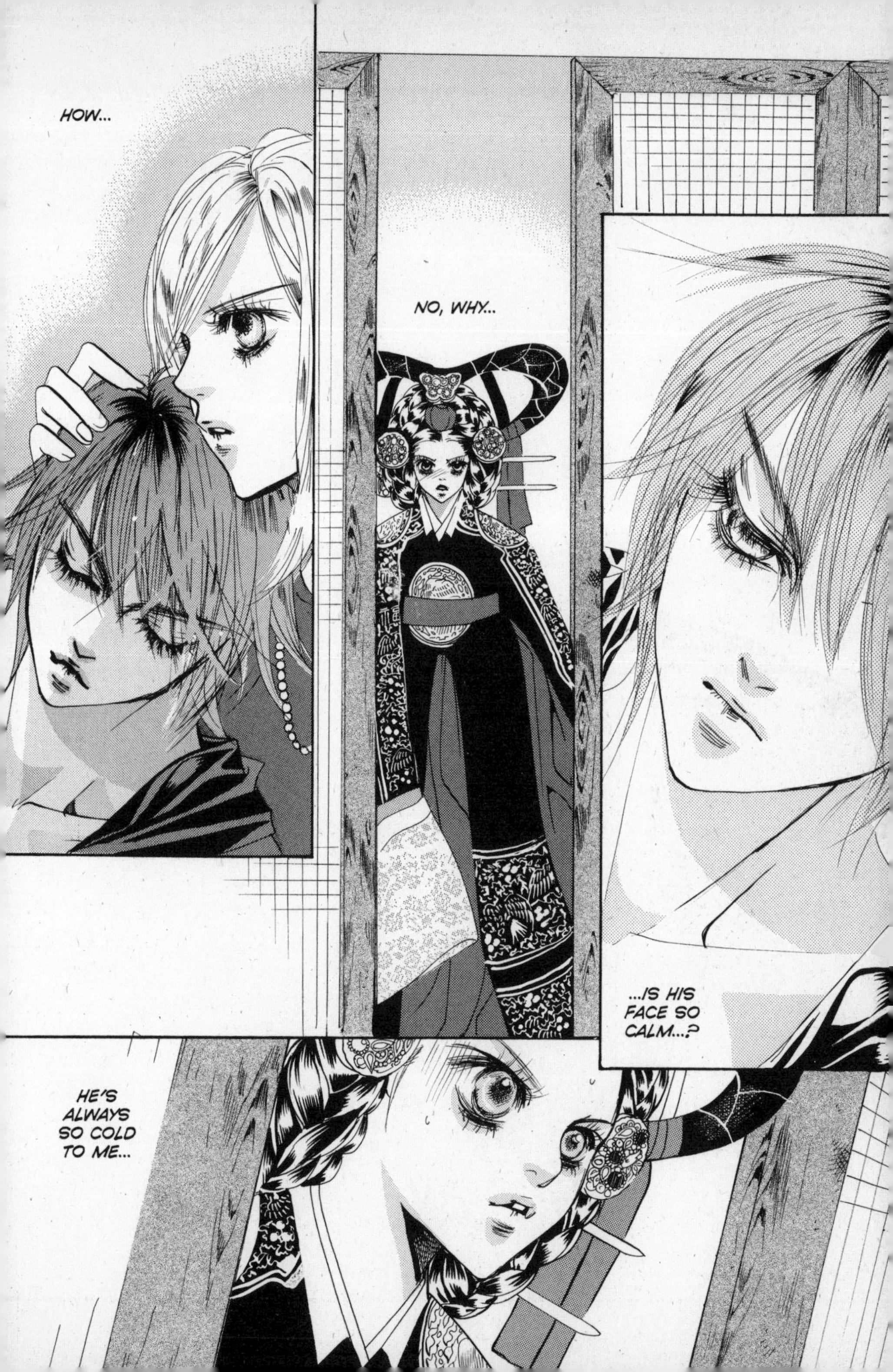
HOW...
NO, WHY...
...IS HIS FACE SO CALM...?
HE'S ALWAYS SO COLD TO ME...

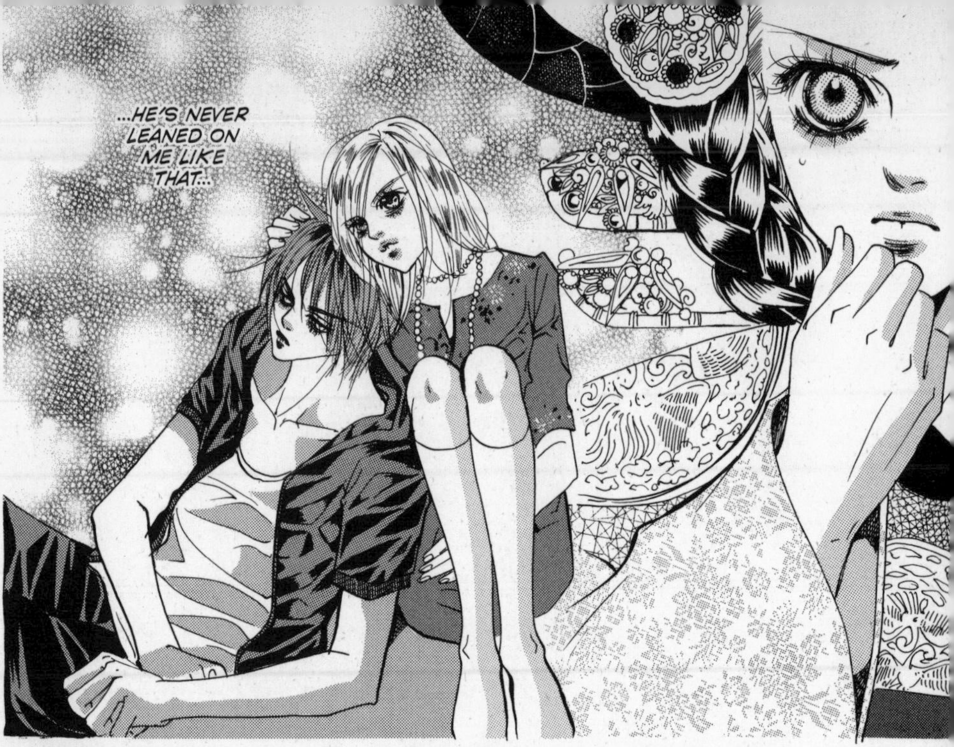
...HE'S NEVER LEANED ON ME LIKE THAT...

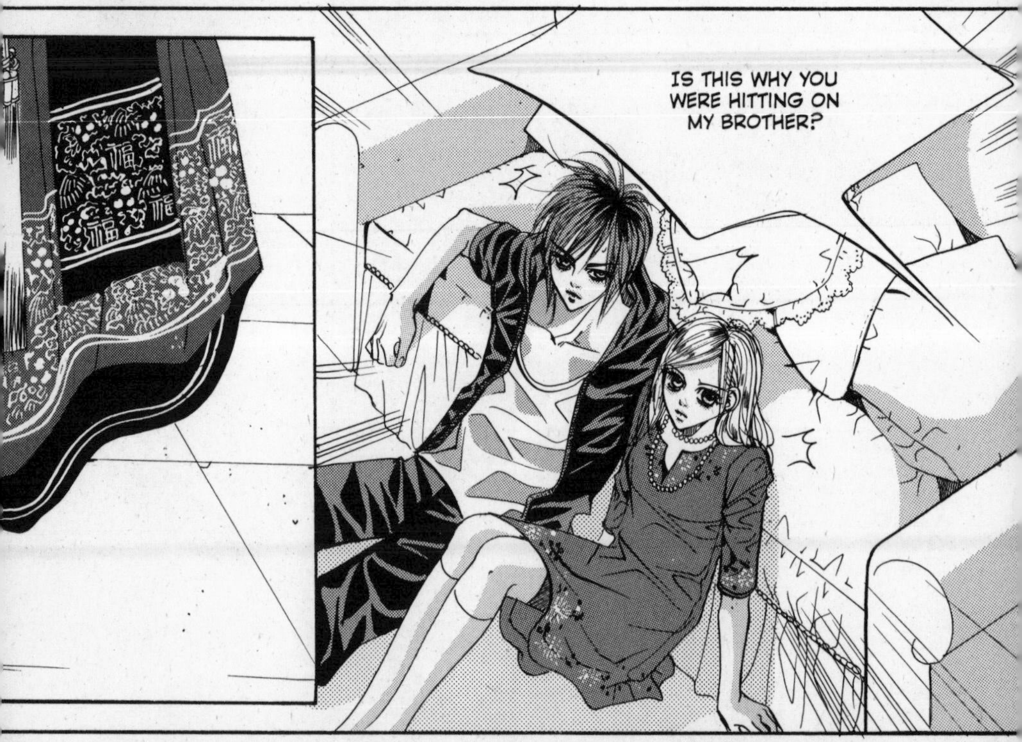
IS THIS WHY YOU WERE HITTING ON MY BROTHER?

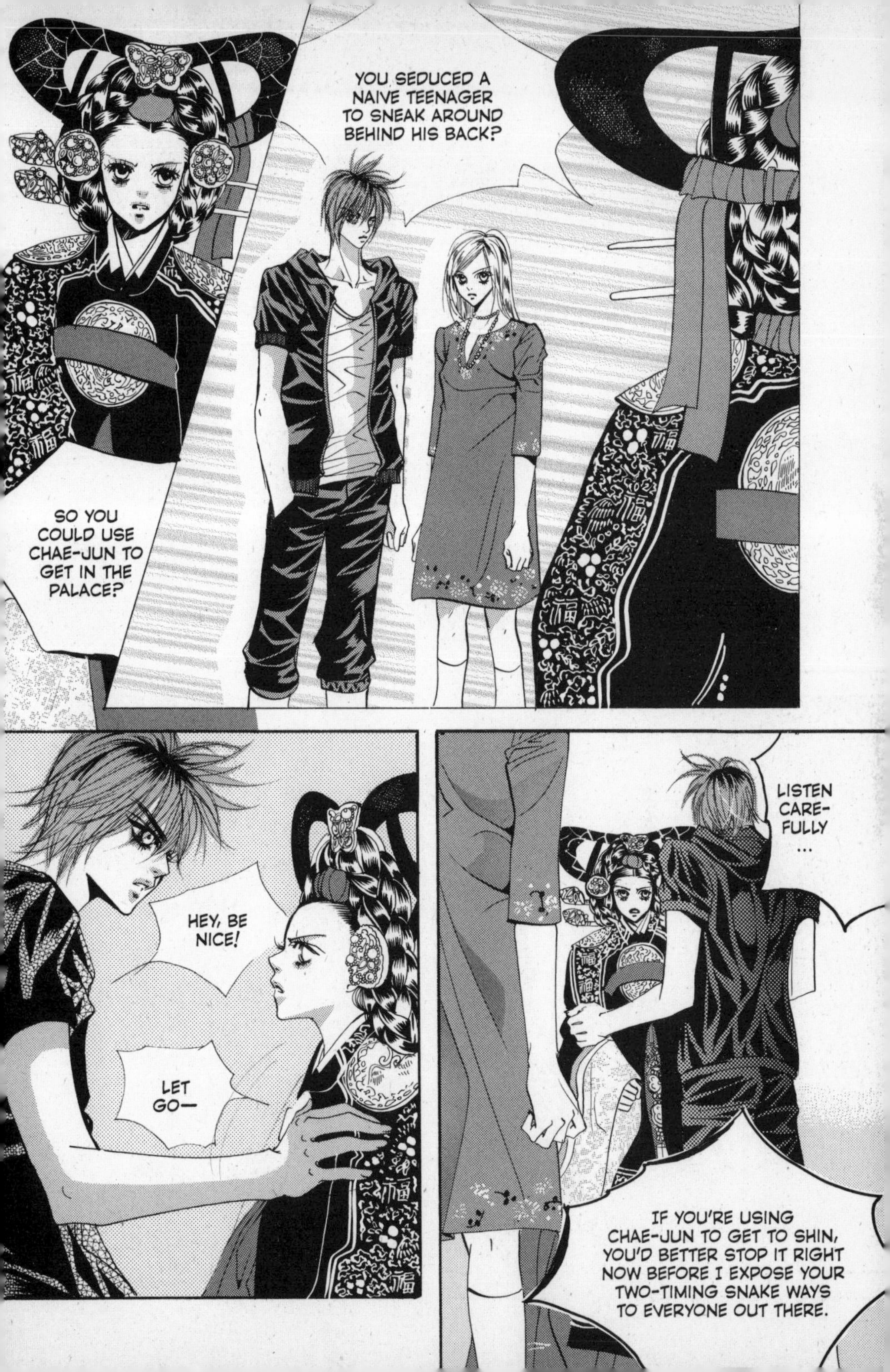
SO YOU COULD USE CHAE-JUN TO GET IN THE PALACE?
YOU SEDUCED A NAIVE TEENAGER TO SNEAK AROUND BEHIND HIS BACK?
HEY, BE NICE!
LET GO—
LISTEN CAREFULLY ...
IF YOU'RE USING CHAE-JUN TO GET TO SHIN, YOU'D BETTER STOP IT RIGHT NOW BEFORE I EXPOSE YOUR TWO-TIMING SNAKE WAYS TO EVERYONE OUT THERE.

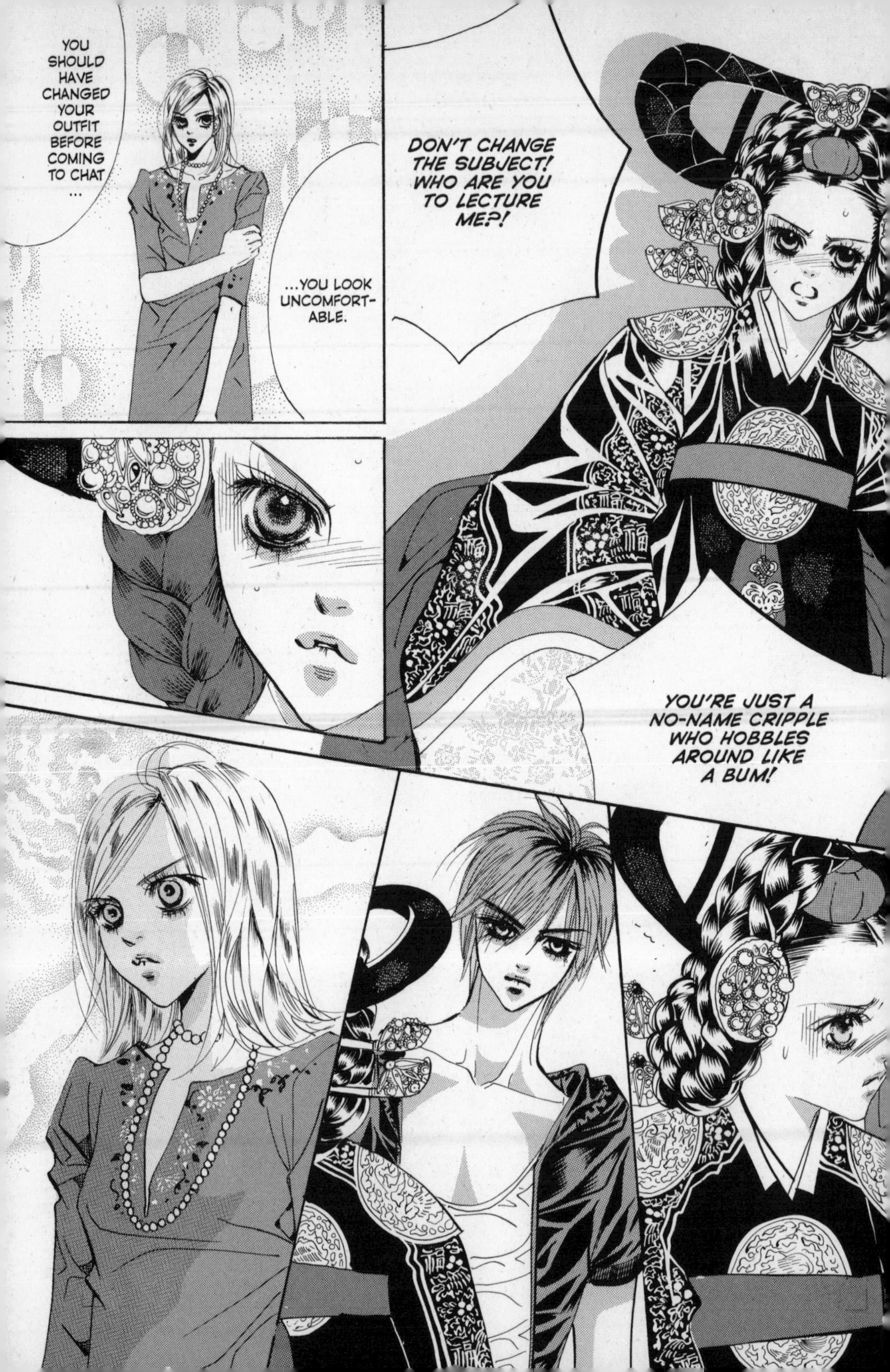
YOU SHOULD HAVE CHANGED YOUR OUTFIT BEFORE COMING TO CHAT ...
...YOU LOOK UNCOMFORTABLE.
DON'T CHANGE THE SUBJECT! WHO ARE YOU TO LECTURE ME?!
YOU'RE JUST A NO-NAME CRIPPLE WHO HOBBLES AROUND LIKE A BUM!

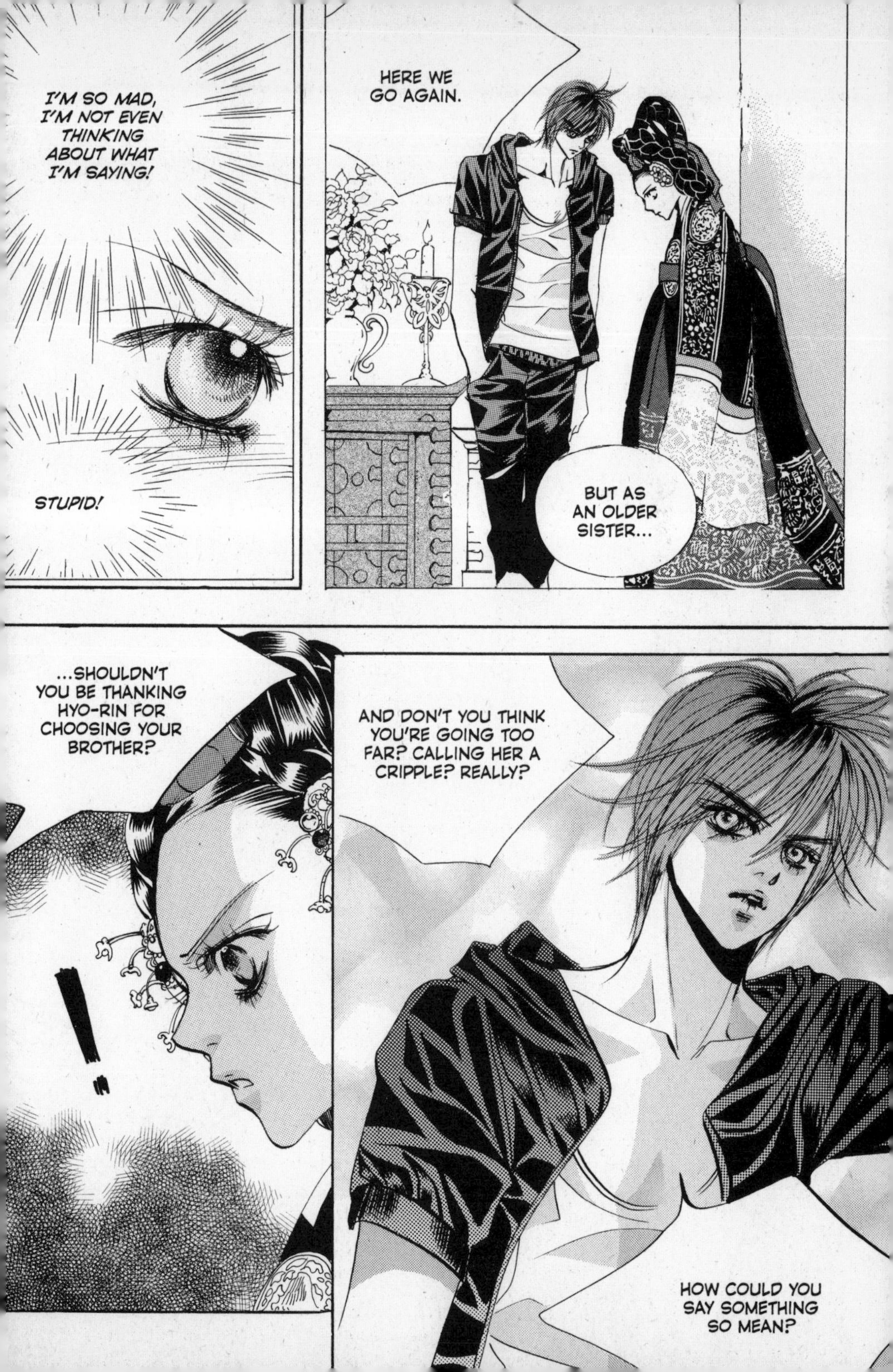
I'M SO MAD, I'M NOT EVEN THINKING ABOUT WHAT I'M SAYING!
STUPID!
HERE WE GO AGAIN.
BUT AS AN OLDER SISTER...
...SHOULDN'T YOU BE THANKING HYO-RIN FOR CHOOSING YOUR BROTHER?
!!
AND DON'T YOU THINK YOU'RE GOING TOO FAR? CALLING HER A CRIPPLE? REALLY?
HOW COULD YOU SAY SOMETHING SO MEAN?

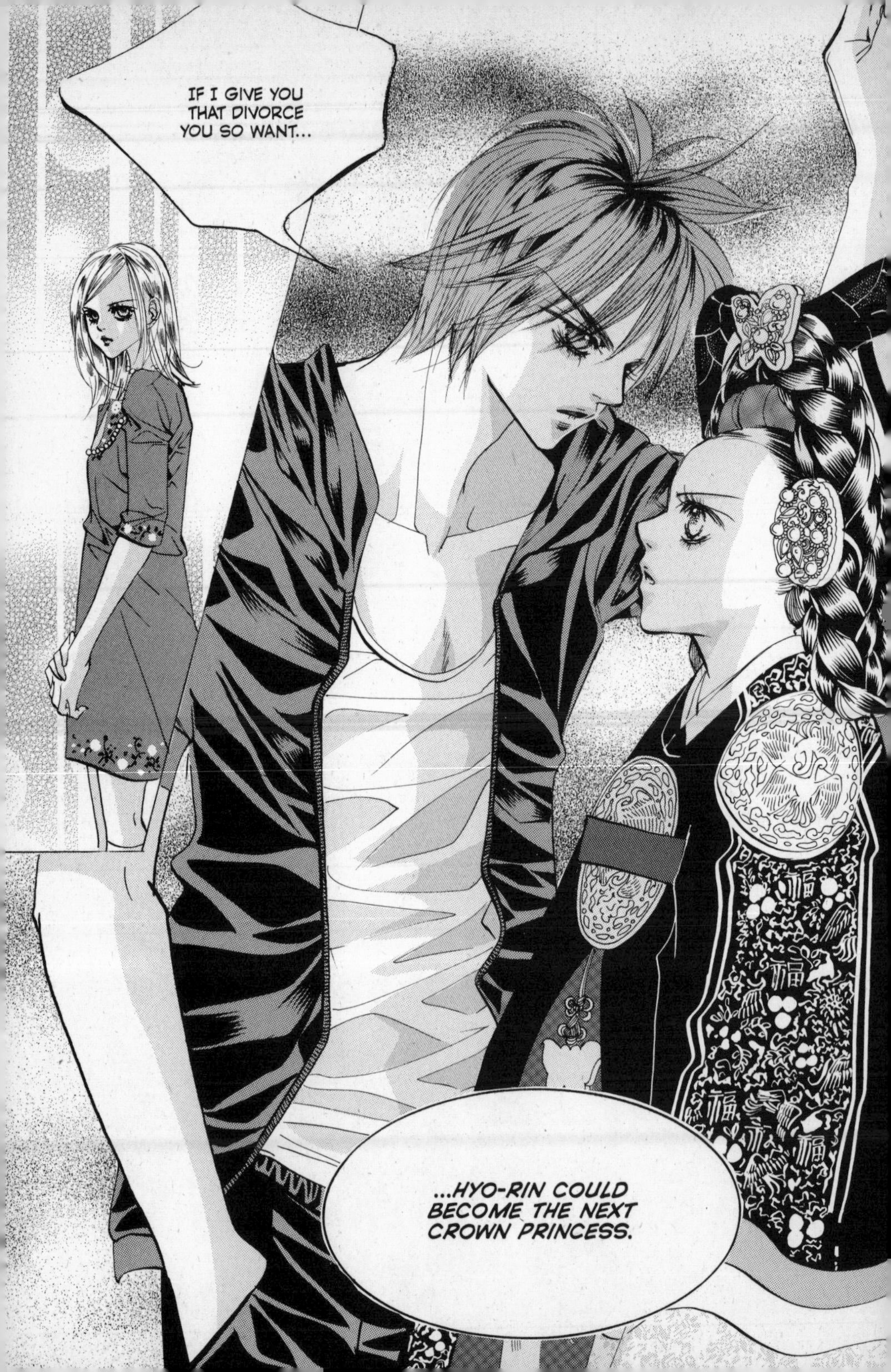
IF I GIVE YOU THAT DIVORCE YOU SO WANT...
...HYO-RIN COULD BECOME THE NEXT CROWN PRINCESS.

The Royal Palace

Goong

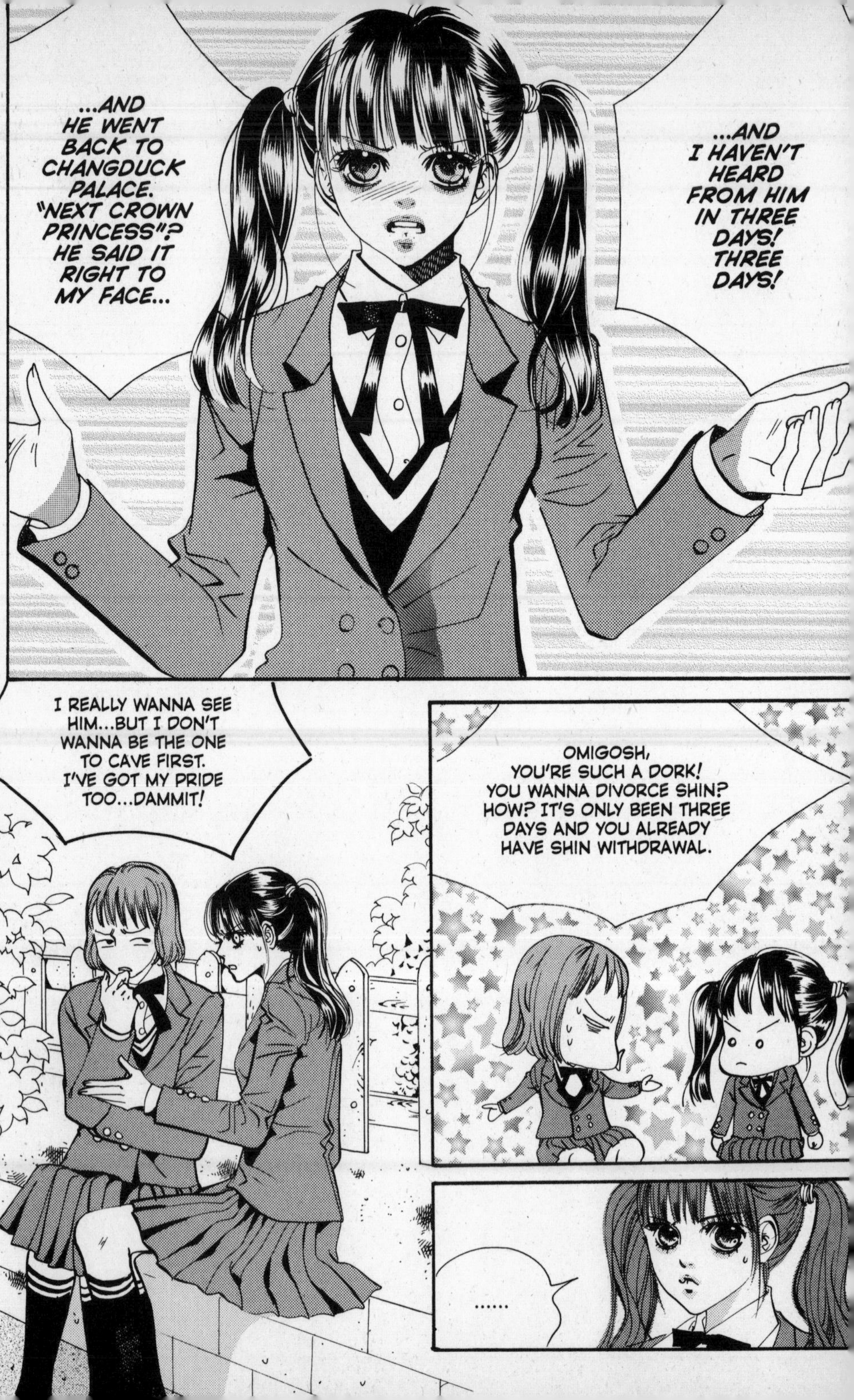
...AND HE WENT BACK TO CHANGDUCK PALACE. "NEXT CROWN PRINCESS"? HE SAID IT RIGHT TO MY FACE...
...AND I HAVEN'T HEARD FROM HIM IN THREE DAYS! THREE DAYS!
I REALLY WANNA SEE HIM...BUT I DON'T WANNA BE THE ONE TO CAVE FIRST. I'VE GOT MY PRIDE TOO...DAMMIT!
OMIGOSH, YOU'RE SUCH A DORK! YOU WANNA DIVORCE SHIN? HOW? IT'S ONLY BEEN THREE DAYS AND YOU ALREADY HAVE SHIN WITHDRAWAL.
......

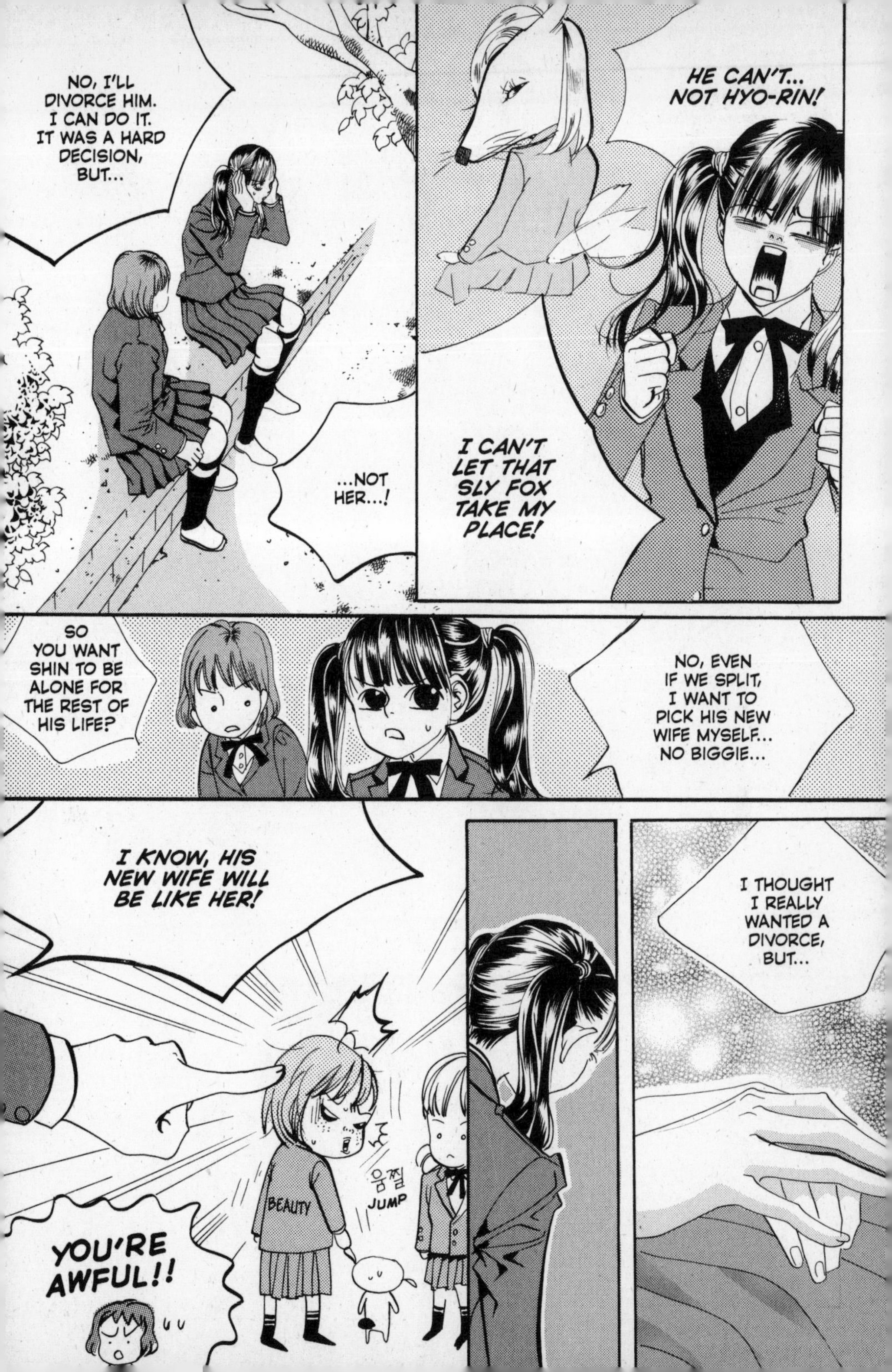
NO, I'LL DIVORCE HIM. I CAN DO IT. IT WAS A HARD DECISION, BUT...
...NOT HER...!
HE CAN'T... NOT HYO-RIN!
I CAN'T LET THAT SLY FOX TAKE MY PLACE!
SO YOU WANT SHIN TO BE ALONE FOR THE REST OF HIS LIFE?
NO, EVEN IF WE SPLIT, I WANT TO PICK HIS NEW WIFE MYSELF... NO BIGGIE...
I KNOW, HIS NEW WIFE WILL BE LIKE HER!
BEAUTY
움찔
JUMP
YOU'RE AWFUL!!
I THOUGHT I REALLY WANTED A DIVORCE, BUT...

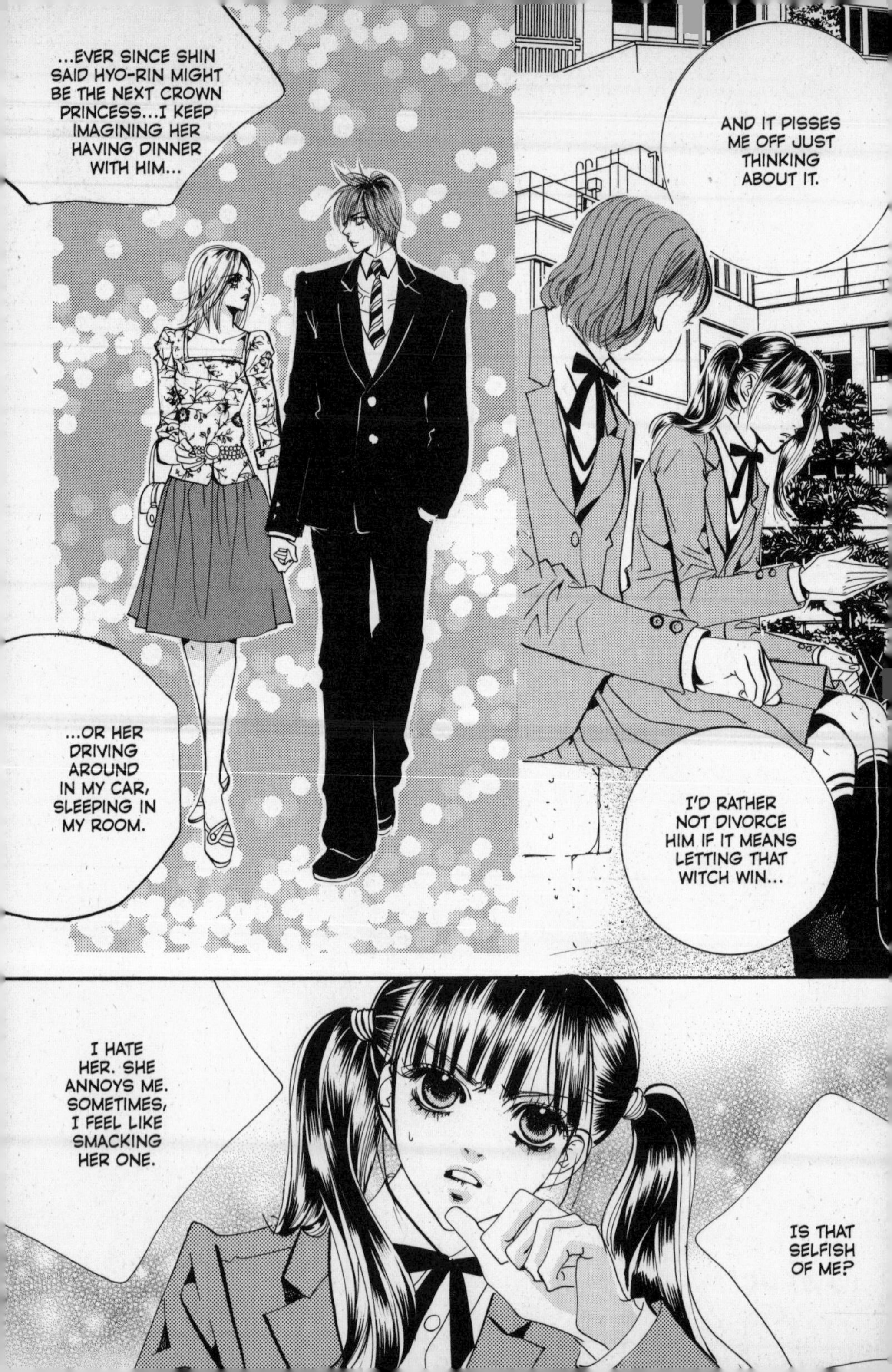
...EVER SINCE SHIN SAID HYO-RIN MIGHT BE THE NEXT CROWN PRINCESS...I KEEP IMAGINING HER HAVING DINNER WITH HIM...
...OR HER DRIVING AROUND IN MY CAR, SLEEPING IN MY ROOM...
AND IT PISSES ME OFF JUST THINKING ABOUT IT.
I'D RATHER NOT DIVORCE HIM IF IT MEANS LETTING THAT WITCH WIN...
I HATE HER. SHE ANNOYS ME. SOMETIMES, I FEEL LIKE SMACKING HER ONE.
IS THAT SELFISH OF ME?

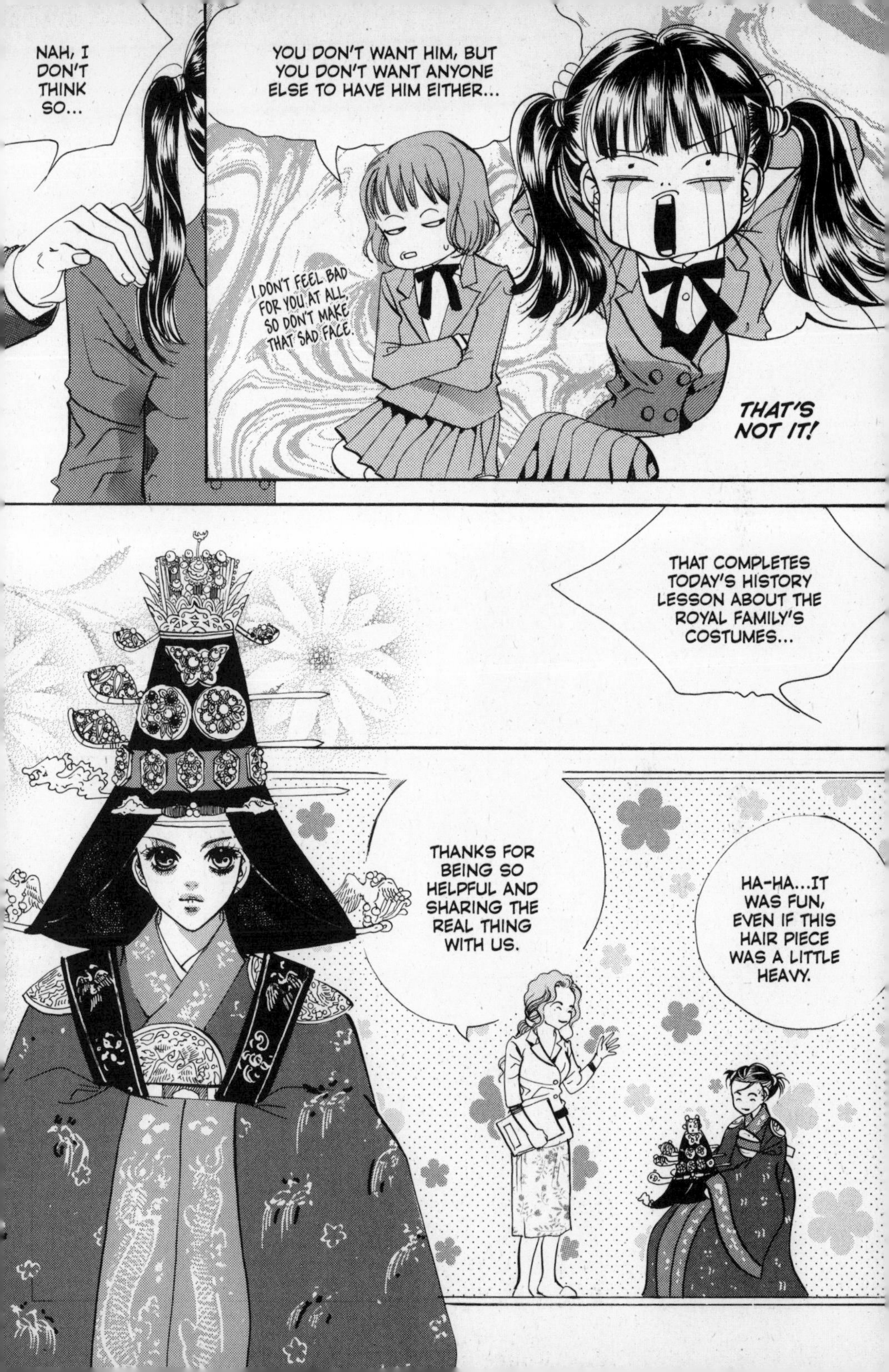
NAH, I DON'T THINK SO...
YOU DON'T WANT HIM, BUT YOU DON'T WANT ANYONE ELSE TO HAVE HIM EITHER...
I DON'T FEEL BAD FOR YOU AT ALL, SO DON'T MAKE THAT SAD FACE.
THAT'S NOT IT!
THAT COMPLETES TODAY'S HISTORY LESSON ABOUT THE ROYAL FAMILY'S COSTUMES...
THANKS FOR BEING SO HELPFUL AND SHARING THE REAL THING WITH US.
HA-HA...IT WAS FUN, EVEN IF THIS HAIR PIECE WAS A LITTLE HEAVY.

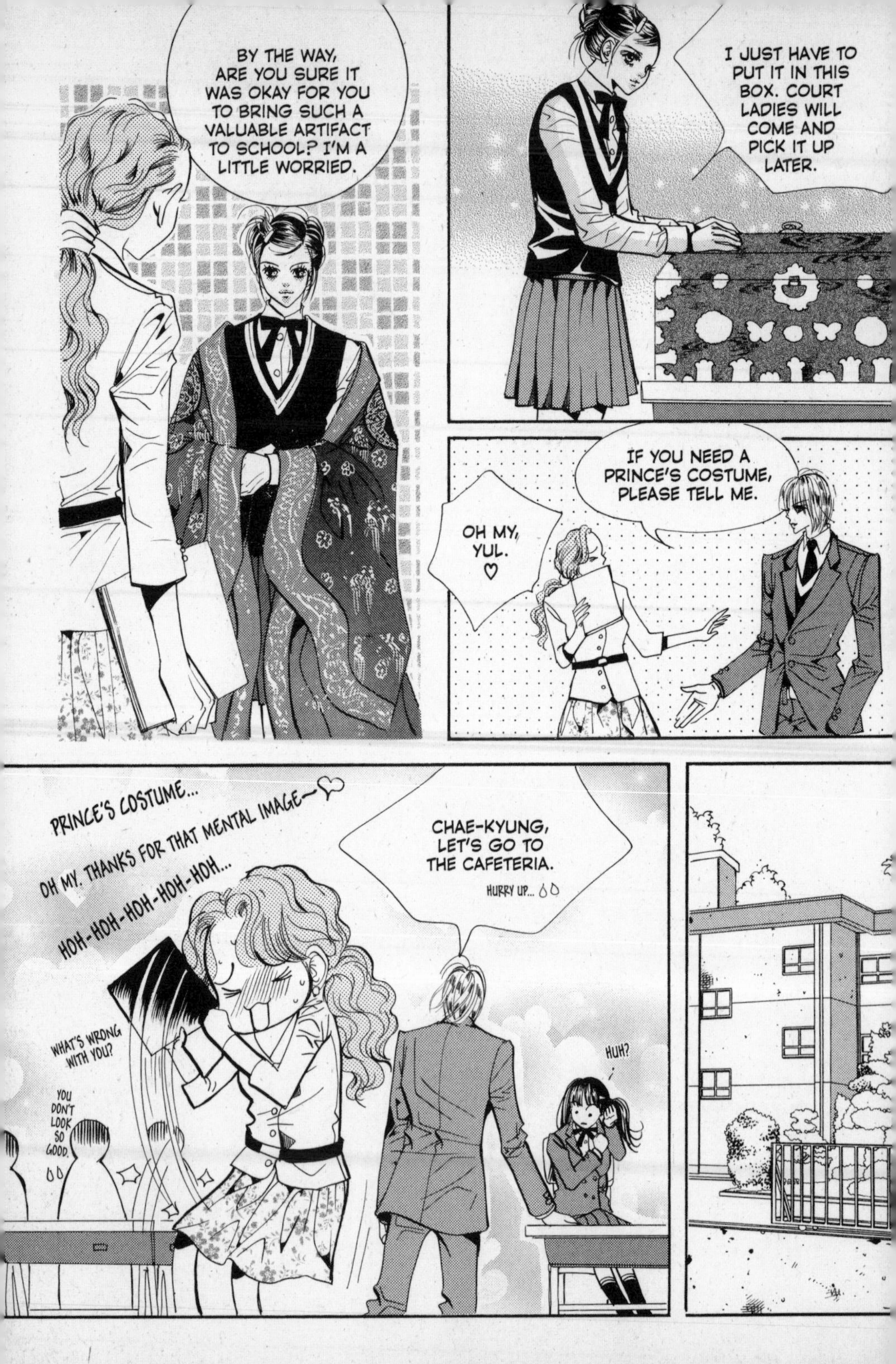
BY THE WAY, ARE YOU SURE IT WAS OKAY FOR YOU TO BRING SUCH A VALUABLE ARTIFACT TO SCHOOL? I'M A LITTLE WORRIED.
I JUST HAVE TO PUT IT IN THIS BOX. COURT LADIES WILL COME AND PICK IT UP LATER.
OH MY, YUL. ♡
IF YOU NEED A PRINCE'S COSTUME, PLEASE TELL ME.
PRINCE'S COSTUME...
OH MY. THANKS FOR THAT MENTAL IMAGE~♡
HOH-HOH-HOH-HOH-HOH...
WHAT'S WRONG WITH YOU?
YOU DON'T LOOK SO GOOD.
CHAE-KYUNG, LET'S GO TO THE CAFETERIA.
HURRY UP...
HUH?

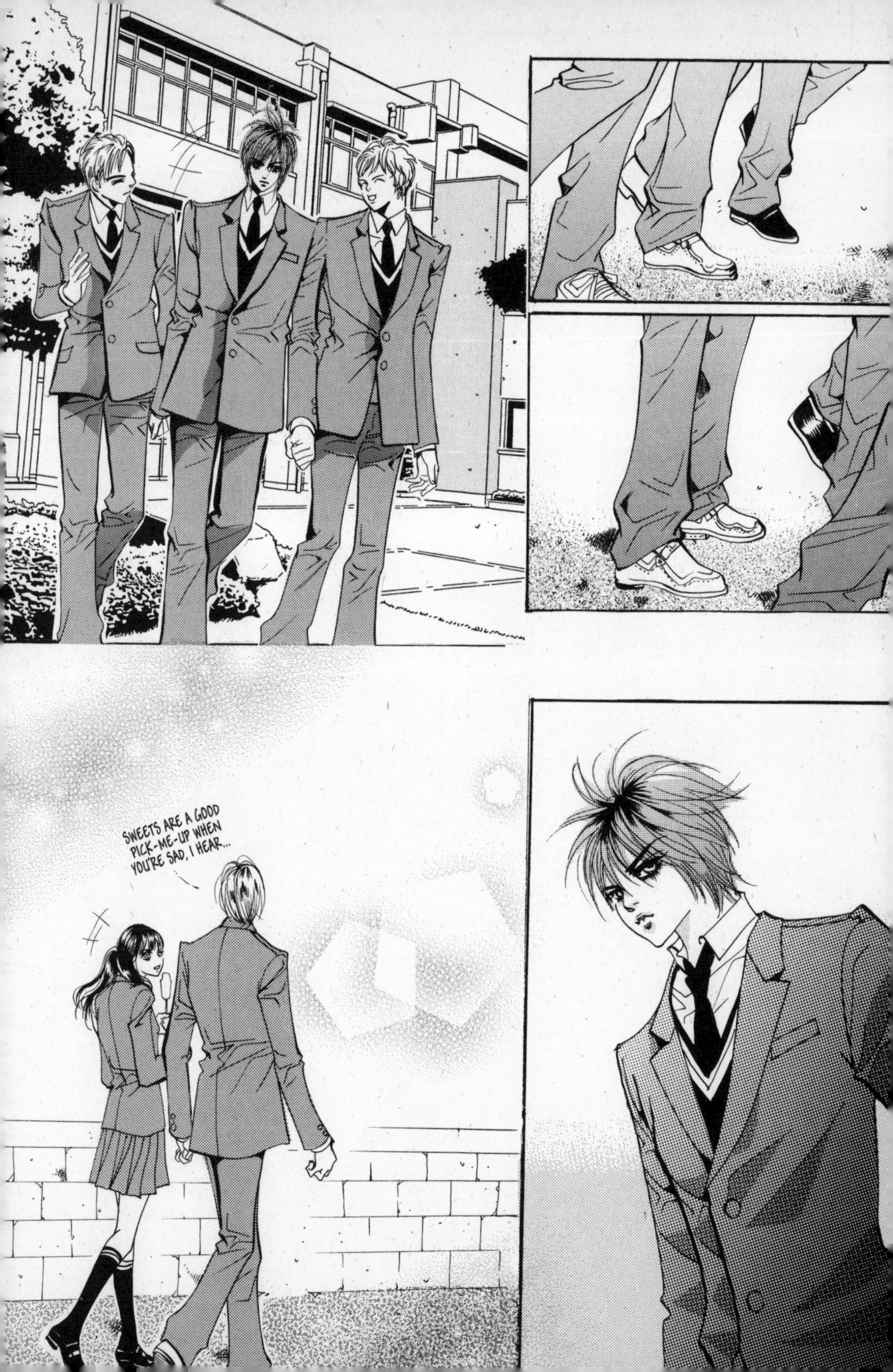
SWEETS ARE A GOOD PICK-ME-UP WHEN YOU'RE SAD, I HEAR...

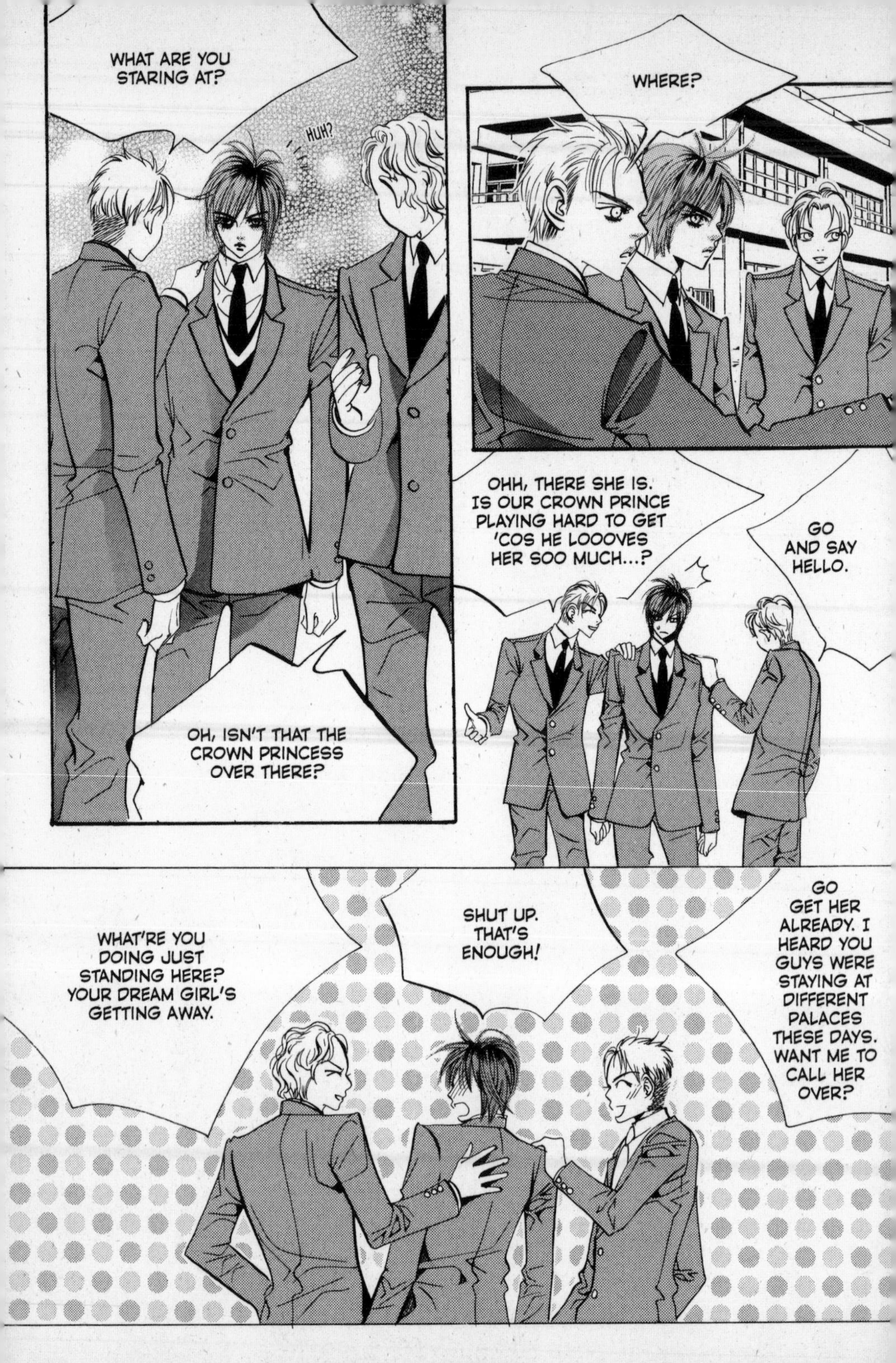
WHAT ARE YOU STARING AT?
HUH?
OH, ISN'T THAT THE CROWN PRINCESS OVER THERE?
WHERE?
OHH, THERE SHE IS. IS OUR CROWN PRINCE PLAYING HARD TO GET 'COS HE LOOOVES HER SOO MUCH...?
GO AND SAY HELLO.
WHAT'RE YOU DOING JUST STANDING HERE? YOUR DREAM GIRL'S GETTING AWAY.
SHUT UP. THAT'S ENOUGH!
GO GET HER ALREADY. I HEARD YOU GUYS WERE STAYING AT DIFFERENT PALACES THESE DAYS. WANT ME TO CALL HER OVER?

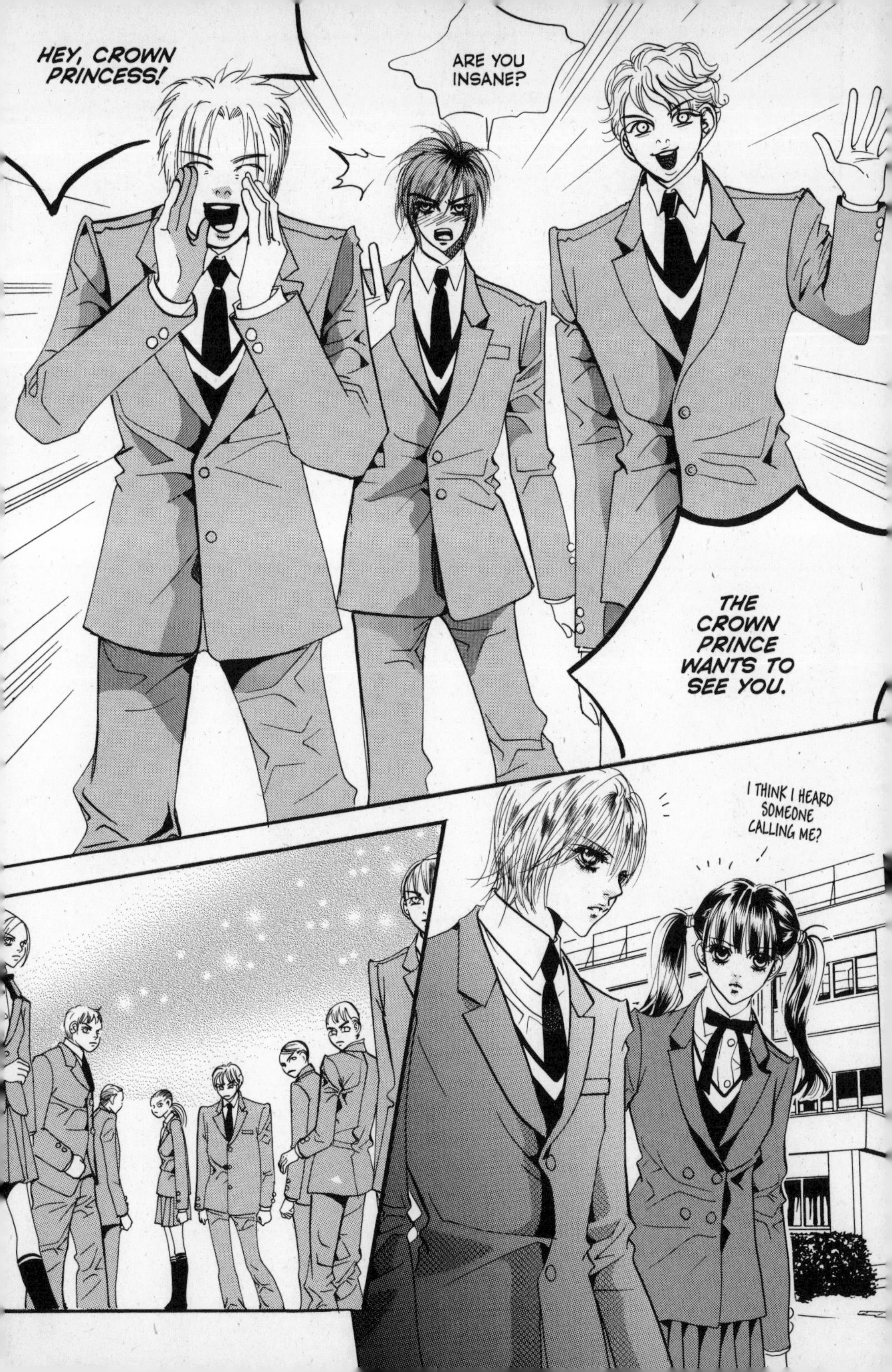
HEY, CROWN PRINCESS!
ARE YOU INSANE?
THE CROWN PRINCE WANTS TO SEE YOU.
I THINK I HEARD SOMEONE CALLING ME?

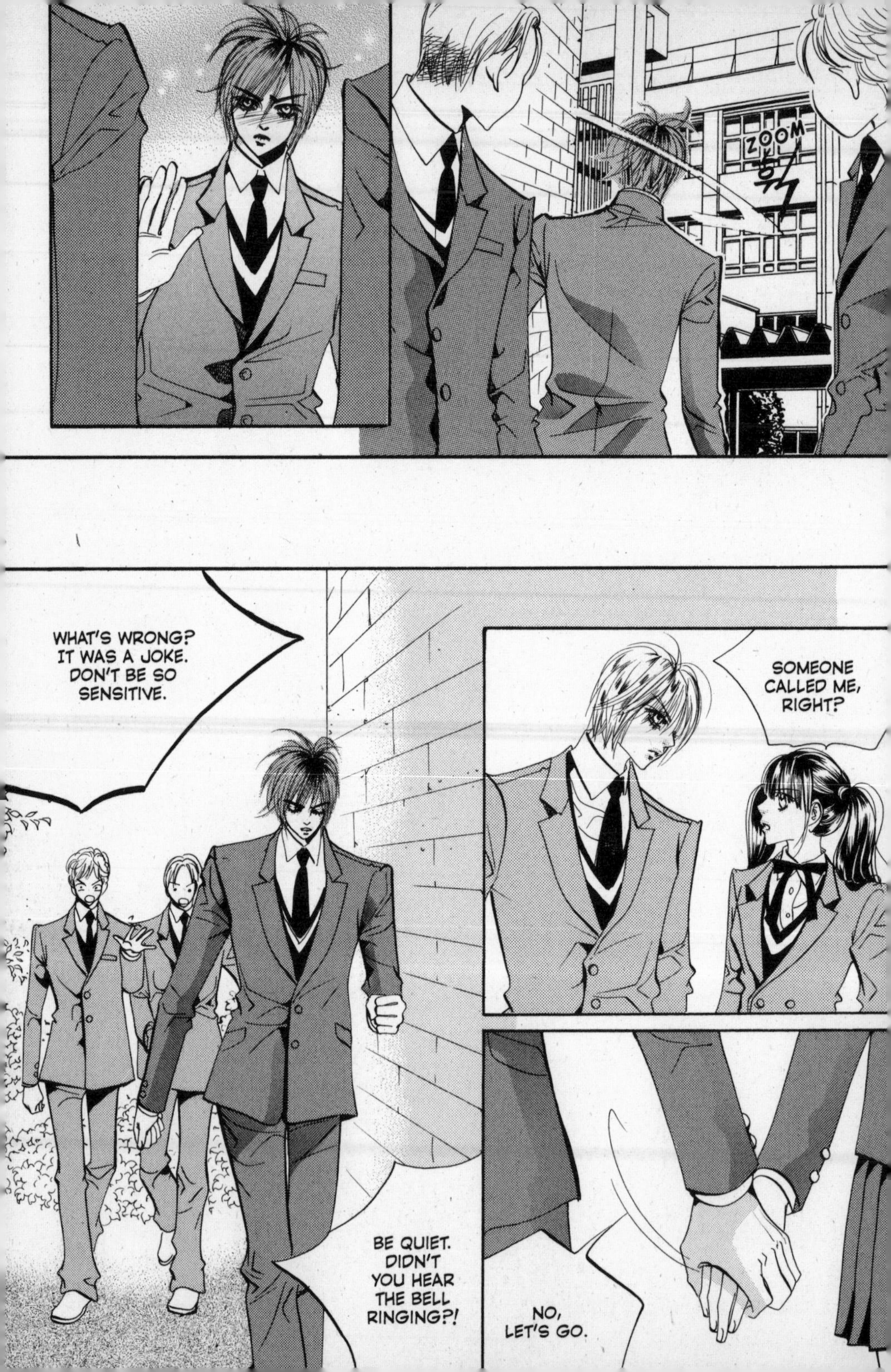
ZOOM
WHAT'S WRONG? IT WAS A JOKE. DON'T BE SO SENSITIVE.
BE QUIET. DIDN'T YOU HEAR THE BELL RINGING?!
SOMEONE CALLED ME, RIGHT?
NO, LET'S GO.

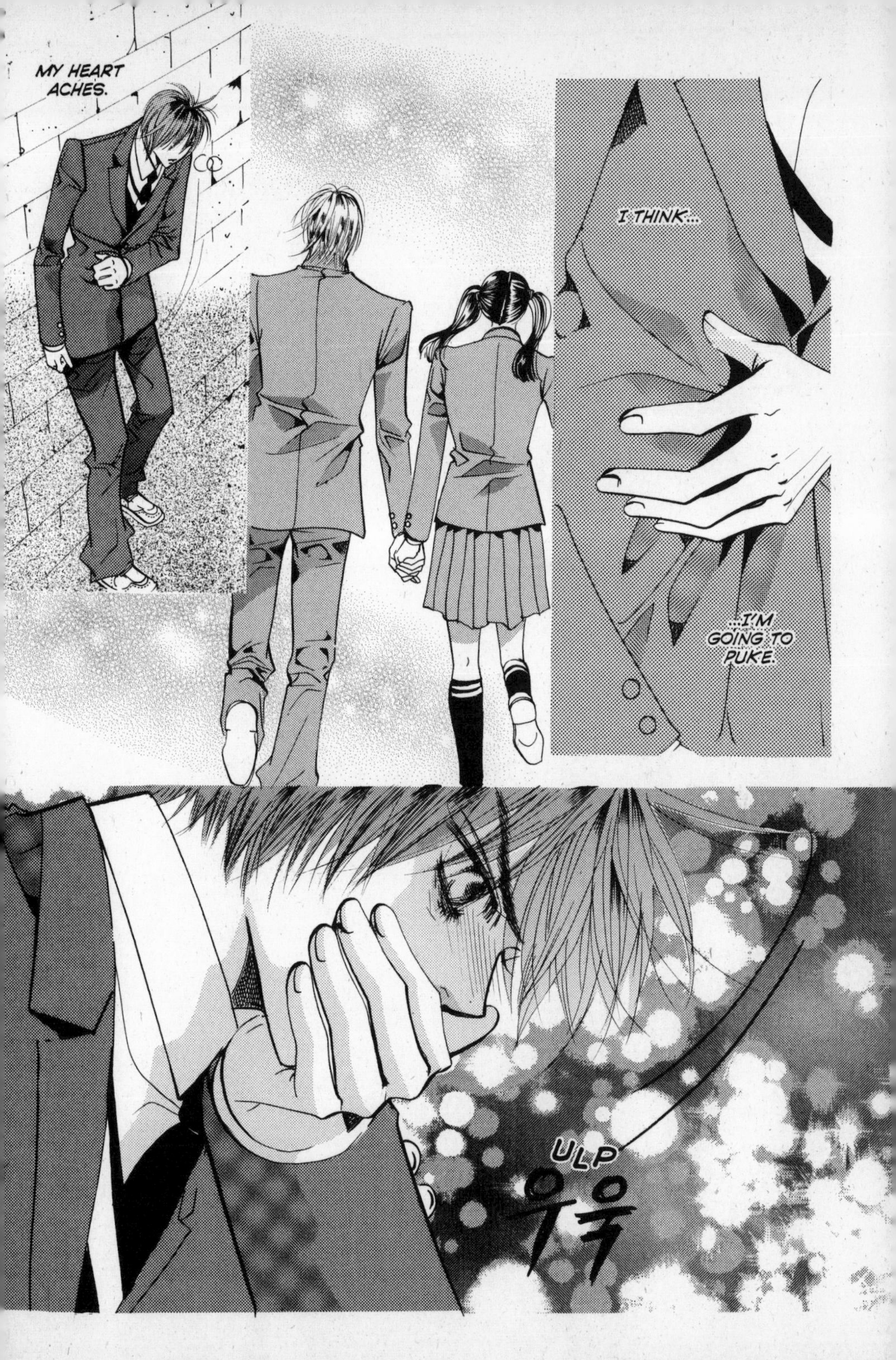
MY HEART ACHES.
I THINK...
...I'M GOING TO PUKE.
ULP
우욱

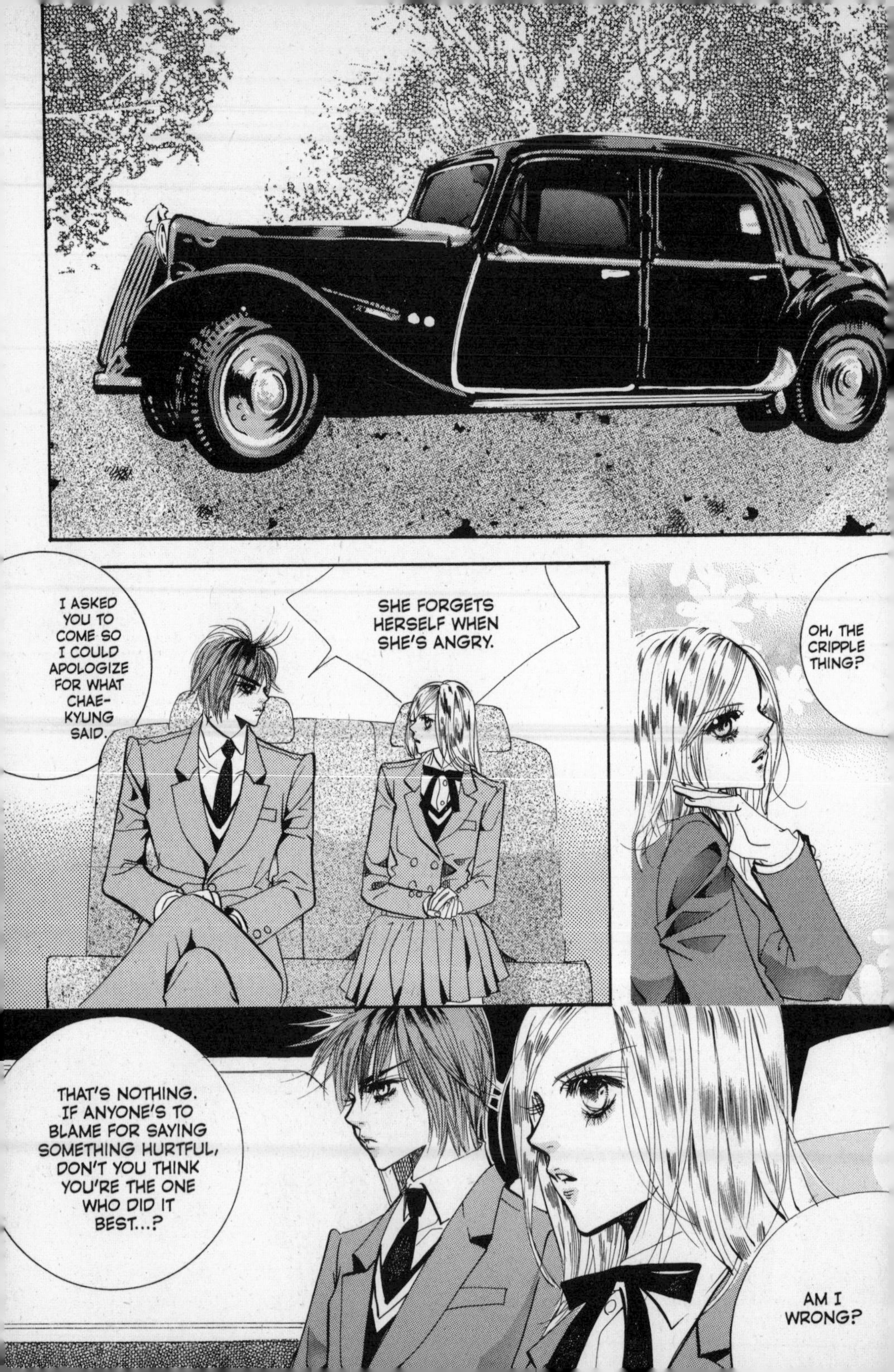
I ASKED YOU TO COME SO I COULD APOLOGIZE FOR WHAT CHAE-KYUNG SAID.
SHE FORGETS HERSELF WHEN SHE'S ANGRY.
OH, THE CRIPPLE THING?
THAT'S NOTHING. IF ANYONE'S TO BLAME FOR SAYING SOMETHING HURTFUL, DON'T YOU THINK YOU'RE THE ONE WHO DID IT BEST...?
AM I WRONG?

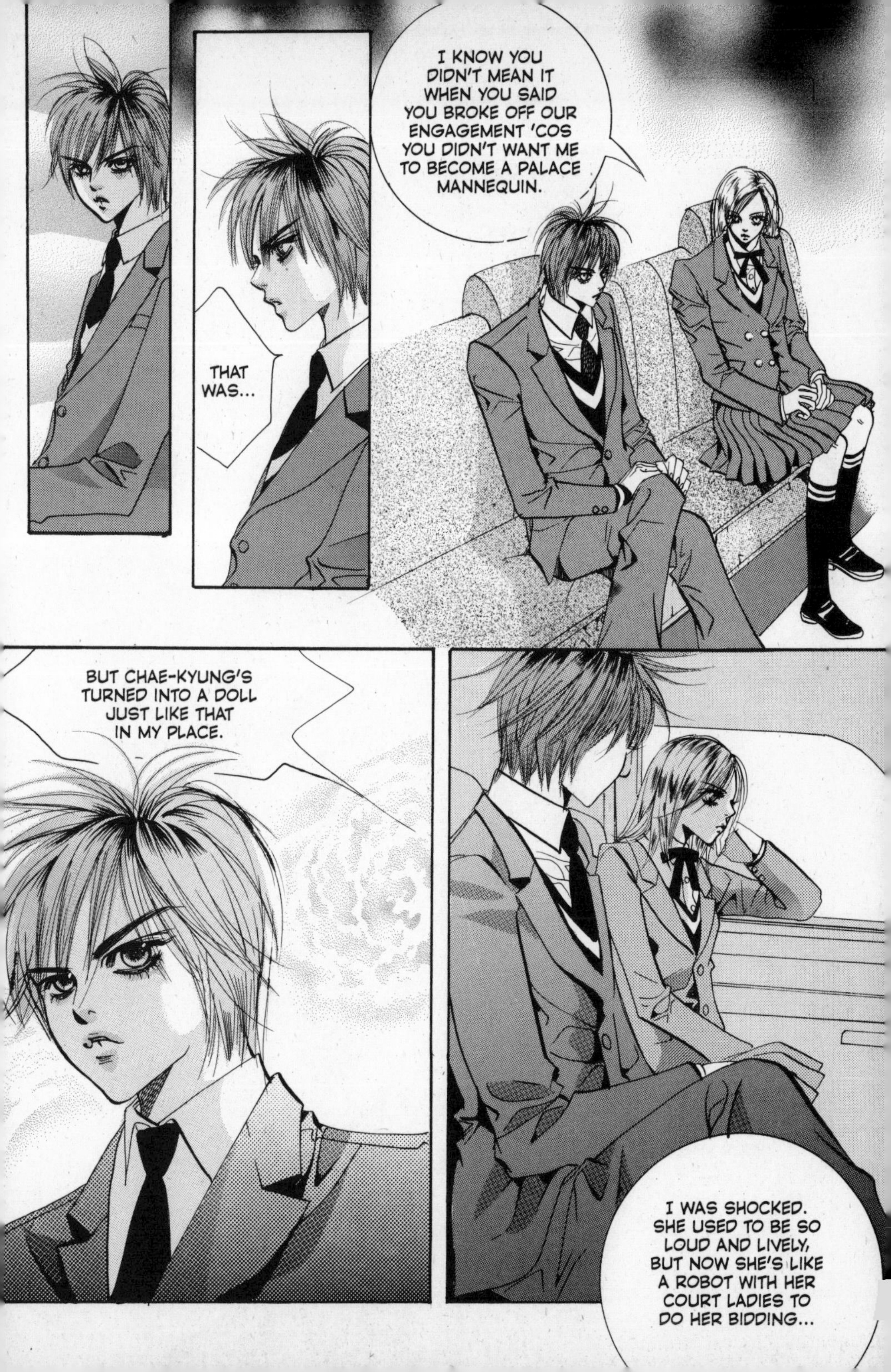
THAT WAS...
I KNOW YOU DIDN'T MEAN IT WHEN YOU SAID YOU BROKE OFF OUR ENGAGEMENT 'COS YOU DIDN'T WANT ME TO BECOME A PALACE MANNEQUIN.
BUT CHAE-KYUNG'S TURNED INTO A DOLL JUST LIKE THAT IN MY PLACE.
I WAS SHOCKED. SHE USED TO BE SO LOUD AND LIVELY, BUT NOW SHE'S LIKE A ROBOT WITH HER COURT LADIES TO DO HER BIDDING...

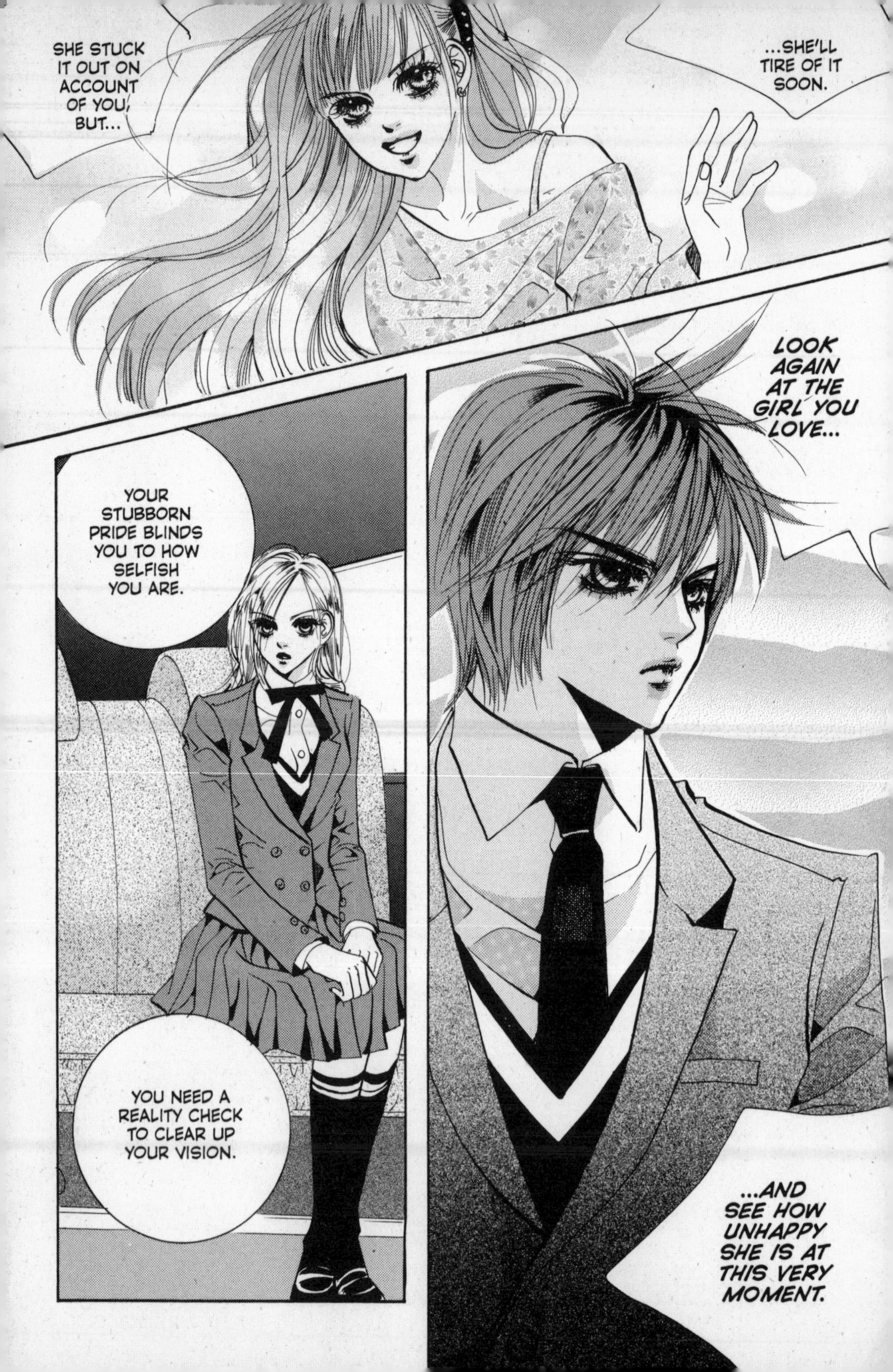
SHE STUCK IT OUT ON ACCOUNT OF YOU, BUT...
...SHE'LL TIRE OF IT SOON.
YOUR STUBBORN PRIDE BLINDS YOU TO HOW SELFISH YOU ARE.
YOU NEED A REALITY CHECK TO CLEAR UP YOUR VISION.
LOOK AGAIN AT THE GIRL YOU LOVE...
...AND SEE HOW UNHAPPY SHE IS AT THIS VERY MOMENT.

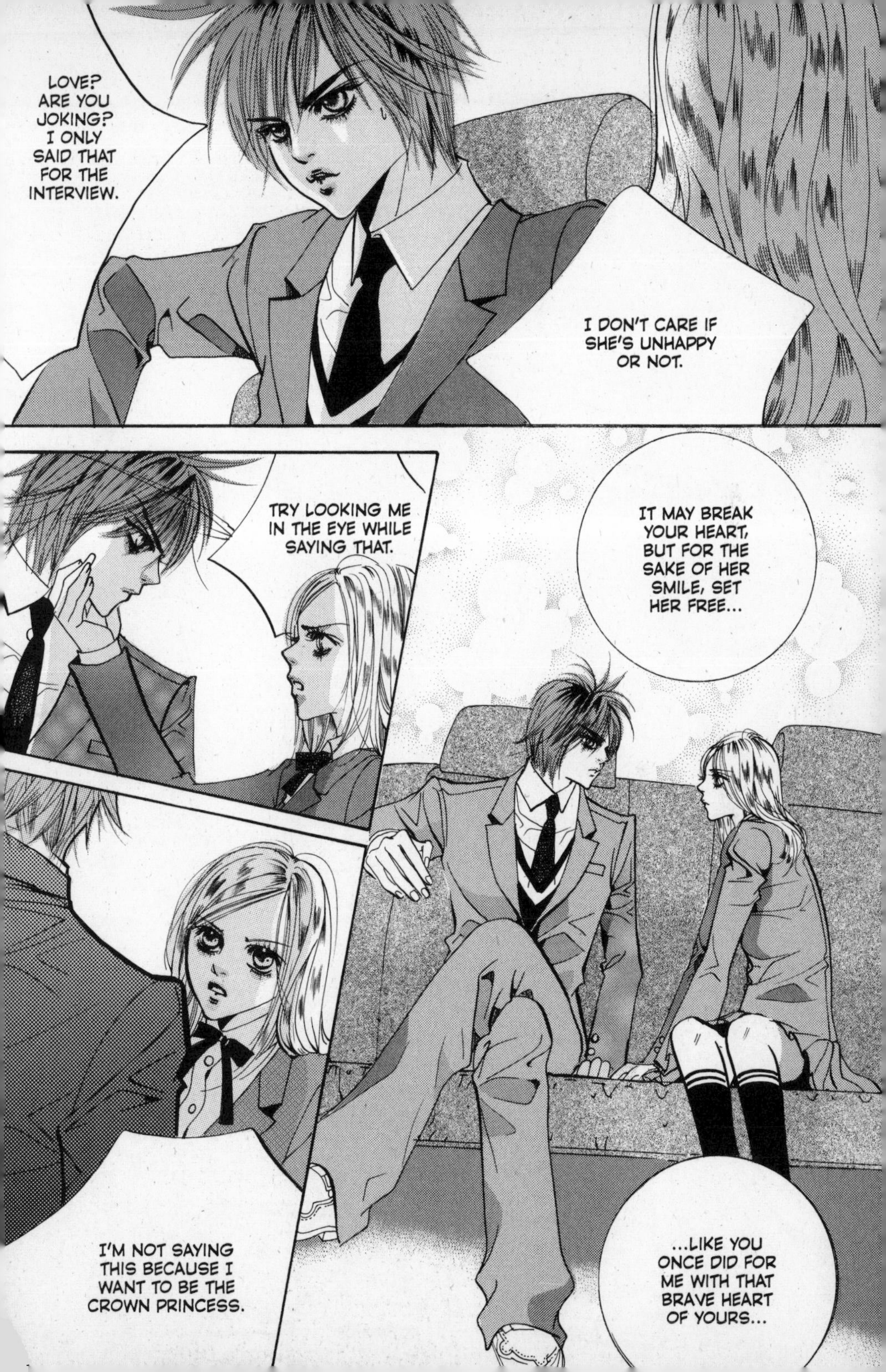
LOVE? ARE YOU JOKING? I ONLY SAID THAT FOR THE INTERVIEW.
I DON'T CARE IF SHE'S UNHAPPY OR NOT.
TRY LOOKING ME IN THE EYE WHILE SAYING THAT.
I'M NOT SAYING THIS BECAUSE I WANT TO BE THE CROWN PRINCESS.
IT MAY BREAK YOUR HEART, BUT FOR THE SAKE OF HER SMILE, SET HER FREE...
...LIKE YOU ONCE DID FOR ME WITH THAT BRAVE HEART OF YOURS...

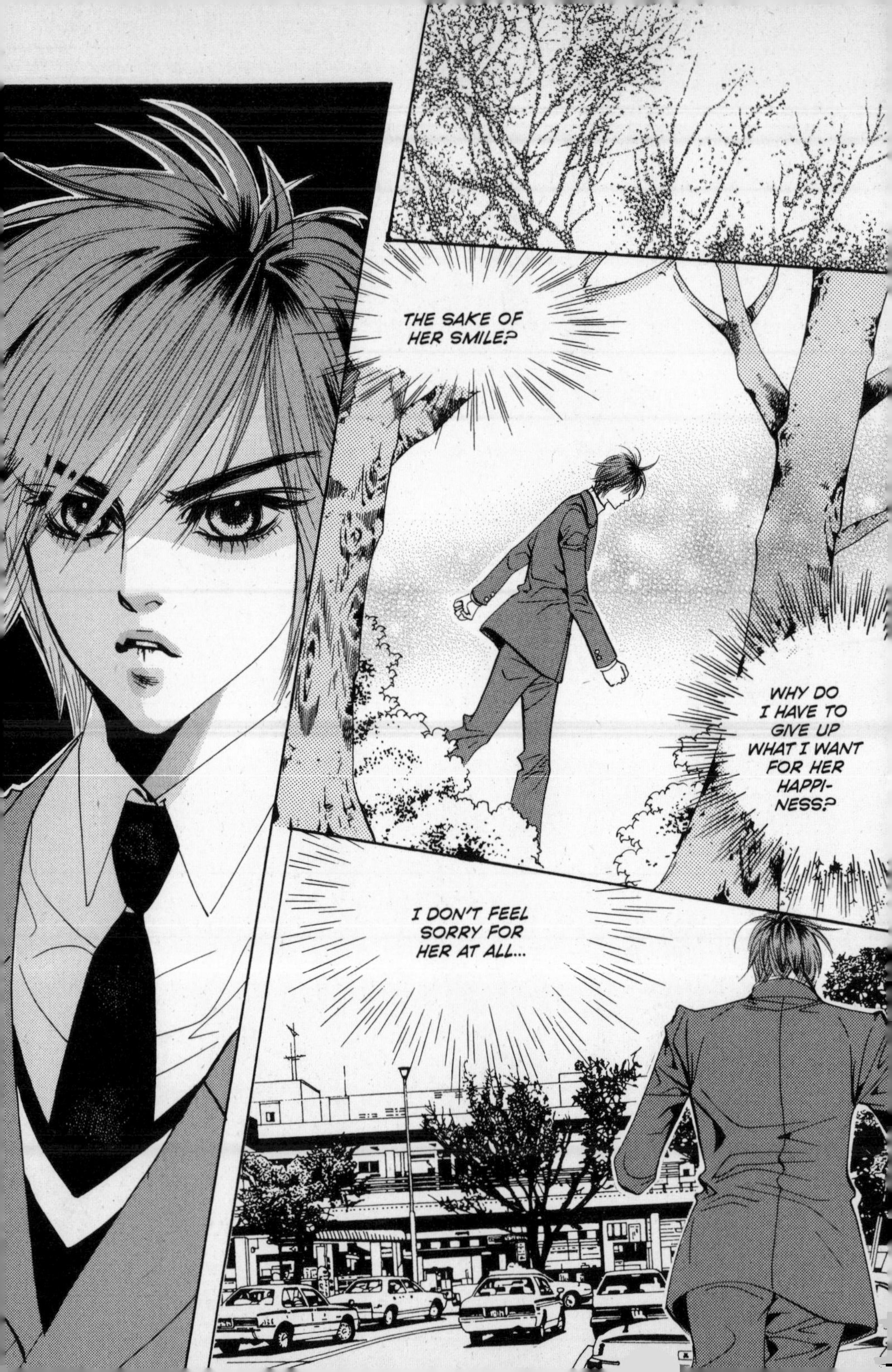
THE SAKE OF HER SMILE?
WHY DO I HAVE TO GIVE UP WHAT I WANT FOR HER HAPPI-NESS?
I DON'T FEEL SORRY FOR HER AT ALL...

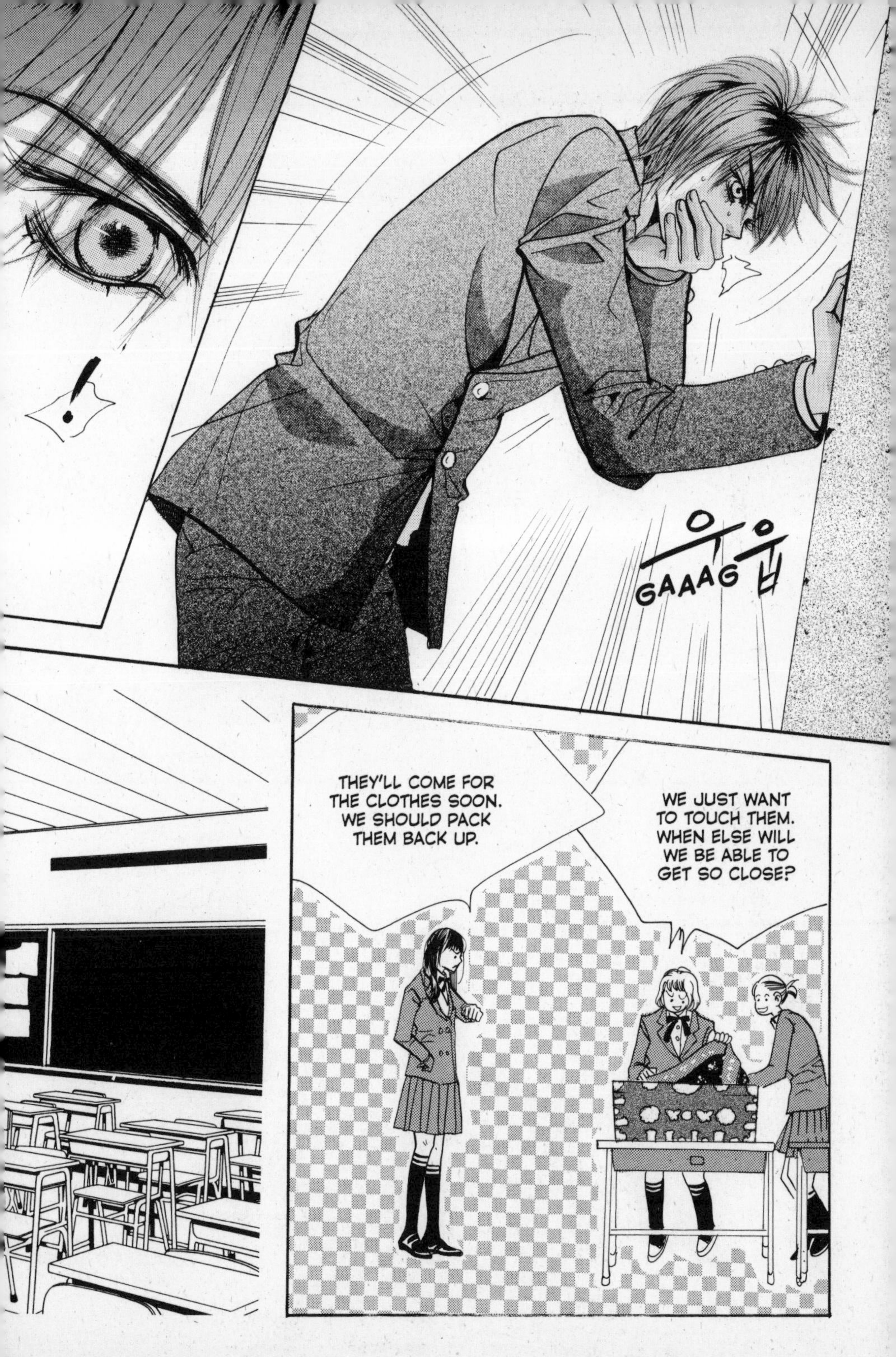
!
우웁
GAAAG
THEY'LL COME FOR THE CLOTHES SOON. WE SHOULD PACK THEM BACK UP.
WE JUST WANT TO TOUCH THEM. WHEN ELSE WILL WE BE ABLE TO GET SO CLOSE?

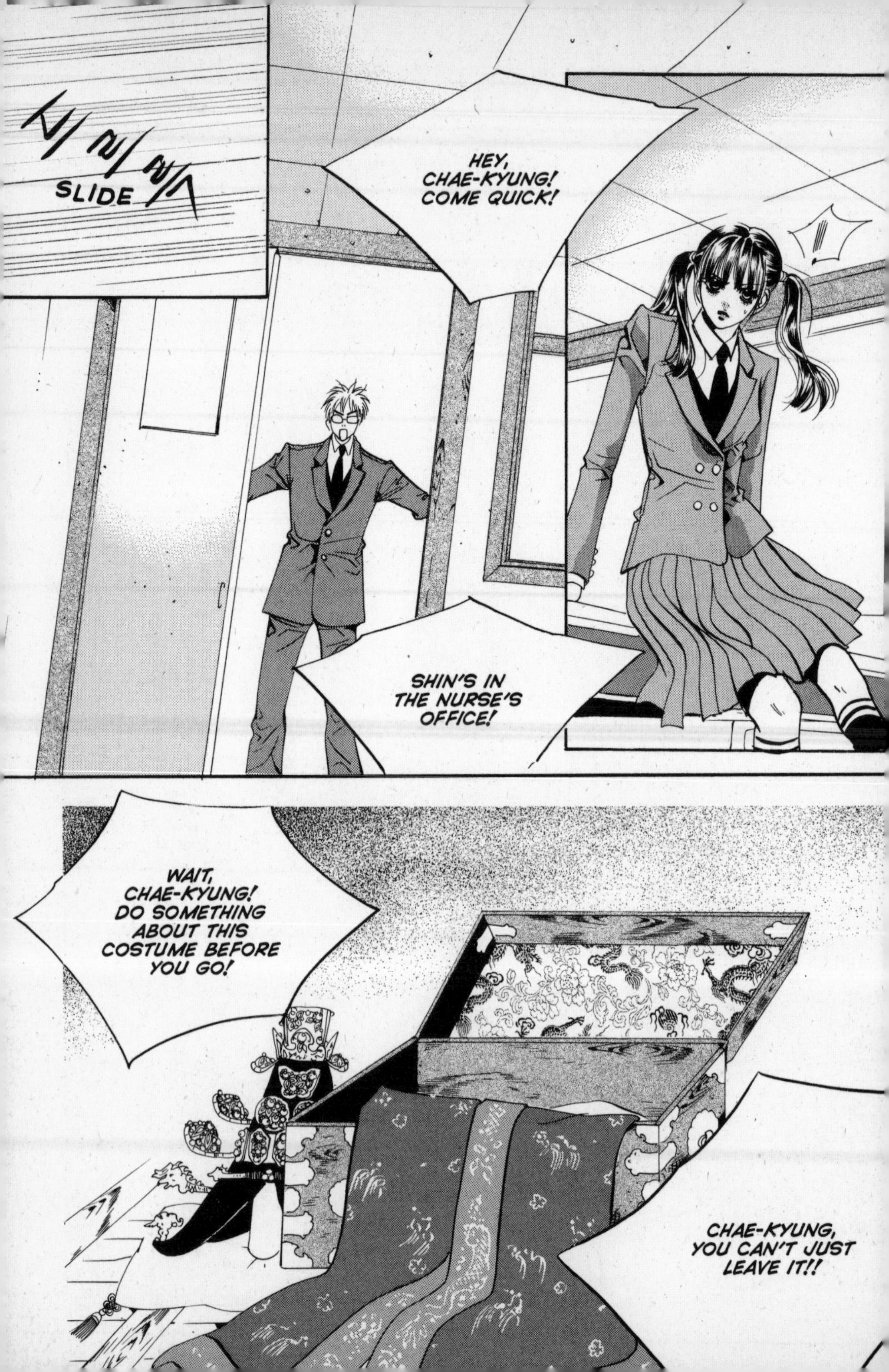
SLIDE
HEY, CHAE-KYUNG! COME QUICK!
!
SHIN'S IN THE NURSE'S OFFICE!
WAIT, CHAE-KYUNG! DO SOMETHING ABOUT THIS COSTUME BEFORE YOU GO!
CHAE-KYUNG, YOU CAN'T JUST LEAVE IT!!

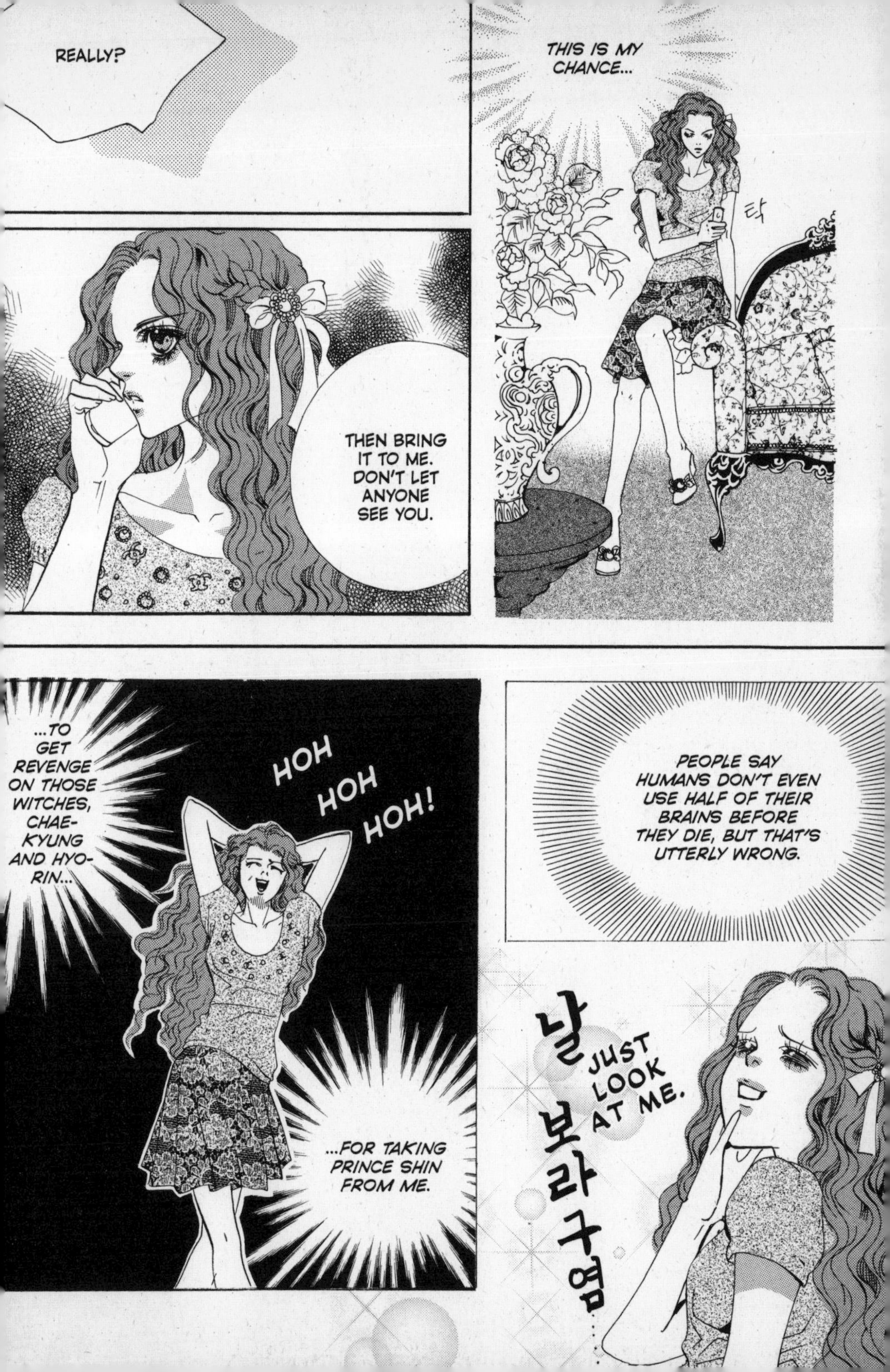
REALLY?
THEN BRING IT TO ME. DON'T LET ANYONE SEE YOU.
THIS IS MY CHANCE...
탁
...TO GET REVENGE ON THOSE WITCHES, CHAE-KYUNG AND HYO-RIN...
HOH HOH HOH!
...FOR TAKING PRINCE SHIN FROM ME.
PEOPLE SAY HUMANS DON'T EVEN USE HALF OF THEIR BRAINS BEFORE THEY DIE, BUT THAT'S UTTERLY WRONG.
날 보라구염...
JUST LOOK AT ME.

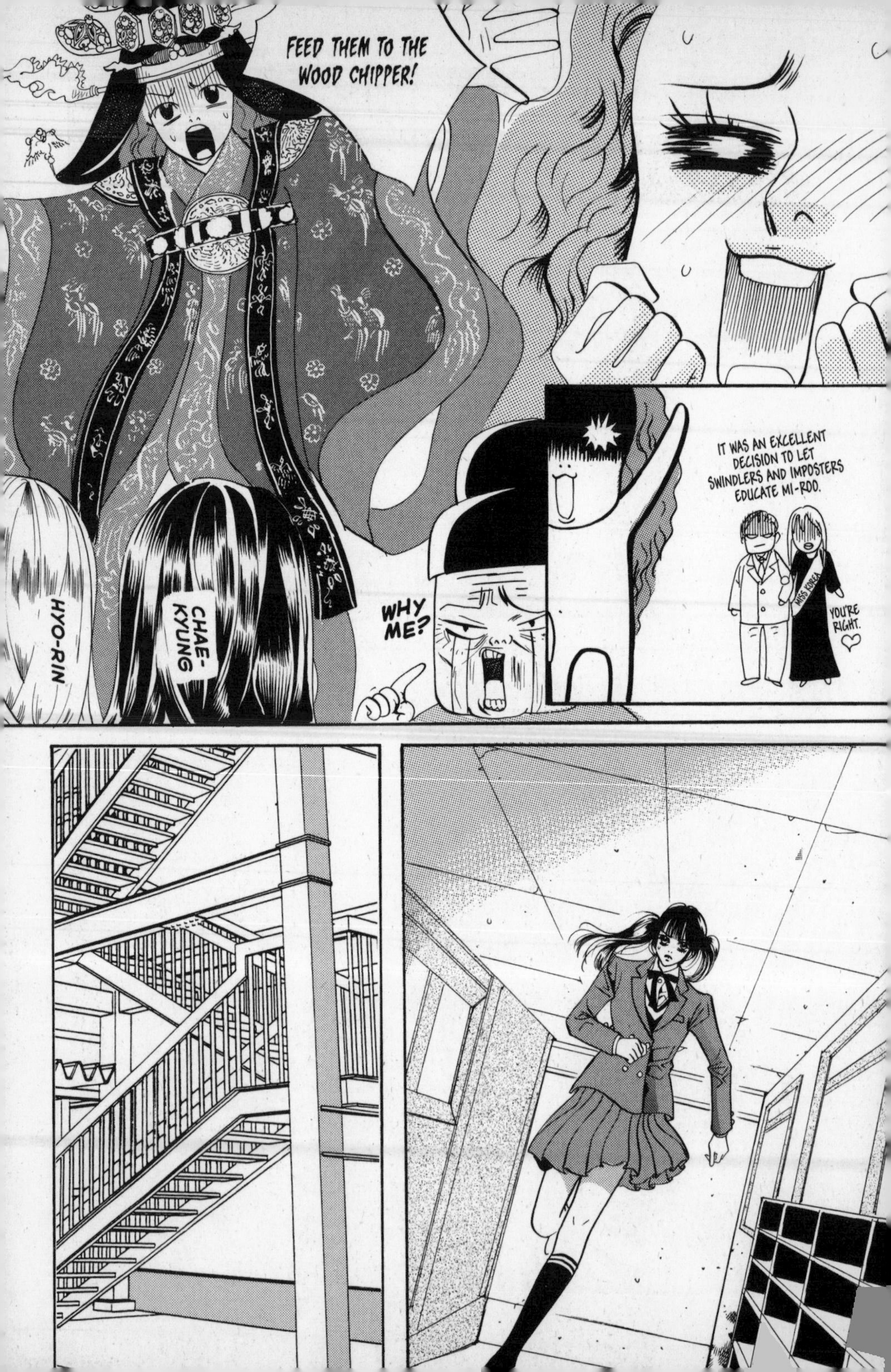
FEED THEM TO THE WOOD CHIPPER!
HYO-RIN
CHAE-KYUNG
WHY ME?
IT WAS AN EXCELLENT DECISION TO LET SWINDLERS AND IMPOSTERS EDUCATE MI-ROO.
MISS KOREA
YOU'RE RIGHT.

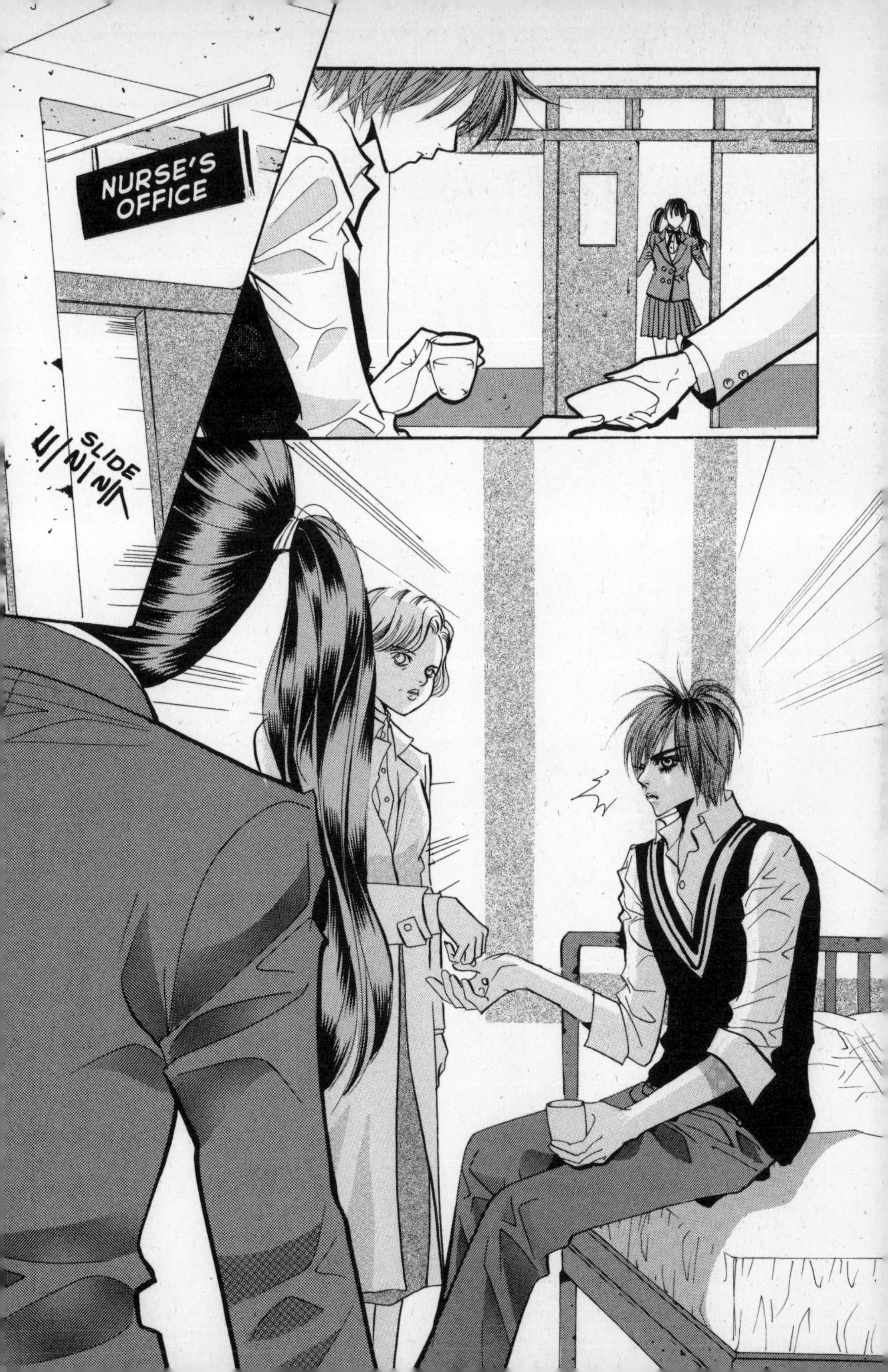
NURSE'S OFFICE
SLIDE

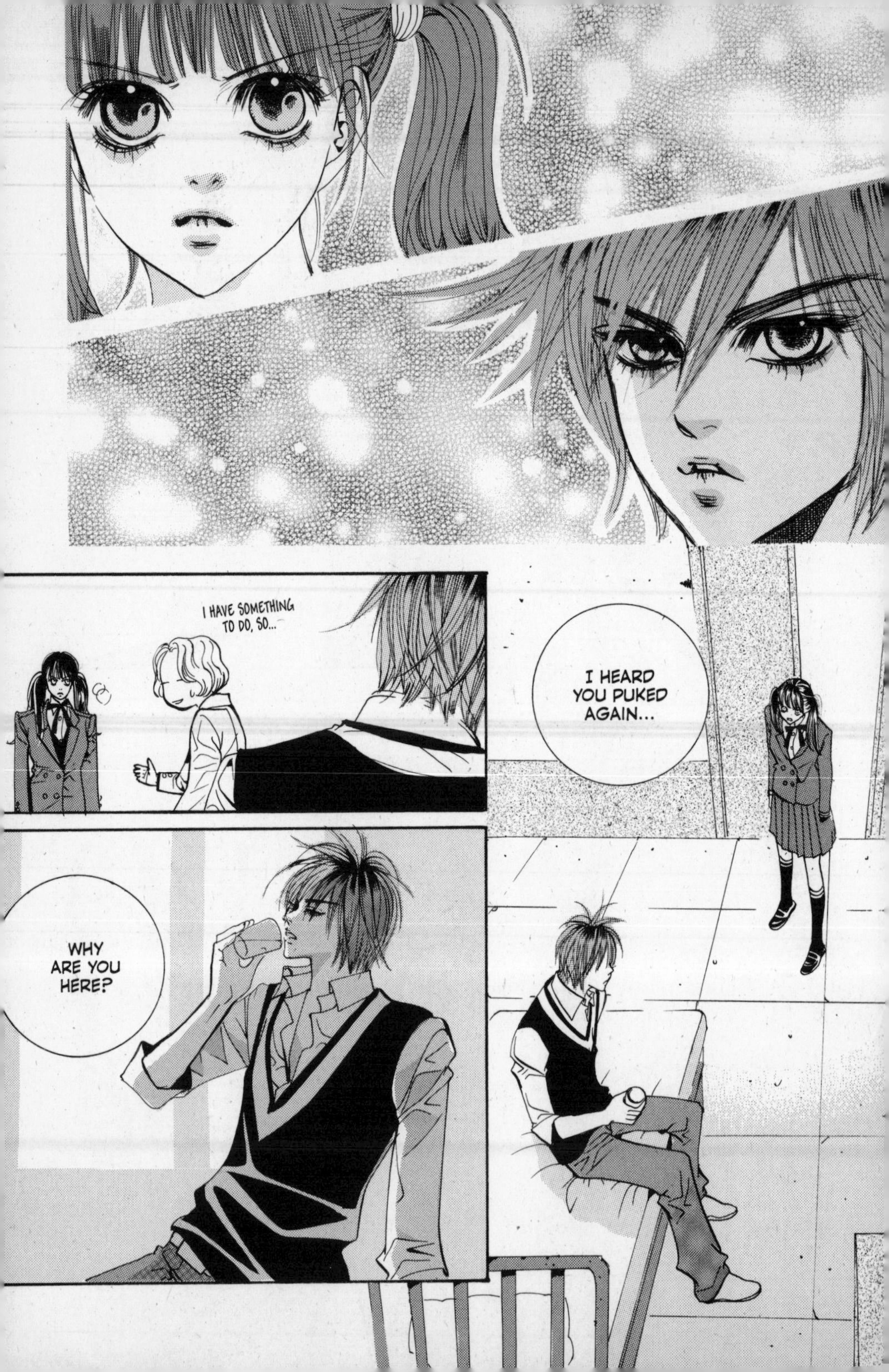
I HAVE SOMETHING TO DO, SO...
WHY ARE YOU HERE?
I HEARD YOU PUKED AGAIN...

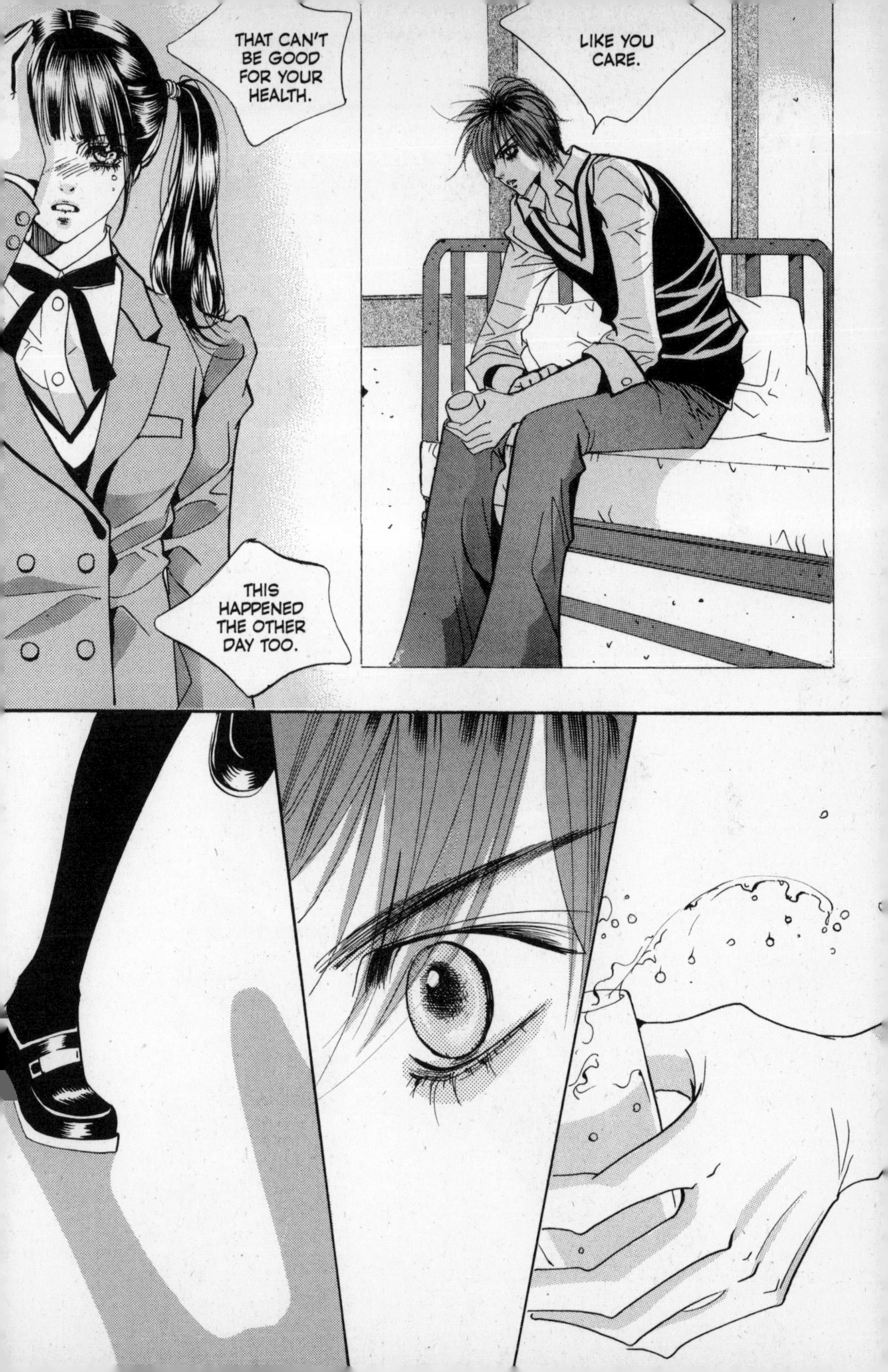
THAT CAN'T BE GOOD FOR YOUR HEALTH.
THIS HAPPENED THE OTHER DAY TOO.
LIKE YOU CARE.

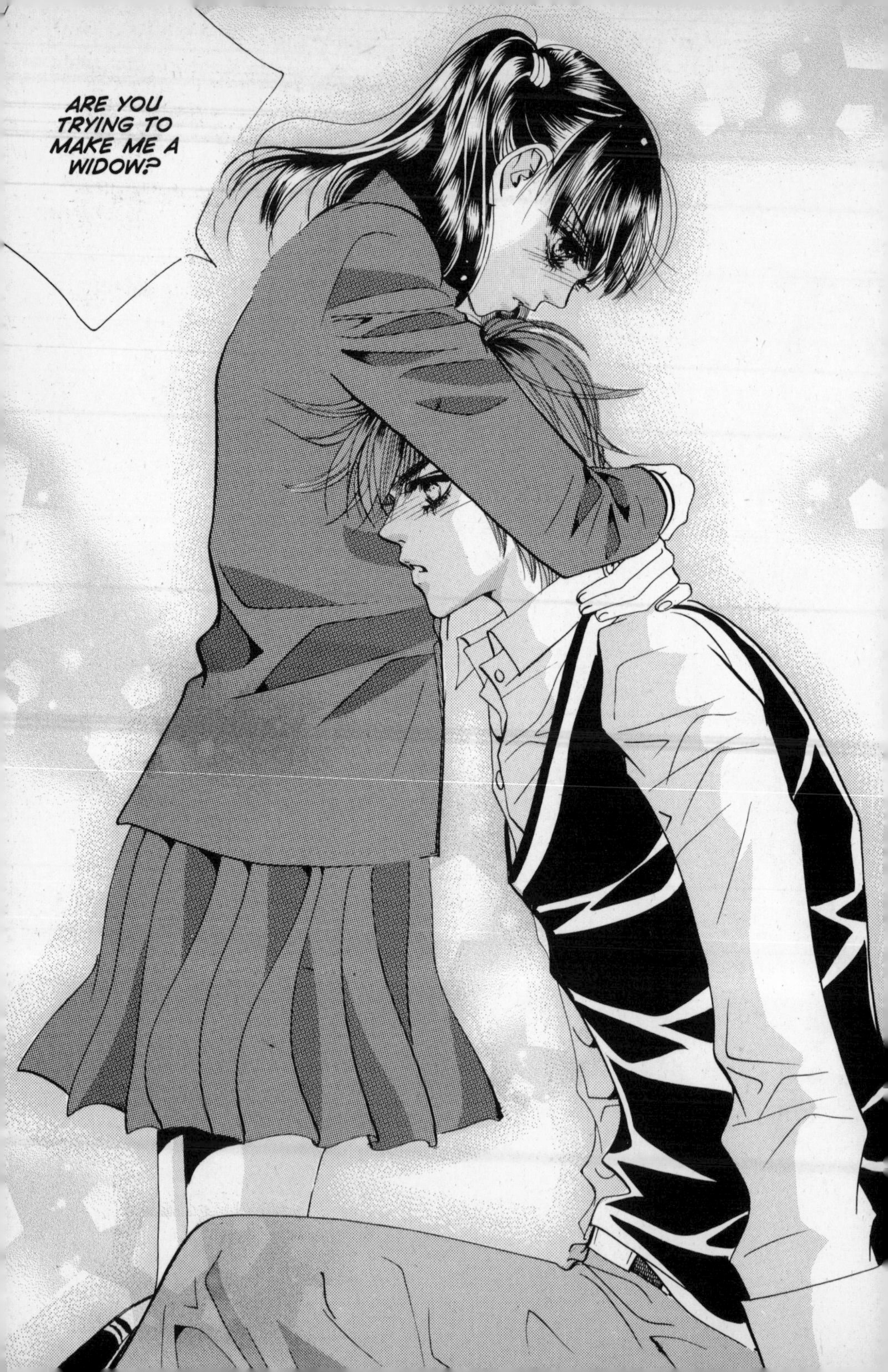
ARE YOU TRYING TO MAKE ME A WIDOW?

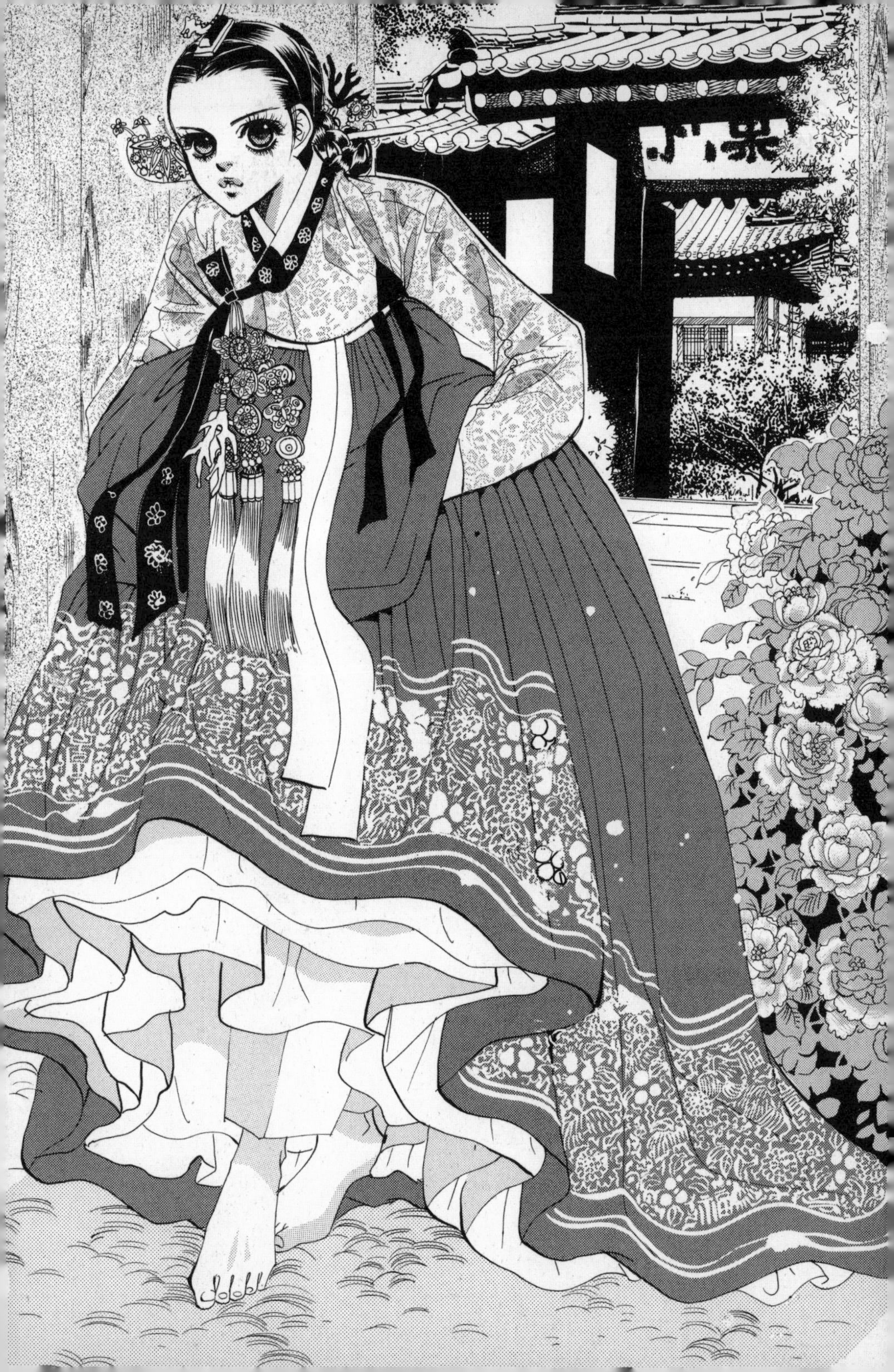

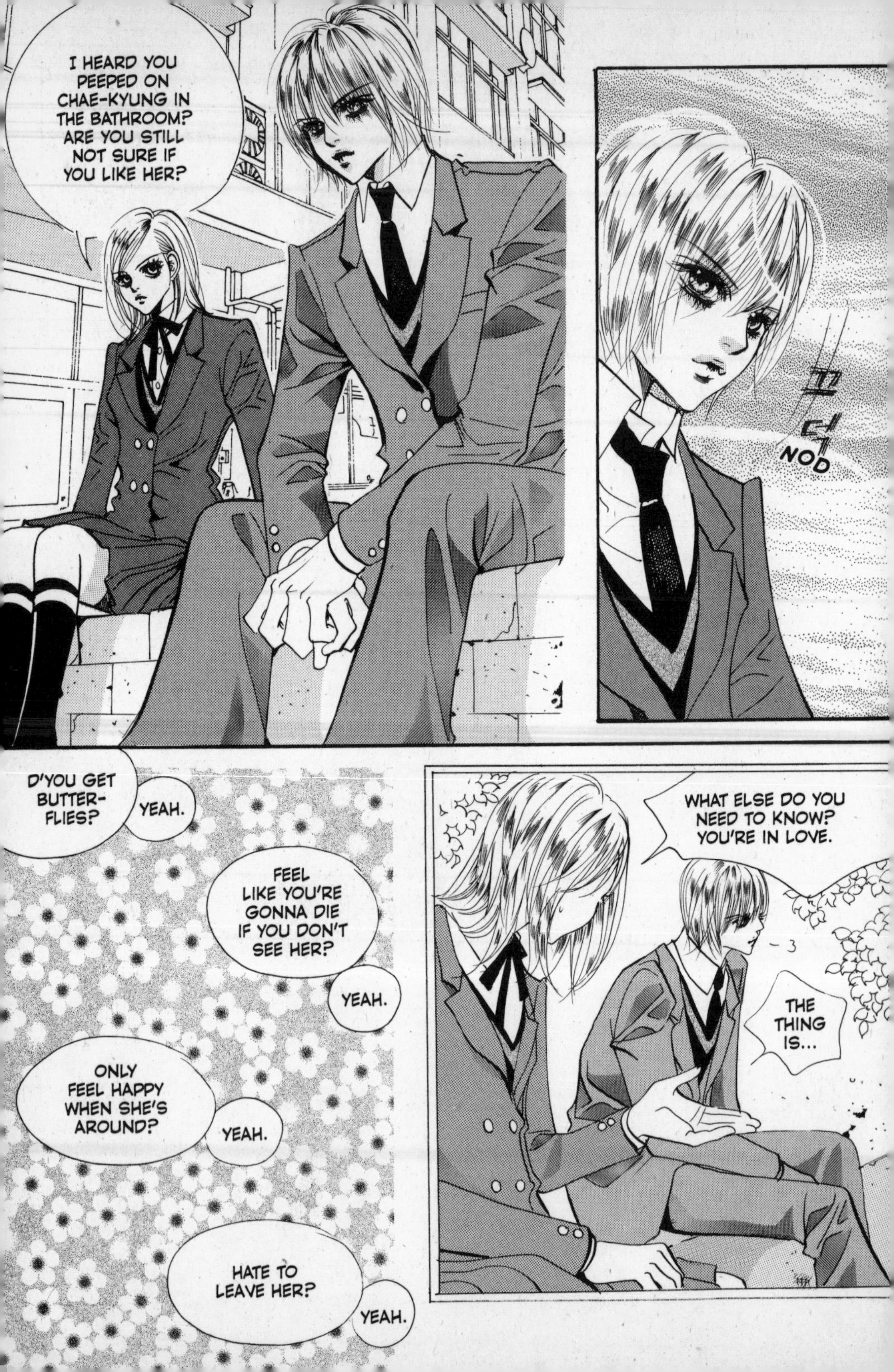
I HEARD YOU PEEPED ON CHAE-KYUNG IN THE BATHROOM? ARE YOU STILL NOT SURE IF YOU LIKE HER?
끄덕
NOD
D'YOU GET BUTTER-FLIES?
YEAH.
FEEL LIKE YOU'RE GONNA DIE IF YOU DON'T SEE HER?
YEAH.
ONLY FEEL HAPPY WHEN SHE'S AROUND?
YEAH.
HATE TO LEAVE HER?
YEAH.
WHAT ELSE DO YOU NEED TO KNOW? YOU'RE IN LOVE.
THE THING IS...

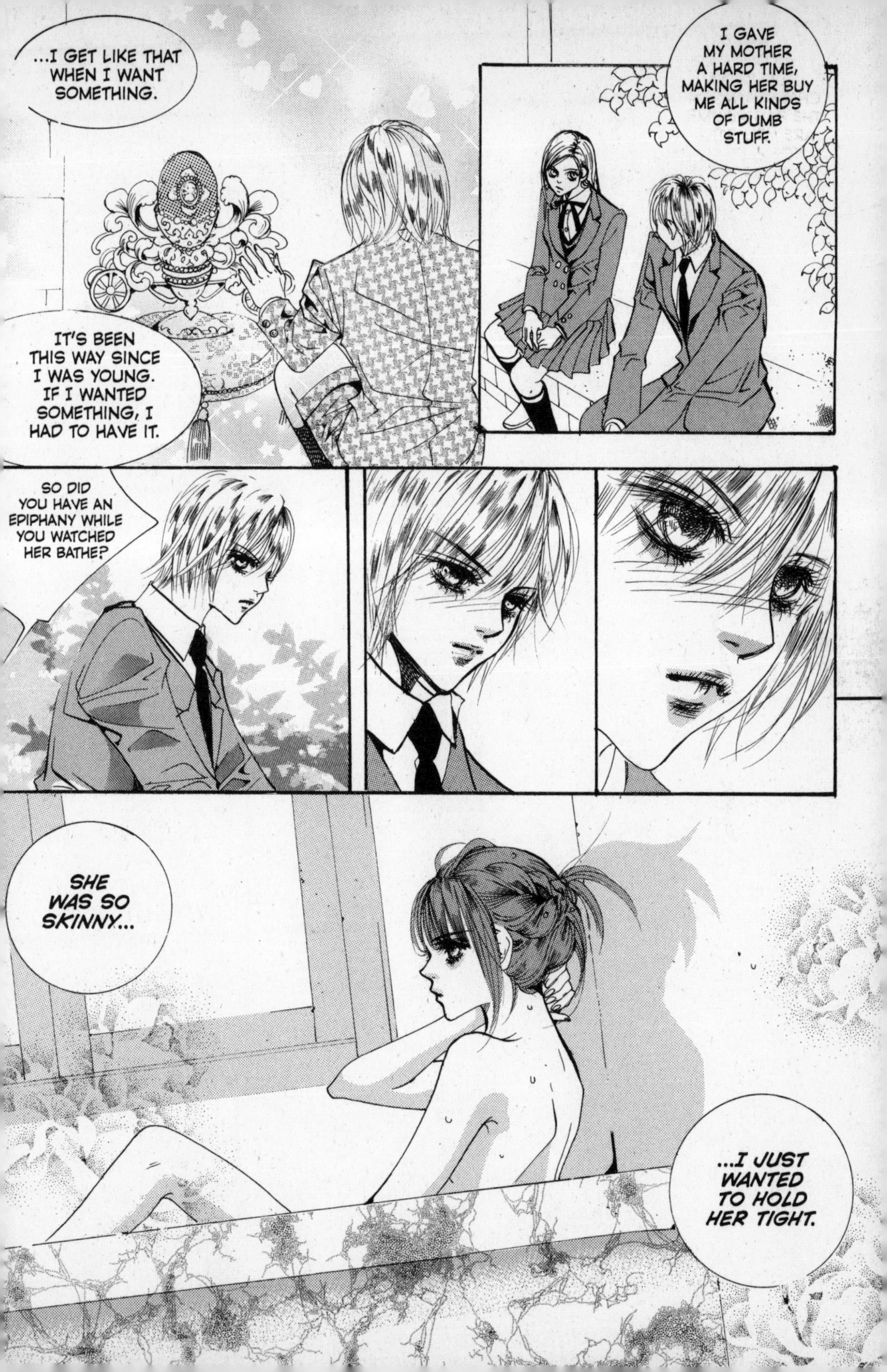
...I GET LIKE THAT WHEN I WANT SOMETHING.
IT'S BEEN THIS WAY SINCE I WAS YOUNG. IF I WANTED SOMETHING, I HAD TO HAVE IT.
I GAVE MY MOTHER A HARD TIME, MAKING HER BUY ME ALL KINDS OF DUMB STUFF.
SO DID YOU HAVE AN EPIPHANY WHILE YOU WATCHED HER BATHE?
SHE WAS SO SKINNY...
...I JUST WANTED TO HOLD HER TIGHT.

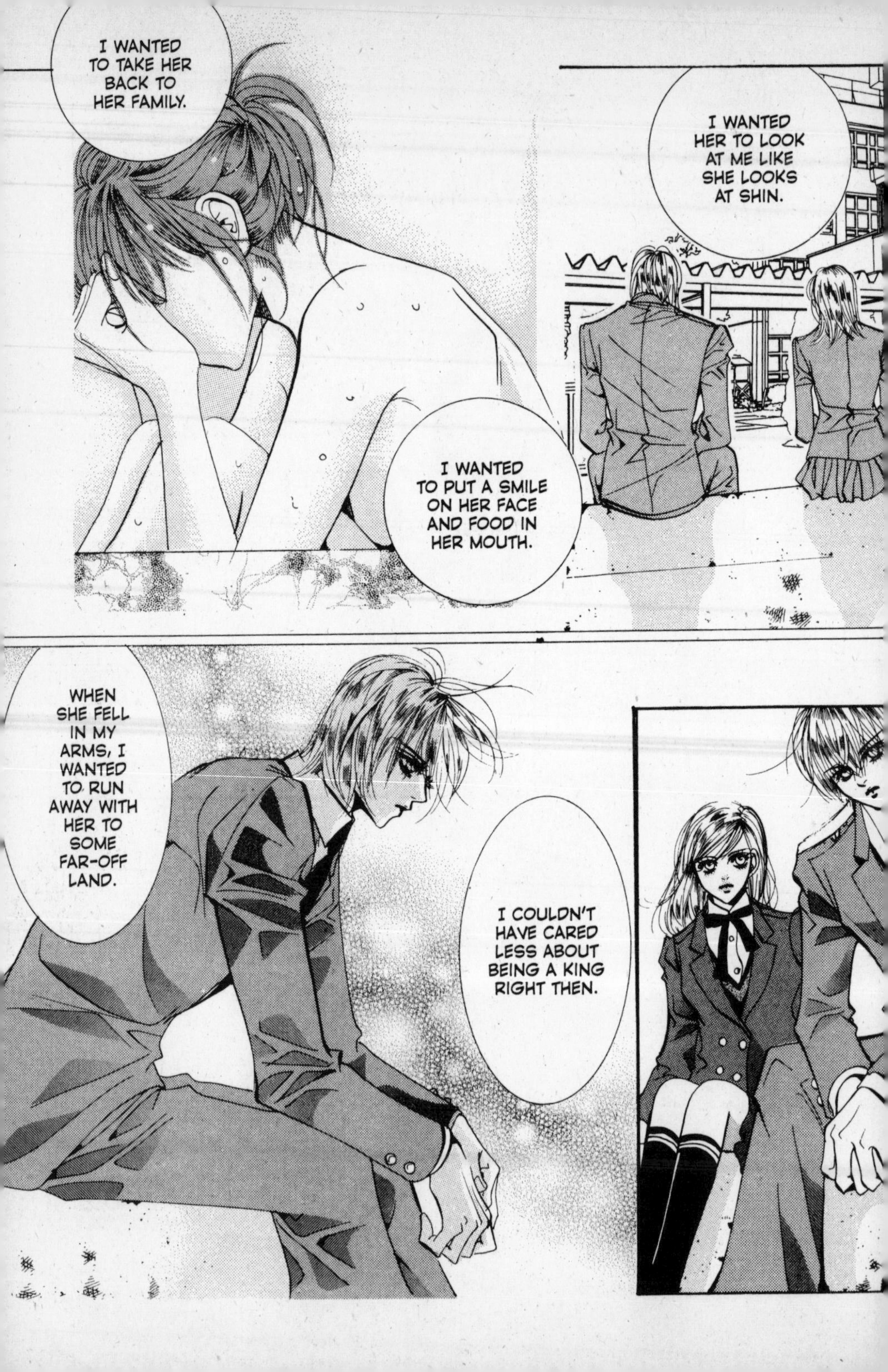
I WANTED TO TAKE HER BACK TO HER FAMILY.
I WANTED TO PUT A SMILE ON HER FACE AND FOOD IN HER MOUTH.
I WANTED HER TO LOOK AT ME LIKE SHE LOOKS AT SHIN.
WHEN SHE FELL IN MY ARMS, I WANTED TO RUN AWAY WITH HER TO SOME FAR-OFF LAND.
I COULDN'T HAVE CARED LESS ABOUT BEING A KING RIGHT THEN.

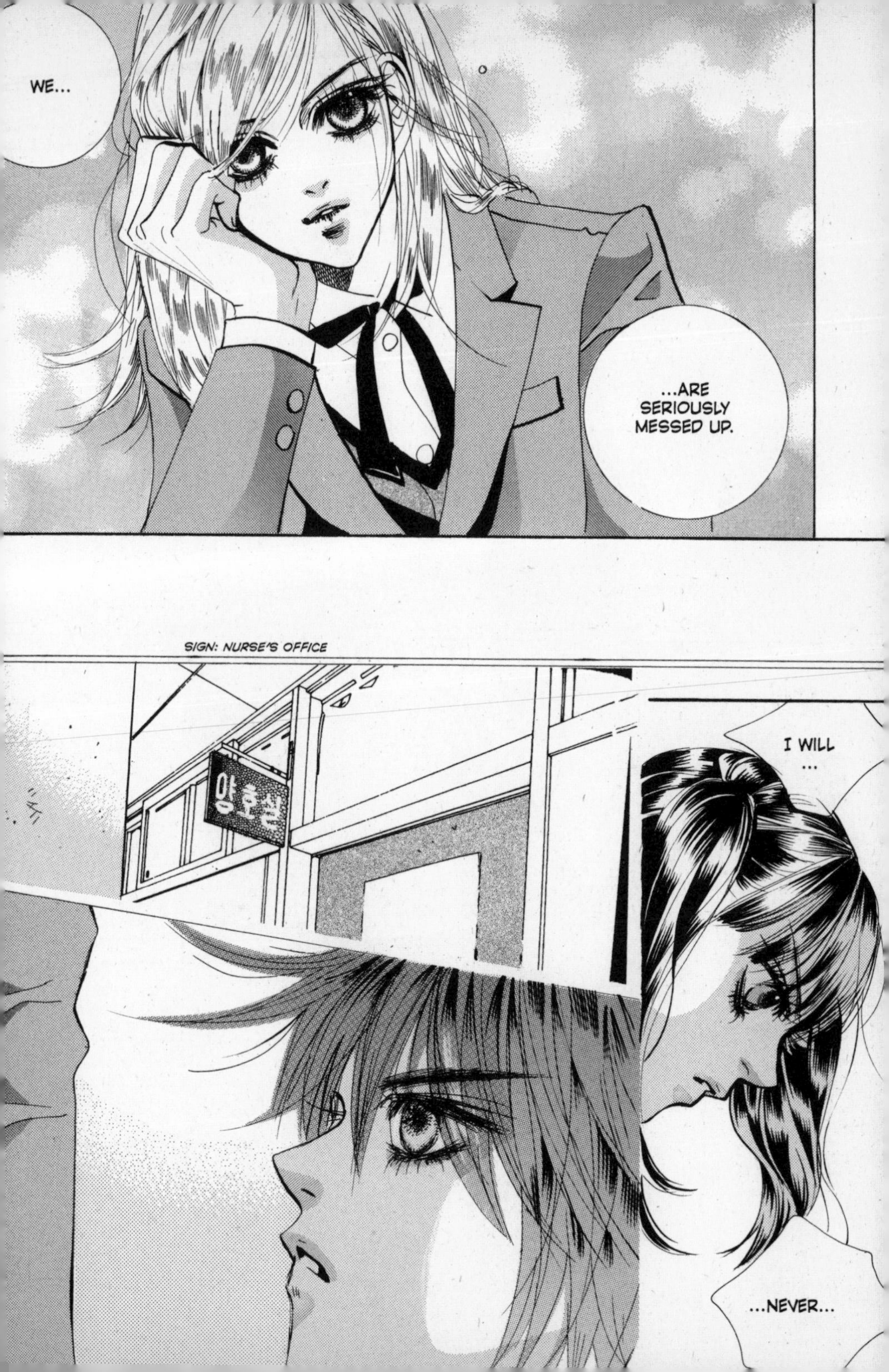
WE...
...ARE SERIOUSLY MESSED UP.
SIGN: NURSE'S OFFICE
양호실
I WILL ...
...NEVER...

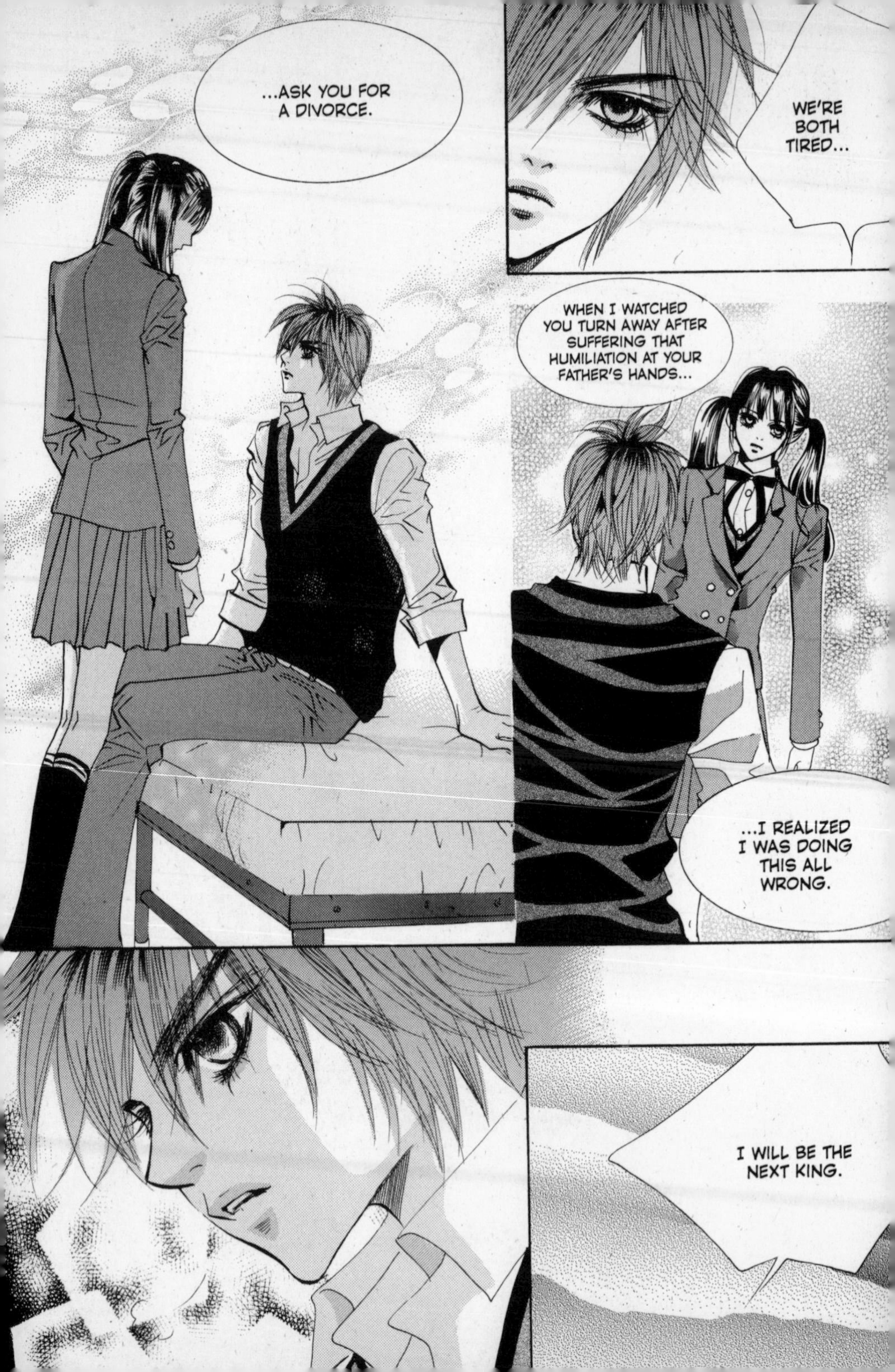
...ASK YOU FOR A DIVORCE.
WE'RE BOTH TIRED...
WHEN I WATCHED YOU TURN AWAY AFTER SUFFERING THAT HUMILIATION AT YOUR FATHER'S HANDS...
...I REALIZED I WAS DOING THIS ALL WRONG.
I WILL BE THE NEXT KING.

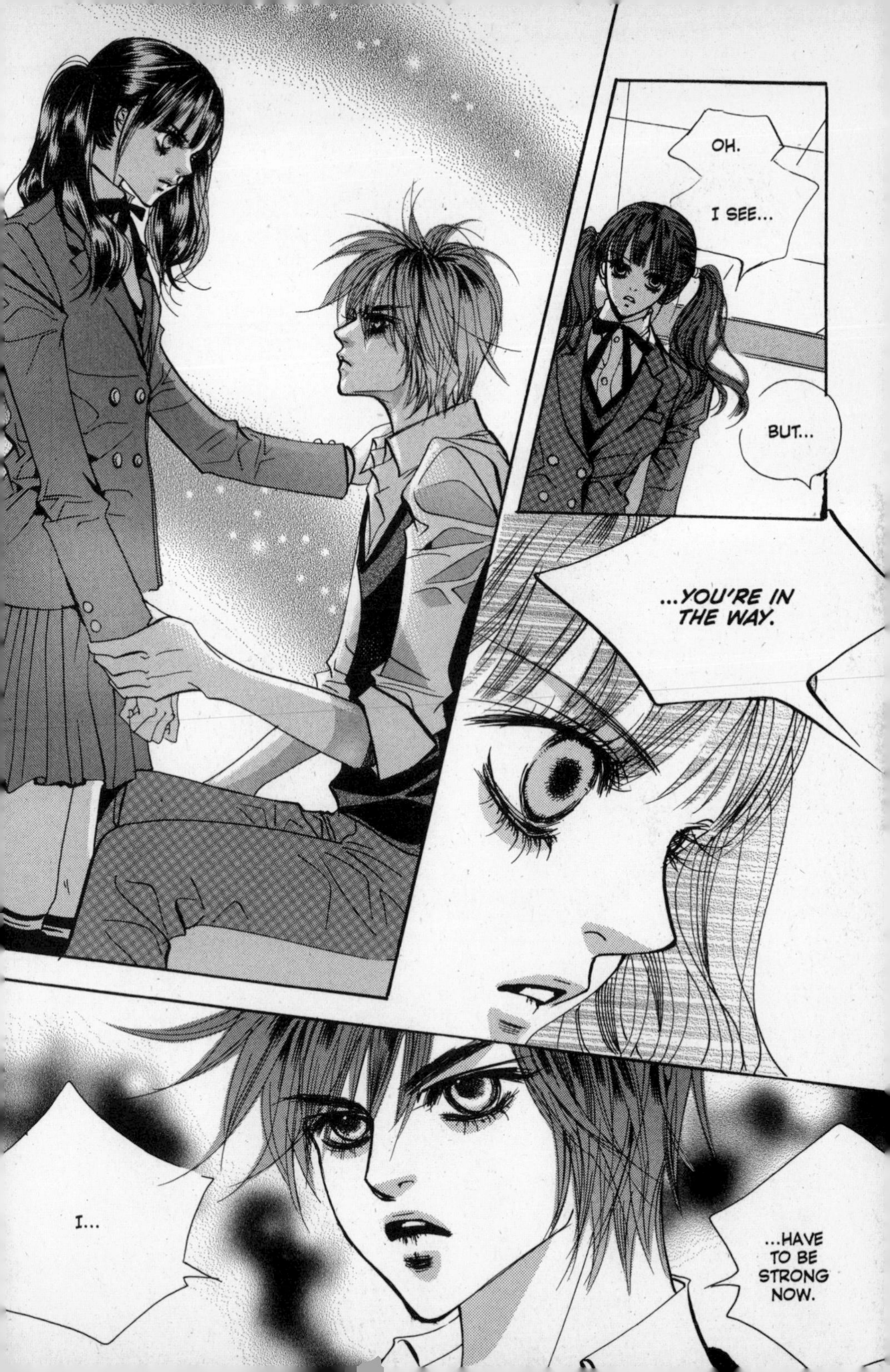
OH.
I SEE...
BUT...
...YOU'RE IN THE WAY.
I...
...HAVE TO BE STRONG NOW.

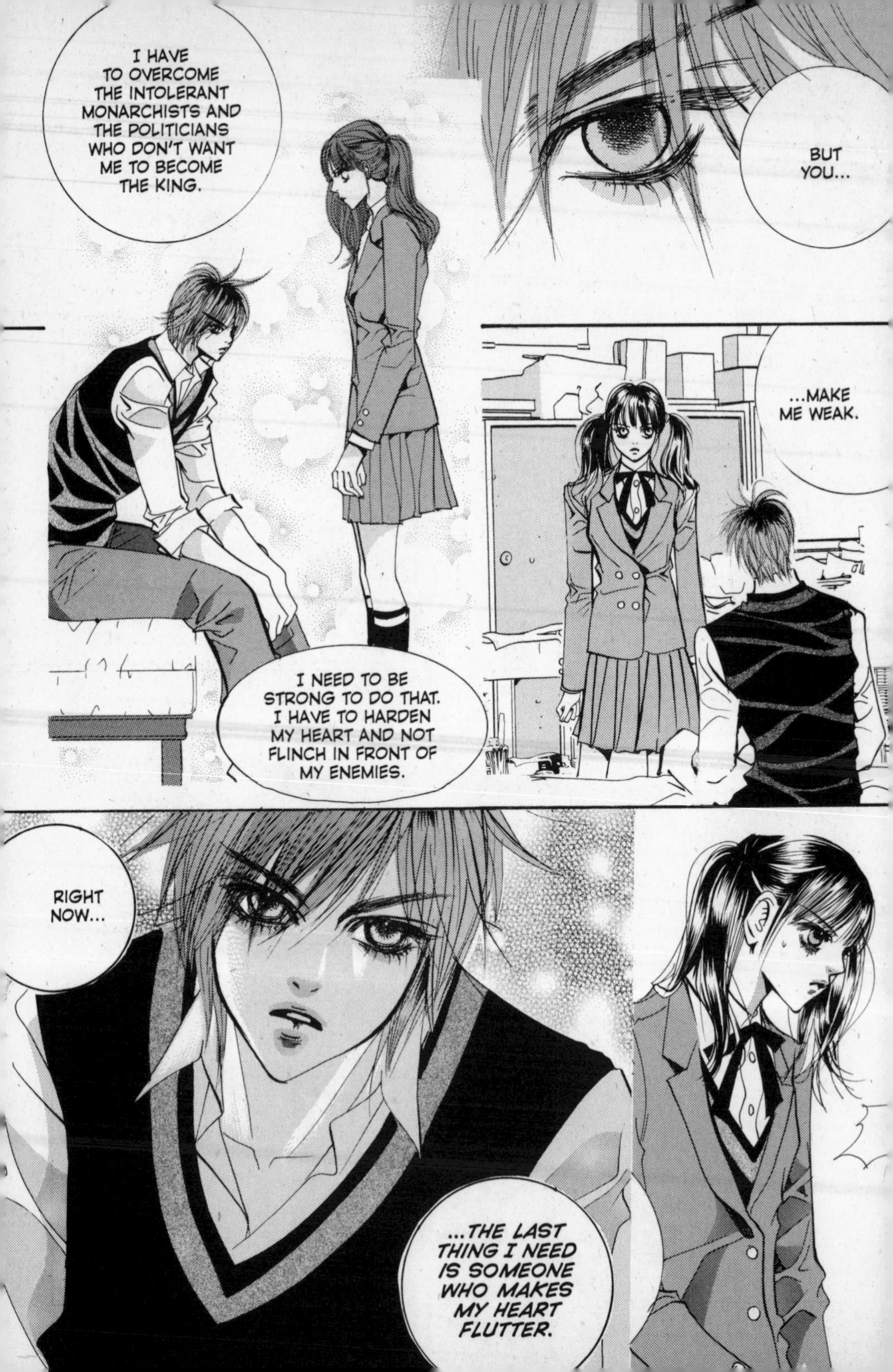

I HAVE TO OVERCOME THE INTOLERANT MONARCHISTS AND THE POLITICIANS WHO DON'T WANT ME TO BECOME THE KING.
I NEED TO BE STRONG TO DO THAT. I HAVE TO HARDEN MY HEART AND NOT FLINCH IN FRONT OF MY ENEMIES.
BUT YOU...
...MAKE ME WEAK.
RIGHT NOW...
...THE LAST THING I NEED IS SOMEONE WHO MAKES MY HEART FLUTTER.

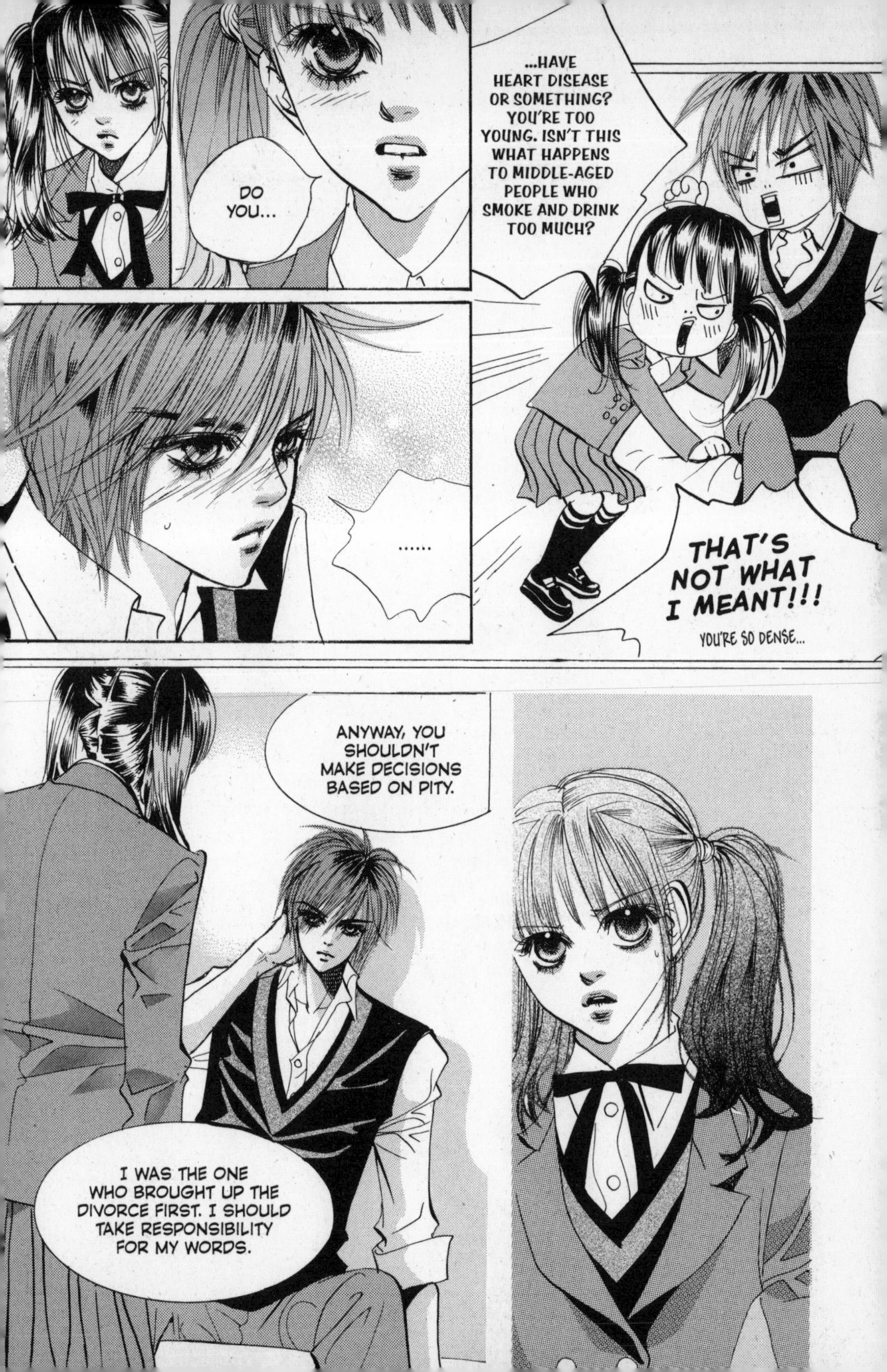
DO YOU...
...HAVE HEART DISEASE OR SOMETHING? YOU'RE TOO YOUNG. ISN'T THIS WHAT HAPPENS TO MIDDLE-AGED PEOPLE WHO SMOKE AND DRINK TOO MUCH?
......
THAT'S NOT WHAT I MEANT!!!
YOU'RE SO DENSE...
ANYWAY, YOU SHOULDN'T MAKE DECISIONS BASED ON PITY.
I WAS THE ONE WHO BROUGHT UP THE DIVORCE FIRST. I SHOULD TAKE RESPONSIBILITY FOR MY WORDS.

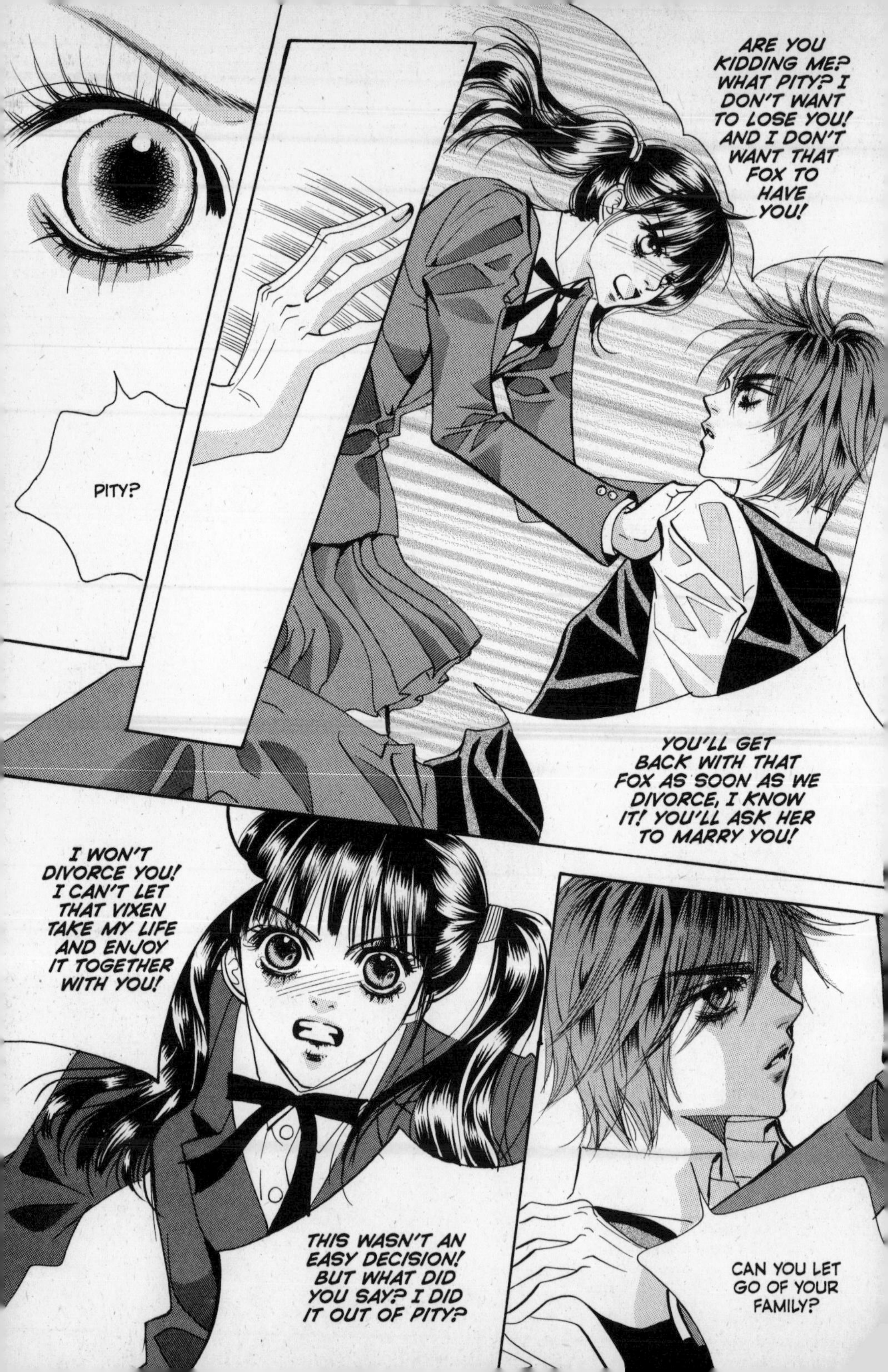
PITY?
ARE YOU KIDDING ME? WHAT PITY? I DON'T WANT TO LOSE YOU! AND I DON'T WANT THAT FOX TO HAVE YOU!
YOU'LL GET BACK WITH THAT FOX AS SOON AS WE DIVORCE, I KNOW IT! YOU'LL ASK HER TO MARRY YOU!
I WON'T DIVORCE YOU! I CAN'T LET THAT VIXEN TAKE MY LIFE AND ENJOY IT TOGETHER WITH YOU!
THIS WASN'T AN EASY DECISION! BUT WHAT DID YOU SAY? I DID IT OUT OF PITY?
CAN YOU LET GO OF YOUR FAMILY?

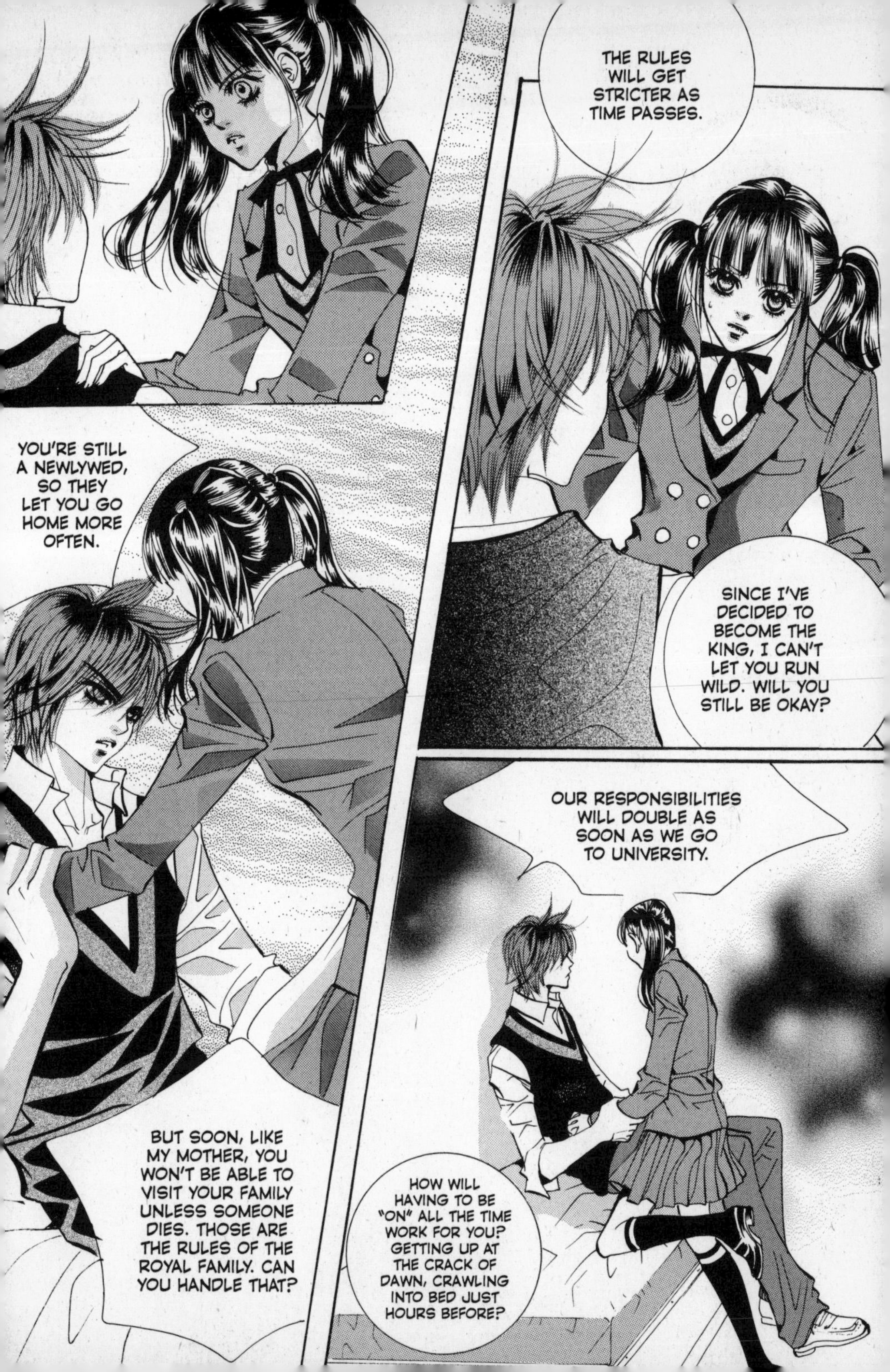
YOU'RE STILL A NEWLYWED, SO THEY LET YOU GO HOME MORE OFTEN.
BUT SOON, LIKE MY MOTHER, YOU WON'T BE ABLE TO VISIT YOUR FAMILY UNLESS SOMEONE DIES. THOSE ARE THE RULES OF THE ROYAL FAMILY. CAN YOU HANDLE THAT?
THE RULES WILL GET STRICTER AS TIME PASSES.
SINCE I'VE DECIDED TO BECOME THE KING, I CAN'T LET YOU RUN WILD. WILL YOU STILL BE OKAY?
OUR RESPONSIBILITIES WILL DOUBLE AS SOON AS WE GO TO UNIVERSITY.
HOW WILL HAVING TO BE "ON" ALL THE TIME WORK FOR YOU? GETTING UP AT THE CRACK OF DAWN, CRAWLING INTO BED JUST HOURS BEFORE?

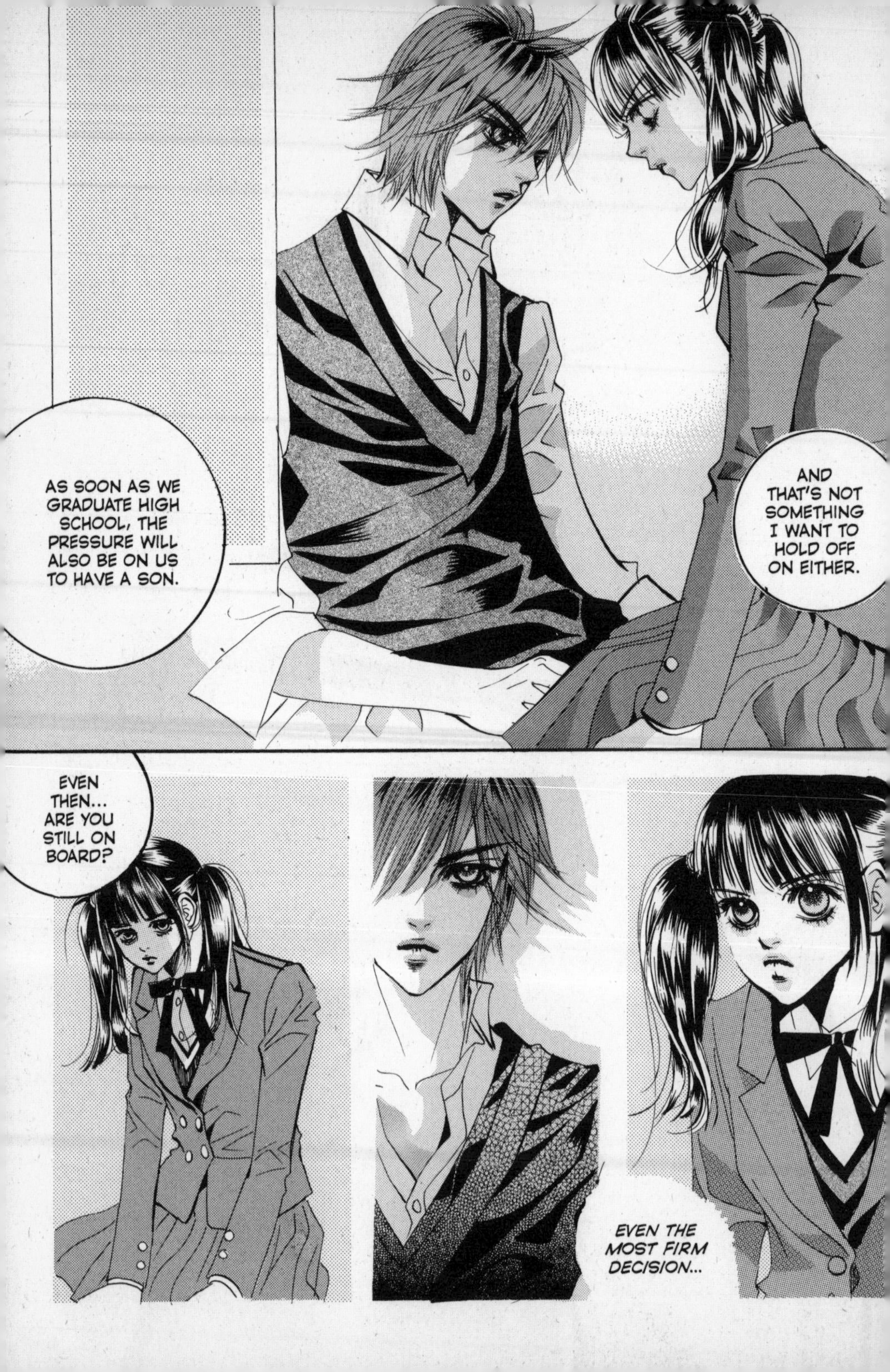
AS SOON AS WE GRADUATE HIGH SCHOOL, THE PRESSURE WILL ALSO BE ON US TO HAVE A SON.
AND THAT'S NOT SOMETHING I WANT TO HOLD OFF ON EITHER.
EVEN THEN... ARE YOU STILL ON BOARD?
EVEN THE MOST FIRM DECISION...

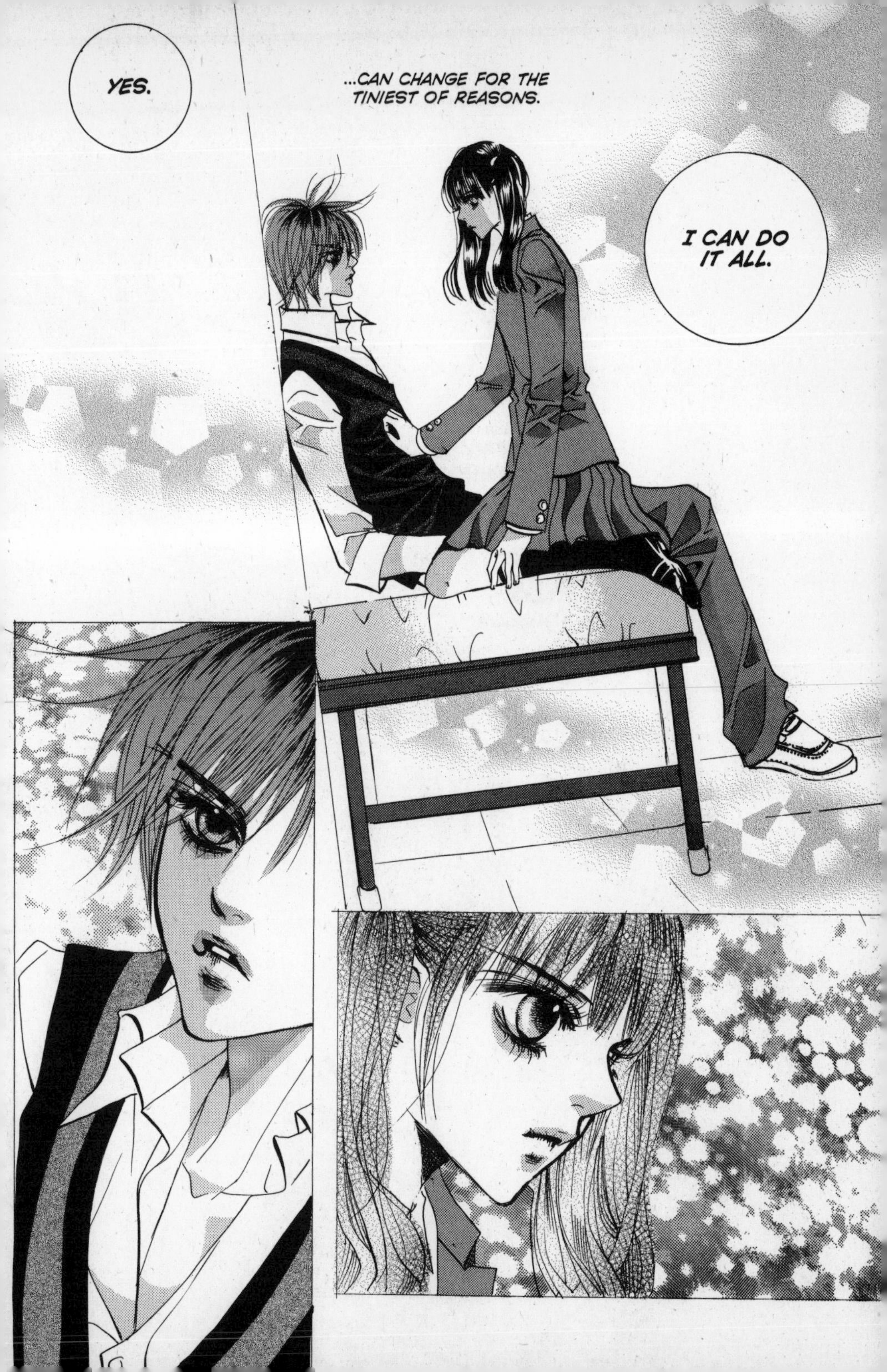
I CAN DO IT ALL.
...CAN CHANGE FOR THE TINIEST OF REASONS.
YES.

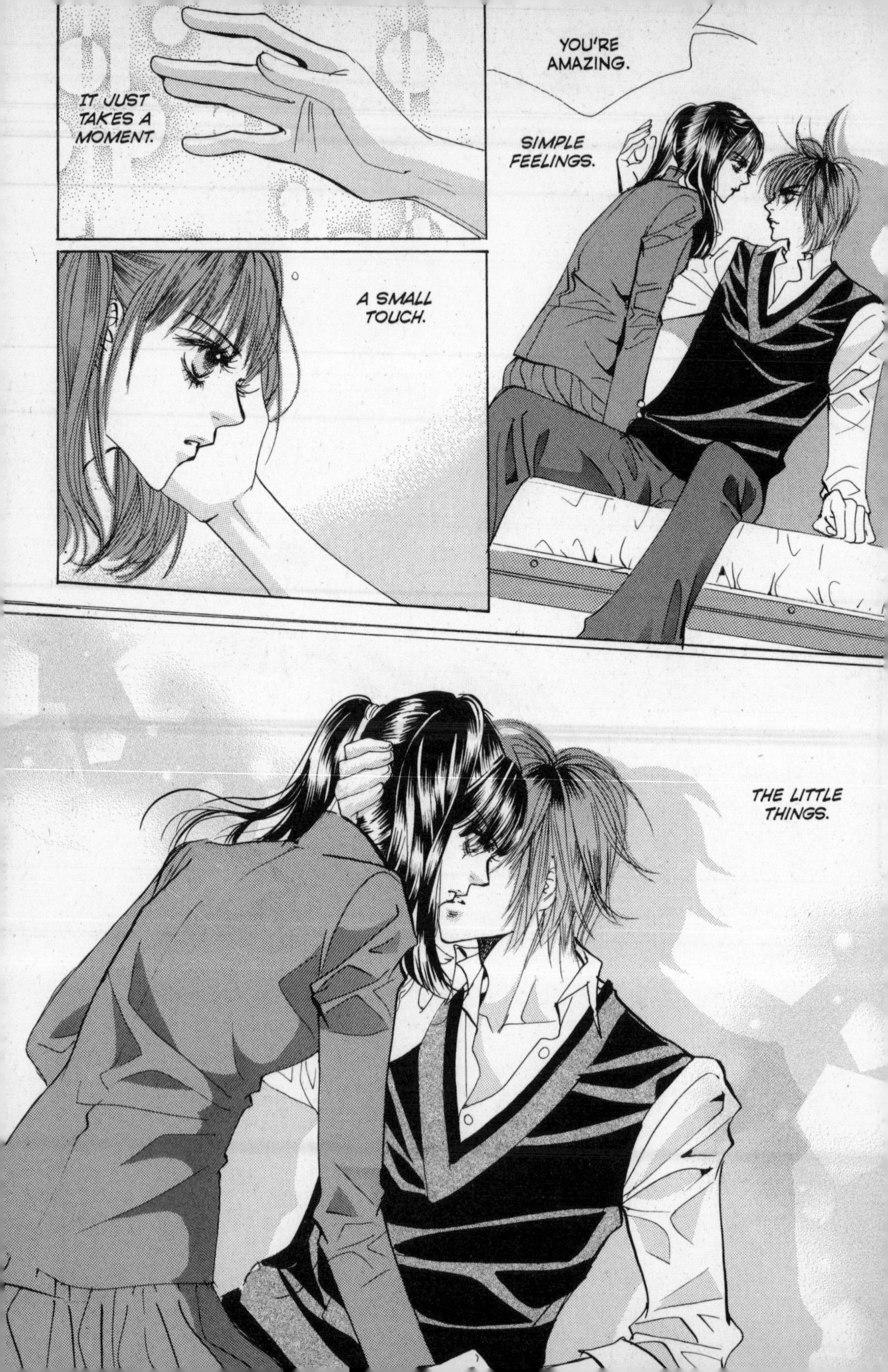
IT JUST TAKES A MOMENT.
A SMALL TOUCH.
YOU'RE AMAZING.
SIMPLE FEELINGS.
THE LITTLE THINGS.

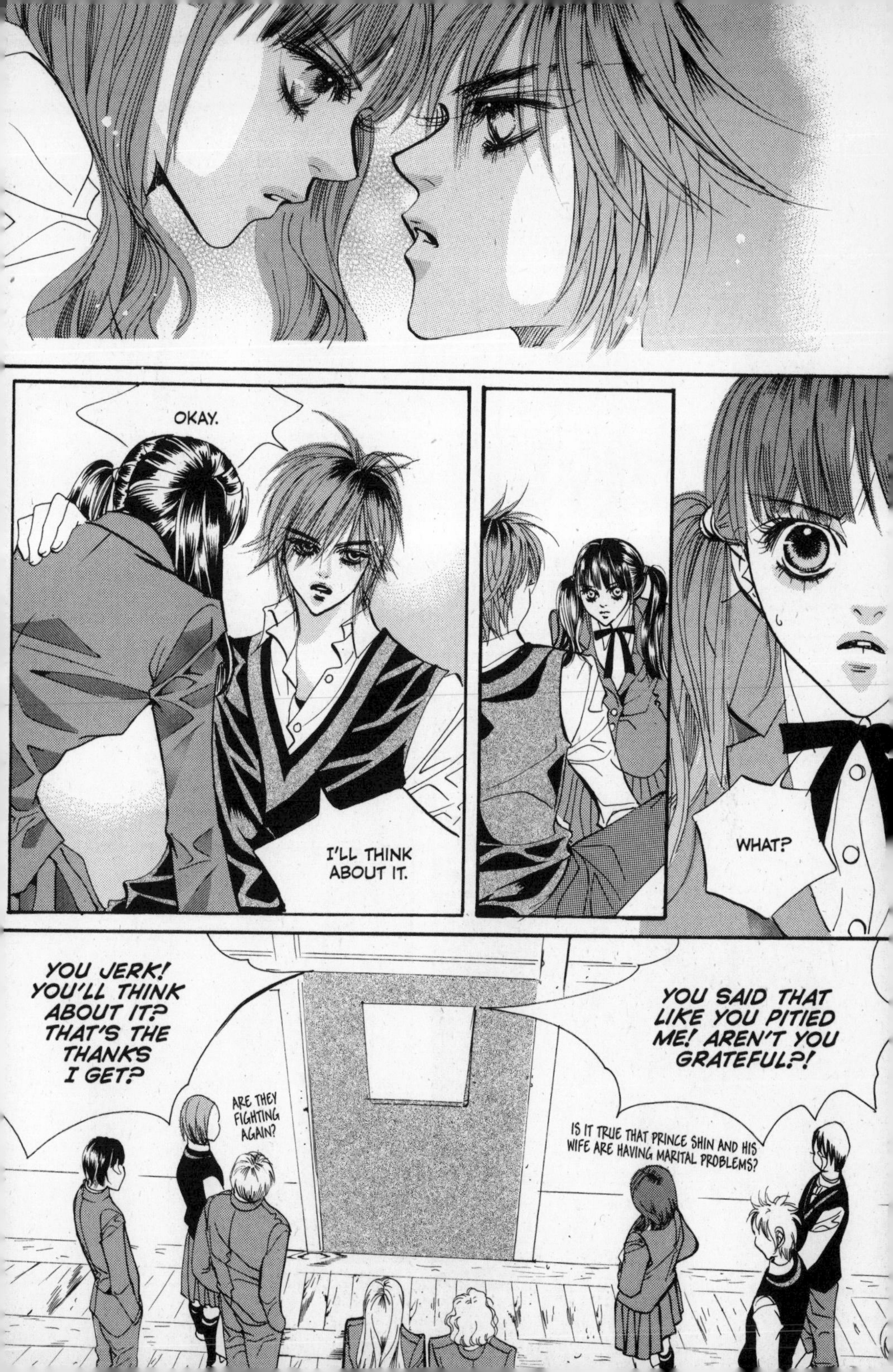

OKAY.
I'LL THINK ABOUT IT.
WHAT?
YOU JERK! YOU'LL THINK ABOUT IT? THAT'S THE THANKS I GET?
ARE THEY FIGHTING AGAIN?
YOU SAID THAT LIKE YOU PITIED ME! AREN'T YOU GRATEFUL?!
IS IT TRUE THAT PRINCE SHIN AND HIS WIFE ARE HAVING MARITAL PROBLEMS?

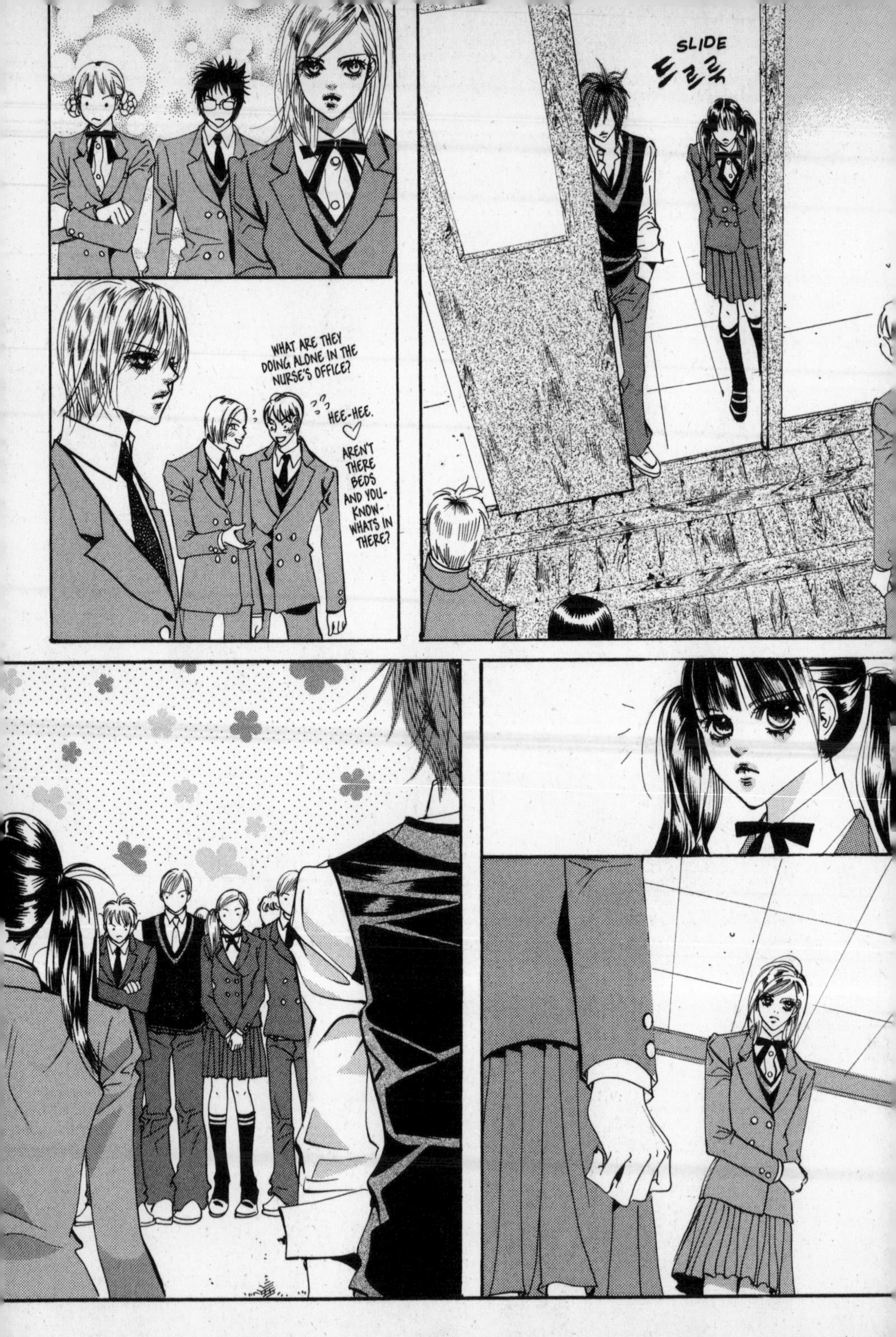
WHAT ARE THEY DOING ALONE IN THE NURSE'S OFFICE?
HEE-HEE. ♡
AREN'T THERE BEDS AND YOU-KNOW-WHATS IN THERE?
SLIDE
드르륵

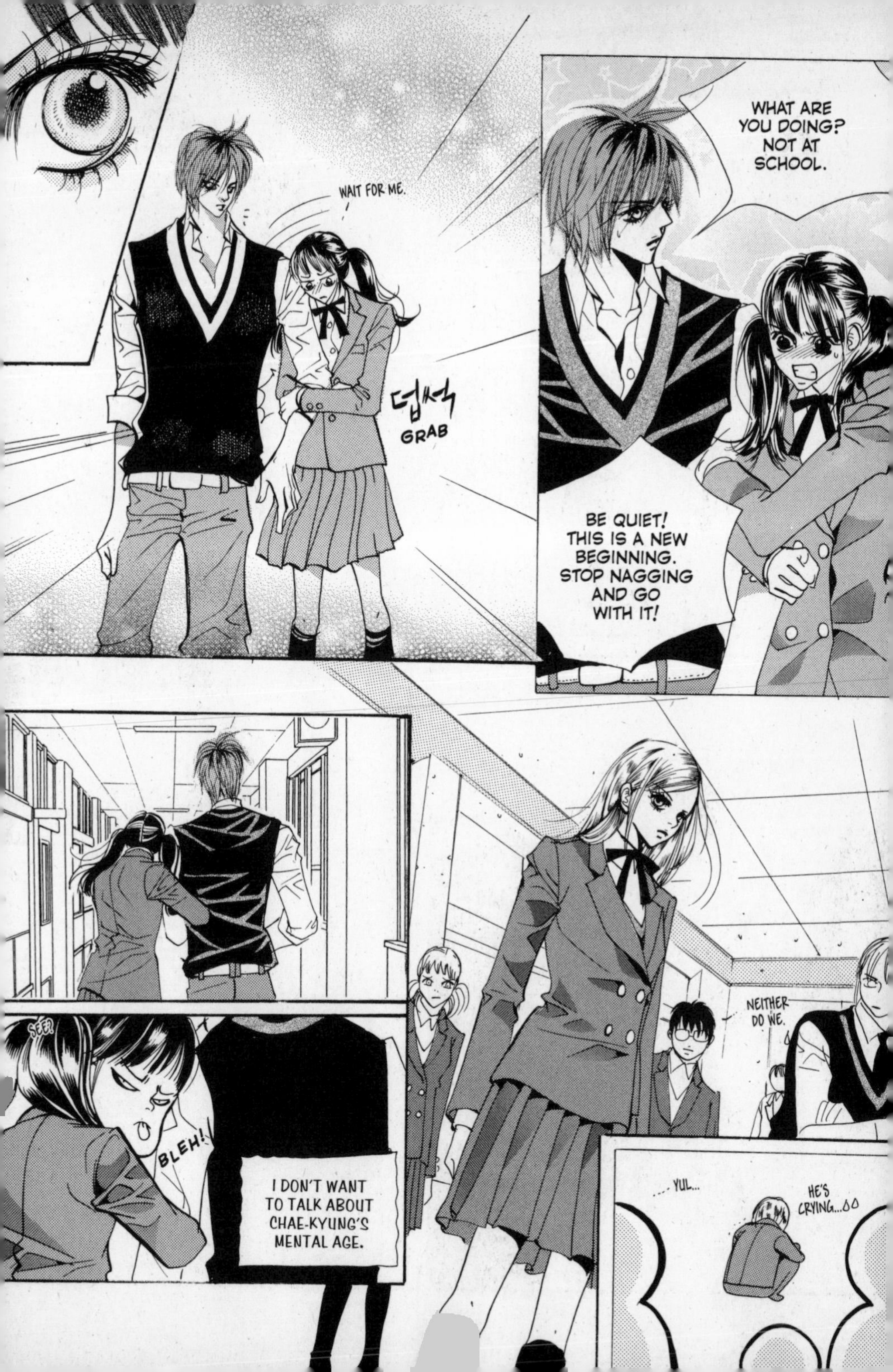
WAIT FOR ME.
덥썩
GRAB
WHAT ARE YOU DOING? NOT AT SCHOOL.
BE QUIET! THIS IS A NEW BEGINNING. STOP NAGGING AND GO WITH IT!
SEE?
BLEH!
I DON'T WANT TO TALK ABOUT CHAE-KYUNG'S MENTAL AGE.
NEITHER DO WE.
... YUL...
HE'S CRYING...

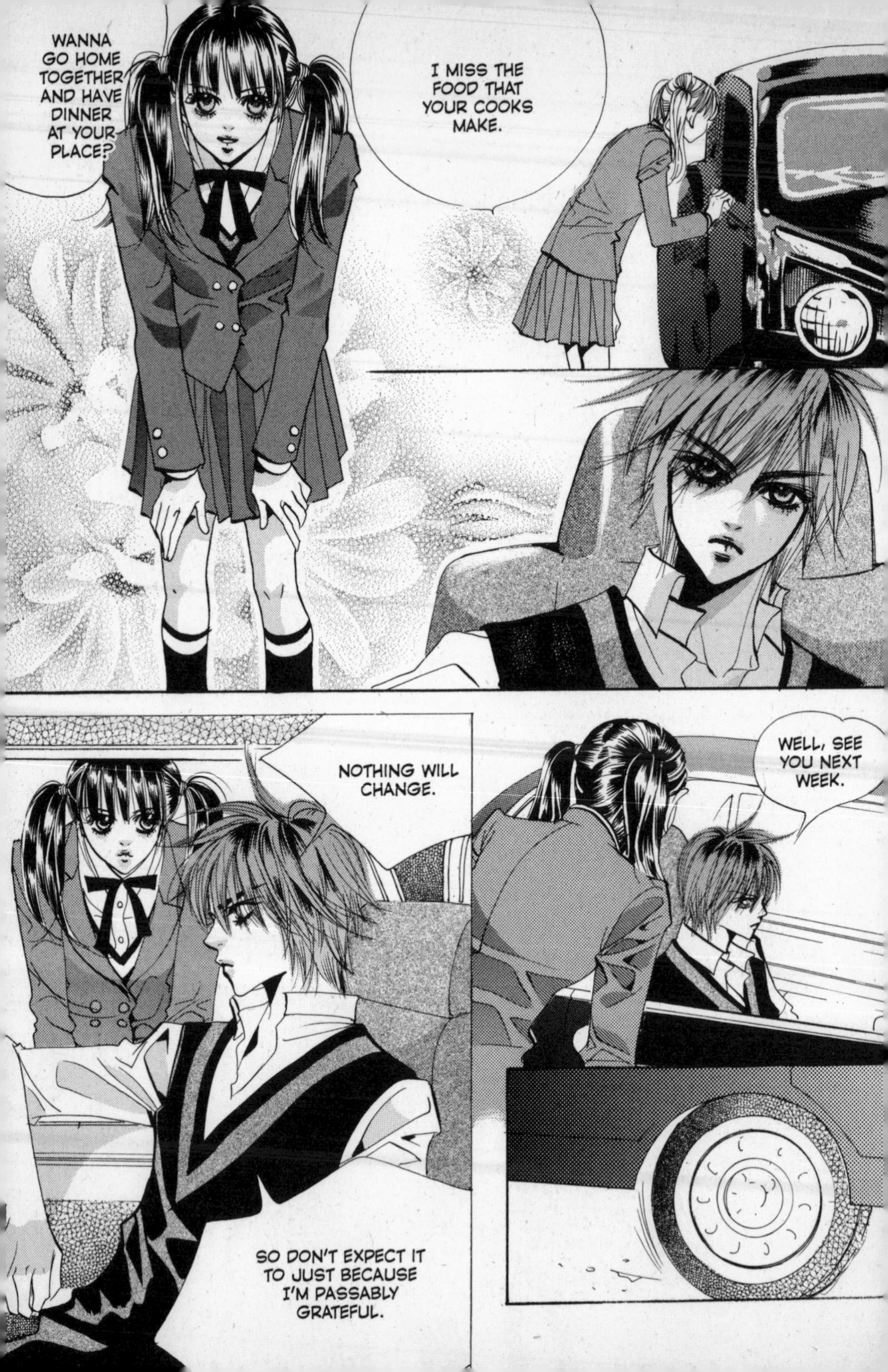
WANNA GO HOME TOGETHER AND HAVE DINNER AT YOUR PLACE?
I MISS THE FOOD THAT YOUR COOKS MAKE.
NOTHING WILL CHANGE.
SO DON'T EXPECT IT TO JUST BECAUSE I'M PASSABLY GRATEFUL.
WELL, SEE YOU NEXT WEEK.

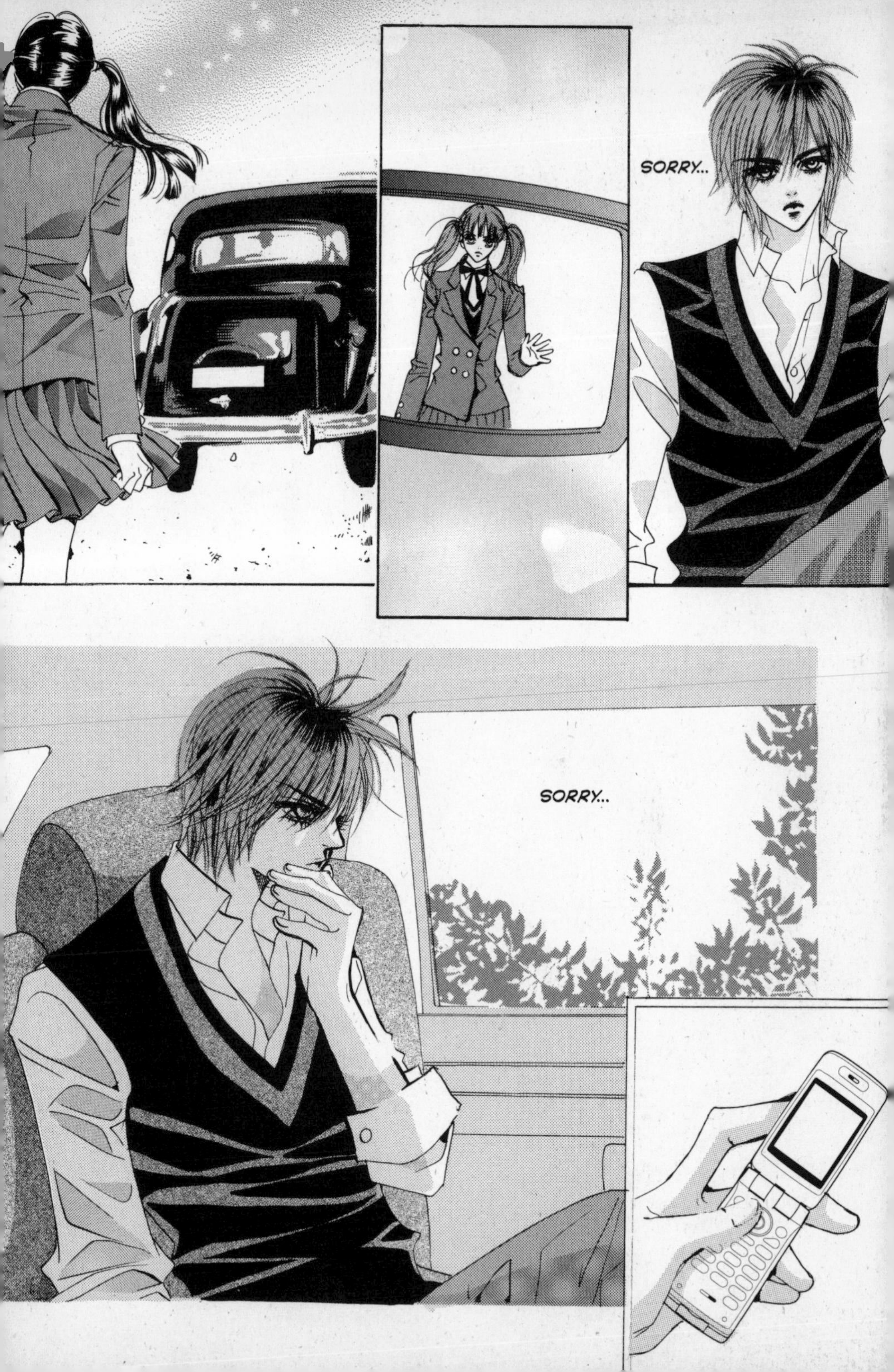
SORRY...
SORRY...

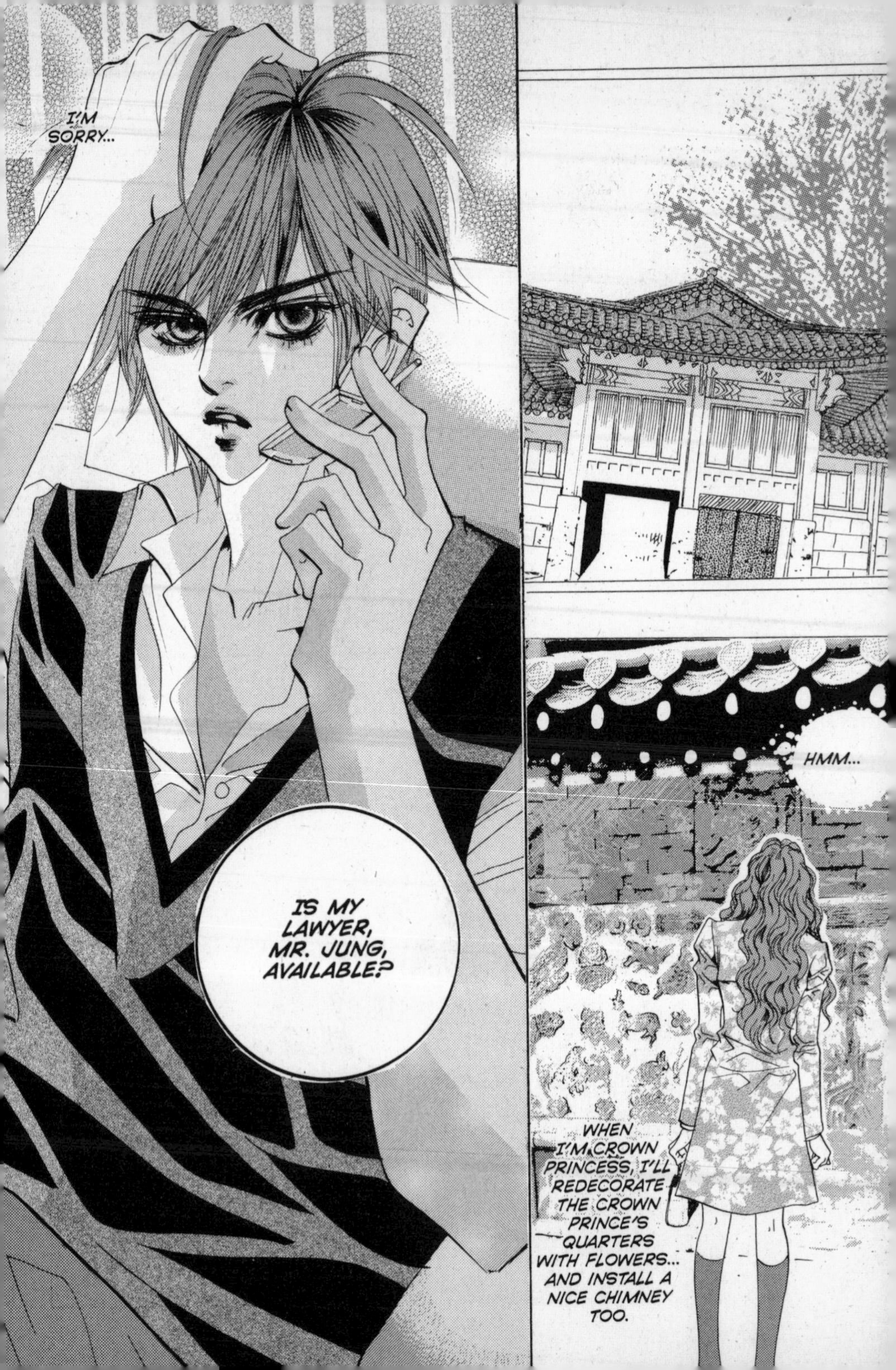
I'M SORRY...
IS MY LAWYER, MR. JUNG, AVAILABLE?
HMM...
WHEN I'M CROWN PRINCESS, I'LL REDECORATE THE CROWN PRINCE'S QUARTERS WITH FLOWERS... AND INSTALL A NICE CHIMNEY TOO.

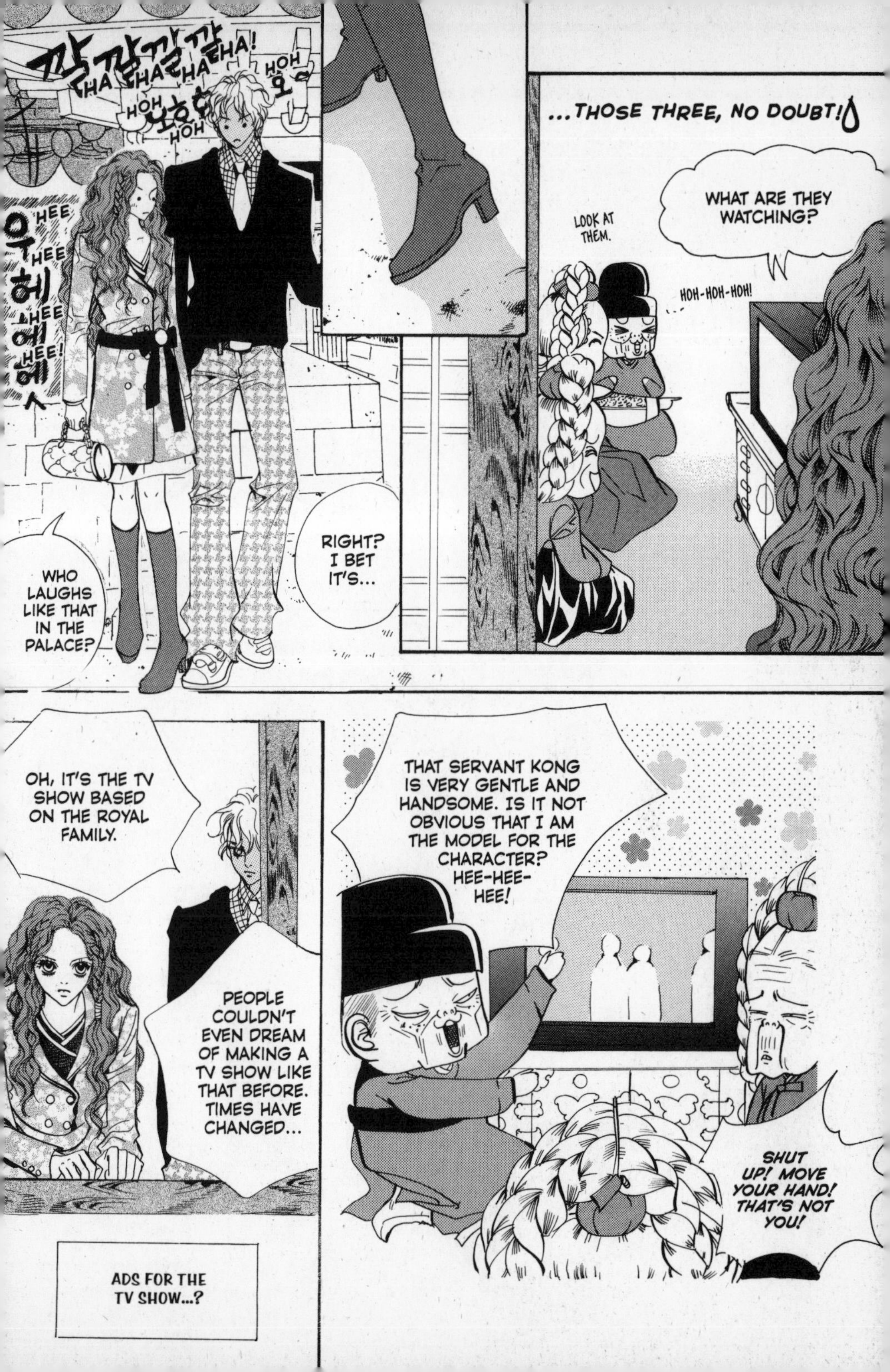
HA HA HA HA HA!
HOH HOH HOH HOH
HEE HEE HEE HEE!
WHO LAUGHS LIKE THAT IN THE PALACE?
RIGHT? I BET IT'S...
...THOSE THREE, NO DOUBT!
LOOK AT THEM.
WHAT ARE THEY WATCHING?
HOH-HOH-HOH!
OH, IT'S THE TV SHOW BASED ON THE ROYAL FAMILY.
PEOPLE COULDN'T EVEN DREAM OF MAKING A TV SHOW LIKE THAT BEFORE. TIMES HAVE CHANGED...
ADS FOR THE TV SHOW...?
THAT SERVANT KONG IS VERY GENTLE AND HANDSOME. IS IT NOT OBVIOUS THAT I AM THE MODEL FOR THE CHARACTER? HEE-HEE-HEE!
SHUT UP! MOVE YOUR HAND! THAT'S NOT YOU!

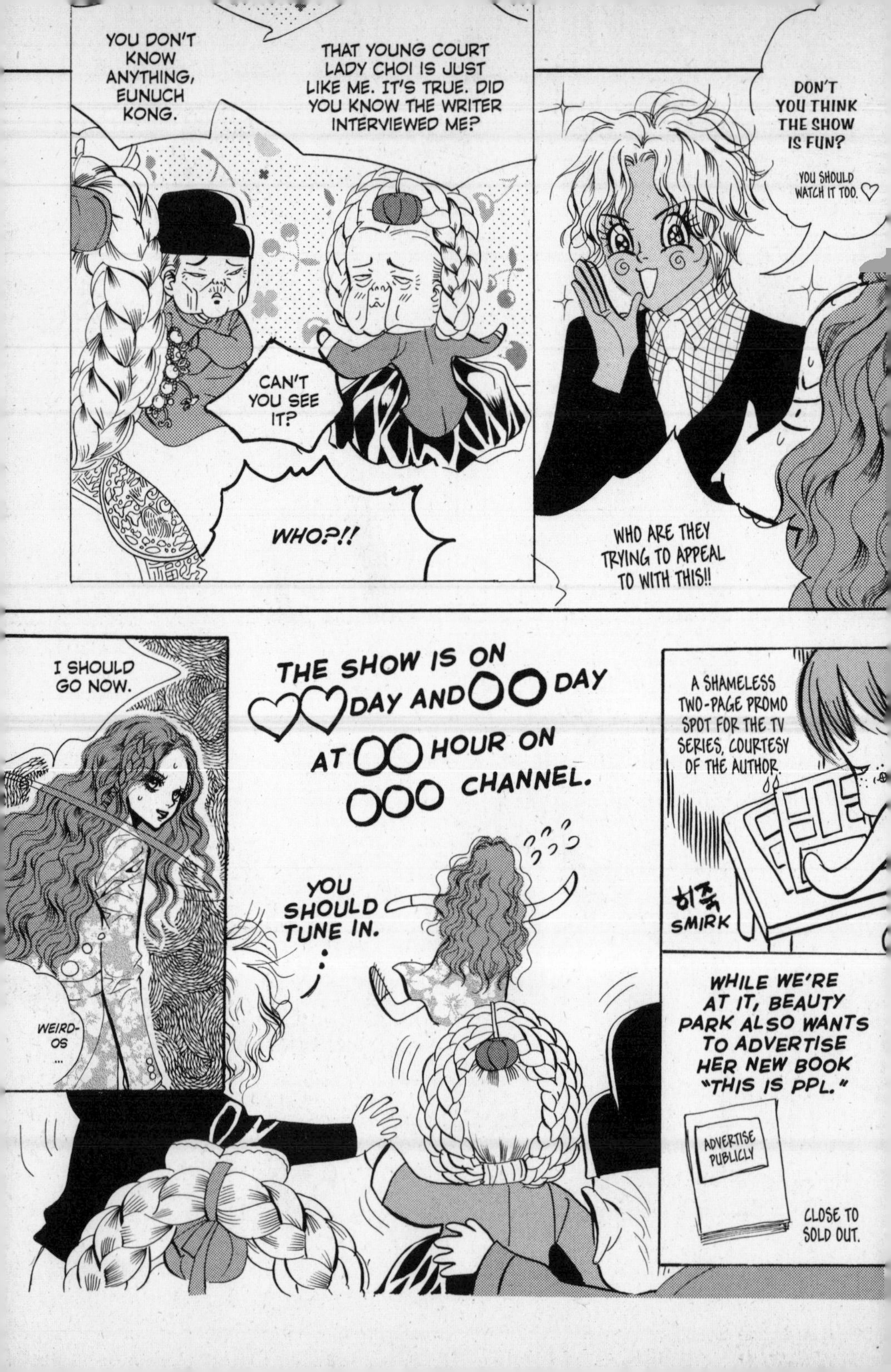
YOU DON'T KNOW ANYTHING, EUNUCH KONG.
THAT YOUNG COURT LADY CHOI IS JUST LIKE ME. IT'S TRUE. DID YOU KNOW THE WRITER INTERVIEWED ME?
CAN'T YOU SEE IT?
WHO?!!
DON'T YOU THINK THE SHOW IS FUN?
YOU SHOULD WATCH IT TOO. ♡
WHO ARE THEY TRYING TO APPEAL TO WITH THIS!!
I SHOULD GO NOW.
WEIRD-OS ...
THE SHOW IS ON ♡♡ DAY AND OO DAY AT OO HOUR ON OOO CHANNEL.
YOU SHOULD TUNE IN.
A SHAMELESS TWO-PAGE PROMO SPOT FOR THE TV SERIES, COURTESY OF THE AUTHOR.
히죽
SMIRK
WHILE WE'RE AT IT, BEAUTY PARK ALSO WANTS TO ADVERTISE HER NEW BOOK "THIS IS PPL."
ADVERTISE PUBLICLY
CLOSE TO SOLD OUT.

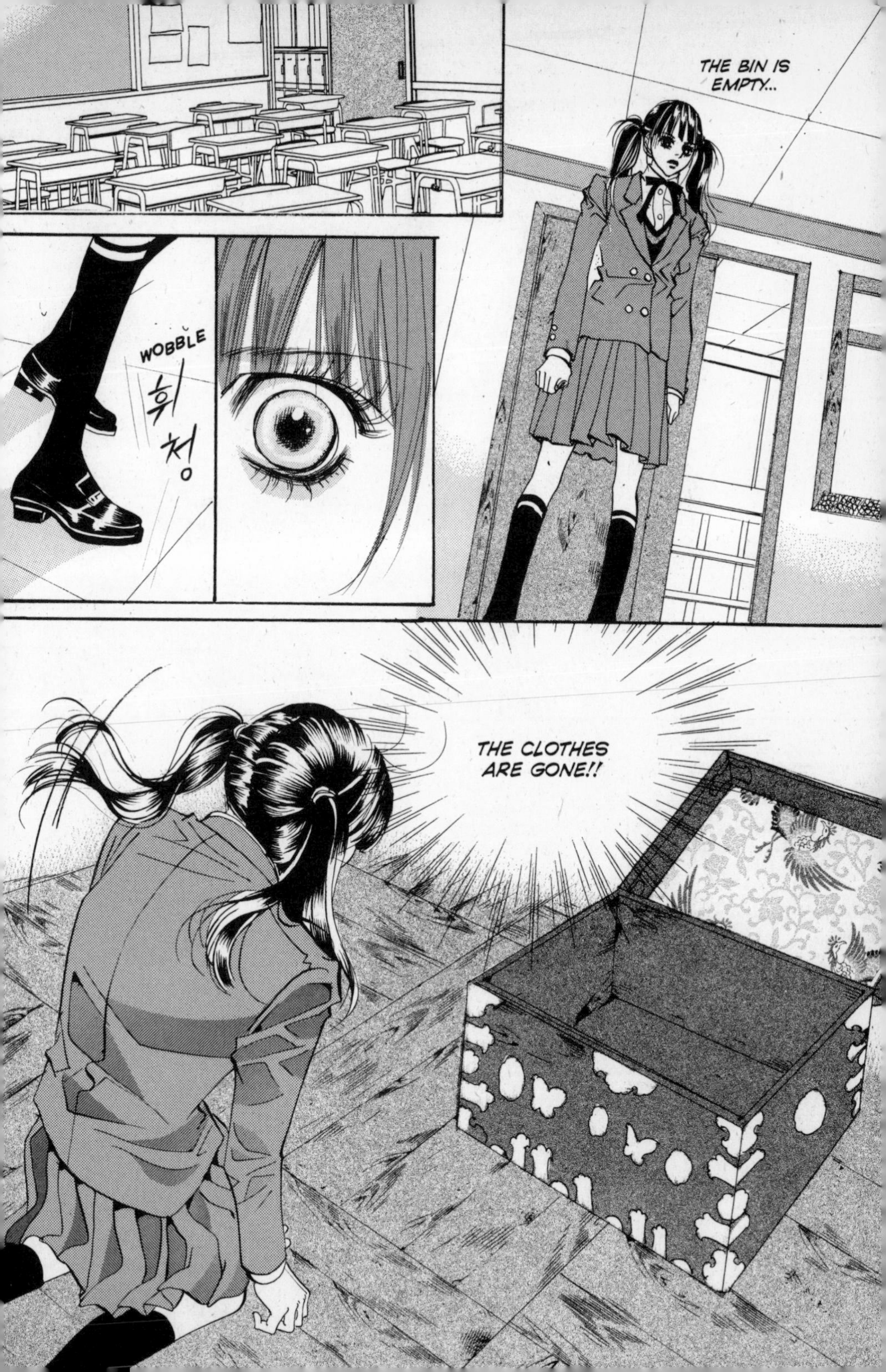
WOBBLE
휘청
THE BIN IS EMPTY...
THE CLOTHES ARE GONE!!

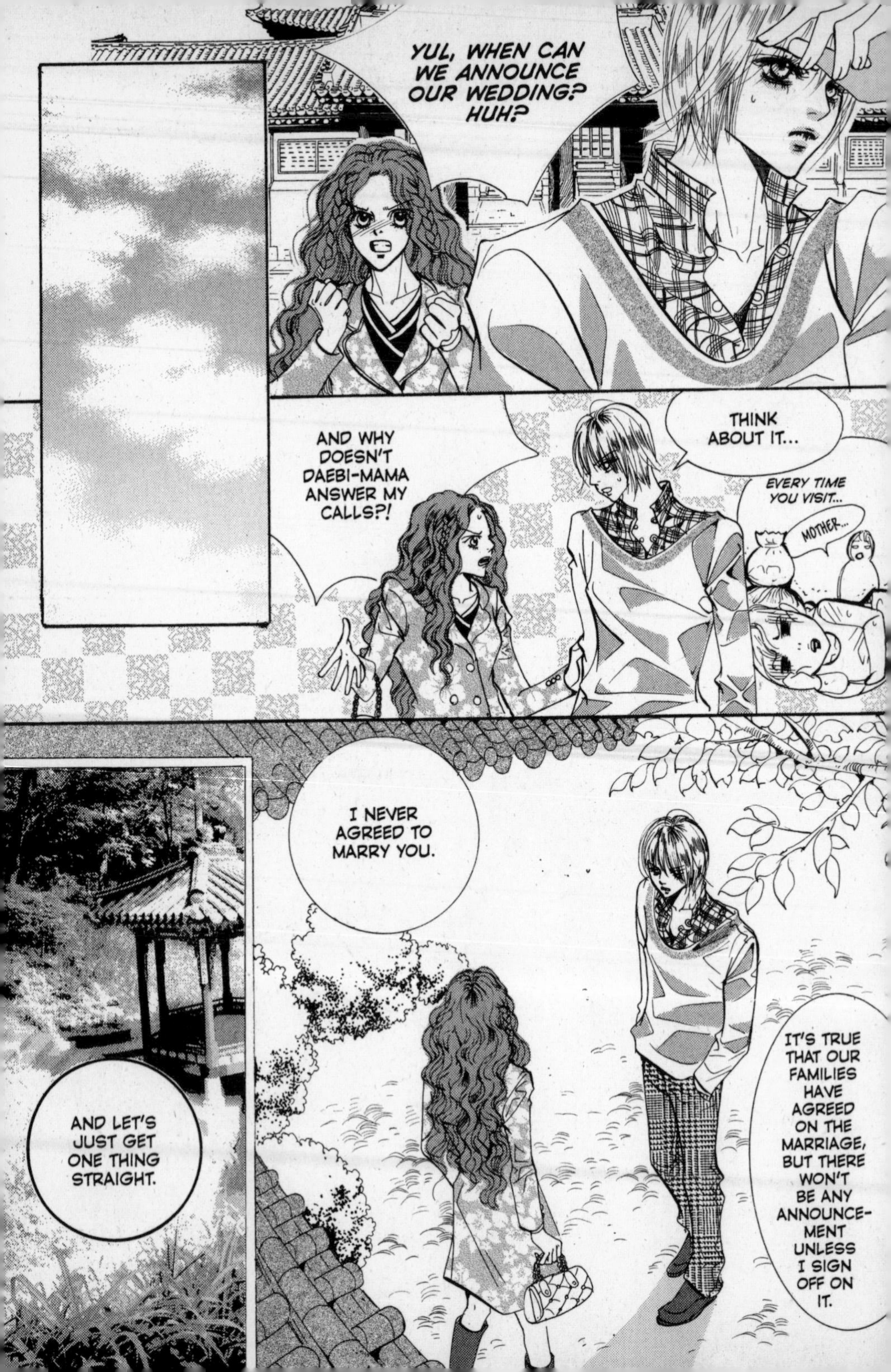
YUL, WHEN CAN WE ANNOUNCE OUR WEDDING? HUH?
AND WHY DOESN'T DAEBI-MAMA ANSWER MY CALLS?!
THINK ABOUT IT...
EVERY TIME YOU VISIT...
MOTHER...
AND LET'S JUST GET ONE THING STRAIGHT.
I NEVER AGREED TO MARRY YOU.
IT'S TRUE THAT OUR FAMILIES HAVE AGREED ON THE MARRIAGE, BUT THERE WON'T BE ANY ANNOUNCEMENT UNLESS I SIGN OFF ON IT.

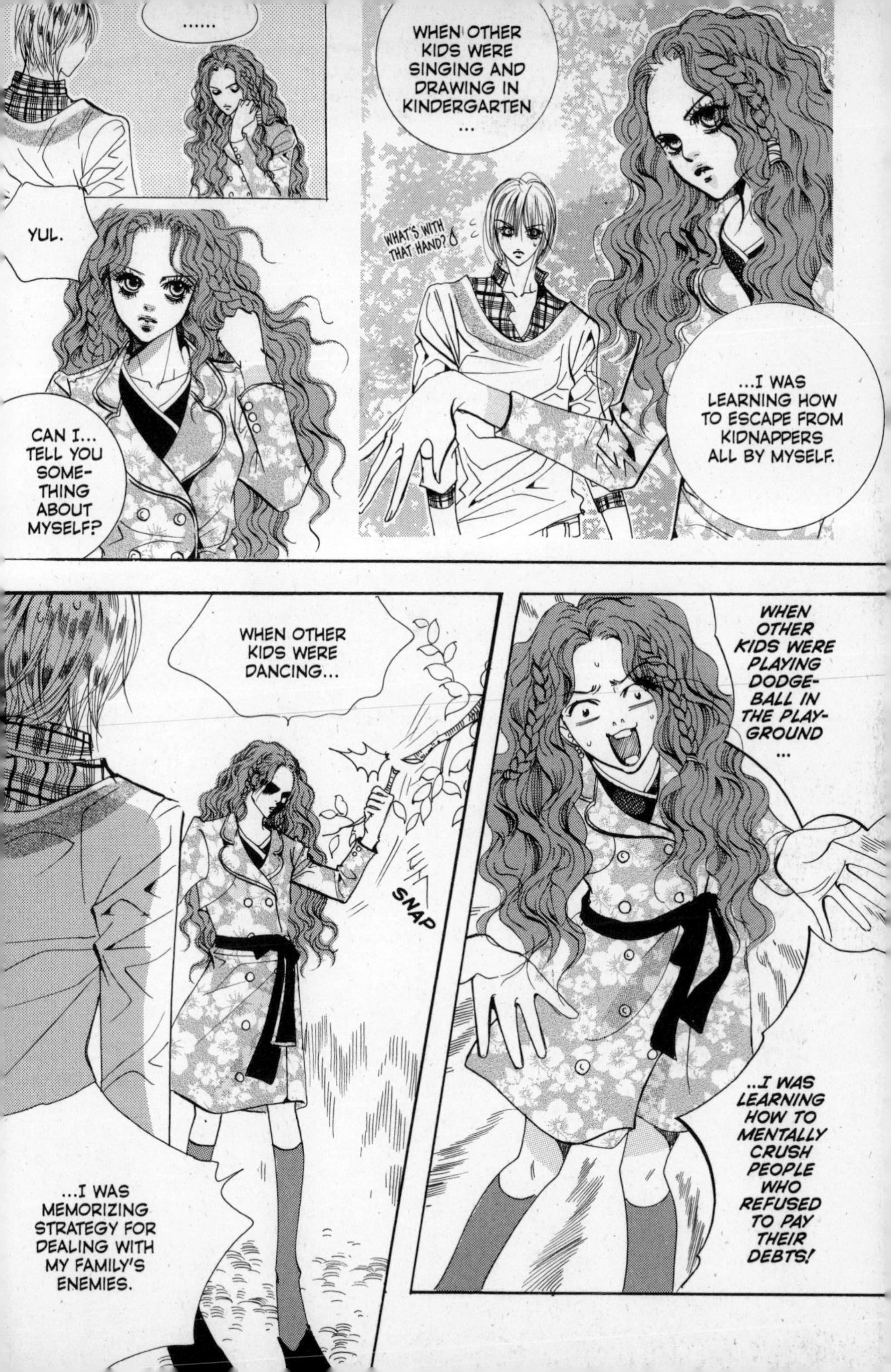
......
YUL.
CAN I... TELL YOU SOME-THING ABOUT MYSELF?
WHEN OTHER KIDS WERE SINGING AND DRAWING IN KINDERGARTEN ...
WHAT'S WITH THAT HAND?
...I WAS LEARNING HOW TO ESCAPE FROM KIDNAPPERS ALL BY MYSELF.
WHEN OTHER KIDS WERE DANCING...
SNAP
...I WAS MEMORIZING STRATEGY FOR DEALING WITH MY FAMILY'S ENEMIES.
WHEN OTHER KIDS WERE PLAYING DODGE-BALL IN THE PLAY-GROUND ...
...I WAS LEARNING HOW TO MENTALLY CRUSH PEOPLE WHO REFUSED TO PAY THEIR DEBTS!

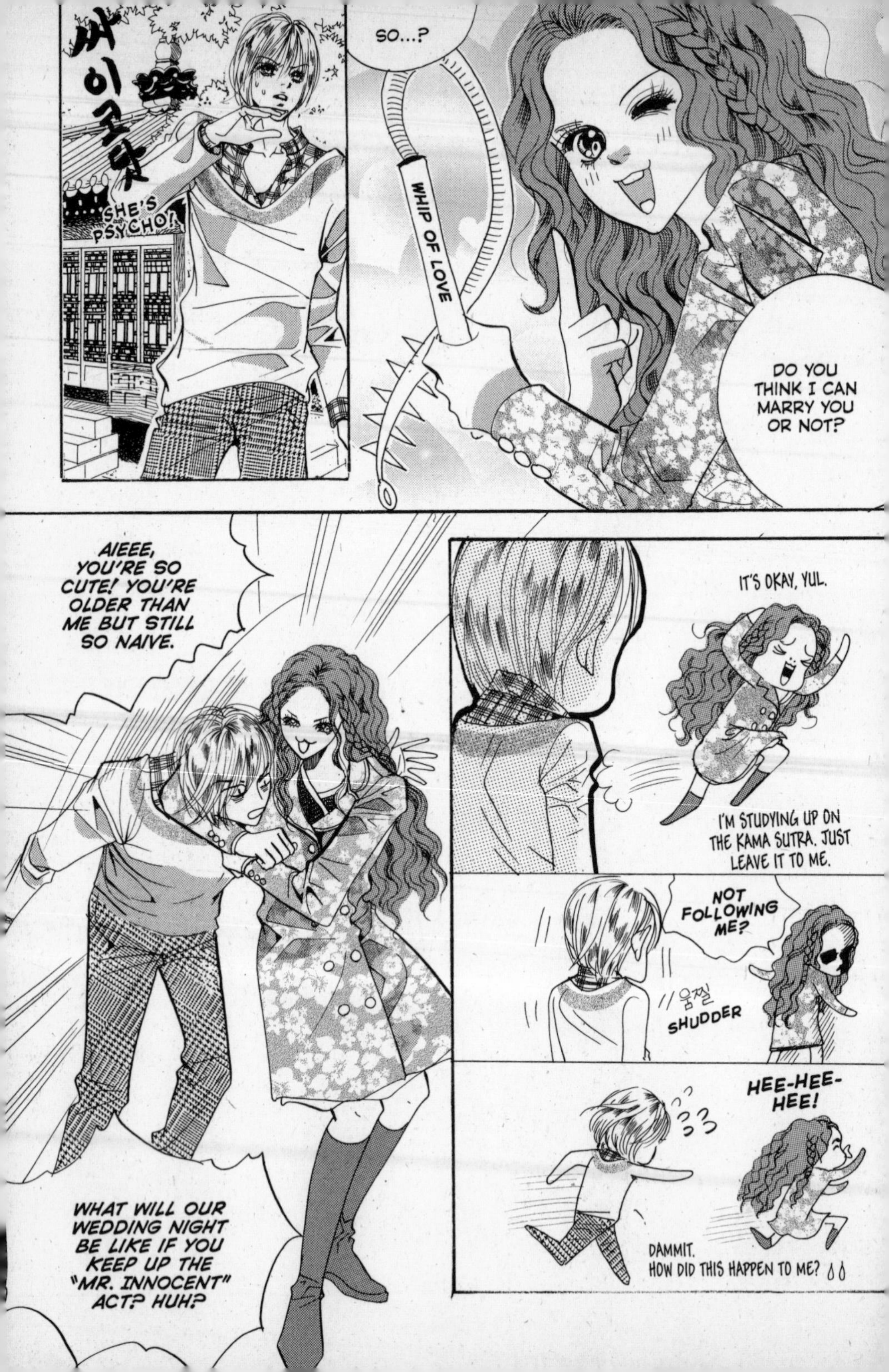
싸이코닷
SHE'S PSYCHO!
SO...?
WHIP OF LOVE
DO YOU THINK I CAN MARRY YOU OR NOT?
AIEEE, YOU'RE SO CUTE! YOU'RE OLDER THAN ME BUT STILL SO NAIVE.
WHAT WILL OUR WEDDING NIGHT BE LIKE IF YOU KEEP UP THE "MR. INNOCENT" ACT? HUH?
IT'S OKAY, YUL.
I'M STUDYING UP ON THE KAMA SUTRA. JUST LEAVE IT TO ME.
NOT FOLLOWING ME?
움찔
SHUDDER
HEE-HEE-HEE!
DAMMIT. HOW DID THIS HAPPEN TO ME?

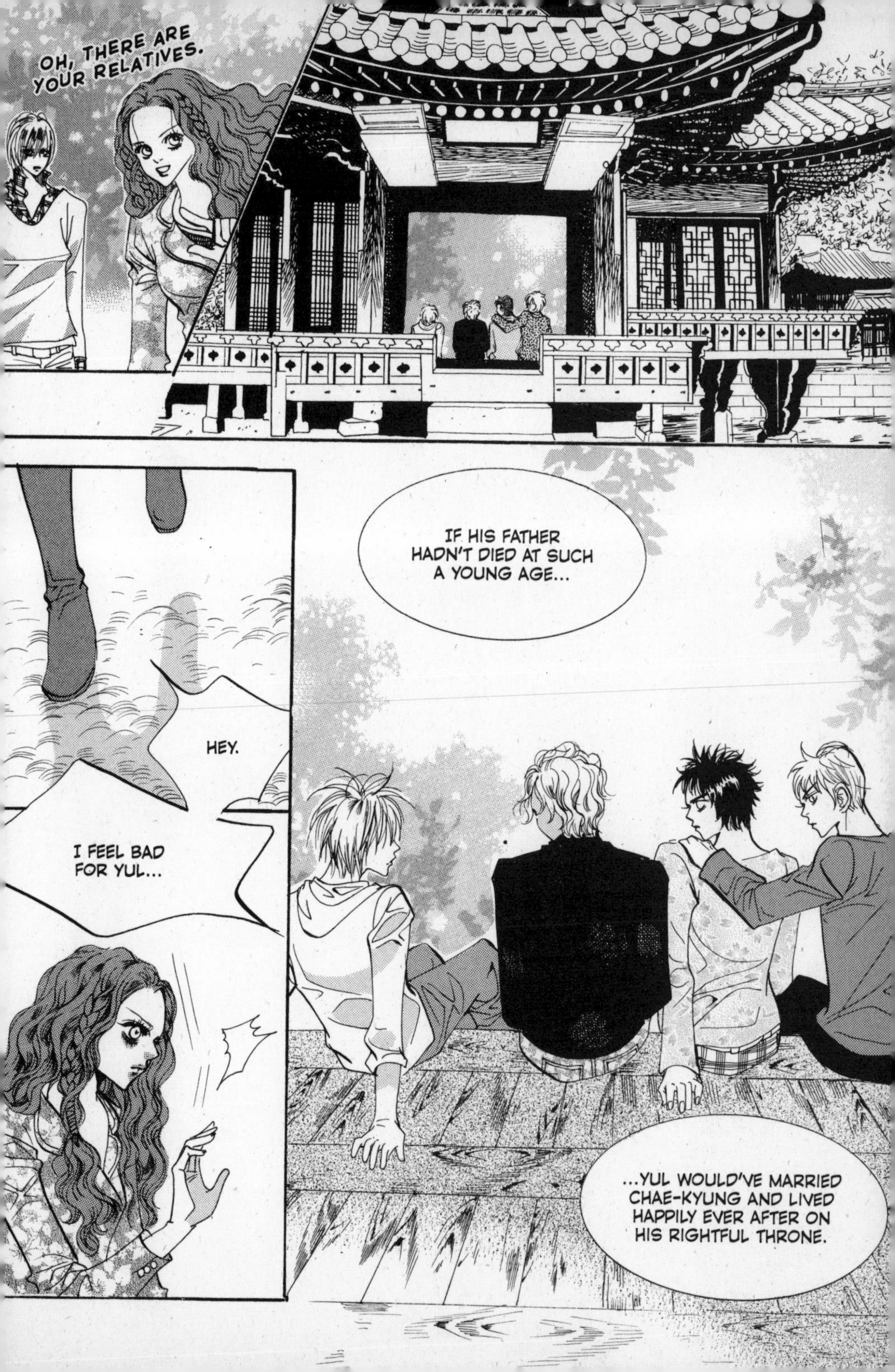
OH, THERE ARE YOUR RELATIVES.
HEY.
I FEEL BAD FOR YUL...
IF HIS FATHER HADN'T DIED AT SUCH A YOUNG AGE...
...YUL WOULD'VE MARRIED CHAE-KYUNG AND LIVED HAPPILY EVER AFTER ON HIS RIGHTFUL THRONE.

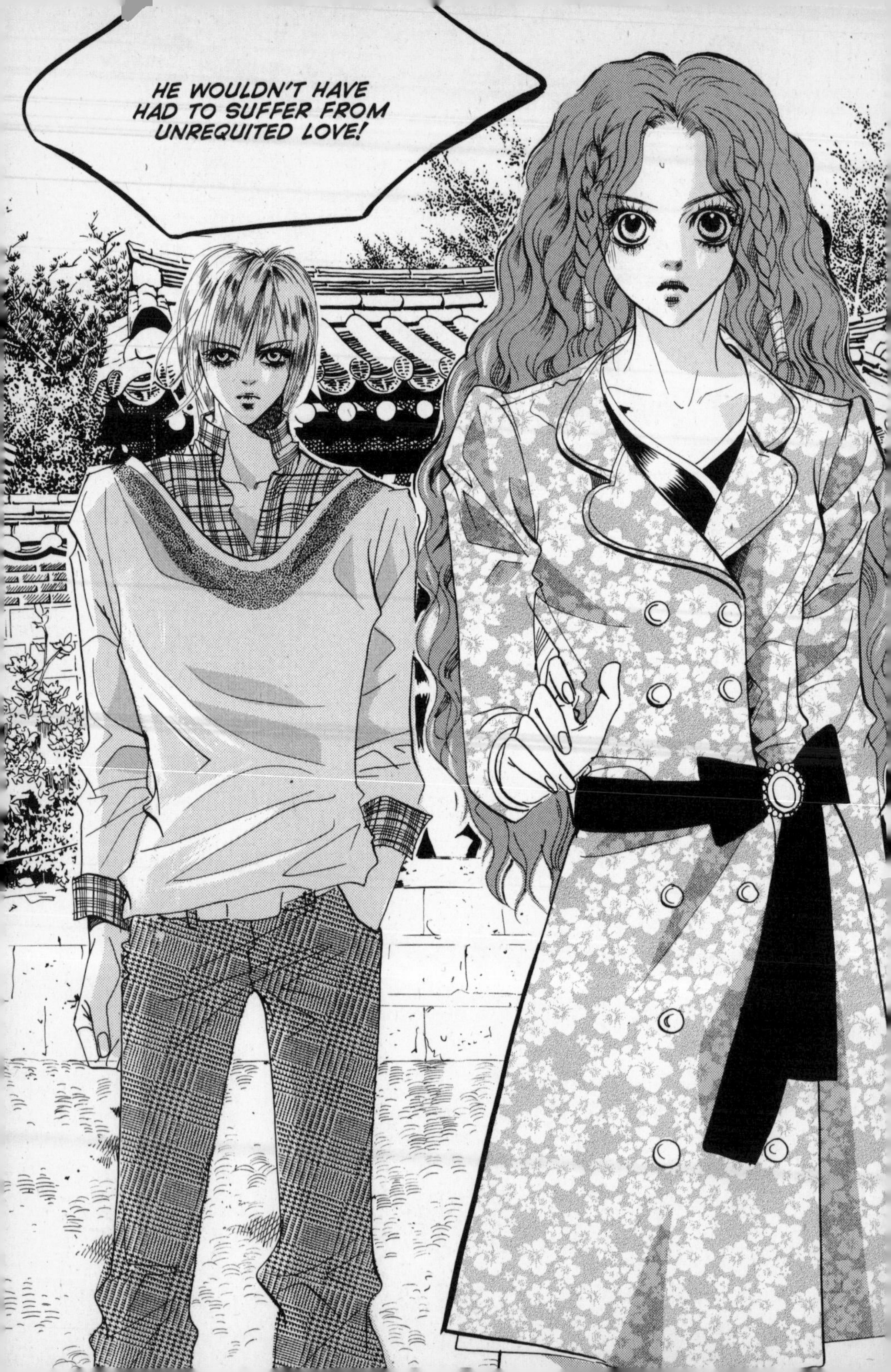
HE WOULDN'T HAVE HAD TO SUFFER FROM UNREQUITED LOVE!

THE ROYAL PALACE

Goong

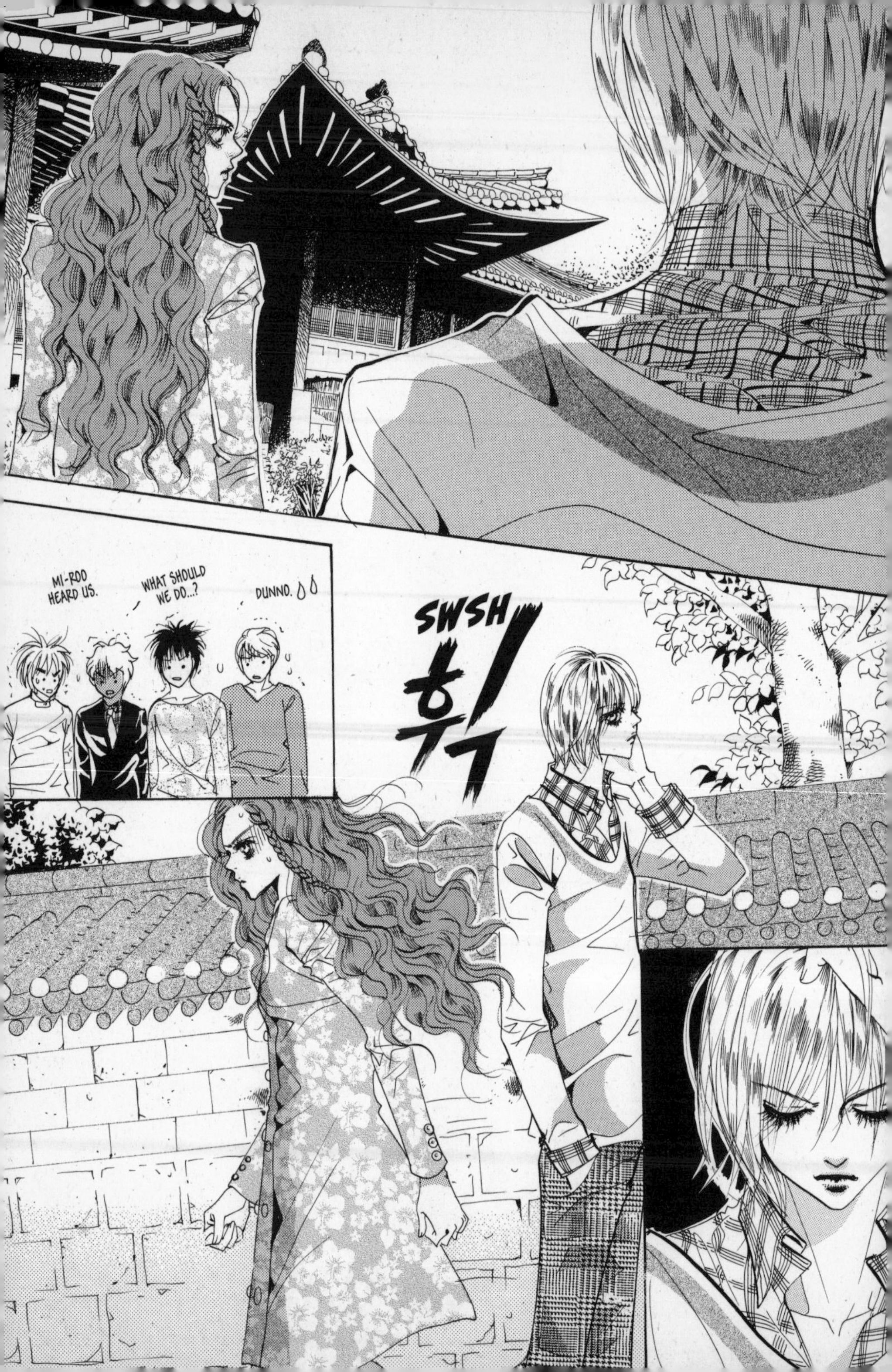
MI-ROO HEARD US.
WHAT SHOULD WE DO...?
DUNNO.
SWSH

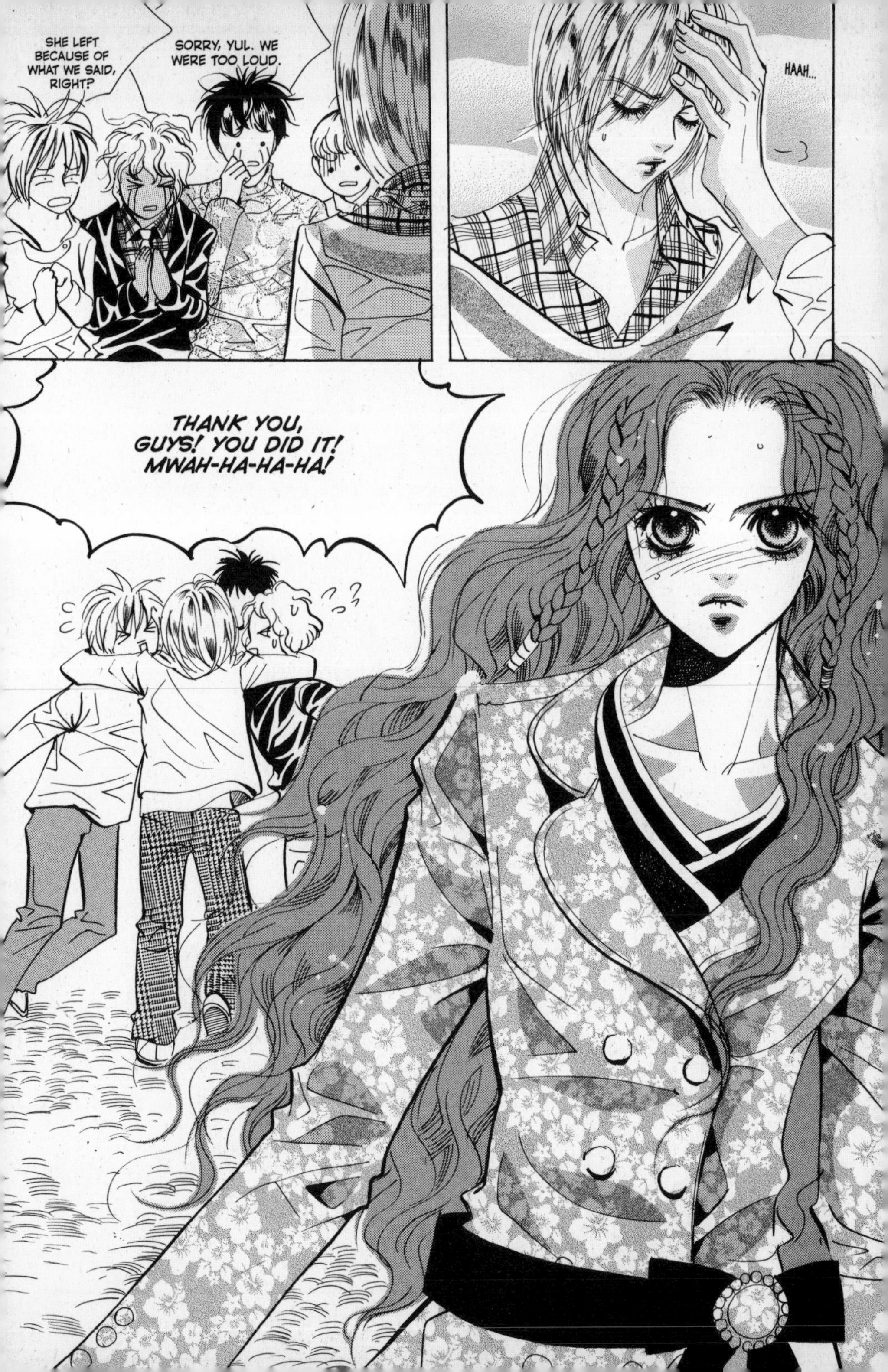
SHE LEFT BECAUSE OF WHAT WE SAID, RIGHT?
SORRY, YUL. WE WERE TOO LOUD.
HAAH...
THANK YOU, GUYS! YOU DID IT! MWAH-HA-HA-HA!

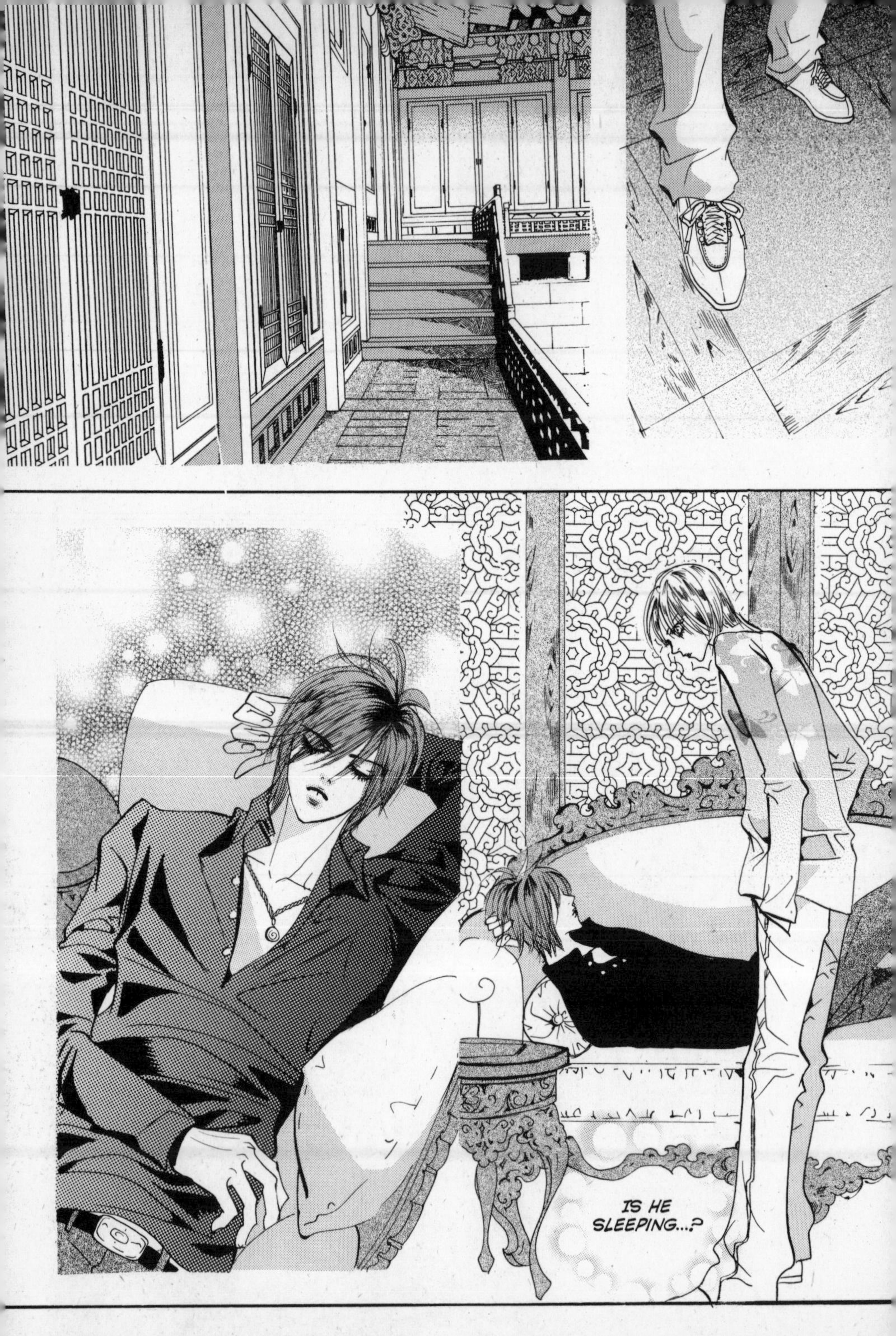
IS HE
SLEEPING...?

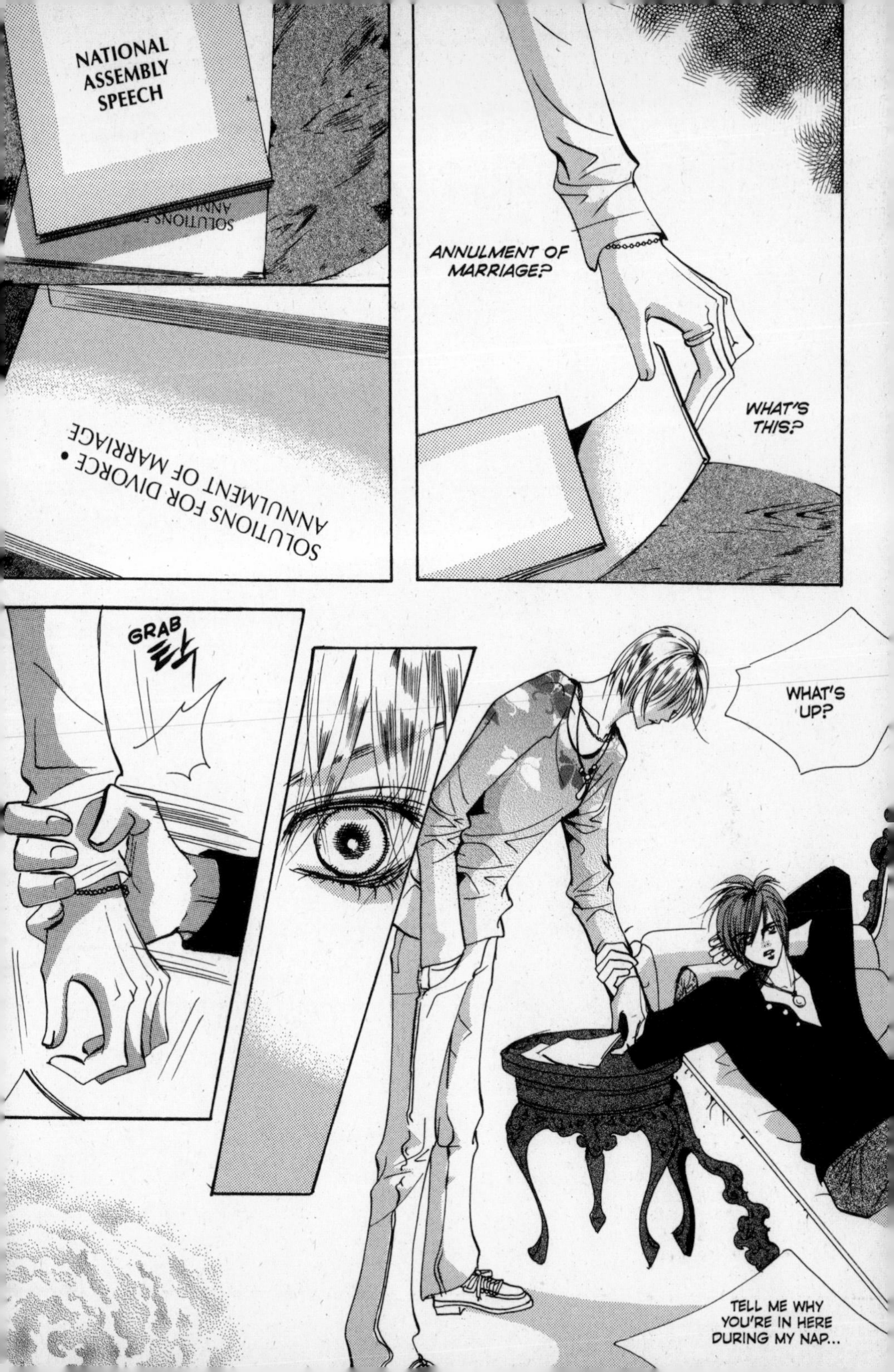
WHAT'S THIS?
ANNULMENT OF MARRIAGE?
NATIONAL ASSEMBLY SPEECH
SOLUTIONS FOR DIVORCE • ANNULMENT OF MARRIAGE
WHAT'S UP?
TELL ME WHY YOU'RE IN HERE DURING MY NAP...
GRAB

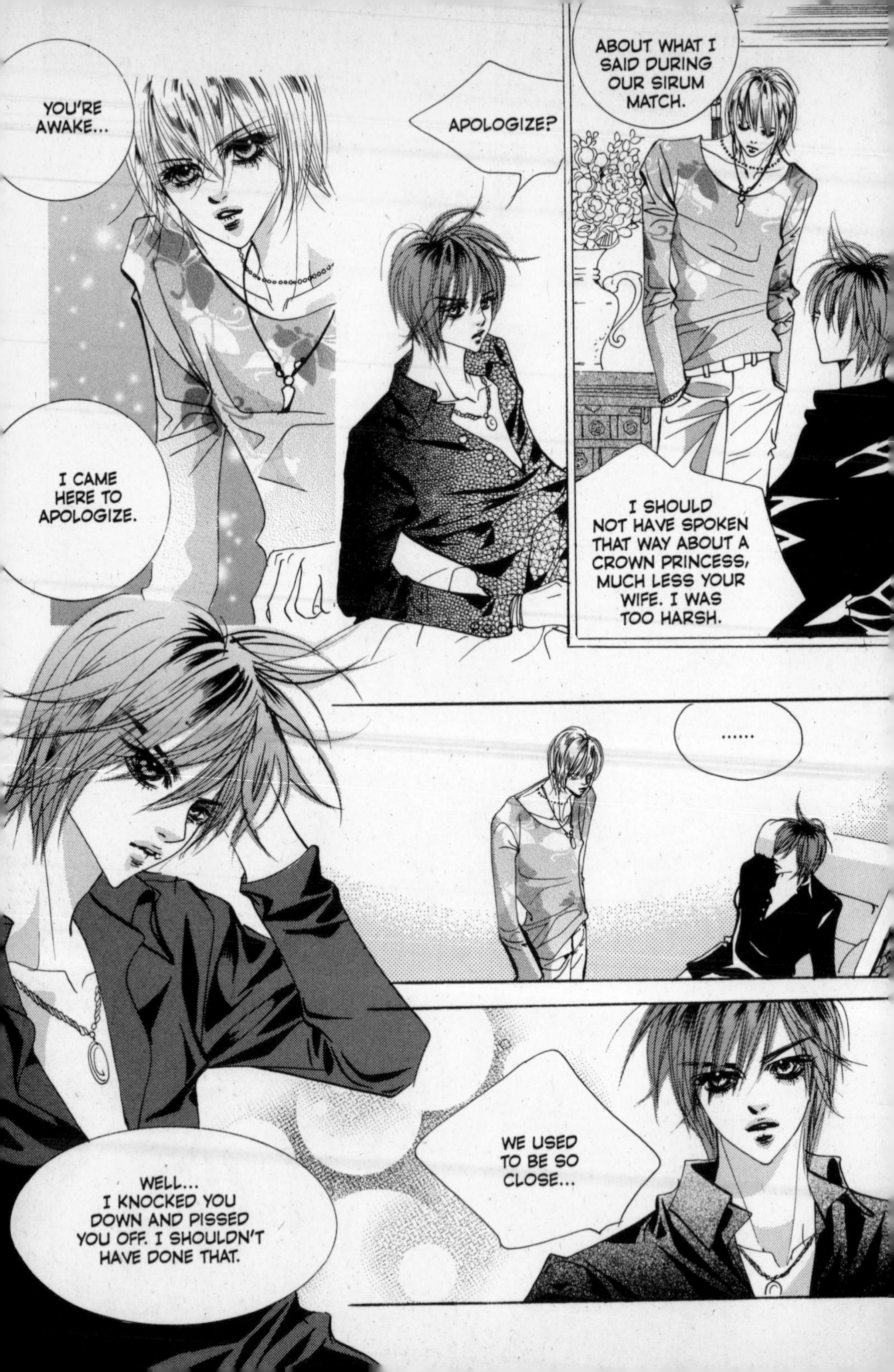
YOU'RE AWAKE...
I CAME HERE TO APOLOGIZE.
APOLOGIZE?
ABOUT WHAT I SAID DURING OUR SIRUM MATCH.
I SHOULD NOT HAVE SPOKEN THAT WAY ABOUT A CROWN PRINCESS, MUCH LESS YOUR WIFE. I WAS TOO HARSH.
WELL... I KNOCKED YOU DOWN AND PISSED YOU OFF. I SHOULDN'T HAVE DONE THAT.
......
WE USED TO BE SO CLOSE...

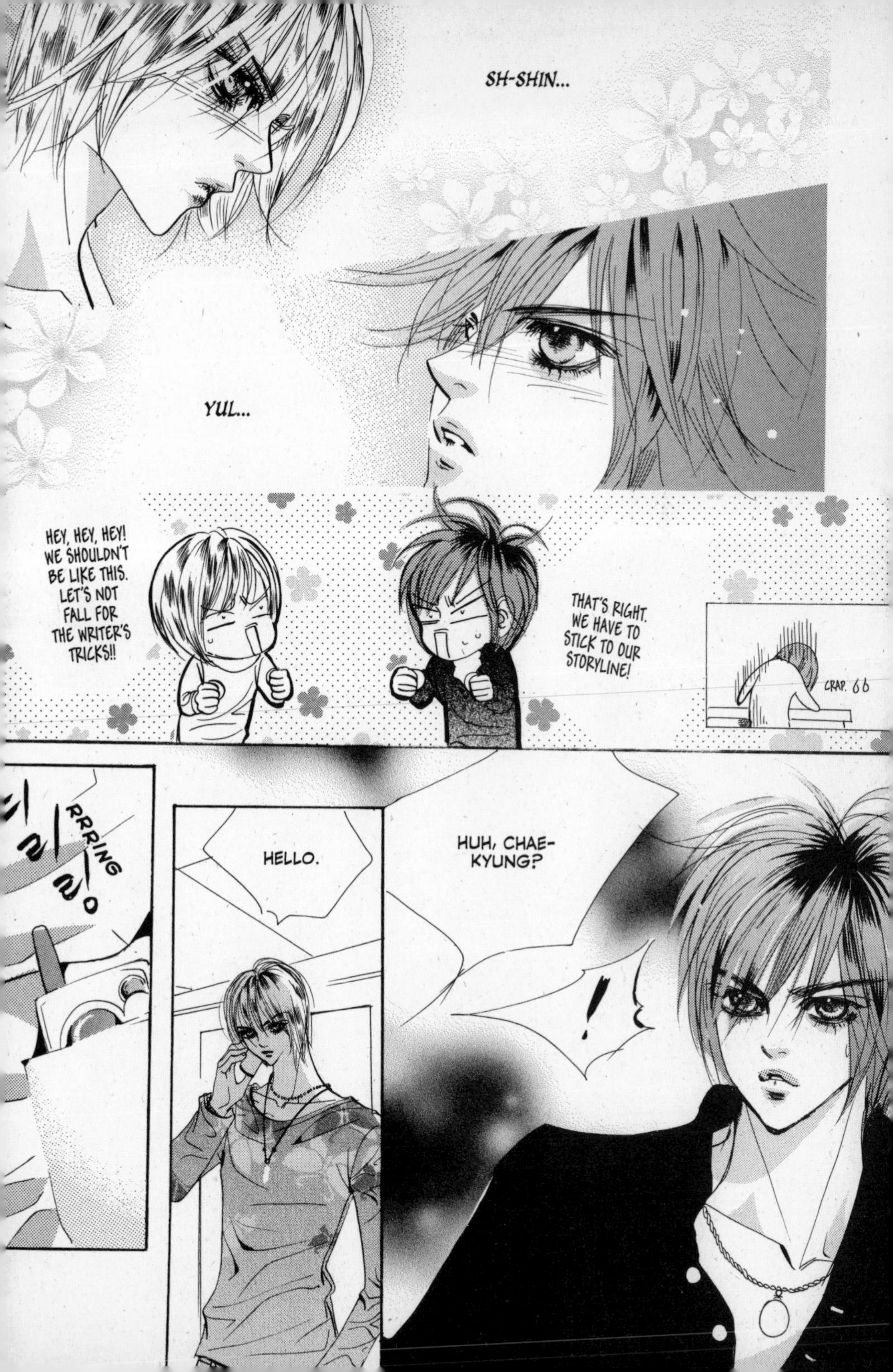
SH-SHIN...
YUL...
HEY, HEY, HEY! WE SHOULDN'T BE LIKE THIS. LET'S NOT FALL FOR THE WRITER'S TRICKS!!
THAT'S RIGHT. WE HAVE TO STICK TO OUR STORYLINE!
CRAP.
RRRING
HELLO.
HUH, CHAE-KYUNG?
!

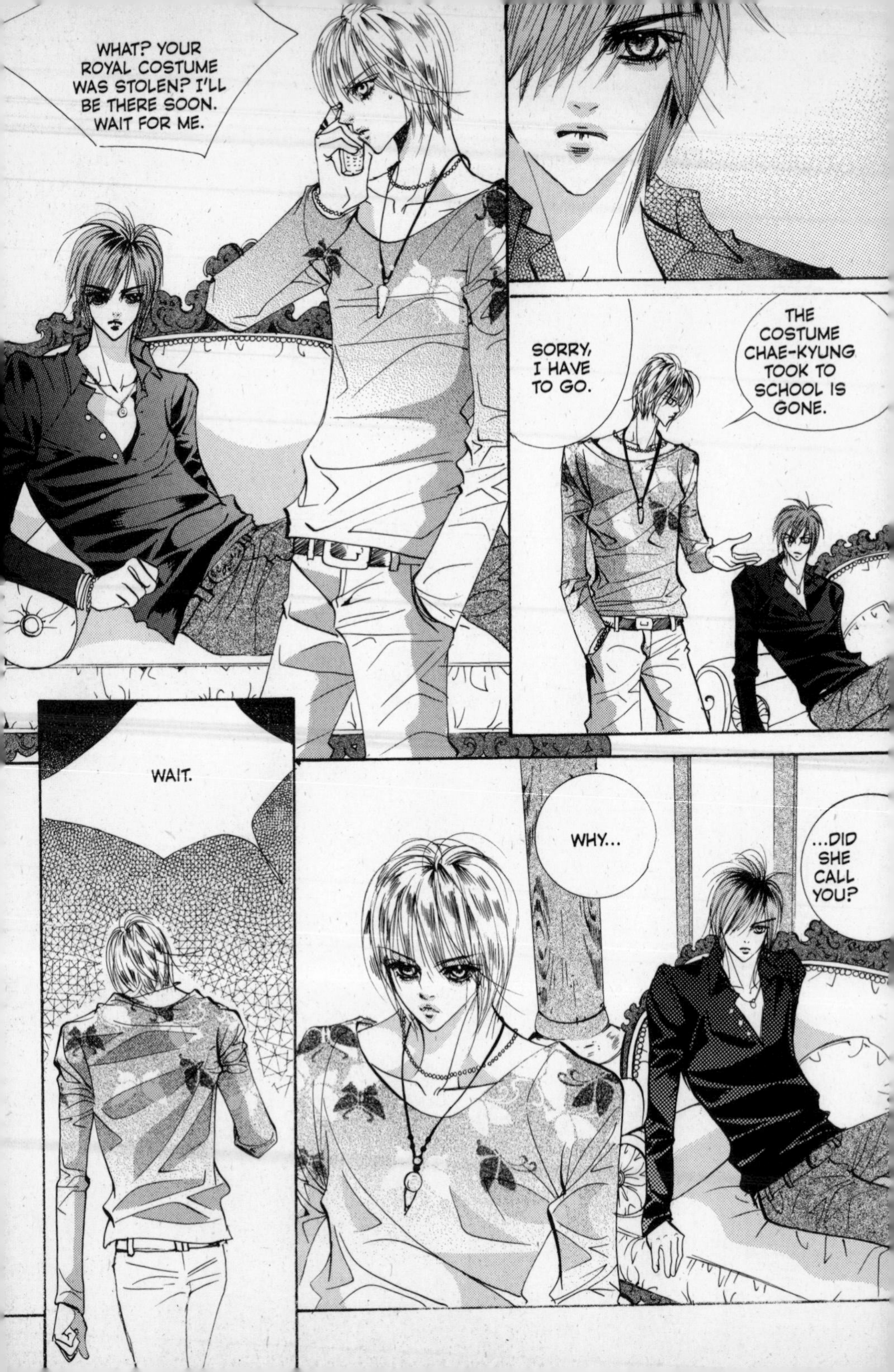
WHAT? YOUR ROYAL COSTUME WAS STOLEN? I'LL BE THERE SOON. WAIT FOR ME.
SORRY, I HAVE TO GO.
THE COSTUME CHAE-KYUNG TOOK TO SCHOOL IS GONE.
WAIT.
WHY...
...DID SHE CALL YOU?

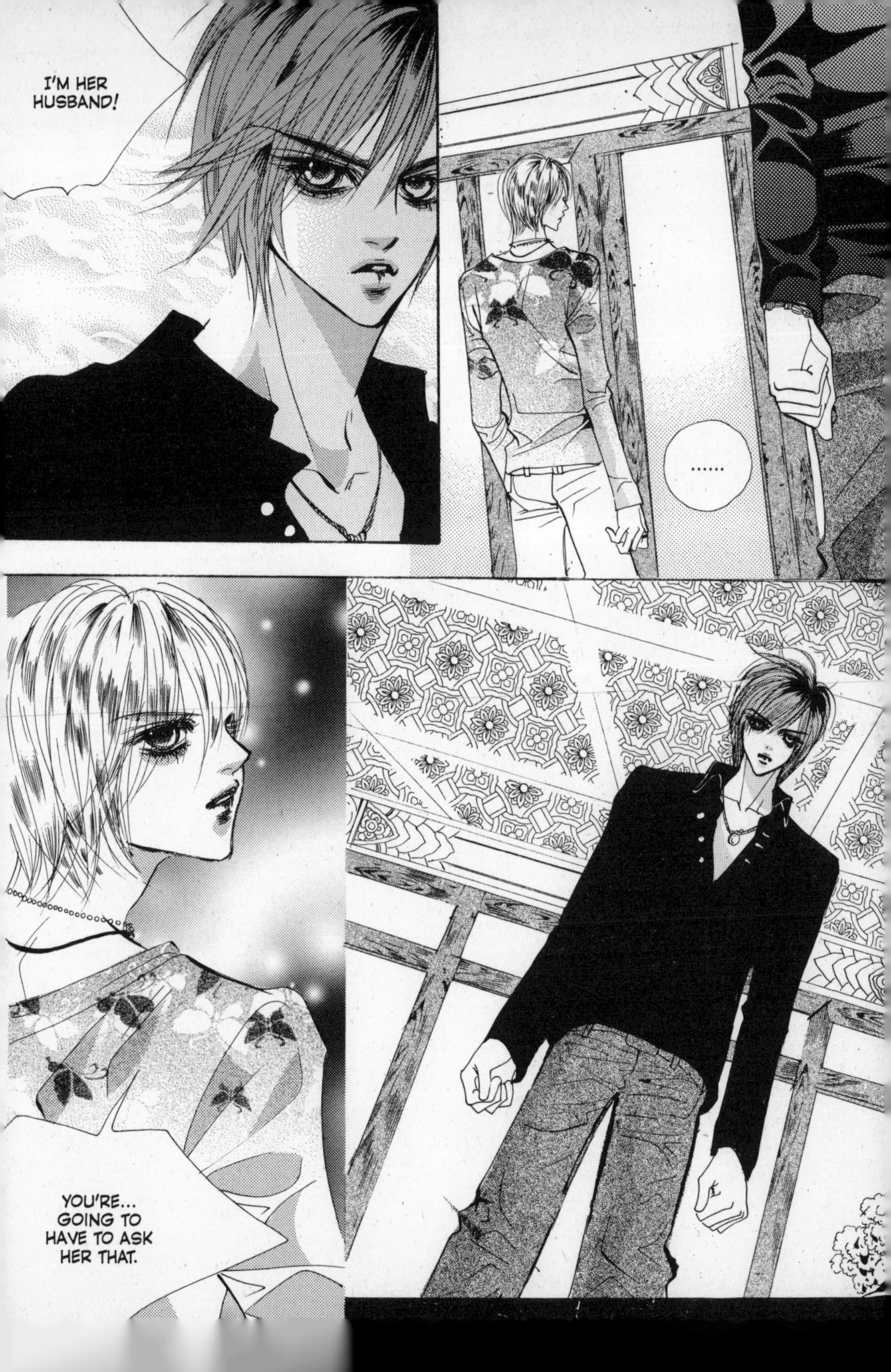
I'M HER HUSBAND!
......
YOU'RE... GOING TO HAVE TO ASK HER THAT.

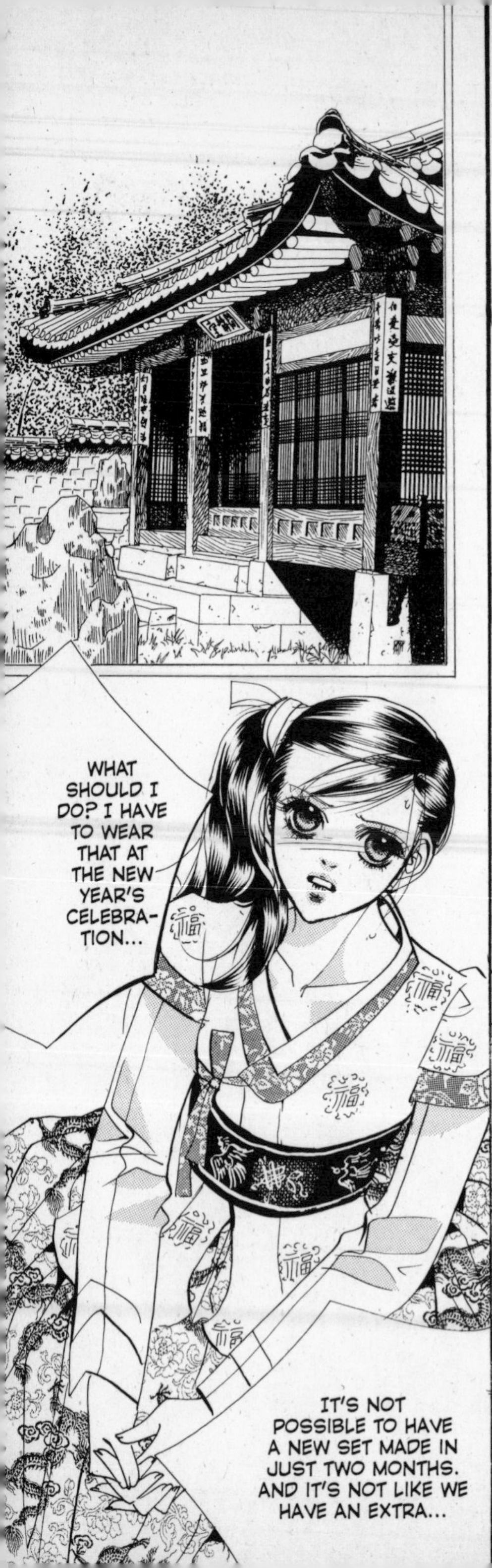
WHAT SHOULD I DO? I HAVE TO WEAR THAT AT THE NEW YEAR'S CELEBRATION...
IT'S NOT POSSIBLE TO HAVE A NEW SET MADE IN JUST TWO MONTHS. AND IT'S NOT LIKE WE HAVE AN EXTRA...
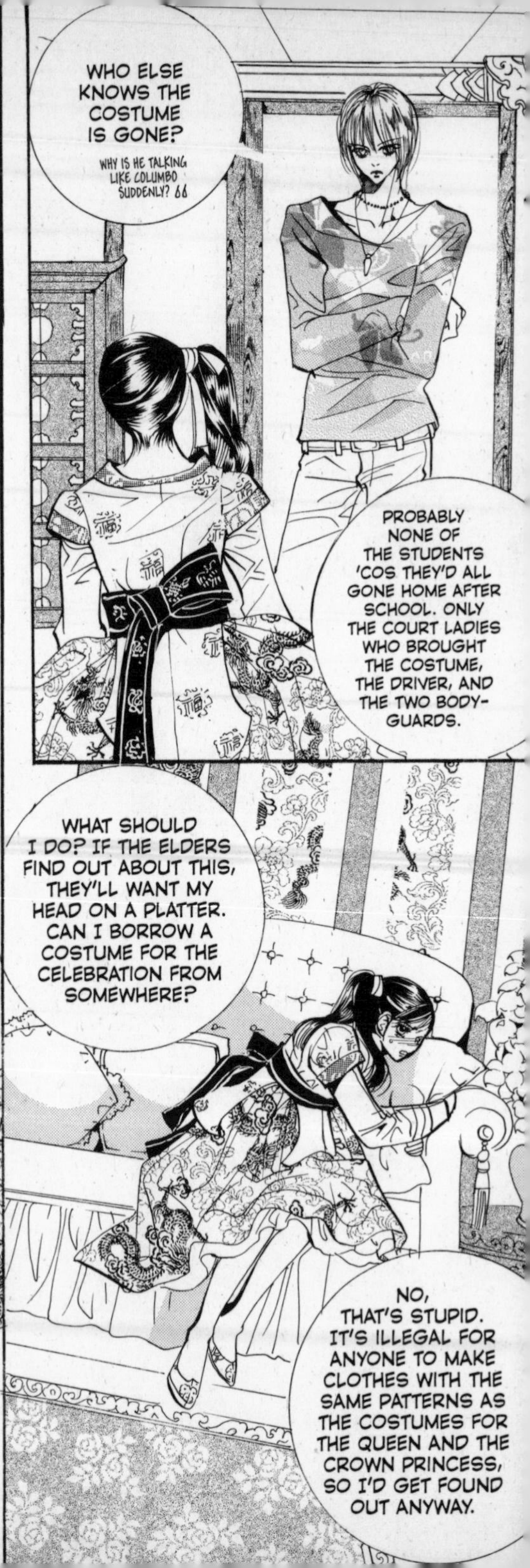
WHO ELSE KNOWS THE COSTUME IS GONE?
WHY IS HE TALKING LIKE COLUMBO SUDDENLY?
PROBABLY NONE OF THE STUDENTS 'COS THEY'D ALL GONE HOME AFTER SCHOOL. ONLY THE COURT LADIES WHO BROUGHT THE COSTUME, THE DRIVER, AND THE TWO BODY-GUARDS.
WHAT SHOULD I DO? IF THE ELDERS FIND OUT ABOUT THIS, THEY'LL WANT MY HEAD ON A PLATTER. CAN I BORROW A COSTUME FOR THE CELEBRATION FROM SOMEWHERE?
NO, THAT'S STUPID. IT'S ILLEGAL FOR ANYONE TO MAKE CLOTHES WITH THE SAME PATTERNS AS THE COSTUMES FOR THE QUEEN AND THE CROWN PRINCESS, SO I'D GET FOUND OUT ANYWAY.

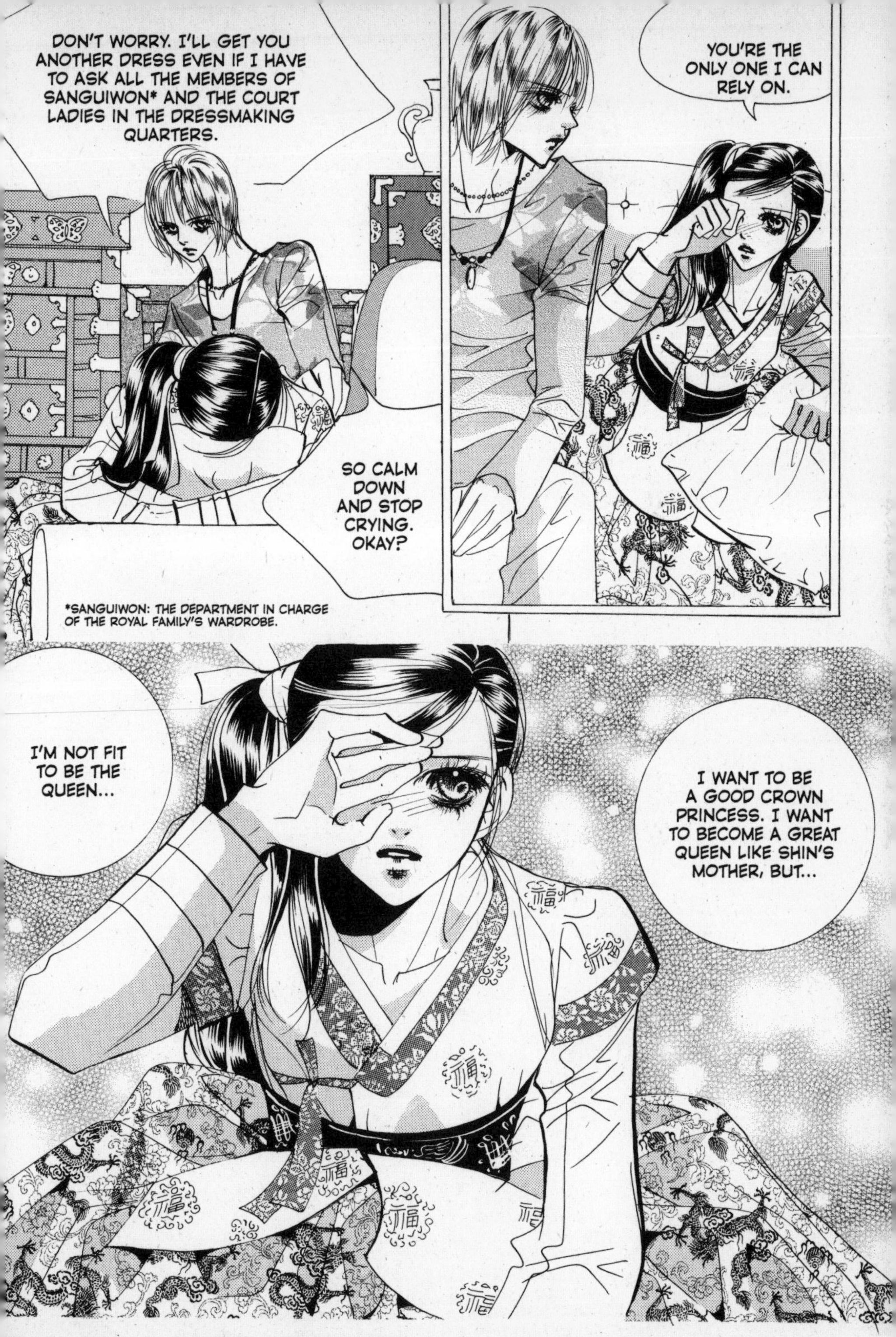
DON'T WORRY. I'LL GET YOU ANOTHER DRESS EVEN IF I HAVE TO ASK ALL THE MEMBERS OF SANGUIWON* AND THE COURT LADIES IN THE DRESSMAKING QUARTERS.
SO CALM DOWN AND STOP CRYING. OKAY?
*SANGUIWON: THE DEPARTMENT IN CHARGE OF THE ROYAL FAMILY'S WARDROBE.
YOU'RE THE ONLY ONE I CAN RELY ON.
I'M NOT FIT TO BE THE QUEEN...
I WANT TO BE A GOOD CROWN PRINCESS. I WANT TO BECOME A GREAT QUEEN LIKE SHIN'S MOTHER, BUT...

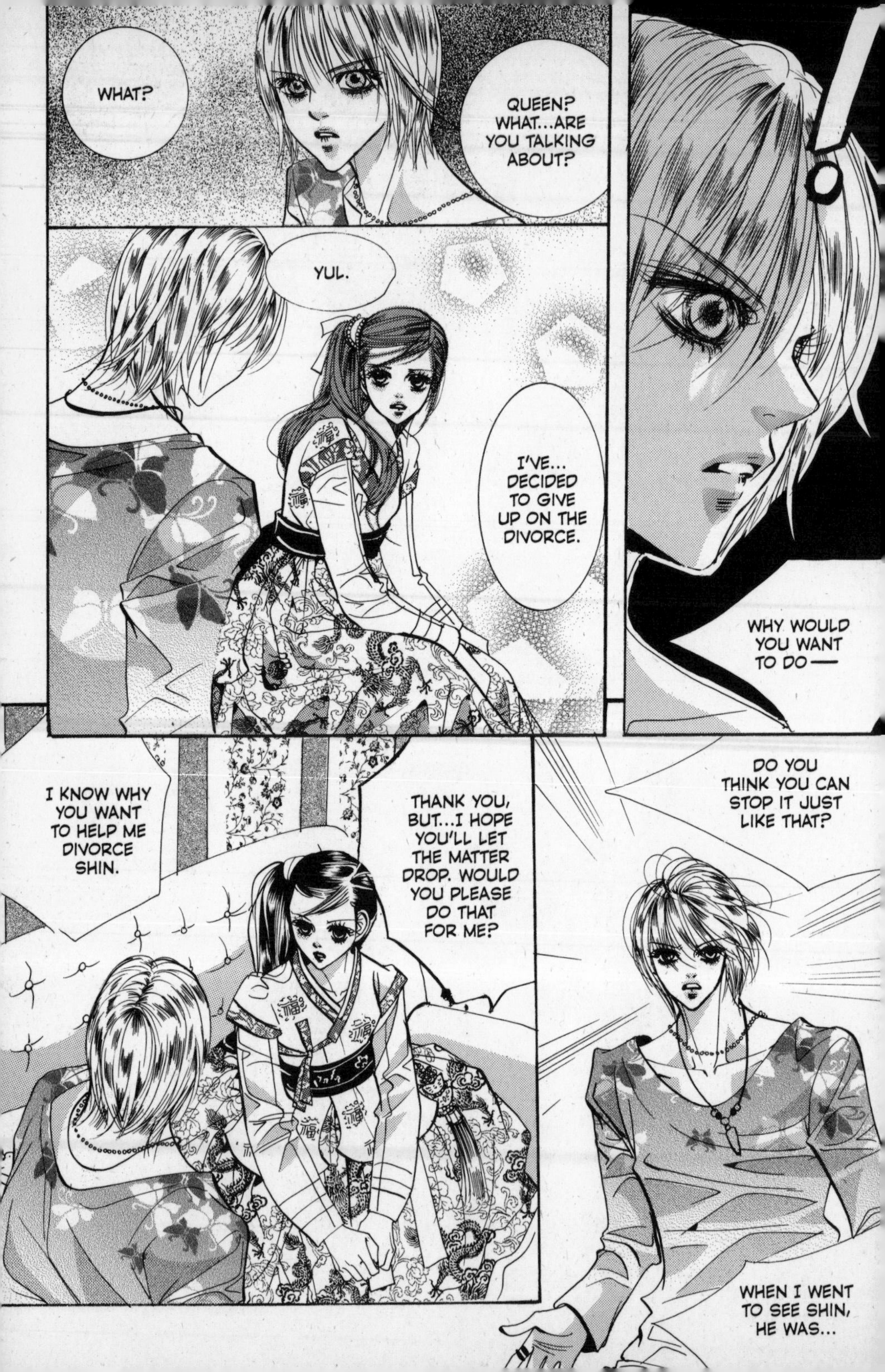
WHAT?
QUEEN? WHAT...ARE YOU TALKING ABOUT?
YUL.
I'VE... DECIDED TO GIVE UP ON THE DIVORCE.
WHY WOULD YOU WANT TO DO—
I KNOW WHY YOU WANT TO HELP ME DIVORCE SHIN.
THANK YOU, BUT...I HOPE YOU'LL LET THE MATTER DROP. WOULD YOU PLEASE DO THAT FOR ME?
DO YOU THINK YOU CAN STOP IT JUST LIKE THAT?
WHEN I WENT TO SEE SHIN, HE WAS...

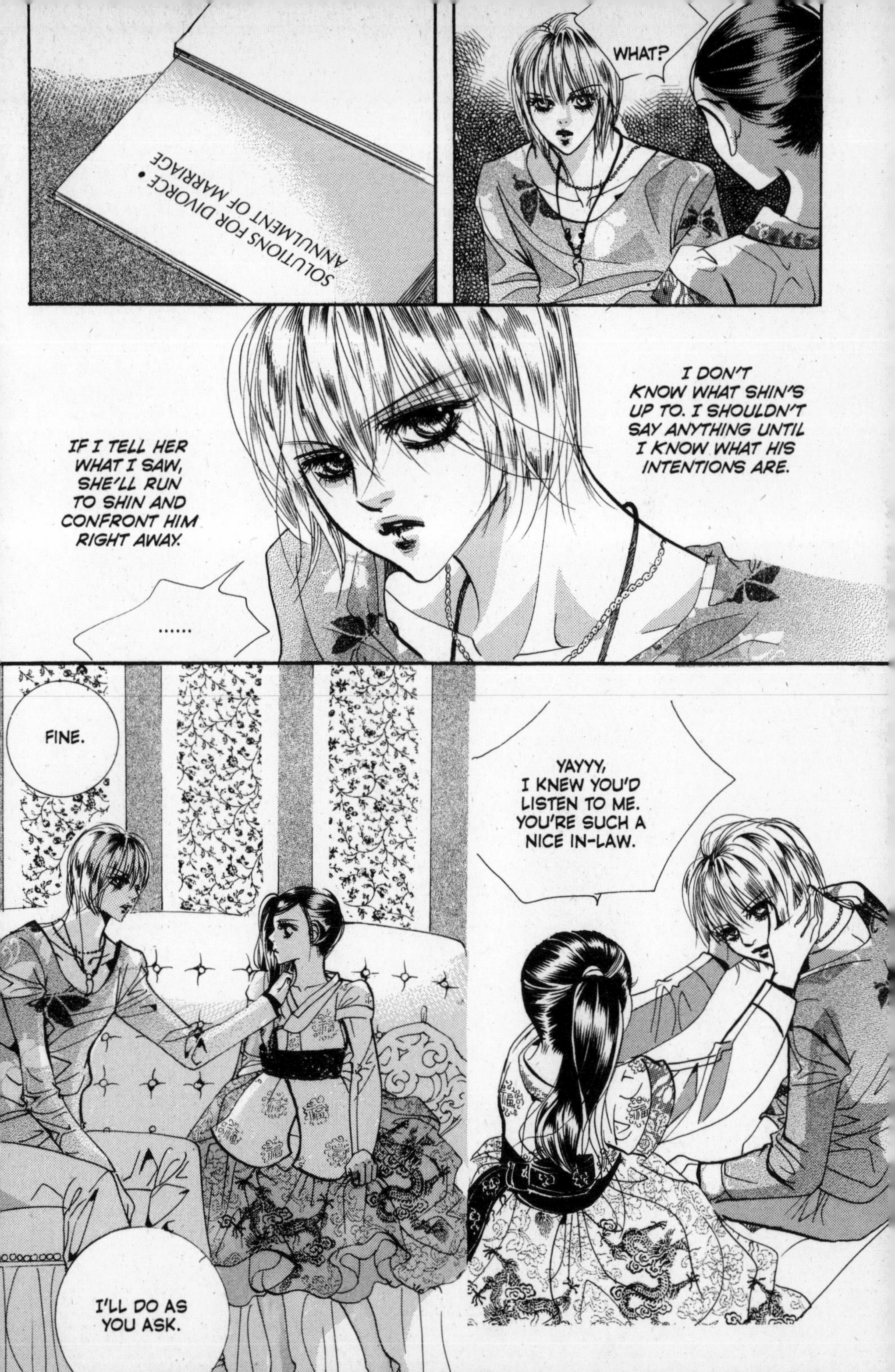
SOLUTIONS FOR DIVORCE •
ANNULMENT OF MARRIAGE
WHAT?
IF I TELL HER WHAT I SAW, SHE'LL RUN TO SHIN AND CONFRONT HIM RIGHT AWAY.
I DON'T KNOW WHAT SHIN'S UP TO. I SHOULDN'T SAY ANYTHING UNTIL I KNOW WHAT HIS INTENTIONS ARE.
......
FINE.
I'LL DO AS YOU ASK.
YAYYY, I KNEW YOU'D LISTEN TO ME. YOU'RE SUCH A NICE IN-LAW.

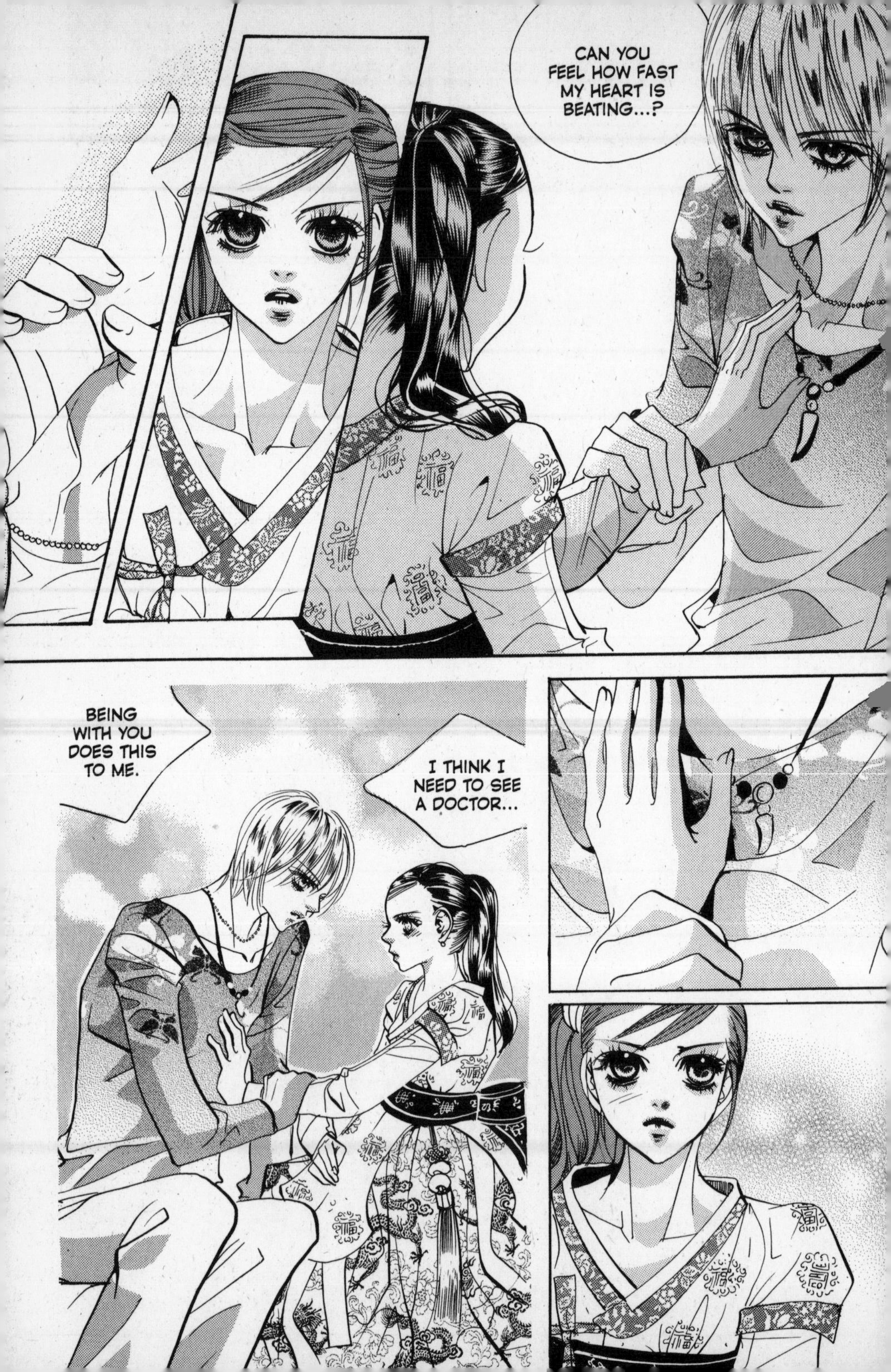
CAN YOU FEEL HOW FAST MY HEART IS BEATING...?
BEING WITH YOU DOES THIS TO ME.
I THINK I NEED TO SEE A DOCTOR...

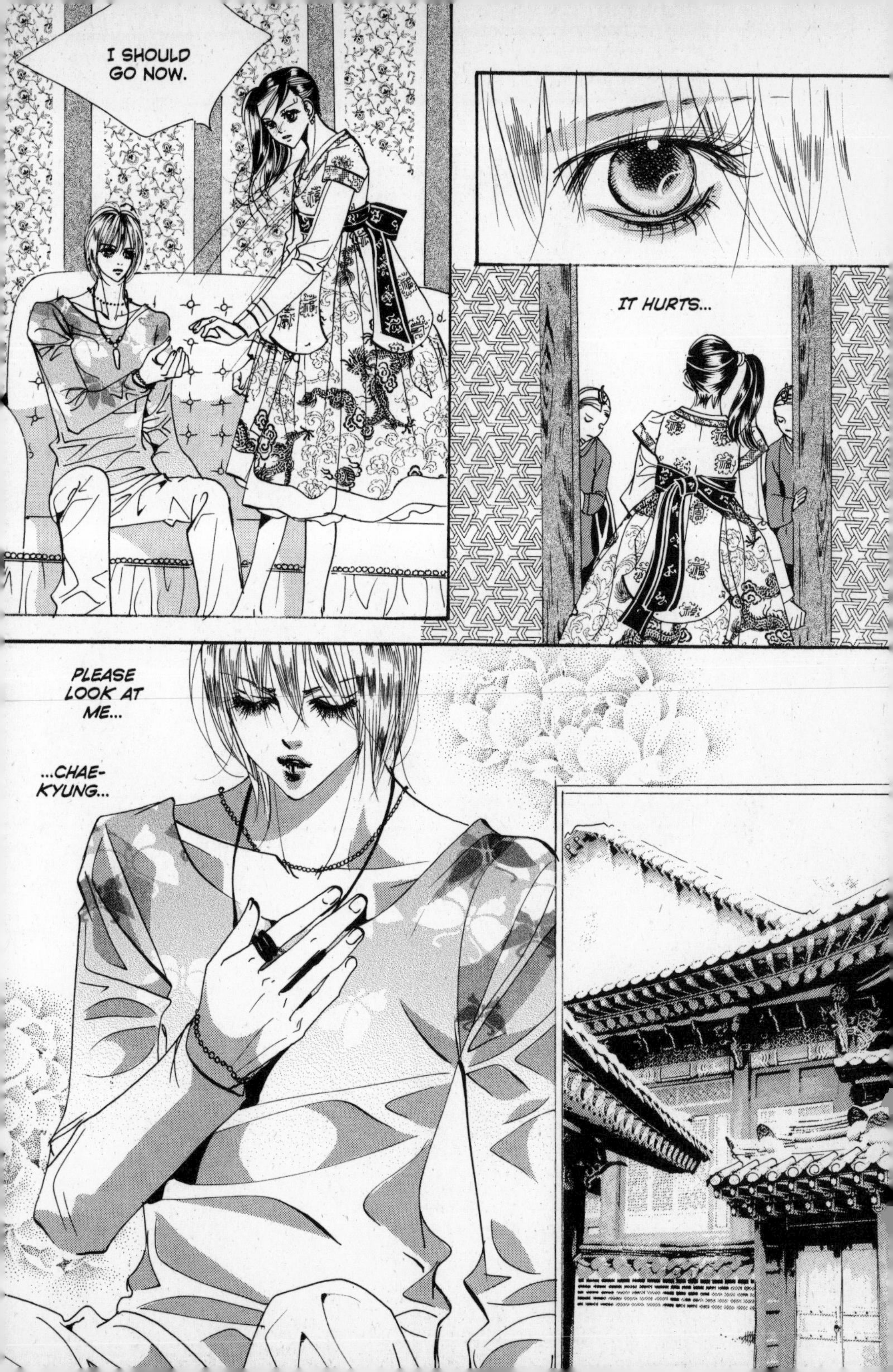
I SHOULD GO NOW.
IT HURTS...
PLEASE LOOK AT ME...
...CHAE-KYUNG...

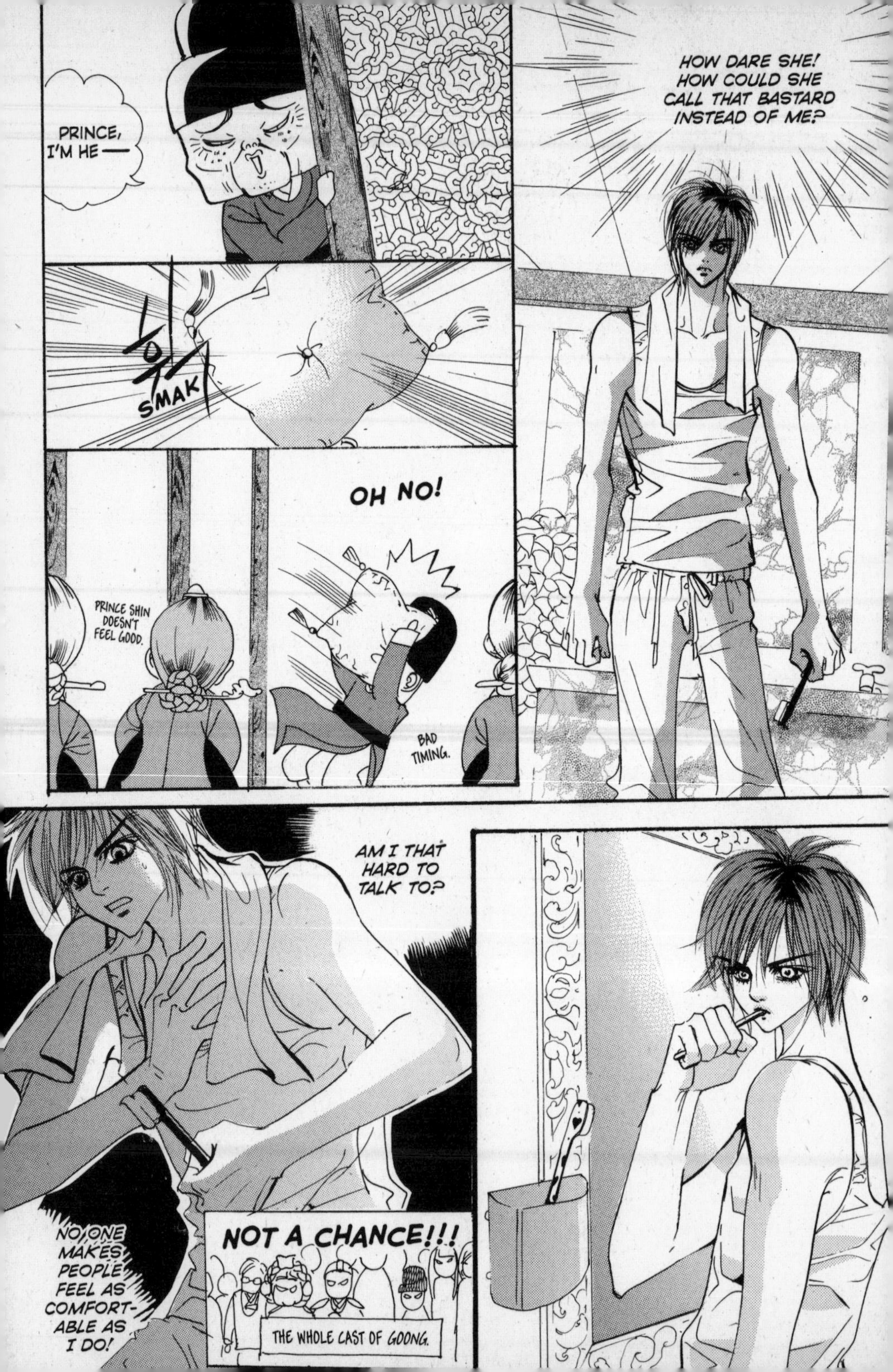
PRINCE, I'M HE—
SMAK
OH NO!
PRINCE SHIN DOESN'T FEEL GOOD.
BAD TIMING.
HOW DARE SHE! HOW COULD SHE CALL THAT BASTARD INSTEAD OF ME?
AM I THAT HARD TO TALK TO?
NO ONE MAKES PEOPLE FEEL AS COMFORT-ABLE AS I DO!
NOT A CHANCE!!!
THE WHOLE CAST OF GOONG.

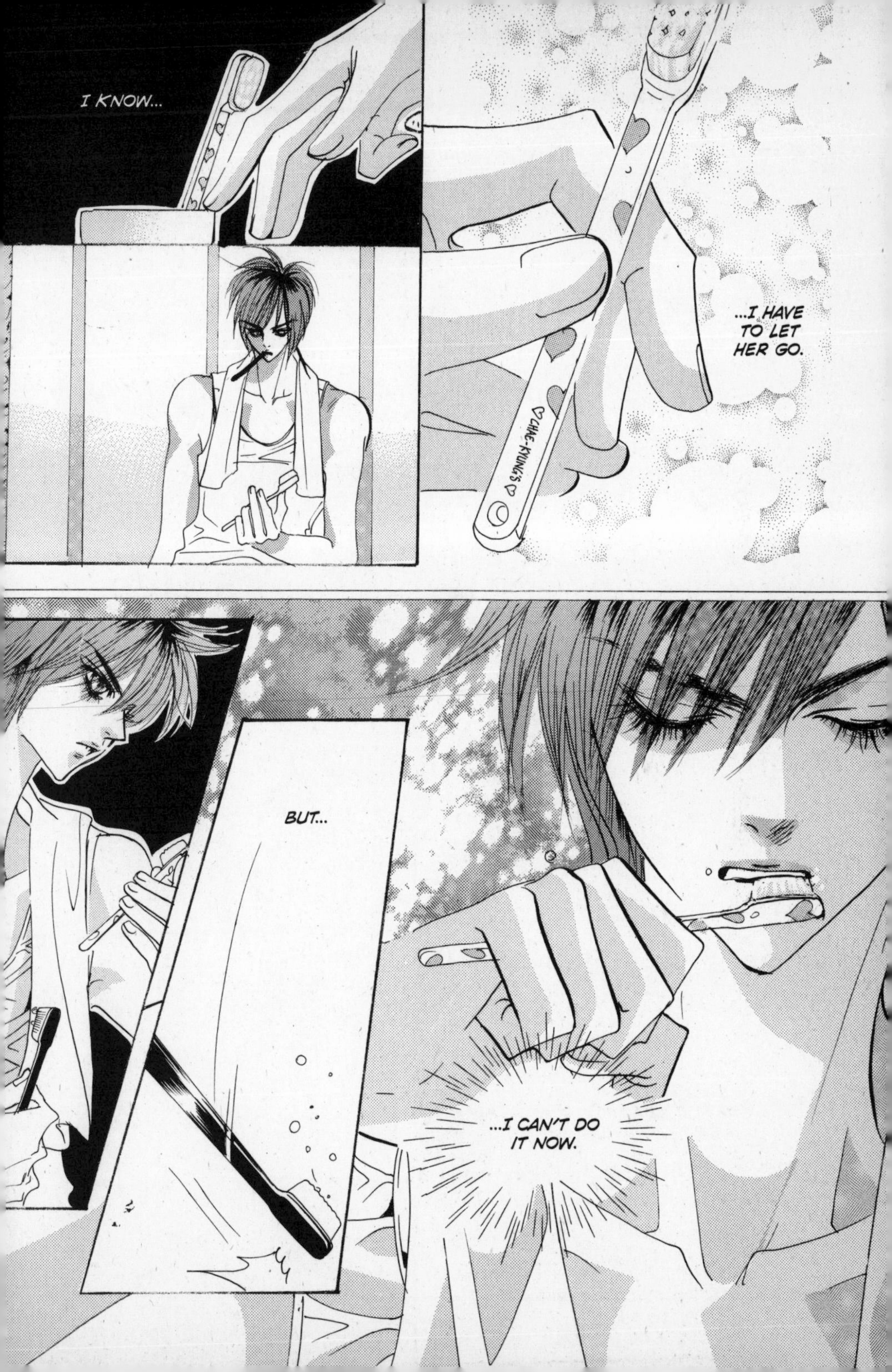
I KNOW...
♡CHAE-KYUNG'S♡
...I HAVE TO LET HER GO.
BUT...
...I CAN'T DO IT NOW.

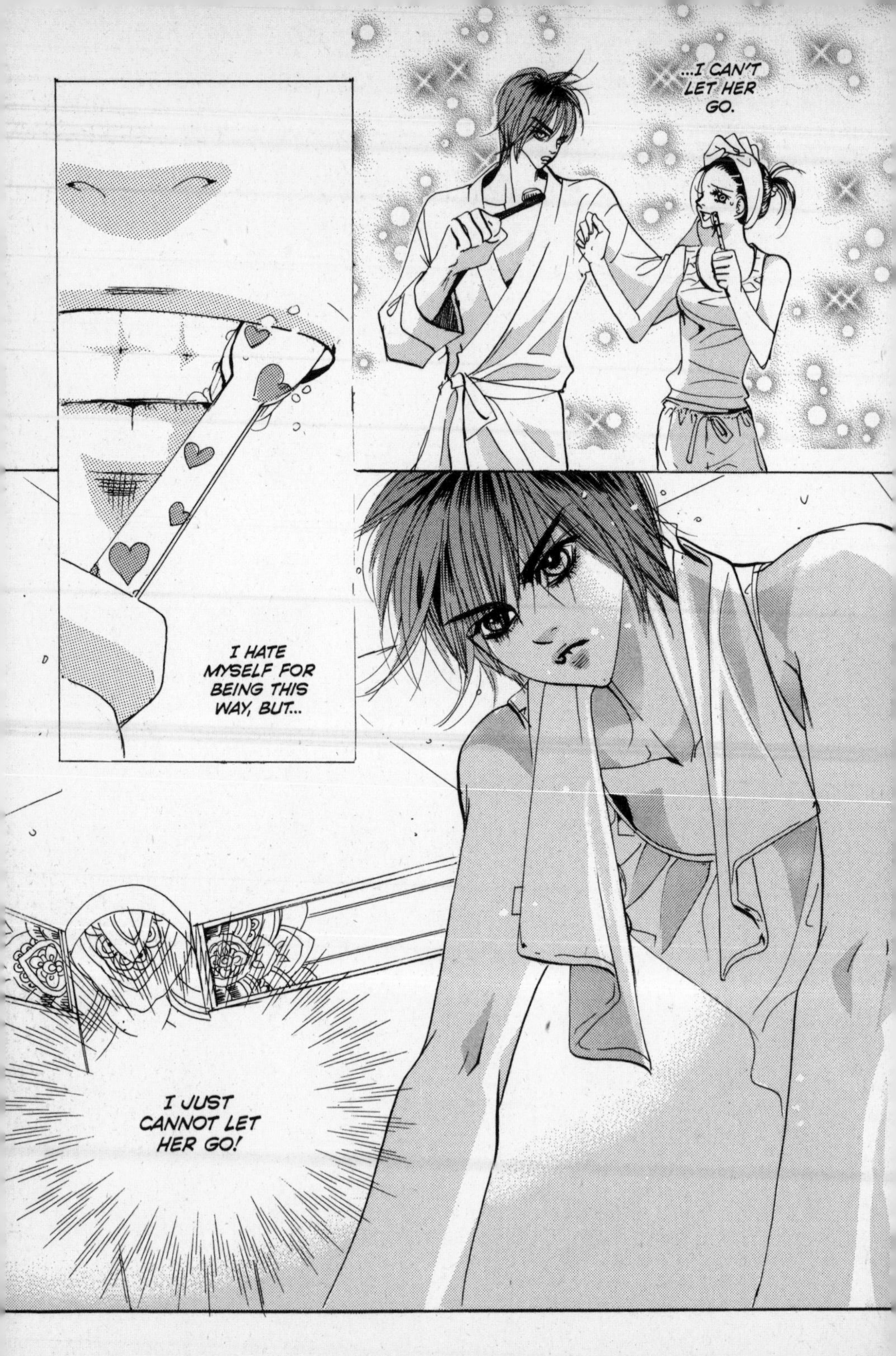
I HATE MYSELF FOR BEING THIS WAY, BUT...
...I CAN'T LET HER GO.
I JUST CANNOT LET HER GO!

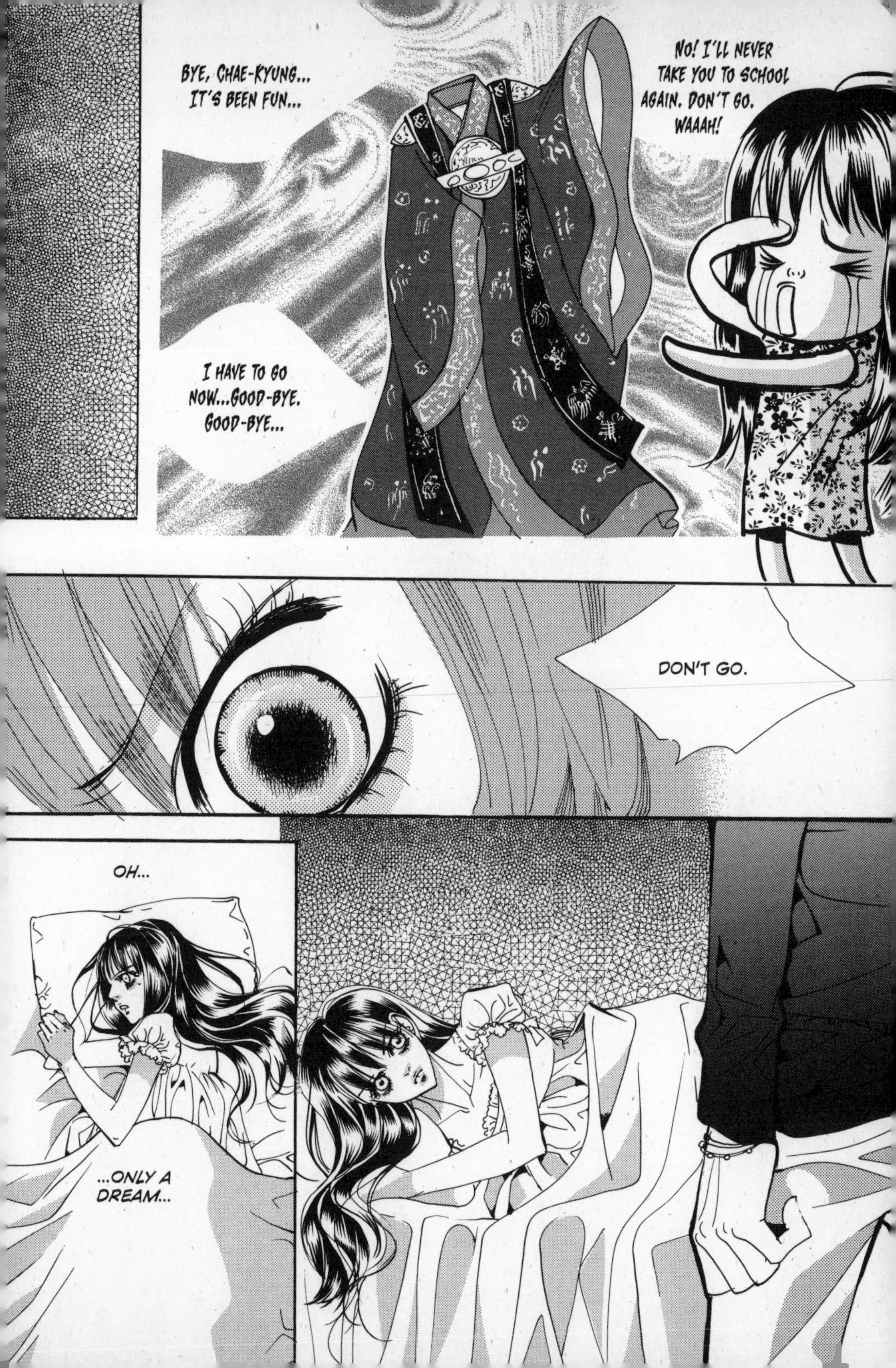
BYE, CHAE-KYUNG... IT'S BEEN FUN...
I HAVE TO GO NOW...GOOD-BYE. GOOD-BYE...
NO! I'LL NEVER TAKE YOU TO SCHOOL AGAIN. DON'T GO. WAAAH!
DON'T GO.
OH...
...ONLY A DREAM...

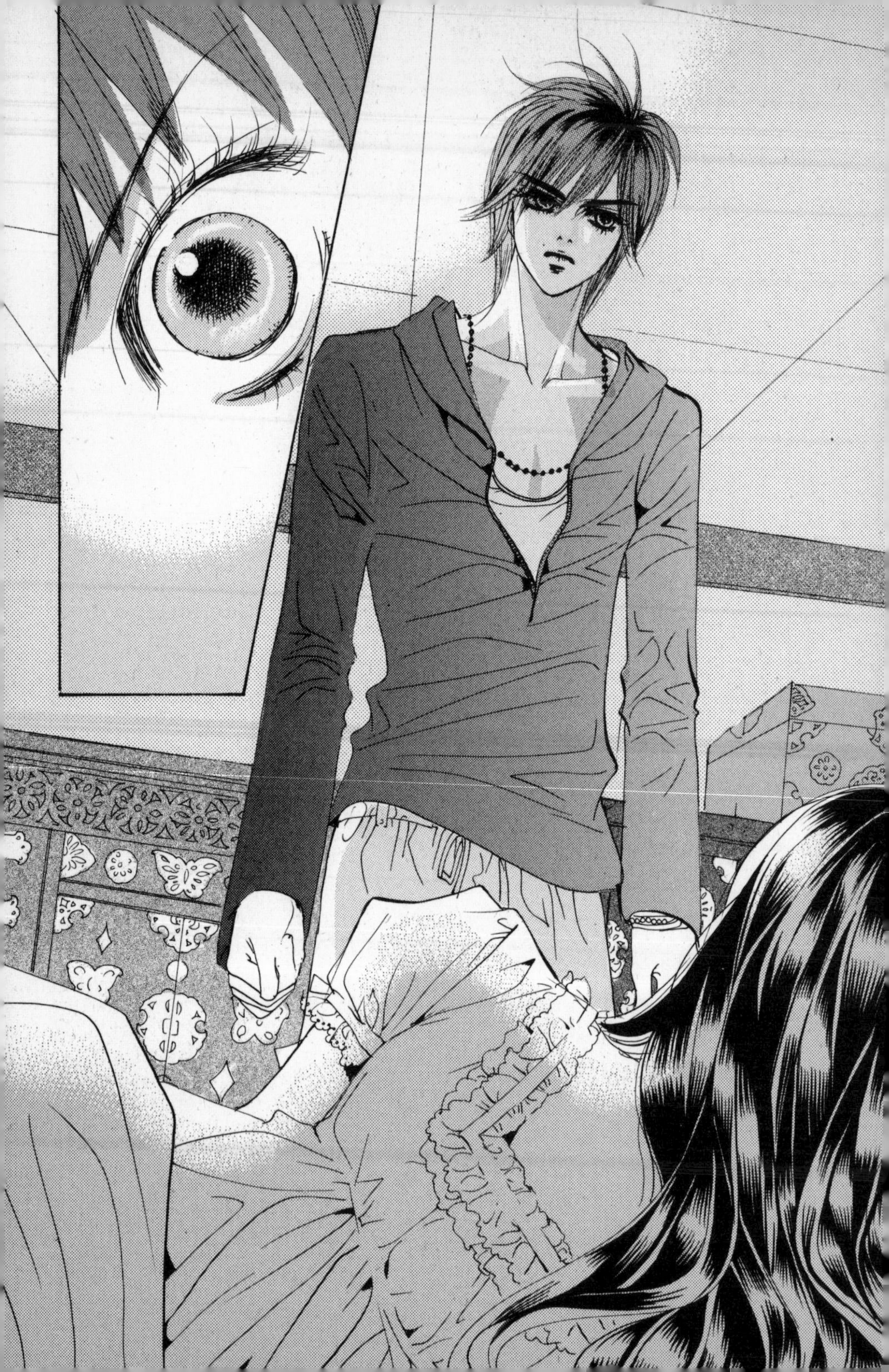

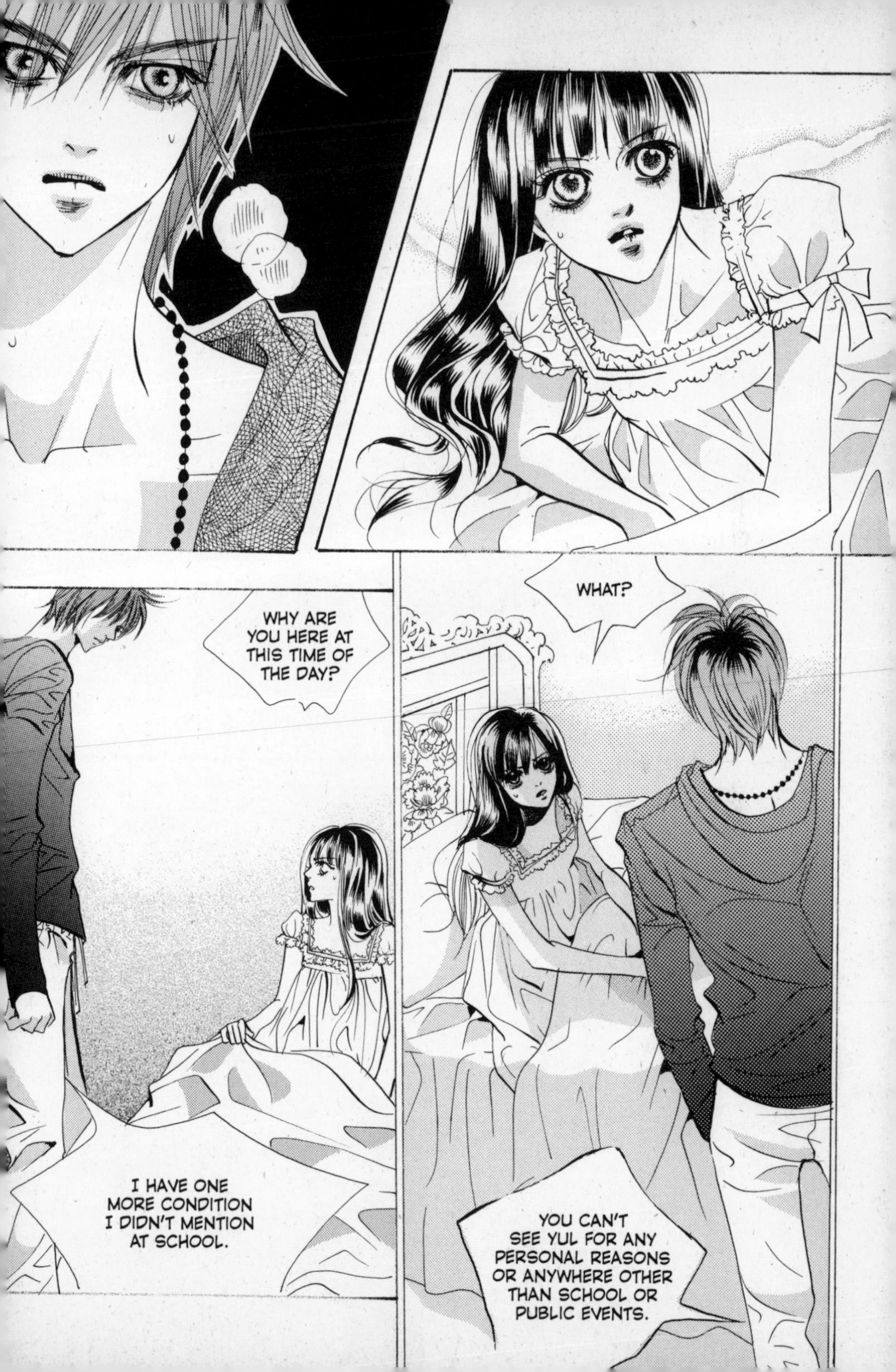
WHY ARE YOU HERE AT THIS TIME OF THE DAY?
WHAT?
I HAVE ONE MORE CONDITION I DIDN'T MENTION AT SCHOOL.
YOU CAN'T SEE YUL FOR ANY PERSONAL REASONS OR ANYWHERE OTHER THAN SCHOOL OR PUBLIC EVENTS.

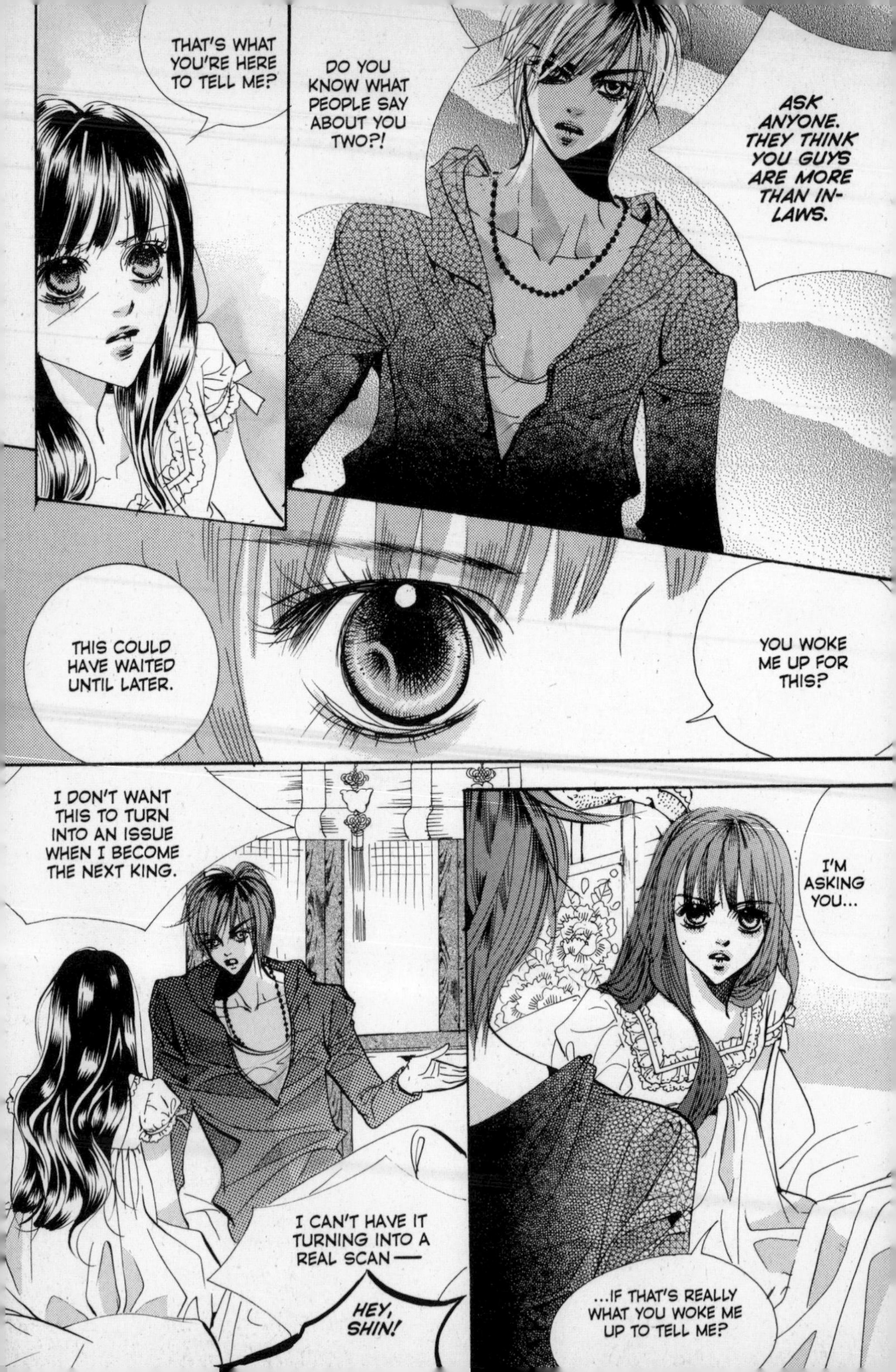
THAT'S WHAT YOU'RE HERE TO TELL ME?
DO YOU KNOW WHAT PEOPLE SAY ABOUT YOU TWO?!
ASK ANYONE. THEY THINK YOU GUYS ARE MORE THAN IN-LAWS.
THIS COULD HAVE WAITED UNTIL LATER.
YOU WOKE ME UP FOR THIS?
I DON'T WANT THIS TO TURN INTO AN ISSUE WHEN I BECOME THE NEXT KING.
I CAN'T HAVE IT TURNING INTO A REAL SCAN—
HEY, SHIN!
I'M ASKING YOU...
...IF THAT'S REALLY WHAT YOU WOKE ME UP TO TELL ME?

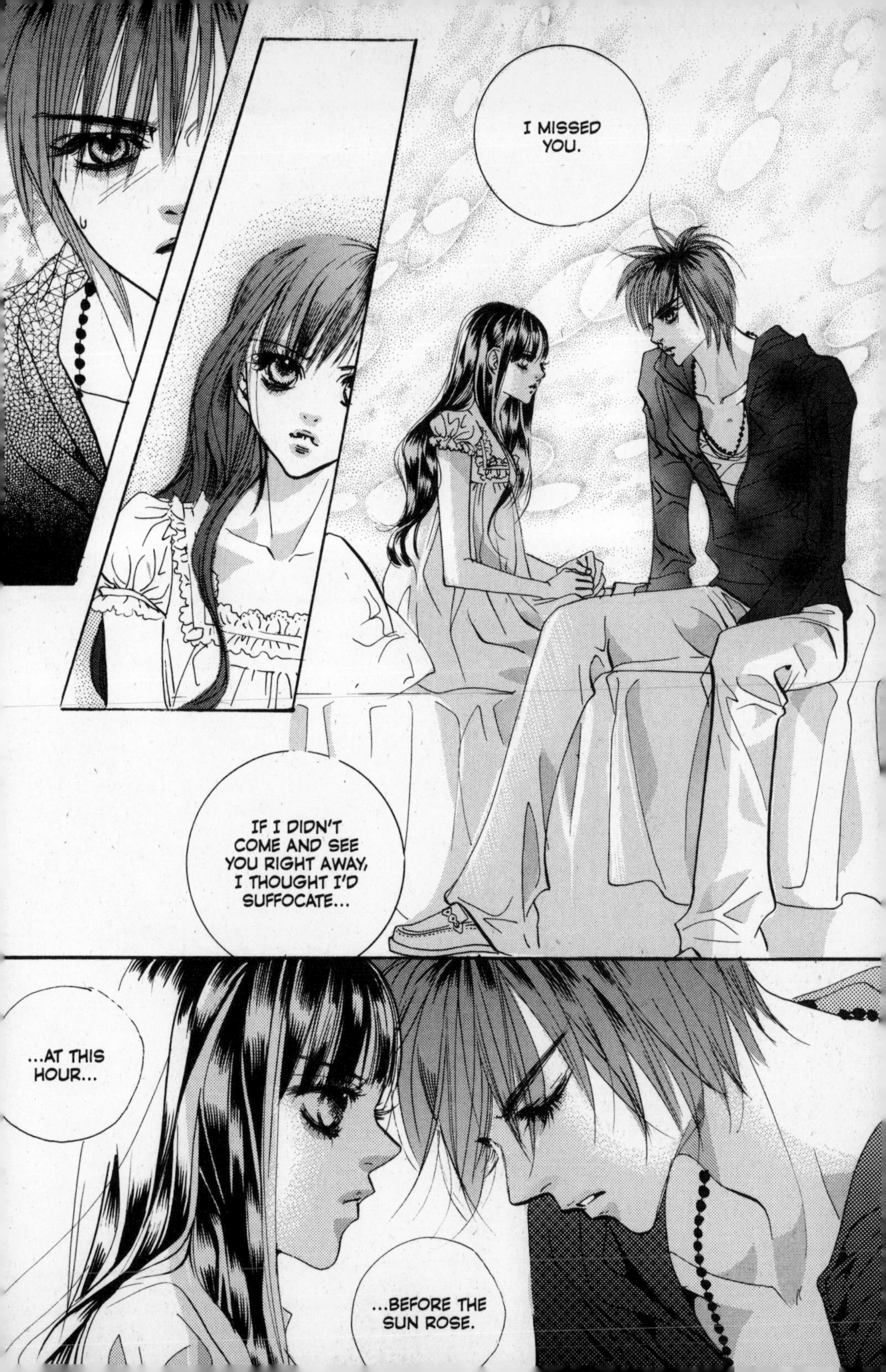
I MISSED YOU.
IF I DIDN'T COME AND SEE YOU RIGHT AWAY, I THOUGHT I'D SUFFOCATE...
...AT THIS HOUR...
...BEFORE THE SUN ROSE.

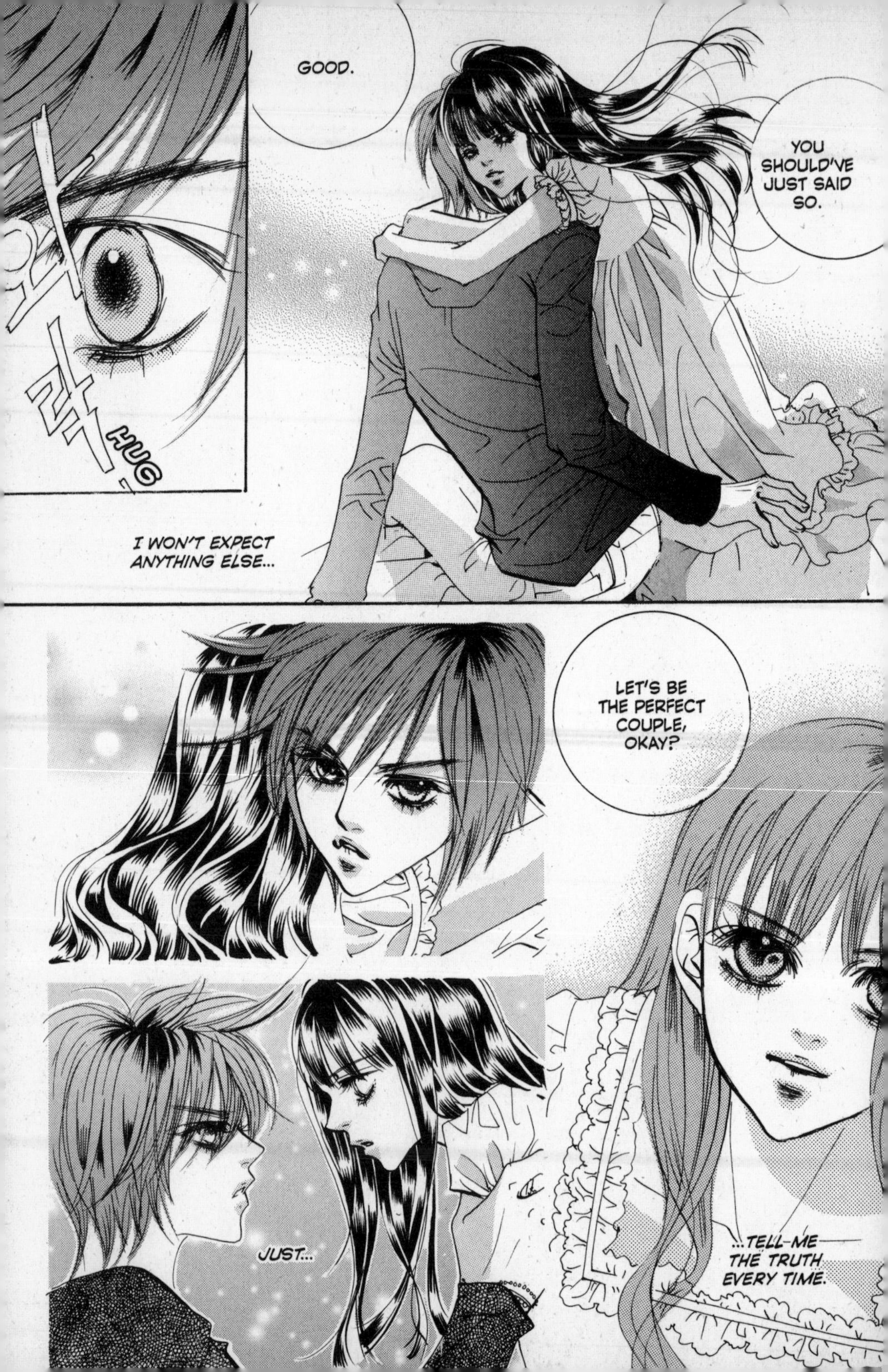
HUG
GOOD.
YOU SHOULD'VE JUST SAID SO.
I WON'T EXPECT ANYTHING ELSE...
JUST...
LET'S BE THE PERFECT COUPLE, OKAY?
...TELL-ME THE TRUTH EVERY TIME.

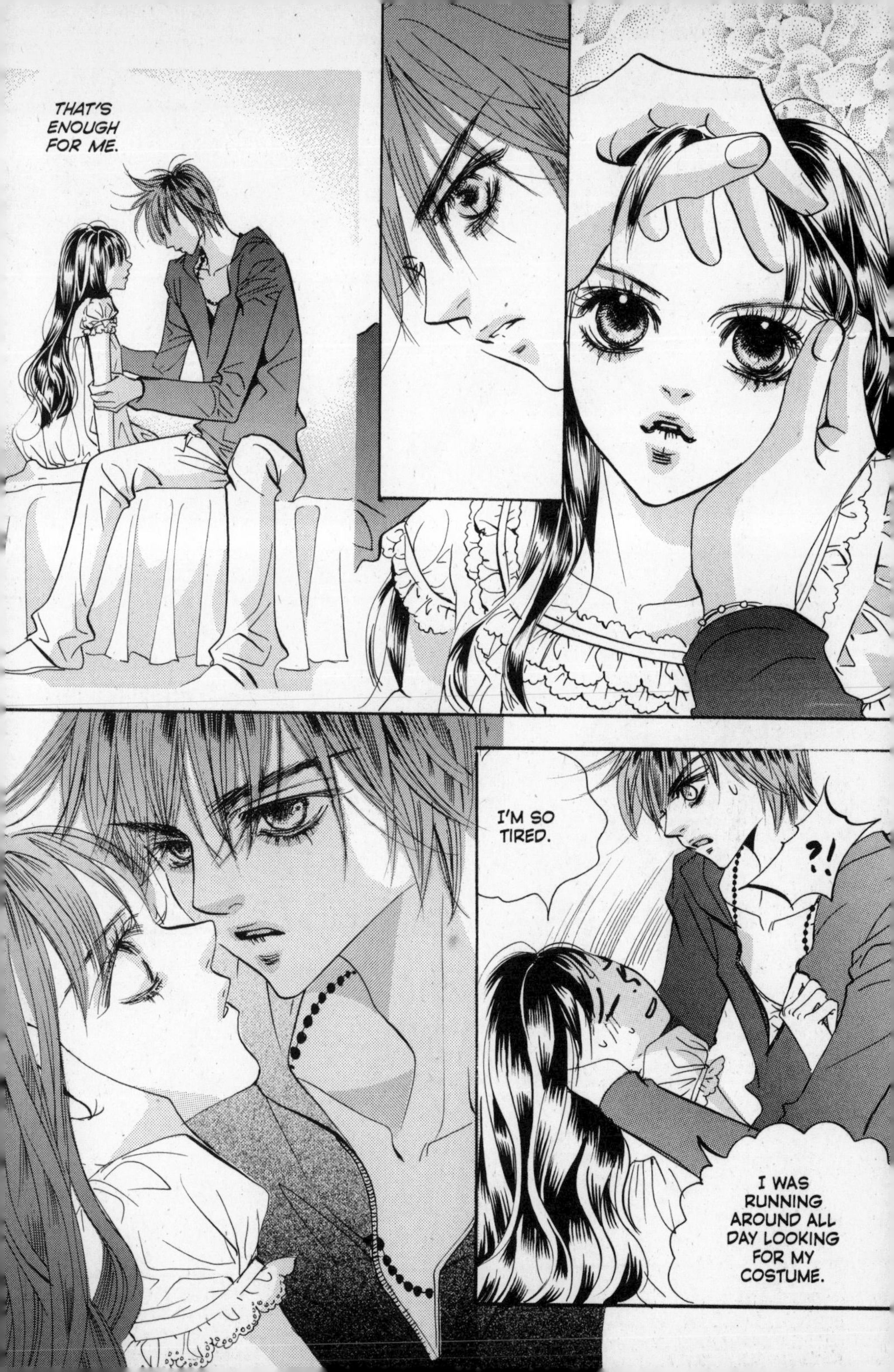
THAT'S ENOUGH FOR ME.
I'M SO TIRED.
?!
I WAS RUNNING AROUND ALL DAY LOOKING FOR MY COSTUME.

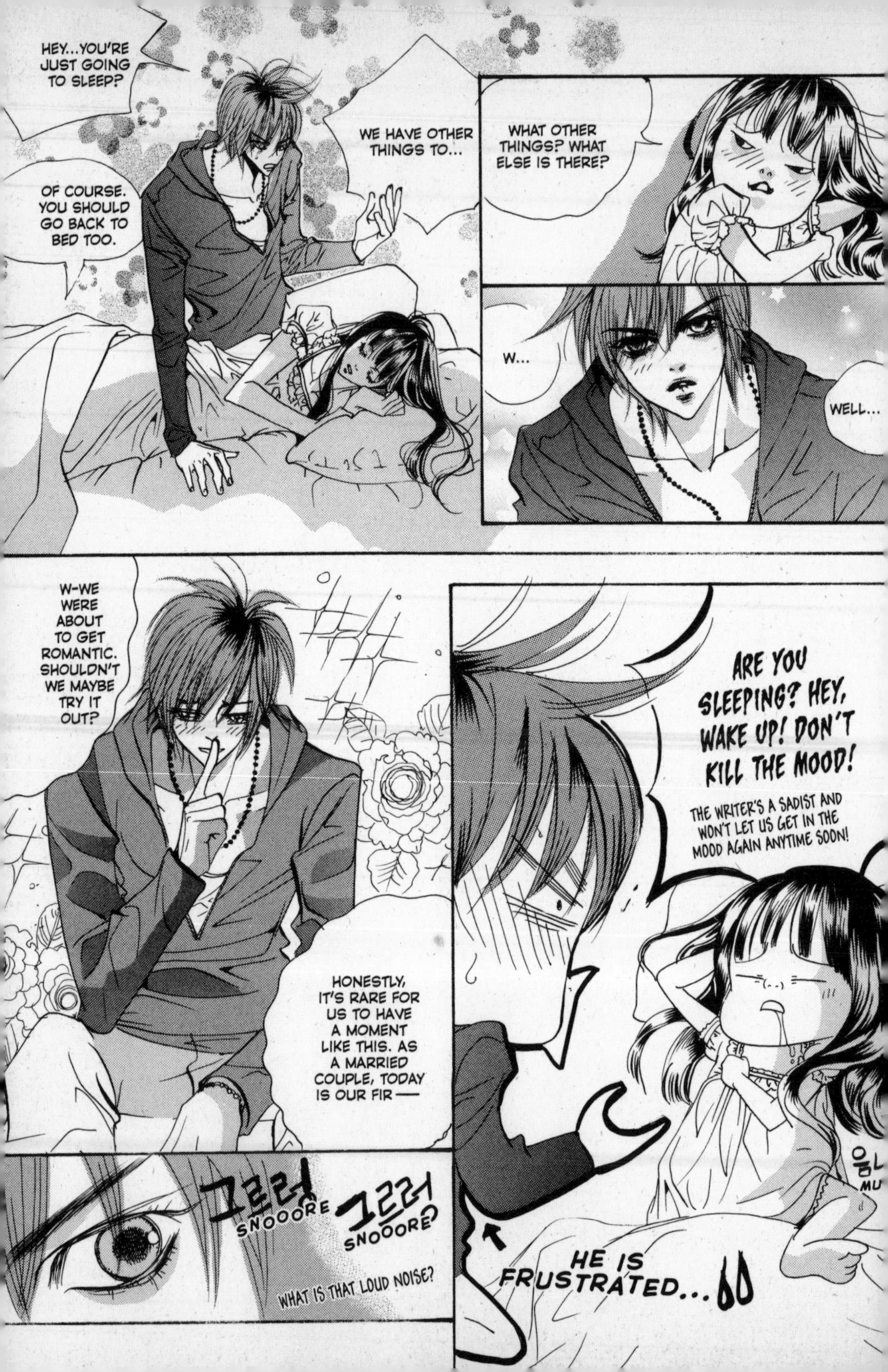

HEY...YOU'RE JUST GOING TO SLEEP?
OF COURSE. YOU SHOULD GO BACK TO BED TOO.
WE HAVE OTHER THINGS TO...
WHAT OTHER THINGS? WHAT ELSE IS THERE?
W...
WELL...
W-WE WERE ABOUT TO GET ROMANTIC. SHOULDN'T WE MAYBE TRY IT OUT?
HONESTLY, IT'S RARE FOR US TO HAVE A MOMENT LIKE THIS. AS A MARRIED COUPLE, TODAY IS OUR FIR—
그르렁 SNOOORE
그르렁 SNOOORE
WHAT IS THAT LOUD NOISE?
ARE YOU SLEEPING? HEY, WAKE UP! DON'T KILL THE MOOD!
THE WRITER'S A SADIST AND WON'T LET US GET IN THE MOOD AGAIN ANYTIME SOON!
음
MU
HE IS FRUSTRATED...

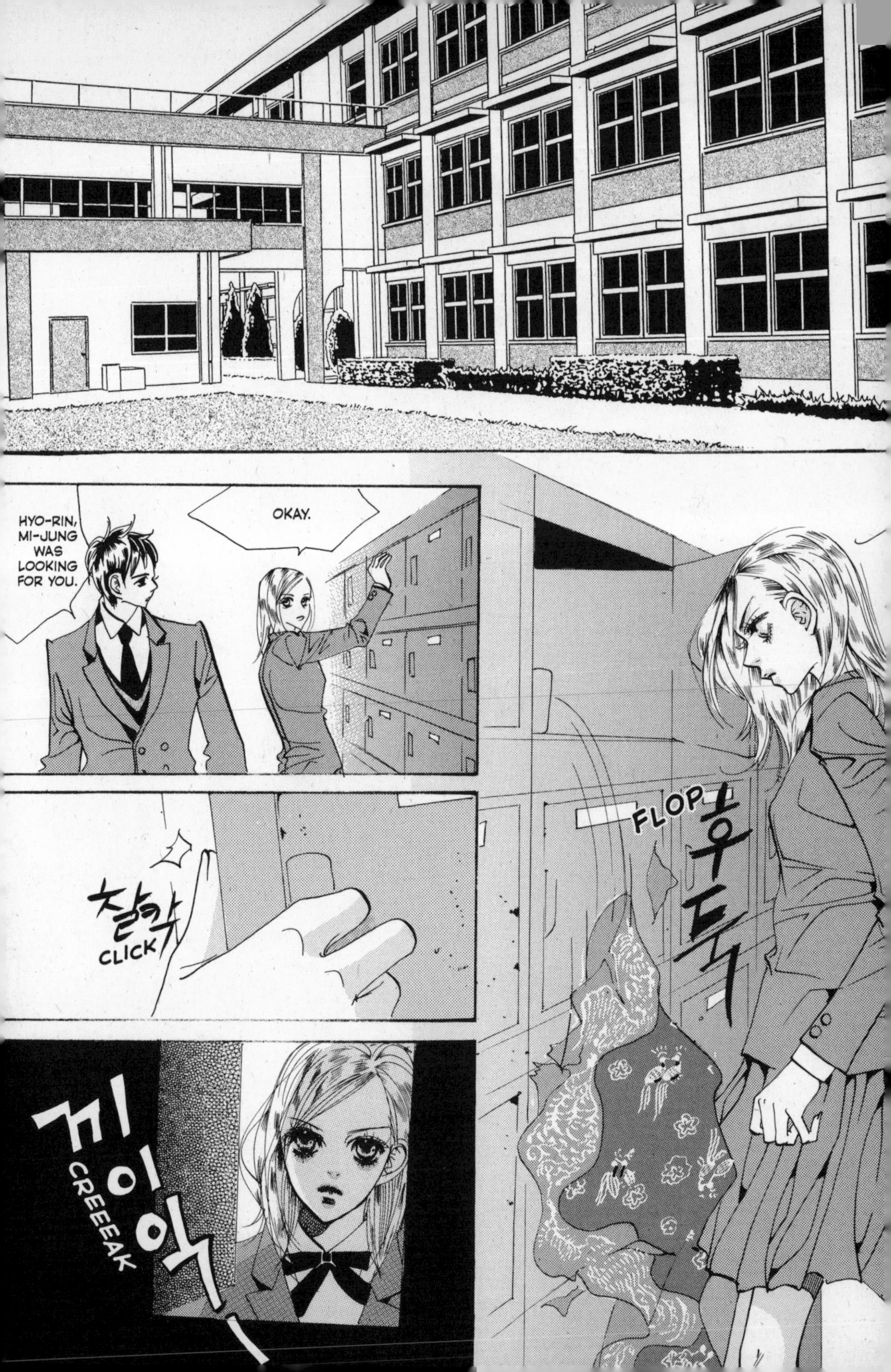
HYO-RIN, MI-JUNG WAS LOOKING FOR YOU.
OKAY.
찰칵
CLICK
끼이익
CREEEAK
FLOP
후드득

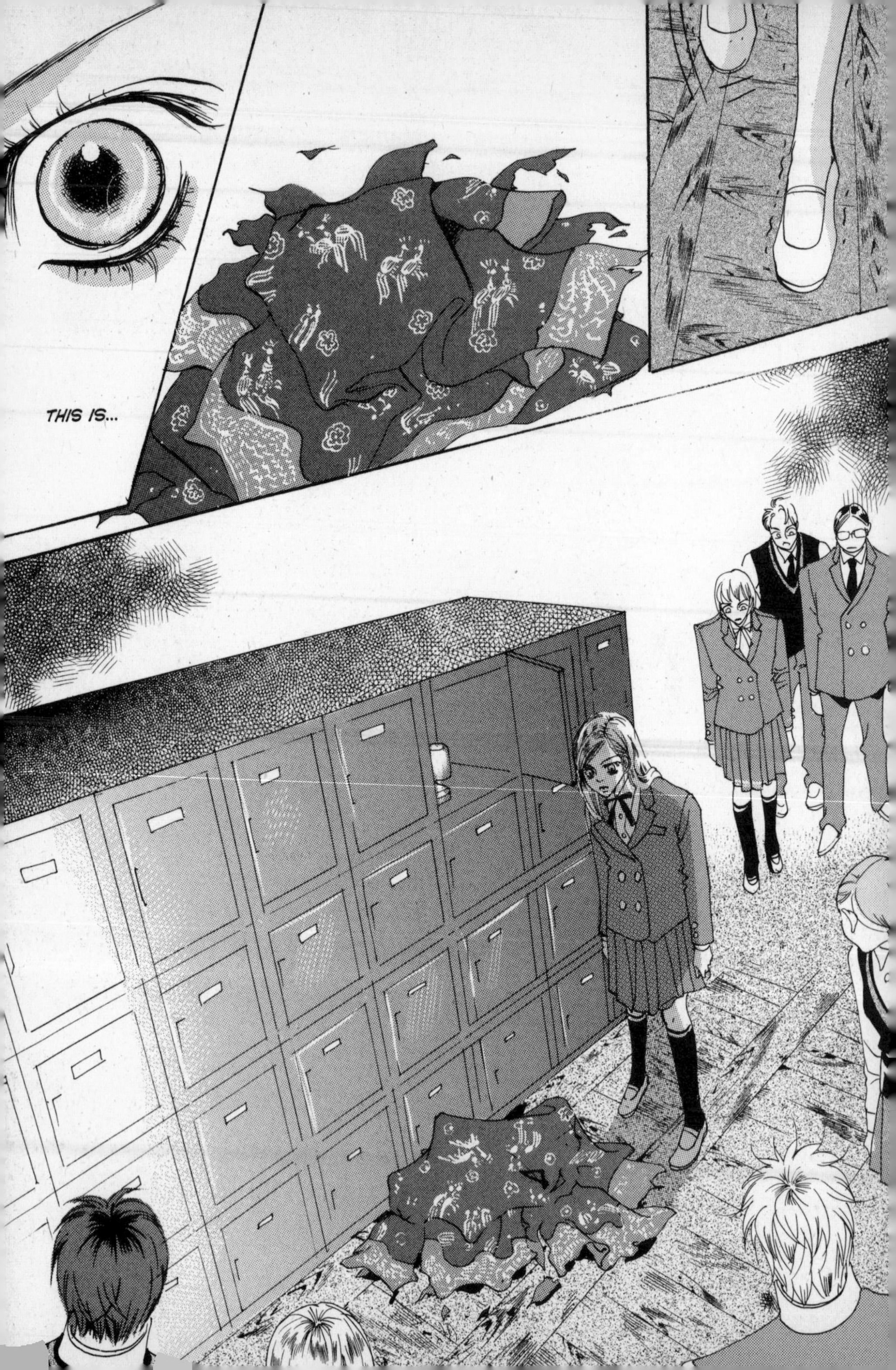
THIS IS...

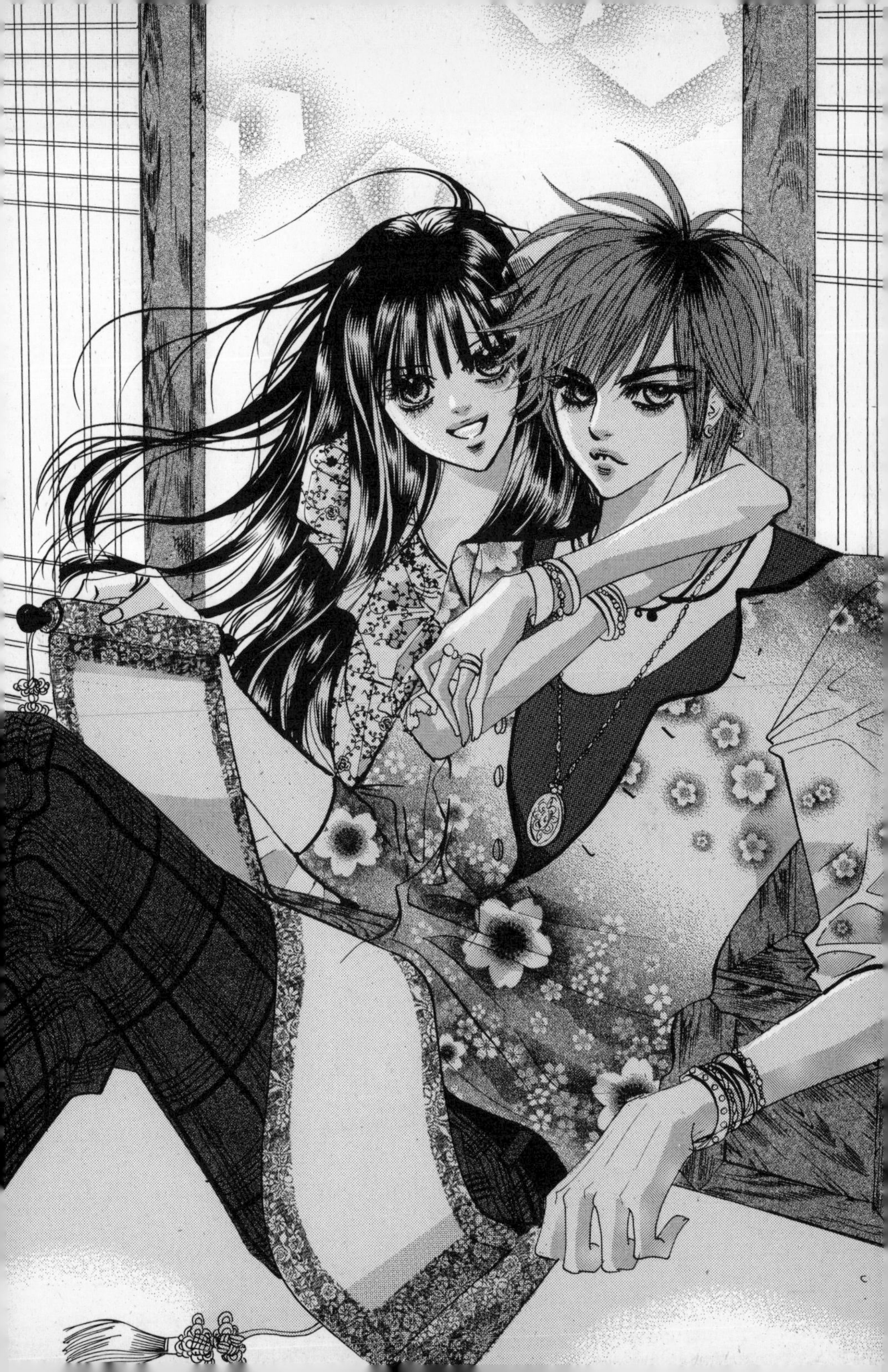

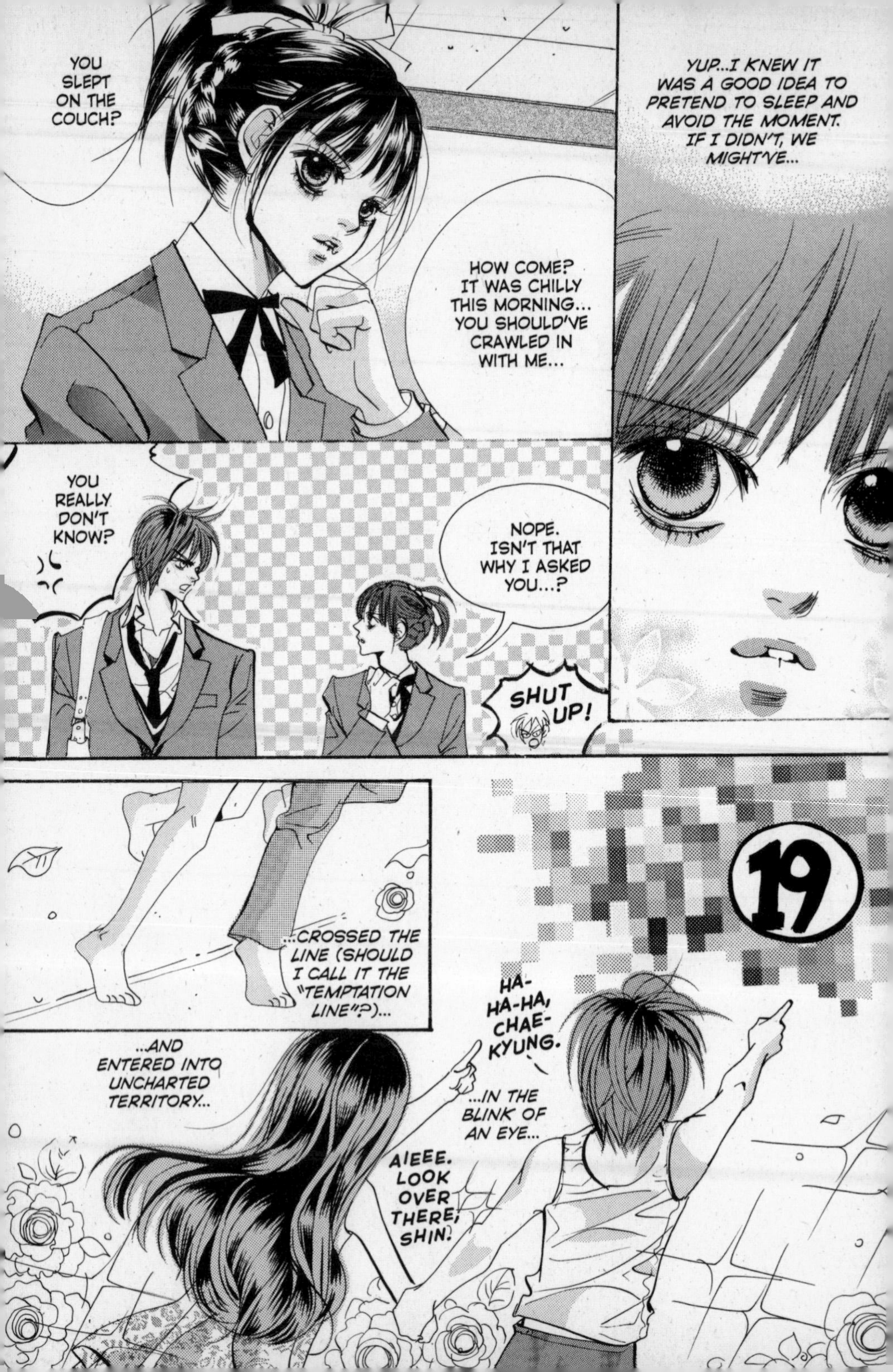
YOU SLEPT ON THE COUCH?
HOW COME? IT WAS CHILLY THIS MORNING... YOU SHOULD'VE CRAWLED IN WITH ME...
YOU REALLY DON'T KNOW?
NOPE. ISN'T THAT WHY I ASKED YOU...?
SHUT UP!
YUP...I KNEW IT WAS A GOOD IDEA TO PRETEND TO SLEEP AND AVOID THE MOMENT. IF I DIDN'T, WE MIGHT'VE...
...CROSSED THE LINE (SHOULD I CALL IT THE "TEMPTATION LINE"?)...
19
...AND ENTERED INTO UNCHARTED TERRITORY...
HA-HA-HA, CHAE-KYUNG.
...IN THE BLINK OF AN EYE...
AIEEE. LOOK OVER THERE, SHIN.

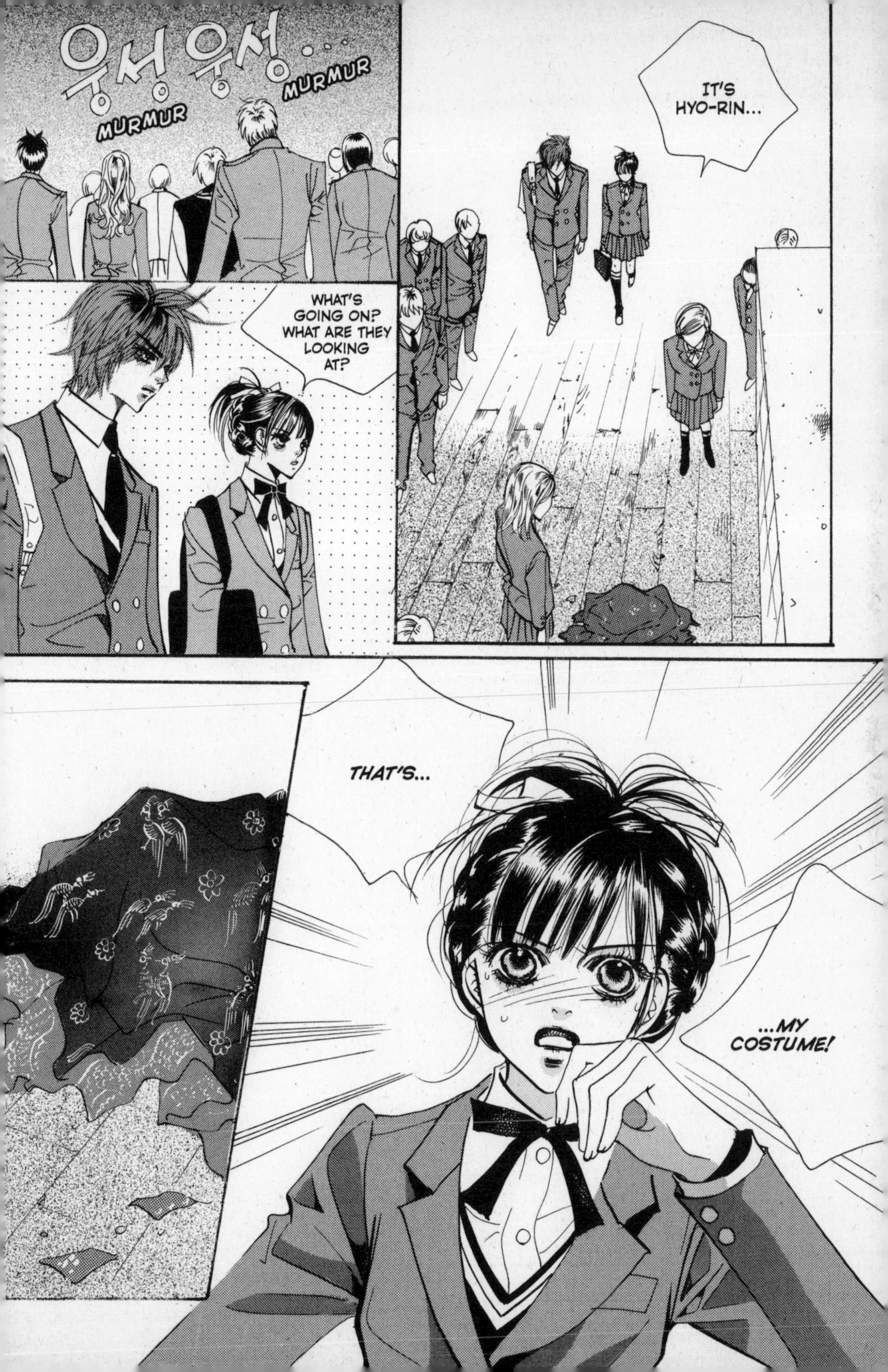

웅성 웅성...
MURMUR
MURMUR
WHAT'S GOING ON? WHAT ARE THEY LOOKING AT?
IT'S HYO-RIN...
THAT'S...
...MY COSTUME!

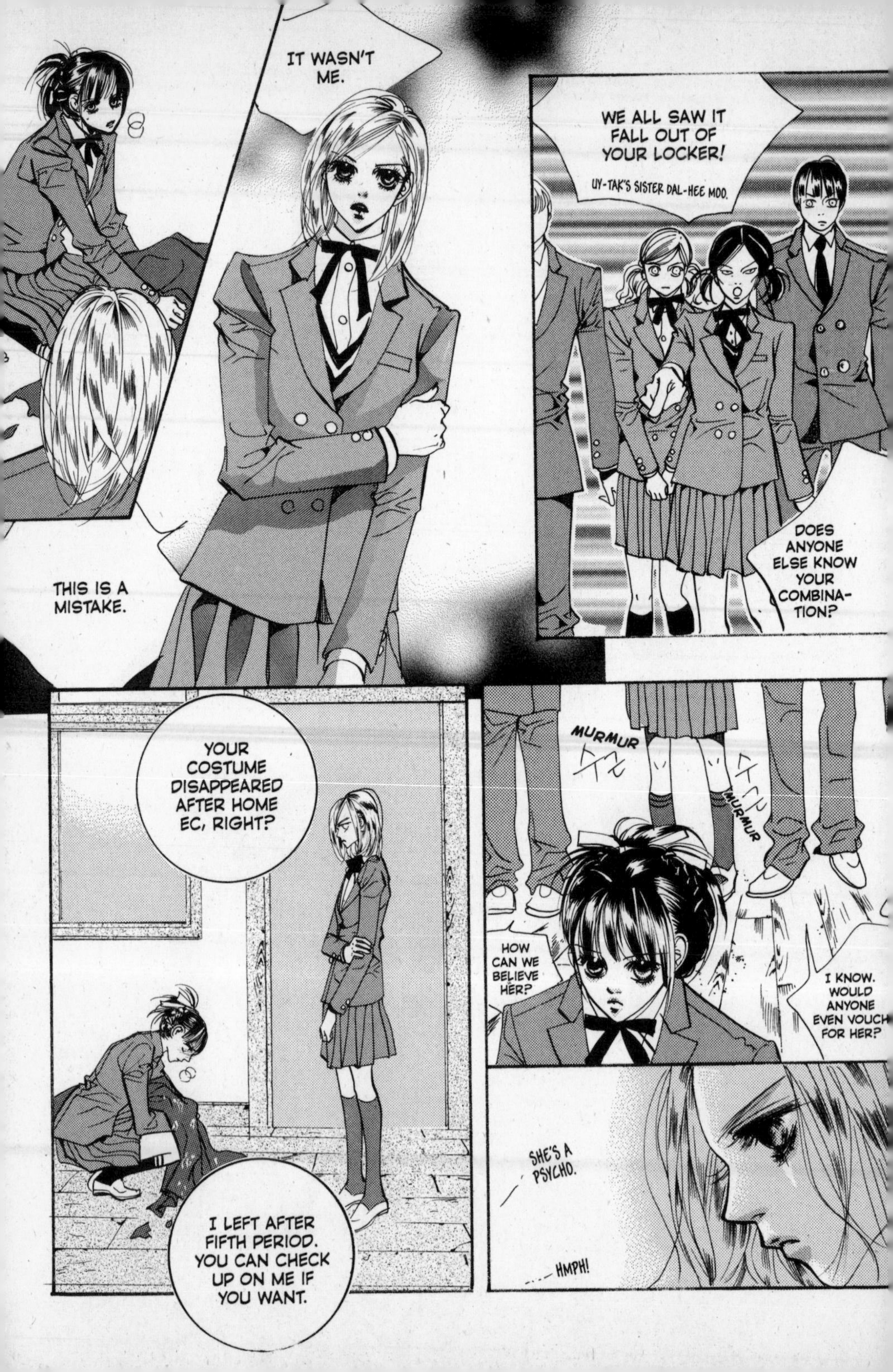
IT WASN'T ME.
THIS IS A MISTAKE.
WE ALL SAW IT FALL OUT OF YOUR LOCKER!
UY-TAK'S SISTER DAL-HEE MOO.
DOES ANYONE ELSE KNOW YOUR COMBINATION?
YOUR COSTUME DISAPPEARED AFTER HOME EC, RIGHT?
I LEFT AFTER FIFTH PERIOD. YOU CAN CHECK UP ON ME IF YOU WANT.
MURMUR
MURMUR
HOW CAN WE BELIEVE HER?
I KNOW. WOULD ANYONE EVEN VOUCH FOR HER?
SHE'S A PSYCHO.
HMPH!

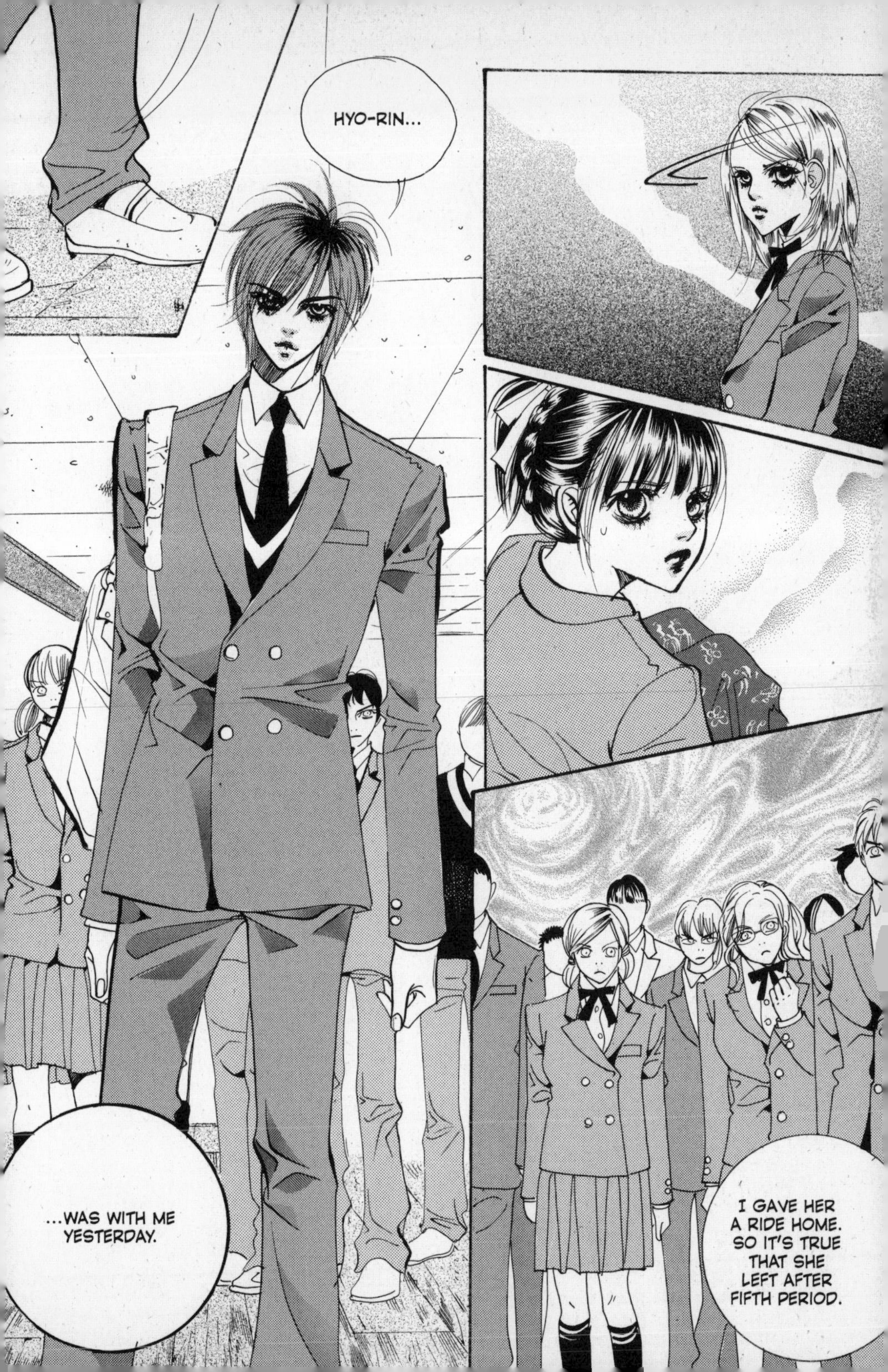
HYO-RIN...
...WAS WITH ME YESTERDAY.
I GAVE HER A RIDE HOME. SO IT'S TRUE THAT SHE LEFT AFTER FIFTH PERIOD.

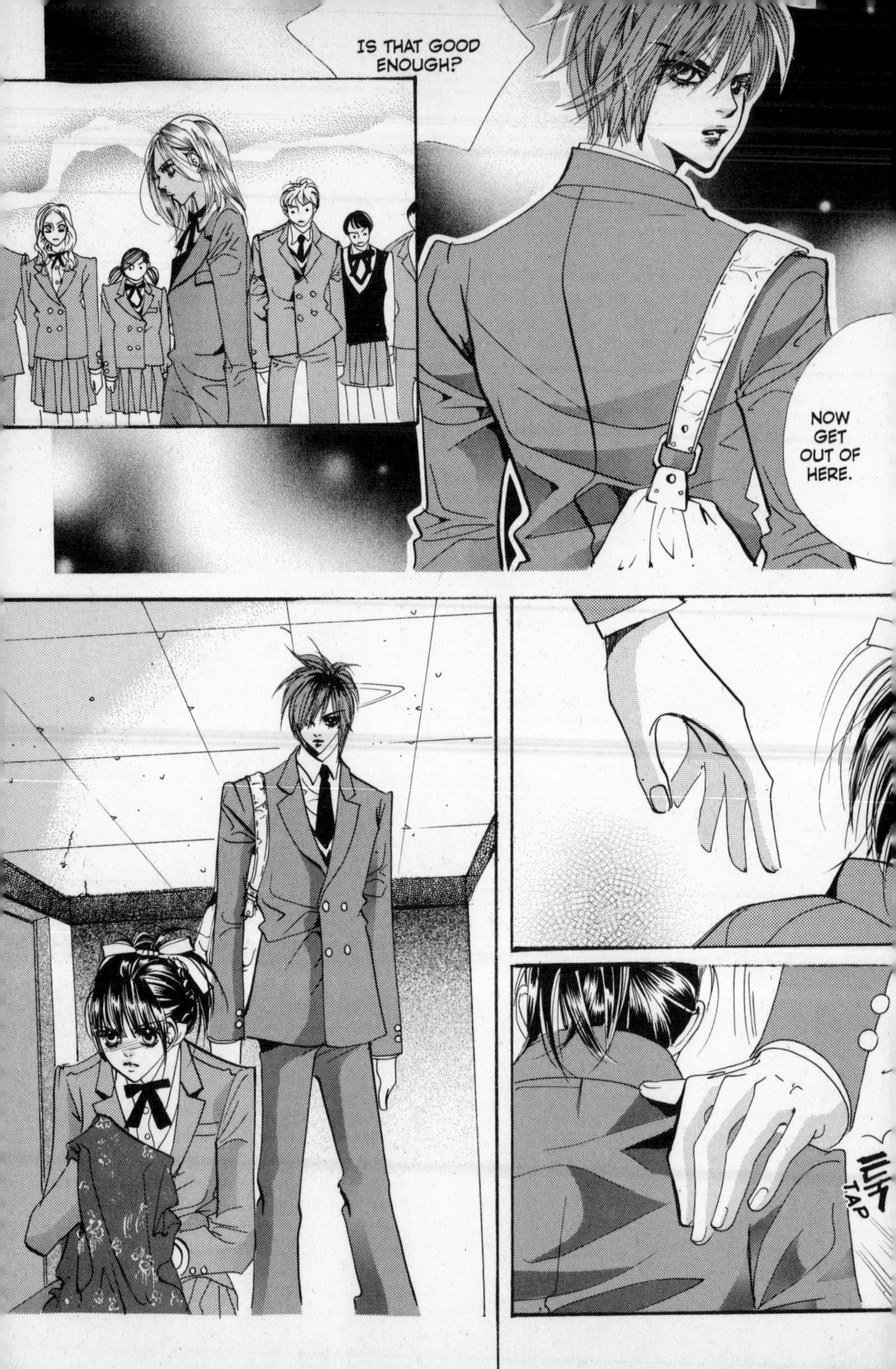
IS THAT GOOD ENOUGH?
NOW GET OUT OF HERE.
TAP

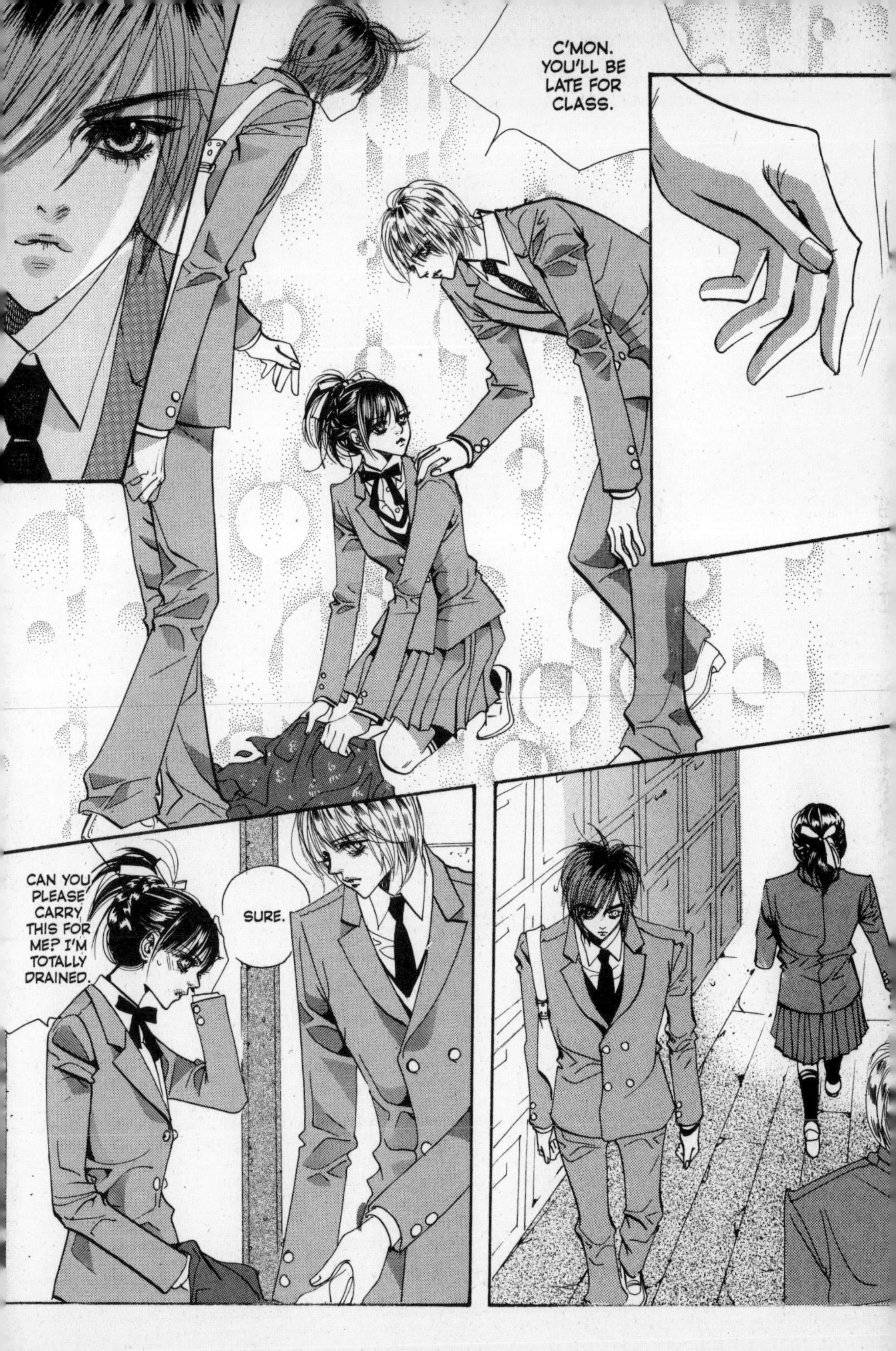
C'MON. YOU'LL BE LATE FOR CLASS.
CAN YOU PLEASE CARRY THIS FOR ME? I'M TOTALLY DRAINED.
SURE.

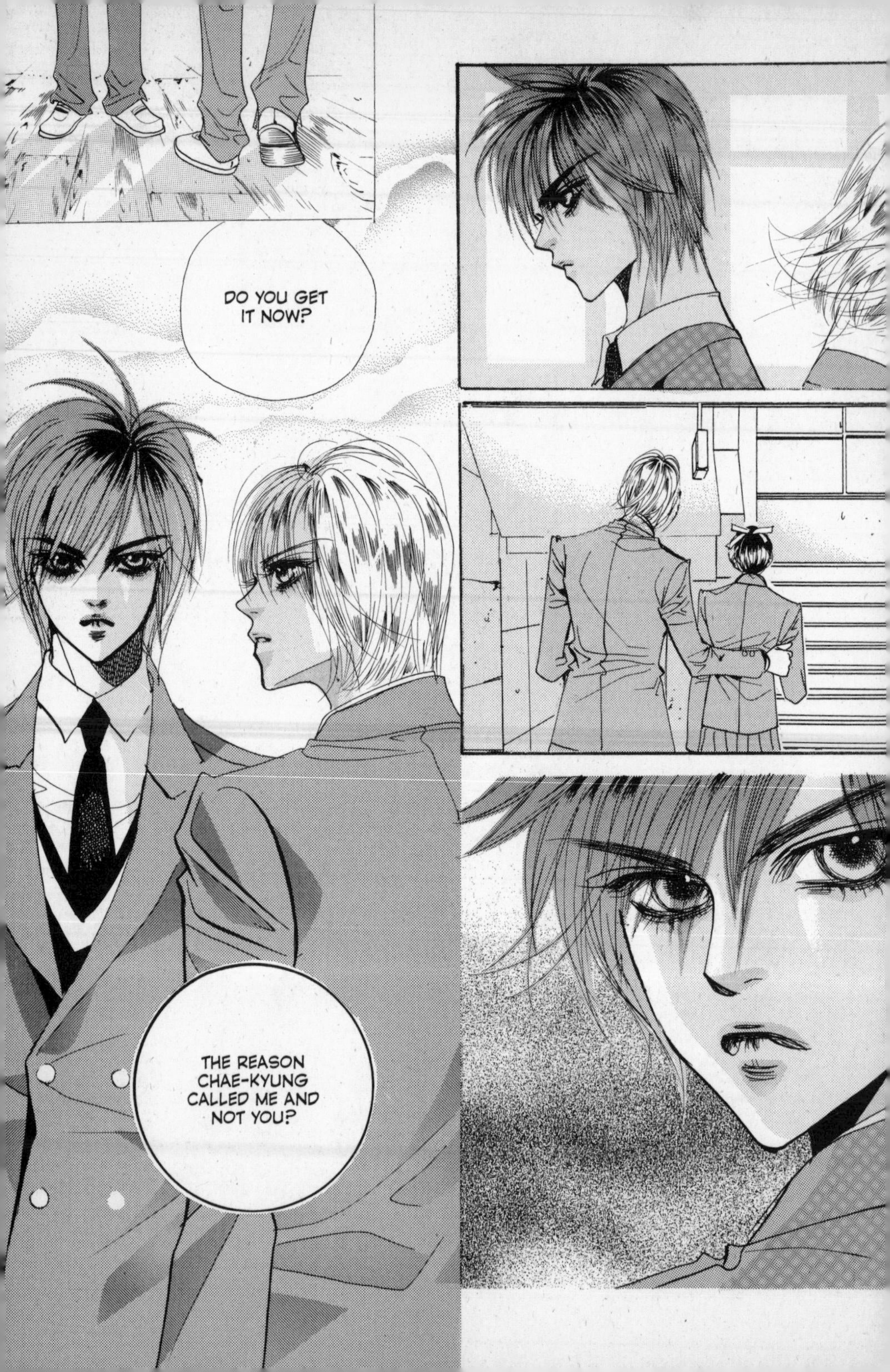
DO YOU GET IT NOW?
THE REASON CHAE-KYUNG CALLED ME AND NOT YOU?

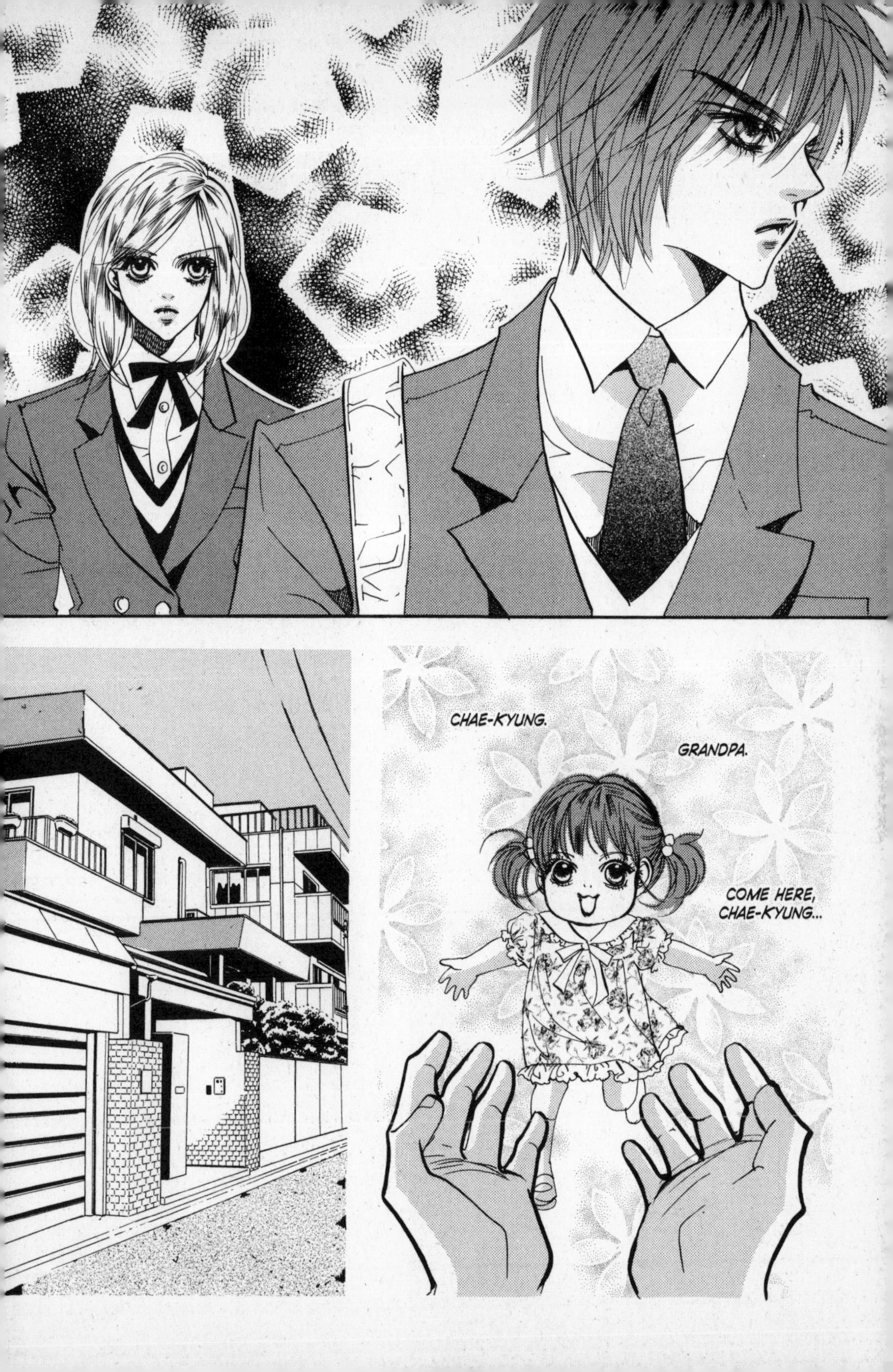
CHAE-KYUNG.
GRANDPA.
COME HERE, CHAE-KYUNG...

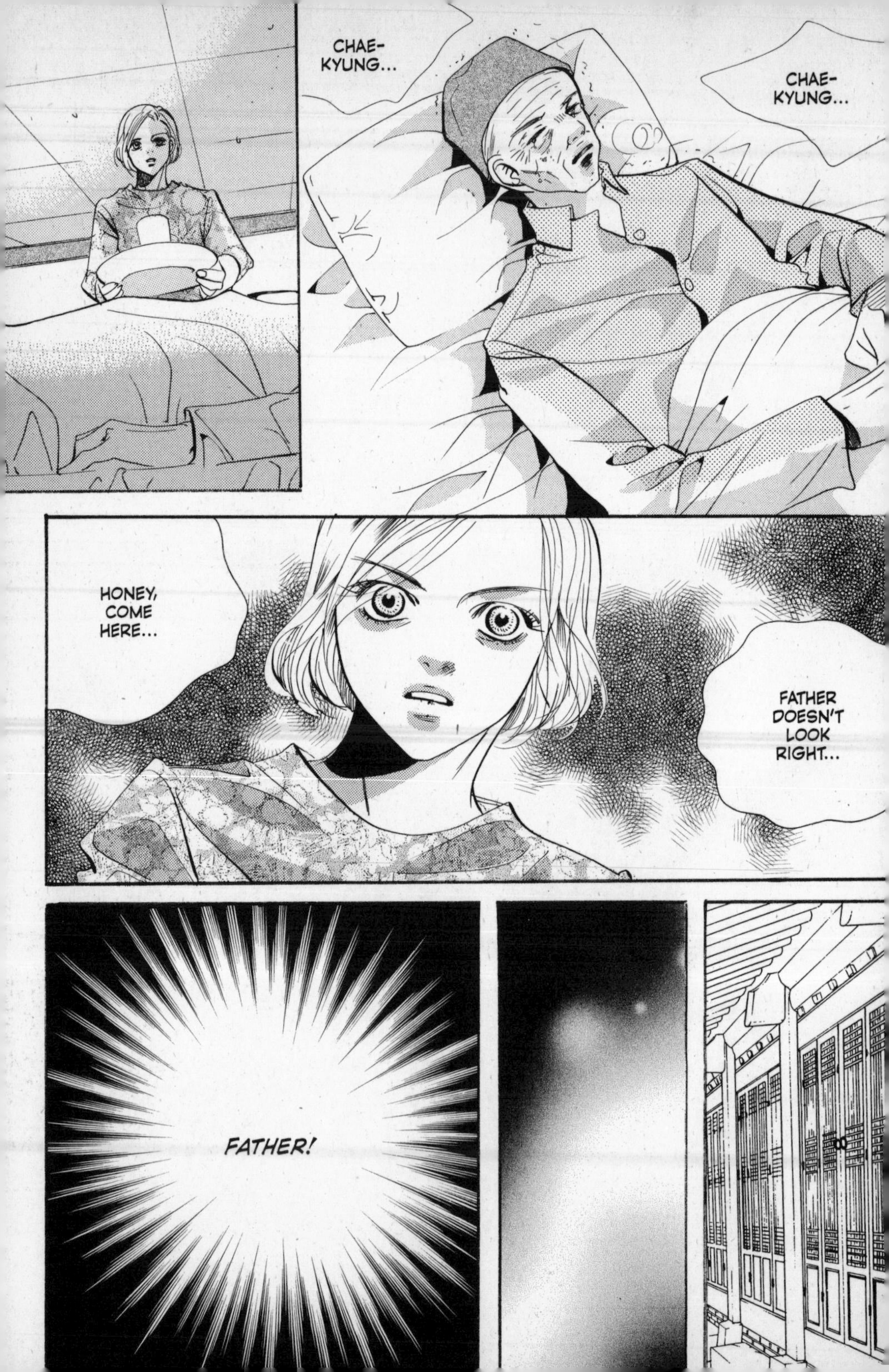
CHAE-
KYUNG...
CHAE-
KYUNG...
HONEY, COME HERE...
FATHER DOESN'T LOOK RIGHT...
FATHER!

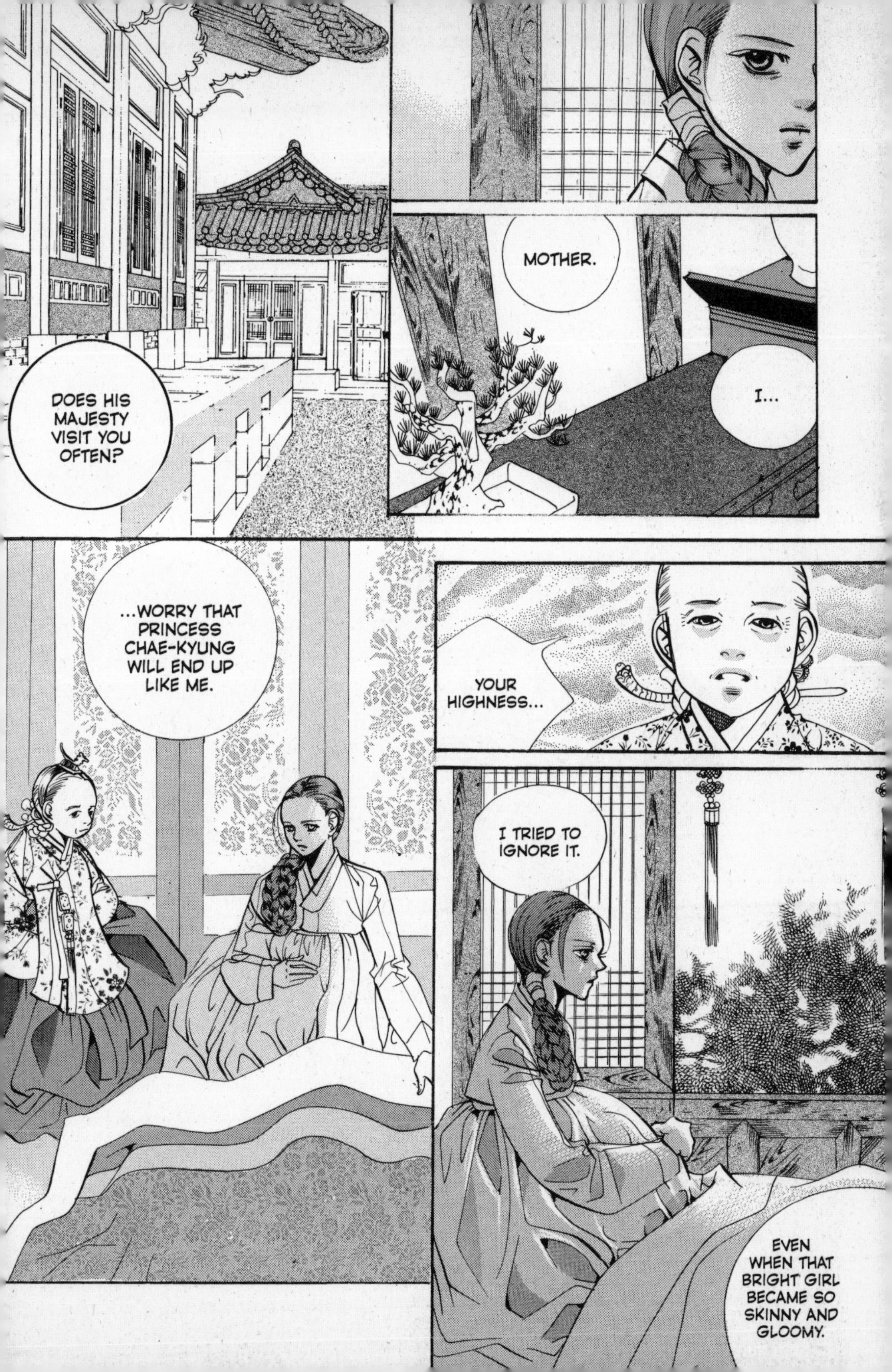
DOES HIS MAJESTY VISIT YOU OFTEN?
MOTHER.
I...
...WORRY THAT PRINCESS CHAE-KYUNG WILL END UP LIKE ME.
YOUR HIGHNESS...
I TRIED TO IGNORE IT.
EVEN WHEN THAT BRIGHT GIRL BECAME SO SKINNY AND GLOOMY.

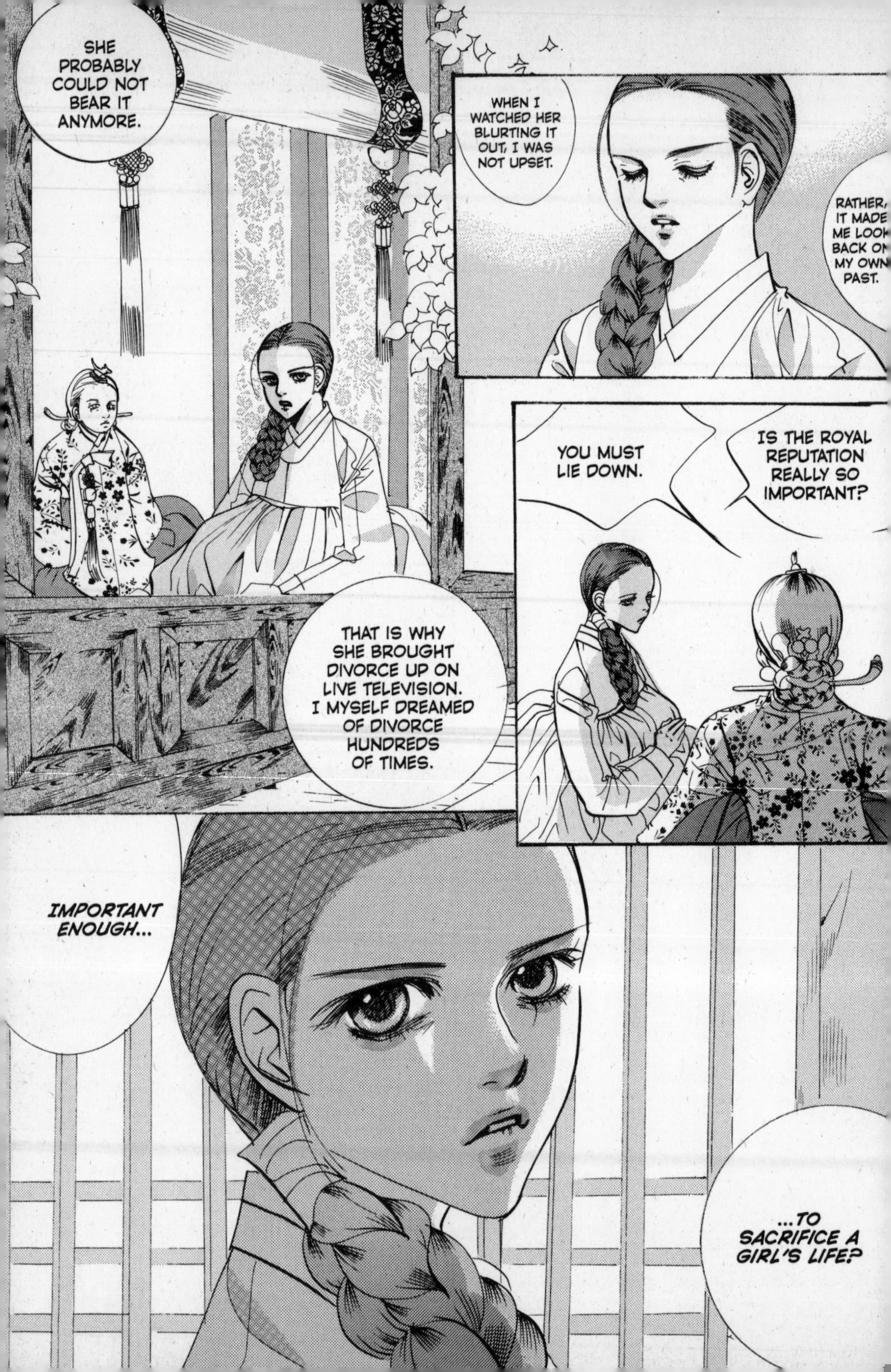
SHE PROBABLY COULD NOT BEAR IT ANYMORE.
THAT IS WHY SHE BROUGHT DIVORCE UP ON LIVE TELEVISION. I MYSELF DREAMED OF DIVORCE HUNDREDS OF TIMES.
WHEN I WATCHED HER BLURTING IT OUT, I WAS NOT UPSET.
RATHER, IT MADE ME LOOK BACK ON MY OWN PAST.
YOU MUST LIE DOWN.
IS THE ROYAL REPUTATION REALLY SO IMPORTANT?
IMPORTANT ENOUGH...
...TO SACRIFICE A GIRL'S LIFE?

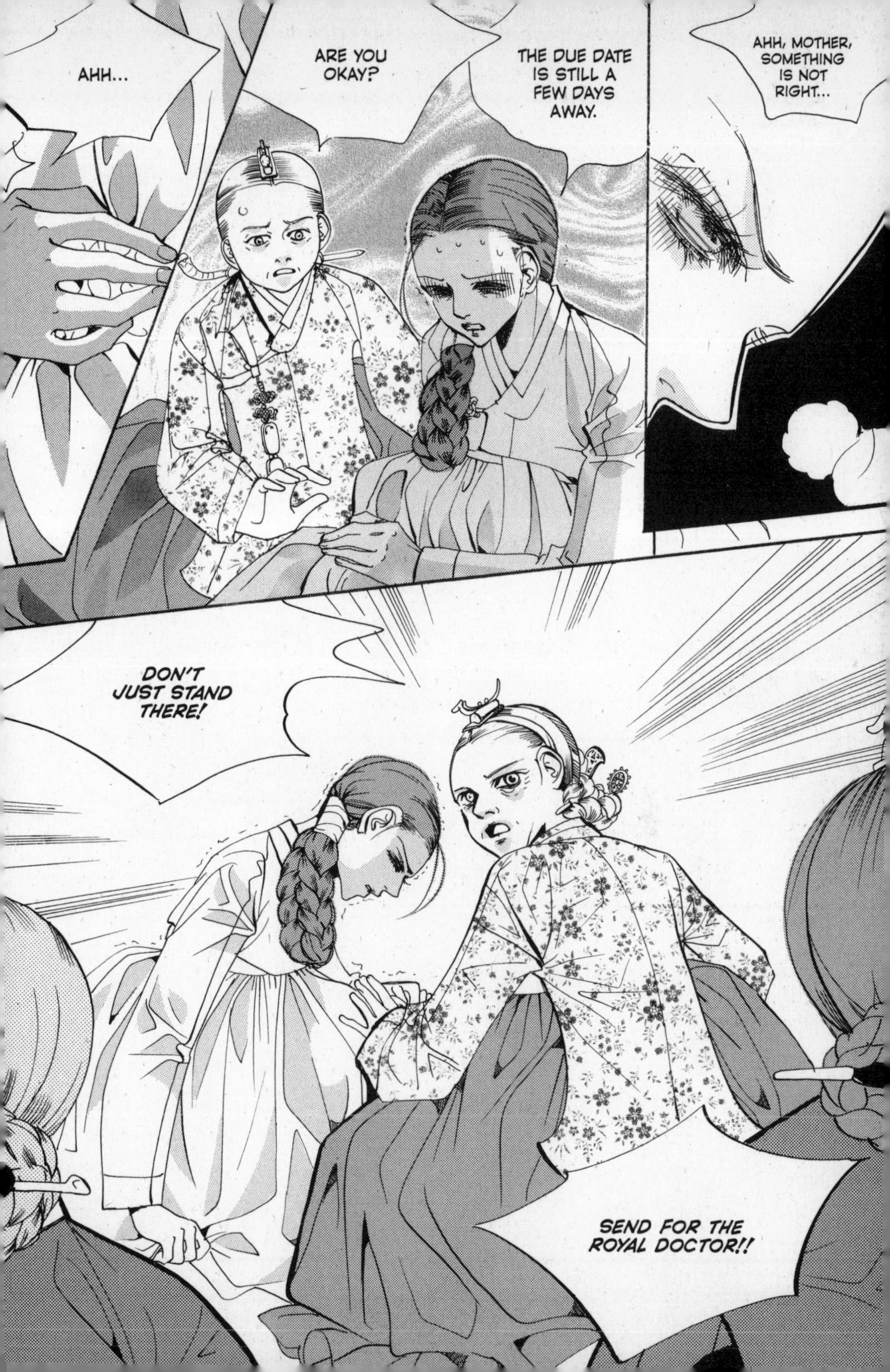
AHH...
ARE YOU OKAY?
THE DUE DATE IS STILL A FEW DAYS AWAY.
AHH, MOTHER, SOMETHING IS NOT RIGHT...
DON'T JUST STAND THERE!
SEND FOR THE ROYAL DOCTOR!!

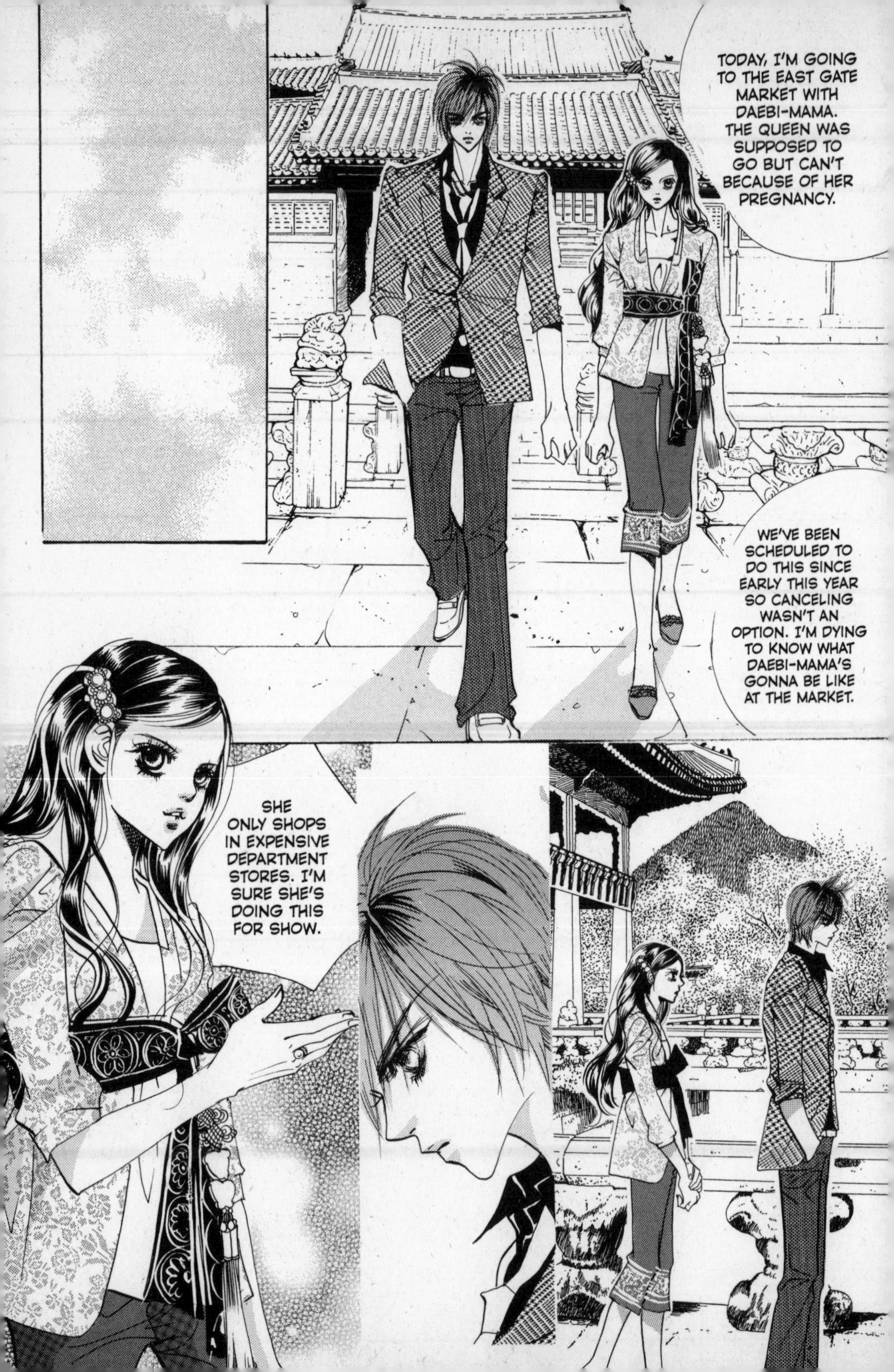
TODAY, I'M GOING TO THE EAST GATE MARKET WITH DAEBI-MAMA. THE QUEEN WAS SUPPOSED TO GO BUT CAN'T BECAUSE OF HER PREGNANCY.
WE'VE BEEN SCHEDULED TO DO THIS SINCE EARLY THIS YEAR SO CANCELING WASN'T AN OPTION. I'M DYING TO KNOW WHAT DAEBI-MAMA'S GONNA BE LIKE AT THE MARKET.
SHE ONLY SHOPS IN EXPENSIVE DEPARTMENT STORES. I'M SURE SHE'S DOING THIS FOR SHOW.

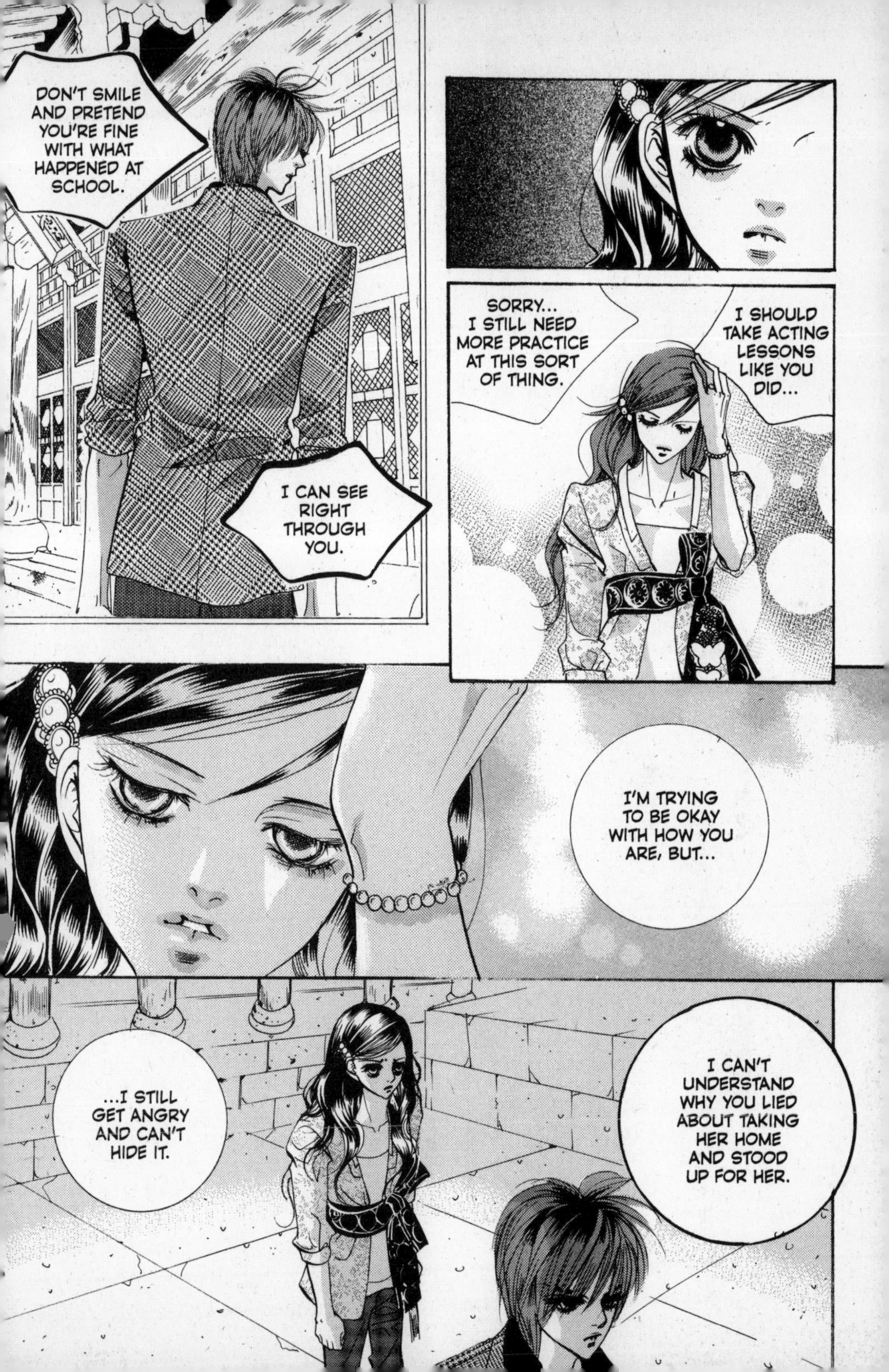
DON'T SMILE AND PRETEND YOU'RE FINE WITH WHAT HAPPENED AT SCHOOL.
I CAN SEE RIGHT THROUGH YOU.
SORRY... I STILL NEED MORE PRACTICE AT THIS SORT OF THING.
I SHOULD TAKE ACTING LESSONS LIKE YOU DID...
I'M TRYING TO BE OKAY WITH HOW YOU ARE, BUT...
...I STILL GET ANGRY AND CAN'T HIDE IT.
I CAN'T UNDERSTAND WHY YOU LIED ABOUT TAKING HER HOME AND STOOD UP FOR HER.

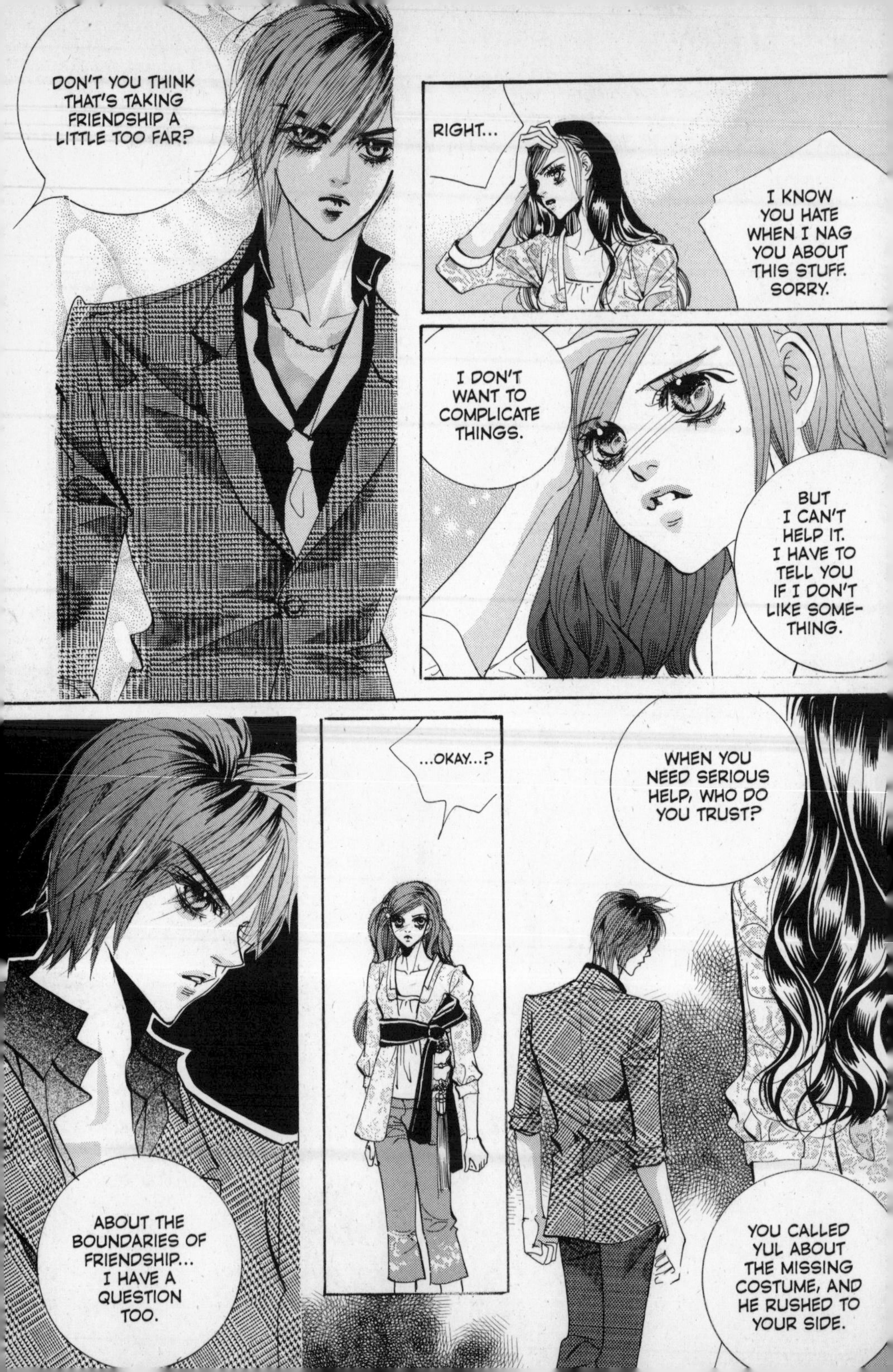
DON'T YOU THINK THAT'S TAKING FRIENDSHIP A LITTLE TOO FAR?
RIGHT...
I KNOW YOU HATE WHEN I NAG YOU ABOUT THIS STUFF. SORRY.
I DON'T WANT TO COMPLICATE THINGS.
BUT I CAN'T HELP IT. I HAVE TO TELL YOU IF I DON'T LIKE SOME-THING.
ABOUT THE BOUNDARIES OF FRIENDSHIP... I HAVE A QUESTION TOO.
...OKAY...?
WHEN YOU NEED SERIOUS HELP, WHO DO YOU TRUST?
YOU CALLED YUL ABOUT THE MISSING COSTUME, AND HE RUSHED TO YOUR SIDE.

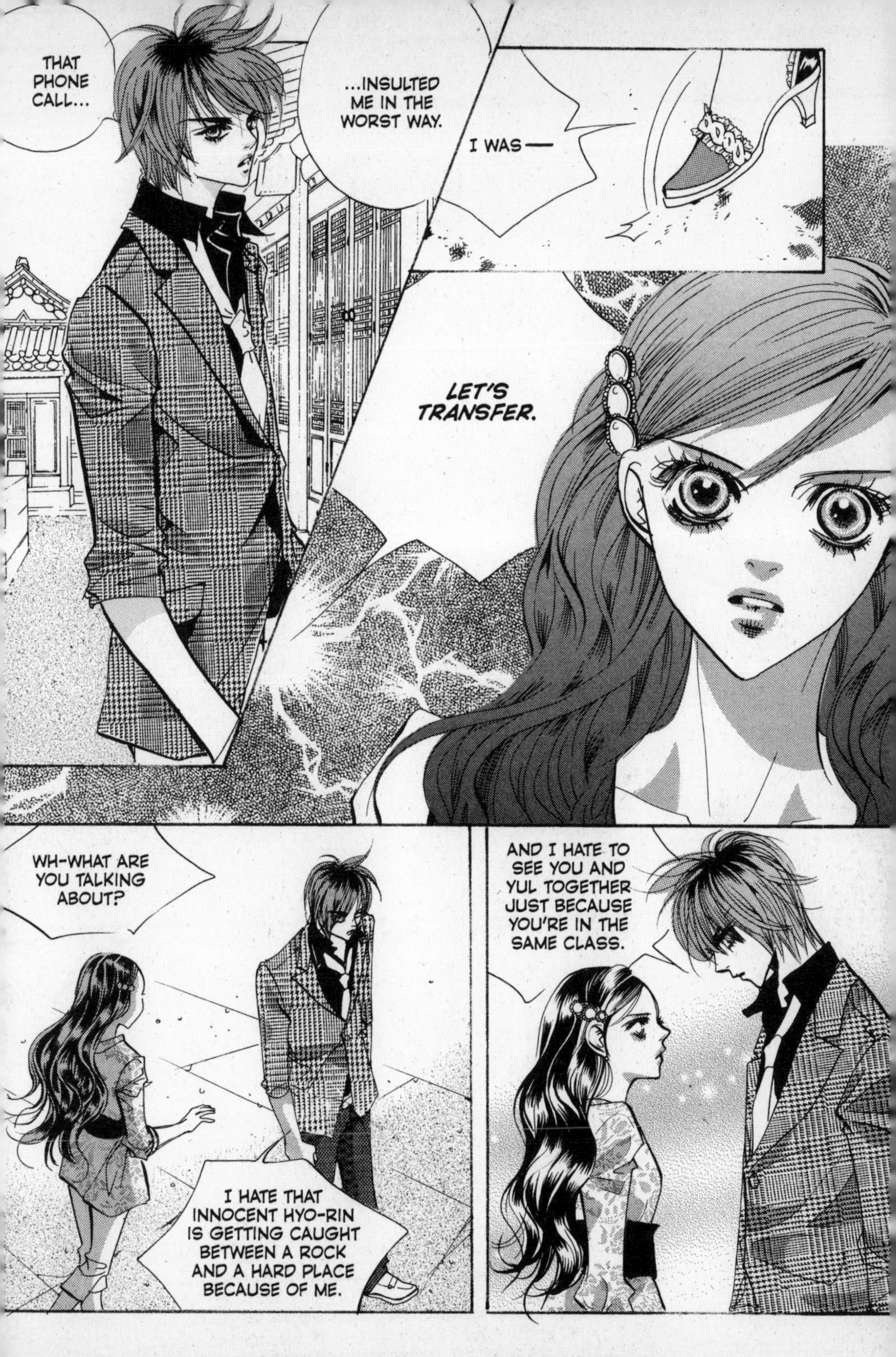
THAT PHONE CALL...
...INSULTED ME IN THE WORST WAY.
I WAS—
LET'S TRANSFER.
WH-WHAT ARE YOU TALKING ABOUT?
I HATE THAT INNOCENT HYO-RIN IS GETTING CAUGHT BETWEEN A ROCK AND A HARD PLACE BECAUSE OF ME.
AND I HATE TO SEE YOU AND YUL TOGETHER JUST BECAUSE YOU'RE IN THE SAME CLASS.

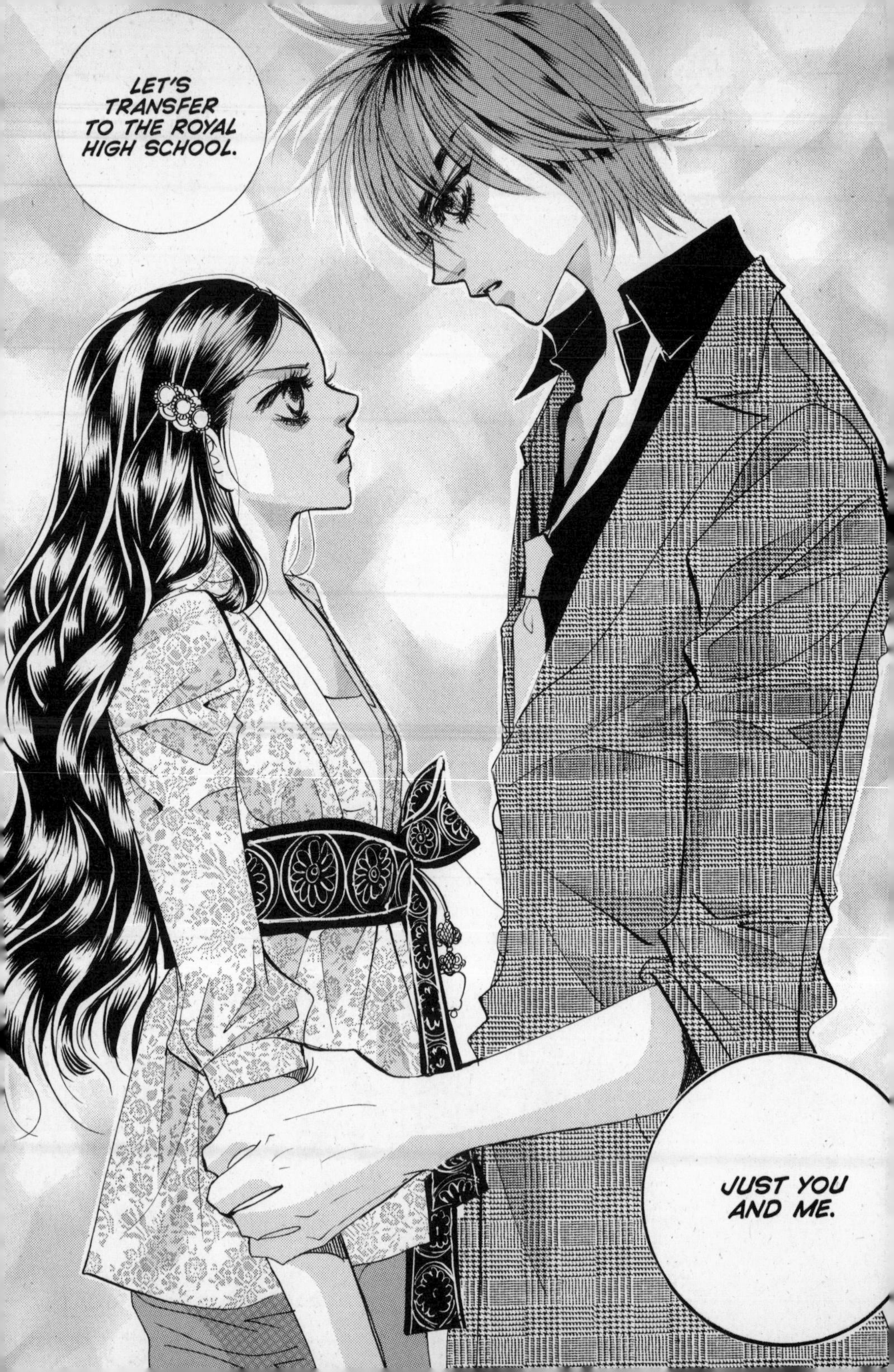
LET'S TRANSFER TO THE ROYAL HIGH SCHOOL.
JUST YOU AND ME.

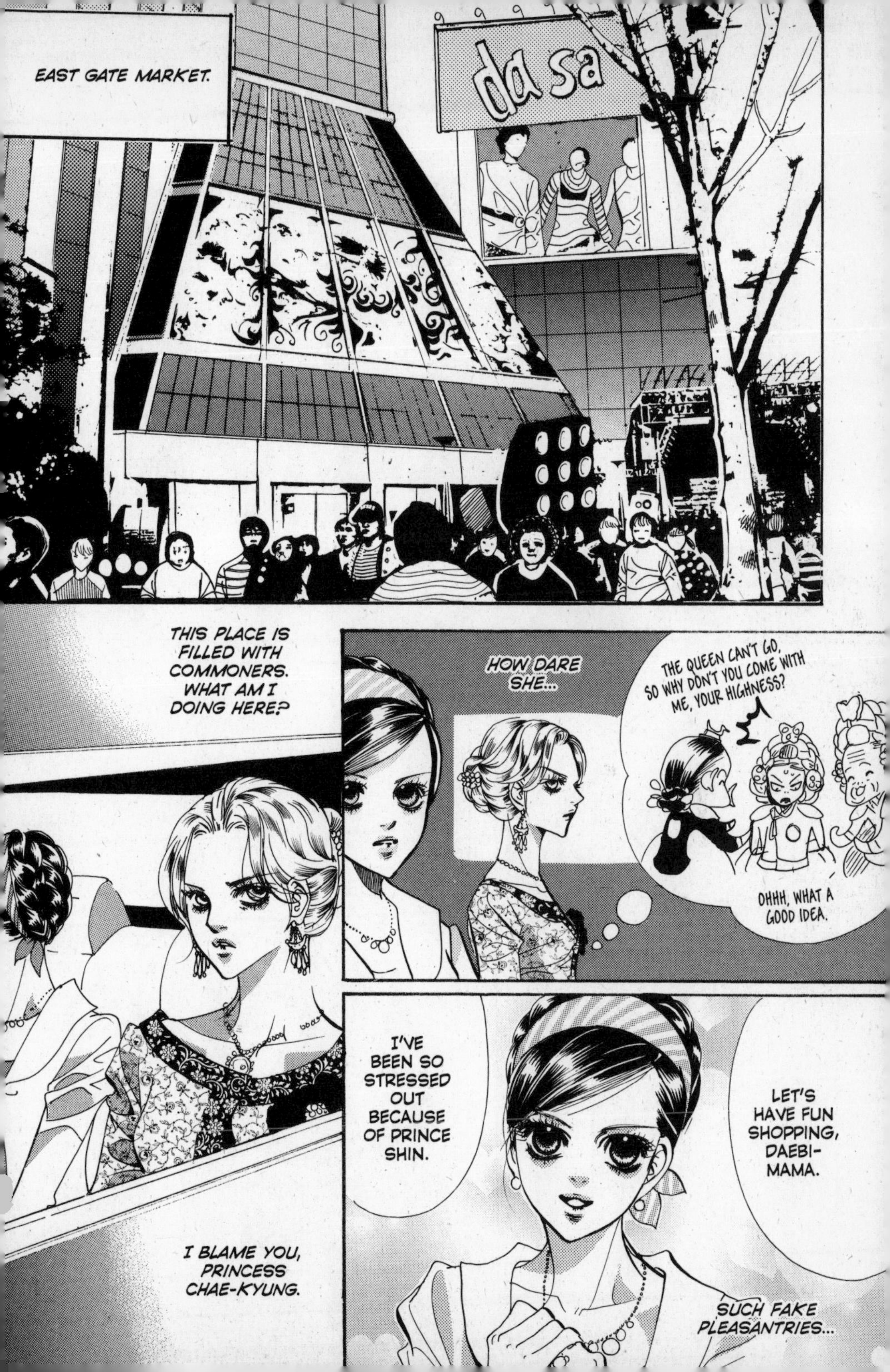
EAST GATE MARKET.
da sa
THIS PLACE IS FILLED WITH COMMONERS. WHAT AM I DOING HERE?
HOW DARE SHE...
THE QUEEN CAN'T GO, SO WHY DON'T YOU COME WITH ME, YOUR HIGHNESS?
OHHH, WHAT A GOOD IDEA.
I BLAME YOU, PRINCESS CHAE-KYUNG.
I'VE BEEN SO STRESSED OUT BECAUSE OF PRINCE SHIN.
LET'S HAVE FUN SHOPPING, DAEBI-MAMA.
SUCH FAKE PLEASANTRIES...

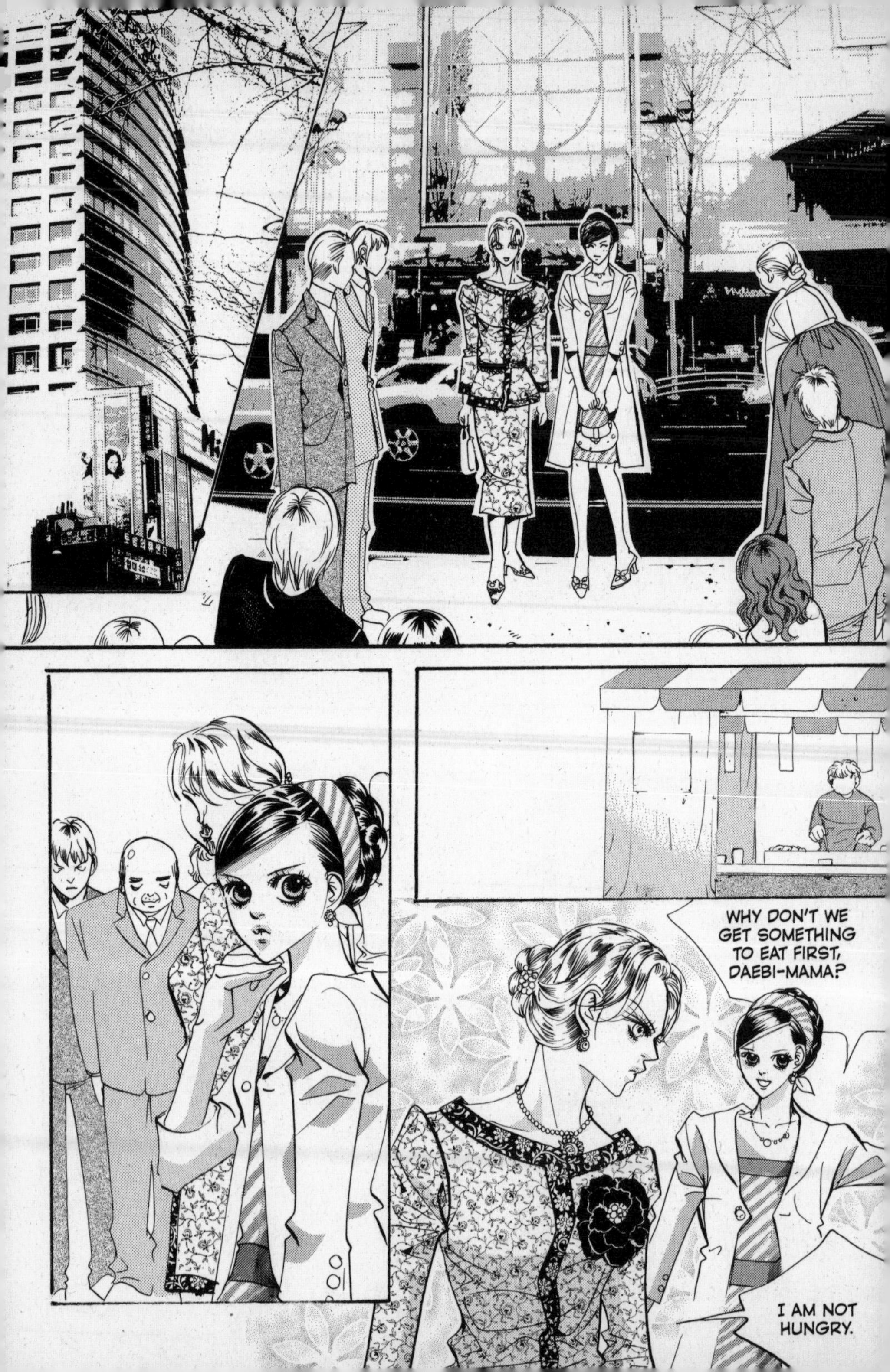
WHY DON'T WE GET SOMETHING TO EAT FIRST, DAEBI-MAMA?
I AM NOT HUNGRY.

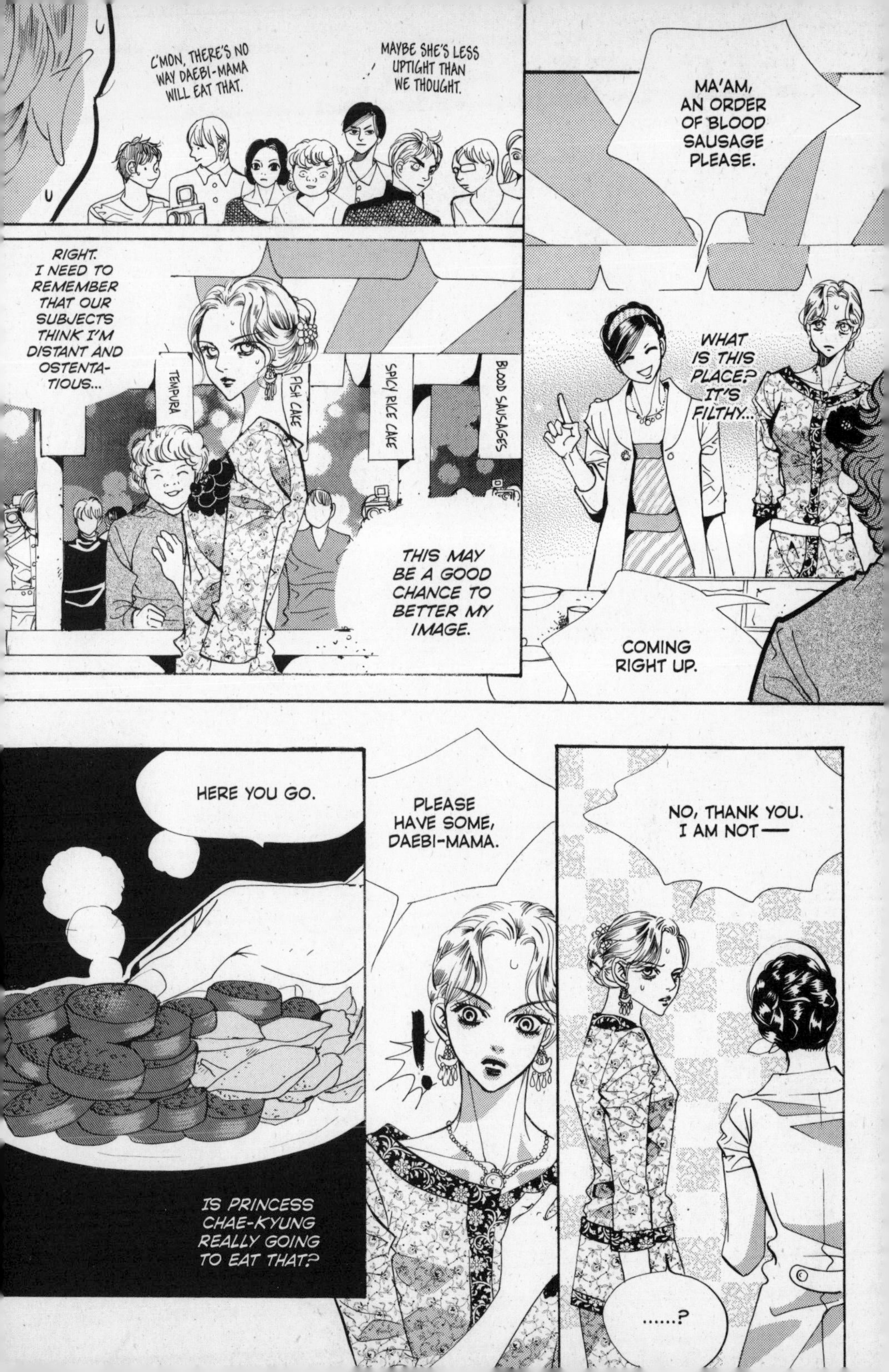
C'MON, THERE'S NO WAY DAEBI-MAMA WILL EAT THAT.
MAYBE SHE'S LESS UPTIGHT THAN WE THOUGHT.
MA'AM, AN ORDER OF BLOOD SAUSAGE PLEASE.
RIGHT. I NEED TO REMEMBER THAT OUR SUBJECTS THINK I'M DISTANT AND OSTENTATIOUS...
TEMPURA
FISH CAKE
SPICY RICE CAKE
BLOOD SAUSAGES
THIS MAY BE A GOOD CHANCE TO BETTER MY IMAGE.
WHAT IS THIS PLACE? IT'S FILTHY...
COMING RIGHT UP.
HERE YOU GO.
IS PRINCESS CHAE-KYUNG REALLY GOING TO EAT THAT?
PLEASE HAVE SOME, DAEBI-MAMA.
NO, THANK YOU. I AM NOT—
......?

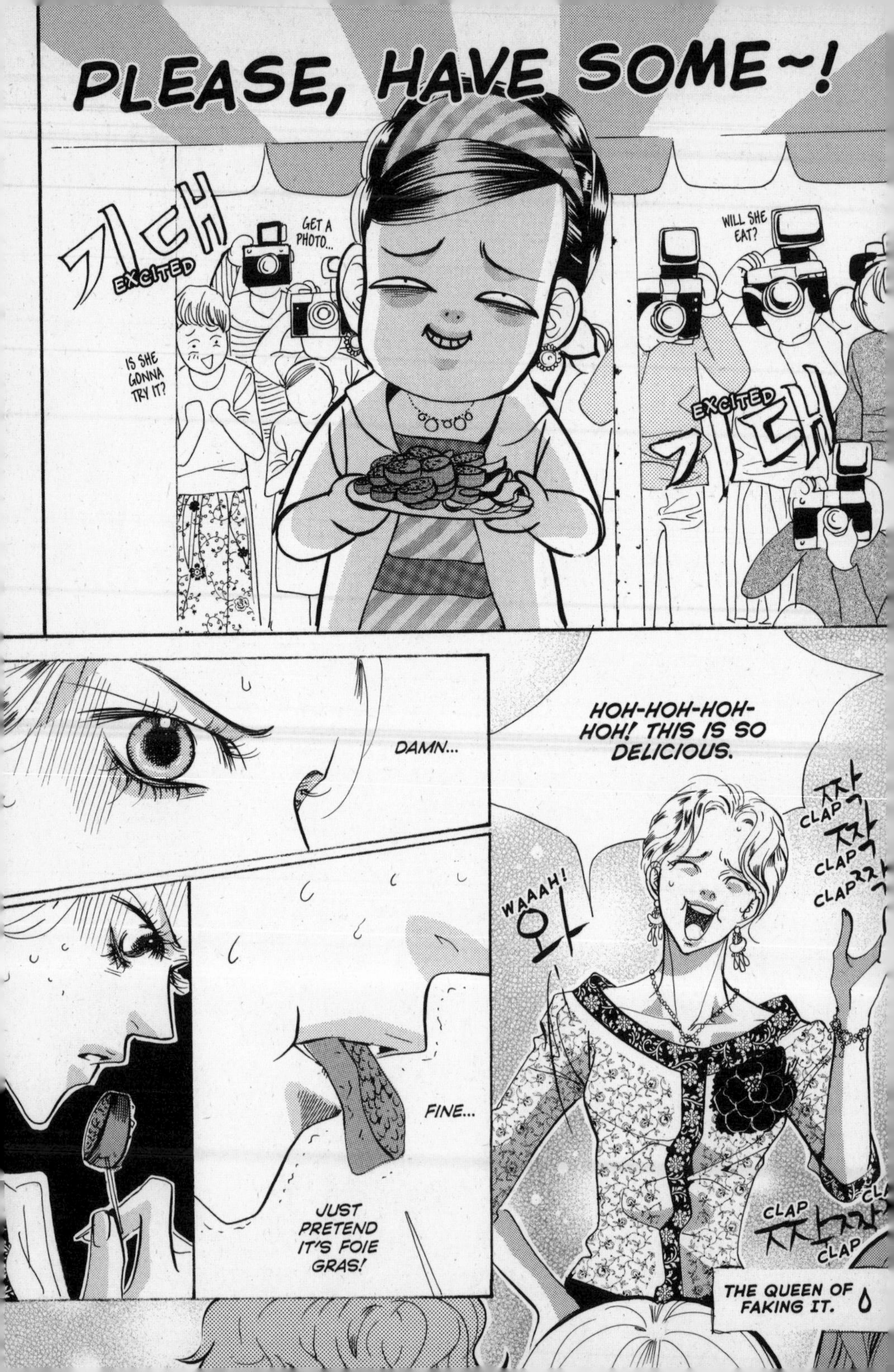
PLEASE, HAVE SOME~!
기대
EXCITED
GET A PHOTO...
IS SHE GONNA TRY IT?
WILL SHE EAT?
EXCITED
기대
DAMN...
FINE...
JUST PRETEND IT'S FOIE GRAS!
HOH-HOH-HOH-HOH! THIS IS SO DELICIOUS.
WAAAH!
와
CLAP 짝
CLAP 짝
CLAP 짝
CLAP
CLAP
CLAP
THE QUEEN OF FAKING IT.

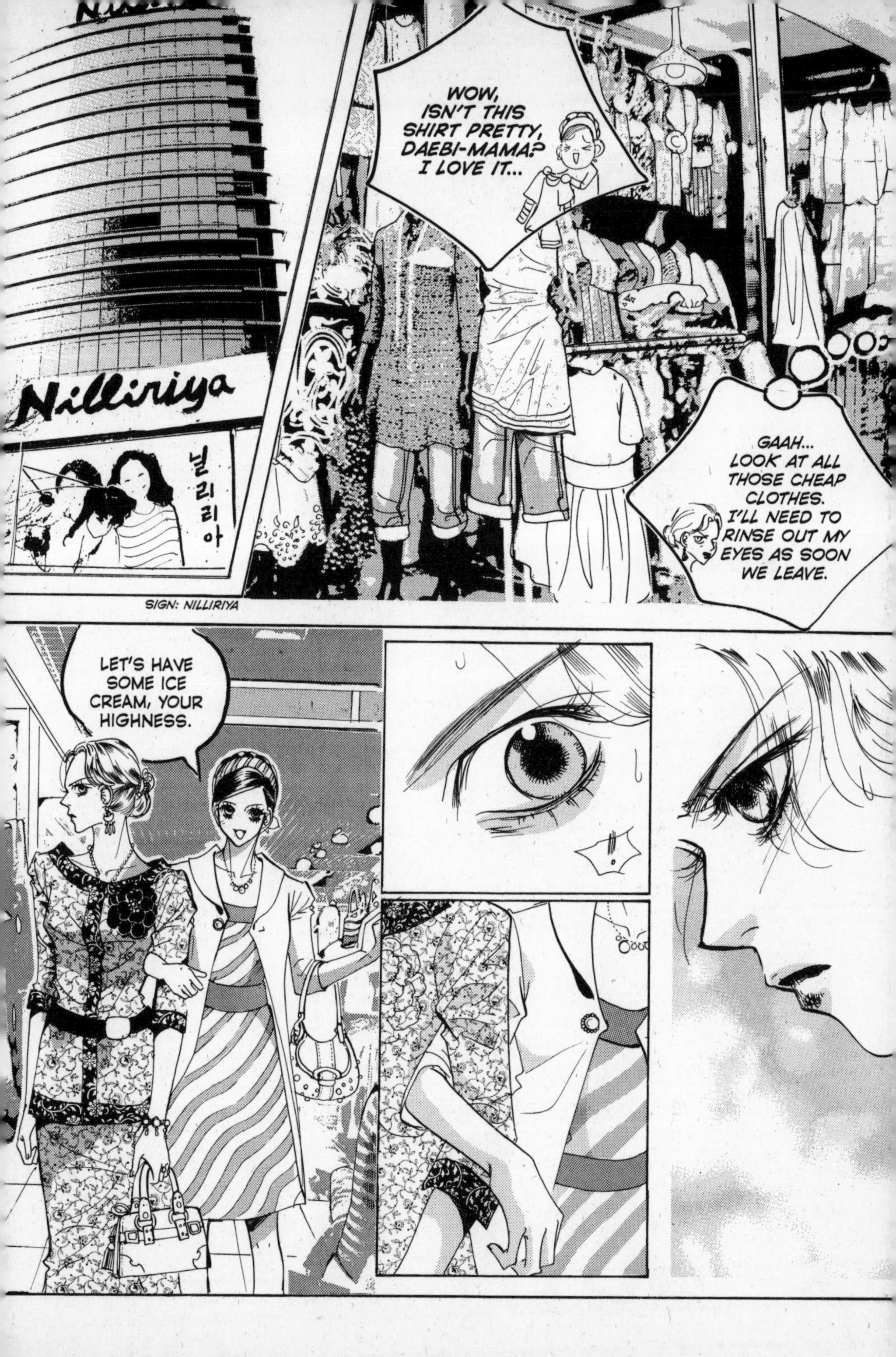
Nilliriya
널리리아
WOW, ISN'T THIS SHIRT PRETTY, DAEBI-MAMA? I LOVE IT...
GAAH... LOOK AT ALL THOSE CHEAP CLOTHES. I'LL NEED TO RINSE OUT MY EYES AS SOON WE LEAVE.
SIGN: NILLIRIYA
LET'S HAVE SOME ICE CREAM, YOUR HIGHNESS.
!!

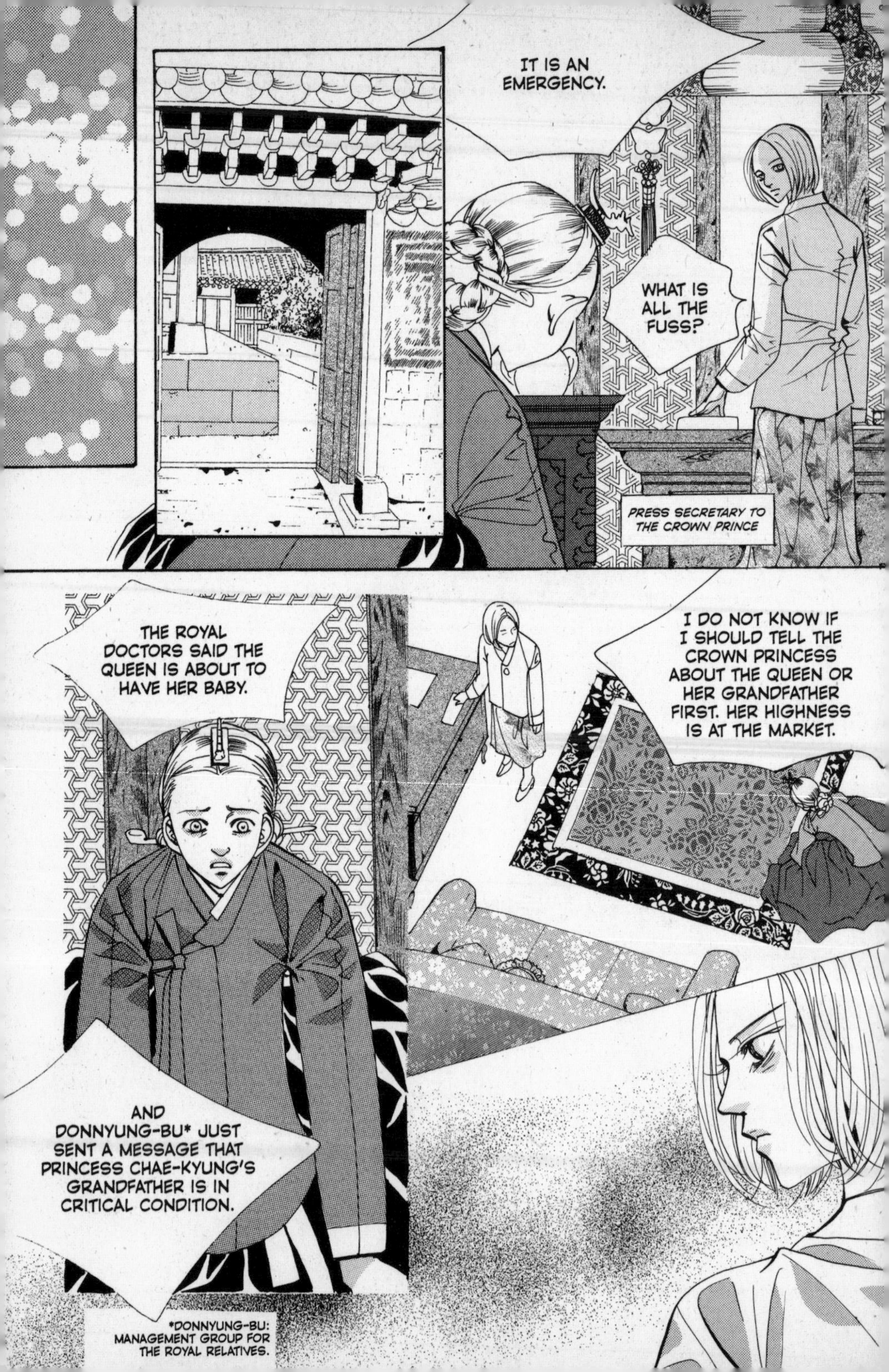
IT IS AN EMERGENCY.
WHAT IS ALL THE FUSS?
PRESS SECRETARY TO THE CROWN PRINCE
THE ROYAL DOCTORS SAID THE QUEEN IS ABOUT TO HAVE HER BABY.
AND DONNYUNG-BU* JUST SENT A MESSAGE THAT PRINCESS CHAE-KYUNG'S GRANDFATHER IS IN CRITICAL CONDITION.
I DO NOT KNOW IF I SHOULD TELL THE CROWN PRINCESS ABOUT THE QUEEN OR HER GRANDFATHER FIRST. HER HIGHNESS IS AT THE MARKET.
*DONNYUNG-BU: MANAGEMENT GROUP FOR THE ROYAL RELATIVES.

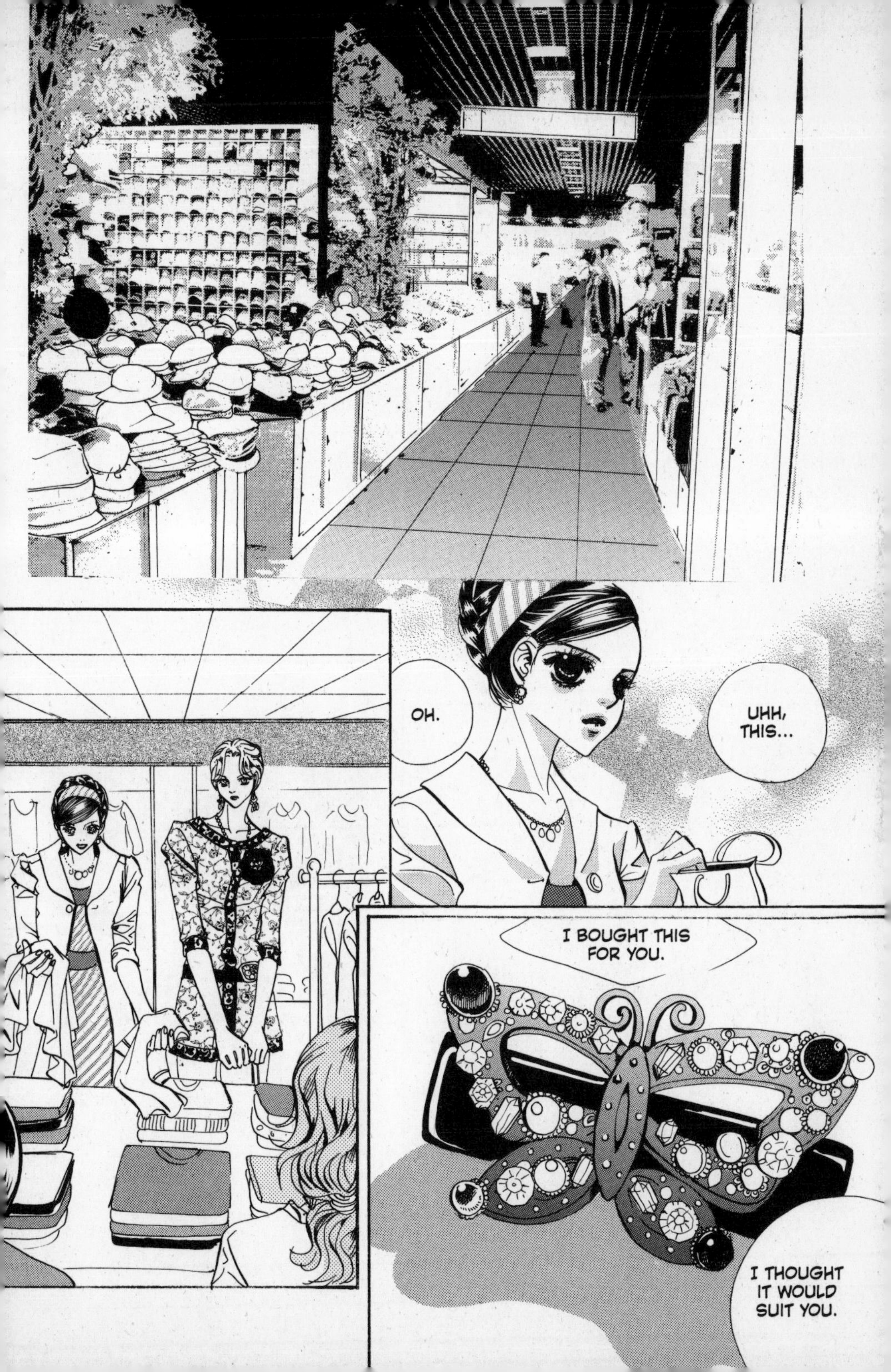
OH.
UHH, THIS...
I BOUGHT THIS FOR YOU.
I THOUGHT IT WOULD SUIT YOU.

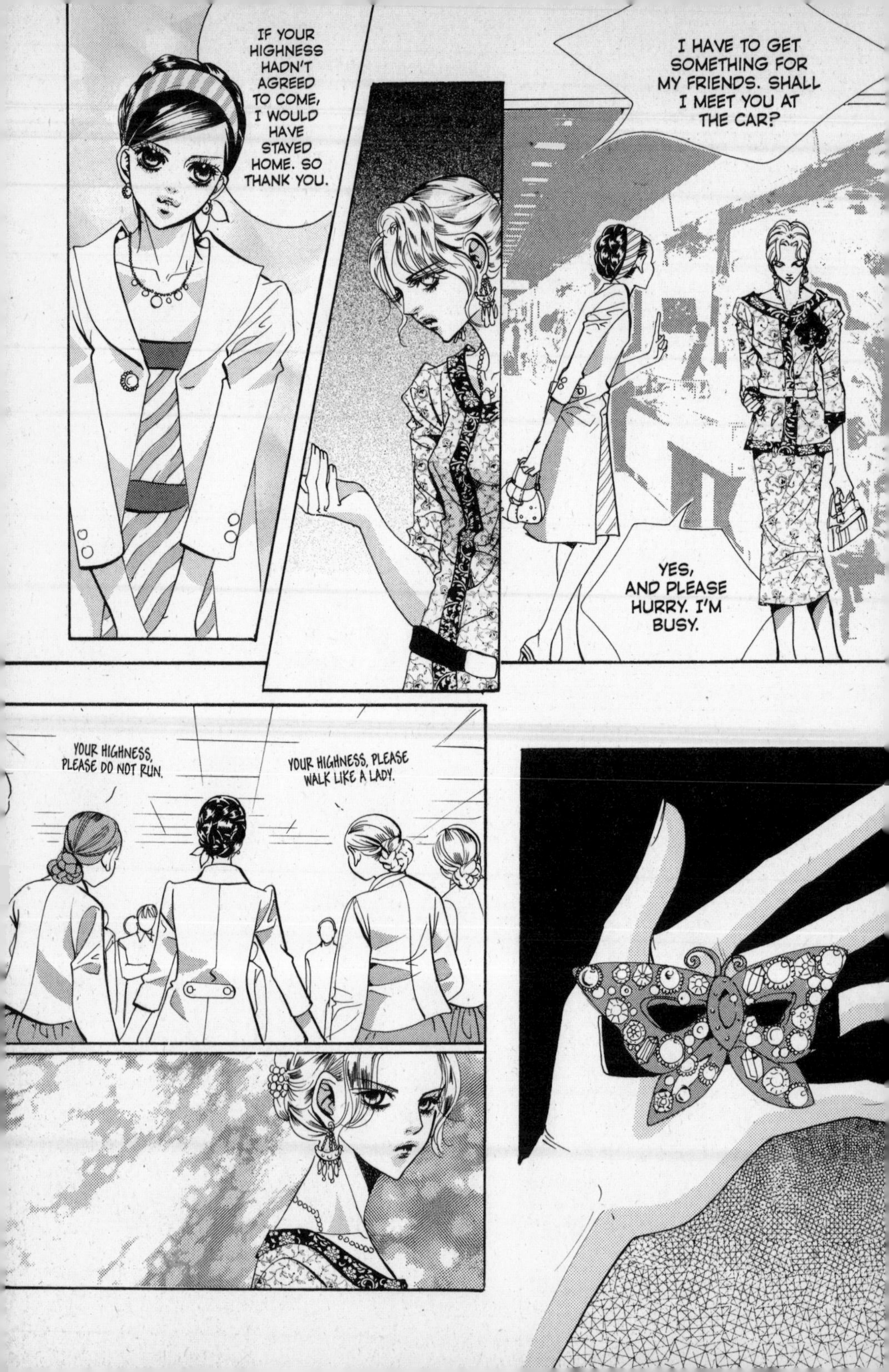
IF YOUR HIGHNESS HADN'T AGREED TO COME, I WOULD HAVE STAYED HOME. SO THANK YOU.
I HAVE TO GET SOMETHING FOR MY FRIENDS. SHALL I MEET YOU AT THE CAR?
YES, AND PLEASE HURRY. I'M BUSY.
YOUR HIGHNESS, PLEASE DO NOT RUN.
YOUR HIGHNESS, PLEASE WALK LIKE A LADY.

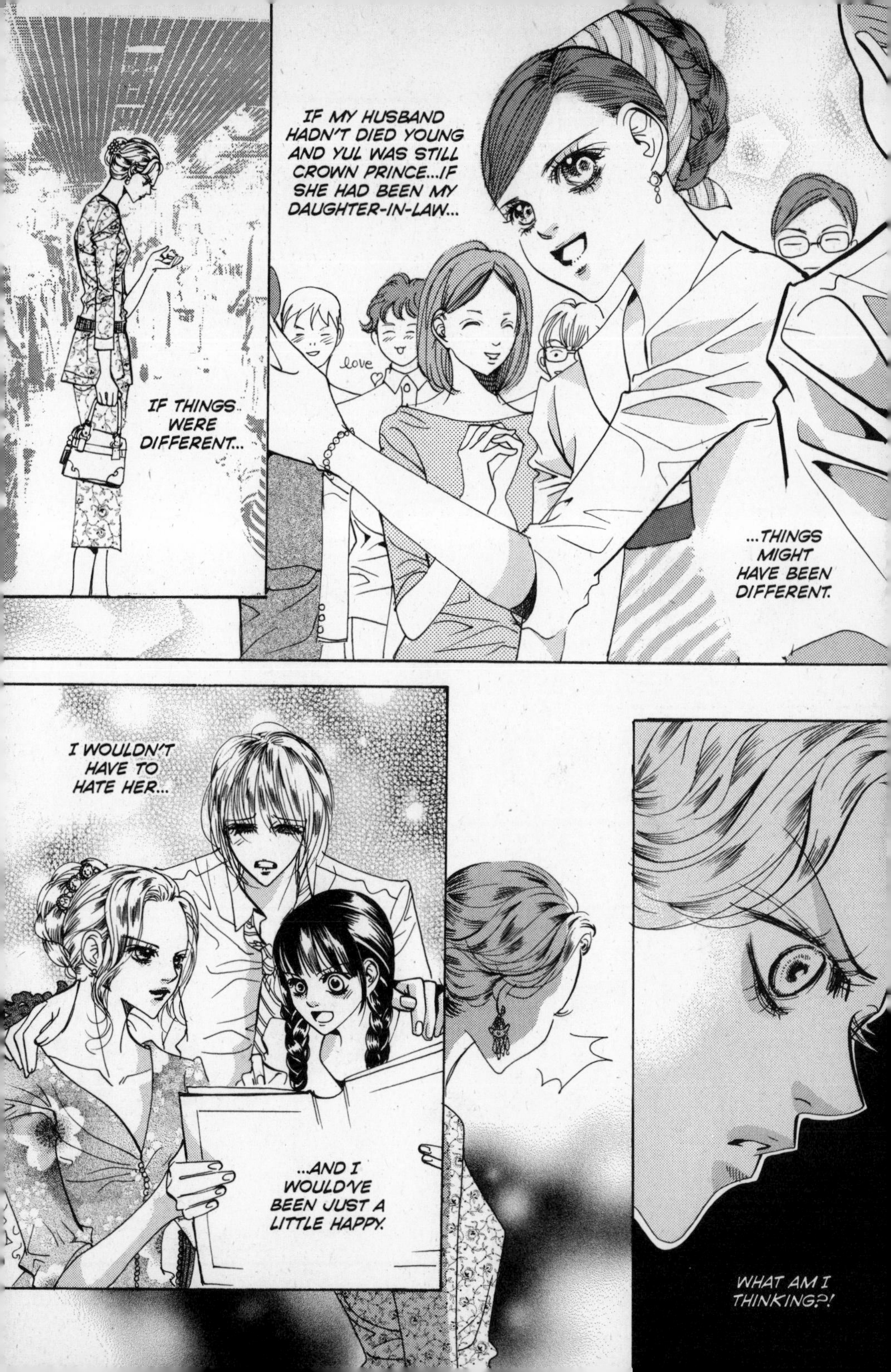
IF THINGS WERE DIFFERENT...
IF MY HUSBAND HADN'T DIED YOUNG AND YUL WAS STILL CROWN PRINCE...IF SHE HAD BEEN MY DAUGHTER-IN-LAW...
love
...THINGS MIGHT HAVE BEEN DIFFERENT.
I WOULDN'T HAVE TO HATE HER...
...AND I WOULD'VE BEEN JUST A LITTLE HAPPY.
WHAT AM I THINKING?!

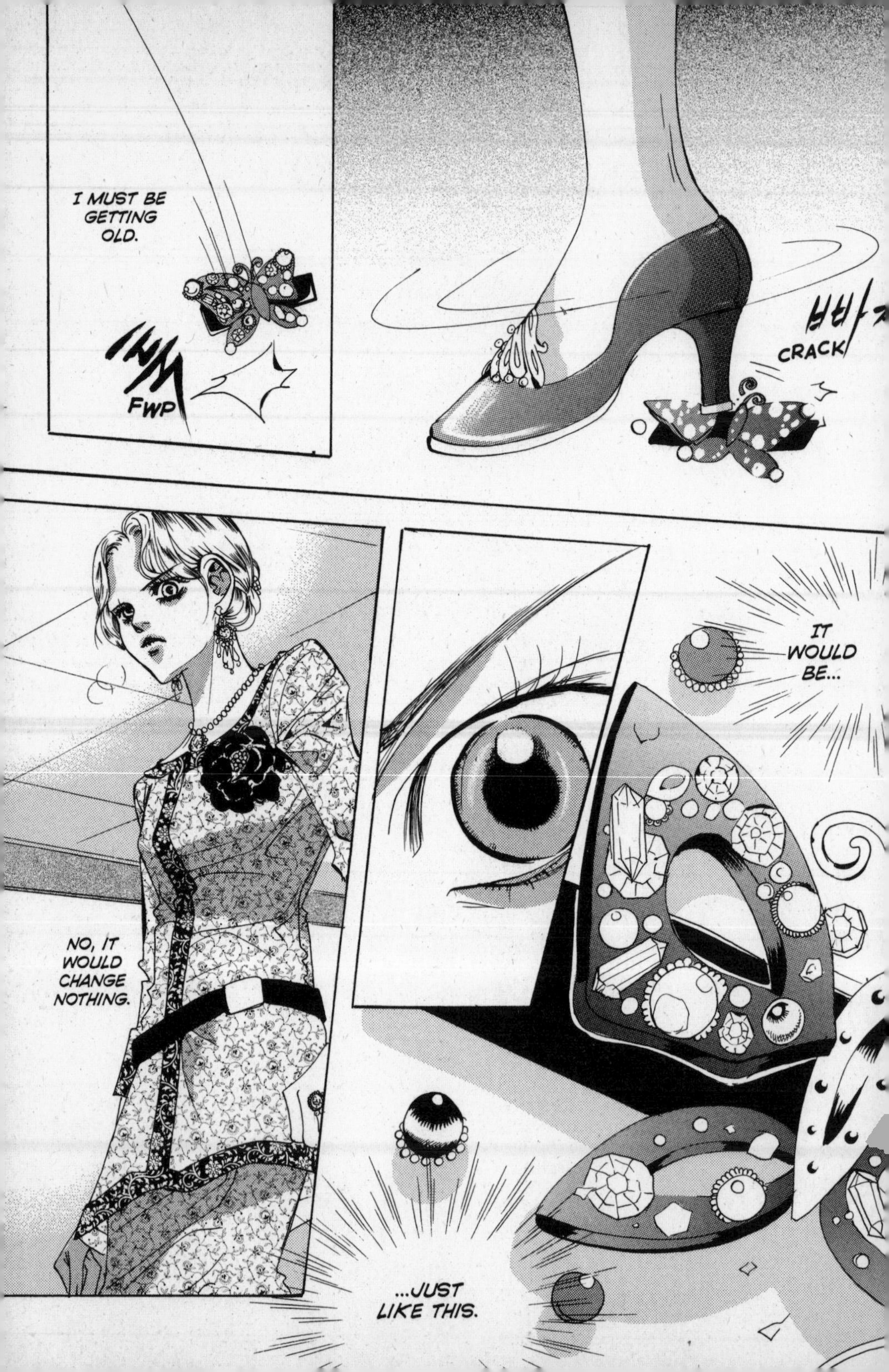
I MUST BE GETTING OLD.
FWP
CRACK
NO, IT WOULD CHANGE NOTHING.
IT WOULD BE...
...JUST LIKE THIS.

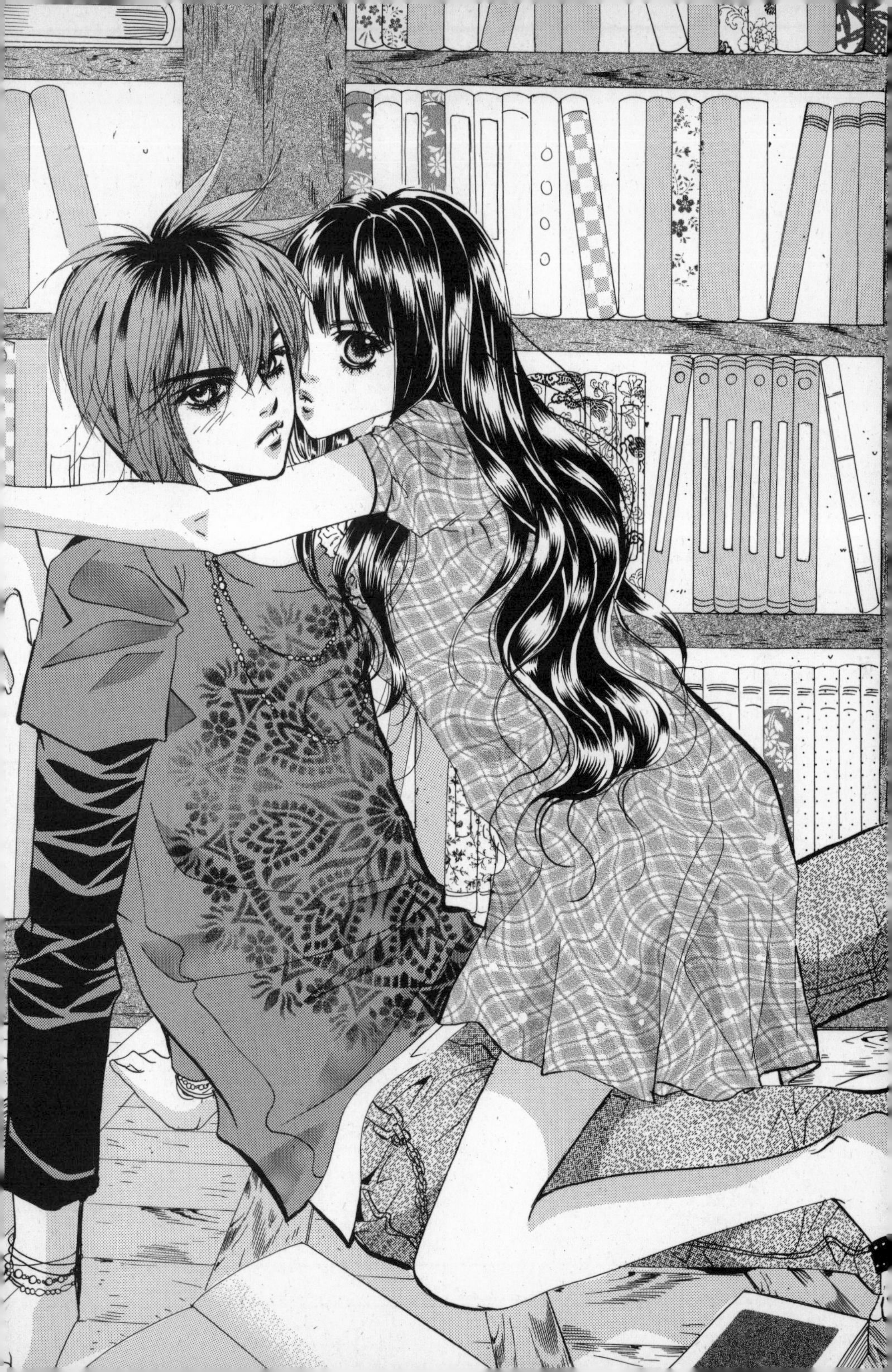

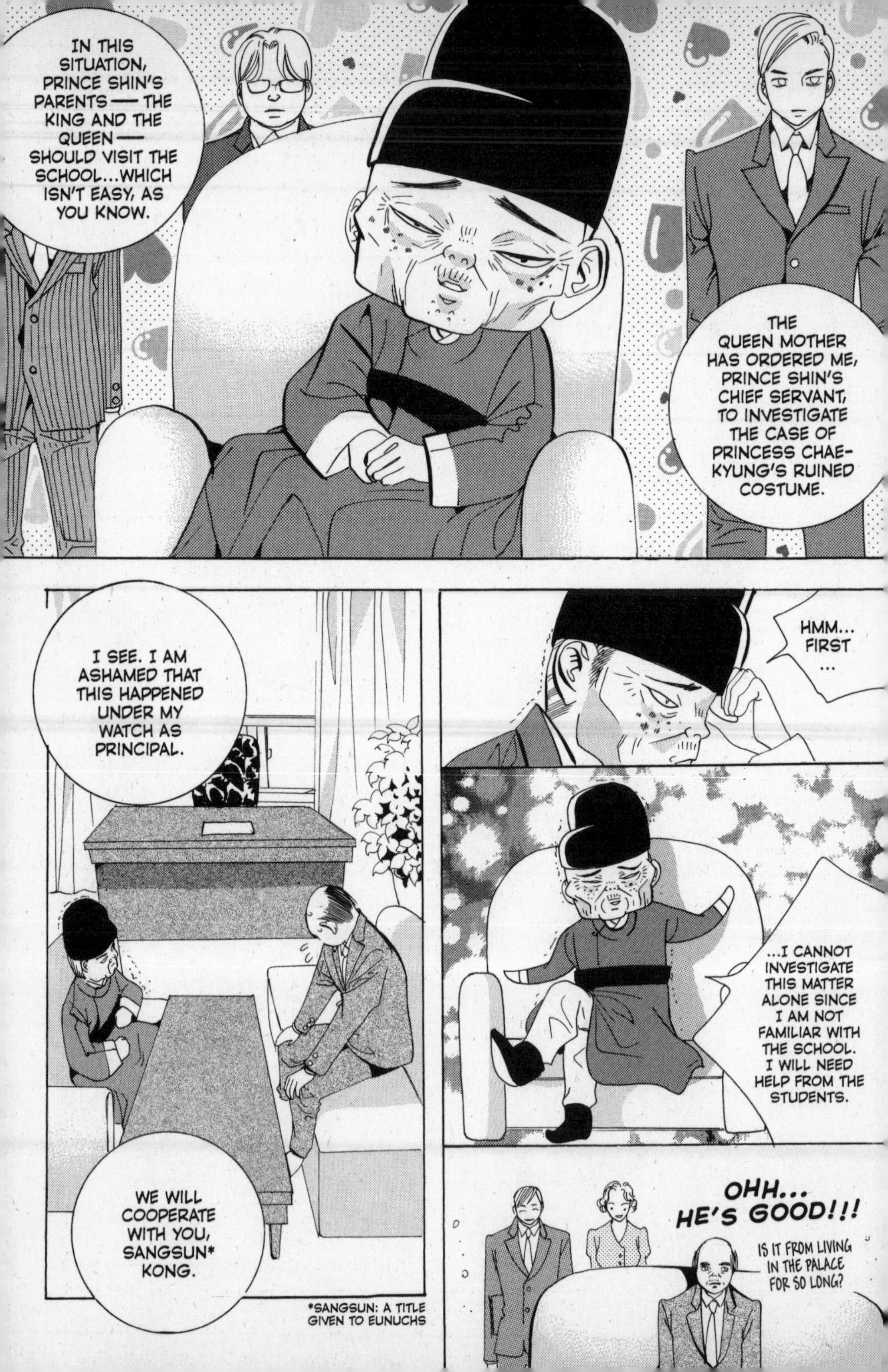
IN THIS SITUATION, PRINCE SHIN'S PARENTS — THE KING AND THE QUEEN — SHOULD VISIT THE SCHOOL...WHICH ISN'T EASY, AS YOU KNOW.
THE QUEEN MOTHER HAS ORDERED ME, PRINCE SHIN'S CHIEF SERVANT, TO INVESTIGATE THE CASE OF PRINCESS CHAE-KYUNG'S RUINED COSTUME.
I SEE. I AM ASHAMED THAT THIS HAPPENED UNDER MY WATCH AS PRINCIPAL.
WE WILL COOPERATE WITH YOU, SANGSUN* KONG.
HMM... FIRST ...
...I CANNOT INVESTIGATE THIS MATTER ALONE SINCE I AM NOT FAMILIAR WITH THE SCHOOL. I WILL NEED HELP FROM THE STUDENTS.
OHH... HE'S GOOD!!!
IS IT FROM LIVING IN THE PALACE FOR SO LONG?

*SANGSUN: A TITLE GIVEN TO EUNUCHS

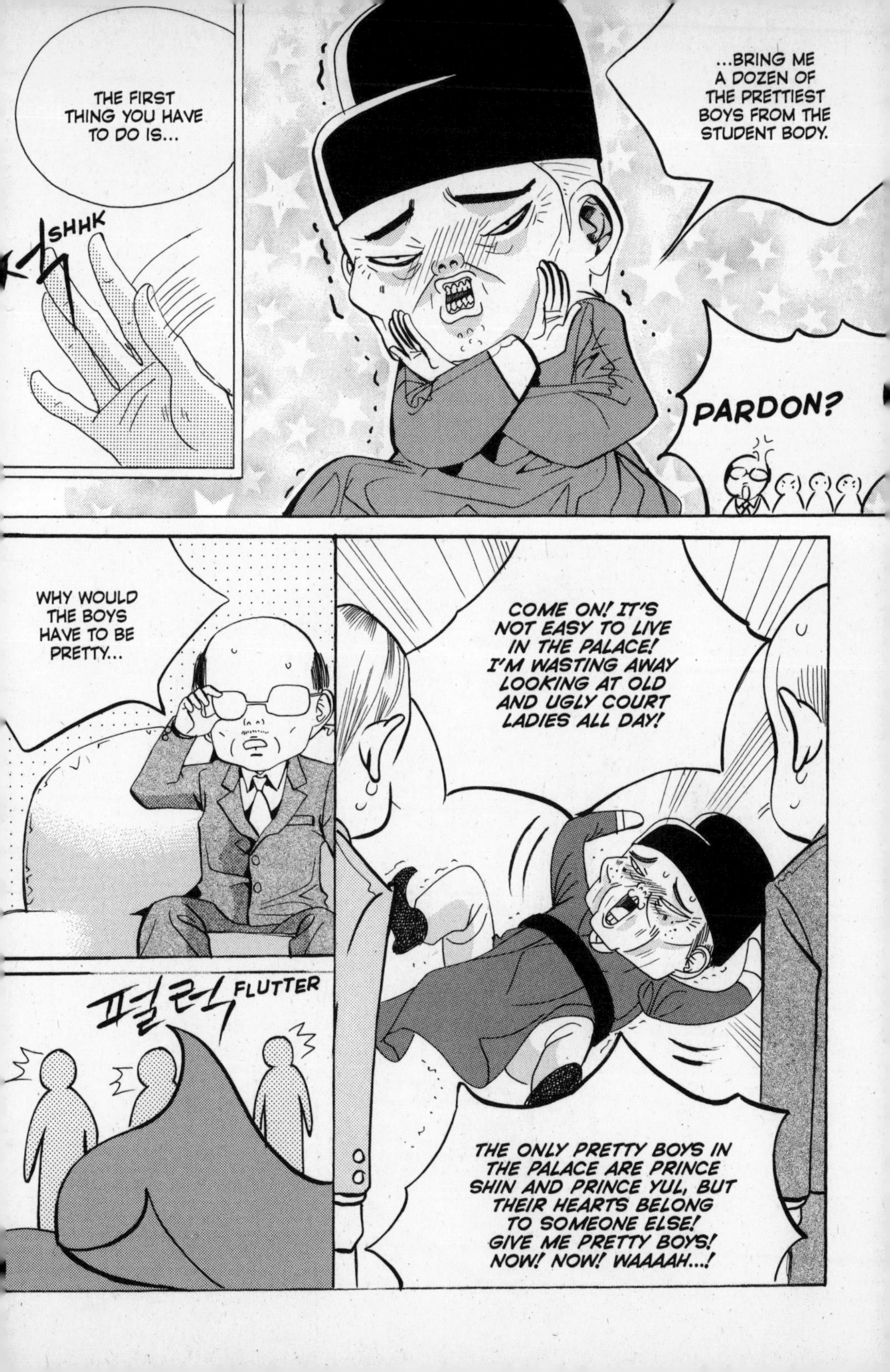
THE FIRST THING YOU HAVE TO DO IS...
SHHK
...BRING ME A DOZEN OF THE PRETTIEST BOYS FROM THE STUDENT BODY.
PARDON?
WHY WOULD THE BOYS HAVE TO BE PRETTY...
펄럭 FLUTTER
COME ON! IT'S NOT EASY TO LIVE IN THE PALACE! I'M WASTING AWAY LOOKING AT OLD AND UGLY COURT LADIES ALL DAY!
THE ONLY PRETTY BOYS IN THE PALACE ARE PRINCE SHIN AND PRINCE YUL, BUT THEIR HEARTS BELONG TO SOMEONE ELSE! GIVE ME PRETTY BOYS! NOW! NOW! WAAAAH...!

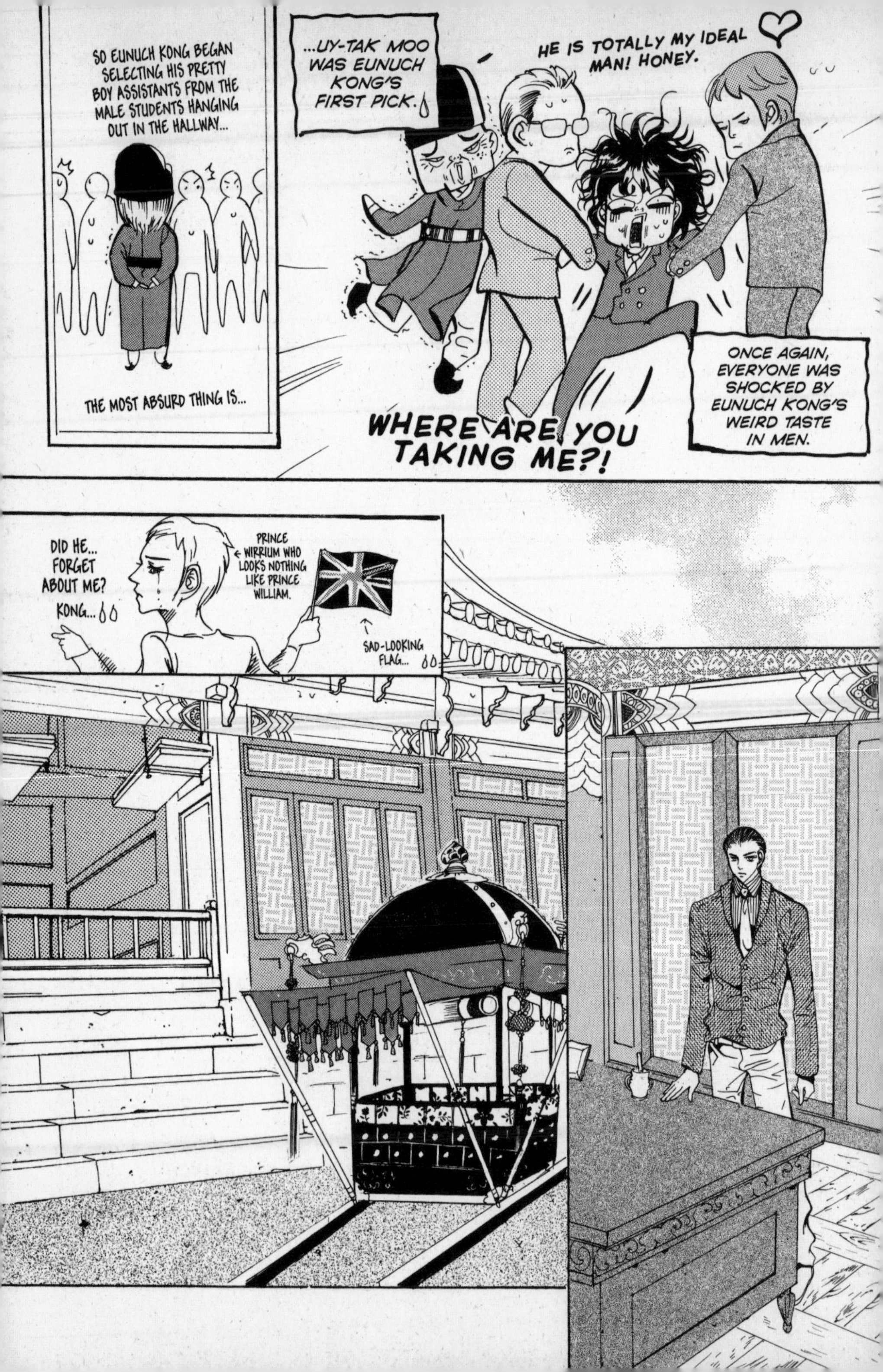
SO EUNUCH KONG BEGAN SELECTING HIS PRETTY BOY ASSISTANTS FROM THE MALE STUDENTS HANGING OUT IN THE HALLWAY...
THE MOST ABSURD THING IS...
...UY-TAK MOO WAS EUNUCH KONG'S FIRST PICK.
HE IS TOTALLY MY IDEAL MAN! HONEY.
WHERE ARE YOU TAKING ME?!
ONCE AGAIN, EVERYONE WAS SHOCKED BY EUNUCH KONG'S WEIRD TASTE IN MEN.
DID HE... FORGET ABOUT ME?
KONG...
PRINCE WIRRIUM WHO LOOKS NOTHING LIKE PRINCE WILLIAM.
SAD-LOOKING FLAG...

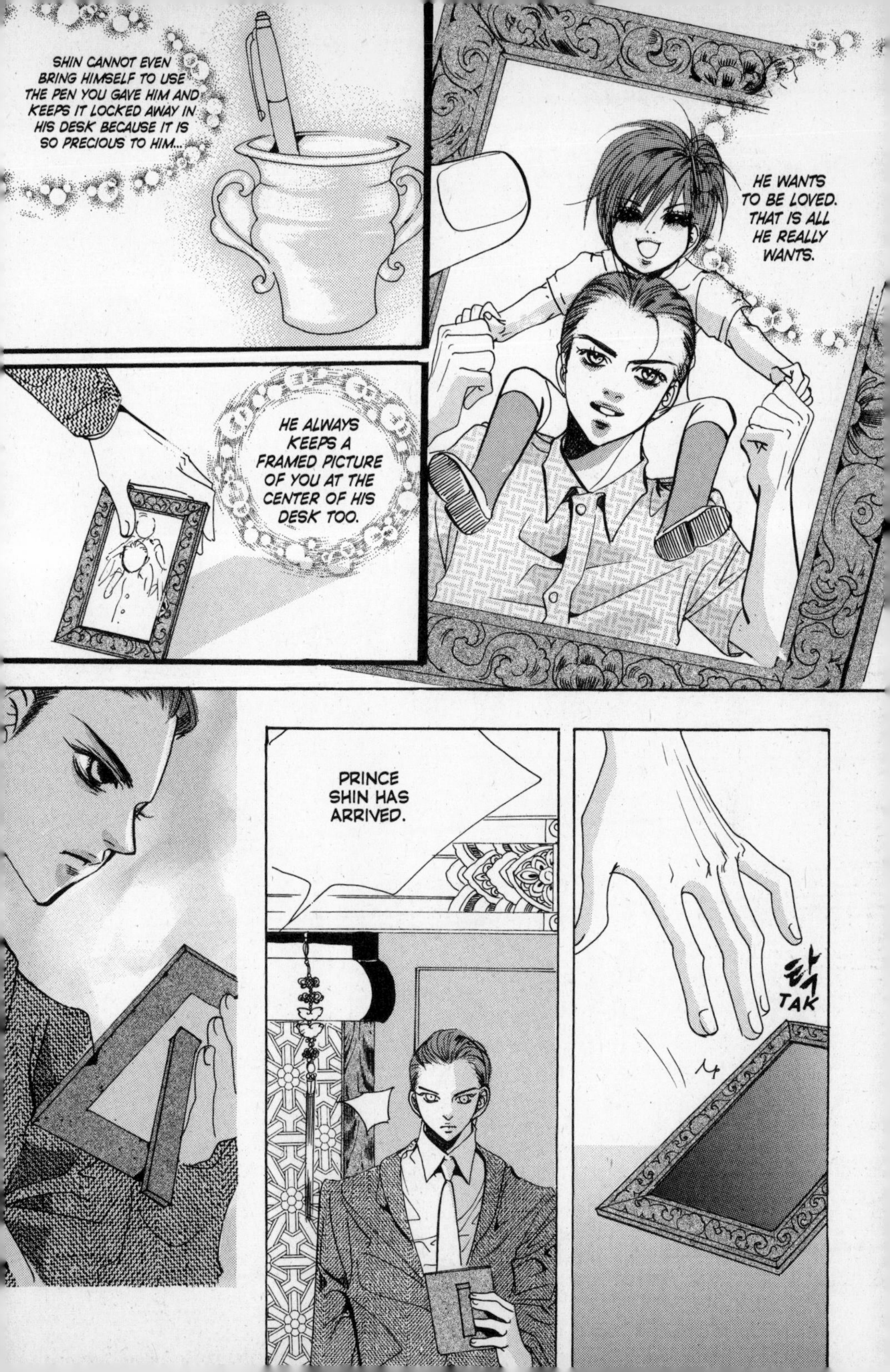
SHIN CANNOT EVEN BRING HIMSELF TO USE THE PEN YOU GAVE HIM AND KEEPS IT LOCKED AWAY IN HIS DESK BECAUSE IT IS SO PRECIOUS TO HIM...
HE WANTS TO BE LOVED. THAT IS ALL HE REALLY WANTS.
HE ALWAYS KEEPS A FRAMED PICTURE OF YOU AT THE CENTER OF HIS DESK TOO.
PRINCE SHIN HAS ARRIVED.
탁
TAK

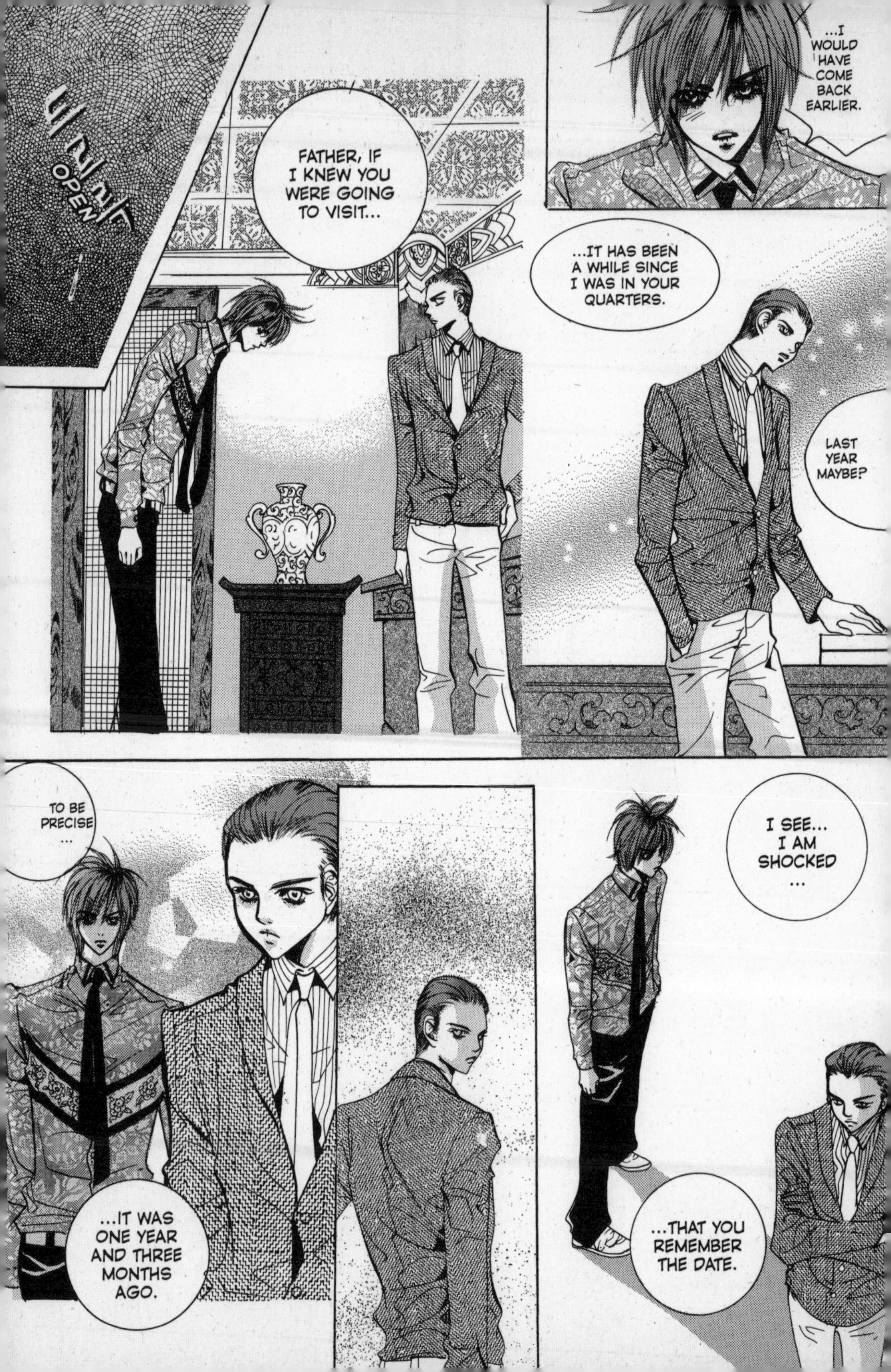
OPEN
FATHER, IF I KNEW YOU WERE GOING TO VISIT...
...I WOULD HAVE COME BACK EARLIER.
...IT HAS BEEN A WHILE SINCE I WAS IN YOUR QUARTERS.
LAST YEAR MAYBE?
TO BE PRECISE ...
...IT WAS ONE YEAR AND THREE MONTHS AGO.
I SEE... I AM SHOCKED ...
...THAT YOU REMEMBER THE DATE.

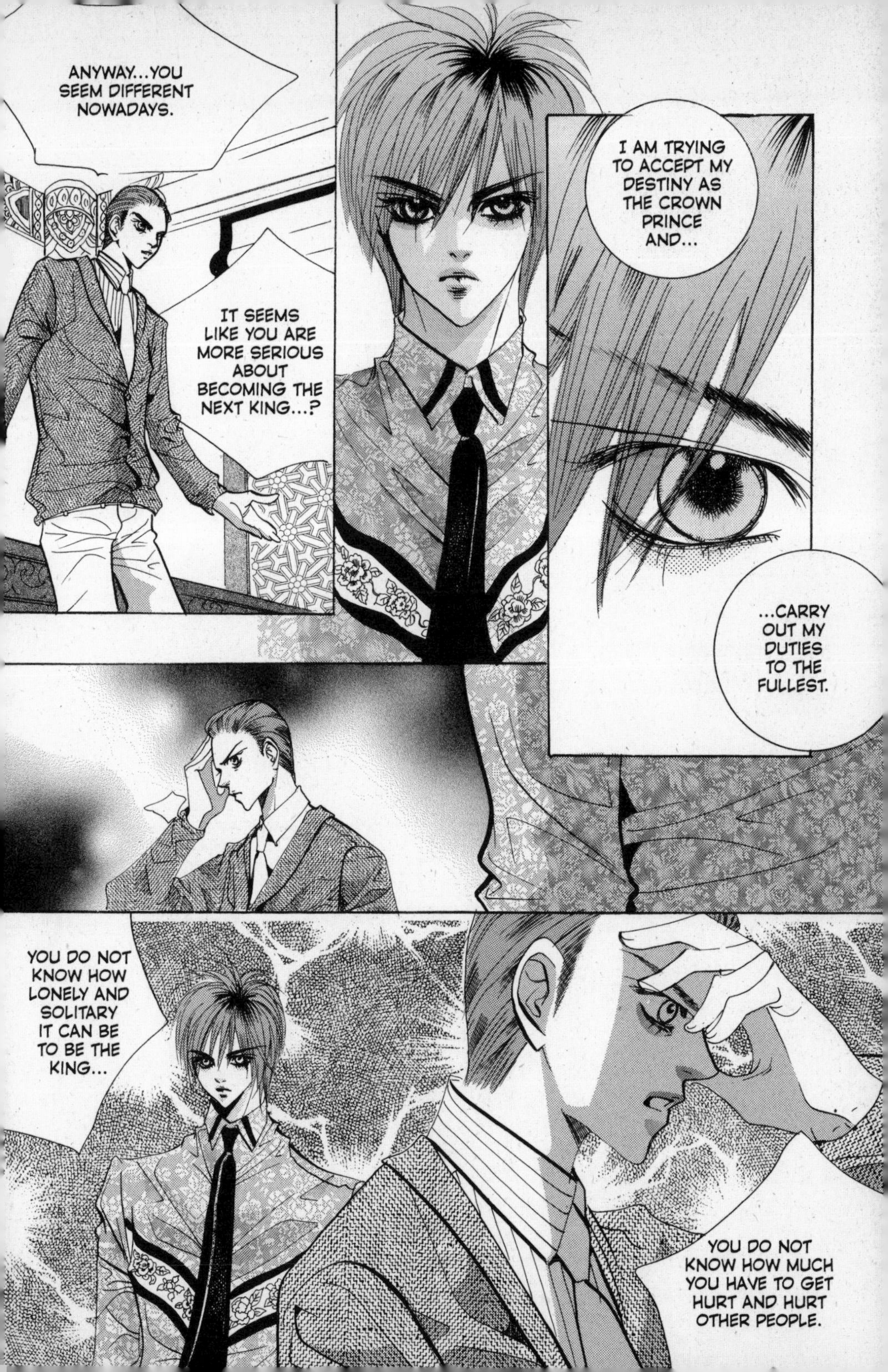
ANYWAY...YOU SEEM DIFFERENT NOWADAYS.
IT SEEMS LIKE YOU ARE MORE SERIOUS ABOUT BECOMING THE NEXT KING...?
I AM TRYING TO ACCEPT MY DESTINY AS THE CROWN PRINCE AND...
...CARRY OUT MY DUTIES TO THE FULLEST.
YOU DO NOT KNOW HOW LONELY AND SOLITARY IT CAN BE TO BE THE KING...
YOU DO NOT KNOW HOW MUCH YOU HAVE TO GET HURT AND HURT OTHER PEOPLE.

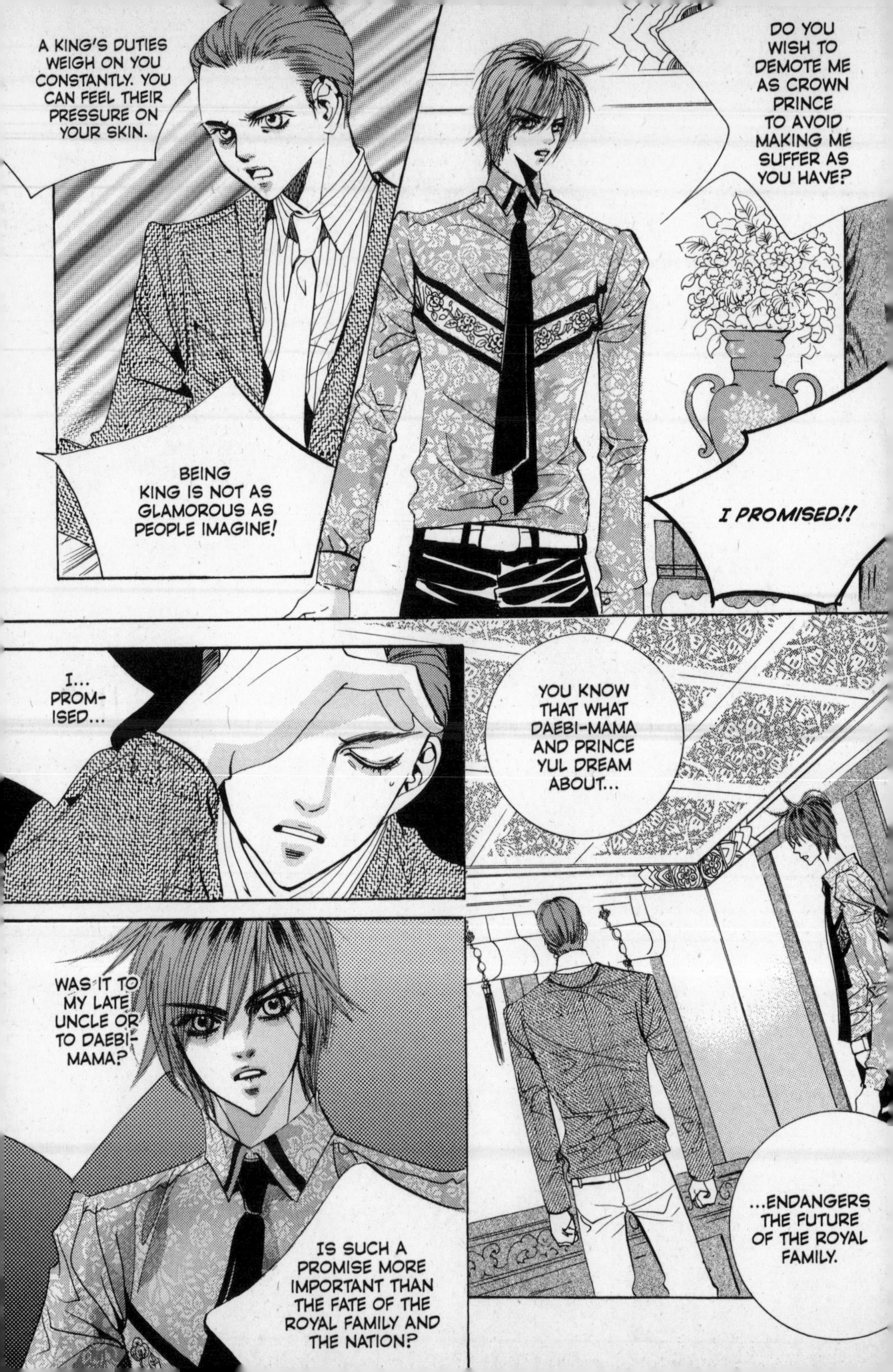
A KING'S DUTIES WEIGH ON YOU CONSTANTLY. YOU CAN FEEL THEIR PRESSURE ON YOUR SKIN.
BEING KING IS NOT AS GLAMOROUS AS PEOPLE IMAGINE!
DO YOU WISH TO DEMOTE ME AS CROWN PRINCE TO AVOID MAKING ME SUFFER AS YOU HAVE?
I PROMISED!!
I... PROM-ISED...
WAS IT TO MY LATE UNCLE OR TO DAEBI-MAMA?
IS SUCH A PROMISE MORE IMPORTANT THAN THE FATE OF THE ROYAL FAMILY AND THE NATION?
YOU KNOW THAT WHAT DAEBI-MAMA AND PRINCE YUL DREAM ABOUT...
...ENDANGERS THE FUTURE OF THE ROYAL FAMILY.

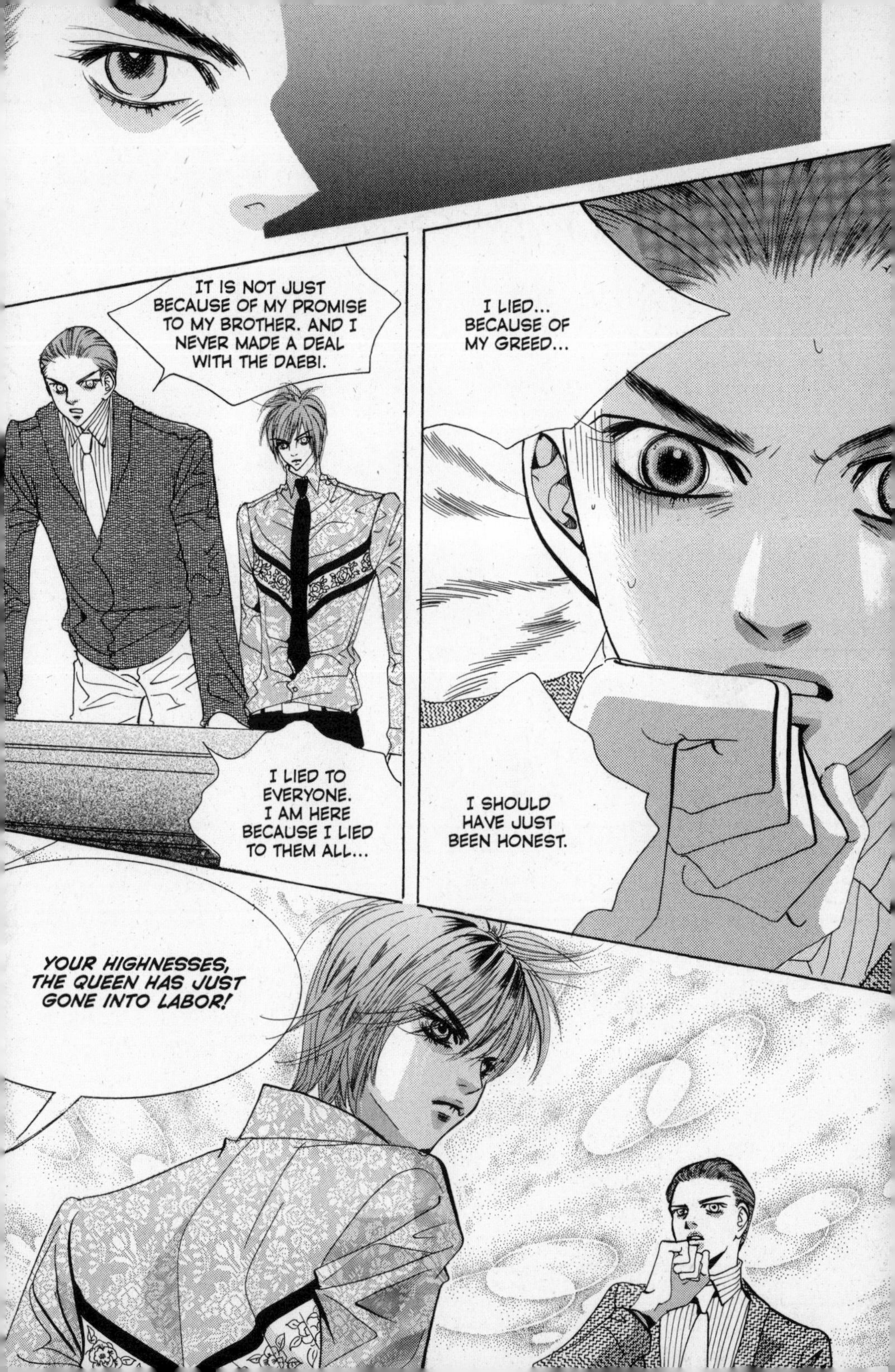
IT IS NOT JUST BECAUSE OF MY PROMISE TO MY BROTHER. AND I NEVER MADE A DEAL WITH THE DAEBI.
I LIED TO EVERYONE. I AM HERE BECAUSE I LIED TO THEM ALL...
I LIED... BECAUSE OF MY GREED...
I SHOULD HAVE JUST BEEN HONEST.
YOUR HIGHNESSES, THE QUEEN HAS JUST GONE INTO LABOR!

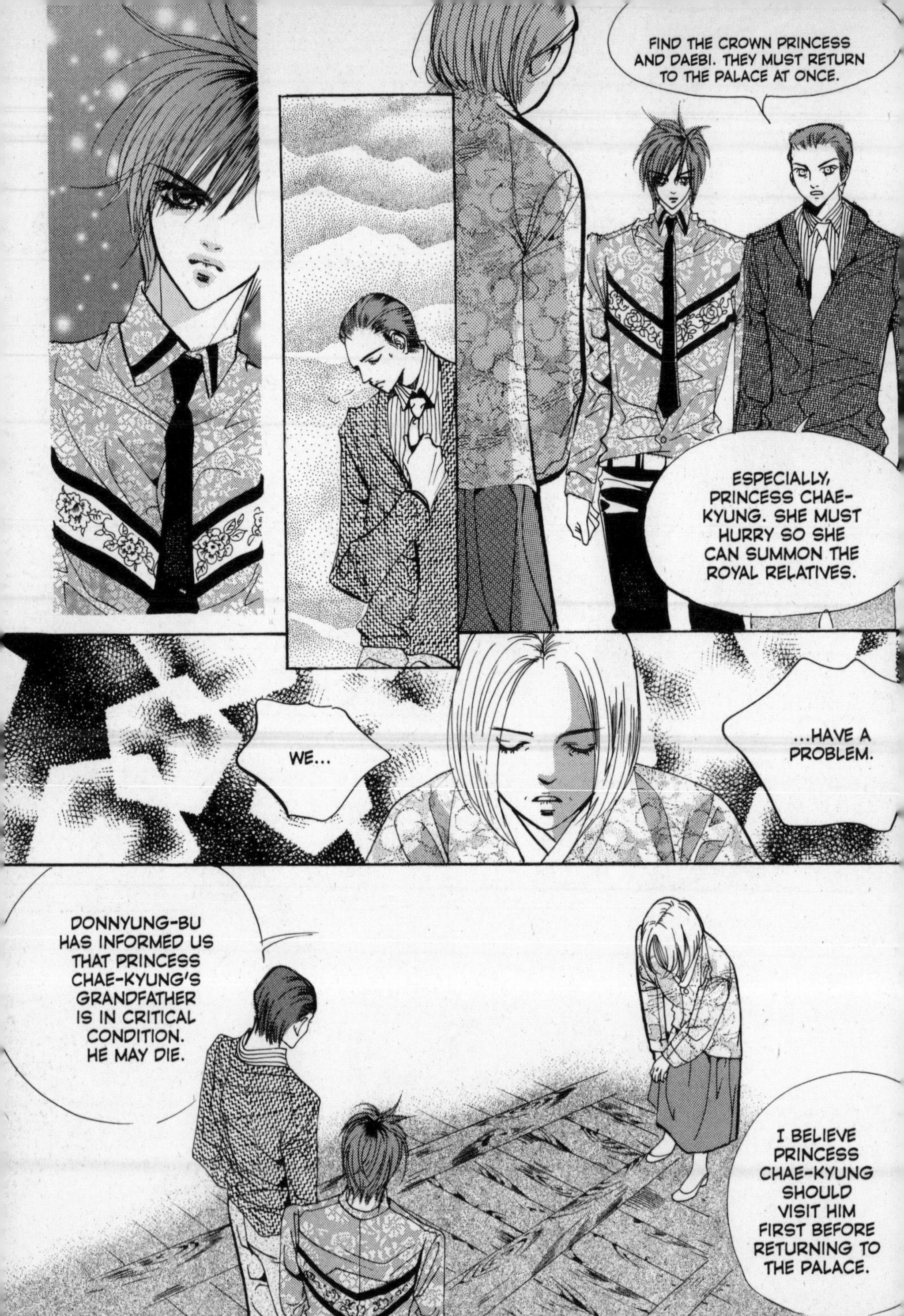
FIND THE CROWN PRINCESS AND DAEBI. THEY MUST RETURN TO THE PALACE AT ONCE.
ESPECIALLY, PRINCESS CHAE-KYUNG. SHE MUST HURRY SO SHE CAN SUMMON THE ROYAL RELATIVES.
WE...
...HAVE A PROBLEM.
DONNYUNG-BU HAS INFORMED US THAT PRINCESS CHAE-KYUNG'S GRANDFATHER IS IN CRITICAL CONDITION. HE MAY DIE.
I BELIEVE PRINCESS CHAE-KYUNG SHOULD VISIT HIM FIRST BEFORE RETURNING TO THE PALACE.

*THE ORGANIZATIONS WHICH DEAL WITH ROYAL RELATIVES ARE THE DONNYUNG-BU (THEY HANDLE IN-LAWS OF THE ROYAL FAMILY), JONGCHIN-BU (ROYAL RELATIVES), AND UIBIN-BU (SON-IN-LAWS OF A KING OR CROWN PRINCE).

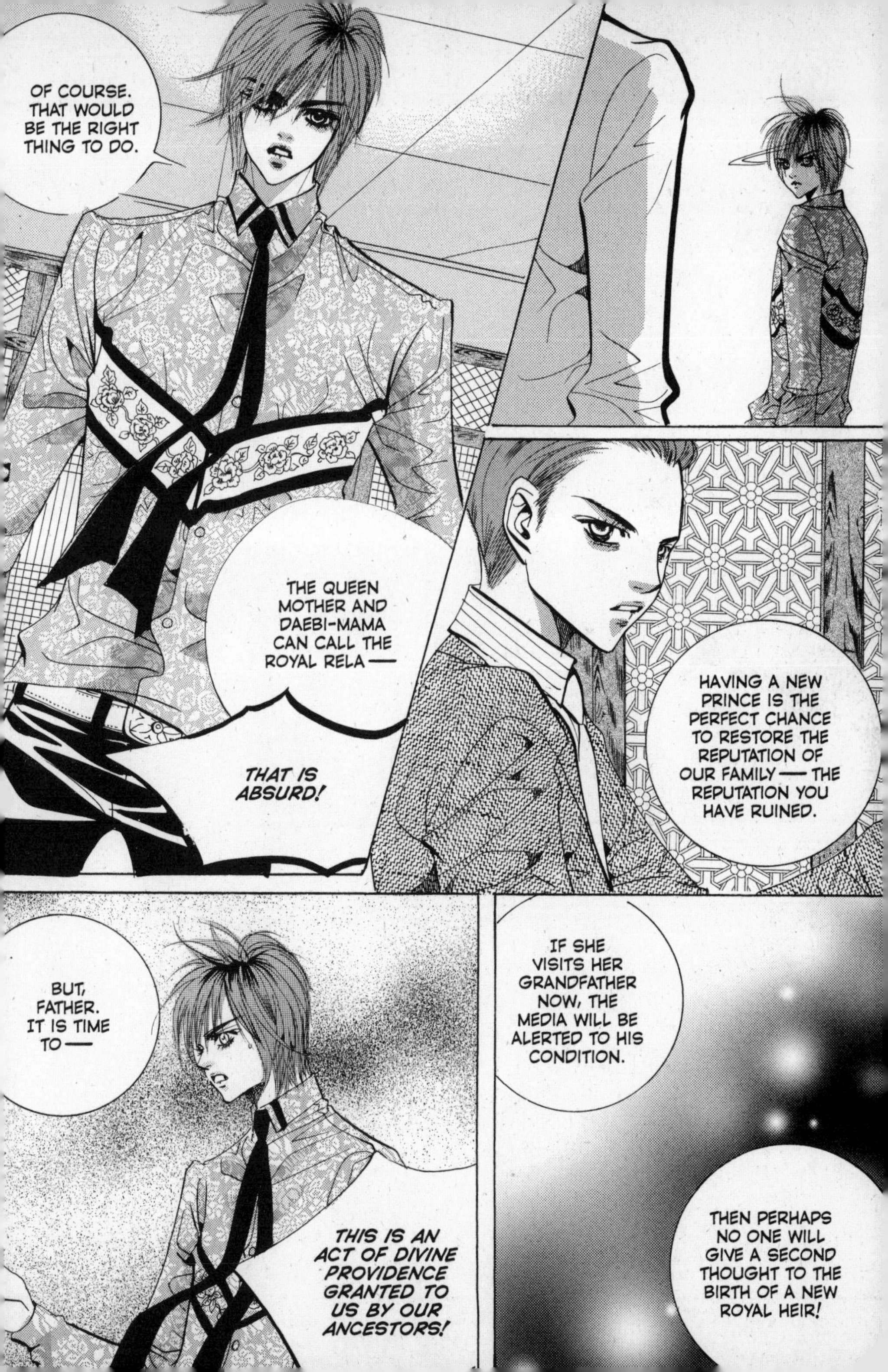
OF COURSE. THAT WOULD BE THE RIGHT THING TO DO.
THE QUEEN MOTHER AND DAEBI-MAMA CAN CALL THE ROYAL RELA—
THAT IS ABSURD!
HAVING A NEW PRINCE IS THE PERFECT CHANCE TO RESTORE THE REPUTATION OF OUR FAMILY— THE REPUTATION YOU HAVE RUINED.
BUT, FATHER. IT IS TIME TO—
THIS IS AN ACT OF DIVINE PROVIDENCE GRANTED TO US BY OUR ANCESTORS!
IF SHE VISITS HER GRANDFATHER NOW, THE MEDIA WILL BE ALERTED TO HIS CONDITION.
THEN PERHAPS NO ONE WILL GIVE A SECOND THOUGHT TO THE BIRTH OF A NEW ROYAL HEIR!

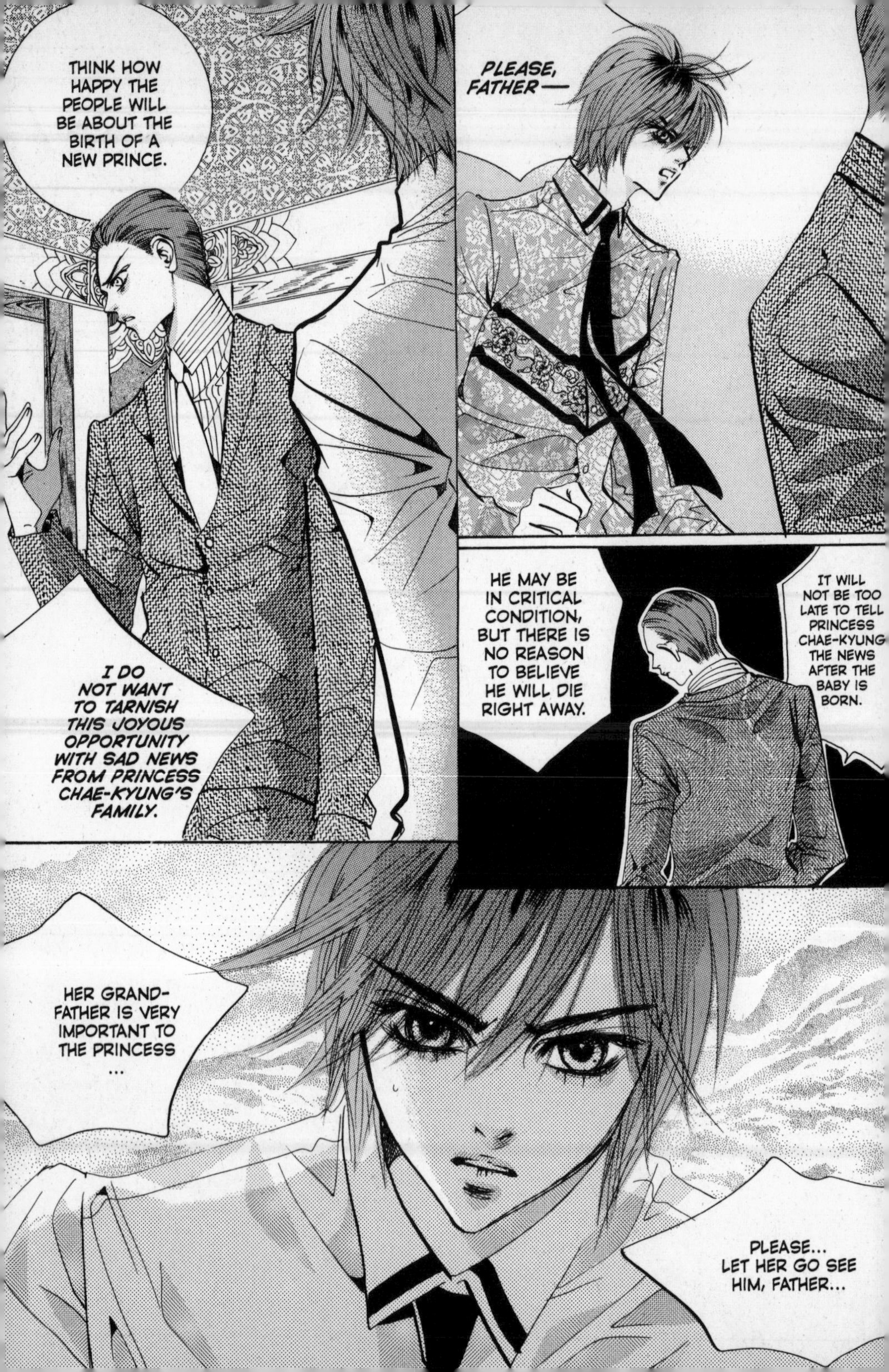
THINK HOW HAPPY THE PEOPLE WILL BE ABOUT THE BIRTH OF A NEW PRINCE.
I DO NOT WANT TO TARNISH THIS JOYOUS OPPORTUNITY WITH SAD NEWS FROM PRINCESS CHAE-KYUNG'S FAMILY.
PLEASE, FATHER—
HE MAY BE IN CRITICAL CONDITION, BUT THERE IS NO REASON TO BELIEVE HE WILL DIE RIGHT AWAY.
IT WILL NOT BE TOO LATE TO TELL PRINCESS CHAE-KYUNG THE NEWS AFTER THE BABY IS BORN.
HER GRAND-FATHER IS VERY IMPORTANT TO THE PRINCESS ...
PLEASE... LET HER GO SEE HIM, FATHER...

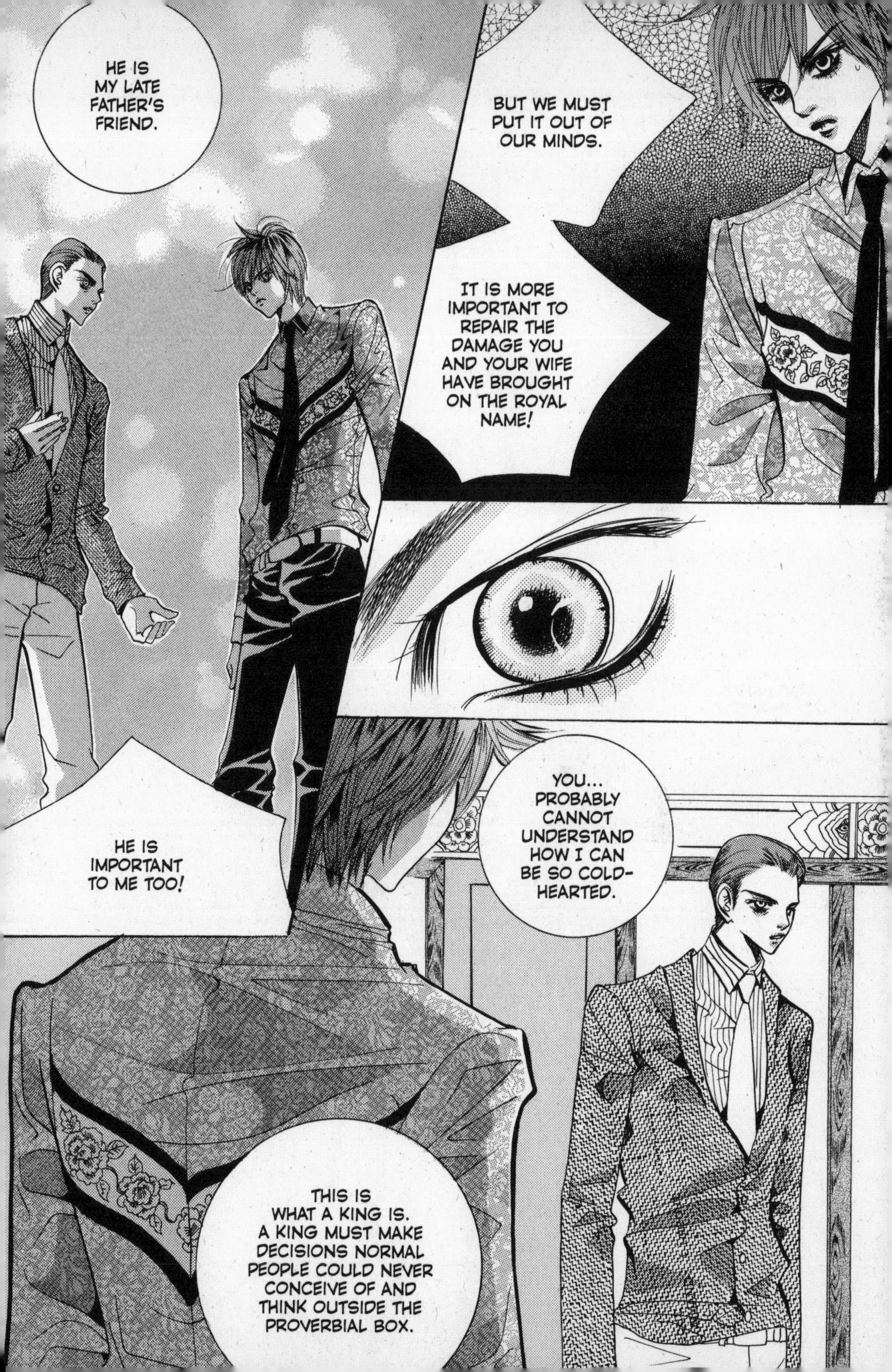
HE IS MY LATE FATHER'S FRIEND.
HE IS IMPORTANT TO ME TOO!
BUT WE MUST PUT IT OUT OF OUR MINDS.
IT IS MORE IMPORTANT TO REPAIR THE DAMAGE YOU AND YOUR WIFE HAVE BROUGHT ON THE ROYAL NAME!
YOU... PROBABLY CANNOT UNDERSTAND HOW I CAN BE SO COLD-HEARTED.
THIS IS WHAT A KING IS. A KING MUST MAKE DECISIONS NORMAL PEOPLE COULD NEVER CONCEIVE OF AND THINK OUTSIDE THE PROVERBIAL BOX.

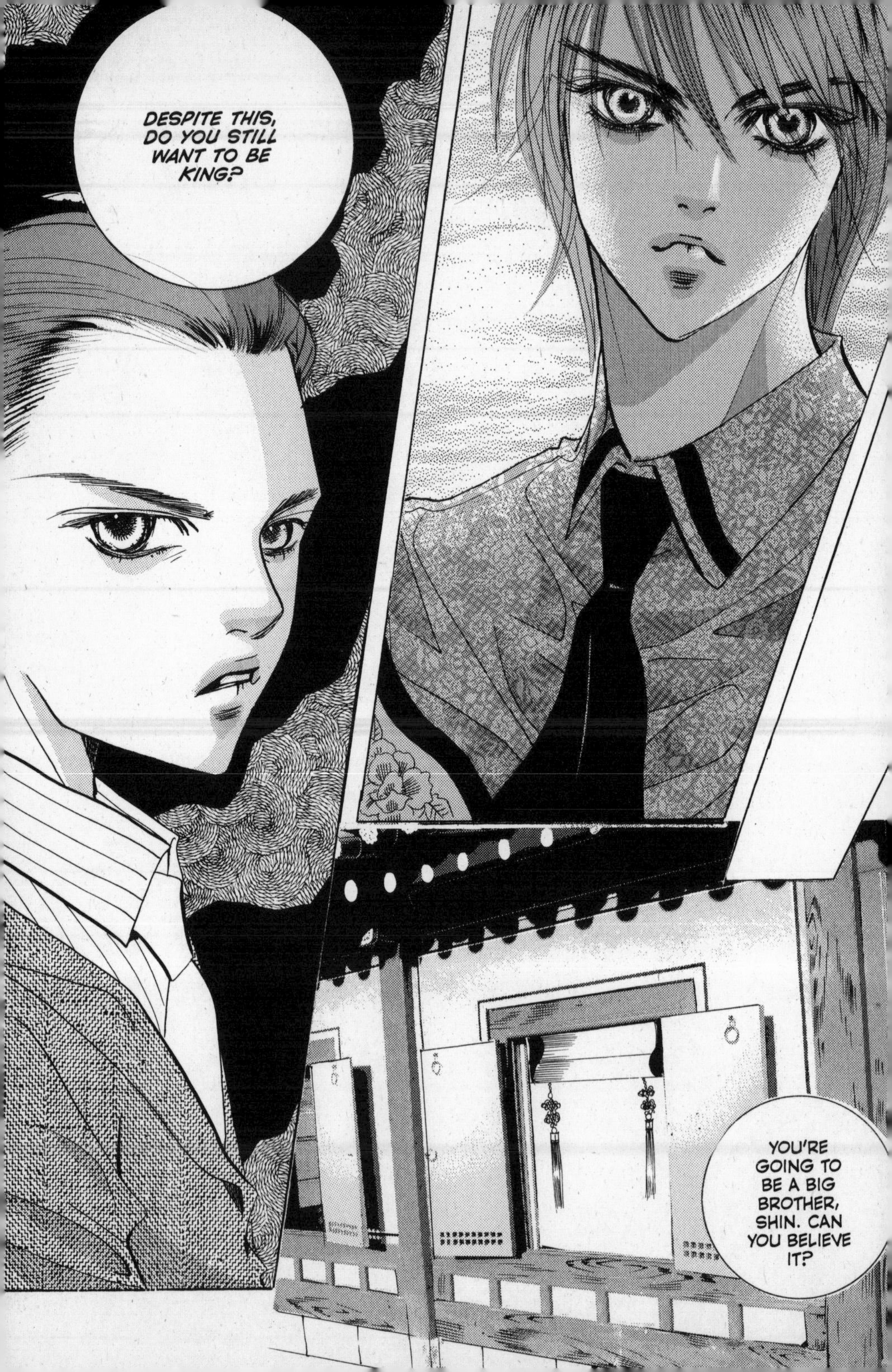
DESPITE THIS, DO YOU STILL WANT TO BE KING?
YOU'RE GOING TO BE A BIG BROTHER, SHIN. CAN YOU BELIEVE IT?

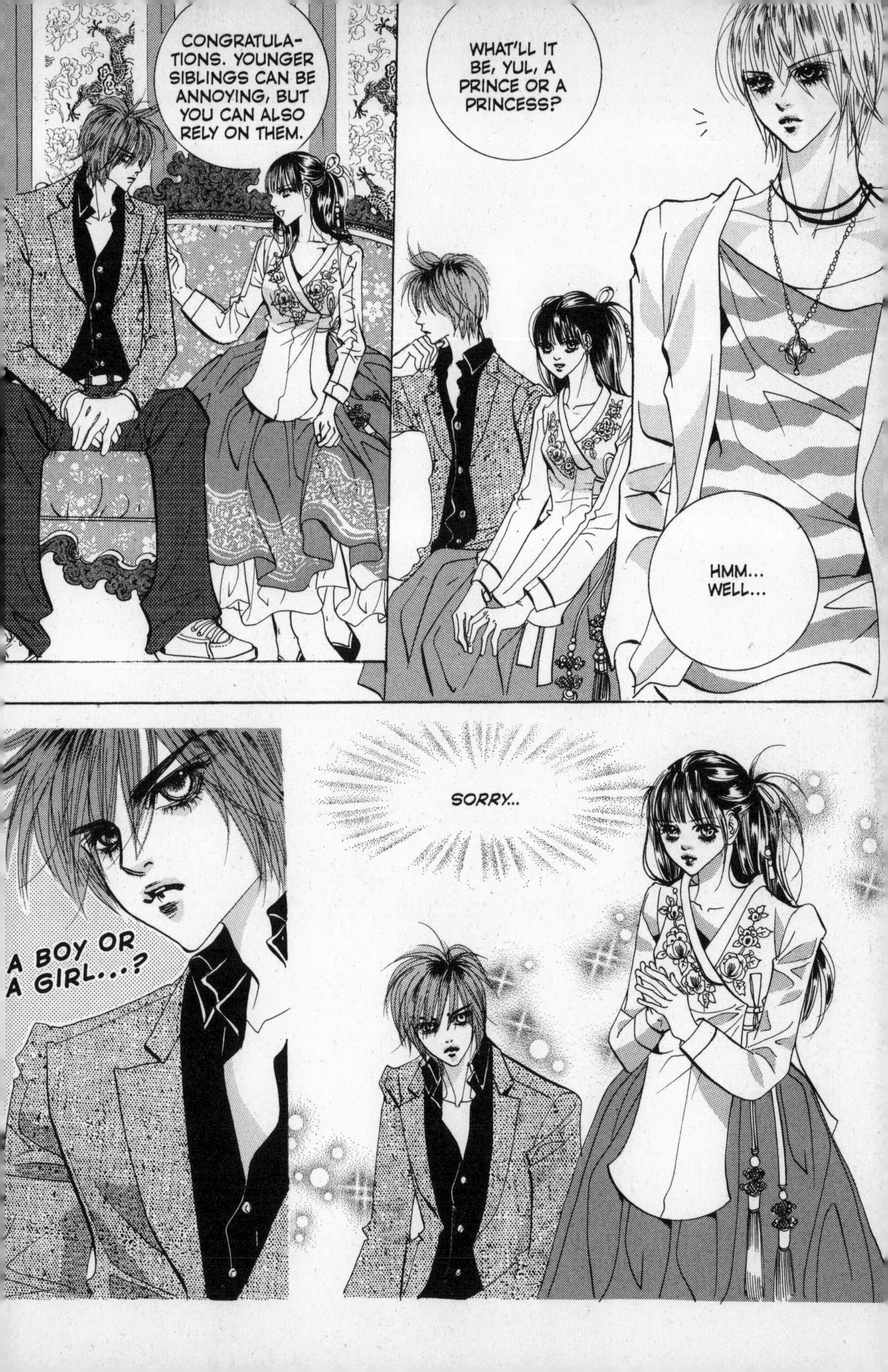
CONGRATULA-TIONS. YOUNGER SIBLINGS CAN BE ANNOYING, BUT YOU CAN ALSO RELY ON THEM.
WHAT'LL IT BE, YUL, A PRINCE OR A PRINCESS?
HMM... WELL...
A BOY OR A GIRL...?
SORRY...

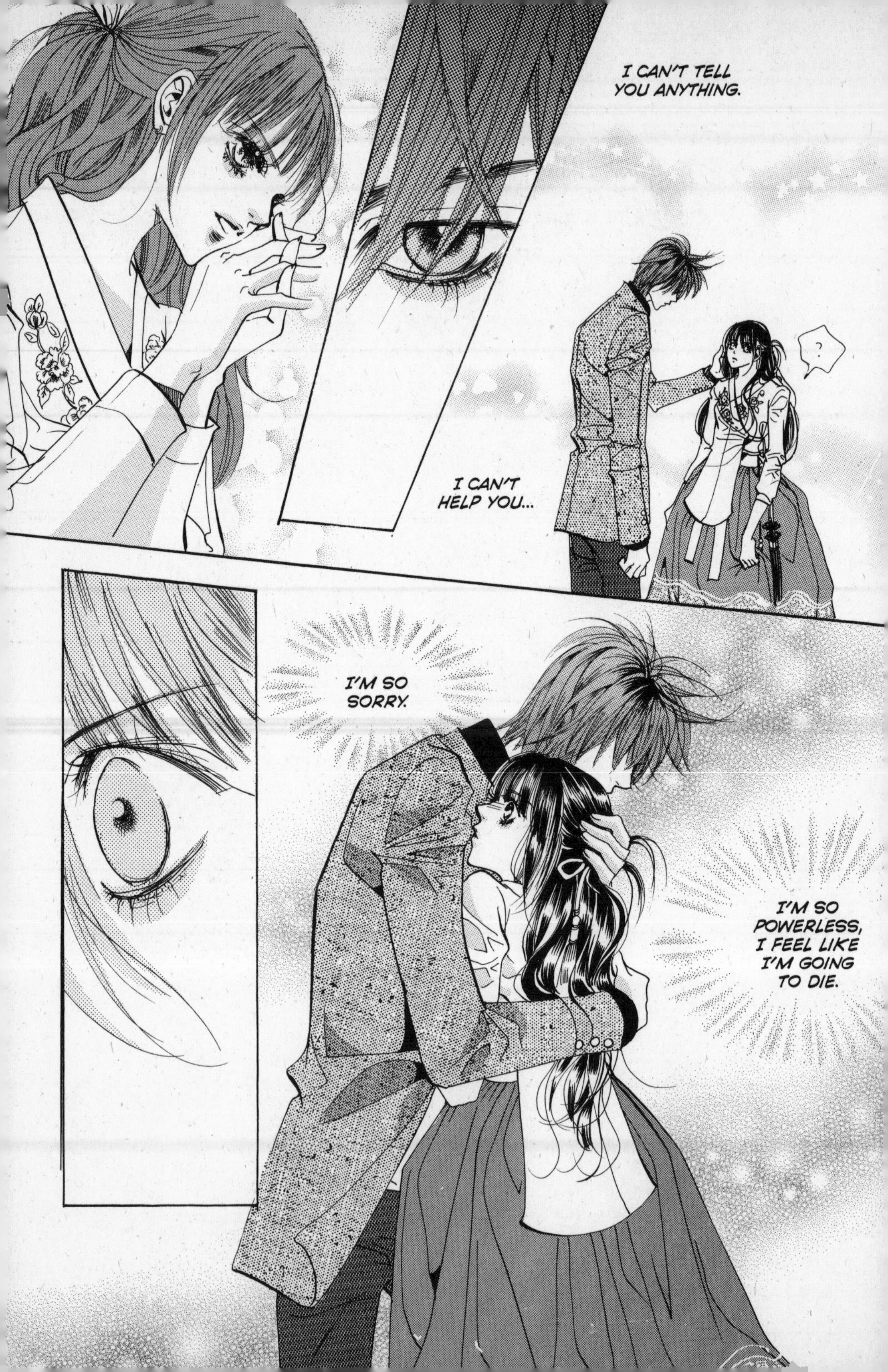
I CAN'T TELL YOU ANYTHING.
I CAN'T HELP YOU...
?
I'M SO SORRY.
I'M SO POWERLESS, I FEEL LIKE I'M GOING TO DIE.

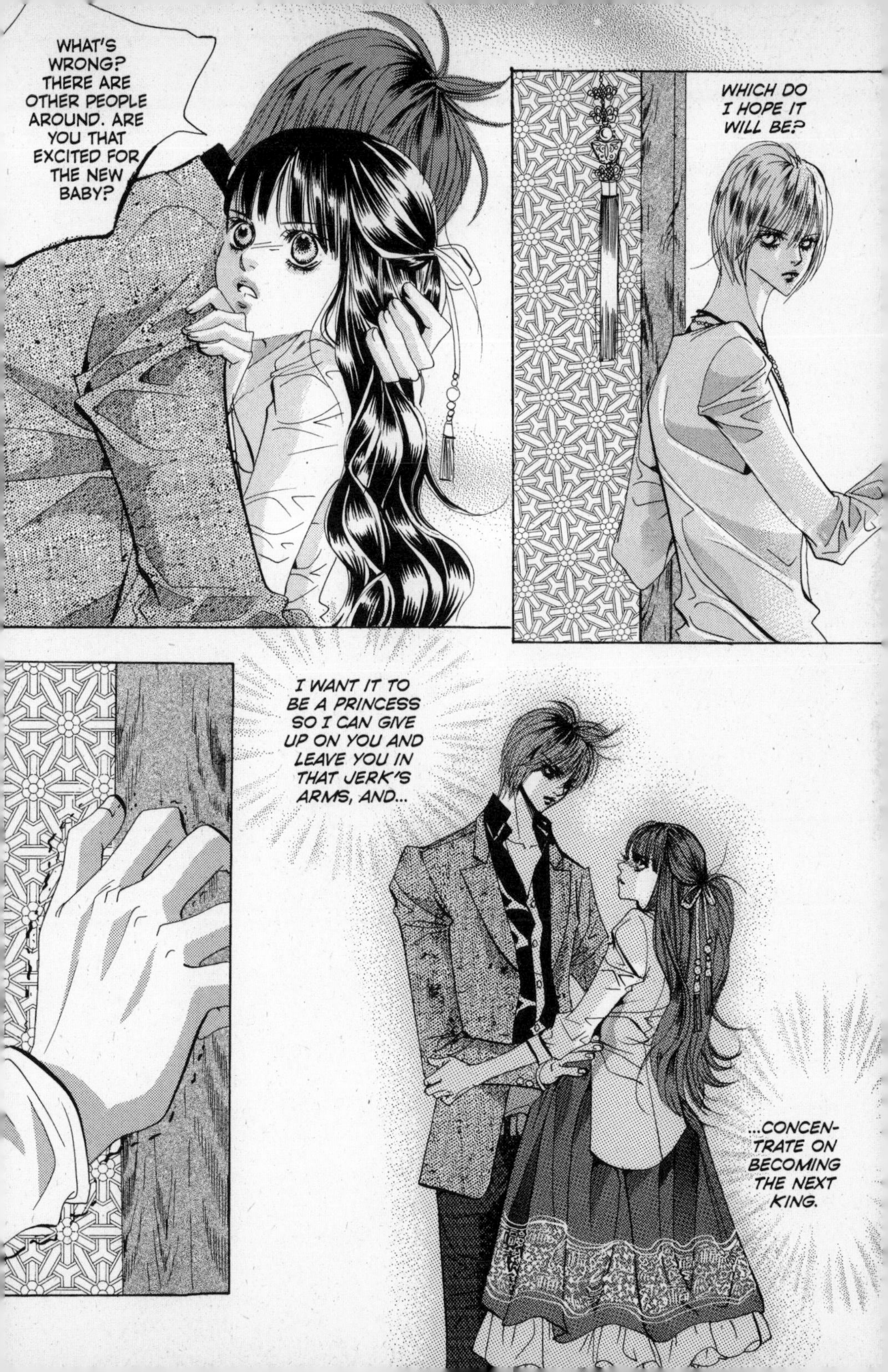
WHAT'S WRONG? THERE ARE OTHER PEOPLE AROUND. ARE YOU THAT EXCITED FOR THE NEW BABY?
WHICH DO I HOPE IT WILL BE?
I WANT IT TO BE A PRINCESS SO I CAN GIVE UP ON YOU AND LEAVE YOU IN THAT JERK'S ARMS, AND...
...CONCEN-TRATE ON BECOMING THE NEXT KING.

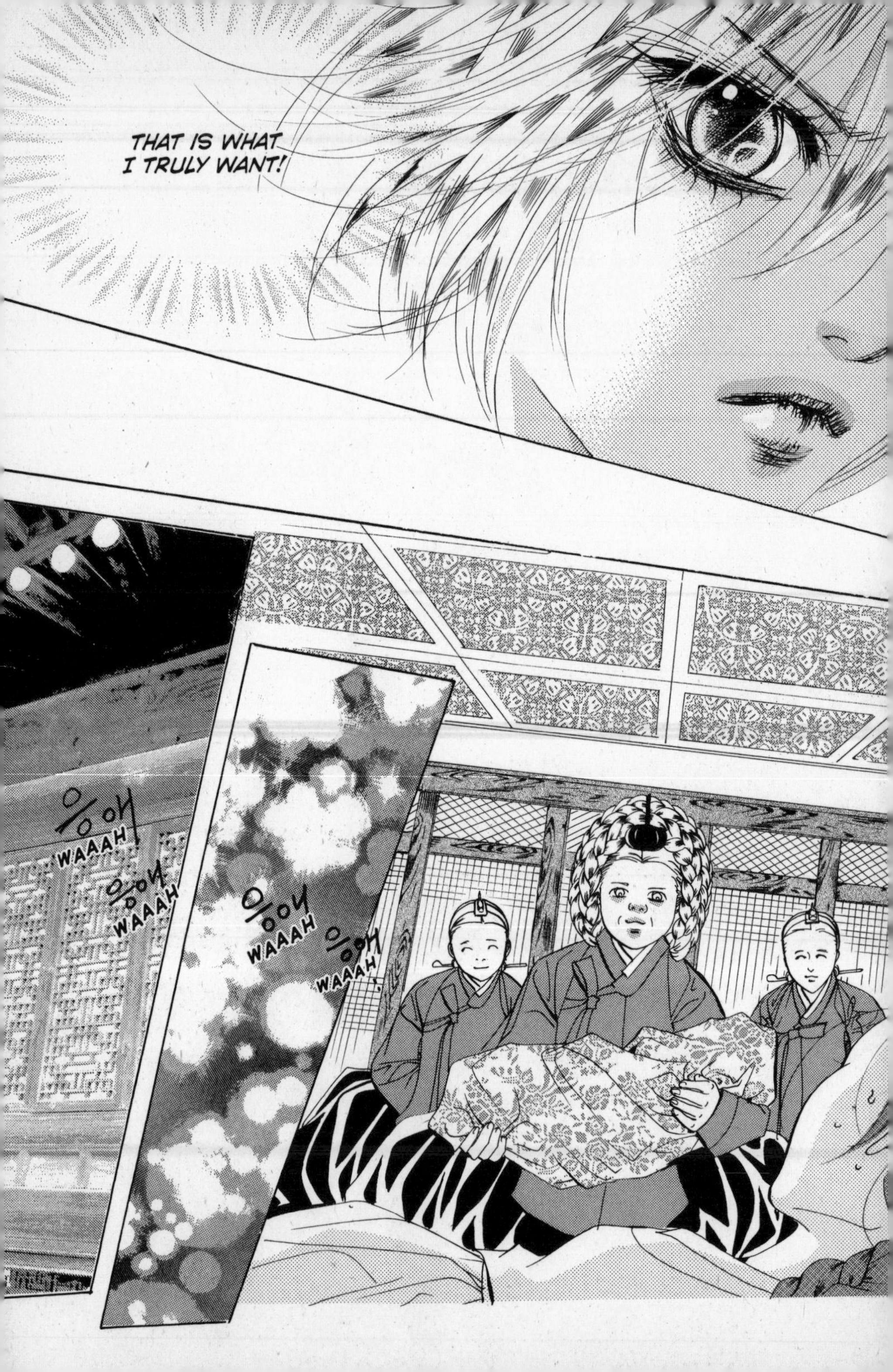
THAT IS WHAT I TRULY WANT!
으앙 WAAAH
으앙 WAAAH
으앙 WAAAH
으앙 WAAAH

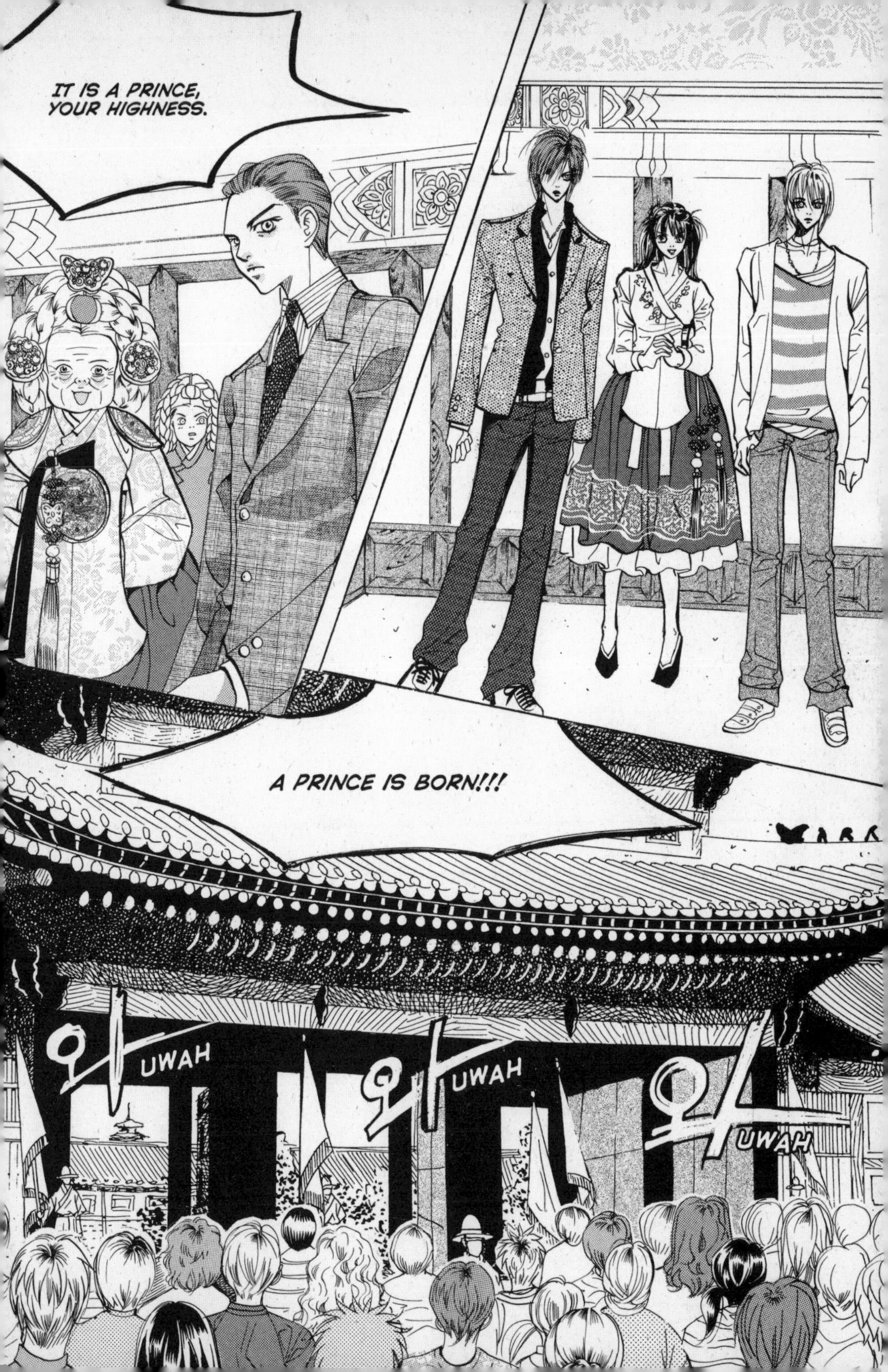
IT IS A PRINCE, YOUR HIGHNESS.
A PRINCE IS BORN!!!
UWAH
UWAH
UWAH

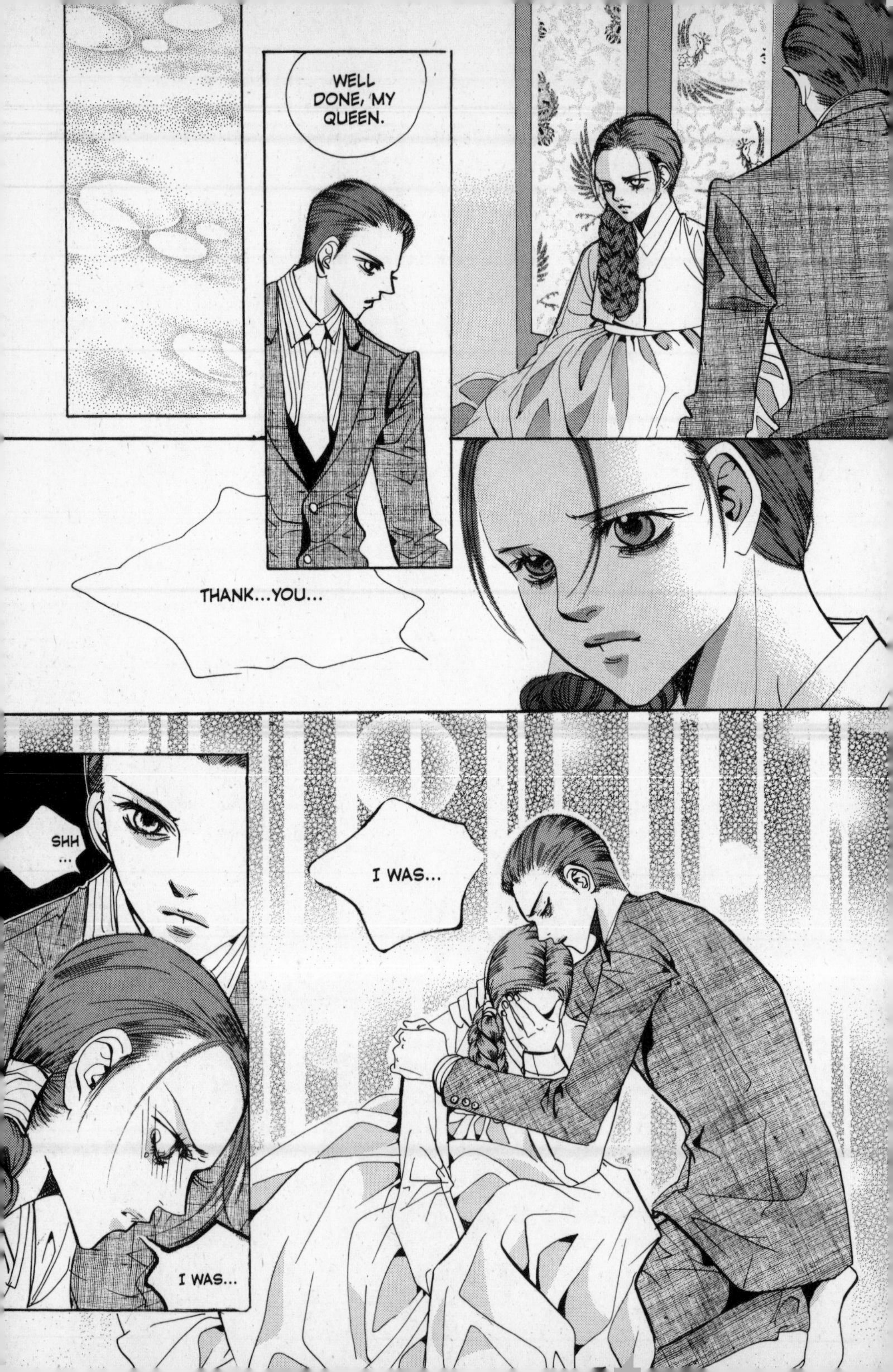
WELL DONE, MY QUEEN.
THANK...YOU...
SHH ...
I WAS...
I WAS...

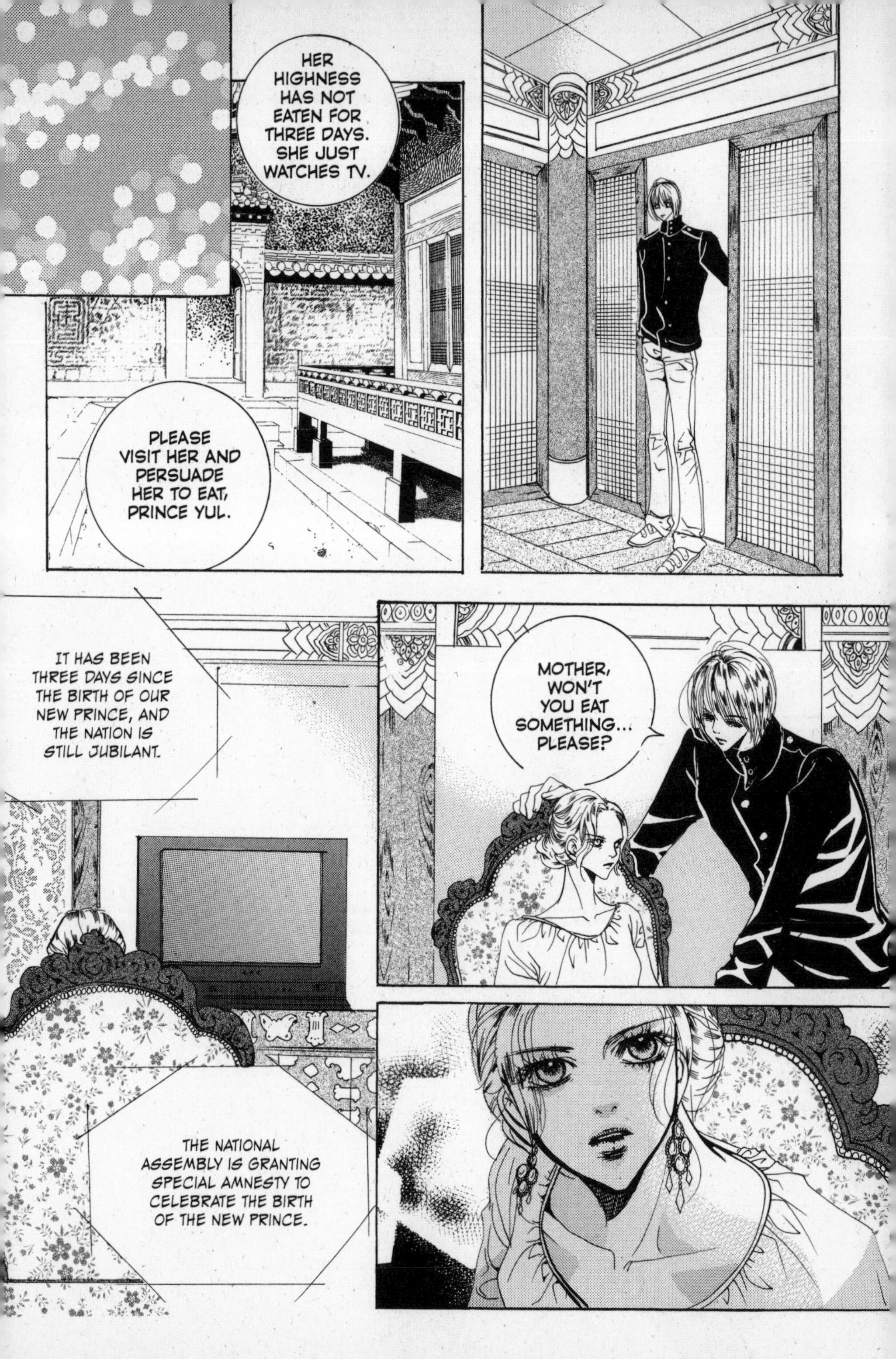
HER HIGHNESS HAS NOT EATEN FOR THREE DAYS. SHE JUST WATCHES TV.
PLEASE VISIT HER AND PERSUADE HER TO EAT, PRINCE YUL.
IT HAS BEEN THREE DAYS SINCE THE BIRTH OF OUR NEW PRINCE, AND THE NATION IS STILL JUBILANT.
MOTHER, WON'T YOU EAT SOMETHING... PLEASE?
THE NATIONAL ASSEMBLY IS GRANTING SPECIAL AMNESTY TO CELEBRATE THE BIRTH OF THE NEW PRINCE.

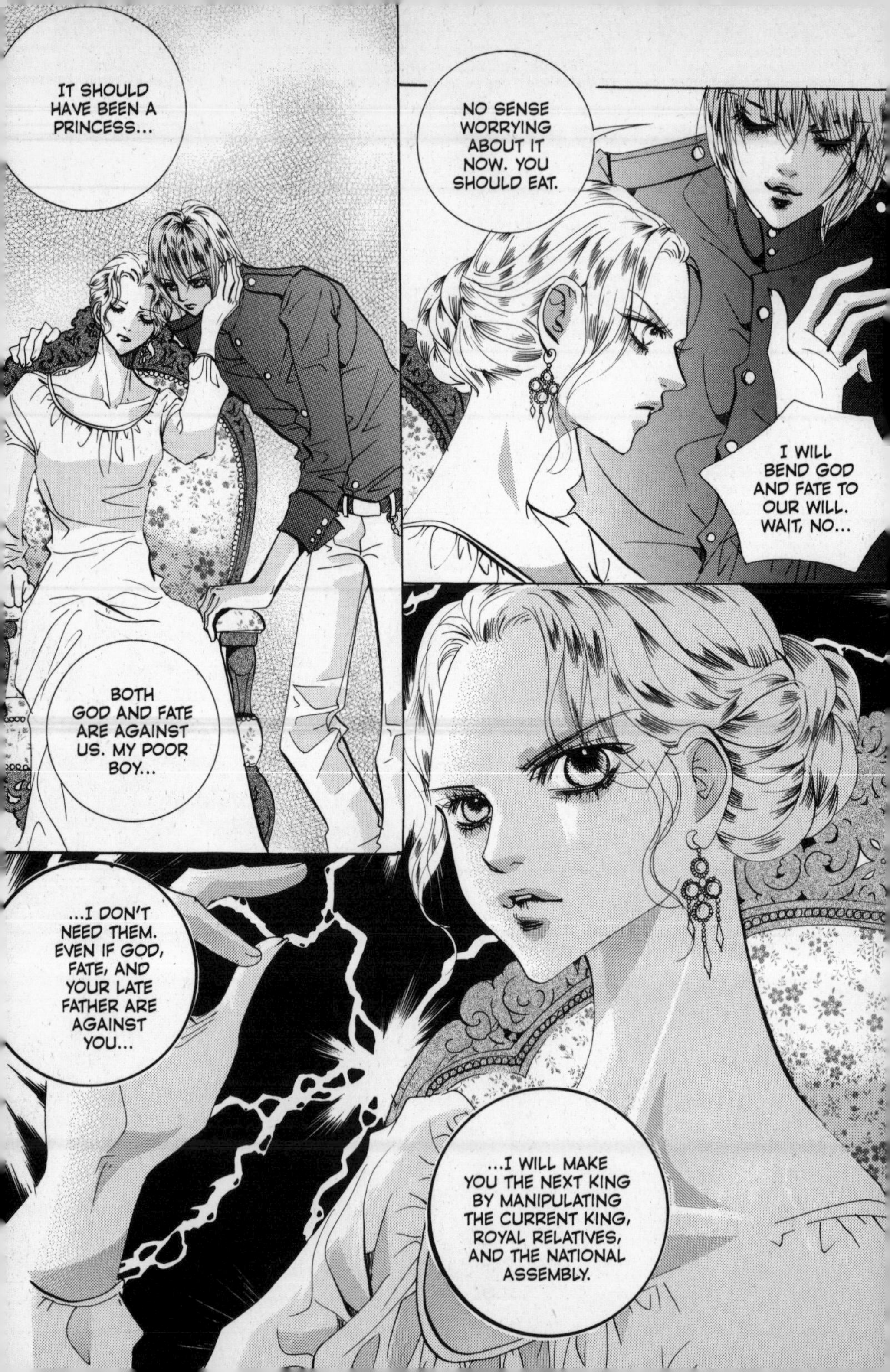
IT SHOULD HAVE BEEN A PRINCESS...
BOTH GOD AND FATE ARE AGAINST US. MY POOR BOY...
NO SENSE WORRYING ABOUT IT NOW. YOU SHOULD EAT.
I WILL BEND GOD AND FATE TO OUR WILL. WAIT, NO...
...I DON'T NEED THEM. EVEN IF GOD, FATE, AND YOUR LATE FATHER ARE AGAINST YOU...
...I WILL MAKE YOU THE NEXT KING BY MANIPULATING THE CURRENT KING, ROYAL RELATIVES, AND THE NATIONAL ASSEMBLY.

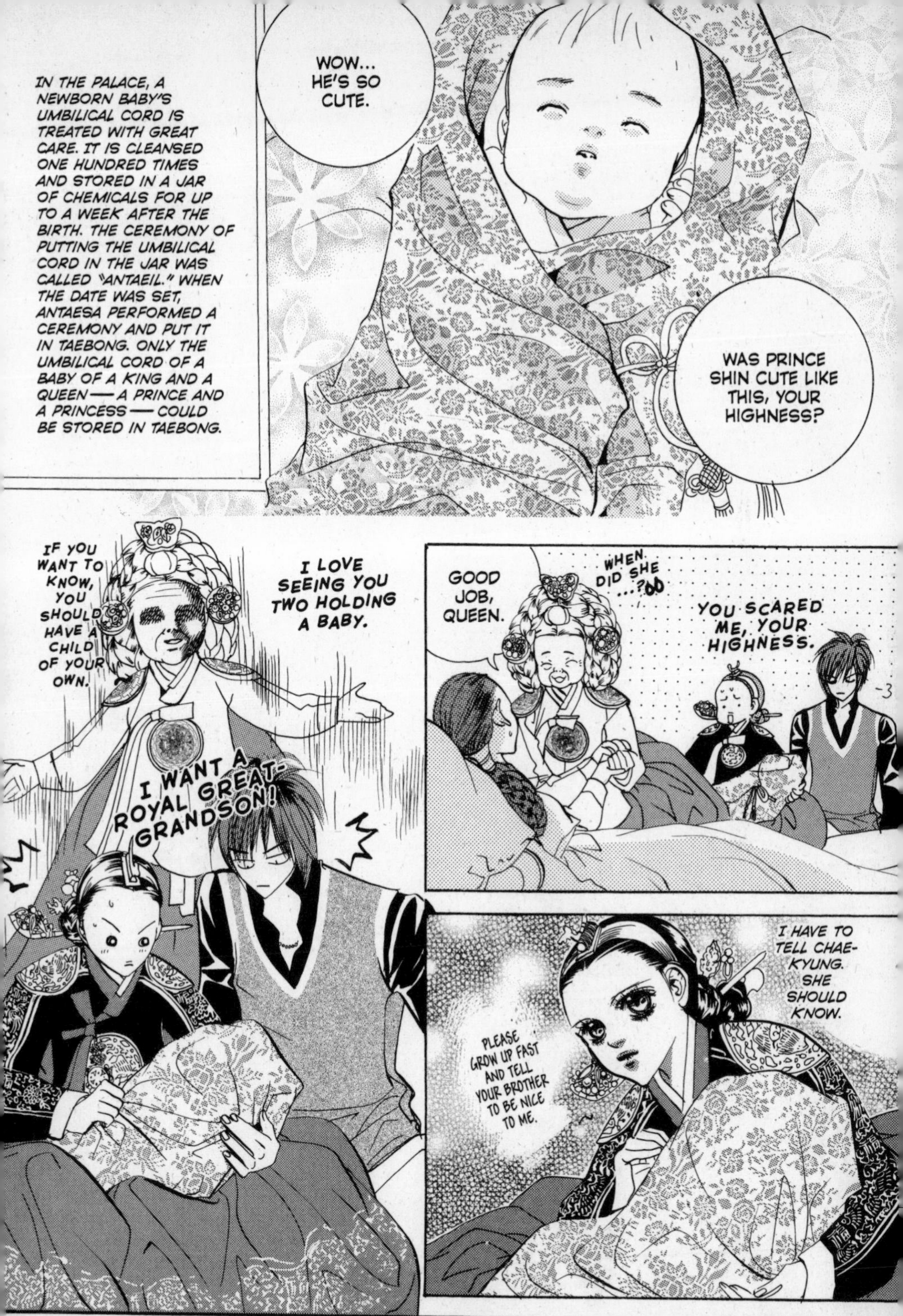
IN THE PALACE, A NEWBORN BABY'S UMBILICAL CORD IS TREATED WITH GREAT CARE. IT IS CLEANSED ONE HUNDRED TIMES AND STORED IN A JAR OF CHEMICALS FOR UP TO A WEEK AFTER THE BIRTH. THE CEREMONY OF PUTTING THE UMBILICAL CORD IN THE JAR WAS CALLED "ANTAEIL." WHEN THE DATE WAS SET, ANTAESA PERFORMED A CEREMONY AND PUT IT IN TAEBONG. ONLY THE UMBILICAL CORD OF A BABY OF A KING AND A QUEEN — A PRINCE AND A PRINCESS — COULD BE STORED IN TAEBONG.
WOW... HE'S SO CUTE.
WAS PRINCE SHIN CUTE LIKE THIS, YOUR HIGHNESS?
IF YOU WANT TO KNOW, YOU SHOULD HAVE A CHILD OF YOUR OWN.
I LOVE SEEING YOU TWO HOLDING A BABY.
I WANT A ROYAL GREAT-GRANDSON!
GOOD JOB, QUEEN.
WHEN DID SHE ...?
YOU SCARED ME, YOUR HIGHNESS.
I HAVE TO TELL CHAE-KYUNG. SHE SHOULD KNOW.
PLEASE GROW UP FAST AND TELL YOUR BROTHER TO BE NICE TO ME.

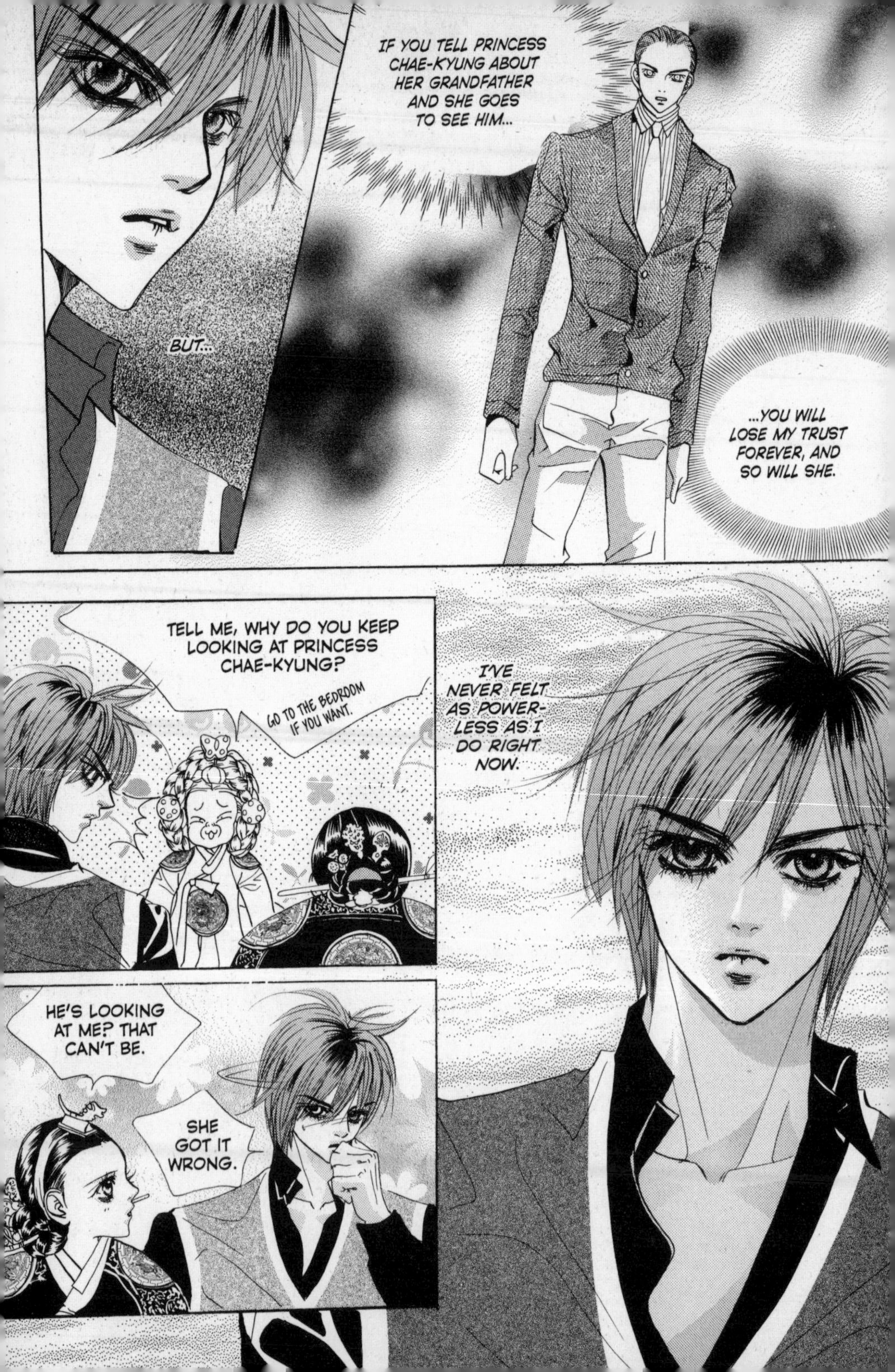
BUT...
IF YOU TELL PRINCESS CHAE-KYUNG ABOUT HER GRANDFATHER AND SHE GOES TO SEE HIM...
...YOU WILL LOSE MY TRUST FOREVER, AND SO WILL SHE.
TELL ME, WHY DO YOU KEEP LOOKING AT PRINCESS CHAE-KYUNG?
GO TO THE BEDROOM IF YOU WANT.
HE'S LOOKING AT ME? THAT CAN'T BE.
SHE GOT IT WRONG.
I'VE NEVER FELT AS POWER-LESS AS I DO RIGHT NOW.

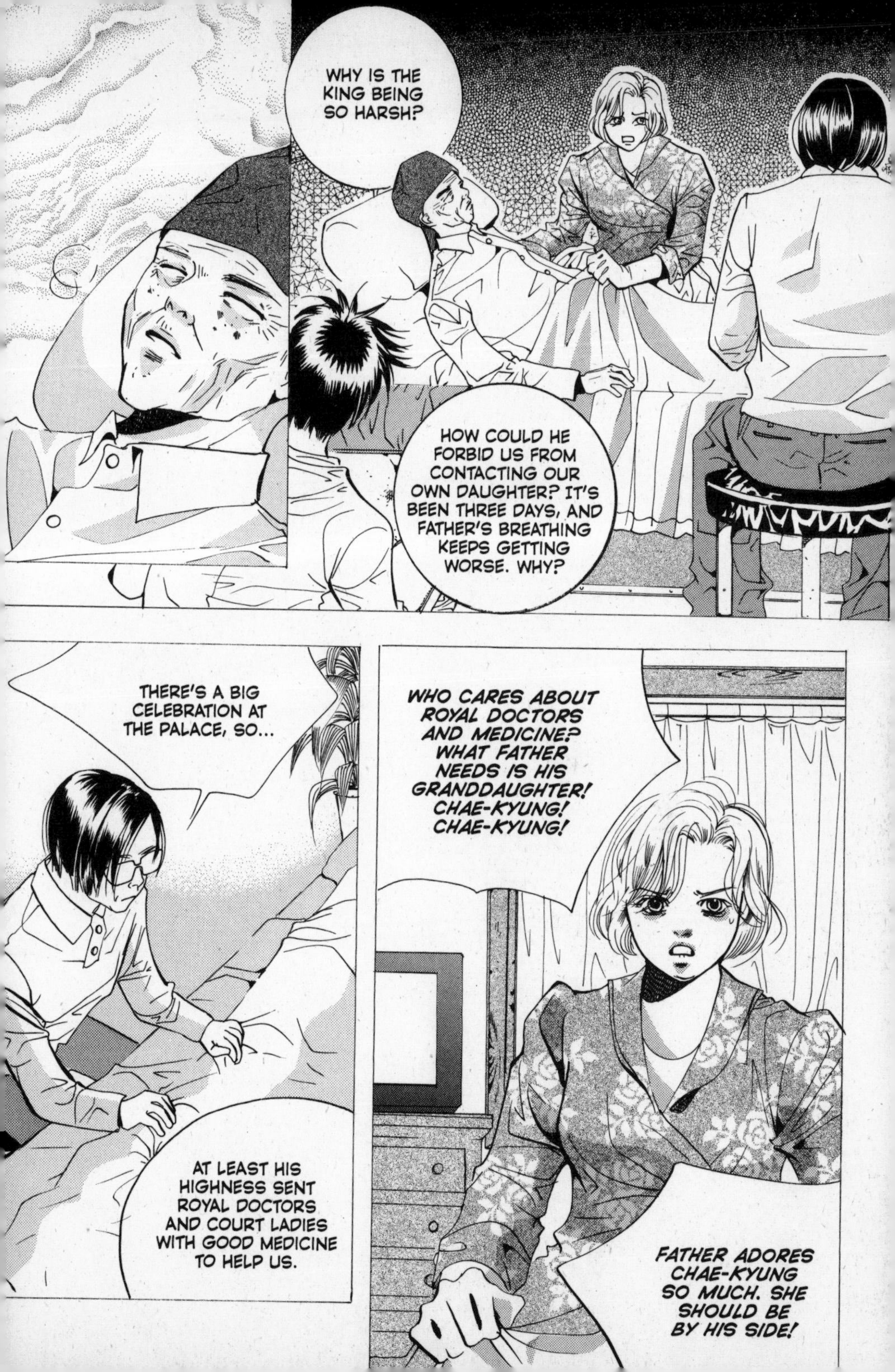
WHY IS THE KING BEING SO HARSH?
HOW COULD HE FORBID US FROM CONTACTING OUR OWN DAUGHTER? IT'S BEEN THREE DAYS, AND FATHER'S BREATHING KEEPS GETTING WORSE. WHY?
THERE'S A BIG CELEBRATION AT THE PALACE, SO...
AT LEAST HIS HIGHNESS SENT ROYAL DOCTORS AND COURT LADIES WITH GOOD MEDICINE TO HELP US.
WHO CARES ABOUT ROYAL DOCTORS AND MEDICINE? WHAT FATHER NEEDS IS HIS GRANDDAUGHTER! CHAE-KYUNG! CHAE-KYUNG!
FATHER ADORES CHAE-KYUNG SO MUCH. SHE SHOULD BE BY HIS SIDE!

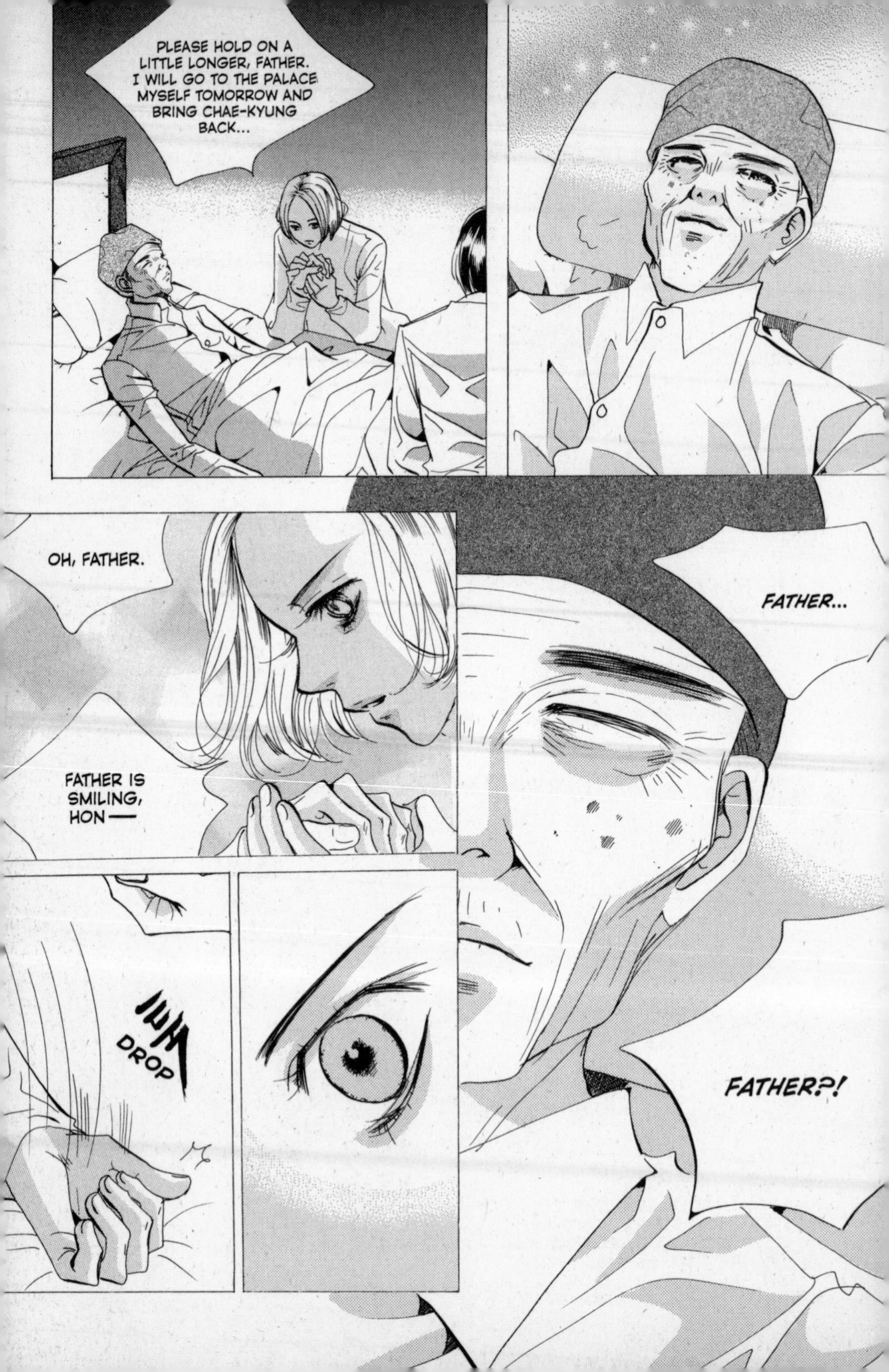
PLEASE HOLD ON A LITTLE LONGER, FATHER. I WILL GO TO THE PALACE MYSELF TOMORROW AND BRING CHAE-KYUNG BACK...
OH, FATHER.
FATHER IS SMILING, HON—
FATHER...
DROP
FATHER?!

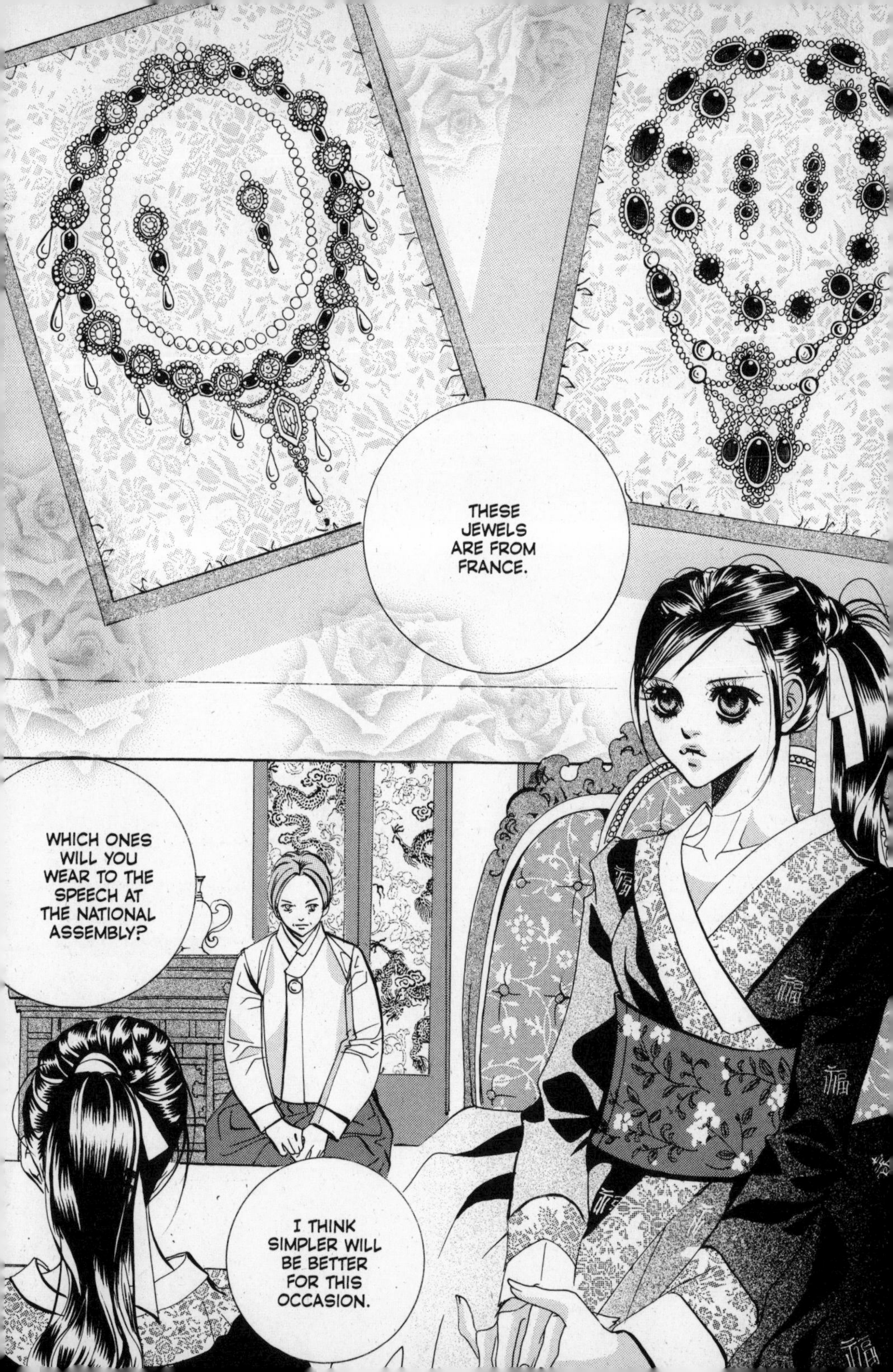
THESE JEWELS ARE FROM FRANCE.
WHICH ONES WILL YOU WEAR TO THE SPEECH AT THE NATIONAL ASSEMBLY?
I THINK SIMPLER WILL BE BETTER FOR THIS OCCASION.

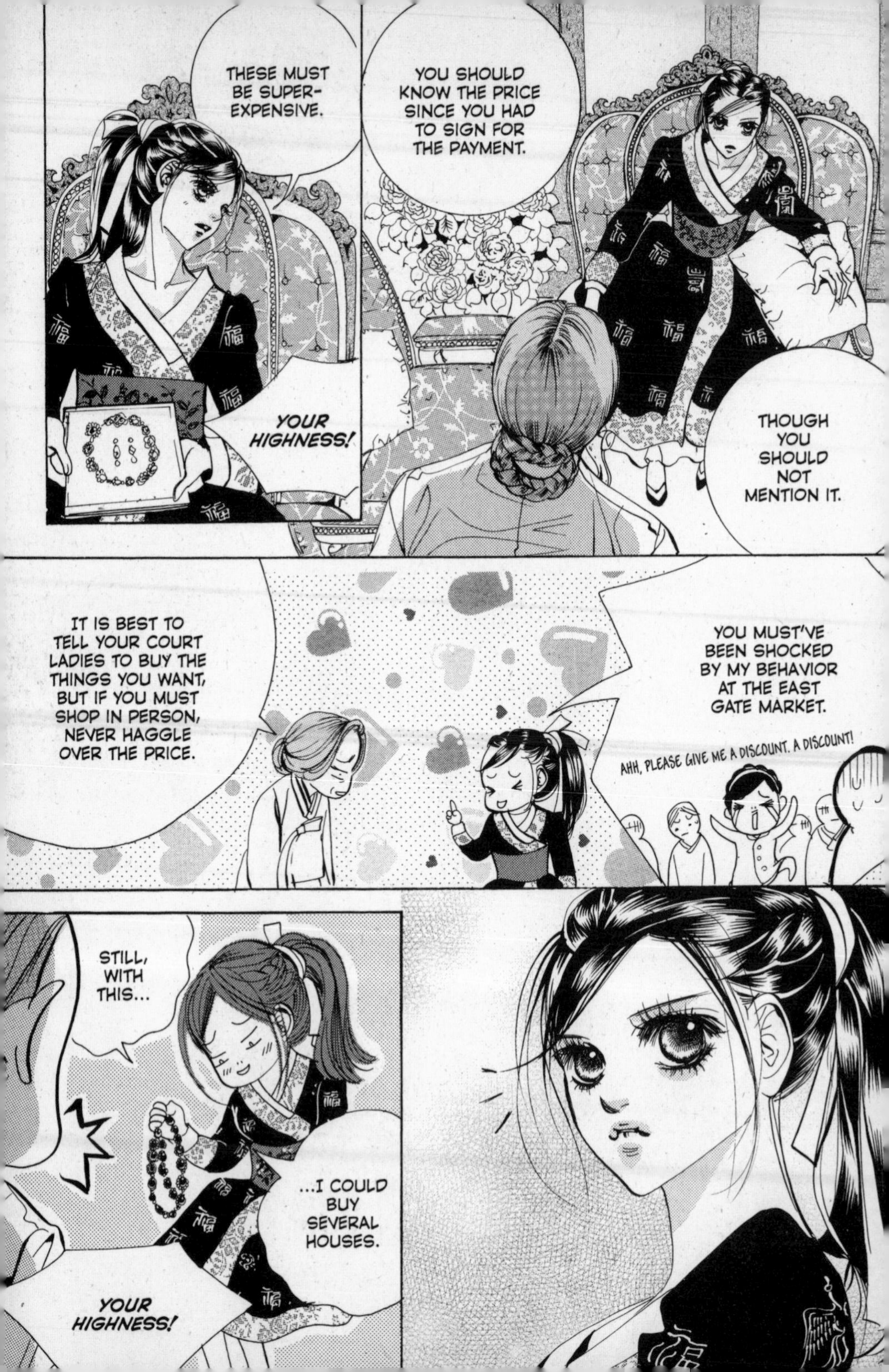
THESE MUST BE SUPER-EXPENSIVE.
YOUR HIGHNESS!
YOU SHOULD KNOW THE PRICE SINCE YOU HAD TO SIGN FOR THE PAYMENT.
THOUGH YOU SHOULD NOT MENTION IT.
IT IS BEST TO TELL YOUR COURT LADIES TO BUY THE THINGS YOU WANT, BUT IF YOU MUST SHOP IN PERSON, NEVER HAGGLE OVER THE PRICE.
YOU MUST'VE BEEN SHOCKED BY MY BEHAVIOR AT THE EAST GATE MARKET.
AHH, PLEASE GIVE ME A DISCOUNT. A DISCOUNT!
STILL, WITH THIS...
...I COULD BUY SEVERAL HOUSES.
YOUR HIGHNESS!

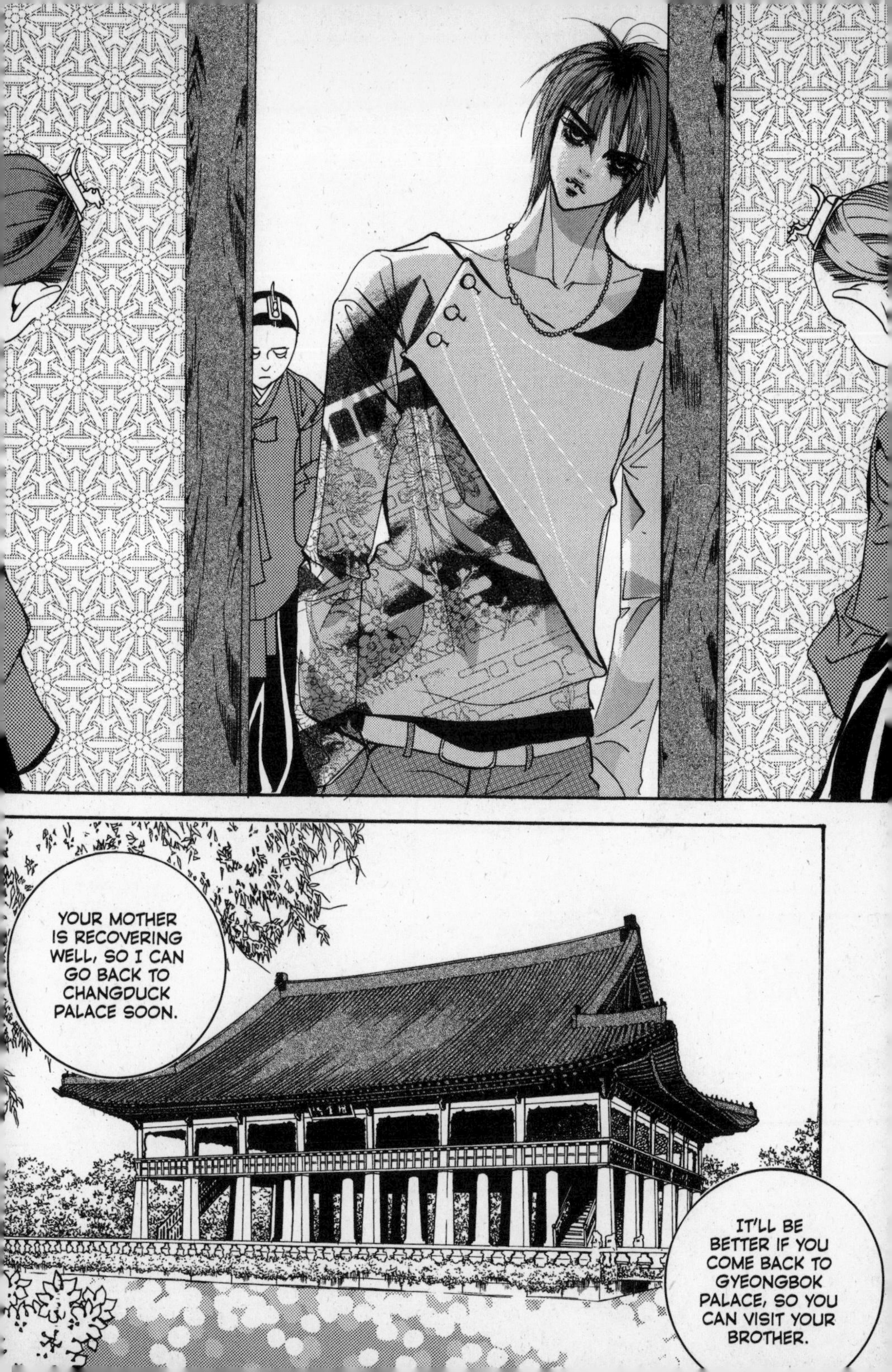
YOUR MOTHER IS RECOVERING WELL, SO I CAN GO BACK TO CHANGDUCK PALACE SOON.
IT'LL BE BETTER IF YOU COME BACK TO GYEONGBOK PALACE, SO YOU CAN VISIT YOUR BROTHER.

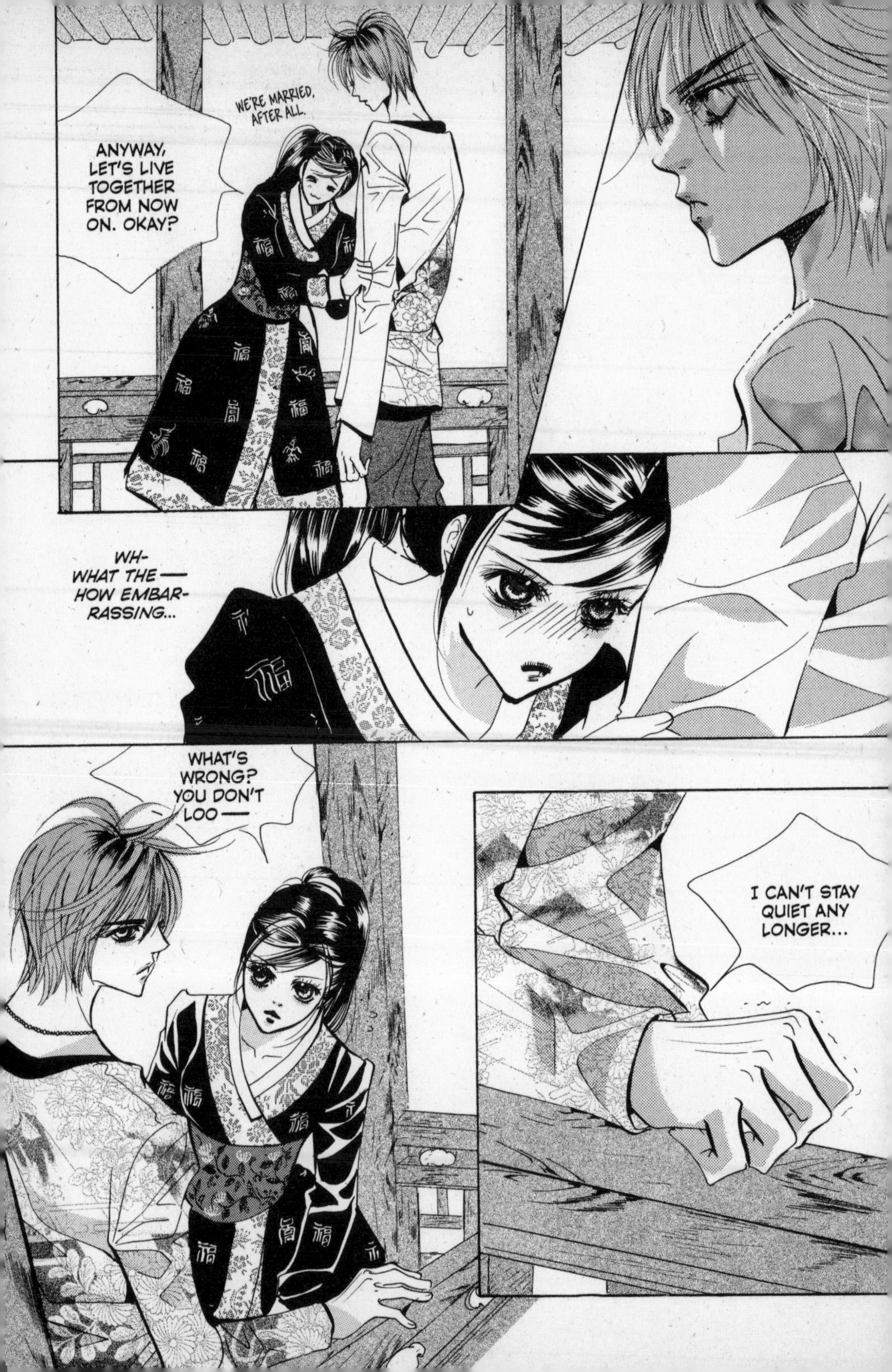
WE'RE MARRIED, AFTER ALL.
ANYWAY, LET'S LIVE TOGETHER FROM NOW ON. OKAY?
WH- WHAT THE— HOW EMBARRASSING...
WHAT'S WRONG? YOU DON'T LOO—
I CAN'T STAY QUIET ANY LONGER...

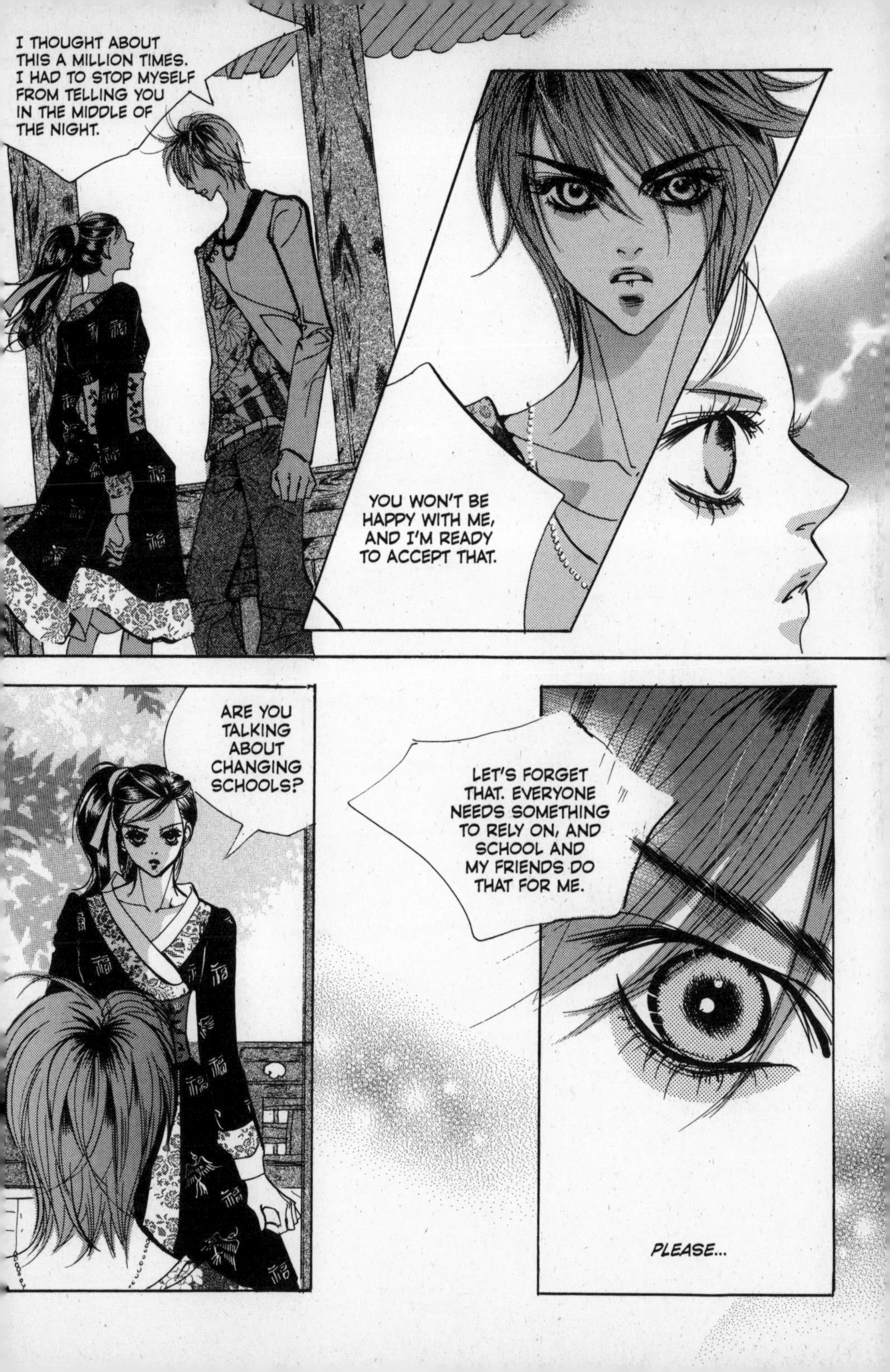
I THOUGHT ABOUT THIS A MILLION TIMES. I HAD TO STOP MYSELF FROM TELLING YOU IN THE MIDDLE OF THE NIGHT.
YOU WON'T BE HAPPY WITH ME, AND I'M READY TO ACCEPT THAT.
ARE YOU TALKING ABOUT CHANGING SCHOOLS?
LET'S FORGET THAT. EVERYONE NEEDS SOMETHING TO RELY ON, AND SCHOOL AND MY FRIENDS DO THAT FOR ME.
PLEASE...

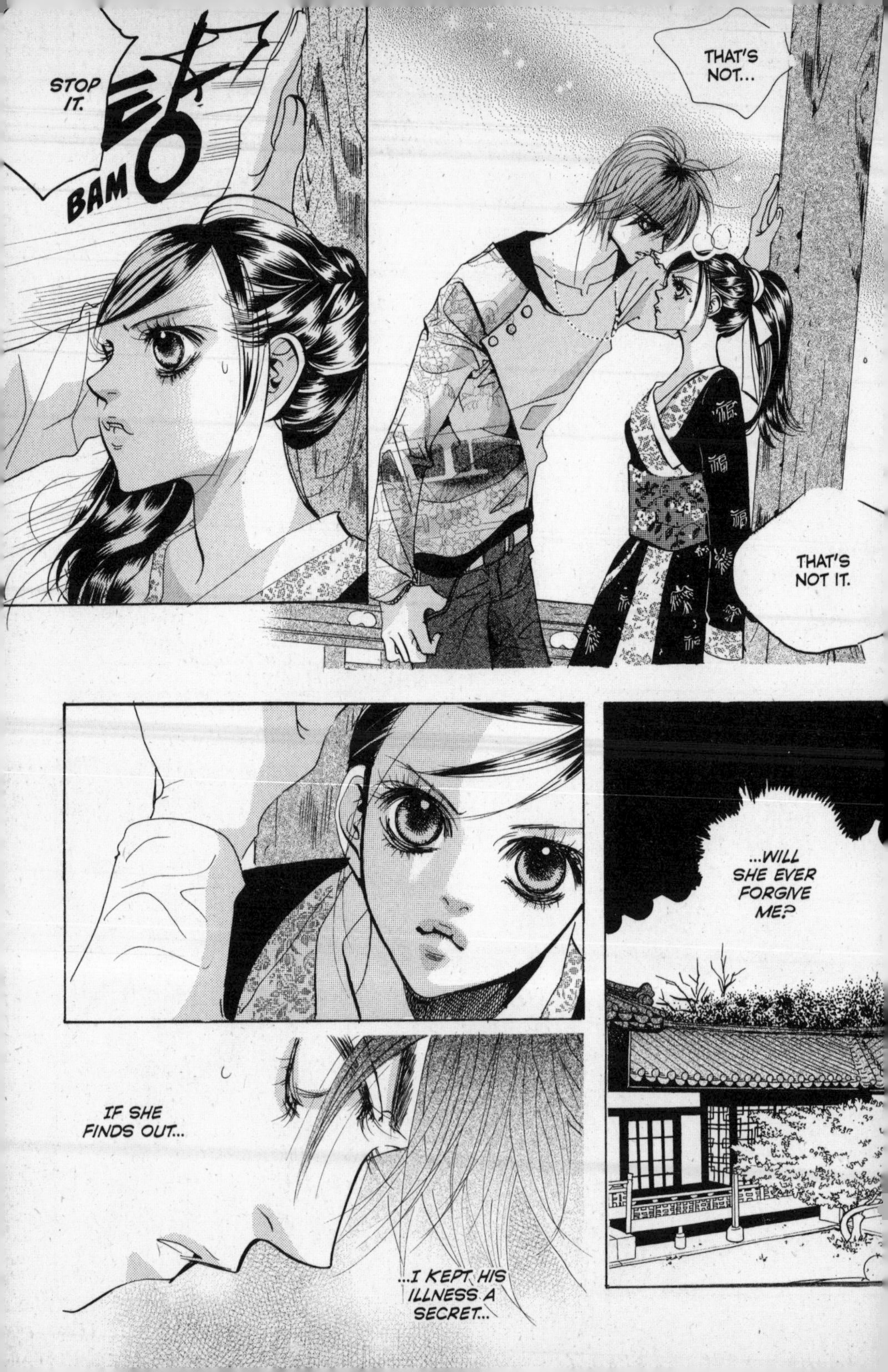
STOP IT.
BAM
THAT'S NOT...
THAT'S NOT IT.
...WILL SHE EVER FORGIVE ME?
IF SHE FINDS OUT...
...I KEPT HIS ILLNESS A SECRET...

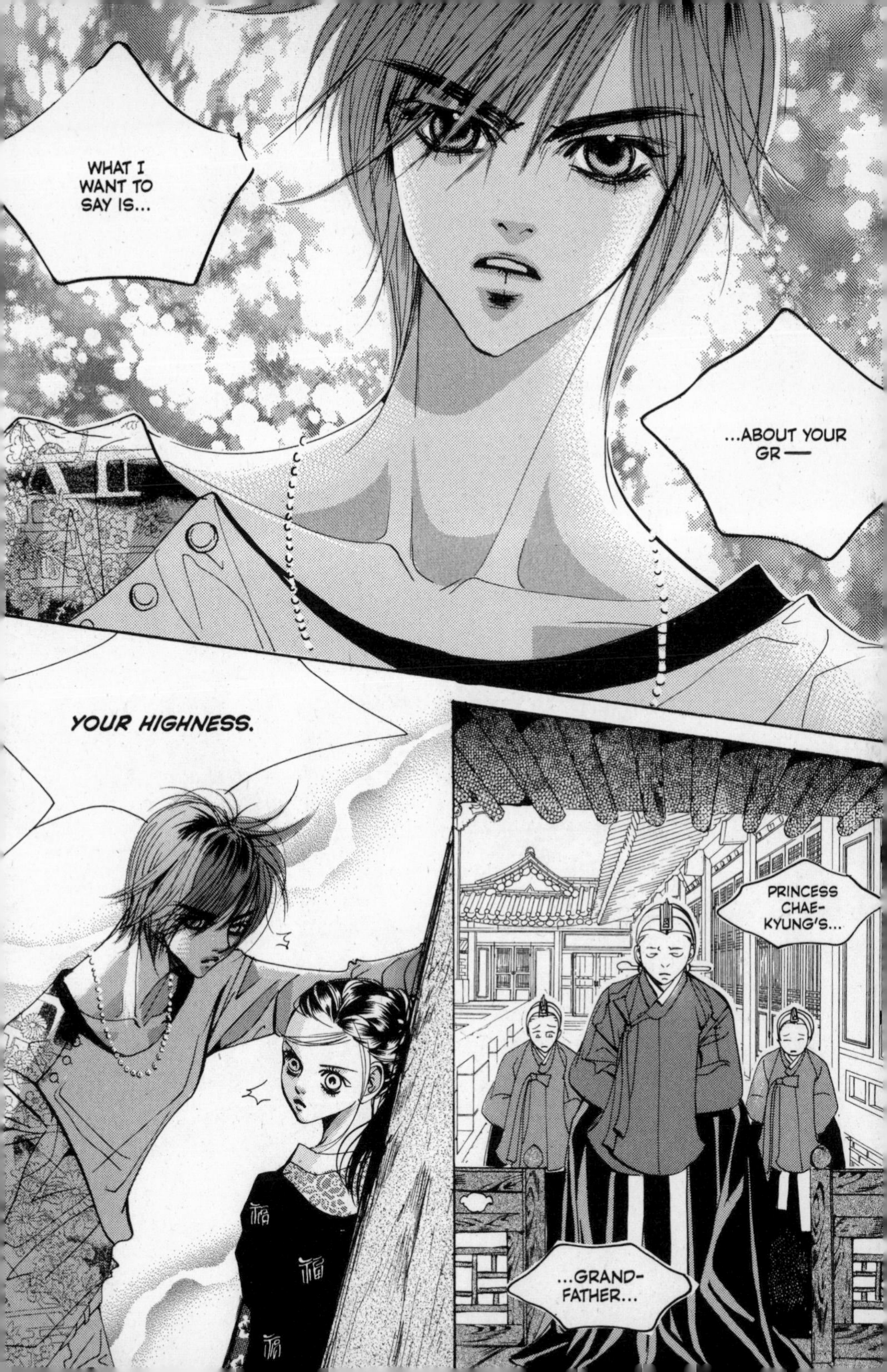
WHAT I WANT TO SAY IS...
...ABOUT YOUR GR—
YOUR HIGHNESS.
PRINCESS CHAE-KYUNG'S...
...GRAND-FATHER...

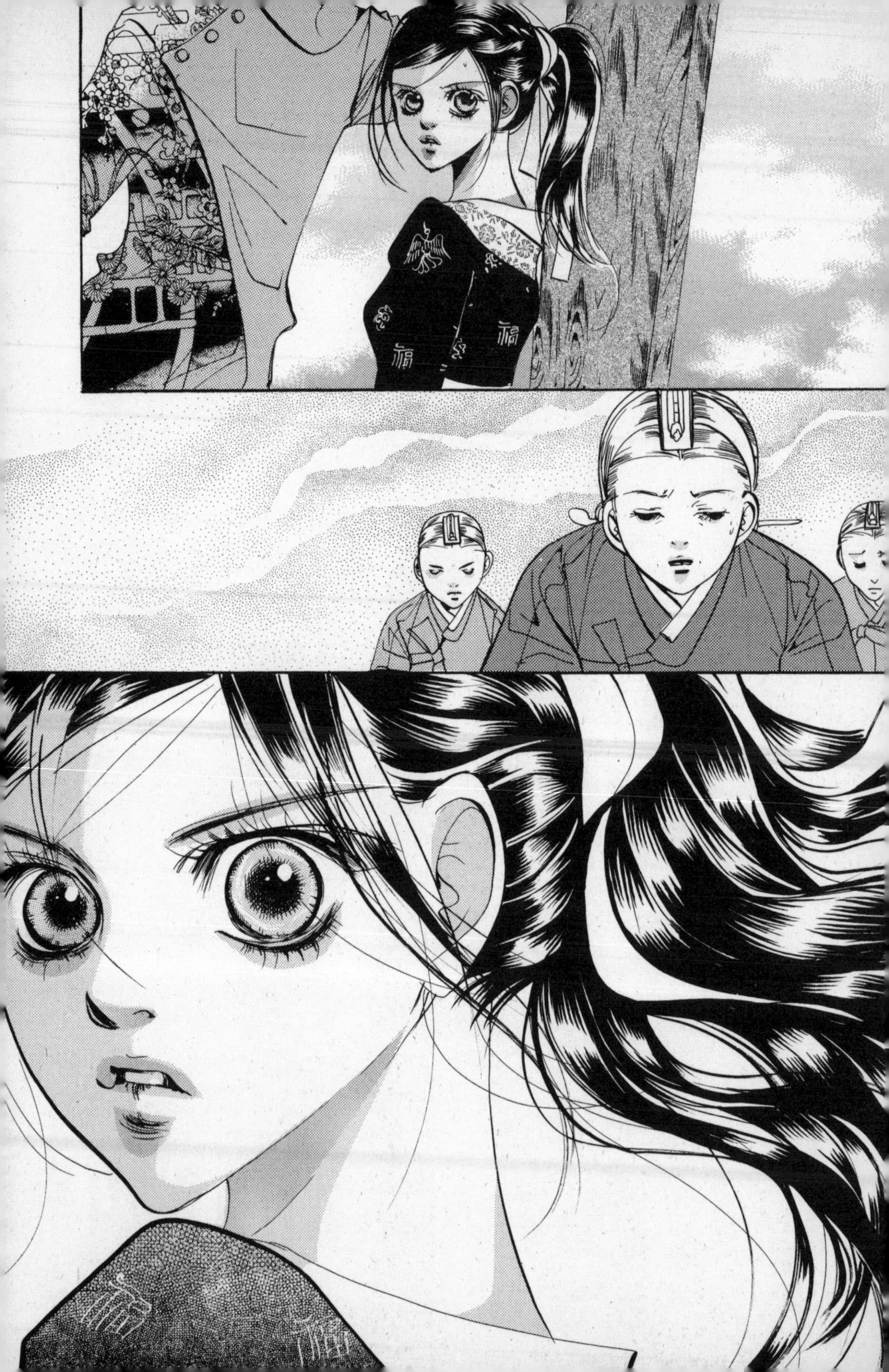

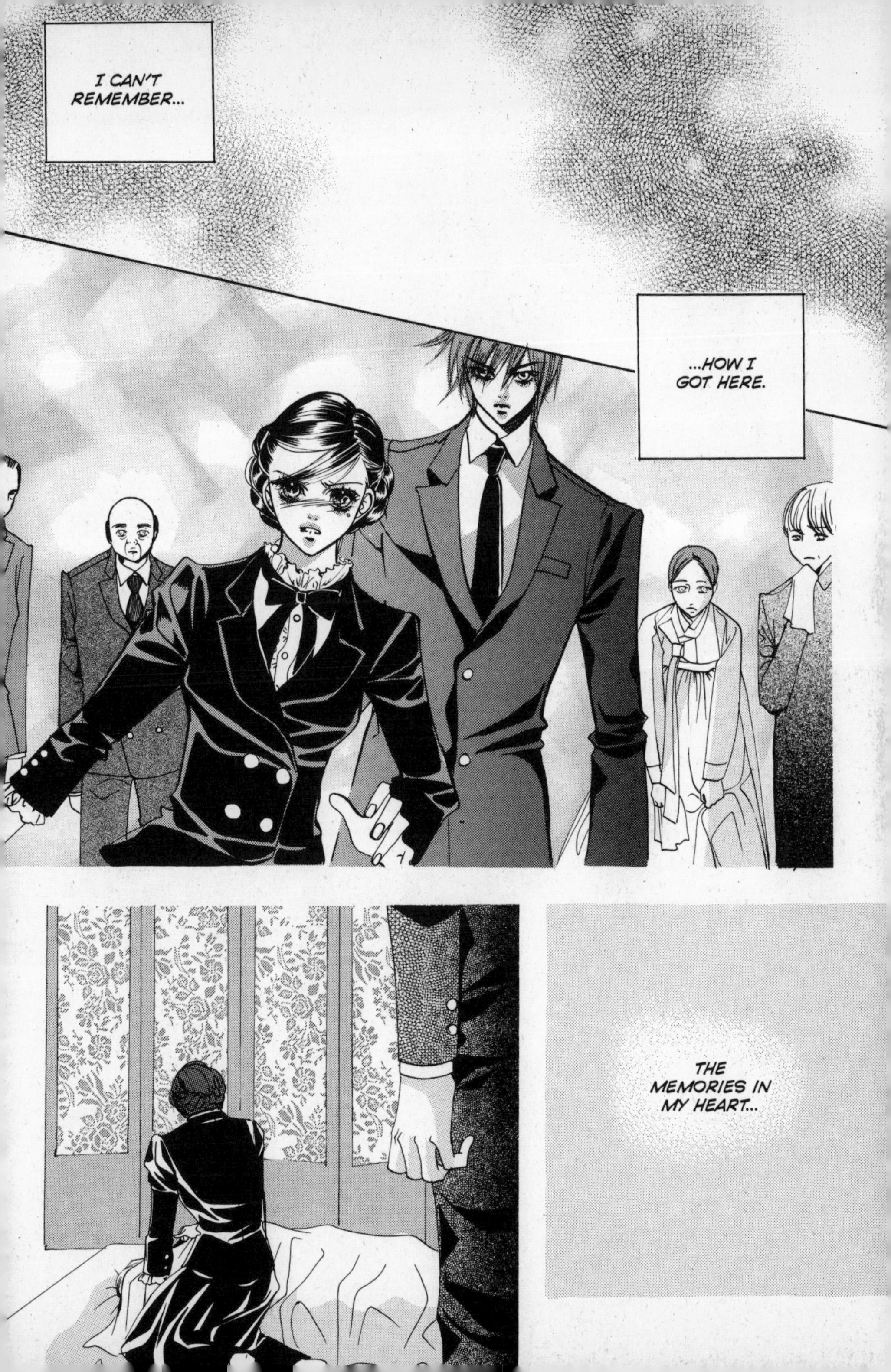
I CAN'T REMEMBER...
...HOW I GOT HERE.
THE MEMORIES IN MY HEART...

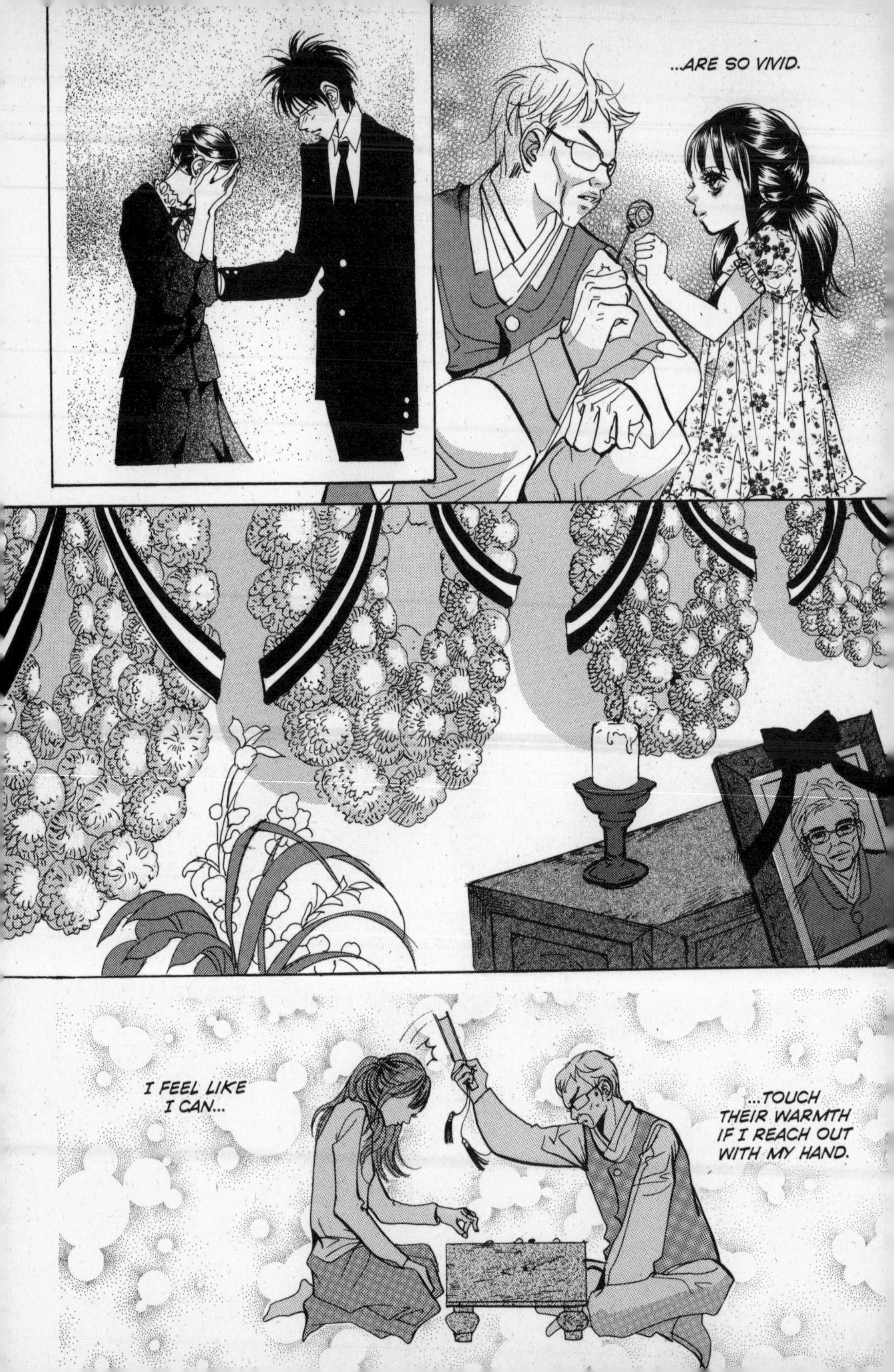
...ARE SO VIVID.
I FEEL LIKE I CAN...
...TOUCH THEIR WARMTH IF I REACH OUT WITH MY HAND.

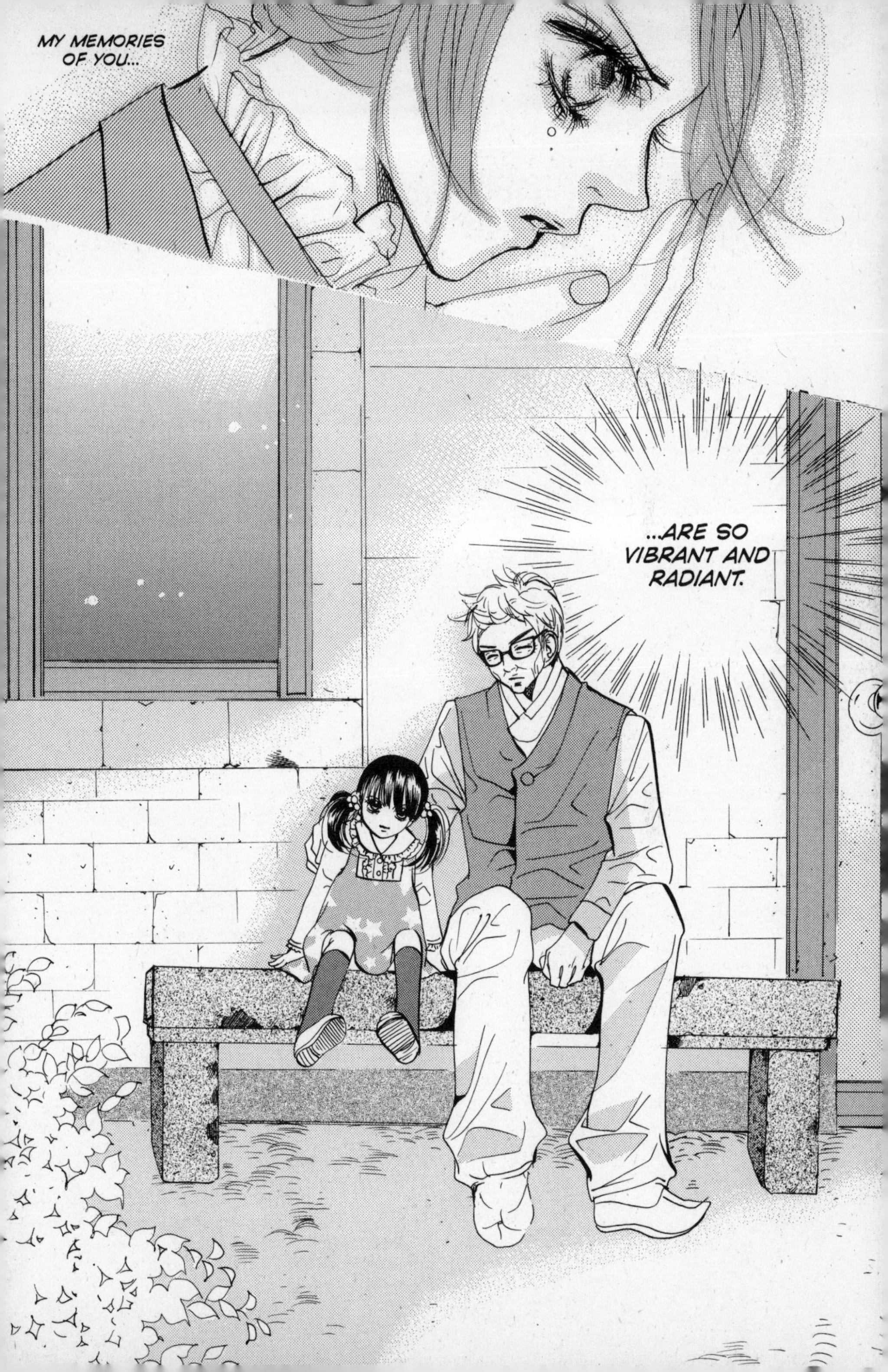
MY MEMORIES OF YOU...
...ARE SO VIBRANT AND RADIANT.

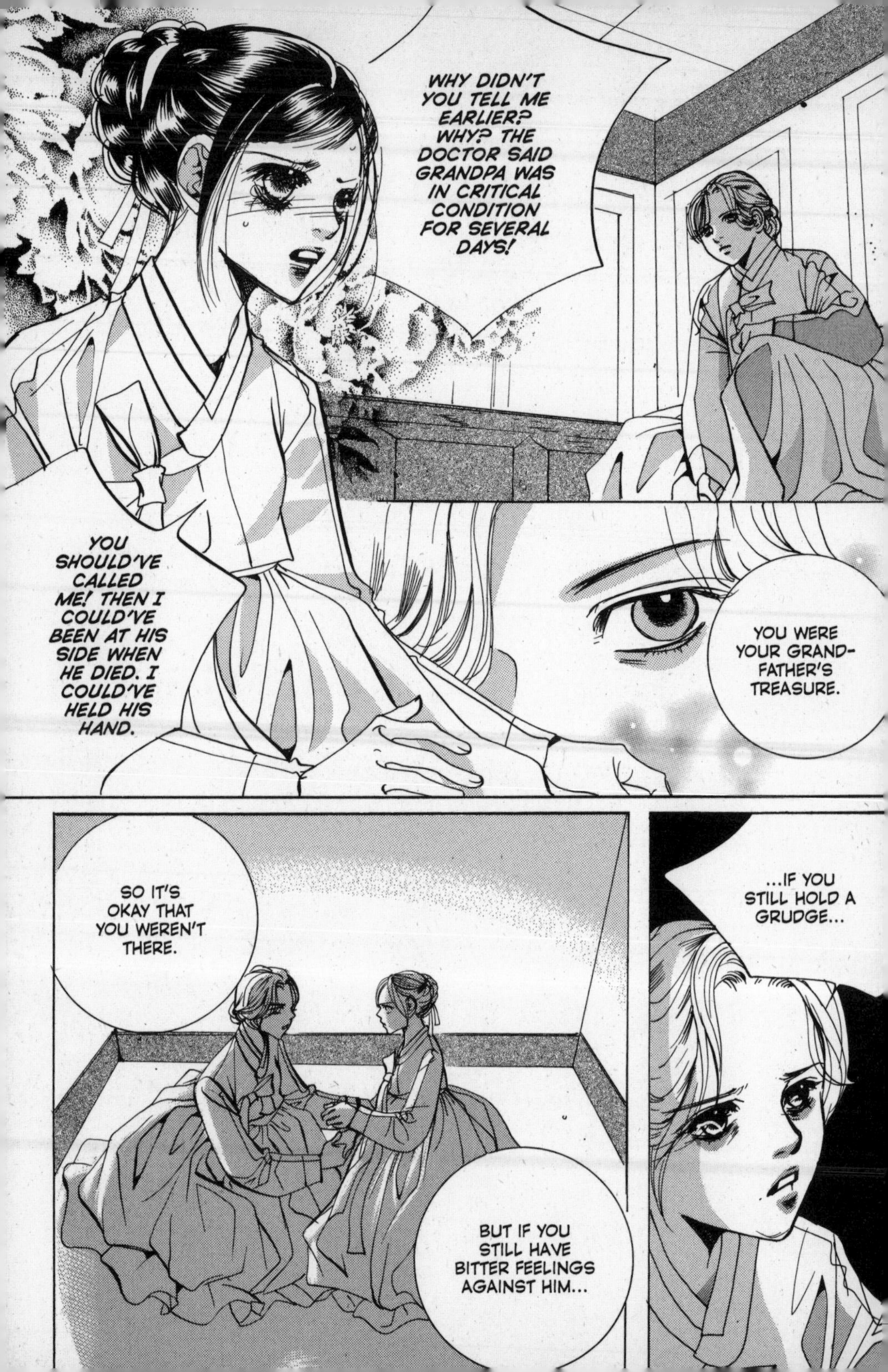
WHY DIDN'T YOU TELL ME EARLIER? WHY? THE DOCTOR SAID GRANDPA WAS IN CRITICAL CONDITION FOR SEVERAL DAYS!
YOU SHOULD'VE CALLED ME! THEN I COULD'VE BEEN AT HIS SIDE WHEN HE DIED. I COULD'VE HELD HIS HAND.
YOU WERE YOUR GRAND-FATHER'S TREASURE.
SO IT'S OKAY THAT YOU WEREN'T THERE.
BUT IF YOU STILL HAVE BITTER FEELINGS AGAINST HIM...
...IF YOU STILL HOLD A GRUDGE...

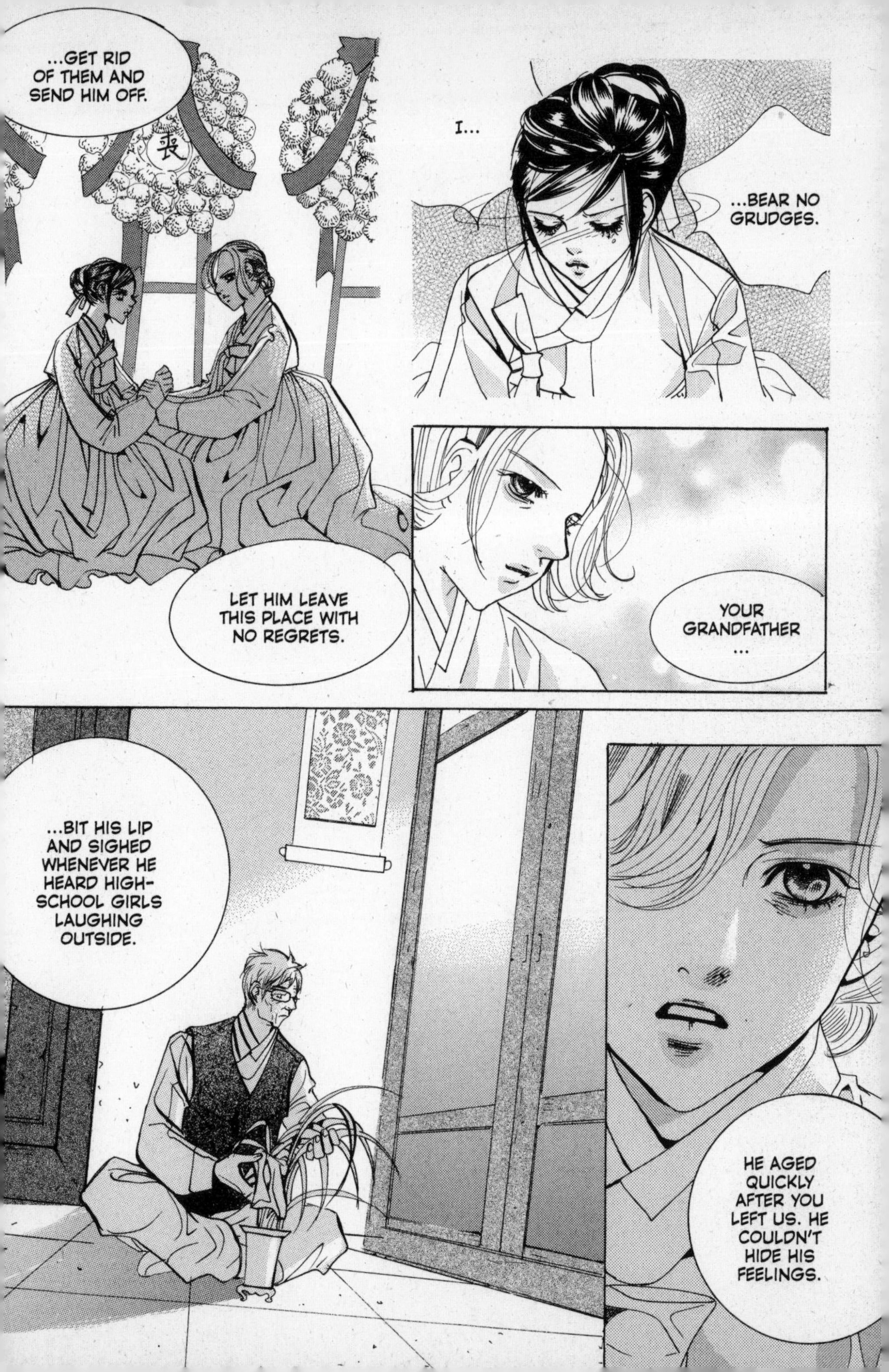
...GET RID OF THEM AND SEND HIM OFF.
I...
...BEAR NO GRUDGES.
LET HIM LEAVE THIS PLACE WITH NO REGRETS.
YOUR GRANDFATHER ...
...BIT HIS LIP AND SIGHED WHENEVER HE HEARD HIGH-SCHOOL GIRLS LAUGHING OUTSIDE.
HE AGED QUICKLY AFTER YOU LEFT US. HE COULDN'T HIDE HIS FEELINGS.

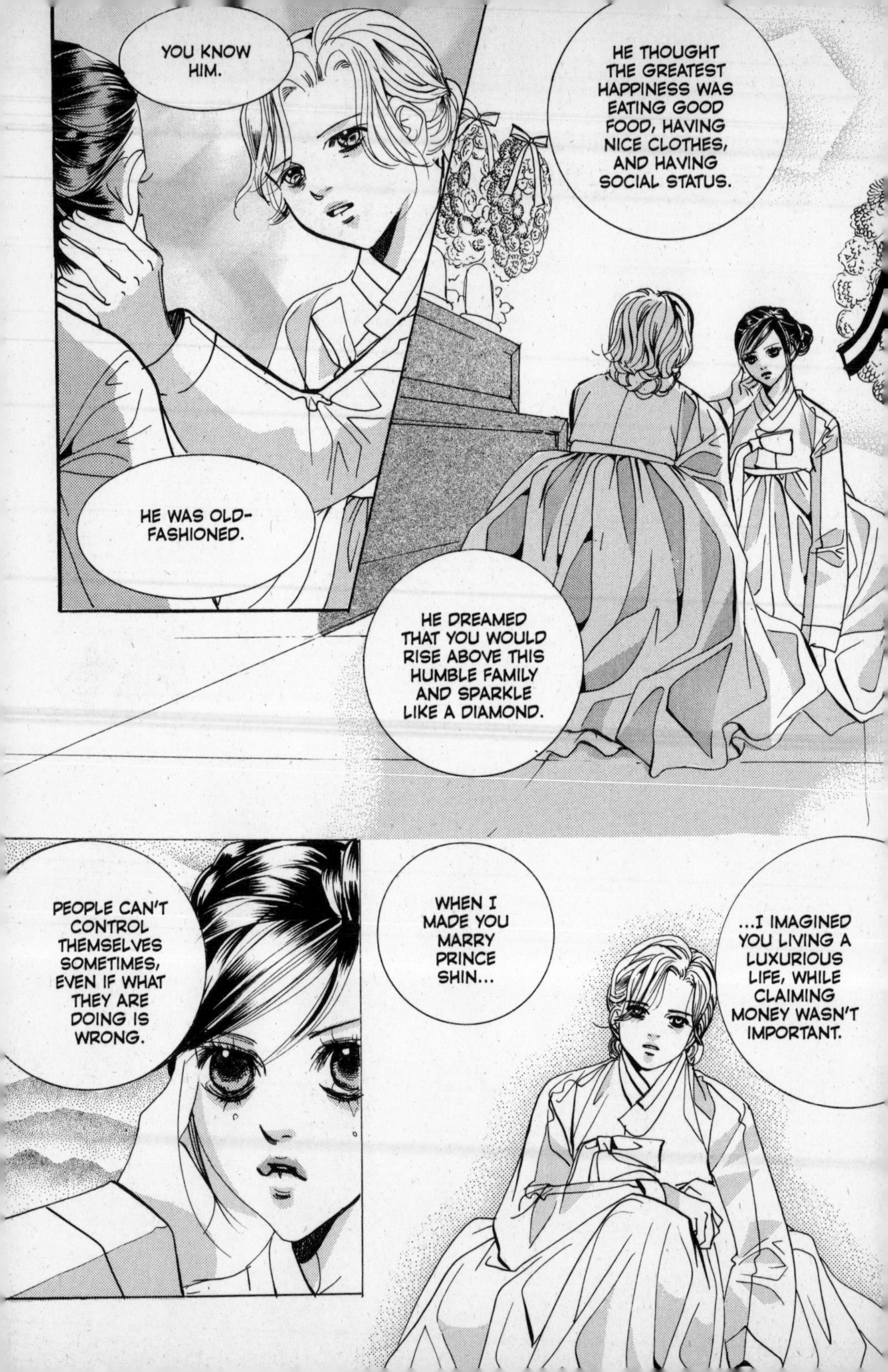
YOU KNOW HIM.
HE WAS OLD-FASHIONED.
HE THOUGHT THE GREATEST HAPPINESS WAS EATING GOOD FOOD, HAVING NICE CLOTHES, AND HAVING SOCIAL STATUS.
HE DREAMED THAT YOU WOULD RISE ABOVE THIS HUMBLE FAMILY AND SPARKLE LIKE A DIAMOND.
PEOPLE CAN'T CONTROL THEMSELVES SOMETIMES, EVEN IF WHAT THEY ARE DOING IS WRONG.
WHEN I MADE YOU MARRY PRINCE SHIN...
...I IMAGINED YOU LIVING A LUXURIOUS LIFE, WHILE CLAIMING MONEY WASN'T IMPORTANT.

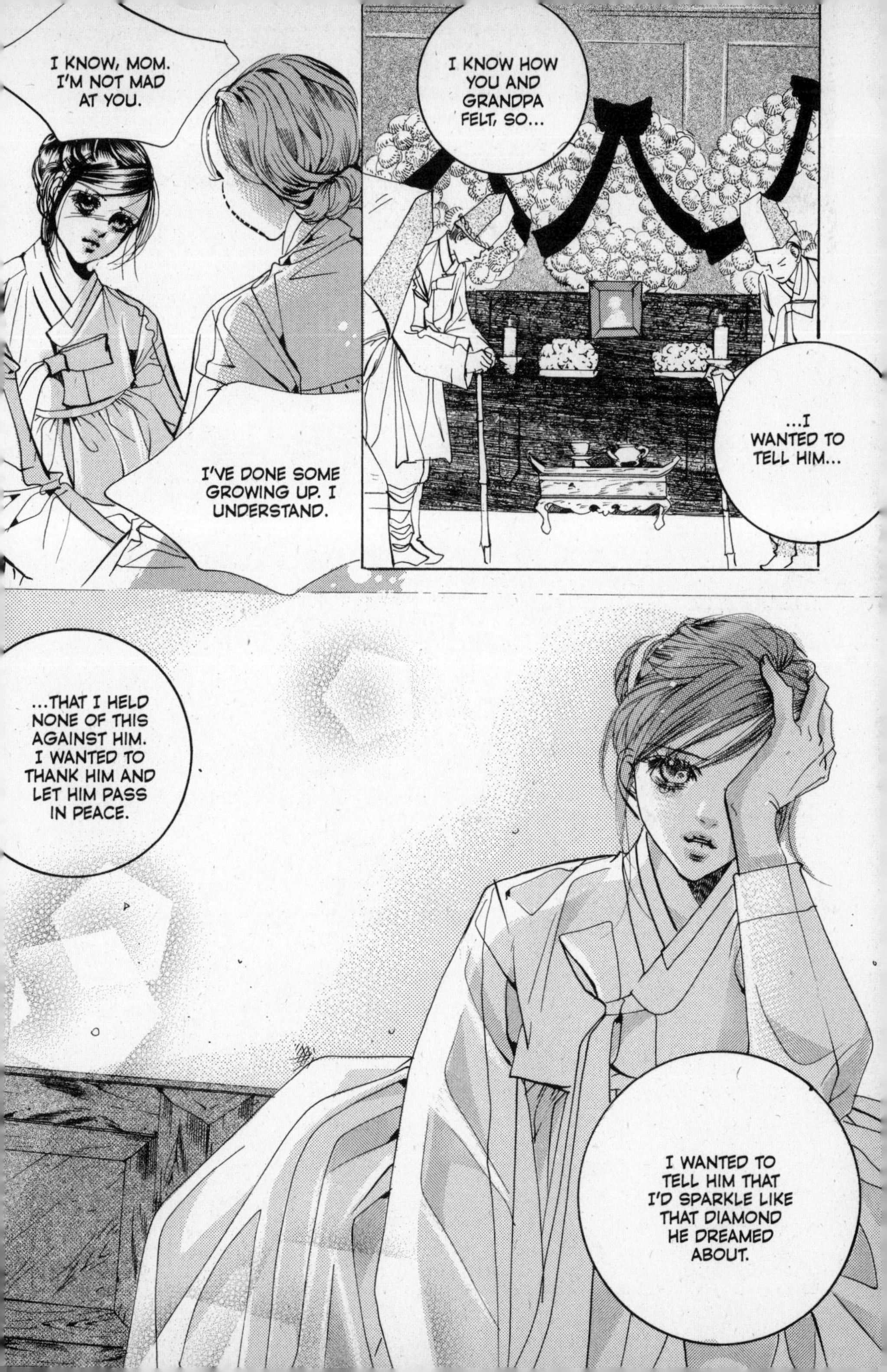
I KNOW, MOM. I'M NOT MAD AT YOU.
I'VE DONE SOME GROWING UP. I UNDERSTAND.
I KNOW HOW YOU AND GRANDPA FELT, SO...
...I WANTED TO TELL HIM...
...THAT I HELD NONE OF THIS AGAINST HIM. I WANTED TO THANK HIM AND LET HIM PASS IN PEACE.
I WANTED TO TELL HIM THAT I'D SPARKLE LIKE THAT DIAMOND HE DREAMED ABOUT.

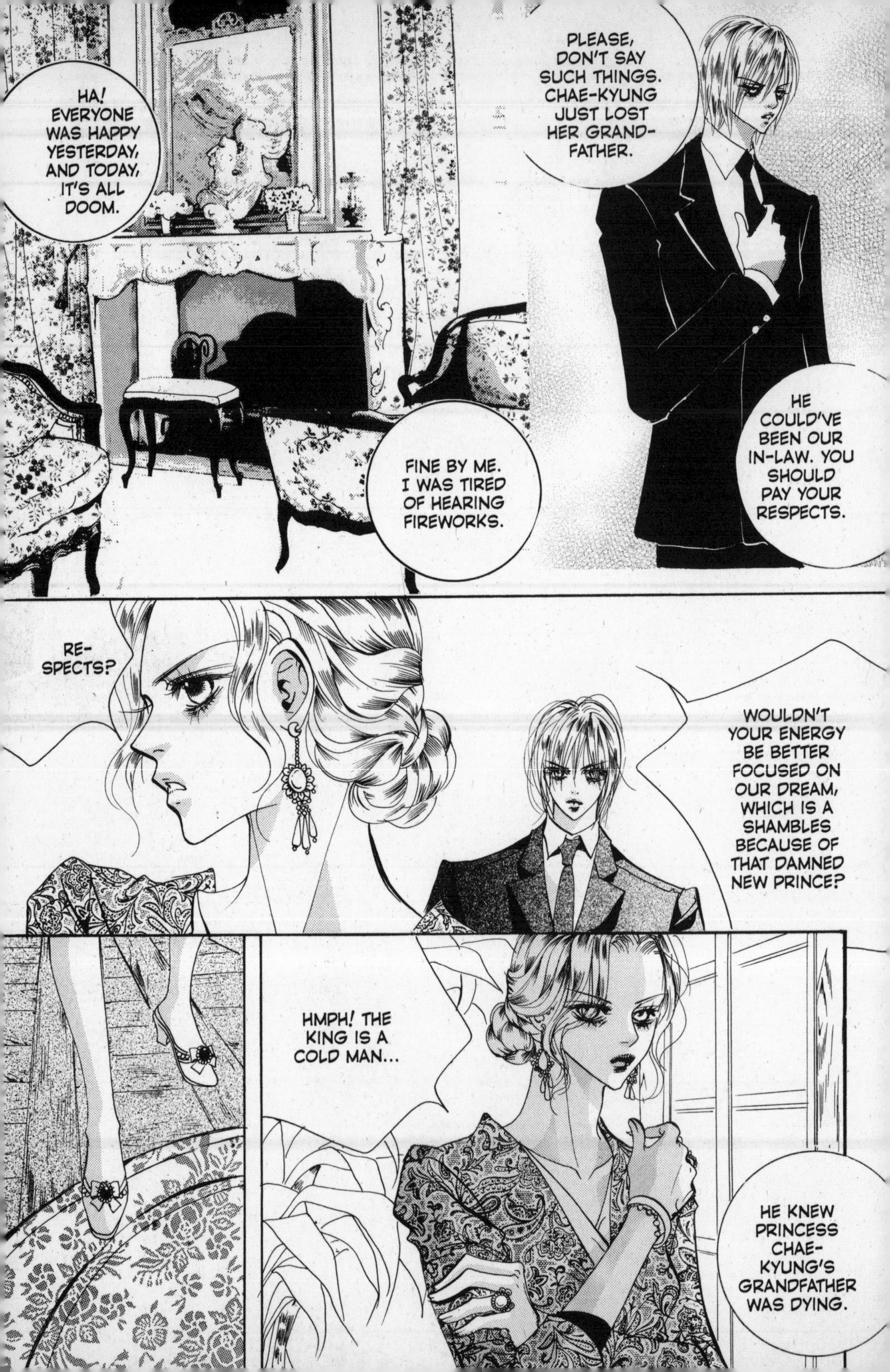
HA! EVERYONE WAS HAPPY YESTERDAY, AND TODAY, IT'S ALL DOOM.
FINE BY ME. I WAS TIRED OF HEARING FIREWORKS.
PLEASE, DON'T SAY SUCH THINGS. CHAE-KYUNG JUST LOST HER GRAND-FATHER.
HE COULD'VE BEEN OUR IN-LAW. YOU SHOULD PAY YOUR RESPECTS.
RE-SPECTS?
WOULDN'T YOUR ENERGY BE BETTER FOCUSED ON OUR DREAM, WHICH IS A SHAMBLES BECAUSE OF THAT DAMNED NEW PRINCE?
HMPH! THE KING IS A COLD MAN...
HE KNEW PRINCESS CHAE-KYUNG'S GRANDFATHER WAS DYING.

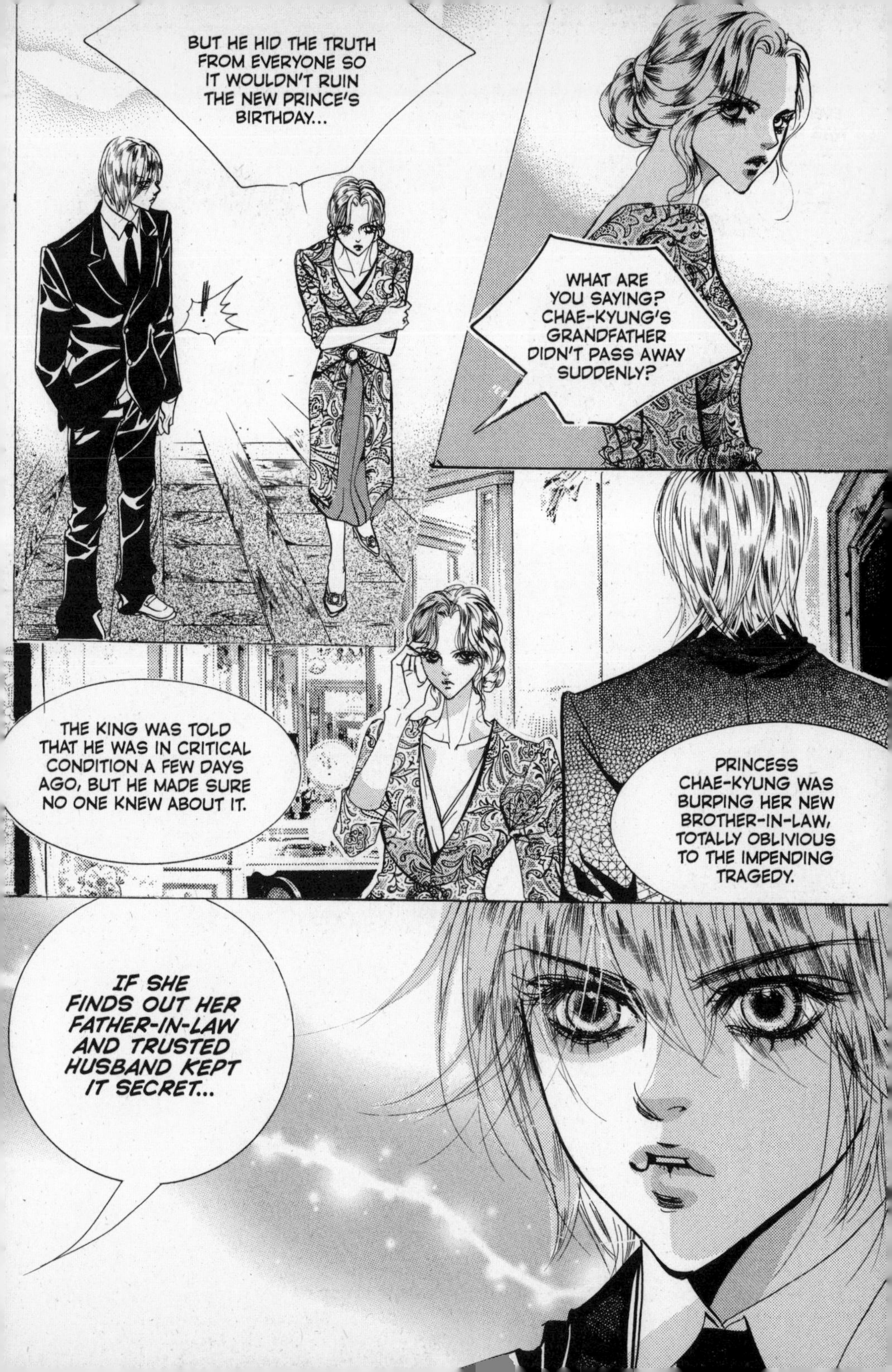
BUT HE HID THE TRUTH FROM EVERYONE SO IT WOULDN'T RUIN THE NEW PRINCE'S BIRTHDAY...
!
WHAT ARE YOU SAYING? CHAE-KYUNG'S GRANDFATHER DIDN'T PASS AWAY SUDDENLY?
THE KING WAS TOLD THAT HE WAS IN CRITICAL CONDITION A FEW DAYS AGO, BUT HE MADE SURE NO ONE KNEW ABOUT IT.
PRINCESS CHAE-KYUNG WAS BURPING HER NEW BROTHER-IN-LAW, TOTALLY OBLIVIOUS TO THE IMPENDING TRAGEDY.
IF SHE FINDS OUT HER FATHER-IN-LAW AND TRUSTED HUSBAND KEPT IT SECRET...

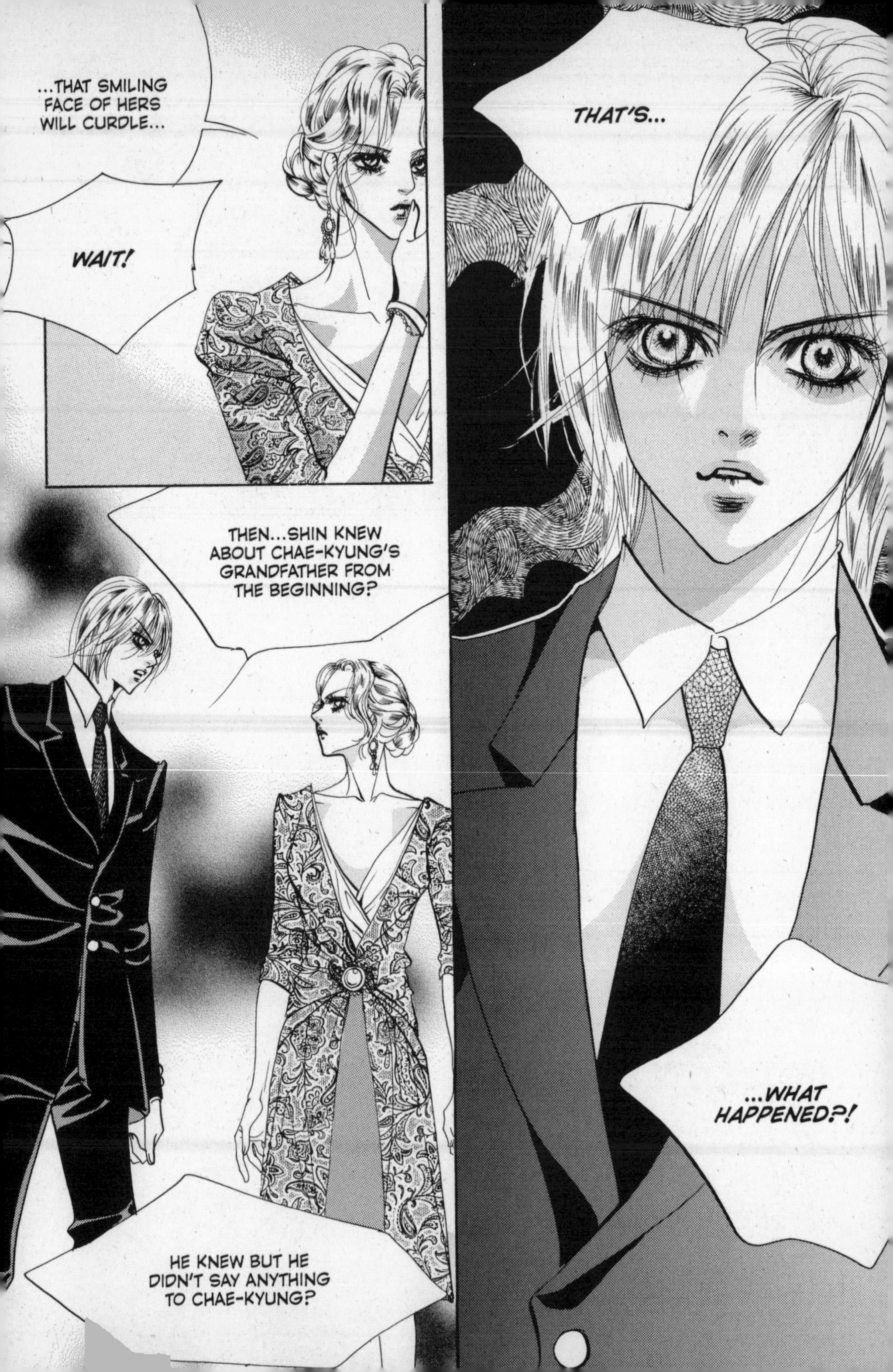
...THAT SMILING FACE OF HERS WILL CURDLE...
WAIT!
THEN...SHIN KNEW ABOUT CHAE-KYUNG'S GRANDFATHER FROM THE BEGINNING?
HE KNEW BUT HE DIDN'T SAY ANYTHING TO CHAE-KYUNG?
THAT'S...
...WHAT HAPPENED?!

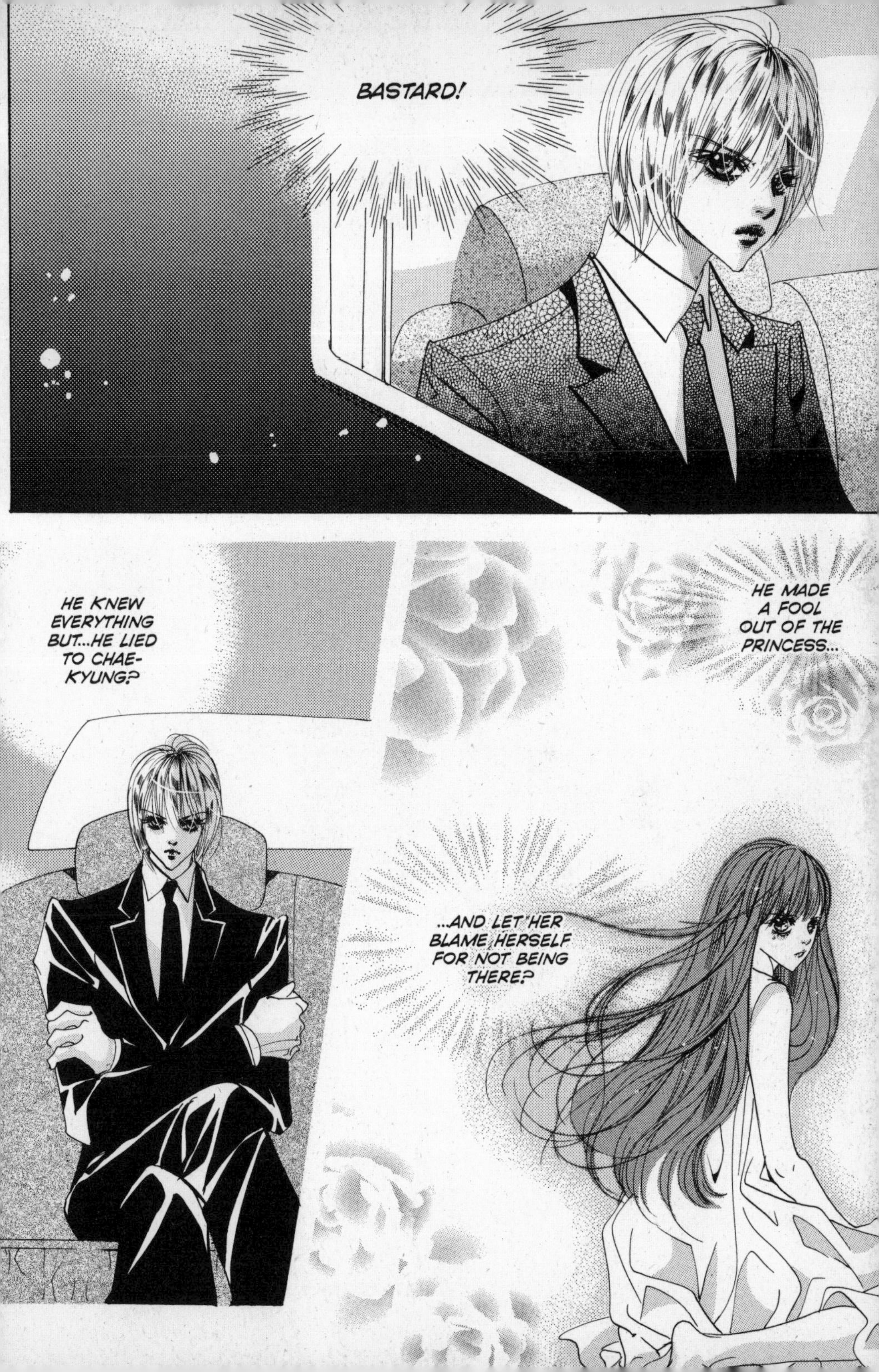
BASTARD!
HE KNEW EVERYTHING BUT...HE LIED TO CHAE-KYUNG?
HE MADE A FOOL OUT OF THE PRINCESS...
...AND LET HER BLAME HERSELF FOR NOT BEING THERE?

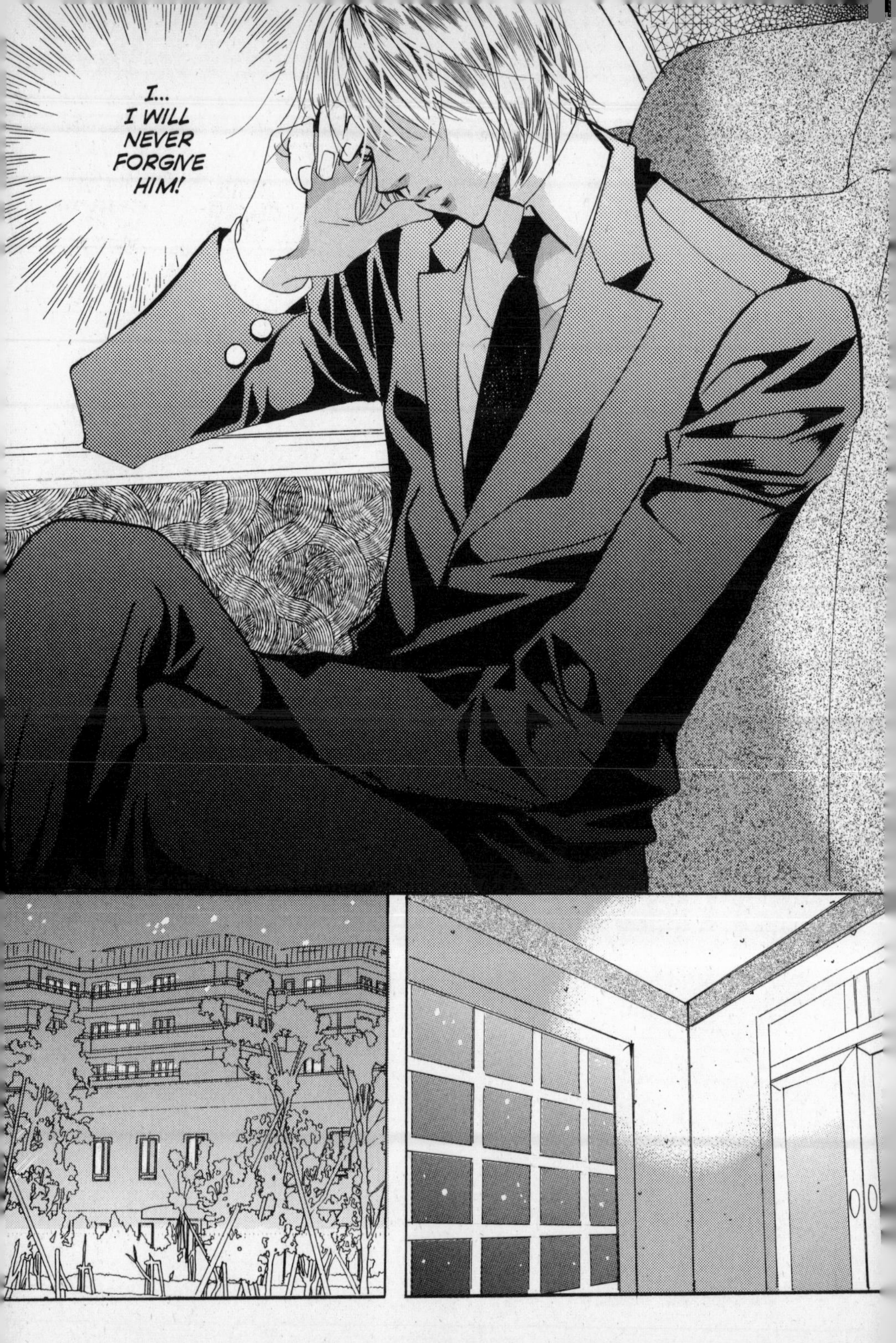
I... I WILL NEVER FORGIVE HIM!

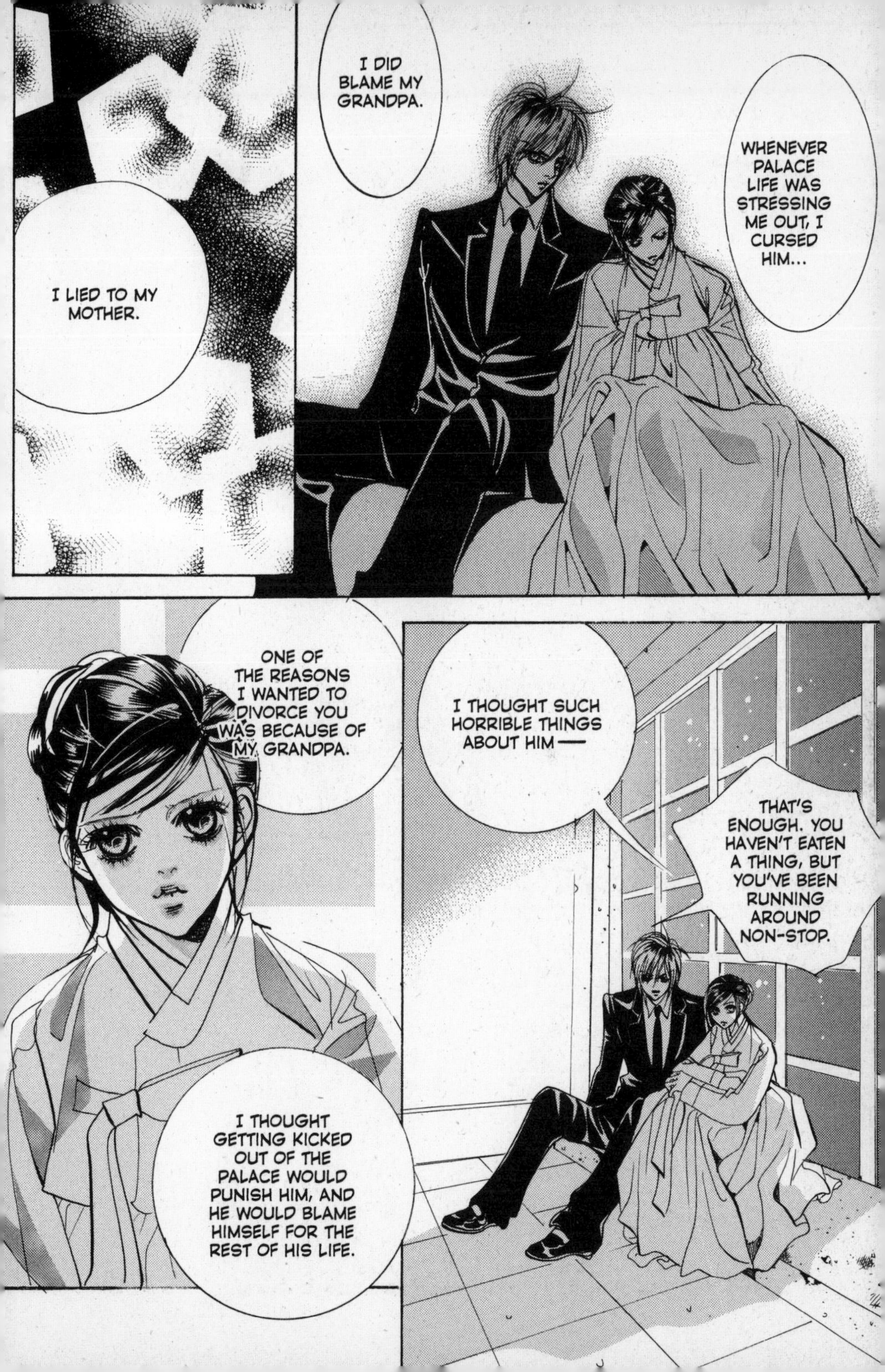
I LIED TO MY MOTHER.
I DID BLAME MY GRANDPA.
WHENEVER PALACE LIFE WAS STRESSING ME OUT, I CURSED HIM...
ONE OF THE REASONS I WANTED TO DIVORCE YOU WAS BECAUSE OF MY GRANDPA.
I THOUGHT GETTING KICKED OUT OF THE PALACE WOULD PUNISH HIM, AND HE WOULD BLAME HIMSELF FOR THE REST OF HIS LIFE.
I THOUGHT SUCH HORRIBLE THINGS ABOUT HIM—
THAT'S ENOUGH. YOU HAVEN'T EATEN A THING, BUT YOU'VE BEEN RUNNING AROUND NON-STOP.

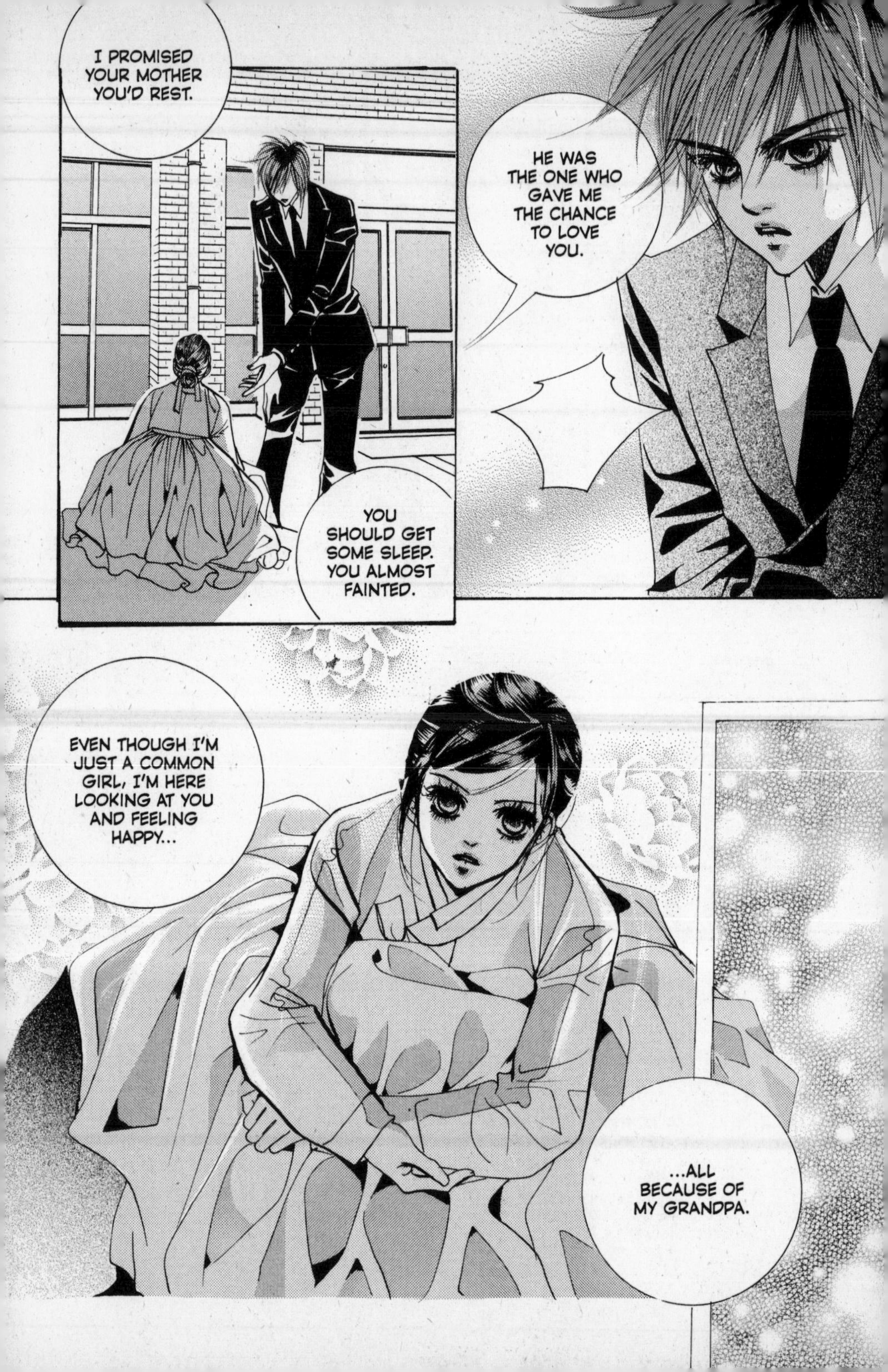
I PROMISED YOUR MOTHER YOU'D REST.
YOU SHOULD GET SOME SLEEP. YOU ALMOST FAINTED.
HE WAS THE ONE WHO GAVE ME THE CHANCE TO LOVE YOU.
EVEN THOUGH I'M JUST A COMMON GIRL, I'M HERE LOOKING AT YOU AND FEELING HAPPY...
...ALL BECAUSE OF MY GRANDPA.

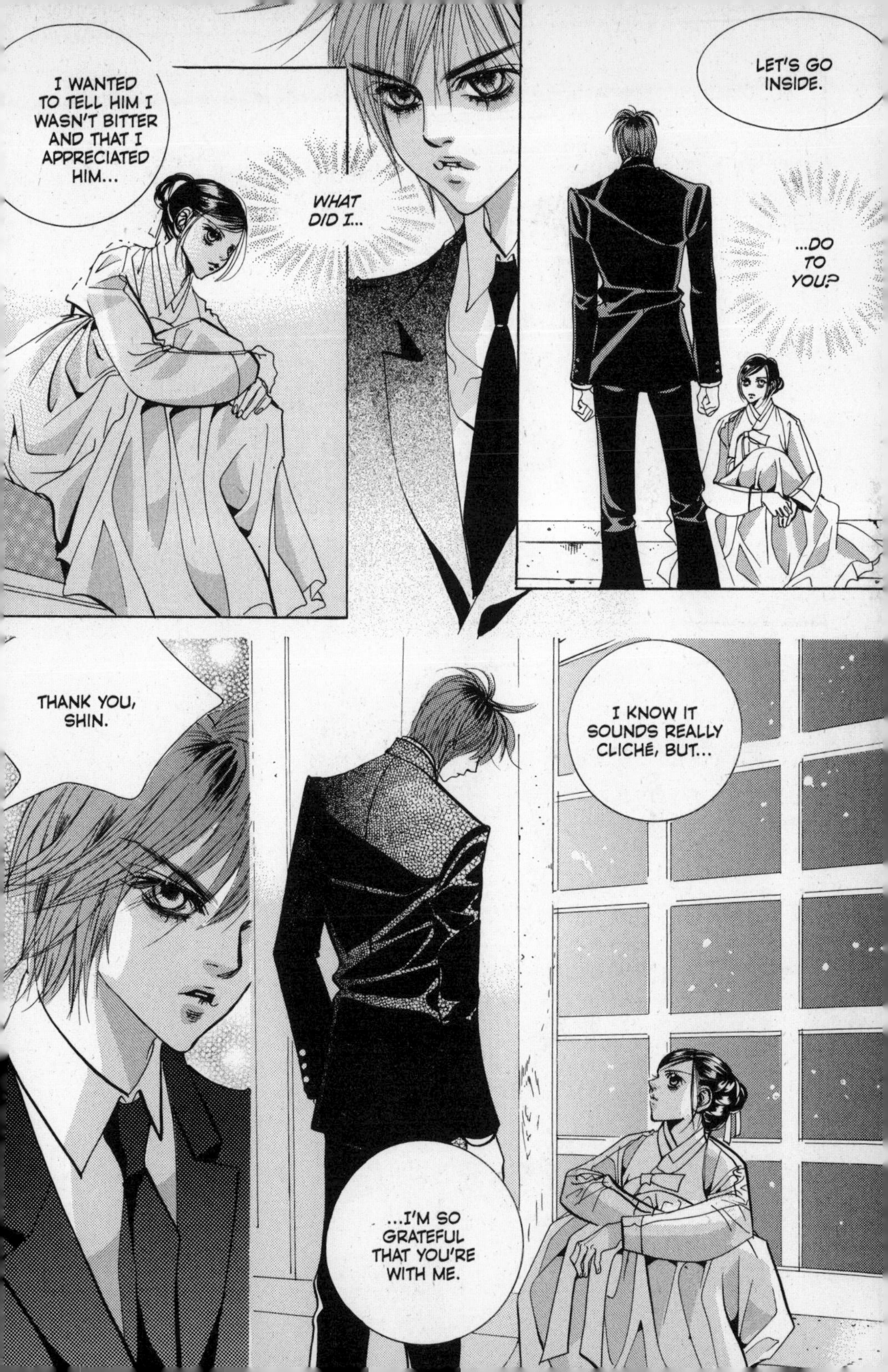
I WANTED TO TELL HIM I WASN'T BITTER AND THAT I APPRECIATED HIM...
WHAT DID I...
LET'S GO INSIDE.
...DO TO YOU?
THANK YOU, SHIN.
I KNOW IT SOUNDS REALLY CLICHÉ, BUT...
...I'M SO GRATEFUL THAT YOU'RE WITH ME.

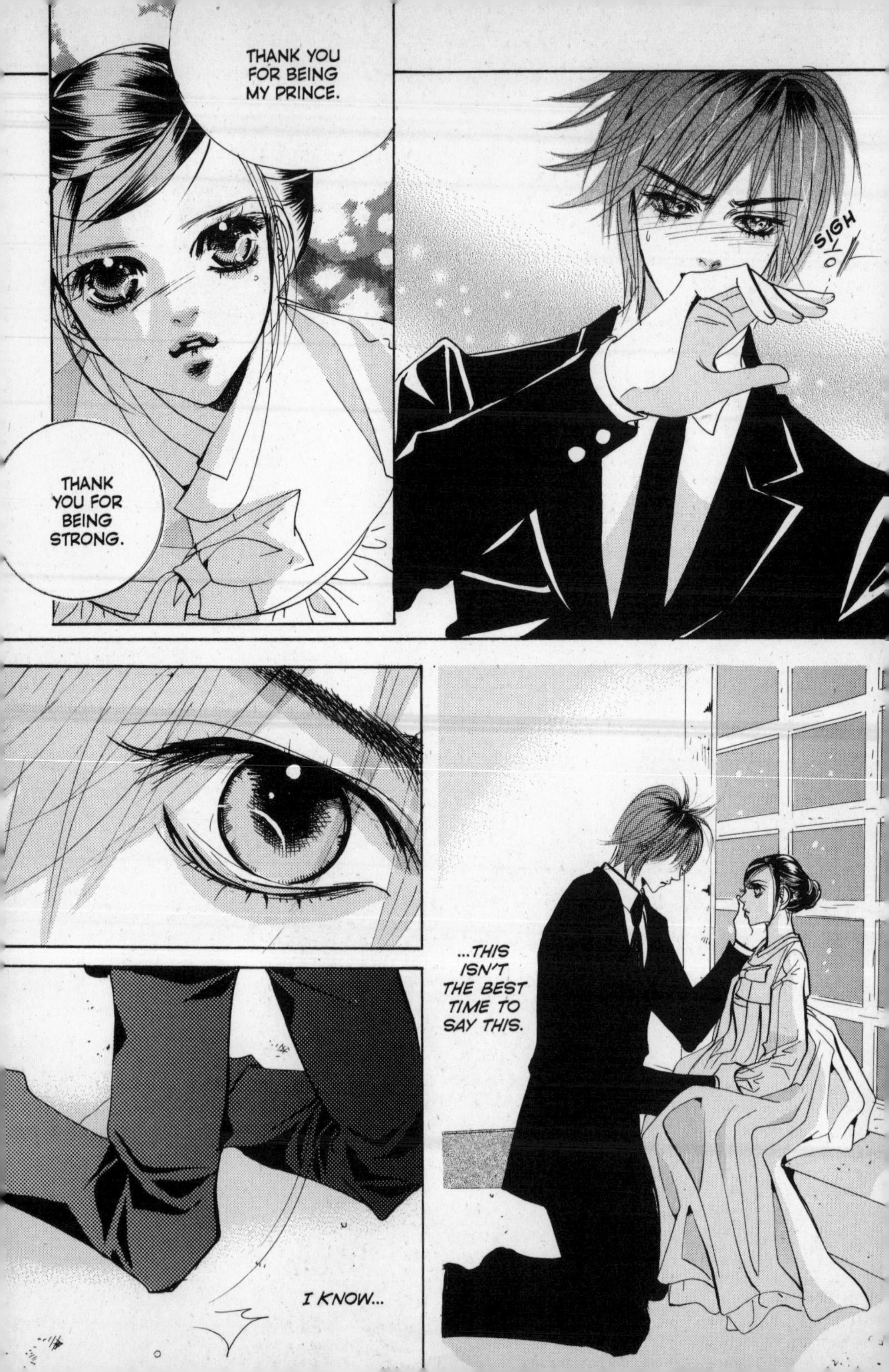
THANK YOU FOR BEING MY PRINCE.
THANK YOU FOR BEING STRONG.
SIGH
I KNOW...
...THIS ISN'T THE BEST TIME TO SAY THIS.

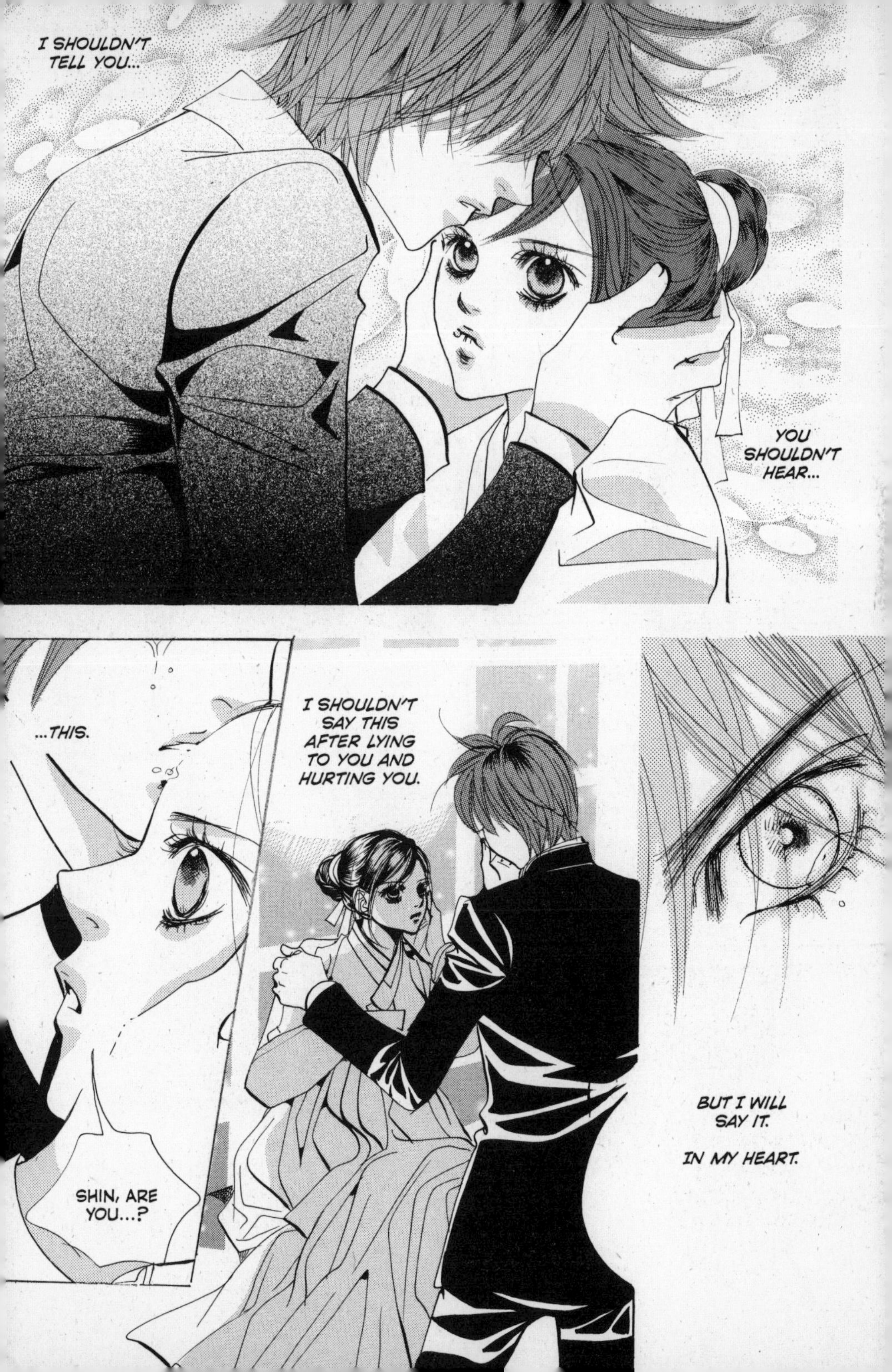
I SHOULDN'T TELL YOU...
YOU SHOULDN'T HEAR...
...THIS.
SHIN, ARE YOU...?
I SHOULDN'T SAY THIS AFTER LYING TO YOU AND HURTING YOU.
BUT I WILL SAY IT.
IN MY HEART.

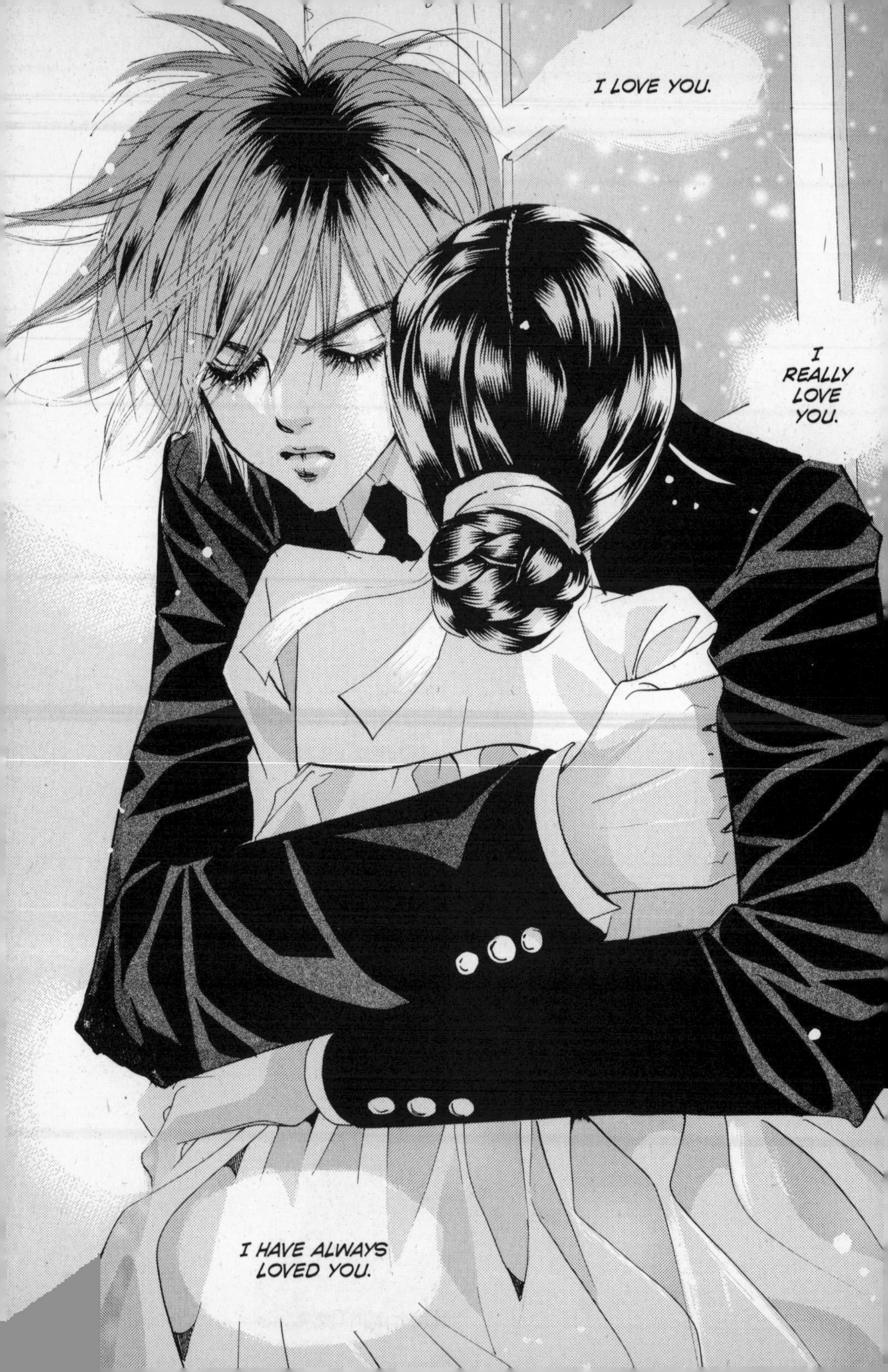
I LOVE YOU.
I REALLY LOVE YOU.
I HAVE ALWAYS LOVED YOU.

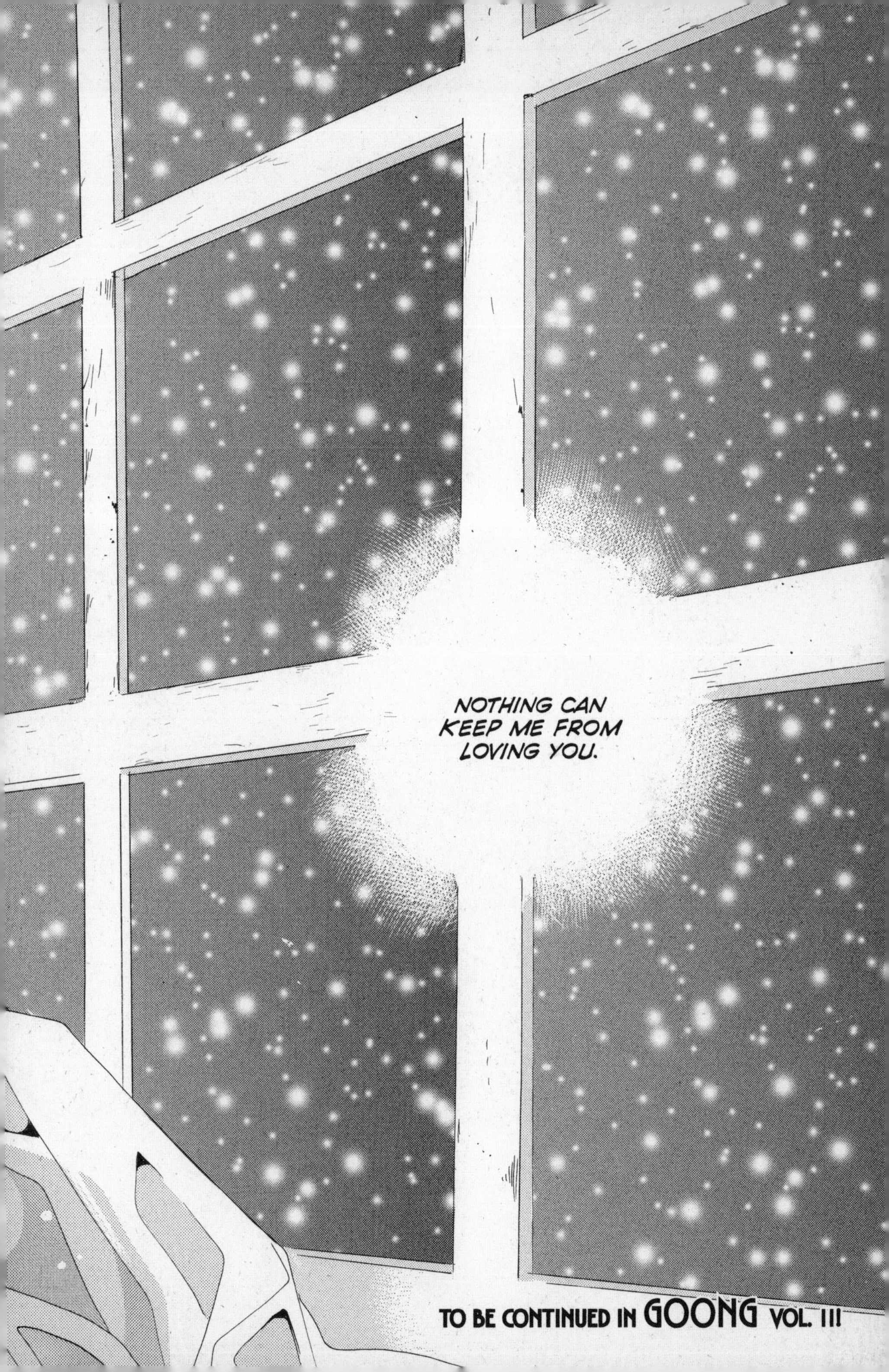
NOTHING CAN KEEP ME FROM LOVING YOU.
TO BE CONTINUED IN GOONG VOL. 11!

REALIZATION WHILE WATCHING TV.

BY BEAUTY PARK

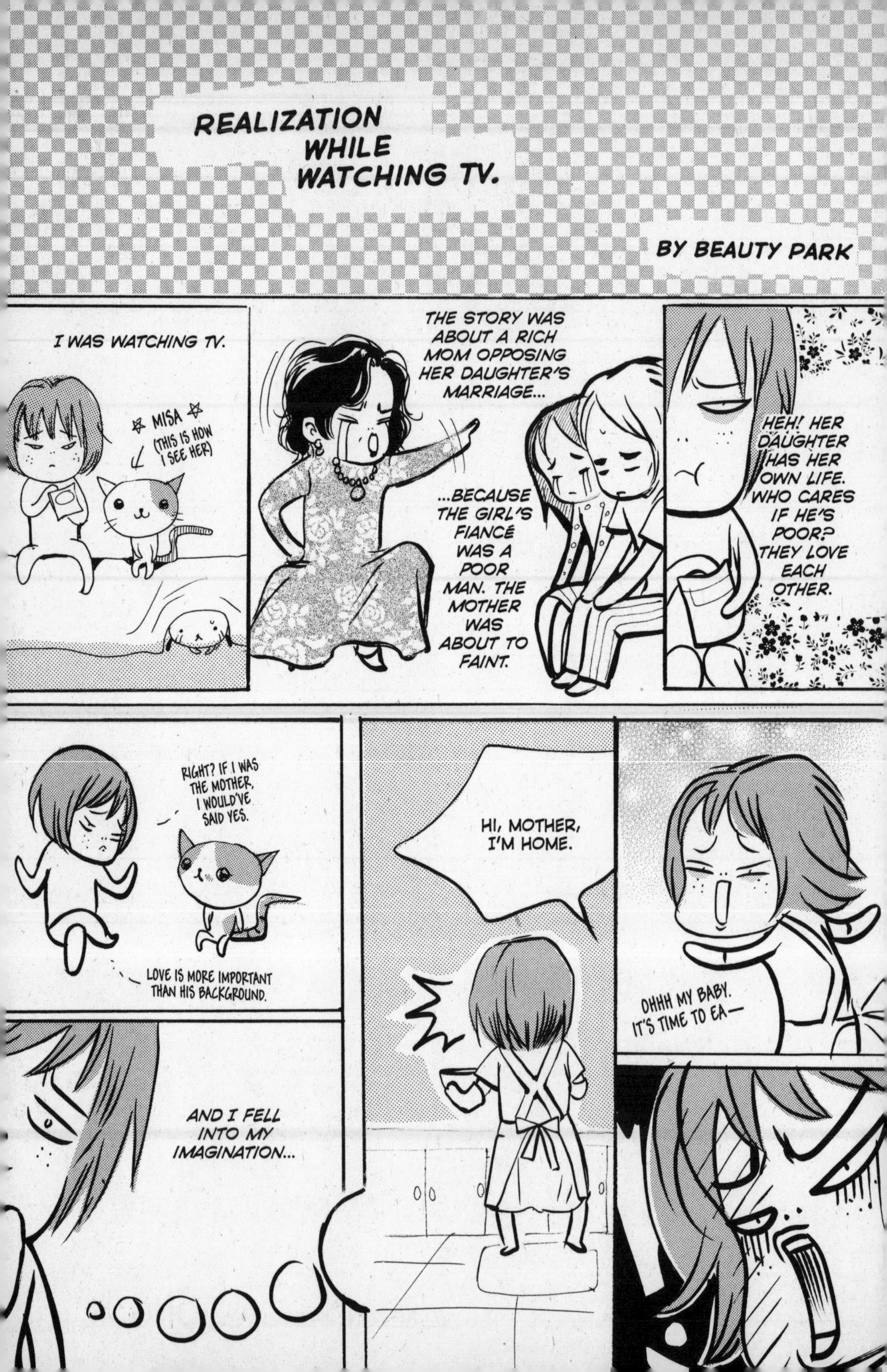
I WAS WATCHING TV.
MISA (THIS IS HOW I SEE HER)
THE STORY WAS ABOUT A RICH MOM OPPOSING HER DAUGHTER'S MARRIAGE...
...BECAUSE THE GIRL'S FIANCÉ WAS A POOR MAN. THE MOTHER WAS ABOUT TO FAINT.
HEH! HER DAUGHTER HAS HER OWN LIFE. WHO CARES IF HE'S POOR? THEY LOVE EACH OTHER.
RIGHT? IF I WAS THE MOTHER, I WOULD'VE SAID YES.
LOVE IS MORE IMPORTANT THAN HIS BACKGROUND.
AND I FELL INTO MY IMAGINATION...
HI, MOTHER, I'M HOME.
OHHH MY BABY. IT'S TIME TO EA—

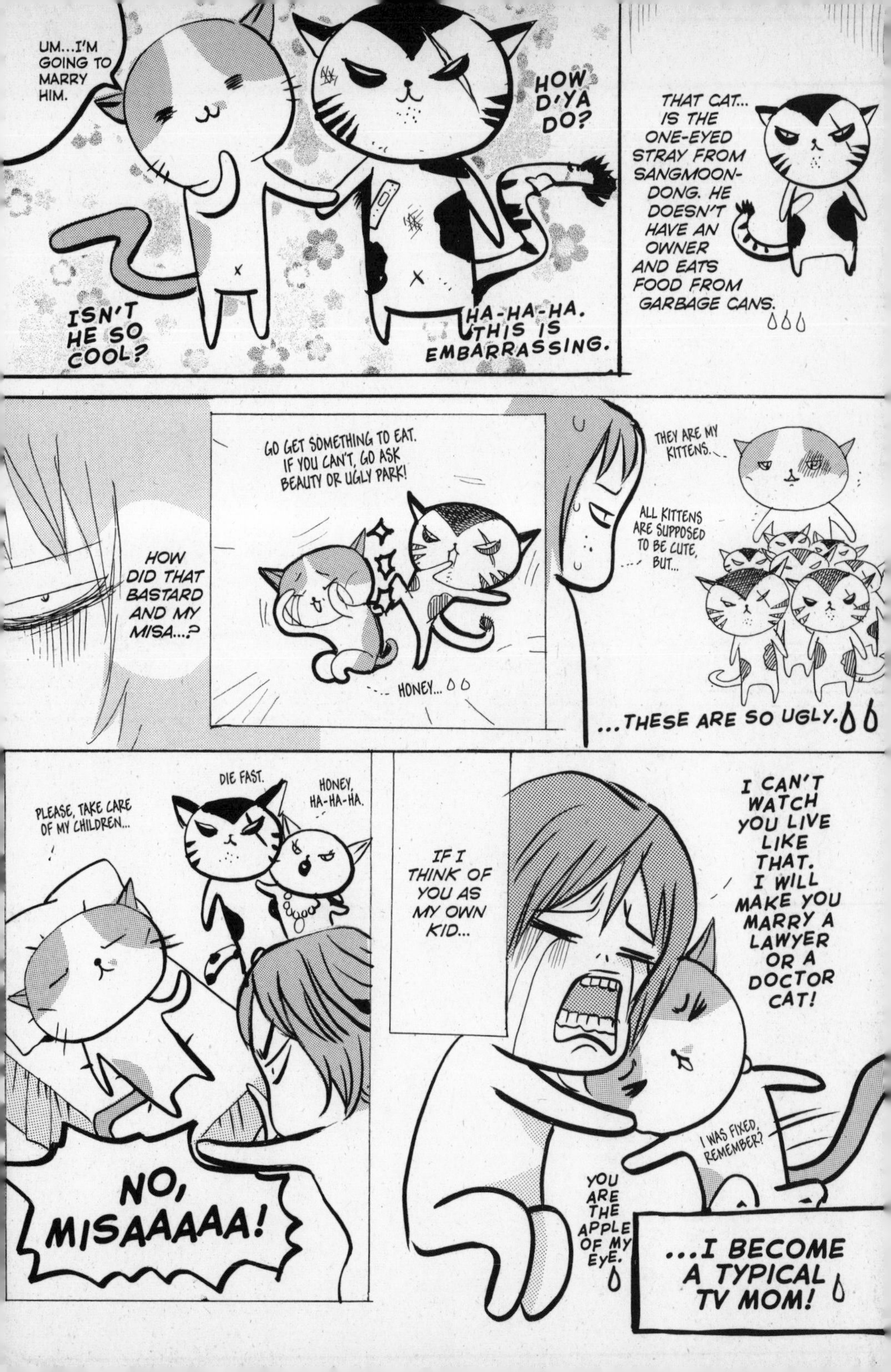
UM...I'M GOING TO MARRY HIM.
HOW D'YA DO?
ISN'T HE SO COOL?
HA-HA-HA. THIS IS EMBARRASSING.
THAT CAT... IS THE ONE-EYED STRAY FROM SANGMOON-DONG. HE DOESN'T HAVE AN OWNER AND EATS FOOD FROM GARBAGE CANS.
HOW DID THAT BASTARD AND MY MISA...?
GO GET SOMETHING TO EAT. IF YOU CAN'T, GO ASK BEAUTY OR UGLY PARK!
HONEY...
THEY ARE MY KITTENS.
ALL KITTENS ARE SUPPOSED TO BE CUTE, BUT...
...THESE ARE SO UGLY.
PLEASE, TAKE CARE OF MY CHILDREN...
DIE FAST.
HONEY, HA-HA-HA.
NO, MISAAAAA!
IF I THINK OF YOU AS MY OWN KID...
I CAN'T WATCH YOU LIVE LIKE THAT. I WILL MAKE YOU MARRY A LAWYER OR A DOCTOR CAT!
I WAS FIXED, REMEMBER?
YOU ARE THE APPLE OF MY EYE.
...I BECOME A TYPICAL TV MOM!

KONG'S HAREM

THE FOURTH BODYBUILDING COMPETITION FOR EUNUCHS

SIX ANGERS OF EUNUCH KONG

WARNING: THIS ISN'T ABOUT EUNUCH KONG'S ANGERS. IT'S MORE ABOUT HOW PEOPLE GET EXTREMELY MAD WHEN THEY SEE THESE DRAWINGS. COPY THIS PAGE AND SEND IT TO PEOPLE YOU DON'T LIKE. IT'S THE BEST!

THE ROYAL PALACE

Goong

Big City Lights, Big City Romance

Jae-Gyu is overwhelmed when she moves from her home in the country to the city. Will she be able to survive in the unforgiving world of celebrities and millionaires?

Gong GooGoo

Sugarholic

Seeking the love promised by destiny . . .
Can it be found in the thirteenth boy?

After eleven
boyfriends,
Hee-So thought
she was through
with love . . .
until she met
Won-Jun, that is . . .

But when
number twelve
dumps her, she's
not ready to
move on to the
thirteenth boy just
yet! Determined to win
back her destined love,
Hee-So's on a mission
to reclaim Won-Jun,
no matter what!

VOLUMES 1-5
IN STORES NOW!

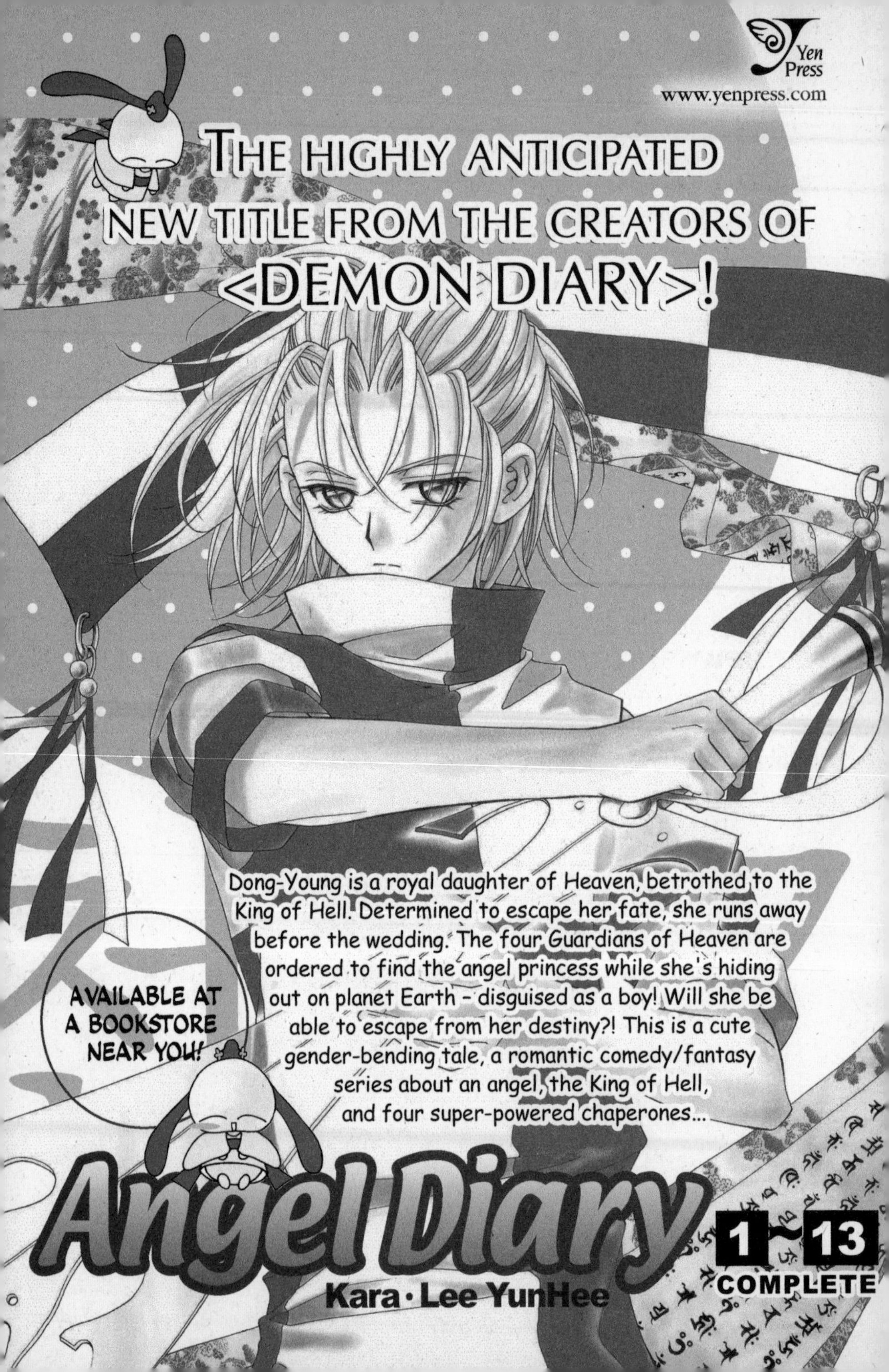
Yen Press
www.yenpress.com
THE HIGHLY ANTICIPATED
NEW TITLE FROM THE CREATORS OF
<DEMON DIARY>!
Dong-Young is a royal daughter of Heaven, betrothed to the King of Hell. Determined to escape her fate, she runs away before the wedding. The four Guardians of Heaven are ordered to find the angel princess while she's hiding out on planet Earth – disguised as a boy! Will she be able to escape from her destiny?! This is a cute gender-bending tale, a romantic comedy/fantasy series about an angel, the King of Hell, and four super-powered chaperones...
AVAILABLE AT A BOOKSTORE NEAR YOU!
Angel Diary
Kara · Lee YunHee
1~13
COMPLETE

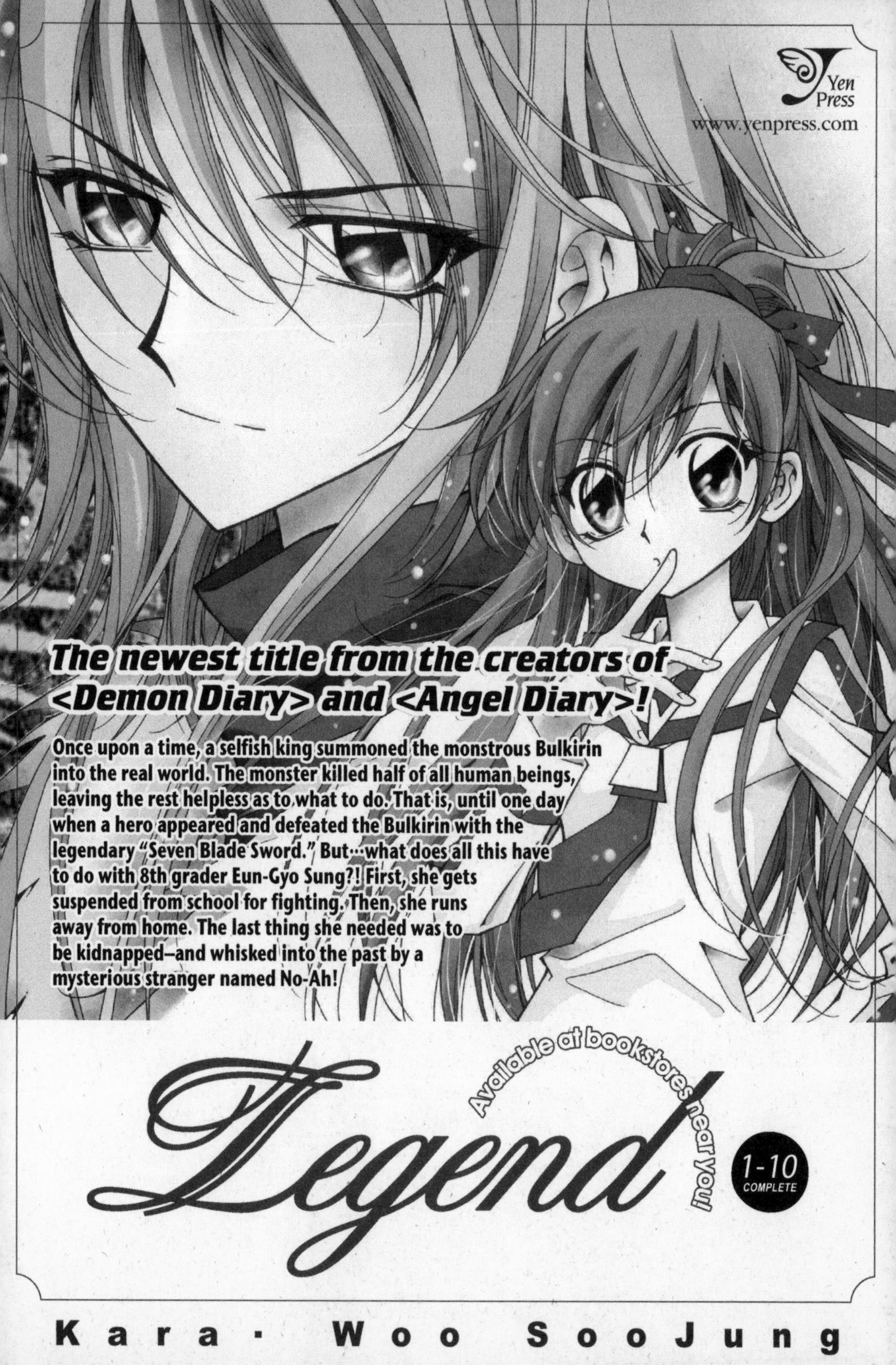
Yen Press
www.yenpress.com
The newest title from the creators of <Demon Diary> and <Angel Diary>!
Once upon a time, a selfish king summoned the monstrous Bulkirin into the real world. The monster killed half of all human beings, leaving the rest helpless as to what to do. That is, until one day when a hero appeared and defeated the Bulkirin with the legendary "Seven Blade Sword." But…what does all this have to do with 8th grader Eun-Gyo Sung?! First, she gets suspended from school for fighting. Then, she runs away from home. The last thing she needed was to be kidnapped–and whisked into the past by a mysterious stranger named No-Ah!
Legend
Available at bookstores near you!
1-10 COMPLETE
Kara · Woo SooJung

Wonderfully illustrated
modern day crossover
fantasy, available at
your local bookstore
or comic shop!

Apart from the fact her
eyes turn red when the moon
rises, Myung-Ee is your average,
albeit boy-crazy, 5th grader. After
picking a fight with her classmate
Yu-Da Lee, she discovers a startling
secret: the two of them are "earth
rabbits" being hunted by the "fox
tribe" of the moon!
Five years pass and Myung-Ee
transfers to a new school in search of
pretty boys. There, she unexpectedly
reunites with Yu-Da. The problem is
he doesn't remember a thing about
her or their shared past!

Moon Boy

얼 요 르 소 년

1~9
COMPLETE

Lee YoungYou

Yen Press
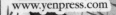
www.yenpress.com

The Antique Gift Shop

Lee Eun

1~10 COMPLETE

Available at bookstores near you!

Yen Press

www.yenpress.com

CAN YOU FEEL THE SOULS OF THE ANTIQUES? DO YOU BELIEVE?

Did you know that an antique possesses a soul of its own?
The Antique Gift Shop specializes in such items that charm and captivate the
buyers they are destined to belong to. Guided by a mysterious and
charismatic shopkeeper, the enchanted relics lead their new owners on a
journey into an alternate cosmic universe to their true destinies.
Eerily bittersweet and dolefully melancholy, The Antique Gift Shop opens up
a portal to a world where torn lovers unite, broken friendships are mended,
and regrets are resolved. Can you feel the power of the antiques?

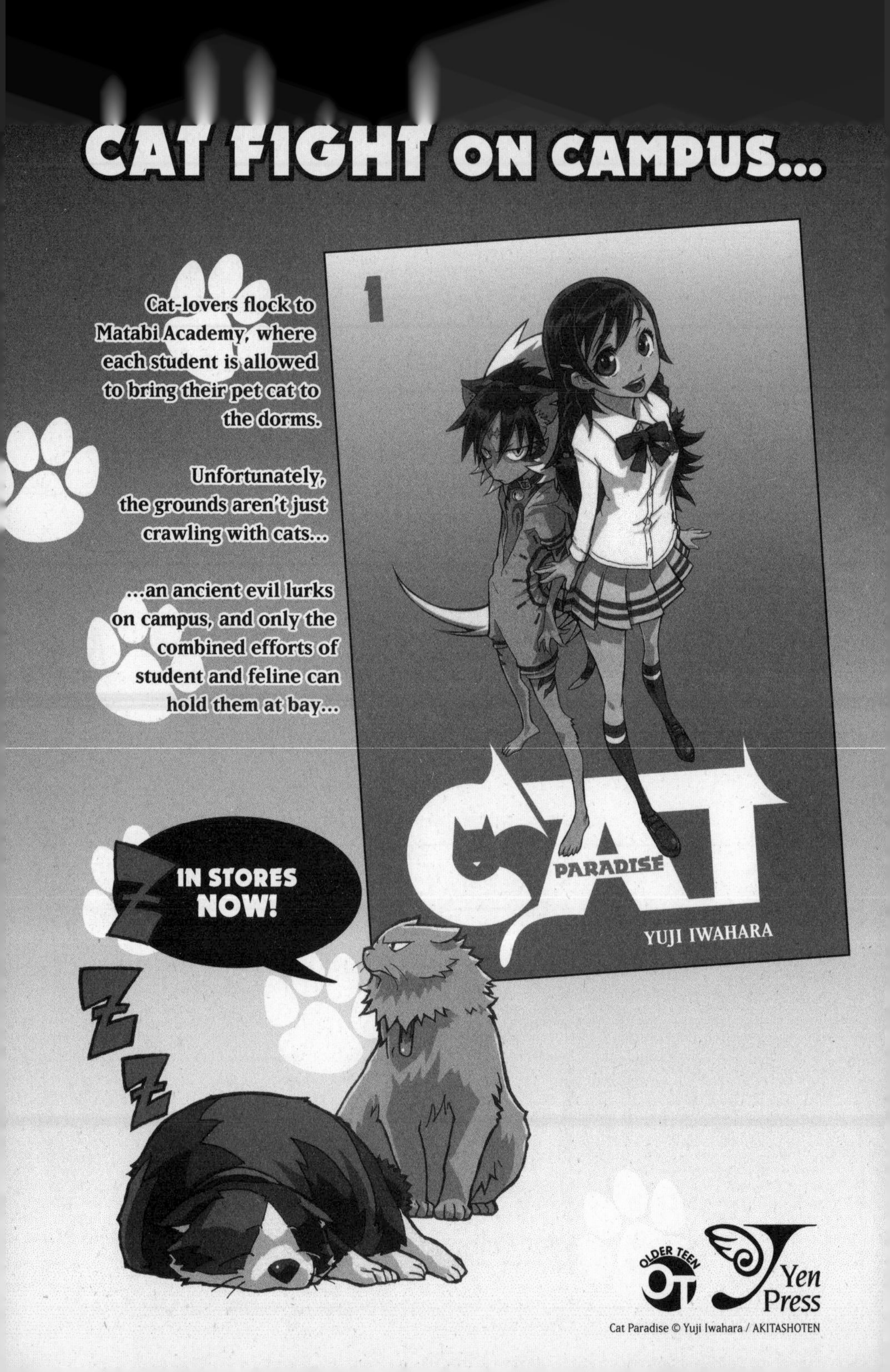

CAT FIGHT ON CAMPUS...
Cat-lovers flock to Matabi Academy, where each student is allowed to bring their pet cat to the dorms.
Unfortunately, the grounds aren't just crawling with cats...
...an ancient evil lurks on campus, and only the combined efforts of student and feline can hold them at bay...
1
CAT PARADISE
YUJI IWAHARA
IN STORES NOW!
Z
Z
Z
OLDER TEEN
OT
Yen Press
Cat Paradise © Yuji Iwahara / AKITASHOTEN

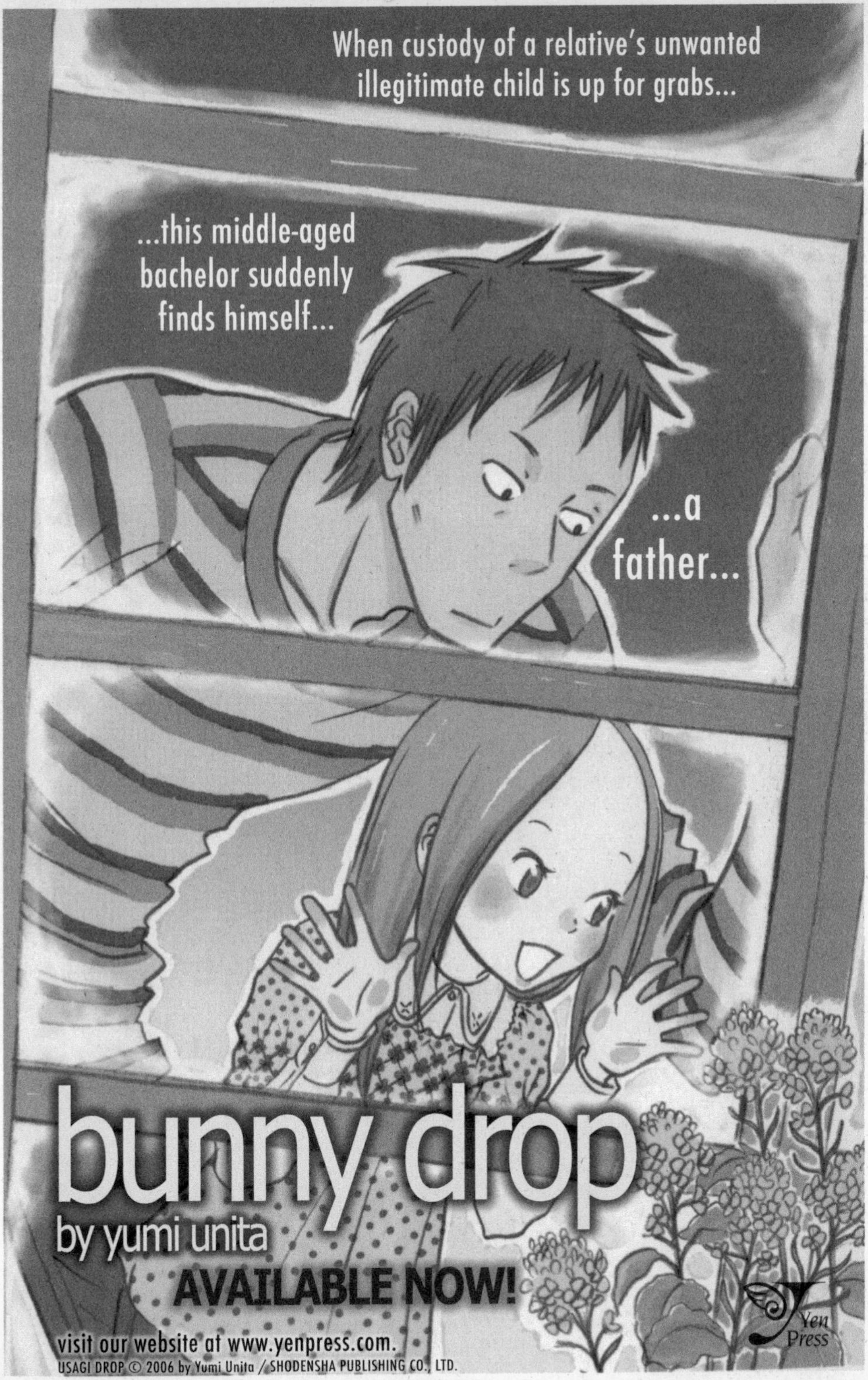

Hello! This is YOTSUBA!

Guess what? Guess what? Yotsuba and Daddy just moved here from waaaay over there!

And Yotsuba met these nice people next door and made new friends to play with!

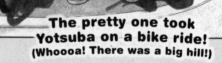

The pretty one took Yotsuba on a bike ride!
(Whoooa! There was a big hill!)

And Ena's a good drawer!
(Almost as good as Yotsuba!)

And their mom always gives Yotsuba ice cream!
(Yummy!)

And...
      And... OHHHH!